# Key Readings in Journalism

# Key Readings in

# Journalism

Edited by

## Elliot King and
## Jane L. Chapman

Routledge
Taylor & Francis Group

NEW YORK AND LONDON

First published 2012
by Routledge
711 Third Avenue, New York, NY 10017

Simultaneously published in the UK
by Routledge
2 Park Square, Milton Park, Abingdon, Oxon OX14 4RN

*Routledge is an imprint of the Taylor & Francis Group, an informa business*

*Library of Congress Cataloging in Publication Data*
Key readings in journalism/edited by Elliot King & Jane Chapman.
    p.cm
  Includes bibliographical references and index
   1. Journalism–United States.   2. Journalists–United states–Biography.
3. Reporters and reporting–United States.   4. American newspaper–History.
I. King, Elliot, 1953–   II. Chapman, Jane, 1950–
   PN4857.K45 2012
   071'.3–dc23
                                2011042328

ISBN: 978-0-415-88027-5 (hbk)
ISBN: 978-0-415-88028-2 (pbk)

Typeset in Perpetua and Bell Gothic
by RefineCatch Limited, Bungay, Suffolk, UK

Printed and bound in the United States of America by Sheridan Books, Inc.(a Sheridan Group company)

# Contents

# Acknowledgments

We would like to thank Laurel Leff, Frank Fee, Nancy Roberts, Joe Cutbirth, Dane Claussen and those who attended the panel at the 2009 Joint Journalism and Communications History Conference that helped generate the structure of the survey on which this book was based. As editor of *Journalism and Mass Communication Educator*, Dane Claussen also published an essay that described the problem that this book is intended to address, for which we are grateful. Parts of the research that form the foundation of this book were presented at the World Journalism Educators conference, the History Division of the Association for Education in Journalism and Mass Communication, and the Joint Journalism and Communication History Conference where the co-editors of the book met. We would like to thank Jim Martin, then the editor of *American Journalism*, that published a snapshot of the survey results. Finally, we would like to thank the nearly 400 journalism educators, in both the United States and the United Kingdom, who responded to the survey from which these selections were generally drawn.

In addition, thanks to the Association of Journalism Educators (AJE) in the UK for giving time at their annual general meeting and subsequent effort to answering questionnaires and making suggestions on the selection for this book. In addition, we are grateful to Deborah Wilson and Nick Nuttall from the School of Journalism, Lincoln University (UK) who provided information about, and extracts from, the works of Martha Gellhorn and Truman Capote respectively. Thanks to Matthew Byrnie for recognizing the merit of this project and a huge thank you to Erica Wetter, Margo Irvin, Georgette Enriquez and the rest of the team at Routledge who have worked continuously to see this book through to completion.

# INTRODUCTION

# WHAT WE SHOULD KNOW

IN 1903, JOSEPH PULITZER, THE PUBLISHER of the *New York World* and one of the most powerful publishers in America asked the *World*'s longtime business manager Don Seitz to join him on a train ride from New York City to one of Pulitzer's homes on Jekyll Island, Georgia. In route, Pulitzer handed Seitz a plan to bequeath to Columbia University $2 million to establish a school of journalism as well as to establish a set of prizes for working journalists along the same lines as the prizes Alfred Nobel had endowed the year before. The sum was more than three times the university's operating budget at the time.

Pulitzer had not always been a proponent of journalism education in colleges and universities. Earlier, when a group of publishers in Missouri had proposed establishing a professorship of journalism, Pulitzer had mocked them, calling the idea absurd. Later he came to the view that while a professor of journalism could potentially teach students the technical aspects of the profession, he (or she) could not create great journalists in the same way that military schools could not produce military geniuses along the lines of Hannibal or Napoleon Bonaparte.

While perhaps grudgingly conceding that a university education in journalism could be of some use, Pulitzer had another goal in endowing a school of journalism. A school of journalism could help increase respect for journalism and journalists, enabling journalists to take what Pulitzer saw as their rightful places alongside the other learned professions like law and medicine. Not long before, Columbia had established a school of mining, so why not a school of journalism?

When Pulitzer asked Seitz what he thought about the plan, Seitz's answer was direct and to the point. "Not much," Seitz said. Endowing the *World* itself would be a much better use of the money than endowing a school of journalism, he suggested.

Since the study of journalism at the university level was introduced by Robert E. Lee at what was then Washington College in the late 1860s, learning about journalism was seen skeptically by journalists themselves and presumably little considered by most of the public, for whom college was out of reach. Within the journalism community, the thought was that people entering the field would do better by finding an entry level position and learning their craft under the tutelage of senior editors and reporters. In any case, as even Pulitzer suggested, many believed that being a great journalist depended on having great talent and was not an activity one could learn except by doing. As for the public at large, in that period of time, reading a newspaper was still, in many ways, a political act. Readers were less concerned with the "professional values" of a particular newspaper than with the politics it espoused.

The divergence of opinion on the value of an education in journalism made its way into the academy itself as journalism programs became more commonplace throughout the twentieth century and then, on many campuses were either joined or merged into broader-based departments of communication. On the one hand, many of the faculty in journalism programs felt it was their primary responsibility to teach entry-level skills to their students, preparing them for jobs in the news industry. The apprenticeship model common in an earlier period was imported into the academy. On the other hand, some faculty felt it was their responsibility to teach their students material that ranged beyond the requisite skill set and explore wider issues associated with communication in general. The former approach to journalism education was often espoused by ex-practitioners who had made their way into the academy, and newspaper editors. The latter was proposed by Ph.D.-holding academics, many, though not all, of whom had some experience in journalism, as well as academic administrators interested in increasing the research productivity of their faculties. The split in approach was captured in a 1967 article called "Green Eyeshades vs. Chi-Squares," which appeared in *The Quill*, the magazine of the Society of Professional Journalists (SPJ). In it, the author Jake Highton argued that editors believed that journalism students should receive a practical education focused on the skills needed to practice journalism while the administrators of journalism programs in colleges and universities were more interested in students learning more theoretical courses and integrating journalism with "communication education." During the 1980s and into the 1990s, the battle lines seemed to be drawn between a more holistic journalism education and an industry-oriented sequence approach.

This split in journalism education, however, side-stepped an important question— what should people entering the field of journalism know about the practice of journalism itself. Regardless of whether people learned entry-level professional skills in a university program or through on-the-job training, was there anything about journalism itself beyond the skill set, such as its history, development, social role, and its practitioners that people entering the field, and the public at large, should know?

Perhaps through the 1980s, that question was irrelevant. In 1970, 77 percent of the adult Americans read weekday newspapers and even in 1985, that number still stood at 64.2 percent. Watching evening news broadcasts, both network and local, were nightly habits for tens of millions of people. In 1980, the network news programs regularly reached more than 36 million households. Reading newspapers and watching broadcast news were routine activities for most people, enabling them to form their sense of the news media and what is news through their own experience with their favorite newspaper or television news broadcast.

That situation has changed dramatically. By 1995, only 23 percent of people under the age of 30 reported that they read newspapers on a regular basis. Viewership of broadcast news was also dropping precipitously. Many students interested in studying journalism and entering the field simply are not that familiar with the current news media. They cannot form their opinions about what news should be and how the news media should operate through their own personal experience because this is insufficient to do so.

A similar process has occurred in the workplace as well: in the past many newspapers, as established institutions, had developed their own local cultures. New employees could learn about the traditions of the *Atlanta Constitution*, perhaps, or the *Chicago Tribune*. They could learn about the founders, the great editors and reporters, and the important stories the newspapers or the news broadcasts broke and covered. In short, news reporters could absorb the culture of journalism through their experience in the workplace.

Even if at some point in the past aspiring journalists and the public at large could understand journalism as an area of practice, an institution, and a social force through their own personal experiences, largely this is no longer the case. The consolidation of newspapers into a few great chains has hurt newspapers' local identification and culture. Senior editorial staff, who could be expected to be the bearers of a newspaper's culture, are transferred from property to property through the chain as they ascend the corporate ranks. The downsizing of newspaper staffs has hit hardest at senior journalists with the most experience in their organizations, who are also the bearers of the organizational history. While young reporters can still theoretically learn how to "do" journalism on the job, there is little chance to learn or think about journalism in any systematic way.

At least two other factors have raised the question—what should the public and aspiring journalists know about journalism? Since the Republican convention that nominated Senator Barry Goldwater for the presidency of the United States at the Cow Palace in San Francisco in 1964, where the attendees erupted in wild applause when President Eisenhower warned delegates not to be divided by those outside "our family," that is "sensation seeking columnists and commentators," conservative politicians have railed against the "liberal" media. From Spiro Agnew's attacks on "nattering nabobs of negativity," a phrase coined by William Safire, a speech writer for President Richard Nixon and then a *New York Times* columnist, through the radio commentator Rush Limbaugh, conservatives have assailed the operation of the mainstream media as biased and misleading. For their part, though perhaps the recipient of less popular attention, liberals and those farther to the left have published a steady attack on mainstream journalism as being biased in the other direction and basically serving as lapdogs to people in power.

The result is that members of the public often have very cynical views of the press, seeing it as biased and more interested in "selling newspapers" than truly reporting the news. In fact, in a 2010 Gallup poll, only 25 percent of the public had confidence in newspapers and even fewer, 22 percent, had confidence in television news. In short, the public knows little about the operation of the news media and journalism itself and what it knows, it doesn't like. These attitudes shape the environment from which students enter the field of journalism and to which they will return after they complete their education, should they ultimately choose journalism as a profession.

The cold hard truth, however, is that many journalism students ultimately will not work in journalism, either in print, broadcast or online, in the short or long run. According to the National Association of Colleges and Employers, that bills itself as the leading source of information about the employment of college graduates, in the spring of 2009, only 24 percent of college graduates looking for jobs in journalism actually received offers, making it the toughest field in which to get a job. With the relatively low pay for many entry level positions, the vicious downsizing of newspaper and broadcast operations, and the uncertainty of Web-based news operations coupled with rising enrolments in journalism programs, the math itself indicates that many students who major in journalism will look for and find jobs elsewhere when they graduate.

Given this reality, the study of journalism in the academy can no longer be conceptualized solely as training for jobs in the media. Instead, journalism must be seen as an academic discipline that stands on its own merits as a rewarding area for students to invest a significant period of time during their undergraduate and even graduate educations in the same way that history or English are seen as worthy academic disciplines regardless of the professional paths those who study those fields might ultimately travel. The study of journalism has to be seen as a worthwhile endeavor in and of itself, as an interesting way to engage and better understand the world in general, in the same way that other liberal arts and social science disciplines allow students to engage and understand the world.

That said, academic disciplines, almost by definition, have boundaries. While those boundaries may be porous at the edges, in virtually all disciplines there is a core of knowledge that everybody said to be educated or knowledgeable in that field holds in common. It is a familiarity of this shared core of knowledge that in some ways defines who is a member of that learned community, or at least who can claim to be educated in the field.

For the past perhaps 50 years, the shared core of knowledge has been the skill set—how to write in an objective fashion; how to make sure stories are credible; how to develop a straightforward unadorned writing style; how to produce good work on a tight deadline. Moreover, the thought was that students should be taught to address significant issues—this despite the rise of celebrity journalism, the proliferation of sports journalism, the lack of attention to the arts and so on. A focus on the skill set may have sufficed when journalism education was seen primarily as a training ground for entry into the profession, but most academic disciplines have a core of knowledge that ranges beyond an acquisition of specific skills. Academic disciplines are defined by what students of that discipline should know and what students of that discipline should have read.

So beyond the skill set, what should journalism students and perhaps the public at large know about journalism to be considered educated in the field? As reflected in the selections in this reader, students of journalism should be knowledgeable in five areas— the development of journalism, the practice of journalism, lasting works produced by journalists, notable practitioners in the field, a critical analysis of journalism and the social impact of journalism.

Each area is significant in its own right and taken as a whole, can result in a well-informed multifaceted understanding of journalism. For example, it is important for students of journalism to understand that the development of the field has always been shaped by shifting economic, political, social and cultural changes in play in the country at large. While the emergence of the Internet as a platform for mass communication is leading to radical changes, those changes are no more severe in many ways than those sparked by the growth of democratic capitalism in the 1830s or the introduction of the telegraph in the 1840s. Journalism's developmental arc has always been conditioned by a wide range of significant factors. The key is identifying and recognizing which of those factors are having a critical impact and how to cope with them.

While the development of journalism has been shaped by social forces, on a daily basis news is reported and written by people. To understand journalism, it is important to understand how journalists go about their work. Those work routines shape the news product created and presented to the public every day. The organization of work plays a significant role in the output of journalism.

The output of journalism, of course, is the production of "texts"—news reports, magazine articles, television broadcasts, books and now blogs and Web sites. A familiarity with the journalism texts that have made a difference is critical to an understanding of journalism itself. In fact, many people in the field feel that the best way to teach people to be great journalists is to have them read great journalism. Others feel that the best way to teach people the history of journalism is to have them read or watch the primary texts produced by journalists—the newspaper and magazine articles and news broadcasts themselves.

Interestingly, it is often easy to identify reporting that made a difference: reporting on the Civil War; 100 years later the civil rights movement; the exposure of Boss Tweed and corruption in New York in the late 1860s and early 1870s; then the exposure of corruption in the Watergate scandal in the 1970s that led to the resignation of President Richard Nixon; reporting on the lead up to the Spanish American war in 1898; then on the war in Viet Nam in the 1960s and the 1970s, the impact of reporting is often cumulative. No single article stands out. For example, the investigative reporter Seymour Hersh's report that Lt. William Calley was under investigation for deliberately killing 109 unarmed civilians at My Lai in Viet Nam in 1968 had huge repercussions as it basically raised the possibility that U.S. soldiers were guilty of war crimes. The story itself, however, took the form of a straight, almost routine dispatch.

As a result, most lasting journalism is frequently found in books, but it is here that the lines between journalism and other disciplines begin to blur. In journalism, many of the exemplary books use techniques often associated with literature. While perhaps not representative of the routine output of journalism, these books generally are examples of the best of journalism, meticulously researched, well-written works that have had a major impact. The line between literature and literary journalism is fuzzy indeed, as well it should be. From the beginning of modern journalism in the 1800s until very recently, journalism was often seen as the first rung of literature.

It is virtually self evident that texts are primarily created by individuals, with the assistance of a support team. As in most fields, certain individuals have come to be seen as role models in the field for the work that they have done. The presence of role models is particularly important in professional fields: they help new entrants understand what is considered good work and what is valued. In journalism, the lives of the luminaries sometimes become the point of entry for understanding changes in the field or the significance of reporting on specific topics. This is only to be expected. While the development of journalism has been shaped in large part by broader social forces, journalism itself consists predominantly of stories about people. Any knowledge of journalism is surely incomplete without knowing about Edward R. Murrow, for example. Whilst the exploits of Robert Woodward and Carl Bernstein drew many people to journalism as a career in the 1970s, now many incoming journalism students can barely name a single prominent journalist, currently working or from the past.

The stakes involved in truly understanding journalism, its practitioners, its output, and its institutions may be higher than they may be for other academic disciplines. Journalism is one of the few professional fields that benefit from constitutional protection: at the heart of the First Amendment is the need to safeguard the right to a robust debate that is essential to democracy. In fact, journalism plays a vital role in establishing and maintaining a democratic and free society. Providing citizens the information they need to be self governing is journalism's paramount goal. Educated students of journalism must understand the relationship of journalism to society.

Since journalism is so critical to democratic life, students must be familiar with the broad criticisms of journalism as well. While ill-informed and slanted criticism has soured many on journalism in general, an astute critique of press performance is most necessary. Students should be equipped to assess the work of the contemporary news media and also be familiar with the assessments that have been made in the past.

If the areas outlined above can serve to broadly define the contours of the academic discipline of journalism, the question "what should students of journalism know in order to claim to be educated about the field?" still remains unanswered. Many other academic disciplines have what could be called core readings or a canon. Students of English, for example, are expected to read some of the plays of William Shakespeare and some of the works of Mark Twain, preferably *The Adventures of Huckleberry Finn*. If they don't, those students cannot be said to be well educated in English. In the same way, most sociology students must read works by Max Weber, Emile Durkheim and Karl Marx. Once again, those thinkers are central to that field.

Building a canon, however, is a tricky business involving issues of power. A great deal of what was called the "culture wars" in the 1980s revolved around what was to be included on the booklist for introductory and advanced English courses. More conservative academics wanted to reserve the canon for works that have been defined as the "best" of their time periods, works that often were the books of dead white men. More liberal academics argued that the definition of "best" did not reflect quality but the power structure in the academic world at the time. They fought to have the canon enlarged to include other, hitherto excluded voices—particularly those of women, people of color and people from non-Western societies. Conservatives argued that the liberals were "diluting" the quality of the canon. Liberals argued that they were widening the scope of the field.

Acknowledging the risks involved, to identify a core literature for journalism, a survey was conducted in the spring of 2009 soliciting respondents to identify books that they felt were essential for all journalism students to have read. Sent to journalism academics and graduate students, 382 people responded. *All the President's Men*, by Carl Bernstein and Bob Woodward, *Public Opinion* by Walter Lippmann and *Discovering the News* by Michael Schudson topped the list. The selections in this volume were drawn from that survey and supplemented by additional choices designed to broaden the book's scope on every dimension including gender, race and nationality.

The books from which the excerpts in this reader were taken do not represent a consensus on a canon. The survey on which they are largely based is not representative; there was no consensus in the survey, as the top voted work received fewer than half the votes; and the leading books on the list do not seem to have the same cultural weight that Shakespeare and Twain have. On the other hand, Shakespeare and Twain probably did not have the same cultural weight when they were still alive as they do today. The problem with developing a canon may be that journalism as an academic discipline is still quite new, perhaps too new. Or, as some of the survey respondents argued, there is no need to develop a canon at all since canons are generally just exercises in authority and control.

Be that as it may, it seems very clear that there is a pressing need to develop a common pool of knowledge among students of journalism, knowledge that goes well beyond teaching the traditional skills and even the traditional values of journalism, values that increasingly seem to be honored more in their breach than in their implementation. With the revolution in the delivery of news, the very definition of who is a journalist has been called into question. Journalists can no longer be defined by the organizations for which they work, their work practices, or the way that they report the news. Instead, journalists must be defined by the lens through which they see the world and people who are educated in journalism will understand what that lens is.

The author Benedict Anderson argued that people imagine themselves to be members of a specific community and their imaginations are shaped by the texts they produce and the texts to which they attend. The selections in this volume identify the texts that should be held in common by the community of those educated about journalism. The works represented in the volume may not be comprehensive, completely inclusive or completely uncontroversial. But readers of these selections and the books from which they are drawn will have a deep understanding of journalism along many of its dimensions. This common ground created by sharing these texts is essential to establishing who a journalist should be and what a journalist should do now and in the future, giving people who do not enter the field professionally a deep and appropriate understanding of journalism as a field of human activity, an education critical to the functioning of democracy itself.

SECTION I

# The Development of Journalism

# INTRODUCTION

**B**OTH THE PRACTICE AND THE BUSINESS of journalism are in the midst of a seismic shift. The collapse of many urban newspapers and the rise of the Internet as a platform for the distribution of news is reshaping the news business and has called into question the very definition of journalism. People still require news, but other crucial issues have become shifting territory, such as who receives what news, how they receive it, who reports the news, and even what constitutes news. As troubling as the changes seem, this is not the first major revolution in journalism. The emergence of the penny press in the 1830s and the second penny press revolution in the 1880s, the fight to include other voices in the media, particularly women and African Americans, and the development of new technologies such as radio and television—also triggered powerful and profound changes in journalism.

This section provides several accounts of key moments in the development of journalism over time, from when James Gordon Bennett and others were reshaping journalism through the launch of the penny press and the creation of truly mass circulation newspapers to the development of the Internet. It does not present a "whiggish" picture of the development of journalism from bad to good—a technique of 19th century conservative and Romantic historiography in which history was viewed as the essence of innumerable biographies that tell the story of the success of great people and the march of progress.

Instead a number of themes emerge from the excerpts and a number of observations and generalizations can be made. First, change can take time and usually involves a difficult struggle. This has certainly been the case for freedom of expression, and for the struggle of women and people of color to win a place in the field of journalism. And the stakes have been high, as Patrick Washburn suggests, for instance, in *The African American Newspaper* when he describes the "Double V" campaign championed by the black press as a forerunner to the drive for equal rights after World War II. Kay Mills also describes a struggle in *A Place in the News*—in this case for women's professional equality in the newsroom. She contends that there is a clear interaction between the women's movement, the presence of women working on American newspapers and coverage of women in the press.

These two excerpts suggest that journalism cannot be viewed in isolation, which is the rationale for Jane L. Chapman's *Comparative Media History*. She argues that social, economic and political factors shape the environment in which the profession operates. The excerpt takes a close look at radio, but the principles remain the same for all media. Chapman believes that the roots of modern journalism lie in the 19th century with the victory of commercialism in the press over allegiance to citizenship. She shares common territory with Michael Schudson who suggests in *The Discovery of the News*, one of the most widely cited books in the field, that the development of the penny press can only be understood within the wider context of democratization of business and politics in the 1830s. The penny press did not emerge because of the "genius" of James Gordon Bennett or the invention of new technology, although new technology did play a role. The success of the penny press rested on a wide variety of social, political and economic forces in play at the time.

On the other hand, while social, political and economic factors play a profound role in shaping the practice and business of journalism, technology remains a key enabler for new forms of journalism. In the excerpt of an essay from his book *Communication as Culture*, James W. Carey explores the impact of the telegraph on community. In the excerpt from *Free for All: The Internet's Transformation of Journalism*, Elliot King asks if the present forms of online journalism are sufficient to build community in the same way that the media of the past did.

Taken as a whole, the section demonstrates that change has been a constant and that it is driven by economics, politics and other social factors. As journalism changes so does society. On the other hand, journalism, at least in free societies, is informed by elements of continuity—the desire to expand the human conversation, a commitment to equality, human dignity and civil rights, freedom of expression, the need to speak out and to uphold a sense of community. In periods of great change, those values often seem under attack. As an old aphorism goes, if you don't know where you are going, any road will get you there. To know where journalism is going—and if and how the core values of journalism can be preserved—it is critical to know the road it has traveled already.

# Chapter 1

# MICHAEL SCHUDSON

# DISCOVERING THE NEWS

I N 1977, IN A POWERFUL ESSAY that became a touchstone in the field, James Carey, a preeminent journalism scholar, decried the state of journalism history and called for a new approach—an approach that embedded the history of journalism within cultural, economic and political contexts. Shortly thereafter, *Discovering the News* provided just that. Based on his Harvard Ph.D. dissertation, in *Discovering the News*, Michael Schudson offers a cultural history of the development of the value of objectivity in journalism. Relatively short and very accessible, the book places the developing notion of objectivity squarely within other social and cultural changes occurring from the 1830s onwards and immediately established Schudson, a sociologist, as a leading historian of journalism.

In the wake of *Discovering the News*, several other scholars including Daniel Schiller, David Mindich and Steven Knowlton took cracks at understanding the emergence of objectivity in the American press, but Schudson's work remains the most widely cited. Nonetheless, *Discovering the News* has had its fair share of critics. In perhaps the most noted attack, Mitchell Stephens at New York University lambasted Schudson for asserting that the penny press of the 1830s "invented the news." Stephens went on to write *The History of News* to demonstrate that an interest in news is deeply rooted in the human experience from ancient times on. The significance of *Discovering the News*, however, does not lay just in the argument it presents but as a model for locating the development in journalism within a larger social, culture and economic context.

In this selection from Chapter 1, Schudson describes the invention of the penny press, the first true mass newspapers in America, in the 1830s. He contends that with the ascendency of the penny press, news and news reports became the point of competition amongst newspapers and newspapers became more commercially independent. Later in the chapter, in a section not included here, Schudson suggests that the penny

press should be understood as a part of the same democratization of business and politics that characterized the Jacksonian period in American history.

## The Revolution in American Journalism in the Age of Egalitarianism: The Penny Press

By birth, education, and marriage, James Fenimore Cooper was an American aristocrat. For him, power and prestige were always near at hand. But he was also an ardent nationalist, a great admirer of Jefferson and even Jackson. His novel *The Bravo* (1831) honored the July Revolution in France. It sought to expose those people in society who were "contending for exclusive advantages at the expense of the mass of their fellow-creatures."[1]

*The Bravo* was written during Cooper's seven-year sojourn in Europe from 1826 to 1833. In that time Cooper developed "a lofty detachment from the fears natural to his own class, and a warm sympathy for the lower classes that in Europe were, and in America might be, deprived of their political rights."[2] But detachment did not last. The America Cooper found on his return seemed far different from the Republic he remembered. Cooper felt that a new breed of individuals seeking only their own ends was threatening the bonds of community. His growing disaffection led him to attack American newspapers. He did so in an extended series of libel suits; in his characteriza-
tion of a newspaper editor, the disgusting Steadfast Dodge who appeared in *Homeward Bound* (1838) and *Home As Found* (1838); and in *The American Democrat* (1838), a short work of political criticism. In that work he wrote:

> If newspapers are useful in overthrowing tyrants, it is only to establish a
> tyranny of their own. The press tyrannizes over publick men, letters, the
> arts, the stage, and even over private life. Under the pretence of protecting
> publick morals, it is corrupting them to the core, and under the semblance
> of maintaining liberty, it is gradually establishing a despotism as ruthless, as
> grasping, and one that is quite as vulgar as that of any christian state known.
> With loud professions of freedom of opinion, there is no tolerance; with a
> parade of patriotism, no sacrifice of interests; and with fulsome panegyrics
> on propriety, too frequently, no decency.[3]

Perhaps this is suggestive of the state of the American press in the 1830s; more surely it represents a protest of established power against a democratized—in this case, middle-
class—social order. Cooper expressed a deep anxiety about the moral influence of the press which appeared to him to be "corrupting," "vulgar," and without decency. It had in his eyes the unwelcome characteristics of a middle-class institution: parochialism, scant regard for the sanctity of private life, and grasping self-interest. Most disturbing of all, it had enormous and unwarranted power over the shaping of opinion. Cooper's fears of a "press-ocracy" were exaggerated, but he was responding to real changes in American journalism. In 1830 the country had 650 weeklies and 65 dailies. The average circulation of a daily was 1,200, so the total daily circulation was roughly 78,000. By 1840 there were 1,141 weeklies and 138 dailies. The dailies averaged 2,200 in circulation for an estimated total daily circulation of 300,000. Population during the same period was also growing, but more slowly—from 12.9 million to 17.1 million, urban population

increasing from .9 million to 1.5 million.[4] But Cooper was not responding to statistics. He knew that newspapers were different, not just more numerous, than the ones he left behind in 1826, and those most different—the "penny papers"—appeared most powerful. The new journals reflected political, social, and technological changes that a thoughtful man might well have been alarmed about. It is now widely agreed that the 1830s, a remarkable decade in so many ways, marked a revolution in American journalism. That revolution led to the triumph of "news" over the editorial and "facts" over opinion, a change which was shaped by the expansion of democracy and the market, and which would lead, in time, to the journalist's uneasy allegiance to objectivity.

## The Revolution of the Penny Press

When Cooper left America, as when Tocqueville visited a few years later, the typical American paper was generally a weekly, but there were already many dailies in seaboard cities. The typical daily was four pages long. Its front page was almost exclusively devoted to advertising, and the fourth page likewise was strictly advertising. These outside pages were like the cover of a book or magazine—one turned to the inside to find the content of the paper. Page two carried the editorial columns. Much of page two and page three detailed the arrival of ships in the harbor and the contents of their cargoes, as well as other marine news. On page two one could find an editorial on politics, as well as short "items" of news. Many of the "items" were lifted directly from other newspapers, with credit generally given. Other items were not distinguished, in layout, typography, or style, from editorial—all were expressions of the editor or his party.

Some newspapers were primarily commercial, others were political. The political papers gave greater emphasis to news of national politics. They were financed by political parties, factions of parties, or candidates for office who dictated editorial policy and sometimes wrote the editorials personally. There was nothing deceptive about this—it was standard practice and common knowledge. The party papers were dependent on political leaders, not only for their initial capital and their point of view, but for maintenance through the paid publication of legal notices when the party they backed held power. Edwin Croswell ran the *Albany Argus*, the organ of the Democratic Party in New York, from 1824 to 1840, during which time he was also official state printer. This was the most lucrative post in the state; Croswell estimated it was worth $30,000 a year. Thurlow Weed of the *Albany Evening Journal* succeeded Croswell as state printer. He stated that he and his two partners grossed $50,000 in 1841, though Croswell put the figure at $65,000.[5]

The commercial press and the party press had several important features in common. First, they were expensive. A paper ordinarily cost the reader six cents an issue at a time when the average daily wage for nonfarm labor was less than eighty-five cents. But a person could not buy one issue at a time except at the printer's office. Newspapers were generally sold only by subscription, and annual subscriptions ranged from eight to ten dollars. Not surprisingly, circulation of newspapers was low, usually just one to two thousand for even the most prominent metropolitan papers. Newspaper readership was confined to mercantile and political elites; it is no wonder, then, that newspaper content was limited to commerce and politics.

This is not to say that these papers were staid or sedate. True, dominated as they were by advertising and shipping news, they appear to have been little more than bulletin boards for the business community. But their editorials, in which they took great pride, were strongly partisan, provocative, and ill-tempered. Editors attacked one another ferociously in print, and this sometimes carried over into fist fights or duels. The New York diarist Philip Hone recorded one such incident in 1831:

> While I was shaving this morning I witnessed from the front windows an encounter in the streets between William Cullen Bryant, one of the editors of the Evening Post, and Wm L Stone, editor of the Commercial Advertiser. The former commenced the attack by striking Stone over the head with a cowskin; after a few blows the parties closed and the whip was wrested from Bryant and carried off by Stone.[6]

Editing a newspaper was an intensely personal matter. Early newspapers were small operations. One man generally served as editor, reporter (insofar as there was any reporting at all), business manager, and printer. But the personal character of these early papers should not be misunderstood. Many editors were subservient to their political masters and, at the same time, very limited in their views on what was acceptable to put in print. "Journalists," wrote New York editor James Gordon Bennett's contemporary biographer, "were usually little more than secretaries dependent upon cliques of politicians, merchants, brokers, and office-seekers for their position and bread. . . ."[7] Not until the revolution in the press of the 1830s did the editor's ability to express himself in his newspaper grow, and then it grew in new directions—the editor made himself known, not only through editorials, but through the industry, enterprise, and innovation in his news gathering. Paradoxically, the newspaper became a more personal instrument at the same time that it began to emphasize news rather than editorial.

We can trace this development in a makeshift way by examining the names of newspapers in different periods. Before the 1830s, when newspapers sought the readership of commercial elites, they named themselves accordingly. In Boston, in 1820, the two dailies were *The Boston Daily Advertiser* and the *Boston Patriot and Daily Mercantile Advertiser*. In Baltimore, the dailies in 1820 were the *American and Commercial Daily Advertiser*, the *Federal Gazette and Baltimore Daily Advertiser*, the *Federal Republican and Baltimore Telegraph* (formerly the *Federal Republican and Commercial Gazette*), the *Morning Chronicle and Baltimore Advertiser*, and finally the *Baltimore Patriot and Mercantile Advertiser*. More than half of all newspapers published weekly or more frequently in New York, Boston, Baltimore, Philadelphia, Washington, Charleston, and New Orleans in 1820 had the words "advertiser," "commercial," or "mercantile" in their titles. But, after 1830, few newspapers were founded which bore such names. Instead, there were a great many papers whose names express a kind of *agency*—names like "critic," "herald," "tribune." One might also include as part of this development the papers named "star" or "sun," for both words suggest active objects which illuminate the world. So newspapers, if we can judge from their titles, became less passive, more self-consciously expressive of the editor's personality and convictions after 1830.[8]

The movement from "advertisers" to "heralds" and "suns" in the 1830s has been called the "commercial revolution" in the American press.[9] The "commercial revolution" refers not to all newspapers in the period but to those which most radically broke with tradition and established the model which the mainstream of American journalism has since followed. These were the "penny papers." As the name suggests, what was most obviously original about them is that they sold for a penny, not six cents. Further, rather than selling by annual subscription, they were hawked in the streets each day by news-boys. Their circulation was correspondingly enormous compared to the six-penny jour-nals. The first penny paper, the *New York Sun*, first published September 3, 1833, had the largest circulation of any paper in the city within a few months—by January, 1834, it claimed a circulation of 5,000. Within two years it was selling 15,000 copies a day. The *Sun* was quickly followed by two other penny papers in New York—the *Evening Transcript* and, on May 6, 1835, James Gordon Bennett's *New York Herald*. In June, 1835, the combined circulation of just these three papers was 44,000; when the *Sun* began in 1833, the combined circulation of all of the city's eleven dailies had been only 26,500.[10]

The penny press spread to the country's other urban, commercial centers—Boston, Philadelphia, and Baltimore. The *Boston Daily Times* appeared February 16, 1836, and within weeks was the city's largest paper, claiming a circulation of 8,000 by the middle of March. In Philadelphia, the *Philadelphia Public Ledger* began March 25, 1836, organized by William Swain and Arunah Abell, New York printers and friends of Benjamin Day, and their partner Azariah Simmons. The *Public Ledger*'s circulation was 10,000 within eight months, and 20,000 after eighteen months, at a time when the largest of the estab-lished dailies in the city sold about 2,000. The *Baltimore Sun* was founded in 1837 by Arunah Abell with the backing of his fellow *Public Ledger* proprietors. Within nine months its circulation was over 10,000, more than triple the circulation of any other Baltimore paper.[11]

The penny papers made their way in the world by seeking large circulation and the advertising it attracted, rather than by trusting to subscription fees and subsidies from political parties. This rationalized the economic structure of newspaper publishing. Sources of income that depended on social ties or political fellow feeling were replaced by market-based income from advertising and sales. Sales moved to a cash basis, and the old complaints of editors about subscribers who would not pay declined. Advertising, as well as sales, took on a more democratic cast. First, advertising in the established jour-nals, which heretofore had addressed the reader only insofar as he was a businessman interested in shipping and public sales or a lawyer interested in legal notices, increasingly addressed the newspaper reader as a human being with mortal needs. Patent medicines became the mainstay of the advertising columns.[12] "Want ads" became a more promi-nent feature of the papers; when P. T. Barnum moved to New York in the winter of 1834–1835 to find a job in a mercantile house, he conducted his job search by reading the "wants" each morning in the *Sun*.[13]

Second, advertising became more strictly an economic exchange, not a moral one: older journals had often refused to print ads for what they believed to be objectionable advertising. The *Journal of Commerce* in New York would not accept advertisements of theaters, lotteries, or "business to be transacted on the Sabbath." The *New England Palladium* in Boston followed a similar policy. The *New York Evening Post* banned lottery advertising and, by the late 1820s, this was fairly common. The penny press, in contrast, was not very fussy about who advertised in its columns. Penny papers were self-righteous in defending their wide-open practices:

> Some of our readers complain of the great number of patent medicines
> advertised in this paper. To this complaint we can only reply that it is for
> our interest to insert such advertisements as are not indecent or improper
> in their language, without any inquiry whether the articles advertised are
> what they purport to be. That is an inquiry for the reader who feels

interested in the matter, and not for us, to make. It is sufficient for our purpose that the advertisements are paid for, and that, while we reserve the right of excluding such as are improper to be read, to the advertising public we are impartial, and show no respect to persons, or to the various kinds of business that fill up this little world of ours. One man has as good a right as another to have his wares, his goods, his panaceas, his profession, published to the world in a newspaper, provided he pays for it.[14]

This comment from the *Boston Daily Times* could not better express a policy and a morality of laissez faire. In this, it was representative of the penny press. With an over-the-shoulder nod to propriety, the penny papers appealed to the equal right of any advertiser to employ the public press, so long as the advertiser paid. The self-righteousness of the penny papers, compared to the established press, was peculiarly inverted: they proudly denied their own authority or responsibility for exercising moral judgment in advertising matters and defended this position, without embarrassment, as consistent with their self-interest.

The six-penny papers criticized the penny press for its advertising policies and centered especially on the large number of patent medicine ads. Bennett's *Herald* was the special butt of this criticism. It became the object of abuse from penny papers as well, including Horace Greeley's penny *New York Tribune*, established in 1841, and Henry Raymond's penny *New York Times*, founded in 1851. These papers, it is fair to surmise, coveted Bennett's readership. Greeley criticized the *Sun* and the *Herald* in 1841 for taking the ads of New York's leading abortionist, Madame Restell. On the other hand, the *Tribune*'s columns were themselves filled with patent medicine advertising, and when a reader complained, Greeley wrote: "He should complain to our advertisers themselves, who are not responsible to us for the style or language (if decent) of their advertisements, nor have we any control over them."[15] In 1852 the *Times* wrote that the *Herald* was "the recognized organ of quack doctors."[16] This was, however, the narcissism of small differences: the same issue of the *Times*, for instance, included ads for "The American Mental Alchemist," Dr. Kellinger's Liniment, Doctor Houghton's Pepsin, and Ayer's Cherry Pectoral; both the *Times* and the *Herald* that day ran about two thirds of a column of medical ads. All the penny papers, to greater or lesser degrees, adopted the language and morality of laissez faire.

No less original than the economic organization of the new journalism was its political position. Most of the penny papers, including all of the pioneers in the field, claimed political independence, something that earlier papers rarely pretended to. James Gordon Bennett felt that this was closely tied to the economic design of the penny paper, the "nonsubscriber plan," as he called it, of selling on the streets. Only the penny press could be a free press, he wrote, "simply because it is subservient to none of its readers—known to none of its readers—and entirely ignorant who are its readers and who are not."[17] The penny papers were not only formally independent of political parties but were, relatively speaking, indifferent to political events. The *New York Sun*'s lead on a short item of congressional news was not unusual: "The proceedings of Congress thus far, would not interest our readers."[18] The *Sun* had announced in its first issue that its object was "to lay before the public, at a price within the means of everyone, all the news of the day, and at the same time afford an advantageous medium for advertising." No mention of politics. Early issues of the *New York Transcript* featured fiction on page one and inside focused on local items that rarely included politics. One issue, for instance, included short paragraphs on attempted rape, riot, attempted suicide, mail robbery, stingless bees from Mexico, and even news of an abandoned child left in a basket on a doorstep.[19] A year later, it should be added, articles were longer, there was more court reporting, and there was more news of national politics.

The *Transcript*, like some other penny papers, advertised its divorce from politics. The paper announced in its inaugural issue that, so far as politics goes, "*we have none.*" The *Boston Daily Times* claimed to be "neutral in politics" and advised political parties to find the way into the newspaper columns by advertising. The *Baltimore Sun* proclaimed:

> We shall give no place to religious controversy nor to political discussions of merely partisan character. On political principles, and questions involving the interests of honor of the whole country, it will be free, firm and temperate. Our object will be the common good, without regard to that of sects, factions, or parties; and for this object we shall labor without fear or partiality.[20]

While some penny papers failed, at least at first, to attend very much to politics at all, others covered politics more completely than the six-penny press, and just as vigorously. But even these papers, like the *New York Herald*, did not identify their mission or their hopes with partisan politics; to some extent, the world of parties became just a part of a larger universe of news. The penny papers were not all determined to be politically neutral. Horace Greeley's aim in establishing the *New York Tribune* in 1841 was to found "a journal removed alike from servile partisanship on the one hand and from gagged, mincing neutrality on the other."[21] But even Greeley's avowal of principled partisan politics supports the general point, for Greeley contrasts the *Tribune* to the "gagged, mincing neutrality" he surely associated with some of his penny rivals.

The penny press was novel, not only in economic organization and political stance, but in its content. The character of this originality is simply put: the penny press invented the modern concept of "news." For the first time the American newspaper made it a regular practice to print political news, not just foreign but domestic, and not just national but local; for the first time it printed reports from the police, from the courts, from the streets, and from private households. One might say that, for the first time, the newspaper reflected not just commerce or politics but social life. To be more precise, in the 1830s the newspapers began to reflect, not the affairs of an elite in a small trading society, but the activities of an increasingly varied, urban, and middle-class society of trade, transportation, and manufacturing. The six-penny papers responded to the penny newcomers with charges of sensationalism. This accusation was substantiated less by the way the penny papers treated the news (there were no sensational photographs, of course, no cartoons or drawings, no large headlines) than by the fact that the penny papers would print "news"—as we understand it—at all. It was common for penny papers, covering a murder trial, to take a verbatim transcript of the trial and spread it across most, or all, of the front page. What the six-penny press decried as immoral was that a murder trial should be reported at all. The typical news story was the verbatim report, whether it be of a presidential address, a murder trial, or the annual statement of the United States Treasury.

News became the mainstay of the daily paper. The penny papers did not depend on the usual trickle of stale news but sought out the news. They took pride in their activity, as the *New York Transcript* made clear in 1834:

There are eleven large and regularly established daily papers in this city; and with the exception of the *Courier and Enquirer*, and perhaps the *Times*, not one of them employs a news reporter, or takes any other pains to obtain accurate and correct local information—on the other hand there are two small daily NEWS papers, (ourselves and our cotemporary,) and those two employ four reporters, exclusively to obtain the earliest, fullest, and most correct intelligence on every local incident; and two of these latter arise at 3 in the morning, at which hour they attend the police courts, and are there employed, with short intermissions, till the close of the office at 8 in the evening, while others are obtaining correct information about the city.[22]

In 1835 the *Herald* joined the *Transcript* and its "cotemporary" the *Sun* and, by the end of 1837, boasted two Washington correspondents, permanent correspondents in Jamaica and Key West; occasional correspondents in London, Philadelphia, and Boston; two Canadian correspondents during the MacKenzie Rebellion of 1837; and a correspondent roving New York State to report on the wheat crop. This was expensive, the *Herald* noted, but it was done to gratify the public.[23] A year later the *Herald* had hired six European correspondents as regular contributors.[24]

The institution of paid reporters was not only novel but, to some, shocking. Until the late 1820s, New York coverage of Washington politics relied mainly on members of Congress writing occasionally to their home papers. Some regular "letter writers" passed on dull reports and summarized speeches. James Gordon Bennett, writing in 1827 and 1828 for the *New York Enquirer*, initiated more lively reporting with his dispatches on "the court of John Q. Adams."[25] Adams never accommodated himself to the impudence of the new journalism. He wrote with disgust in his diary in 1842 that sons of President Tyler "divulged all his cabinet secrets to a man named Parmalee and John Howard Payne, hired reporters for Bennett's *Herald* newspaper in New York. . . ."[26] His use of "hired" to qualify "reporters" suggests how new, and perhaps disreputable, the institution of a reportorial staff was.

One way to see the dominance of the newspaper by news, which the penny press initiated, is to regard it as the decline of the editorial. This is much less than the whole story, but it was one of the ways in which contemporaries understood the change they were witnessing. In an article in *North American Review* in 1866, Horace Greeley's biographer James Parton sought to explain the phenomenal success and influence of James Gordon Bennett's *New York Herald*. Parton reviewed current opinion about the *Herald*. One view was that the *Herald* rose to prominence because it was a very bad newspaper, pandering to the bad taste of the public. A second view, and Parton's own view, was that the *Herald* succeeded because it was a very good newspaper—but that the newspaper had become something different from what the *Herald*'s critics assumed it to be. Parton argued that people who thought the *Herald* a bad paper spoke mainly of its editorials which, he admitted, were execrable. Bennett was ornery, prejudiced, misanthropic, and opportunistic, and his editorials reflected his nature. But, Parton went on, the editorial is dying and only the news is the "point of rivalry" between papers. The success of a journal had come to depend "wholly and absolutely upon its success in getting, and its skill in exhibiting, the news. The word *newspaper* is the exact and complete description of the thing which the true journalist aims to produce."[27]

News was, indeed, the point of rivalry with the penny papers. We have so completely identified the concept of "news" with the newspaper itself that it may be difficult to understand how dramatic a change the penny press represented. Until the 1830s, a newspaper provided a service to political parties and men of commerce; with the penny press a newspaper sold a product to a general readership and sold the readership to advertisers. The product sold to readers was "news," and it was an original product in several respects. First, it claimed to represent, colorfully but without partisan coloring, events in the world. Thus the news product of one paper could be compared to that of another for accuracy, completeness, liveliness, and timeliness. The *Herald* in 1840 crowed over the accuracy and fullness of its report of a speech by Daniel Webster and ridiculed a Mr. Stansbury, reporting for a six-penny paper, who "knows nothing of stenography and wrote out some thirty or forty pages of small quarto foolscap, in long hand."[28] The *Herald* patted itself on the back, on one occasion, for having had the only reporter on the school-visiting trip of the City Council and School Fund commissioners and, on another, for having been the only paper in the city to print the United States Treasurer's report in full.[29] As for the timeliness of news, the *Herald* and the *Sun* rivaled each other in printing "extras" and praising themselves for it. The *Herald*, for instance, boasted on November 21, 1840, of its extra on the day before announcing the arrival of British forces in Canton: "*No other newspaper establishment in New York had the news at that time, nor could they get it, they are so inefficient and lazy.*"[30]

During the first decades of the nineteenth century, newspapers had increasingly tried to be up-to-date, especially in reporting the arrival of ships and in printing the news they brought with them. The New York papers began to send out small boats to incoming ships to gather up news; in the late 1820s, several papers formed an association which bought a fast boat to meet the ships for all association members. But only with the penny press was the competition for news "beats" firmly established as the chief basis of the newspaper business. Thanks to James Gordon Bennett, even advertising became more timely. Until the 1840s advertisers paid a flat fee, often on an annual basis, to place the same notice in a paper day after day. In 1847 Bennett announced that, beginning January 1, 1848, all ads in the *Herald* would have to be resubmitted daily. This encouraged changing ad copy so that Bennett's managing editor, Frederic Hudson, exclaimed in his history of American journalism:

> . . . the advertisements form the most interesting and practical city news. They are the hopes, the thoughts, the joys, the plans, the shames, the losses, the mishaps, the fortunes, the pleasures, the miseries, the politics, and the religion of the people. Each advertiser is therefore a reporter, a sort of penny-a-liner, he paying the penny. What a picture of the metropolis one day's advertisements in the *Herald* presents to mankind![31]

The penny papers' concept of news not only created news as a marketable product whose attributes—particularly timeliness—could be measured, it invented a genre which acknowledged, and so enhanced, the importance of everyday life. In literature until the eighteenth century, aristocratic conventions had dictated that the common aspects of everyday life could receive only comic treatment, if they were dealt with at all.[32] A similar convention appears to have prevailed in journalism—newspapers simply did not report on the lives of ordinary people. Although the War of 1812 ended the almost exclusive dominance of foreign news in the American press, local or hometown news, before the penny papers, remained a minor feature. The commercial press proved less reliable in reporting local prices of commodities or stocks than in reporting foreign news and shipping news.[33] The penny press, in contrast, focused on the nearby and the everyday, and for the first time hired reporters on a regular basis to cover local news. Reporters were assigned to the police, the courts, the commercial district, the churches, high society, and sports. The penny papers made the "human interest story" not only an important part of daily journalism but its most characteristic feature.

The penny papers saw news in ordinary events where no one had seen anything noteworthy before. This is nowhere better indicated than in those moments when even the most aggressive penny papers had a hard time claiming there had been any news. In an item headed "The News of the Week," the *Herald* of March 12, 1837 wrote:

> THE NEWS OF THE WEEK
> Is not of very much importance. Yet the most insignificant events can be swelled to matters of great moment, if they are traced up eternity to their causes, or down eternity to their consequences. Not a single incident—not the slightest event that does not become a part of the time past or the time to come, and thus mix with the greatest everlasting both in time and in space. The news of a day—of a week—is supposed by the superficial blockheads who conduct newspapers and govern nations—or cheat the public—or sell quack medicine—or stir up politics—or shave in Wall Street, to be of trifling moment. And so it is to them. To the philosopher who dips deeply into things, it is different.[34]

The penny papers inaugurated this democratic attitude toward the happenings of the world: any event, no matter how apparently trivial, might qualify for print in a newspaper.

The attention to everyday life did not necessarily mean attention to the familiar. The penny papers printed much that would appeal to the ordinary middle-class reader precisely because it was exotic—it concerned the everyday lives of other classes. Benjamin Day at the *Sun* pioneered the coverage of the criminal, especially in reporting police news. Bennett, from the *Herald*'s earliest days, reported on the social affairs of the elite of New York and Saratoga. As was usual with Bennett, he advertised his own innovation:

> No one ever attempted till now to bring out the graces, the polish, the elegancies, the bright and airy attributes of social life. We never can be an indepennent [*sic*], a happy, an original people, unless we rely on our resources, either for fashion, gaiety, politics, potatoes, flour, or manufactures. Our purpose has been, and is, to give to the highest society of New York a life, a variety, a piquancy, a brilliancy, an originality that will entirely outstrip the worn out races of Europe, who have been degenerating for the last twenty generations.[35]

Diarist Philip Hone recorded the presence of a *Herald* reporter at a fancy dress ball he attended in 1840. The host consented to the presence of the reporter, Hone wrote, because this imposed on the reporter "a sort of obligation . . . to refrain from abusing the house, the people of the house, and their guests, which would have been done in case of a denial." Hone continued: "But this is a hard alternative; to submit to this kind of surveillance is getting to be intolerable, and nothing but the force of public opinion will correct the insolence. . . ."[36] Public opinion was in no such mood. Bennett devoted most of page one to this ball, suggesting that it "created a greater sensation in the fashionable world than anything of the kind since the creation of the world, or the fall of beauteous woman, or the frolic of old Noah, after he left the ark and took to wine and drinking."[37]

The attention to the everyday, and particularly the focus on the social life of the rich, helped obscure the division of public and private life. For an editor like Bennett, little was privileged, personal, or private—though he was cautious enough in his reports on high society to use initials rather than names. Penny papers introduced news of family squabbles and scandals. While notices of marriages and deaths were familiar in newspapers, printing birth announcements was not. When the *Pittsburgh Daily Express* advocated the propriety of recording births in the papers, Bennett's sarcastic comment in the *Herald* indicated his approval, while protecting his flank of propriety: "Why, the practice would rouse up all the Miss Squeamishes in the country. It is no argument that they do such things in England; they do a great many things in England that would not suit here!"[38]

In February, 1848, a Washington correspondent for the *New York Tribune*, writing under the name "Persimmon," sketched the luncheon habits of Representative William Sawyer of Ohio. His article detailed how each day at two o'clock Sawyer moved from his seat in the House to a place behind and to the left of the Speaker's chair, near the window, and proceeded to take out his lunch. He would unfold a greasy paper and eat the bread and sausage it contained, wipe his hands on the paper, and throw the paper out the window. He used his jackknife for a toothpick and his pantaloons and coatsleeves for a napkin. Sawyer objected to this coverage and his friends succeeded in passing a resolution (119 to 46) ousting all *Tribune* reporters from their seats or desks on the House floor. "What was the offense of the 'Tribune,' after all?" asked the *Tribune* correspondent in a later article. "Nothing in the world but stating a few facts, not against the moral character of anybody, but about the personal habits of a member of the House."[39]

Shortly before this incident, the House had failed to censure the organ of the Democratic administration for calling a member of the House a liar. That was a kind of journalism they were used to. The new journalism of the penny press, on the other hand, ushered in a new order, a shared social universe in which "public" and "private" would be redefined. It is no wonder that this should have appalled those who believed the early days of the American Republic had re-established the elevated public realm of the Greek city-states and the Roman Forum. Something new was threatening this idyll, something Hannah Arendt refers to as the creation of *society*, "that curiously hybrid realm where private interests assume public significance."[40] Both meanings of interest—self-aggrandizement and curiosity—seem fitting here. With the growth of cities and of commerce, everyday life acquired a density and a fascination quite new, "society" was palpable as never before, and the newspapers—especially the penny papers—were both agent and expression of this change.

Granting that this fairly describes the changes in American journalism in the 1830s, what can account for it? Why did it happen? More precisely, why did it happen when and where it did? Recapitulating, what took place is that a cheap press originated in the 1830s in New York, a city which was already the national hub of interurban trade, transportation, and communication.[41] It quickly spread to the other leading urban centers—Boston, Philadelphia, and Baltimore. The new press was distinctive economically—in selling cheaply, in its distribution by newsboys, and in its reliance on advertising;

politically—in its claims to independence from party; and substantively—in its focus on news, a genre it invented. What accounts for all this?

These changes in journalism were closely connected to broad social, economic, and political change which I shall refer to as the rise of a "democratic market society." This meant the expansion of a market economy and political democracy or, put another way, the democratization of business and politics sponsored by an urban middle class which trumpeted "equality" in social life. To show that this is what was happening in the 1830s and to relate it to journalism is to do more than conclusive and compact evidence will allow. But there is much to make the case persuasive. It becomes all the more appealing when the inadequacies of likely alternative explanations are made plain. The two that require most attention are the technological argument and the literacy argument.

## Notes

1.  James Fenimore Cooper, *A Letter to His Countrymen* (New York: John Wiley, 1834), p. 11.
2.  George Dekker and Larry Johnston, "Introduction" in James Fenimore Cooper, *The American Democrat* (Baltimore: Penguin Books, 1969), p. 26.
3.  James Fenimore Cooper, *The American Democrat*, edited with an Introduction by George Dekker and Larry Johnston (Baltimore: Penguin Books, 1969), p. 183. Originally published 1838.
4.  Statistics on journalism in this period are from Alfred McClung Lee, *The Daily Newspaper in America* (New York: Macmillan, 1937), pp. 705–753.
5.  Glyndon G. Van Deusen, *Thurlow Weed* (Boston: Little, Brown, 1947), pp. 108, 360.
6.  Philip Hone, *The Diary of Philip Hone*, ed. Bayard Tuckerman, 2 vols. (New York: Dodd, Mead, 1889), I: 30 (April 20, 1831). Lambert A. Wilmer cataloged duels and fights between editors in his diatribe on the American press, *Our Press Gang* (Philadelphia: J. T. Lloyd, 1859), pp. 294–325.
7.  Isaac Clark Pray, *Memoirs of James Gordon Bennett* (New York: Stringer and Townsend, 1855), p. 84. Pray wrote this biography of Bennett under the name, "A Journalist." On Pray and his relation to Bennett, see William A. Croffut, *An American Procession 1855–1914* (Boston: Little, Brown, 1931), pp. 9–23.
8.  Newspaper names and dates of publication for this period can be found in Clarence S. Brigham, *History and Bibliography of American Newspapers 1690–1820* (Worcester, Mass.: American Antiquarian Society, 1947); and S. N. D. North, *The Newspapers and Periodical Press* (Washington: Government Printing Office, 1884).
9.  Walter Lippmann, "Two Revolutions in the American Press," *Yale Review* 20 (March 1931): 433–441.
10. Willard G. Bleyer, *Main Currents in the History of American Journalism* (Boston: Houghton Mifflin, 1927), p. 166.
11. Ibid., pp. 171–180. Bleyer's information comes from the newspapers' own claims of their circulation and so surely overestimates the actual circulation.
12. See James Harvey Young, *The Toadstool Millionaires* (Princeton: Princeton University Press, 1961); and James Harvey Young, *The Medical Messiahs* (Princeton: Princeton University Press, 1967), for a history of patent medicines in America.
13. P. T. Barnum, *Struggles and Triumphs: Or, Forty Years' Recollections of P. T. Barnum* (New York: American News, 1871), p. 67.
14. *Boston Daily Times*, October 11, 1837, quoted in Bleyer, *Main Currents*, p. 175.
15. *New York Tribune*, December 20, 1841, quoted in Bleyer, *Main Currents*, p. 217.
16. *New York Times*, July 17, 1852.
17. *New York Herald*, November 21, 1837.
18. *New York Sun*, December 9, 1833.
19. *New York Transcript*, July 4, 1834.
20. *Baltimore Sun*, quoted in Bleyer, *Main Currents*, p. 180.

21. Horace Greeley, *Recollections of a Busy Life* (New York: J. B. Ford, 1868), p. 137.

22. *New York Transcript*, June 23, 1834, quoted in Bleyer, *Main Currents*, p. 165. The "cotemporary" referred to is the *New York Sun*.

23. *New York Herald*, December 8, 1837.

24. Pray, *Memoirs*, p. 251.

25. James Gordon Bennett, quoted in Frederic Hudson, *Journalism in the United States* (New York: Harper and Brothers, 1872), p. 286. Bennett's self-report of his innovation is corroborated in Ben: Perley Poore's recollections, which recall Bennett's "lively" letters which "abounded in personal allusions" about politicians and their families as an important new development in Washington correspondence. Ben: Perley Poore, *Perley's Reminiscences of Sixty Years in the National Metropolis*, 2 vols. (Philadelphia: Hubbard Brothers, 1886), I:58.

26. John Quincy Adams, *The Diary of John Quincy Adams*, ed. Allan Nevins (New York: Frederick Ungar Publishing, 1969), p. 543.

27. James Parton, "The New York Herald," *North American Review* 102 (April 1866): 376.

28. *New York Herald*, September 30, 1840. Stansbury is Arthur J. Stansbury, an important figure in the early development of Washington correspondence, who wrote out his accounts of speeches with his own contractions of longhand. See L. A. Gobright, *Recollections of Men and Things at Washington During the Third of a Century* (Philadelphia: Claxton, Remson, and Haffelfinger, 1869), p. 401.

29. *New York Herald*, December 24, 1841.

30. *New York Herald*, November 21, 1840.

31. Hudson, *Journalism*, p. 470.

32. Erich Auerbach, *Mimesis* (Princeton: Princeton University Press, 1953), p. 31.

33. Frank Luther Mott, *American Journalism: A History 1690–1960* (New York: Macmillan, 1962), pp. 196–197.

34. *New York Herald*, March 12, 1837.

35. *New York Herald*, March 17, 1837.

36. Hone, *The Diary*, II:13. (February 25, 1840.)

37. *New York Herald*, March 2, 1840.

38. *New York Herald*, December 28, 1837.

39. Gobright, *Recollections of Men and Things*, pp. 73–76.

40. Hannah Arendt, *The Human Condition* (Garden City, N.Y.: Doubleday Anchor Books, 1958), p. 33.

41. New York's position as the focal point of the nation's commerce, transportation, and communication is documented in Allan R. Pred, *Urban Growth and the Circulation of Information: The United States System of Cities, 1790–1840* (Cambridge: Harvard University Press, 1973).

# Chapter 2

## KAY MILLS

## A PLACE IN THE NEWS

IN 1988, KAY MILLS, THEN AN EDITORIAL WRITER for *The Los Angeles Times* and a former assistant press secretary for Senator Edmond Muskie of Maine, published *A Place in the News*. It is a history of the role of women in journalism from 1783, starting when Elizabeth Timothy took over the *South Carolina Gazette* after the death of her husband, through to the 1980s. The book opens with an anecdote from 1966, when a man at *Newsweek* magazine implied to Mills that women were unsuited to be professional journalists because journalists needed to be able to pursue stories anywhere including being able to chase potential sources into men's rooms, if necessary. The ability to chase men into the bathroom or the locker room was an ongoing metaphor used to exclude women from certain beats.

A carefully researched work, *A Place in the News* documents women's long struggle to achieve professional equality in newsrooms. Mills argues that "There is a clear and current interaction between the women's movement, the presence of women on American newspapers, and the coverage of women by American newspapers." That interaction is the focus of the book. As women play an increasingly large role in the news and as women represent a larger and larger percentage of journalism students, it is essential to be aware of this history.

The excerpt surveys some of the women who were prominent in journalism before the door to the newsroom was pushed open more fully by women journalists of the 1970s and 1980s. Those featured range from the dozen or more women who printed newspapers in colonial times to Dorothy Thompson, the first woman to head a foreign news bureau and one of the preeminent foreign correspondents and columnists in America in the 1930s and 1940s. In fact, Thompson holds the badge of distinction of being the first American journalist to be expelled by Adolf Hitler in 1934.

## Publishers and Pundits

Debating women's place was a luxury few could afford in the American colonies and the young United States. Work was a family affair. Later, machinery took many jobs out of the home and into factories and offices. Labor was divided then—men outside the home, women inside. Wars, economics, education, and birth control eventually broke down some of that division.

In the eighteenth, nineteenth, and early twentieth centuries, women were always in the newspaper business, unlike some other fields. But they were so rare that the same names pop up over and over again in the histories. Elizabeth Timothy. Margaret Fuller. Jane Croly. Ida Wells Barnett. Nellie Bly. Dorothy Thompson. Cissy Patterson.

Contemporary scholars are restoring these and other women to the collective memory of the profession. This outline of their work illustrates that women entering the profession today are not standing on thin air. There is a foundation beneath them that has been laid by independent-minded women who felt the attraction of newspaper work, recognized how they could contribute to public information, and sometimes offered perceptive analyses of women's roles.

In journalism past as in journalism present, there were publishers and then the rest of us. Until recently, virtually no woman who was a publisher achieved that rank without being born into a publishing family or marrying into one. Men also inherited their publishing empires, like the Sulzbergers and Chandlers, Hearsts and McClatchys, or married into them, like Philip Graham and the first Chandler publisher. The critical difference is that men started those empires. Only when there were no male candidates did women become their leaders.

As America was being settled, as fields were cleared, communities built, businesses started, clothing stitched, and candles made, women worked alongside men. Work was split somewhat along gender lines, but it was done together, around the home. Newspapering could be family work, and in an era when disease and death struck early and often, it was sometimes women's work entirely.

More than a dozen women printed newspapers in colonial times, including Anna Maul Zenger, widow of John Peter Zenger, famous for his early defense of freedom of the press. The first American woman journalist was publisher Elizabeth Timothy. She and her husband Lewis, a French Huguenot, arrived in Philadelphia in 1731 from Rotterdam, and Lewis Timothy, who knew printing, went into business with Benjamin Franklin. In 1734, Franklin sent the Timothy family off to Charleston, South Carolina, to help with his developing journalistic empire there. Lewis Timothy was named editor of *The South Carolina Gazette*. His wife was busy with educating her growing family, which by 1738 included eight children. Then smallpox struck. Lewis Timothy died in December 1738. The next month the newspaper carried a notice that, in their son Peter's name, Elizabeth Timothy was taking over the paper. She hoped to make the paper "as entertaining and correct as may reasonably be expected." The widow Timothy was not the compositor her husband had been, but Ben Franklin found her a far better business partner. Her accounts were clearer, she collected on more bills, and she cut off advertisements if payments were not current. The *Gazette*'s content was much like that of other papers of its day: speeches by the governor, sermons, ship arrivals, local events, foreign correspondence (literally—it came by mail), and advertisements.

In November 1740, a devastating fire ripped through Charleston. The *Gazette* covered the event and for days thereafter served as a community bulletin board, carrying announcements of relocated businesses and pleas for housing for the homeless. In May 1746, Elizabeth Timothy turned full-time operation of the paper over to Peter. After he died in 1781, his widow Ann continued the family tradition by running the paper.[1]

Historians have paid little attention to the family contexts of American newspaper dynasties—especially to women who have worked alongside their better-remembered husbands. Eliza Otis, wife of the founder of the *Los Angeles Times* chain of leadership that has continued for a hundred years, often stepped in for her husband, Harrison Gray Otis, as his newspaper career developed. Studying Eliza as a "journalistic comrade," historian Susan Henry of California State University, Northridge, found that Otis's wife in essence ran *The Santa Barbara Press* for her husband when he became a U.S. Treasury agent in the Seal Islands off Alaska in 1879.[2] Her writing had already been appearing in the paper for three years, although she had little practical newspaper experience.

Eliza Otis believed in hard work, both to ease her lonely heart while her husband was away and to keep from being "a mere domestic machine." In the late nineteenth century, it became increasingly acceptable for women to write; that acceptability, combined with the necessity for frontier publishing families to work together setting type, folding newspapers, and selling advertisements, helps explain Eliza Otis's emergence as a partner in her husband's newspaper enterprises.

The couple moved to Los Angeles, where Otis was hired as editor and then became owner of the *Times*, while Eliza Otis wrote poetry for the paper as well as doing local reporting, a regular travel column, editorials, and household advice. Their daughter married a *Times* man, Harry Chandler, and the Chandler name has been on the paper's masthead ever since.

A handful of modern publishers also started with family ties to publishing. Helen Rogers was social secretary to Elizabeth Reid, wife of the publisher of *The New York Tribune*. She wed the Reids' son Ogden. Ogden inherited the *Tribune*, and Helen busied herself with the New York women's suffrage campaign. Soon, however, she started selling ads for the *Tribune* and proved to have far better managerial skills than her husband, an alcoholic.

Helen Rogers Reid became vice president of the newspaper and helped bring Walter Lippmann to the *Tribune*. "It was not politics, though," writes *Tribune* chronicler Richard Kluger, "but Helen Reid's lifelong feminism that provided the main conduit for her liberating and liberalizing influence on the Tribune."[3] She hired food writer Clementine Paddleford, whose descriptions made readers taste the food she was discussing and whose consumer suggestions helped them in practical matters. Helen Reid also made sure there were women in other departments, including Irita Van Doren as book editor. She brought Dorothy Thompson to the paper and later approved sending Marguerite Higgins to Europe during World War II. Reid's husband died in 1947. She was president of the company for six years until she turned the post over to her son.

Helen Reid had married into her newspaper dynasty; Eleanor (Cissy) Patterson was born into hers. Her grandfather, Joseph Medill, directed the *Chicago Tribune*; her father and brother were both editors of the *Tribune*. Brother Joe Patterson also founded the New York *Daily News* with her cousin, Col. Robert (Bertie) McCormick, who took over the *Tribune*. Cissy Patterson grew up to be a spoiled rich kid and fell in love with a handsome Polish nobleman. She married him despite his reputation as a philanderer but soon realized that she couldn't live with his indifference. Returning to America, she took up a dizzying party life in Washington but at 49 decided she wanted to do more with her life than exchange insults with Alice Roosevelt Longworth.

In 1930, she persuaded William Randolph Hearst to let her run *The Washington Herald*. Her only previous newspaper experience, other than listening to her beloved grandfather, her father, and her brother talk about their papers, had been in covering a murder trial for the New York *Daily News*. In a front-page editorial, she wrote that having a woman as editor shouldn't be odd. "Men have always been bossed by women anyway, although most of them don't know it." In a radio talk she added, "Perhaps a woman editor is resented because an editor is supposed to possess wisdom, and something in the masculine mind objects to the suggestion that a woman can know anything except what she has already been told by a man. . . . There is . . . no part of a newspaper management that need necessarily be beyond her power to control."[4]

In an era when newspapers were becoming more and more alike, Patterson's *Herald* had a distinctive voice, wrote her biographer, Ralph Martin. She created a gossipy feature, "Page 3," to which Washingtonians turned to "find out who was doing what to whom." In less than two years after Patterson took over the *Herald*, she was able to tell Hearst that she had built the paper into the largest morning circulation in Washington, some ten thousand papers ahead of her nearest competition. Hearst made her publisher as well as editor.

In 1932, as the Depression got worse, Patterson herself went out to see how the poor lived. She put on her shabbiest clothes—hard to find in a fashion plate's wardrobe—and was dropped by her limousine near the Salvation Army at 11:45 at night. She worked ten days on the series and got so caught up in her alter ego that she cried during job interviews. That series led her to undertake other investigations such as checking on hungry children and on the problems of the Bonus Army of veterans camping in Anacostia Flats.

She continued to hire women and urged them to do more. "Women are the best reporters in the world," she once said. "In regards to feature writing—by which I mean emotional writing—women from the very start have headed for first flight. I think men have shoved them out of many a position in which, to my mind, they could prove themselves superior."[5] Always insecure, Patterson turned increasingly to drugs and alcohol, Martin writes, and slowly her interest in her paper diminished. She died on July 14, 1948, at 67.

Her niece Alicia Patterson's career began more conventionally. Unable to talk his daughter out of going into the newspaper business, Joe Patterson gave her a job on the New York *Daily News* as a cub reporter. She muffed a divorce story—she got the names wrong—and as a result the paper faced a libel suit. She dabbled in journalism through the 1930s but concentrated more on flying and writing about it. She married Harry Guggenheim, heir to a paper fortune. Together they bought *The Nassau Daily Journal* in Hempstead on Long Island, New York.

Alicia Patterson was in full charge of the editorial side of the paper, which was renamed *Newsday* in a contest. (She joked that she wanted to call in the *Courier-Irritant*.) Its first issue appeared in 1940, the paper was thus in position when the New York suburbs boomed after World War II. It covered local news intensely and irreverently and investigated everything. In 1954 the newspaper won a Pulitzer Prize for exposing a construction union shakedown at Long Island harness racing tracks.[6]

Originally aimed at 15,000 circulation, *Newsday* had 375,000 readers by mid-1963, when Alicia Patterson died of bleeding ulcers. Journalists remember Alicia Patterson today for creating a fund for fellowships to permit them to travel and study.

At the same time, in Manhattan, Dorothy Schiff's *New York Post* was advocating "honest unionism, social reform and humane government programs." Schiff was devoted to politics—she switched from the Republican to the Democratic Party after hearing Franklin D. Roosevelt's "Rendezvous with Destiny" speech in 1936. Her devotion was reflected not only in the editorials but also in the coverage of news. Schiff was a working publisher who for several years wrote her own column, one of many in the *Post*. She had bought the paper at the suggestion of her husband, George Backer, in 1939, and became the *Post*'s publisher in 1942; in 1976, she announced the sale of the paper to Rupert Murdoch.[7]

In California, two women whose papers held opposite political views were propelled into their jobs through family connections, Eleanor McClatchy and Helen Copley. McClatchy had trained to be a playwright but became president of the McClatchy Newspapers—*The Sacramento Bee, The Fresno Bee, The Modesto Bee*, and later *The Anchorage Daily News*—in 1936, after her father died. A reticent woman, she used her papers to champion liberal causes and candidates. She died in 1980.[8]

Helen Copley, a secretary, married her boss and succeeded him as publisher of the arch-Republican *San Diego Union* and other Copley papers upon his death in 1973. Feeling shy and ill-equipped for her new role, Copley hired a speech instructor to drill her for public appearances. She thereafter worked on shifting the flagship San Diego paper into a more moderate political stance.

At her first national publishers' convention, Helen Copley received a call in her hotel room from Katharine Graham of *The Washington Post*. "I know what you're doing because I used to do the same thing. You're staring at the wall and planning to have dinner in your room," Graham said. They ate together that evening and talked about shared experiences.[9]

Katharine Graham moved into the publishing ranks after the death of her husband, Philip Graham. Her father had picked Philip Graham and not his daughter to succeed him at the helm of the *Post*. Phil Graham, a bright young man around Washington and adviser to Presidents, killed himself in 1965. Kay Graham, who had worked as a reporter in San Francisco after graduating from the University of Chicago, slowly emerged from her deferential shell and guided the paper through its severest test, Watergate. She has been president of the American Newspaper Publishers Association and was the first woman on the Associated Press Board of Directors. She remained chairman of the *Post*'s board after she turned the publishing job over to her son Donald in 1979.[10] If Americans know the name of one woman in journalism today, it is likely to be Kay Graham's.

These women did not get their jobs by reading the classified ads. They were clearly unlike the vast majority of working women. Until recently, many employed women worked only until they got married or because they were impoverished immigrant or minority women or genteel poor whose husbands had died. Or they were unmarried women whose families had no money to support them. They could aspire to becoming teachers, nurses, or secretaries; many were restricted to work as domestics or waitresses.

A few women, all of an especially independent strain, broke society's restraints, often with the inadvertent help of fathers who had educated them too well to be content with embroidering doilies. Some of these women were early feminist leaders like Elizabeth Cady Stanton. Others were journalists.

Margaret Fuller's dour father saw to it that she was widely read. Timothy Fuller had his daughter reading Latin when she was six and Shakespeare at eight. She learned Greek,

French, Italian, and German. Her knowledge was not wasted. When her father died in 1835, Margaret Fuller went to work teaching at Bronson Alcott's progressive, experimental school in Boston.

Fuller was soon moving among the intellectual giants of the day—Ralph Waldo Emerson, William Ellery Changing, Theodore Parter, Henry David Thoreau. This group held endless discussions on moral and literary topics; the editor of its journal, *The Dial*, a woman treated with equality in a circle of intellectual men, was Margaret Fuller. Fuller also presided over philosophical conversations in women's homes. In her book *Woman in the Nineteenth Century*, Fuller wrote that women, like men, should be educated and have the same opportunities. A mild plea today, it was radical in its age.

More than her feminism and social analysis, however, her colorful descriptions and her interview style caught the eye of pioneering *New York Tribune* editor Horace Greeley, who hired her as his paper's literary editor. Initially, Greeley criticized Fuller for writing in a ponderous Germanic style. Eventually, he called her "the most remarkable, and in some respects, the greatest, woman America has yet known."[11] Central Park was a goat pasture when Margaret Fuller arrived in New York. She soon became a reporter as well as the *Tribune*'s literary editor. She wrote about conditions for prostitutes imprisoned at Sing Sing or the insane shunted away in corners at the asylum on Blackwell's Island. When Fuller's long-sought chance to travel abroad finally came, she was not as excited as she might have been earlier in her life, feeling that her mind and character were already formed. Nonetheless, she recognized the importance of a foreign tour. "I feel that, if I persevere, there is nothing to hinder my having an important career even now. But it must be in the capacity as a journalist, and for that I need this new field of observation."[12]

At 36, Margaret Fuller sailed for Europe. From England, she wrote home about the new parks and public libraries for the workers of Manchester. She observed that there was a woman "nominally, not really" in charge of a Liverpool education institute. In France she inspected the crèches of Paris—day-care centers where working mothers could leave their children. Her most sustained foreign coverage was of the Italian edition of the revolutions of 1848. Despite the political ferment and despite her personal ferment in a romance with an Italian marchese, Giovanni Angelo Ossoli, whom she may or may not have married (that tidbit of history has never been clear), Fuller did not neglect observations about women.

Anticipating feminists' frustrations a century later, Fuller said in a dispatch from Rome: "I am very tired of the battle with giant wrongs, and would like to have some one younger and stronger arise to say what ought to be said, still more to do what ought to be done. Enough! If I felt these things in privileged America, the cries of mothers and wives beaten at night by sons and husbands by their diversion after drinking, as I have repeatedly heard them these past months . . . have sharpened my perception as to the ills at woman's condition and the remedies that must be applied. Had I but genius, had I but energy, to tell what I know as it ought to be told! God grant them to me, or some other more worthy woman, I pray."[13]

Fuller covered politics and war in Italy, writing of class conflicts sure to come as Italy became a state and of the Pope's loss of political influence within Italy. Fuller survived the shelling of Rome by the French but drowned with Ossoli and their young son in a shipwreck within sight of Fire Island, New York, on a trip home.

Jane Cunningham Croly became a journalist and reformer under the pen name Jennie June. Like Fuller, she received her early education from her father, in his library in Wappinger's Falls, New York. Like Fuller, Cunningham had to go to work after her father died and left her virtually penniless at 25. And like Fuller, Cunningham wrote her first newspaper articles for *The New York Tribune*. She used the name Jennie June to hide her real identity—journalism was still no place for a lady.

Her husband was sickly and there was not enough money for their large family, so Jennie June wrote fashion, drama, straight news, and advice over the next forty years. She concentrated much of her editorial advice on sensible fashions and proper eating habits for women as well as on opening new careers for women in bookkeeping, teaching, nursing, and secretarial work. "It is somewhat ironic," writes historian Sharon M. Murphy, "that she used her influence to promote as careers for women the very types at work in which many modern-day women now find themselves trapped. But at the time she was writing, she was pressing for horizons then unfamiliar to many of her readers."[14]

When Charles Dickens visited New York City in 1868, the New York Press Club held a banquet at Delmonico's for the famous author. Jennie June, by then one of the country's best-known writers, was denied a ticket. In reaction, June and other literary women formed their own club, Sorosis. One hundred years later, Jennie June's feminist descendants were still fighting for admission to male-only groups like the National Press Club.

Jennie June insisted on being judged on the quality of her work alone, saying, "There is no sex in labor, and I want my work taken as the achievement of an individual with no qualifications, no indulgence, no extenuations simply because I happen to be a woman, working along the same line with men."[15]

For years, if there was a woman on a newspaper who didn't write on fashion and food, she was the paper's "stunt girl." The most legendary stunt girl of them all was Elizabeth Cochrane Seaman—pen name, Nellie Bly.

Born in 1865, Elizabeth Cochrane lived with her mother in a series of boarding houses in Pittsburgh after her father died; there Cochrane learned life was hard for women alone. Reading a *Pittsburgh Dispatch* editorial arguing that girls should stay home and not seek careers or the vote, Cochrane wrote a rebuttal that women had a right to seek interesting lives. The editor printed her article. She then wrote another—on divorce, not a popular topic in those days—and the editor hired her at five dollars a week in 1885. She called herself Nellie Bly, after a Stephen Foster song, "She was a reformer who wanted to go out among the poor, into the tenements and factories, first-hand, talking with people, especially immigrants," writes historian Madelon Golden Schilpp.[16]

Later, for *The New York World*, Bly feigned insanity to expose conditions at the mental asylum on Blackwell's Island. She checked into a seedy hotel, pretended that she had just arrived from Cuba and spoke little English, and became so irrational that the matron called the police. Three medical experts found she was suffering from dementia, so off she went to Blackwell's Island. Other papers carried the story of her commitment, not knowing it was a gimmick by the *World*.

In the asylum, Bly was appalled at the way patients were treated. Buckets of ice water were thrown on patients for a bath, and the food was garbage. After a week, publisher Joseph Pulitzer's lawyer finally sprang her. Then she did a front-page finale to the story, calling the asylum a "human rat trap."[17] She also posed as a poor working girl to expose sweatshops. She stole fifty dollars from a woman's purse to see how women were treated in jail. She even played a chorus girl, complete with scanty outfit.

Bly's most famous stunt was her attempt to beat the fictional record "set" in *Around the World in 80 Days*. Her editors were reluctant to let a lone woman undertake such a journey. They relented but then worried that she would need too much baggage. Bly took one satchel and a pocket watch set to New York time. With headlines blaring about a "Feminine Phileas Fogg," Bly set off on November 14, 1889. She became America's sweetheart, a merchandiser's bonanza worthy of E. T. There were, historian Schlipp notes, Nellie Bly games, Nellie Bly clothes, Nellie Bly songs. After twenty-four days the *World* received her first cheerful dispatch about her seven-day sail across the Atlantic. From England, she detoured to Amiens in France to meet Fogg's creator, Jules Verne, at his elegant estate.

Off she hurried to the Mediterranean, Port Said, Ceylon, Singapore, and Hong Kong. Monsoon rains buffeted her ship en route. The *World*'s circulation rose as readers followed her bargaining in the markets, looking at Buddhist relics, witnessing a Chinese funeral. Then came the turbulent trip home, when some in the crew wanted to throw Bly's pet monkey overboard. They considered it a jinx. Finally the ship steamed into San Francisco Bay. Nellie Bly and the monkey headed for the welcoming reception, then boarded a special train that the *World* had hired to take her east. When Bly arrived in Jersey City, the timers called out "Seventy-two days, six hours, ten minutes, and eleven seconds."

It was a hard act to follow. Bly kept reporting, doing stories on anarchist Emma Goldman and on the Pullman strike in Chicago. She left the newspaper business when she married Robert Seaman, a wealthy man more than twice her age. Less than ten years later, Seaman died. His widow took over his hardware business, only to lose it to dishonest employees. After World War I, the Nellie Bly byline reappeared because the widow Seaman badly needed money. Hired by her old friend Arthur Brisbane, Nellie Bly worked quietly in a corner, handling a column on abandoned children for *The New York Evening Journal*. She died three years later of pneumonia. In her obituary the *Evening Journal* said simply, "She was the best reporter in America."[18]

There were stunt girls and there were sob sisters. One of the first of the latter breed was Annie Laurie, whose real name was Winifred Black. Her first story for the *San Francisco Examiner* in 1889 was overwritten. Her editor told her, "We don't want fine writing in a newspaper. There's a gripman on the Powell Street line—he takes his car out at three o'clock in the morning, and while he's waiting for the signals he opens the morning paper. It's still wet from the press, and by the light of his grip he reads it. Think of him when you're writing a story. Don't write a single word he can't understand and wouldn't read."[19]

Soon, like Nellie Bly, Winifred Black was dressing as a bag lady (before anyone coined the phrase) to check on conditions among women at a San Francisco hospital. In preparation, she asked a doctor she knew to drop belladonna into her eyes so that she would look desperate. (Belladonna, a drug made from the deadly nightshade plant, was used as a narcotic and dilated the pupils.) Black then wandered along Kearny Street and fell to the ground. She was tossed roughly into a prison horse cart, bounced at full speed over cobblestones, pulled from the wagon, and dragged into the hospital. After being treated with an emetic of mustard and hot water, she was pushed back on the street. Her story brought a furious reaction from the hospital, a governor's inspection, the firing of many on the hospital staff, and the beginning of ambulance service in San Francisco.[20] Black also did stories on a leper colony in Molokai and on conditions in cotton mills and fruit canneries—all in punchy sentences with emotional impact. She was the first reporter from outside to reach Galveston after it was struck by a tidal wave that washed away much of the city. Disguising herself as a boy because she knew no woman could get through, she stepped over bodies and wrote about people so dazed they barely knew what had happened. She helped organize relief efforts. Later, she was in Denver when she saw headlines about the San Francisco earthquake. A succinct telegram from her boss, William Randolph Hearst, read: "Go."[21]

Trials brought out women reporters in force. Winifred Black missed few in forty years. One of the most famous was the trial of Harry Thaw, who was accused of killing famed architect Stanford White for his attentions to his wife, Evelyn Nesbit Thaw. Dorothy Dix, Ada Patterson, and Nixola Greeley-Smith covered that trial with Black. At this trial, according to Ishbel Ross, a famous phrase was born: "A cynical colleague, looking a little wearily at the four fine-looking girls who spread their sympathy like jam, injected a scornful line into his copy about the 'sob sisters.' " The sob sisters' function, as Ross defined it in *Ladies of the Press*, "was to watch for the tear-filled eye, the widow's veil, the quivering lip, the lump in the throat, the trembling hand. They did it very well."[22]

Dorothy Dix not only covered trials, she was an early "Dear Abby," writing one of the first personal advice columns. Her real name was Elizabeth Meriwether Gilmer, and she was another who as a girl was encouraged to use her family's fine library, making her a confirmed bookworm. Her husband developed an incurable mental illness, so she went to work freelancing and was hired by *The New Orleans Picayune*. William Randolph Hearst, who in his neverending battles to boost circulation advanced women's careers as much as anyone in the early days of the twentieth century, hired her away from the *Picayune*. She covered Carrie Nation's saloon-smashing tour of Kansas as well as murder trials. In her columns, Dix counseled people to take charge of their own lives, supported women's right to vote, and campaigned for women's education and employment.[23]

However one defined it, news received a different slant from some women from their earliest professional days. In part, that was because women could get into places where men would have been suspect. They could get victims to talk more readily. So they had different information and wrote different stories. Those who succeeded also dared to be different because they had little to lose and they weren't going to get the job or be able to do it if they didn't have a gimmick such as going around the world or exploring the seamy side of life.

The press was blatantly biased; objectivity was rarely prized. If people didn't like what they read in one paper, they could buy another. Big cities had four, five, sometimes even ten competing papers. Reporters—male and female—readily adopted causes, and for some those became more important than their careers.

Ida Wells-Barnett was the daughter of an emancipated slave and grew up in Holly Springs, Mississippi. She challenged segregation early, at 22: a train conductor tried to make her go into a smoking car with the rest of the black passengers. She refused and bit the conductor's hand. She sued over her treatment and won in circuit court, but the state supreme court reversed the decision.

Like many women of the era, Wells-Barnett got into journalism by freelancing. She wrote an article for a black church weekly about her fight with the railroad. The editor of the Negro Press Association hired her to write for his paper, and she went to Washington. Then she was offered a share in the ownership as well as the editorship of a small paper in Memphis, *The Free Speech and Headlight*. She wrote about poor conditions in black schools and was fired from a teaching job, so she went into journalism full time. In 1892, three black Memphis grocery store operators were lynched—mutilated and shot to death—possibly because their store was draining off business from white store owners. Wells-Barnett wrote outraged articles. While she was out of town, local racists ransacked and destroyed her newspaper office.

Friends warned her that her life would be in danger if she went back to Memphis. So she started working for *The New York Age* but vowed to fight against lynching all her life. She did. She was a founder of the National Association for the Advancement of Colored People and a suffragist.[24]

Josephine Herbst's life paralleled the intellectual currents of the twentieth century. She was a bohemian in the 1920s, knee deep in Communist Popular Front activity in the 1930s, withdrawn from public life in the 1940s and 1950s, and ultimately revived by the social turmoil of the 1960s. In radical literary circles in New York in the 1920s, Herbst wrote mainly fiction at first, producing a trilogy of novels that only thinly disguised her own family history. In the 1930s she gave more time to journalism, writing about the midwestern farmers' strikes, an uprising in Cuba, German resistance to Hitler, and the Spanish Civil War for publications as varied as the *New York Post* and *New Masses*.[25]

Call it social notes or call it gossip, but intrigues and innuendoes have always been rich newspaper content. Washington and Hollywood are the richest mines, places that thrive on personalities as well as politics. Gossip has a long lineage in Washington, going back to the days of Anne Royall, considered by many historians one of the first women to establish her own reportorial reputation.

After finding a niche as a travel writer to "new" places like Alabama, Royall settled in Washington in 1830 to publish a four-page newspaper. She was already notorious from being tried the year before on charges of being a common scold—she had sworn at a group of evangelists harassing her. Now Royall turned her paper's attention to exposing Washington nepotism and scandal. The stories bore Royall's unmistakable gossipy style. Few people were neutral about her reporting.[26]

Not were residents of the other intrigue center—Hollywood—neutral about the reporting of Louella Parsons and Hedda Hopper decades later. Parsons started in Chicago, then went to New York and in 1923 became movie editor for *The New York American*, owned by William Randolph Hearst. Two years later he made her movie editor for his Universal News Service, and she moved to Hollywood in 1926.

Parsons became powerful because she had Hearst's influence behind her. She could make or break stars; her columns talked about their private lives as well as their public careers. She considered her two greatest scoops to be the breakup of the marriage of Douglas Fairbanks and Mary Pickford in 1935 and Ingrid Bergman's pregnancy in 1949 as a result of her affair with Italian director Roberto Rossellini. Parsons's power faded in the late 1950s, when she lost touch with the younger film stars and the rock music world that was changing the tone of the times.[27]

Hedda Hopper, Parsons's chief rival, started as an actress; she ran away from home to join a theatrical troupe after the eighth grade. She appeared in many of the hastily made films of the 1920s for M-G-M and then took up writing because the studio executives wanted to create competition for Louella Parsons. They thought Hopper could be controlled.

Benign at first, Hopper's column took off when it started reporting scandals and divorces. Hopper scooped Parsons on the divorce announcement of James Roosevelt, the President's eldest son. She called her house in Beverly Hills "the house that fear built." Known for her flamboyant hats, Hopper got her tips where she could. She learned, for example, that Clark Gable was entering the Air Force from the dentist who was fixing his teeth so he could pass the physical. After the war, Hopper became increasingly conservative and urged a boycott of films by writers, actors, and directors with Communist connections. She helped persuade Richard Nixon to run against Helen Gahagan Douglas for Congress in the race that launched his national political career. She praised J. Edgar Hoover and Ronald Reagan so often that some newspapers refused to run her column, saying that it was supposed to be about movies and not politics.[28]

Gossip and gore weren't women's only realm. Although there were still many stubborn holdouts that refused to hire women, some papers had at least one woman reporter, a few of whom covered politics, social issues, and foreign affairs. Among them were Sigrid Arne, Genevieve Herrick, and Dorothy Thompson.

Sigrid Arne grew up in Cleveland and knew at age 6 that she wanted to be a writer. By high school she had focused her attention on newspaper writing. In the 1920s Arne worked for papers in Muskogee, Oklahoma, Oklahoma City, Detroit, and Cleveland, then joined the Associated Press in Washington in 1933.

While she was working in Oklahoma City, Arne set out to expose that babies were being peddled like groceries. Using a marked fifty-dollar bill, she "bought" a twenty-four-hour-old baby boy and then wrote a series of articles exposing the racket. She hoped the Oklahoma legislature would appropriate money for child care to allow women to keep their children. Instead, she wrote, "They voted $100,000 for tick eradication." Long before John Steinbeck's *The Grapes of Wrath* took the Joads from Oklahoma to California, Arne wrote a fourteen-part series in 1929 showing the plight of real people in real places. At the start of the New Deal, Arne went to Washington. She wrote about National Recovery Administration codes governing various industries and about the Social Security Act. Studying the NRA code for the textile industry, she realized that textile prices would increase dramatically, so she went out and bought a huge supply of linens, curtains, and other household products—a supply she was still using years later. For her Social Security Act stories, she pasted up sheets and sheets of paper to chart how much money workers might expect to receive. She had hundreds of questions for government officials, who had to study Arne's chart themselves before they could give her answers.

She covered the Bretton Woods international monetary conference in July 1944 and the United Nations conference in 1945 for the AP. She wrote everything from a comprehensive study of postwar planning to the annual Christmas fiction story. As it customarily did with women, the Associated Press retired Sigrid Arne at 55. Beth Campbell Short, who worked with Arne, called her the model of a conscientious, smart reporter.[29]

Genevieve Forbes Herrick covered police and politics and showed that the woman's angle could be front page news. Herrick consistently paid attention to women in politics, and according to historians Linda Steiner and Susanne Gray of Governors State University in Chicago, "her work was instructive to newly enfranchised women readers trying to define their political goals and responsibilities."

Herrick became a reporter for the *Chicago Tribune* in 1921. To investigate conditions on Ellis Island, Herrick disguised herself as an immigrant and traveled from Ireland to America. The *Tribune* published a splashy thirteen-part series on her trip that led to a House investigation of corruption and cruelty within the U.S. Immigration Service.

Best known for her crime reporting, Herrick covered such headline events as the 1924 Leopold-Loeb trial. But she also did a series of articles on Rep. Ruth Hanna McCormick, who ran for the Senate in 1930, and about women delegates to national political conventions. In 1928 she wrote a twelve-part series on the intersection of society and politics in the nation's capital, calling it "Washington—Democracy's Drawing Room." Ultimately, her friendship with Eleanor Roosevelt got her in trouble with *Tribune* publisher Robert McCormick. He accused her of being "socially subsidized" by Mrs. Roosevelt, whose politics he abhorred. Herrick quit and turned to magazine writing.

Herrick's contribution was to explain to readers the ambitions of activist women, according to Steiner and Gray. "Presumably these articles promoted understanding on the part of male readers unused to seeing women active in political life apart from specific reform movements."[30]

Dorothy Thompson's name appears on any list of the most famous women in American journalism. She was sufficiently famous and forthright to be the subject of *New Yorker* cartoons, to be the first reporter thrown out of Hitler's Germany, and to help make the political candidacy of Wendell Willkie in 1940. Dorothy Thompson's professional skills and force of personality created that fame. Yet sometimes she could not reconcile her public role with the role of happy wife that she thought she wanted. Throughout three marriages—including one to author Sinclair Lewis—she wrestled with conflicting desires to throw her things in a suitcase and undertake new adventures or to foster an environment in which creative men could work. The former won out more often.

After graduation in 1914 from Syracuse University—where she was notorious for what became a lifelong habit of monopolizing conversations—Thompson worked for the suffrage movement. In 1920 she and a friend sailed for Europe, where Thompson worked for the Red Cross and freelanced for the *New York Post* and *The Christian Science Monitor*. She wrote articles without pay from Vienna for *The Philadelphia Public Ledger* until she had done so many pieces that the paper hired her as a full-time correspondent. She covered nine European countries and always seemed to be at the right place at the right time. Or so she told people, promoting her own legend. She disguised herself as a Red Cross nurse to interview the grandnephew of Franz Joseph, who wanted to reestablish the Hapsburg throne. By 1924 she was the *Ledger*'s Berlin bureau chief, covering the swirling economic and political controversies of the Weimar Republic. She was the first woman to head a major American news bureau overseas.

After a brief retirement during her marriage to Lewis, Thompson returned to Europe and interviewed Adolf Hitler, who was not yet chancellor but already the Nazi Party leader. She wrote a book about the experience, beginning it by saying, "When I walked into Hitler's salon, I was convinced that I was meeting the future dictator of Germany. In less than 50 seconds I was sure I was not. It took me just that time to measure the startling insignificance of this man who had set the world agog." She said Hitler was "inconsequent and voluble, ill-poised, insecure."[31] But Thompson soon changed her judgment of Hitler and started warning Americans of fascism and decrying American isolationism.

William Shirer, reporting from Berlin at the time, recalled Thompson's expulsion from Germany by Hitler in 1934. Thompson was taken to the train station under police escort and sent out of the country because Hitler was enraged about what she had written in her book.[32] Thompson returned to the United States and wrote on fascism for *Foreign*

*Affairs*. In 1936 she began writing a column for *The New York Herald-Tribune* at Helen Reid's insistence. A cover story in *Time* magazine proclaimed Thompson and Eleanor Roosevelt "undoubtedly the most influential women in the U.S."

At odds with President Roosevelt's liberal New Deal social policies, Thompson boosted Wendell Willkie's nomination for President in 1940; then she changed her mind because she decided that Roosevelt's world leadership was more important than his faulty domestic policies. The *Herald-Tribune*, which was pledged to Willkie's candidacy, cancelled her contract the next year.

Thompson's greatest contributions to journalism seemed to be behind her. Marion Sanders, her biographer, feels that Thompson lost her greatest cause once the United States entered the war. "Politically," a friend of Thompson's told Sanders, "she was like a great ship left stranded on the beach after the tide has gone out."[33]

Little ties together these women in the history of journalism except the fact of their being separate from the rest of women in their day, of their being different from other journalists. But their stories form an important backdrop against which to observe the emergence of women in journalism that accelerated in the 1930s through today.

---

## Everyday Indignities

Flora Lewis, now a foreign affairs columnist for *The New York Times,* was covering the first meeting of the United Nations Security Council in London years ago. "A big issue was the U.S. effort to make the Soviet forces withdraw from Azerbaijan (northern Iran), and there was tension between the U.S. and the Soviets.

"Edward Stettinius, then secretary of state, suddenly got up from the table and strode out. Several of us in the press gallery went running downstairs to follow him, thinking there might be an important development. I chased down the hall with the others and saw them go through a door. It was only at the last moment that I noticed it had a sign, 'MEN.'

"My male colleagues roared with laughter when I complained that they had taken unfair advantage. A couple were good enough to brief me on the meaningless things Stettinius had said."

---

## Notes

1.  Schlipp and Murphy, *Great Women*, pp. 1–11.
2.  Susan Henry, "Journalistic Comrade: Eliza Otis and the Beginnings of a Newspaper Dynasty" (Paper prepared for the Association for Education in Journalism and Mass Communication, August 1986).
3.  Kluger, *The Paper*, p. 286. See also Alden Whitman's article on Helen Reid in *Notable American Women: The Modern Period* (Cambridge, Mass: The Belknap Press of Harvard University Press, 1980), pp. 574–75.
4.  Ralph Martin, *Cissy* (New York: Simon and Schuster, 1979), p. 272.
5.  Ibid., p. 338.
6.  "Alicia Patterson Is Dead at 56," *The New York Times*, July 3, 1963, p. 27; "Alicia Patterson," *The New York Times* editorial, July 6, 1963; "This Is The Life I Love," by Alicia Patterson as told to Hal Burton, *The Saturday Evening Post*, February 21, 1959, p. 19; *Editor and Publisher*,

July 13, 1963, p. 11; *Current Biography*, 1955, pp. 474–76; and James Boylan's entry on Alicia Patterson in *Notable American Women*, pp. 529–31.

7. *Current Biography*, 1965, pp. 364–66; Deirdre Carmody, "Dorothy Schiff Agrees to Sell Post to Murdoch, Australian Publisher," *The New York Times*, Nov. 20, 1976, p. 1; Wolfgang Saxon, "The New York Post Has a Long History," *The New York Times*, Nov. 20, 1976, p. 29.

8. *Time*, Nov. 3, 1980, p. 103; Richard West, "Grace McClatchy Dies; Headed Papers," *Los Angeles Times*, Oct. 18, 1980, p. 24 (McClatchy's full name was Grace Eleanor McClatchy).

9. Gail Sheehy, "Cinderella West: California's Unknown New Queen of the Press," *New West*, May 24, 1976, pp. 50–69. See also Alexander Auerbach, "Helen Copley: Novice Takes Firm Control," *Los Angeles Times*, Jul. 19, 1975, p. 1; and Terry Christensen and Larry Gerston, "The Rise of the McClatchys and Other California Newspaper Dynasties," *The Californians*, Sept.–Oct. 1983, pp. 8–24.

10. David Halberstam wrote at length about Kay and Philip Graham in *The Powers That Be* (New York: Alfred A. Knopf, 1979). See also Jane Howard's "The Power That Didn't Corrupt," *Ms.*, Oct. 1974, p. 47.

11. Schlipp and Murphy, *Great Women*, p. 49, quoting from William Harlan Hale's 1950 biography, *Horace Greeley: Voice of the People*.

12. Letter from Margaret Fuller to Samuel Ward, March 3, 1845, cited in Bell Gale Chevigny, *The Woman and the Myth* (Old Westbury, N.Y.: The Feminist Press, 1976), p. 295.

13. Ibid., p. 465.

14. Schlipp and Murphy, *Great Women*, p. 88.

15. Ibid., p. 93.

16. Ibid., p. 135.

17. Ibid., p. 138.

18. Ibid., p. 147. Ross's *Ladies of the Press* also discusses Nellie Bly at length.

19. Schlipp and Murphy, *Great Women*, p. 149.

20. Ibid., p. 150.

21. Ross, *Ladies*, p. 63.

22. Ibid., p. 65–66.

23. Schlipp and Murphy, *Great Women*, pp. 112–20. See also Margaret Culley's article on Dorothy Dix in *Notable American Women*, pp. 275–77.

24. Schlipp and Murphy, *Great Women*, pp. 121–32.

25. Elinor Langer, *Josephine Herbst* (Boston: Atlantic–Little Brown, 1983), as well as Langer's article on Herbst in *Notable American Women*, pp. 333–35.

26. Schlipp and Murphy, *Great Women*, pp. 21–36.

27. Paula Fass on Parsons in *Notable American Women*, pp. 527–529. See also Dorothy Townsend, "Louella Parsons, 1st Hollywood Gossip Queen, Dies at 91," *Los Angeles Times*, Dec. 10, 1972, p. 1; Murray Illson, "Louella Parsons, Gossip Columnist, Dies," *The New York Times*, Dec. 10, 1972; *Current Biography*, 1942, pp. 631–32.

28. George Eells's entry on Hedda Hopper in *Notable American Women*, pp. 350–51. See also *Current Biography*, 1942, pp. 391–92; "Hedda Hopper, Columnist, Dies; Chronicled Gossip of Hollywood," *The New York Times*, Feb. 2, 1966, p. 32.

29. Jack O'Brien, "She Does What She Always Wanted to Do," Associated Press, Oct. 20, 1943; Associated Press, "Sigrid Arne Has Covered Seven World Conferences," Apr. 21, 1945; *Current Biography*, 1945, pp. 15–16.

30. Linda Steiner and Susanne Gray, "Genevieve Forbes Herrick: A Front Page Reporter 'Pleased to Write About Women,' " *Journalism History* 12 (Spring 1985), pp. 8–16. See also Ross, *Ladies*, pp. 539–42.

31. William Shirer, *The Nightmare Years 1930–1940*. (Boston: Little, Brown, 1984), p. 118.

32. Ibid., p. 118.

33. Marion K. Sanders, *Dorothy Thompson: A Legend in Her Times* (New York: Avon Books, 1973), p. 330. Sources on Dorothy Thompson include Vincent Sheean, *Dorothy and Red* (Boston: Houghton Mifflin, 1963); Ross, *Ladies*, pp. 360–66; Schlipp and Murphy, *Great Women*; Kluger, *The Paper*; Jo R. Mengedoht, in *Dictionary of Literary Biography*, Vol. 29, *American Newspaper Journalists, 1926–1950*. Edited by Perry J. Ashley. (Detroit: Bruccoli Clark, 1984), pp. 343–50; and Paul Boyer's entry on Thompson in *Notable American Women*, pp. 683–86.

# Chapter 3

# JAMES W. CAREY

# TECHNOLOGY AND IDEOLOGY: THE CASE OF THE TELEGRAPH

OVER A LONG AND DISTINGUISHED CAREER, James Carey was director of the University of Illinois at Urbana-Champaign Institute for Communication Research, and later Dean of the College of Communication. He also held prominent positions at the University of Iowa and Columbia University Graduate School of Journalism. He played a fundamental role in establishing a cultural perspective for the study of mass communications and modern communications technology, maintaining that communication is not merely the transmission of information—but is a critical process in the constitution of community and culture. By stressing the importance of "mythic", "ritual" and anthropological elements in cultural formations he broadened his definition of the field to include the drawing-together of a people—for he maintained that life is an ongoing conversation.

Carey questioned the American tradition of focusing only on mass communication's function as a means of social and political control, replacing this with a broader mission, "to enlarge the human conversation by comprehending what others are saying." In "Technology and Ideology: The Case of the Telegraph," which is excerpted here, Carey argued that the telegraph marked the separation of "communication" and "transportation" and its impact was multifaceted and complex, changing everything from the workings of the market to the conception of time. In fact, the telegraph, through the grid of time, coordinated the workings of the industrial nation.

I take the neglect of the telegraph to be unfortunate for a number of reasons. First, the telegraph was dominated by the first great industrial monopoly—Western Union, the first communications empire and the prototype of the many industrial empires that were to follow. The telegraph, in conjunction with the railroad, provided the setting in which modern techniques for the management of complex enterprises were first worked out, though for the telegraph in what was eventually monopolistic circumstances.[1] Although the telegraph did not provide the site for the first of the titanic nineteenth-century patent struggles (that prize probably goes to Elias Howe's sewing machine) it led to one of the most significant of them in the rewriting of American law, particularly in the great "telegraph war" between Jay Gould and the Vanderbilt interests for control of the Edison patents for the quadraplex telegraph system, the innovation that Gould rightly prized as the "nerve of industry."

Second, the telegraph was the first product—really the foundation—of the electrical goods industry and thus the first of the science- and engineering-based industries. David Noble's *America by Design: Science, Technology and the Rise of Corporate Capitalism* (1977) implies throughout a sharp distinction between forms of engineering, such as civil engineering, grounded in a handicraft and guild tradition, and chemical engineering and electrical engineering, which were science-based from the outset. Much that is distinctive about the telegraph, from the organization of the industry to the rhetoric that rationalized it, derives from the particular nature of the engineering it brought into being. More to the point, the telegraph was the first electrical engineering technology and therefore the first to focus on the central problem in modern engineering: the economy of a signal.

Third, the telegraph brought about changes in the nature of language, of ordinary knowledge, of the very structures of awareness. Although in its early days the telegraph was used as a toy—as was the computer, which it prefigured—for playing long-distance chess, its implications for human knowledge were the subject of extended, often euphoric, and often pessimistic debate. Adams saw the telegraph as a demonic device dissipating the energy of history and displacing the Virgin with the Dynamo, whereas Thoreau saw it as an agent of trivialization. An even larger group saw the telegraph as an agency of benign improvement—spiritual, moral, economic, and political. Now that thought could travel by "the singing wire," a new form of reporting and a new form of knowledge were envisioned that would replace traditional literature with a new and active form of scientific knowledge.

Fourth, and partly for the foregoing reasons, the telegraph was a watershed in communication, as I hope to show later. Now, it is easy to overemphasize the revolutionary consequences of the telegraph. It is not an infrequent experience to be driving along an interstate highway and to become aware that the highway is paralleled by a river, a canal, a railroad track, or telegraph and telephone wires. In that instant one may realize that each of these improvements in transportation and communications merely worked a modification on what preceded it. The telegraph twisted and altered but did not displace patterns of connection formed by natural geography: by the river and primitive foot and horse paths and later by the wooden turnpike and canal.

But the innovation of the telegraph can stand metaphorically for all the innovations that ushered in the modern phase of history and determined, even to this day, the major lines of development of American communications. The most important fact about the telegraph is at once the most obvious and innocent: It permitted for the first time the effective separation of communication from transportation. This fact was immediately recognized, but its significance has been rarely investigated. The telegraph not only allowed messages to be separated from the physical movement of objects; it also allowed communication to control physical processes actively. The early use of the telegraph in railroad signaling is an example: telegraph messages could control the physical switching of rolling stock, thereby multiplying the purposes and effectiveness of communication. The separation of communication from transportation has been exploited in most subsequent developments in communication down to computer control systems.

When the telegraph reached the West Coast eight years in advance of a transcontinental railroad, the identity of communication and transportation was ended in both fact and symbol. Before the telegraph, "communication" was used to describe transportation as well as message transmittal for the simple reason that the movement of messages was dependent on their being carried on foot or horseback or by rail. The telegraph, by ending the identity, allowed symbols to move independently of and faster than transportation. To put it in a slightly different way, the telegraph freed communication from the constraints of geography. The telegraph, then, not only altered the relation between communication and transportation; it also changed the fundamental ways in which communication was thought about. It provided a model for thinking about communication—a model I have called a transmission model—and displaced older religious views of communication even as the new technology was mediated through religious language. And it opened up new ways of thinking about communication within both the formal practice of theory and the practical consciousness of everyday life. In this sense the telegraph was not only a new tool of commerce but also a thing to think with, an agency for the alteration of ideas.
[. . .]

## III

In the balance of this chapter I wish to concentrate on the effect of the telegraph on ordinary ideas: the coordinates of thought, the natural attitude, practical consciousness, or, less grandly, common sense. As I have intimated, I think the best way to grasp the effects of the telegraph or any other technology is not through a frontal assault but, rather, through the detailed investigation in a couple of sites where those effects can be most clearly observed.

Let me suggest some of the sites for those investigations—investigations to be later integrated and referred for elucidation to some general theoretical notions. First, much additional work needs to be done on the effects of the telegraph on language and journalism. The telegraph reworked the nature of written language and finally the nature of awareness itself. There is an old saw, one I have repeated myself, that the telegraph, by creating the wire services, led to a fundamental change in news. It snapped the tradition of partisan journalism by forcing the wire services to generate "objective" news, news that could be used by papers of any political stripe (Carey, 1969: 23–38). Yet the issue is deeper than that. The wire services demanded a form of language stripped of the local, the regional; and colloquial. They demanded something closer to a "scientific" language, a language of strict denotation in which the connotative features of utterance were under rigid control. If the same story were to be understood in the same way from Maine to California, language had to be flattened out and standardized. The telegraph, therefore, led to the disappearance of forms of speech and styles of journalism and story telling—the tall story, the hoax, much humor, irony, and satire—that depended on a more traditional use of the symbolic, a use I earlier called the fiduciary. 'The origins of objectivity may be sought, therefore, in the necessity of stretching language in space over the long lines of Western Union. That is, the telegraph changed the forms of social relations mediated by language. Just as the long lines displaced a personal relation mediated by speech and correspondence in the conduct of trade and substituted the mechanical coordination of buyer and seller, so the language of the telegraph displaced a fiduciary relationship between writer and reader with a coordinated one.

Similarly, the telegraph eliminated the correspondent who provided letters that announced an event, described it in detail, and analyzed its substance, and replaced him with the stringer who supplied the bare facts. As words were expensive on the telegraph, it separated the observer from the writer. Not only did writing for the telegraph have to be condensed to save money—telegraphic, in other words—but also from the marginal notes and anecdotes of the stringer the story had to be reconstituted at the end of the telegraphic line, a process that reaches high art with the news magazines, the story divorced from the story teller.

But as every constraint is also an opportunity, the telegraph altered literary style. In a well-known story, "cablese" influenced Hemingway's style, helping him to pare his prose to the bone, dispossessed of every adornment. Most correspondents chafed under its restrictiveness, but not Hemingway. "I had to quit being a correspondent," he told Lincoln Steffens later. "I was getting too fascinated by the lingo of the cable."[2] But the lingo of the cable provided the underlying structure for one of the most influential literary styles of the twentieth century.

There were other effects—some obvious, some subtle. If the telegraph made prose lean and unadorned and led to a journalism without the luxury of detail and analysis, it also brought an overwhelming crush of such prose to the newsroom. In the face of what was a real glut of occurrences, news judgment had to be routinized and the organization of the newsroom made factory-like. The reporter who produced the new prose moved into prominence in journalism by displacing the editor as the archetype of the journalist. The spareness of the prose and the sheer volume of it allowed news—indeed, forced news—to be treated like a commodity: something that could be transported, measured, reduced, and timed. In the wake of the telegraph, news was subject to all the procedures developed for handling agricultural commodities. It was subject to "rates, contracts, franchising, discounts and thefts."[3]

A second site for the investigation of the telegraph is the domain of empire. Again, it is best not to assault the problem as an overarching theory of imperialism but, rather, to examine specific cases and specific connections: the role of the telegraph in coordinating military, particularly naval, operations; the transition from colonialism, where power and authority rested with the domestic governor, to imperialism, where power and authority were reabsorbed by the imperial capital; the new forms of political correspondence that came about when the war correspondent was obliged to use the telegraph; and the rise of the first forms of international business that could be called multinational.

While the growth of empire and imperialism have been explained by virtually every possible factor, little attention has been paid to telegraphy in generating the ground conditions for the urban imperialism of the mid-nineteenth century and the international imperialism later in the century.[4] It is probably no accident that the words "empire" and "imperialism" entered the language in 1870, soon after the laying of the transatlantic cable. Although colonies could be held together with printing, correspondence, and sail, the hold, as the American experience shows, was always tenuous over great distance. Moreover, in colonial arrangements the margin had as much power as the center. Until the transatlantic cable, it was difficult to determine whether British colonial policy was being set in London or by colonial governors in the field—out of contact and out of control. It was the cable and telegraph, backed, of course, by sea power, that turned colonialism into imperialism: a system in which the center of an empire could dictate rather than merely respond to the margin.[5] The critical change lay in the ability to secure investments. There was no heavy overseas investment until the control made possible by the cable. The innovation of the telegraph created, if not the absolute impetus for imperial expansion, then at least the wherewithal to make the expansion theoretically tenable. But it also created a tension between the capability to expand and the capacity to rule.

With the development of the railroad, steam power, the telegraph and cable, a coherent empire emerged based on a coherent system of communication. In that system the railroad may be taken as the overland extension of the steamer or vice versa, and the telegraph and cable stood as the coordinating, regulating device governing both.[6]

Although the newspaper and imperial offices are among the best sites at which to look for the effects of the telegraph, there are humbler locations of equal interest. It surely is more than an accident that many of the great nineteenth-century commercial empires were founded in the humble circumstances of the telegraph operator's shack. The case of Richard B. Sears of North Redwood, Minnesota, is instructive. One must not forget that Edison and Carnegie began the same way and that the genius of Jay Gould lay in his integration of the telegraph with the railroad. The significance of the telegraph in this regard is that it led to the selective control and transmission of information. The telegraph operator was able to monopolize knowledge, if only for a few moments, along a route; and this brought a selective advantage in trading and speculation. But it was this same control of information that gave the telegraph a central importance in the development of modern gambling and of the business of credit. Finally, it was central to the late nineteenth-century explosion in forms of merchandising, such as the mail-order house.[7]

In the balance of this essay I want to cut across some of these developments and describe how the telegraph altered the ways in which time and space were understood in ordinary human affairs and, in particular, to examine a changed form in which time entered practical consciousness. To demonstrate these changes I wish to concentrate on the developments of commodity markets and on the institutionalization of standard time. But first let me reiterate the basic argument.

The simplest and most important point about the telegraph is that it marked the decisive separation of "transportation" and "communication." Until the telegraph these words were synonymous. The telegraph ended that identity and allowed symbols to move independently of geography and independently of and faster than transport. I say decisive separation because there were premonitions earlier of what was to come, and there was, after all, pre-electric telegraphy—line-of-sight signaling devices.

Virtually any American city of any vintage has a telegraph hill or a beacon hill reminding us of such devices. They relied on shutters, flaps, disks, or arms operating as for semaphoric signaling at sea. They were optical rather than "writing at a distance" systems and the forerunners of microwave networks, which rely on relay stations on geographic high points for aerial transmissions.

Line-of-sight telegraphy came into practical use at the end of the eighteenth century. Its principal architect was a Frenchman, Claude Chappe, who persuaded the Committee of Public Instruction in post-Revolutionary France to approve a trial. Joseph Lakanal, one of its members, reported back to the committee on the outcome: "What brilliant destiny do science and the arts not reserve for a republic which by its immense population and the genius of its inhabitants, is called to become the nation to instruct Europe" (Wilson, 1976: 122).

The National Convention approved the adoption of the telegraph as a national utility and instructed the Committee of Public Safety to map routes. The major impetus to its development in France was the same as the one that led to the wave of canal and railroad building in America. The pre-electric telegraph would provide an answer to Montesquieu and other political theorists who thought France or the United States too big to be a republic. But even more, it provided a means whereby the departments that had replaced the provinces after the Revolution could be tied to and coordinated with the central authority (Wilson, 1976: 123).

The pre-electric telegraph was also a subject of experimentation in America. In 1800, a line-of-sight system was opened between Martha's Vineyard and Boston (Wilson, 1976: 210). Between 1807 and 1812, plans were laid for a telegraph to stretch from Maine to New Orleans. The first practical use of line-of-sight telegraphy was for the transmission of news of arriving ships, a practice begun long before 1837 (Thompson, 1947: 11). But even before line-of-sight devices had been developed, alterations in shipping patterns had led to the separation of information from cargo, and that had important consequences for international trade. I shall say more on this later.

Despite these reservations and qualifications, the telegraph provided the decisive and cumulative break of the identity of communication and transportation. The great theoretical significance of the technology lay not merely in the separation but also in the use of the telegraph as both a model of and a mechanism for control of the physical movement of things, specifically for the railroad. That is the fundamental discovery: not only can information move independently of and faster than physical entities, but it also can be a simulation of and control mechanism for what has been left behind. The discovery was first exploited in railroad dispatching in England in 1844 and in the United States in 1849. It was of particular use on the long stretches of single-track road in the American West, where accidents were a serious problem. Before the use of the telegraph to control switching, the Boston and Worcester Railroad, for one example, kept horses every five miles along the line, and they raced up and down the track so that their riders could warn engineers of impending collisions (Thompson, 1947: 205–06). By moving information faster than the rolling stock, the telegraph allowed for centralized control along many miles of track. Indeed, the operation of the telegraph in conjunction with the railroad allowed for an integrated system of transport and communication. The same principle realized in these mundane circumstances governs the development of all modern processes in electrical transmission and control from guided gun sights to simple servo mechanisms that open doors. The relationship of the telegraph and the railroad illustrates the basic notion of systems theory and the catch phrase that the "system is the solution," in that the integrated switched system is more important than any of its components.

The telegraph permitted the development, in the favorite metaphor of the day, of a thoroughly encephalated social nervous system in which signaling was divorced from musculature. It was the telegraph and the railroad—the actual, painful construction of an integrated system—that provided the entrance gate for the organic metaphors that dominated nineteenth-century thought. Although German romanticism and idealism had their place, it is less to the world of ideas and more to the world of actual practice that we need to look when trying to figure out why the nineteenth century was obsessed with organicism.

The effect of the telegraph on ideology, on ordinary ideas, can be shown more graphically with two other examples drawn from the commodities markets and the development of standard time. The telegraph, like most innovations in communication down through the computer, had its first and most profound impact on the conduct of commerce, government, and the military. It was, in short, a producer good before it was a consumer good. The telegraph, as I said earlier, was used in its early months for the long-distance playing of chess. Its commercial significance was slow to be realized. But once that significance was determined, it was used to reorganize commerce; and from the patterns of usage in commerce came many of the telegraph's most profound consequences for ordinary thought. Among its first effects was the reorganization of commodity markets.

It was the normal expectation of early nineteenth-century Americans that the price of a commodity would diverge from city to city so that the cost of wheat, corn, or whatever would be radically different in, say, Pittsburgh, Cincinnati, and St. Louis. This belief reflected the fact that before the telegraph, markets were independent of one another, or, more accurately, that the effect of one market on another was so gradually manifested as to be virtually unnoticed. In short, the prices of commodities were largely determined by local conditions of supply and demand. One of the leading historians of the markets has commented, "To be sure in all articles of trade the conditions at all sources of supply had their ultimate effect on distant values and yet even in these the communication was so slow that the conditions might change entirely before their effect could be felt" (Emery, 1896: 106).

Under such circumstances, the principal method of trading is called arbitrage: buying cheap and selling dear by moving goods around in space. That is, if prices are higher in St. Louis than in Cincinnati, it makes sense to buy in Cincinnati and resell in St. Louis, as long as the price differential is greater than the cost of transportation between the two cities. If arbitrage is widely practiced between cities, prices should settle into an equilibrium whereby the difference in price is held to the difference in transportation cost. This result is, in turn, based on the assumption of classical economics of perfect information—that all buyers and sellers are aware of the options available in all relevant markets—a situation rarely approached in practice before the telegraph.

Throughout the United States, price divergence between markets declined during the nineteenth century. Arthur H. Cole computed the average annual and monthly price disparity for uniform groups of commodities during the period 1816–1842, that is, up to the eve of the telegraph. Over that period the average annual price disparity fell from 9.3 to 4.8; and the average monthly disparity, from 15.4 to 4.8 (Cole, 1938: 94–96, 103). The decline itself is testimony to improvements in communication brought about by canal and turnpike building. The steepness of the decline is probably masked somewhat because Cole grouped the prices for the periods 1816–1830 and 1830–1842, whereas it was late in the canal era and the beginnings of large-scale railroad building that the sharpest declines were felt.

Looked at from one side, the decline represents the gradual increase in the effective size of the market. Looked at from the other side, it represents a decline in spatially based speculative opportunities—opportunities, that is, to turn trade into profit by moving goods between distinct markets. In a sense the railroad and canal regionalized markets; the telegraph nationalized them. The effect of the telegraph is a simple one: it evens out markets in space. The telegraph puts everyone in the same place for purposes of trade; it makes geography irrelevant. The telegraph brings the conditions of supply and demand in all markets to bear on the determination of a price. Except for the marginal exception here and there, it eliminates opportunities for arbitrage by realizing the classical assumption of perfect information.

But the significance of the telegraph does not lie solely in the decline of arbitrage; rather, the telegraph shifts speculation into another dimension. It shifts speculation from space to time, from arbitrage to futures. After the telegraph, commodity trading moved from trading between places to trading between times. The arbitrager trades Cincinnati for St. Louis; the futures trader sells August against October, this year against next. To put the matter somewhat differently, as the telegraph closed down spatial uncertainty in prices it opened up, because of improvements in communication, the uncertainty of time. It was not, then, mere historic accident that the Chicago Commodity Exchange, to this day the principal American futures market, opened in 1848, the same year the telegraph reached that city. In a certain sense the telegraph invented the future as a new zone of uncertainty and a new region of practical action.

Let me make a retreat from that conclusion about the effects of the telegraph on time because I have overdrawn the case. First, the opportunities for arbitrage are never completely eliminated. There are always imperfections in market information, even on the floor of a stock exchange: buyers and sellers who do not know of one another and the prices at which the others are willing to trade. We know this as well from ordinary experience at auctions, where someone always knows a buyer who will pay more than the auctioned price. Second, there was a hiatus between arbitrage and the futures market when time contracts dominated, and this was a development of some importance. An approximation of futures trading occurred as early as 1733, when the East India Company initiated the practice of trading warrants. The function of a warrant was to transfer ownership of goods without consummating their physical transfer. The warrant did not represent, as such, particular warehoused goods; they were merely endorsed from person to person. The use of warrants or time contracts evolved rapidly in the United States in the trading of agricultural staples. They evolved to meet new conditions of effective market size and, as importantly, their evolution was unrestrained by historic practice.

The critical condition governing the development of time contracts was also the separation of communication from transport. Increasingly, news of crop conditions reached the market before the commodity itself. For example, warrant trading advanced when cotton was shipped to England by sail while passengers and information moved by steamer. Based on news of the crop and on samples of the commodity, time contracts or "to-arrive" contracts were executed. These were used principally for transatlantic sales, but after the Mississippi Valley opened up to agricultural trade, they were widely used in Chicago in the 1840s (Baer and Woodruff, 1935: 3–5).

The telegraph started to change the use of time contracts, as well as arbitrage. By widely transmitting knowledge of prices and crop conditions, it drew markets and prices together. We do not have good before-and-after measures, but we do have evidence, cited earlier, for the long-run decline in price disparities among markets. Moreover, we have measures from Cincinnati in particular. In the 1820s Cincinnati lagged two years behind Eastern markets. That meant that it took two years for disturbances in the Eastern market structure to affect Cincinnati prices. By 1840 the lag was down to four months; and by 1857—and probably much earlier—the effect of Eastern markets on Cincinnati was instantaneous. But once space was, in the phrase of the day, annihilated, once everyone was in the same place for purposes of trade, time as a new region of experience, uncertainty, speculation, and exploration was opened up to the forces of commerce.

A back-door example of this inversion of space and time can be drawn from a later episode involving the effect of the telephone on the New York Stock Exchange. By 1894 the telephone had made information time identical in major cities. Buyers and sellers, wherever they were, knew current prices as quickly as traders did on the floor of the exchange. The information gap, then, between New York and Boston had been elimi- nated and business gravitated from New York to Boston brokerage firms. The New York exchange countered this movement by creating a thirty-second time advantage that ensured New York's superiority to Boston. The exchange ruled that telephones would not be allowed on the floor. Price information had to be relayed by messenger to an area off the floor of the exchange that had been set aside for telephones. This move destroyed the temporal identity of markets, and a thirty-second monopoly of knowledge was created that drew business back to New York (Emery, 1896: 139).

This movement of commodities out of space and into time had three other conse- quences of great importance in examining the effect of the telegraph. First, futures trading required the decontextualization of markets; or, to put it in a slightly different way, markets were made relatively unresponsive to local conditions of supply and demand. The telegraph removed markets from the particular context in which they were historically located and concentrated on them forces emanating from any place and any time. This was a redefinition from physical or geographic markets to spiritual ones. In a sense they were made more mysterious; they became everywhere markets and everytime markets and thus less apprehensible at the very moment they became more powerful.

Second, not only were distant and amorphous forces brought to bear on markets, but the commodity was sundered from its representations; that is, the development of futures trading depended on the ability to trade or circulate negotiable instruments inde- pendently of the actual physical movement of goods. The representation of the commodity became the warehouse receipts from grain elevators along the railroad line. These instruments were then traded independently of any movement of the actual goods. The buyer of such receipts never expected to take delivery; the seller of such receipts never expected to make delivery. There is the old joke, which is also a cautionary tale, of the futures trader who forgot what he was up to and ended up with forty tons of wheat on his suburban lawn; but it is merely a joke and a tale. The futures trader often sells before he buys, or buys and sells simultaneously. But the buying and selling is not of goods but of receipts. What is being traded is not money for commodities but time against price. In short, the warehouse receipt, which stands as a representation of the product, has no intrinsic relation to the real product. But in order to trade receipts rather than goods, a third change was necessary. In futures trading products are not bought or sold by inspection of the actual product or a sample thereof. Rather, they are sold through a grading system. In order to lend itself to futures trading, a product has to be mixed, standardized, diluted in order to be reduced to a specific, though abstract, grade. With the coming of the telegraph, products could no longer be shipped in sepa- rate units as numerous as there were owners of grain. "The high volume sales required impersonalized standards. Buyers were no longer able personally to check every lot" (Chandler, 1977: 211). Consequently, not all products are traded on the futures market because some resist the attempt to reduce them to standardized categories of quality.

The development of the futures markets, in summary, depended on a number of specific changes in markets and the commodity system. It required that information move independently of and faster than products. It required that prices be made uniform in space and that markets be decontextualized. It required, as well, that commodities be separated from the receipts that represent them and that commodities be reduced to uniform grades.

There were, it should be quickly added, the conditions that underlay Marx's analysis of the commodity fetish. That concept, now used widely and often indiscriminately, was developed in the *Grundrisse* and *Das Kapital* during the late 1850s, when futures trading became the dominant arena for the establishment of agricultural values. In particular, Marx made the key elements in the commodity fetish the decontextualization of markets, the separation of use value from exchange value brought about by the decline in the representative function of the warehouse receipt, and the abstraction of the product out of real conditions of production by a grading system. In the *Grundrisse* he comments, "This locational movement—the bringing of the product to market which is a necessary condition of its circulation, except when the point of production is itself a market—could more precisely be regarded as the transformation of the product into a commodity" (Marx, 1973: 534).

Marx's reference is to what Walter Benjamin (1968) would later call the "loss of aura" in his parallel analysis of the effect of mechanical reproduction on the work of art. After the object is abstracted out of the real conditions of its production and use and is transported to distant markets, standardized and graded, and represented by fully contingent symbols, it is made available as a commodity. Its status as a commodity represents the sundering of a real, direct relationship between buyer and seller, separates use value from exchange value, deprives objects of any uniqueness (which must then be returned to the object via advertising), and, most important, masks to the buyer the real conditions of production. Further, the process of divorcing the receipt from the product can be thought of as part of a general social process initiated by the use of money and widely written about in contemporary semiotics; the progressive divorce of the signifier from the signified, a process in which the world of signifiers progressively overwhelms and moves independently of real material objects.

To summarize, the growth of communications in the nineteenth century had the practical effect of diminishing space as a differentiating criterion in human affairs. What Harold Innis called the "penetrative powers of the price system" was, in effect, the spread of a uniform price system throughout space so that for purposes of trade everyone was in the same place. The telegraph was the critical instrument in this spread. In commerce this meant the decontextualization of markets so that prices no longer depended on local factors of supply and demand but responded to national and international forces. The spread of the price system was part of the attempt to colonize space. The correlative to the penetration of the price system was what the composer Igor Stravinsky called the "statisticalization of mind": the transformation of the entire mental world into quantity, and the distribution of quantities in space so that the relationship between things and people becomes solely one of numbers. Statistics widens the market for everything and makes it more uniform and interdependent. The telegraph worked this same effect on the practical consciousness of time through the construction of standard time zones.

## IV

Our sense of time and our activities in time are coordinated through a grid of time zones, a grid so fixed in our consciousness that it seems to be the natural form of time, at least until we change back and forth between standard and daylight saving time. But standard time in the United States is a relatively recent invention. It was introduced on November 18, 1883.

Until that date virtually every American community established its own time by marking that point when the sun reached its zenith as noon. It could be determined astronomically with exactitude; but any village could do it, for all practical purposes, by observing the shortest shadow on a sundial. Official local time in a community could be fixed, as since time immemorial, by a church or later by a courthouse, a jeweler, or later still the railroad stationmaster; and a bell or whistle could be rung or set off so that the local burghers could set their timepieces. In Kansas City a ball was dropped from the highest building at noon and was visible for miles around, a practice still carried out at the annual New Year's Eve festivities in New York City's Times Square (Corliss, 1952).

Not every town kept its own time; many set their clocks in accord with the county seat or some other nearby town of commercial or political importance. When the vast proportion of American habitats were, in Robert Wiebe's (1967) phrase, "island communities" with little intercourse with one another, the distinctiveness of local time caused little confusion and worry. But as the tentacles of commerce and politics spread out from the capitals, temporal chaos came with them. The chaos was sheerly physical. With every degree of longitude one moved westward, the sun reached its zenith four minutes later. That meant that when it was noon in Boston it was 11:48 a.m. in Albany; when it was noon in Atlanta it was 11:36 a.m. in New Orleans. Put differently, noon came a minute later for every quarter degree of longitude one moved westward, and this was a shorter distance as one moved north: in general thirteen miles equaled one minute of time.

The setting of clocks to astronomically local time or, at best, to county seat time led to a proliferation of time zones. Before standard time Michigan had twenty-seven time zones; Indiana, twenty-three; Wisconsin, thirty-nine; Illinois, twenty-seven. The clocks in New York, Boston, and Philadelphia, cities today on identical time, were several minutes apart (Corliss, 1952: 3). When it was 12:00 in Washington, D.C., it was 11:30 in Atlanta, 12:09 in Philadelphia, 12:12 in New York, 12:24 in Boston, and 12:41 in Eastport, Maine.

As the railroads spread across the continent, the variety of local times caused enormous confusion with scheduling, brought accidents as trains on different clocks collided, and led to much passenger irritation, as no one could easily figure when a train would arrive at another town. The railroads used fifty-eight local times keyed to the largest cities. Moreover, each railroad keyed its clocks to the time of a different city. The Pennsylvania Railroad keyed its time to that of Philadelphia, but Philadelphia's clocks were twelve minutes behind New York's and five minutes ahead of Baltimore's. The New York Central stuck to New York City time. The Baltimore and Ohio keyed its time to three cities: Baltimore; Columbus, Ohio; and Vincennes, Indiana (Bartky and Harrison, 1979: 46–53).

The solution, which was to establish standard time zones, had long attracted the interest of scholars. The pressure to establish such zones was felt more strongly in North America, which averaged eight hours of daylight from Newfoundland to western Alaska. Although standard time was established earlier in Europe, the practical pressure there was less. There is only a half-hour variance in sun time across England; and France, while larger, could be run on Paris time. But England, for purposes of empire, had long been interested in standard time. The control of time allows for the coordination of activity and, therefore, effective social control. In navigation, time was early fixed on English ships according to the clock of the Greenwich observatory; and no matter where a ship might be in the Atlantic, its chronometer always registered Greenwich time. Similarly, Irish time was regulated by a clock set each morning at Big Ben, carried by rail to Holyhead, ferried across the Irish sea to Kingstown (now Dun Laoghaire), and then carried again by rail to Dublin, where Irish clocks were coordinated with English time (Schivelbusch, 1978: 39).

And so it was no surprise when in 1870 a New Yorker, Charles Dowd, proposed a system of standard time zones that fixed Greenwich as zero degrees longitude and laid out the zones around the world with centers 15 degrees east and west from Greenwich. As 15 degrees equals one hour, the world was laid out in twenty-four zones one hour apart.

Dowd's plan was a wonderful example of crackpot realism. The lines were laid out with geometric exactness and ignored geography, topography, region, trade, or natural affinity. Maine and Florida were put in separate time zones. It is a wonderful example of the maxim that the grid is the geometry of empire. Dowd recommended the plan to the railroads, which adopted it provisionally and created an index out of it so that the traveler could convert railroad time to local time by adding or subtracting so many minutes to or from the railroad schedule.

For thirteen years the Dowd system was debated but never officially adopted by the General Time Convention. The railroads tried during that period to get Congress to adopt it as a uniform time system, but Congress would not and for an obvious reason: standard time offended people with deeply held religious sentiments. It violated the actual physical working of the natural order and denied the presence of a divinely ordained nature. But even here religious language was a vanishing mediator for political sentiments; standard time was widely known as Vanderbilt's time, and protest against it was part of the populist protest against the banks, the telegraph, and the railroad.

In 1881, the Philadelphia General Time Convention turned the problem over to William Frederick Allen, a young civil engineer; two years later he returned a plan. It was based on Dowd's scheme but with a crucial difference: it allowed for the adjustment of time zones for purposes of economy and ecology. In his scheme time boundaries could be shifted up to 100 miles away from the geometric lines in order to minimize disruption. Most important, he recommended that the railroads abandon the practice of providing a minute index and that they simply adopt standard time for regulating their schedules and allow communities and institutions to adjust to the new time in any manner they chose.

In the Allen plan the United States was divided into four time zones, with centers on the 75th, 90th, 105th, and 120th meridians: Philadelphia, St. Louis, Denver, and Reno were the approximate centers. The zones extended seven and a half degrees to either side of the center line. November 18, 1883, was selected as the date for the changeover from local to standard time, and an ambitious "educational" campaign was mounted to help citizens adjust to the new system. On that date Chicago, the railroad hub, was tied by telegraph to an observatory in Allegheny, Pennsylvania. When it reached one o'clock over the center of the Eastern time zone, the clocks were stopped at noon in Chicago and held for nine minutes and thirty two seconds until the sun centered on the 90th meridian. Then they were started again, with the railroad system now integrated and coordinated through time.

The changeover was greeted by mass meetings, anger, and religious protest but to no avail. Railroad time had become standard time. It was not made official U.S. time until the emergency of World War I. But within a few months after the establishment of railroad time, the avalanche of switches to it by local communities was well under way. Strangely enough, the United States never did go to 24-hour time and thus retained some connection between the diurnal cycle of human activity and the cycle of the planets.

The boundaries of the time zones have been repeatedly adjusted since that time. In general they have been made to follow state borders, but there are a number of exceptions. The western edge of the Eastern time zone was once in eastern Ohio, but now it forms a jagged line along the Illinois–Indiana border. Boise, Idaho, was moved from Pacific to Mountain time, and recently twelve thousand square miles of Arizona was similarly moved. The reasons for such changes tell us much about America's purposes. One gets the distinct feeling, for example, that the television networks would prefer a country with three time zones: east, central, and west.

Standard time zones were established because in the eyes of some they were necessary. They were established, to return to the point of this chapter, because of the technological power of the telegraph. Time was sent via the telegraph wire; but today, thanks to technical improvements, it is sent via radio waves from the Naval observatory in Maryland. The telegraph could send time faster than a railroad car could move; and therefore it facilitated the temporal coordination and integration of the entire system. Once that was possible, the new definitions of time could be used by industry and government to control and coordinate activity across the country, infiltrate into the practical consciousness of ordinary men and women, and uproot older notions of rhythm and temporality.

The development of standard time zones served to overlay the world with a grid of time in the same way the surveyor's map laid a grid of space on old cities, the new territories of the West, or the seas. The time grid could then be used to control and coordinate activities within the grid of space.


## V

When the ecological niche of space was filled, filled as an arena of commerce and control, attention was shifted to filling time, now defined as an aspect of space, a continuation of space in another dimension. As the spatial frontier was closed, time became the new frontier. Let me mention, in closing, two other dimensions of the temporal frontier.

An additional time zone to be penetrated once space was exhausted was sacred time, in particular the sabbath. The greatest invention of the ancient Hebrews was the idea of the sabbath, though I am using this word in a fully secular sense: the invention of a region free from control of the state and commerce where another dimension of life could be experienced and where altered forms of social relationship could occur. As such, the sabbath has always been a major resistance to state and market power. For purposes of communication, the effective penetration of the sabbath came in the 1880s with the invention of the Sunday newspaper. It was Hearst with his New York Sunday *World* who popularized the idea of Sunday newspaper reading and created, in fact, a market where none had existed before—a sabbath market. Since then the penetration of the sabbath has been one of the "frontiers" of commerical activity. Finally, when the frontier in space was officially closed in 1890, the "new frontier" became the night, and since then there has been a continuous spreading upward of commercial activity. Murray

Melbin (1987) has attempted to characterize "night as a frontier." In terms of communication the steady expansion of commerical broadcasting into the night is one of the best examples. There were no 24-hour radio stations in Boston, for example, from 1918 through 1954; now half of the stations in Boston operate all night. Television has slowly expanded into the night at one end and at the other initiated operations earlier and earlier. Now, indeed, there are 24-hour television stations in major markets.

The notion of night as frontier, a new frontier of time that opens once space is filled, is a metaphor, but it is more than that. Melbin details some of the features common to the spatial and temporal frontiers: they both advance in stages; the population is more sparsely settled and homogeneous; there is solitude, an absence of social constraints, and less persecution; settlements are isolated; government is decentralized; lawlessness and violence as well as friendliness and helpfulness increase; new behavioral styles emerge. That is, the same dialectic between centralization and decentralization occurs on the temporal frontier as on the spatial frontier. On the one hand, communication is even more privatized at night. On the other hand, social constraints on communication are relaxed because the invasive hand of authority loosened.

The penetration of time, the use of time as a mechanism of control, the opening of time to commerce and politics has been radically extended by advances in computer technology. Time has been redefined as an ecological niche to be filled down to the microsecond, nanosecond, and picosecond—down to a level at which time can be pictured but not experienced. This process and the parallel reconstruction of practical consciousness and practical activity begins in those capacities of the telegraph which prefigure the computer. The telegraph constructed a simulacrum of complex systems, provided an analogue model of the railroad and a digital model of language. It coordinated and controlled activity in space, often behind the backs of those subject to it.

E. P. Thompson finds it ominous that the young Henry Ford should have created a watch with two dials: one for local time and another for railroad time. "Attention to time in labour depends in large degree upon the need for the synchronization of labour" (Thompson, 1967: 70). Modern conceptions of time have rooted into our consciousness so deeply that the scene of the worker receiving a watch at his retirement is grotesque and comic. He receives a watch when the need to tell time is ended. He receives a watch as a tribute to his learning the hardest lesson of the working man—to tell time.

As the watch coordinated the industrial factory; the telegraph via the grid of time coordinated the industrial nation. Today, computer time, computer space, and computer memory, notions we dimly understand, are reworking practical consciousness coordinating and controlling life in what we glibly call the postindustrial society. Indeed, the microcomputer is replacing the watch as the favored gift for the middle class retiree. In that new but unchanging custom we see the deeper relationship between technology and ideology.

## Notes

1. See Chandler (1977), esp. Part II.
2. Steffens (1958: 834). For a memoir that discusses the art and adversity of writing for the cable, see Shirer (1976: 282 ff.).
3. The quotation is from an as yet unpublished manuscript by Douglas Birkhead of the University of Utah. Birkhead develops these themes in some detail.

4. On urban imperialism, see Schlesinger (1933) and Pred (1973).
5. Among the few studies on the telegraph and empire, the most distinguished is Fortner (1978); see also Field (1978: 644–68).
6. In making these remarks I am much indebted to the work of Fortner and Field.
7. On these matters there are useful suggestions in Boorstin (1973).

## Bibliography

Boorstin, Daniel J. (1973). *The Americans: The Democratic Experience*. New York: Random House.

Chandler, Alfred D. (1977). *The Visible Hand: The Managerial Revolution in American Business*. Cambridge, MA: Harvard University Press.

Field, James A. (1978). "American Imperialism: The Worst Chapter in Almost Any Book." *American Historical Review*, 83 (3), 644–83.

Fortner, Robert (1978). "Messiahs and Monopolists: A Cultural History of Canadian Communication Systems, 1846–1914." Ph.D. Dissertation, University of Illinois.

Pred, Alan (1973). *Urban Growth and the Circulation of Information: The United States System of Cities, 1790–1840*. Cambridge, MA: Harvard University Press.

Schlesinger, Arthur Sr. (1933). *The Rise of the City, 1878–1898*. New York: Macmillan.

Shirer, William I. (1976). *20th Century Journey: The Start: 1904–1930*. New York: Simon and Schuster.

Steffens, Lincoln (1958). *The Autobiography of Lincoln Steffens*. New York: Harcourt, Brace and World.

# Chapter 4

## PAT WASHBURN

# THE AFRICAN AMERICAN NEWSPAPER

THE AFRICAN AMERICAN NEWSPAPER documents the rise and ultimate decline of the African American newspaper in the United States. With the launch of *The Freedom Journal* in 1827, the black press struggled against fierce inequality and discrimination to provide the African American community with the news it needed and wanted. In fact, since for decades the white press refused to cover news in the black community whatsoever, the black press was the primary medium of news of everyday life in their communities across the nation.

The black press also emerged as a leading voice for equality and civil rights. As Washburn documents, it was in the black press that Ida B. Wells-Barnett conducted her long struggle against lynching. The black press tirelessly crusaded for the integration of professional sports and provided much of the early coverage of the Civil Rights movement in the early 1950s. In this selection, Washburn chronicles *Pittsburgh Courier*'s Double V campaign during World War II, which called for victory over the Nazis in Europe and victory over segregation in the United States. He suggests that the Double V campaign, which was supported by the black press throughout the country, was historically as important as Ida B. Wells-Barnett's crusade against lynching and Robert Abbott's call for African Americans in the South to migrate to the North. In some ways, the campaign presaged the role that returning African American veterans would play in the drive for equal rights that followed the end of the war.

A winner of the Tankard Award for Journalism History, Washburn's *The African American Newspaper* offers an important introduction, overview and analysis of the history of the black press.

## Word War II

> *War may be hell for some, but it bids fair to open up the portals of heaven for us.*
> —Joseph D. Bibb, *Pittsburgh Courier*

On January 31, 1942, less than two months after the United States entered World War II, the *Pittsburgh Courier* ran a letter from James G. Thompson, a twenty-six-year-old black cafeteria worker at the Cessna Aircraft Corporation in Wichita, Kansas. He expressed his feelings on patriotism:

> Like all true Americans, my greatest desire at this time . . . is for a complete victory over the forces of evil which threaten our existence today. Behind that desire is also a desire to serve this, my country, in the most advantageous way.
>
> Most of our leaders are suggesting that we sacrifice every other ambition to the paramount one, victory. With this I agree, but I also wonder if another victory could not be achieved at the same time. . . . Being an American of dark complexion . . . these questions flash through my mind: "Should I sacrifice my life to live half American?" "Will things be better for the next generation in the peace to follow?" "Would it be demanding too much to demand full citizenship rights in exchange for the sacrificing of my life?" "Is the kind of America I know worth defending?" "Will America be a true and pure democracy after this war?" "Will colored Americans suffer still the indignities that have been heaped upon them in the past?" . . .
>
> I suggest that while we keep defense and victory in the forefront that we don't lose sight of our fight for true democracy at home.
>
> The V for victory sign is being displayed prominently in all so-called democratic countries which are fighting for victory over aggression, slavery and tyranny. If this V sign means that to those now engaged in this great conflict, then let we colored Americans adopt the double VV for a double victory. The first V for victory over our enemies from without, the second V for victory over our enemies from within. For surely those who perpetuate these ugly prejudices here are seeking to destroy our democratic form of government just as surely as the Axis forces.

Thompson's letter, which arguably is the most famous ever run by a black paper, had a huge impact. It resulted in the *Courier* immediately launching a high-profile Double V campaign, which ranked historically in importance with Ida B. Wells's vigorous anti-lynching crusade and Robert Abbott's extraordinary call for blacks to leave the South. Other black newspapers quickly joined in, continually pushing for a "double victory" for the remainder of the war. This time there would be no controversial "close ranks" editorial by black newspapers like the one W. E. B. Du Bois had written toward the end of World War I. Blacks wanted more rights, and they wanted them now; they saw no reason to wait until the war was over. And, as events would show, blacks would make enormous gains by the time Germany surrendered in May 1945, followed by Japan three months later. *Courier* columnist Joseph D. Bibb had been right on October 10, 1942, when he had predicted: "When the war ends the colored American will be better off financially, spiritually and economically. War may be hell for some, but it bids fair to open up the portals of heaven for us."

With the bombing of the U.S. Pacific Fleet at Pearl Harbor, which united the country with patriotism and a fervor that had not been seen since the sinking of the battleship *Maine* in 1898, blacks assumed that many discriminatory barriers would vanish quickly in the push to win the war. But they were wrong. When they tried to enlist in the Marines, the Coast Guard, and the Army Air Corps, they were turned away because those services had never had blacks. Meanwhile, the Navy was willing to take them, but only if they agreed to work as messboys in the kitchens, and the Army, which was deliberately 10 percent black to coincide with their percentage in the population, only accepted one black for every nine nonblacks. Furthermore, the extraordinary heroism of a black messboy was tainted by the Navy, at least in the view of the black press, and this escalated black anger. Dorie Miller, who was on one of the ships at Pearl Harbor, had dashed from the kitchen onto the deck during the attack, moved his wounded captain to safety, and then fired a machine gun at the Japanese airplanes until he ran out of ammunition. Learning what he had done, the *Pittsburgh Courier* angrily attacked the Navy's discriminatory policies on January 3, 1942: "Is it fair, honest or sensible that this country, with its fate in the balance, should continue to bar Negroes from service except in the mess department of the Navy, when at the first sign of danger they so dramatically show their willingness to face death in defense of the Stars and Stripes?" The paper campaigned for Miller to receive the Congressional Medal of Honor, and it was not pleased when he was not decorated until May and only then got the Navy Cross, which was that service's highest honor.

Things were no better for blacks outside of the armed services. The Red Cross, for example, refused at first to take blood from blacks. Black newspapers criticized this policy heavily during December 1941 and January 1942, correctly pointing out that scientists had conclusively proven that a certain type of blood from a black was no different than the same type from a white. The Red Cross relented and began accepting blood from black donors, but it still refused to give that blood to whites. In a letter to the *Courier*, one infuriated woman wrote, "I bet the same person who would refuse a transfusion of Negro blood would gladly accept a monkey gland transplanted into his carcass to restore his manhood." At the same time, violence against blacks erupted. After a white policeman struck a black soldier with a club on January 9, 1942, a riot broke out in Alexandria, Louisiana, and twelve black soldiers were shot. But nothing riveted blacks more than what occurred in Sikeston, Missouri, on January 25, when 600 whites seized Cleo Wright, a black who was in jail after being charged with attempting to rape a white woman. They tied him to a car, dragged him at high speeds, and then hanged him before throwing gasoline on his body and burning him. This resulted in a widely noted editorial cartoon in the *Baltimore Afro-American* on January 31 that showed Germany's Adolf Hitler and a Japanese soldier grinning on the other side of an ocean as a white mob lynched Wright. The caption for the drawing said, "Defending America Our Way."

In the midst of this turmoil, which caused the black press to be even more critical of black inequities than it had been before the United States entered the war, the NAACP's *The Crisis* was praised by black newspapers for declaring in its January issue that it was not returning to its "close ranks" position of 1918. *The Crisis* explained its new position as follows:

> *The Crisis* would emphasize with all its strength that now is the time not to be silent about the breaches of democracy here in our own land. Now is the time to speak out, not in disloyalty, but in the truest patriotism, the patriotism with an eye—now that the die is cast—single to the peace which must be won.
>
> Of course, between the declaration of war and the making of a just peace there lies the grim necessity of winning the conflict. To this task the

Negro American quickly pledged his fullest support. Be it said once more that black Americans are loyal Americans; but let there be no mistake about the loyalty. It is loyalty to the democratic ideal as enunciated by America and by our British ally; it is not loyalty to many of the practices—which have been—and are still—in vogue here and in the British empire. . . .

If all the people are called to gird and sacrifice for freedom, and the armies to march for freedom, then it must be for freedom for everyone, everywhere, not merely for those under the Hitler heel.

This was followed with a prediction by a black journalist in *Common Ground* that any editor who printed a "close ranks" editorial would lose influence with black readers.

Clearly the *Pittsburgh Courier*'s Double V campaign, which began in early February 1942, did not advocate a "close ranks" position, and blacks immediately embraced it wholeheartedly. Over the next six months, the paper received hundreds of letters and telegrams praising the campaign, and by mid-July it had signed up 200,000 Double V members. Part of the reason for this success was the timing. While the campaign expressed nothing radically new, it came at a time when the government was desperately stressing the need for a united home front in order to win the war, and blacks assumed that discrimination against them, particularly in the South, could no longer be ignored and thus would be eliminated. As it turned out, they were only partially correct.

The *Courier* introduced the campaign on February 7 with a drawing that became familiar to readers: It contained an American eagle and the words, "Democracy. Double VV victory. At home—abroad." Then, a week later, in a sign of the commitment that the paper would make to the campaign in the coming months, it allotted five and a half times more space to it. Thompson's theme was restated in a box at the top of page one in an obvious effort to convince whites that the paper was not suggesting blacks should be unpatriotic: "Americans all are involved in a gigantic war effort to assure victory for the cause of freedom. . . . We, as colored Americans, are determined to protect our country, our form of government, and freedoms which we cherish for ourselves and for the rest of the world, therefore, we adopted the Double 'V' War Cry. . . . Thus, in our fight for freedom, we wage a two-pronged attack against our enslavers at home and those abroad who would enslave us. WE HAVE A STAKE IN THIS FIGHT. . . . WE ARE AMERICANS, TOO!"

Accompanying the Double V campaign from the beginning was a torrent of photographs of smiling blacks. Besides a standard pose of one or more blacks making two V's with their fingers, there were pictures of women wearing clothes with a Double V sewn into them, women with two V's woven into their hair (a style known as a "doubler"), a woman holding a Double V quilt, a soldier forming two V's with his hands and two military flags, and children selling war bonds and stamps while flashing two V's. By late March, the *Courier* also began selecting and running pictures of Double V beauty queens. Particularly standing out in the photographs were celebrities who supported the campaign. Among the blacks were singers Marian Anderson and Etta Moten; bandleader Lionel Hampton; New York City Councilman Adam Clayton Powell Jr.; NAACP Assistant Secretary Roy Wilkins; and boxer Joe Louis's wife, Marva. Although their numbers were never large, famous whites also were pictured, including politicians Wendell Wilkie and Thomas Dewey; columnist and broadcaster Dorothy Thompson; novelist Sinclair Lewis; comedian Eddie Cantor; CBS's William Paley and

NBC's David Sarnoff; and movie stars Humphrey Bogart, Ingrid Bergman, and Gary Cooper.

Accompanying these photographs were hundreds of letters from across the country congratulating the *Courier* on its campaign and its goals. Some of them were extremely positive while others were strikingly blunt. On March 7, when the paper ran fifteen letters, "a 19-year-old Colored Boy" from Columbus, Ohio, wrote:

> If and when the American White Man loses this war, I am wondering if he will think why he did not give the colored man a chance with the white in the Navy? It may be too late for he may not have the Navy himself! He may ask why he did not give the colored man a bigger part to play in the war. He may say, "We could have used the colored man but we didn't. Why didn't I give more jobs in the factories, where he was much needed at the time? We have found that we could have won the war with his aid, that we couldn't win without him. Why didn't we let more of these colored men into the Army and the Marine Corps? Why didn't we let him do more than flunky work? That is all too late now. We were only thinking of ourselves." Your Double V campaign will help to avoid the above situation.

Others letters were equally grim. A Texas woman labeled the campaign important "because many Americans are more dangerous to us [blacks] than some of our enemies abroad." And a Baptist minister in Ohio said the Double V "will teach the Mr. Charlie of the South a new lesson and will shake the foundations of the hypocritical North."

Not content to make its point with just photographs and letters from readers, the *Courier* continually played up the Double V in editorials, editorial cartoons, and columns. Columnist Frank Bolden, noting that the paper would continue the campaign until its goals were reached, summed up his views on discrimination against blacks in capital letters on March 7: "THOSE WHO DO NOT WANT COLORED PEOPLE TO FULLY PARTICIPATE IN THE WAR EFFORT SHOULD BE CLASSED AS TRAITORS TO THE CAUSE OF DEMOCRACY, BECAUSE THEY ARE BLOCKING THE ASSISTANCE OF A POWERFUL ALLY THAT HAS NEVER SHOWN A SHORTAGE OF COURAGE AND SACRIFICE—COLORED AMERICANS!"

While the paper was quite willing to unleash its stable of famed columnists, who were noted for being outspoken and fearless, it nevertheless sometimes countered their tough statements with calmer comments, apparently concerned that whites, particularly those in the government, might become jittery over what was being written. For example, on March 21, the paper said, "The 'Double V' combines . . . the aims and ideals of all men, black as well as white, to make this a more perfect union of peace-loving men and women, living in complete harmony and equality." It also referred to blacks as "the most loyal segment of the American population." Then, three weeks later, it wrapped itself in patriotism with a Double V Creed across the top of the front page in large type: "We pledge allegiance to the United States of America . . . to its all-out victory over the forces of our enemies on the battle-fronts in every section of the world. We pledge allegiance to the principles and tenets of democracy as embodied in the Constitution of the United States and in the Bill of Rights. To full participation in the fruits of this victory . . . victory both at home and abroad . . . we pledge our all!"

Meanwhile, the *Courier* was filling as much as 13 percent of its available newshole each week with an amazing variety of Double V events. There were Double V dances, flag-raising ceremonies, gardens, and professional baseball games between black teams, with a drum and bugle corps forming a giant Double V on the field before one of the games. The paper also encouraged readers to form clubs and sold Double V pins for 5 cents apiece. The clubs participated in such activities as writing congressmen to protest poll taxes, which were designed to keep poor blacks from voting; contacting radio networks, asking that two programs popular with blacks, "Southernaires" and "Wings over Jordan," not be broadcast at the same time, so that listeners could hear both; meeting with businessmen to promote nondiscriminatory hiring; and sending such things as books, cigarettes, shoe polish, candy, and cookies to military camps. There was even a Double V song, "A Yankee Doodle Tan," which Lionel Hampton's band performed on an NBC radio national program in May. The paper noted that it was heard by 2 million listeners, and two weeks later, the paper was selling sheet music for the song for 30 cents a copy.

As the campaign roared onward, the *Courier* ingeniously played it up in numerous ways. For example, it began replacing the standard straight rules between articles with two long dashes and a "VV" between them. Suddenly, wherever readers looked in the paper, they were confronted with the Double V. It also started filling small spaces at the ends of stories with a boldface filler: "Fifteen million people with one unified thought, 'Double V;' Victory at Home and Abroad."

But through all the hoopla, the paper never forgot the reason that it had a campaign: the letter written by Thompson. Thus, in April, it sent columnist George Schuyler to interview him. The opening paragraph of the story set the tone by almost breathlessly portraying him as a hero:

> For 900 miles by airplane and train from Pittsburgh to Wichita, Kansas, I had been wondering what manner of person was James Gratz Thompson, whose stirring letter to The Pittsburgh Courier had launched the nation-wide "Double V" campaign. I knew that he was young and endowed with unusual gifts of expression. I knew that in his memorable letters he had expressed the feelings of millions of Negroes, young and old, from the Atlantic to the Pacific. It was clear he was a thoughtful young man and his photograph indicated that he was handsome and upstanding. Now, as 1 pressed the buzzer at the front door of the five-room one-story house the Thompsons own at 1239 Indiana Avenue, my curiosity was to be satisfied. At last I was to see and talk with the Negro youth whose words had thrilled a million COURIER readers.

After pointing out that Thompson had quit working at the cafeteria because he had been denied a five-cent-an-hour raise, Schuyler called him "the idol of Wichita's 6,000 Negro citizens."

With such adulation, it should have surprised no one when the paper hired Thompson two months later as head of its Double V campaign. This led a minister in Hopkinsville, Kentucky, to base a sermon on Thompson and the campaign. "Jesus Christ, our 'Double V' Friend, kissed the idea [of the campaign] when he kneeled and prayed in the Garden of Gethsemane," said Rev. L. S. Grooms. "The idea of 'Double Victory' did not leave the earth, it simply remained silent until the selected person [Thompson] was notified and the time pronounced." Thompson directed the paper's campaign for eight months until he joined the service in February 1943.

Going hand in hand with the Double V was the continuing drumbeat by black newspapers about specific instances of injustices against blacks. One of the frequent targets of criticism was the Army, which on the day after the bombing of Pearl Harbor met with a group of black editors, publishers, and columnists and angered them by saying it was not going to be a "sociological laboratory" and change its racial policies during the war. According to historian John Morton Blum, such "unchanging policies" by the military, particularly the Army, were the reason for considerable black discontent: "Angry about military segregation, blacks detested the harassment they suffered from Military Police, the abuses they suffered from civilians in towns near cantonments, especially in the South, and the Army's endorsement of Jim Crow regulations in cities frequented by troops on liberty. Segregation on Southern trains and buses especially irritated northern blacks in training camps in Dixie."

Black problems at Army camps, which frequently involved black soldiers and white military policemen shooting at each other, were among the stories played up heavily on the front pages of the black papers. From August 1941 until June 1942, there were racial disturbances, and sometimes riots, at Fort Dix in New Jersey, Fort Bragg and Camp Davis in North Carolina, Fort Benning in Georgia, and Mitchel Field in New York. A Military Intelligence report did not blame the black press for the problems, but it complained that some of the black newspapers' articles about racial incidents in the camps, as well as other more general problems in the Army, were "beyond the normal agitational behavior of the press" and were not improving black soldiers' allegiance to the country. One article that angered the Army was from the black *People's Voice* in New York, which managed to sneak a reporter into a barracks at Fort Dix on April 3 to cover a gun battle between blacks and whites. The reporter predicted that more race riots would follow in the Army camps, and he belittled an official statement that the shooting was not racially motivated. Military Intelligence, in noting the influence among black troops of black newspapers, such as the *Pittsburgh Courier* and the five papers in the *Afro-American* chain (of which the Baltimore paper was the largest), concluded: "As long as these papers carry on their efforts for the purpose of racial betterment they cannot be termed as subversive organs. They do, however, at times appear to achieve the same result as outright subversive publications."

That comment from Military Intelligence was at the core of a crucial problem for the government in the first half of 1942. It was not sure that it could win the war without the support of the entire country, and there was a fear that critical articles by the black newspapers, whether justified or not, might harm black morale. If that occurred, blacks, who made up 10 percent of the population, might be persuaded, at best, to ignore the war effort, or, at worst, to become internal saboteurs and do such things as blow up railroad lines or power plants. Such concerns led on May 22 to a discussion at a presidential cabinet meeting of the critical nature of the black press as part of an overall assessment of black attitudes toward the war, which everyone agreed were not good. This conclusion was supported by an Office of Facts and Figures report on the same day noting that many articles and editorials in black newspapers were playing up discrimination and that this was hurting black morale. President Franklin D. Roosevelt suggested to Attorney General Francis Biddle and Postmaster General Frank Walker that they should talk to black editors in order to, in Biddle's words, "see what could be done about preventing their subversive language."

Roosevelt probably wanted to only scare the black press into toning down instead of actually suppressing it under the Espionage Act, which had once again gone into effect when the United States entered the war. After all, he appreciated the important part that blacks had played in his reelection in 1940, and he would not have wanted to offend them by publicly attacking the black newspapers. Furthermore, he was not a racist, and blacks made immense strides during his presidency. But as a politician, he was aware that contact with blacks might offend southern voters, and so he used others to interact with them, such as his wife, Eleanor. When asked whether this practice might still lead to criticism of him, he countered, "I can always say, 'Well, that's my wife. I can't do anything about her.' " Thus, asking Biddle and Walker to see the black editors was characteristic of the way he operated.

There is no evidence that Walker had more than a brief, polite conversation with any of the black editors, preferring instead to have his aides handle something that controversial. But Biddle did not avoid the confrontation, and he came into it with a definite familiarity with the black newspapers and what they were writing. Since early spring, the Justice Department had been heavily investigating the country's print media, and the black newspapers particularly posed a thorny problem. Their articles and editorials clearly were more critical of the government and outspoken about injustices than most of the mainstream white-owned papers, but they were far less so than the radical fascist press. That left the Justice Department with a dilemma—it was unsure of whether it could successfully prosecute the black press under the Espionage Act.

The Justice Department addressed the problem in June 1942 when the Post Office asked if an issue of the *Chicago World*, whose weekly circulation of 28,000 made it one of the country's ten largest black newspapers, could be declared unmailable because of its criticism of the treatment of blacks. "What is tyranny in one imperium should not be a blessing in another," the paper wrote in May. "If segregation is the curse of Hitlerism then segregation is the curse of any nation that indulges in it." The Justice Department said the question was whether a publication could combine "all-out united" support of the war with denunciations of discrimination against blacks, which resulted in criticism of the government. It said it relied generally on a statement by legal expert Zechariah Chafee Jr., who had written: "[I]n our anxiety to protect ourselves from foreign tyrants, [the country should not] imitate some of their worst acts, and sacrifice in the process of national defense the very liberties which we are defending." Applying that principle, as well as others from cases that had been decided by the Supreme Court, the Justice Department concluded that the *World* was "basically neither defeatist nor obstructionist nor divisionist"; instead, it was merely pointing out factually what blacks considered to be unfair treatment. "If such utterances [as in the *World*] do not fall within the traditional constitutional immunities for freedom of speech," it said in declaring what the paper wrote as within the law, "categories long established will have to be formulated anew."

While that was a liberal interpretation of freedom of the press in wartime, which was not surprising because Biddle did not think that First Amendment rights shrunk even if the life of the republic was at stake—a belief that he conveyed to those who worked for him—the black newspapers had no way of knowing that was the tack the Justice Department was taking. Consequently, John Sengstacke, who had taken over the *Chicago Defender* in 1940 when his uncle, Robert Abbott, died and who had quickly established himself as the country's leading black publisher, nervously asked for a meeting with Biddle in June 1942. The reason was simple: The black publishers were worried that the government might try to shut down one or more of the papers, and he hoped to forestall any such move.

Biddle readily agreed to see him, and when Sengstacke was shown into a Justice Department conference room in Washington, he found numerous black newspapers, including the *Defender*, the *Pittsburgh Courier*, and the *Baltimore Afro-American*, spread out on a table. All of them had headlines about clashes between whites and blacks in Army camps. Biddle said bluntly that such articles were hurting the war effort, and if the papers did not change their tone quickly, he was going to take them to court for being seditious. Then, turning specifically to the *Defender*, he said a number of its articles were close to being seditious, and the paper was being watched closely by the Justice Department.

Sengstacke, who was just as tough as Biddle, denied that the black newspapers were detrimental to the war effort. He pointed out that they had been fighting against black injustices for more than a hundred years, and then he said firmly, looking Biddle in the eyes, "You have the power to close us down, so if you want to close us, go ahead and attempt it." However, he continued, there was a possibility of a compromise. More than forty years later, he recalled what he said next:

> "I've been trying to get an appointment to see [Henry] Stimson [the secre-tary of war]. . . . I've been trying to get in touch with everybody else [in the government]. Nobody will talk with us. So, what do you expect us to publish? We don't want to publish the wrong information. . . . We want to cooperate with the war effort. . . . But if we can't get information from the heads of the various agencies, we have to do the best we can."
>
> So, he said, "Well, I didn't know that." I said, "That is correct." . . . He said, "Well, look, I'll see if I can help you in that way. . . . And what I'll do is make arrangements for you to see some of these people." So, he called Secretary [Frank] Knox [of the Navy] and made an appointment for me to see him.
>
> Then, at the end of the hour-long meeting, Biddle executed an abrupt 180-degree turn from the meeting's beginning, almost surely because he had never had any intention of going after the black publishers with the Espionage Act. He promised that none of them would be indicted for sedi-tion during the war if they did not write anything more critical than what they already had carried, and, in fact, said he hoped they would tone down. Sengstacke replied that he could not promise that would be the case, but added that if the black papers could interview top government officials, they would be "glad" to support the war effort.

Sengstacke promptly went out and told other black publishers what had occurred, particularly that there would be no Espionage Act indictments, but none of them ever told their readers, and apparently they told few on their staffs. Bolden, who was a war correspondent for the *Pittsburgh Courier*, recalled that his executive editor told him the news confidentially by the end of the summer of 1942, and he was not surprised at Biddle's decision. "We didn't think we were doing anything unconstitutional," he said. "Of course, that may have been debatable. But we had confidence in our government that it wouldn't do anything silly like shutting down the black press. There was just too much pressure on the government to do that."

# Chapter 5

# JANE L. CHAPMAN

# COMPARATIVE MEDIA HISTORY

**C**OMPARATIVE MEDIA HISTORY POSITIONS the development of journalism in relationship to media developments in a global context, tracing the emergence of international media institutions across countries and across industries. The
study compares Anglo-American scholarship to original research from France, Japan
and Germany and juxtaposes the development of journalism alongside that of film,
music and advertising. The book discusses the emergence of globalization as well as
the continuities and disruptions in transnational media development, providing readers
with a broader, international perspective of change. Chapman argues that the main
roots of modern journalism lie in the 19th century, as newspapers increasingly encouraged consumerism over citizenship. In 20th-century wars, governments increasingly
intruded into media via propaganda efforts.

The extracts below address radio—an often neglected journalistic platform—and
connect its development and significance to events in media history, other platforms
and media. The excerpts not only trace radio's development internationally, but also
show how political and economic contexts shape the environment in which news media
operate. Radio, Chapman argues, was more than a precursor to television. It provided
an important breakthrough for journalism, introducing "live" coverage and, in terms
of the way news was received, a new culture of domestic intimacy for the audience.
Over the years, radio has survived as changes in technology have allowed the medium
to regularly reinvent itself.

Urbanization and greater mobility, combined with the impact of the First World War on
both technology and changing attitudes, had led to a new social environment with
demand for improved communication systems. Now that experimentation had produced
valve receivers and loudspeakers, and electricity was being extended throughout the
Western world, continuous wave radio found a mass market. Wireless sets could be

produced and marketed on a large scale. Early radio had been a solitary activity requiring a crystal set with headphones, but between the wars people enjoyed radio in groups, at work or as a family sitting round a smart, large piece of furniture called a 'wireless'; social life was now increasingly centred on family and home.

The spread of radio was accompanied by a rapid institutional growth in a new form of media organization: broadcasters, who were communicating the radio transmissions. Radio's take-off was swift, and public enthusiasm for it peaked during the 'golden age' of the 1930s and 1940s. Collective amnesia concerning radio's heritage has not been helped by the fact that most radio history books until recently have tended to concentrate either on technological breakthroughs or on nostalgic accounts of 'classic' programmes, to the exclusion of political, economic and social factors.

Scholars now argue not only that radio can be seen as 'the most important electronic invention of the century', rivalling cinema in its influence, but also that it helped to support community and cultural identity. 'In speaking to us as a nation during a crucial period of time it helped to shape our cultural consciousness and to define us as people in ways that were certainly not unitary but cut deeply across individual, class, racial, and ethnic experience'. This relationship between national consciousness and radio was shared by every country studied here.

It is also argued that, in the United States, the dominant ideology of big business influenced radio's history, for power to dominate an important medium also brings with it the power to shape historical perception. 'Close analysis of radio begins to unravel the mask that US commercial media have created for themselves: as a naturally arising, consensus-shaped, and unproblematic reflection of a pluralistic society, rather than the conflicting, tension-ridden site of the ruthless exercise of cultural hegemony, often demonstrating in its very effort to exert control the power and diversity of the alternative popular constructions that oppose and resist it'.

According to one historian, three factors influenced the form and content of American radio: the desire for national broadcasting; the choice of a specific technology – wired networks – to provide the service; and dislike and mistrust of radio advertising on the part of both listeners and businesses. The continuing protests over this last, and the programming forms and organizational structure that responded to them, influenced television. The same relevance for television can also be argued in the case of Great Britain, particularly as the BBC had a monopoly on both media for a long time, and for Japan and France.

## Radio Take-off American Style: Influences and Patterns for the Future

US federal (i.e., government) control had been considered just after the Great War, but 'the strong position of the radio companies, the government's disposition to influence rather than directly regulate, and the geography of the United States all worked against the form of centralized broadcasting so widespread in other parts of the world'. Americans had experienced the private operation of telegraphs, railroads, electric light and telephones, all of which had set an organizational precedent. Here cost determined the nature of development: not only receivers but also broadcasting wired networks had to make a profit because network radio entailed the expense of renting wires. Programming became centralized in order to attract advertisers and for cost efficiency, therefore radio emerged as a means of selling products so that 'most programs merely filled the time between commercials'. The American public were hugely enthusiastic for the magic of broadcasting and desired a national network system that would unite and connect the country and give them programmes from far away. Farmers, for instance, saw radio as a means of breaking their isolation. This concept appeared earlier than the idea of radio as a commercial system, which was not inevitable: at first local stations were widespread, and during the 1920s the advertising industry itself doubted that advertisements over radio would work.

Furthermore, there was not agreement: broadcasting was a product of resistance as well as of a few large companies, most notably AT&T. The technology of wired networks that AT&T supported was easily understandable to the public and favoured by President Hoover, who saw his role as being to facilitate the speedy growth of a new industry – which benefited AT&T and its technical monopoly.

National audiences were collectively supplied with a range of programmes. Evangelists used radio extensively and were among the first to own stations, with radio preachers setting the scene for the later rise of the electronic church on television. Programming diversity was impressive: comedy, variety and quiz shows, Westerns and detective dramas, as well as soap operas. In addition, Presidents Harding and Coolidge in the 1920s and President Roosevelt in the 1930s all used radio for political broadcasts.

In Britain and continental Europe, populations had experienced a high level of government intervention in their lives during the war, and the ideal of public service was strong, so attitudes favoured a proactive role for the state to create 'a land fit for heros to live in' after the hardship of the 1914–18 period. This provided the context for the broadcasting model, whereas in America conditions for commercial expansion prevailed.

## Broadcasting Structures and Impact

Although countries all used the same technology, each evolved its own structures for dealing with broadcasting at local, regional and national level. What emerged reflected social, cultural and economic influences as well as political pragmatism, but what they all shared in common was the realization that there was a scarcity of wavelengths, which necessitated some form of regulation. The way that radio became established institutionally and the style of programming that this entailed in the United States and Britain provided role models for other countries, which opted for their own combination of structural elements.

While political broadcasts became a feature everywhere, political structures for broadcasting varied. Systems do not simply have to be either privatized or state-sponsored – there were, and still are, many different variables and combinations within cultural, geographical and technological contexts. In Australia a mixed system of government and private stations evolved, but fewer stations were needed there than in America, because so much of the population was concentrated around six cities. Despite the fact that, in North America, the United States took eighty-nine out of the ninety-five wavelengths, Canadian broadcasting still blossomed, apparently undeterred by fewer stations and no major manufacturing companies to encourage privatization. The Canadian National Railroad started a national service using government telegraph lines, and Canadian Radio Broadcasting was established in 1930 as a forerunner to the Canadian Broadcasting Commission, controlled by central government.

In Britain and France it appeared that, given the scarcity of wavelengths, a state-influenced institution was more appropriate. *The Times* described the British system as 'an independent monopoly with public service as the motive'. The BBC aimed to reach wide audiences in order to sell wireless sets, whereas in America stations sought to attract the largest possible audiences for specific programmes financed by commercial sponsorship.

## The Drama of Radio News

Although the use of radio was integral to the conflict worldwide, at first, in 1939, its performance was far from confident. During the early period of the 'phoney war', audiences in Britain became bored by the BBC's interminable diet of organ music, broadcast because of censorship restrictions on news. However, by the end of August that year, as both the public and the authorities readjusted, three-quarters of those surveyed in a poll found the BBC more reliable than newspaper news. Although wartime radio became identified with news, in the United States news was a relatively late starter. Nevertheless, influential and talented commentators such as H. V. Kalternborn and William Shirer, backed by the CBS director of European operations Edward R. Murrow, had already made Europe's conflict and the real-life drama of Munich 'the greatest show yet heard on American radio'. When war broke out in the Pacific, Japan's NHK immediately carried news flashes on the start of hostilities, while its domestic service was limited to national network broadcasts from Tokyo; most other programmes were suspended, including weather reports. The authorities took control immediately.

As total war progressed, radio came into its own, well illustrated by the BBC's rise to pre-eminence. The extraordinary conflict situation allowed the BBC to argue that, if their radio broadcasting was restricted, national prestige and public morale would be jeopardized and people would turn to German stations. Nevertheless, there was a wartime embargo system, permitting the morning and evening papers to break news. The tone of the BBC was always less over-optimistic and more circumspect than that of the press (in 1941, two-thirds of those questioned in a poll found the BBC 100 per cent reliable), and it continued complete national wavelength coverage throughout, increasingly ignoring embargos. For instance, because the BBC sought out a second opinion for agency feeds, such stories were no longer considered agency 'property'. In addition the corporation broadcast anything that had already been broadcast on foreign stations, without any embargo restrictions.

The BBC was also improving its range of presentational styles – proof in itself of considerable press freedom. There were more eye-witness reports and American-style drama-documentary techniques in topical war features, and increased emphasis on commentary and explanation. Reporters broadcast with the latest technology from as near to the front lines as possible, and the BBC's war reporting unit of sixty-two was given priority access for D-Day coverage. More than 50 per cent of the population continued to switch on to *War Report*, the nightly news programme. In July 1945 the BBC unilaterally ended its scheduling agreement with the press that dated back to pre-war years, and confidently planned eleven daily bulletins across two networks, starting at 7 a.m. The press and broadcasting were now both independent news providers for the first time.

In Japan, by government direction, the same frequencies were to be used throughout the country with the aim of boosting air defence via a radio-wave control headquarters, run by government and representatives of the armed forces as part of an operating programme entitled 'Essentials of Emergency Structure for Domestic Broadcasting'. Further control reduced radio's role to one of raising national morale. Although wireless was the only way of receiving information during the intensification of air raids over the country, both production and supply of receivers fell during the war, declining to 7.5 million by 1945. Meanwhile, the directional antenna technology developed by Yagi for television before the outbreak of war was used by the British army in Singapore in 1940 against the Japanese forces. US navy forces in the Pacific used radar called 'YAGI array' to detect and attack Japanese warships, but were unaware of its significance.

In addition to news broadcasts to back up American intervention, short-wave propaganda from the United States was aimed at Nazi Europe, and the American Forces Radio Service (AFRS) broadcasts were used to boost morale. Wartime AFRS also influenced trends in radio: it used pre-recorded items, reinforcing the technical feasibility of editing and discs, whereas previously the networks had prided themselves on live items only. AFRS also deleted commercial references and advertising, retitling programmes that carried a sponsor's name. Goebbels had no such integrity: in 1942 he spearheaded a decree forcing radio stations to allocate 70 per cent of their broadcasting to light music – which he hoped would then deliver a large number of listeners for the political broadcasts.

The role of radio was at its most dramatic in France, also carrying significance for the future. During the occupation, the Nazis seized people's radio sets. From 1940, as many of the population fled their homes in the north, through to liberation in 1944, the radio airways in France were the scene of a verbal war between Nazi, Vichy and resistance propaganda. The roles of the French resistance, of General de Gaulle's exile in London and of the Free French 'Ici Londres' broadcasts from the BBC, which were so vital for passing information to the active resistance movement, have all been well aired. De Gaulle was unique among the military in his early appreciation and exploitation of the medium:

> the political personality of de Gaulle, which was decades later to be the foundation stone of the broadcasting structure, was created at that moment by the transmitters of the BBC. It was at that time that he first realised, more powerfully and more skilfully than any other world leader, the political potential of broadcasting and its particular applicability to the chaotic conditions of the French nation.

Churchill was also superbly adept at radio performance: despite his unease about the BBC's quasi-autonomy, as prime minister, Churchill more than any other British politician successfully exploited the medium of radio with classic broadcasts. The most moving and famous was his uplifting talk over the airways on 18 June 1940: 'if the British Empire and its Commonwealth last for a thousand years, men will still say: "This was their finest hour" '. That same day General de Gaulle's first Free French broadcast was also transmitted by the BBC from London, going down in the annals of French broadcasting history to such an extent that streets in France are named in commemoration of the date.

## Fact, Fiction, Truth and Propaganda

It was only at the outbreak of war that the democracies realized the need for propaganda, but British attitudes this time round were coloured by the experience of the First World War, when exaggeration and lies about German atrocities had been heavily criticized. This previous experience caused an initial reluctance to exploit Nazi barbarism for propaganda purposes, so, for instance, the full extent of concentration camps and the genocide of Jews in the Holocaust was not fully appreciated until the end of the war. At first officials adopted a policy of 'no news is good news', maintaining military secrecy over the arrival of British troops in France; newspapers were seized for reporting the event and newsreel coverage was banned. There was also an initial ban on all photography of military subjects, but later this was lifted. Although the popularity of newsreels slumped temporarily because of lack of news, for the rest of the war period they were very popular indeed. Cinemas were closed temporarily in anticipation of a short airborne conflict with clusters of population as bombing targets. By 1940 the British government recognized the need to integrate censorship with propaganda functions by merging the Press and Censorship Bureau with the Ministry of Information (MOI). News was given top priority in the encouragement of the war effort by press, broadcasting services and film, to the extent that the BBC's Sir John Reith, who was influential in developing the idea of 'propaganda with truth', called news 'the shocktroops of propaganda'. The MOI's news division aimed to 'tell the truth, nothing but the truth and, as near as possible, the whole truth'. Bad news was issued only gradually, like a drip feed, and the worst casualty statistics from the Battle of the Atlantic were never released.

Nevertheless, the BBC succeeded in maintaining the delicate balance between avoiding giving information to the enemy on the one hand, and maintaining an image of free honesty on the other. Officials set a high priority not only on pre-censorship but also on public trust, avoiding disbelief and feelings of manipulation by a more subtle approach that still provided people with facts. This achievement enhanced the BBC's reputation for accuracy and reliability both at home and abroad. As George Orwell commented, from about 1940 the corporation's prestige was such that the saying 'I heard it on the radio' was almost equivalent to 'I know it must be true'.

## Media Production Influenced by Cold War Politic

McCarthy himself became an astute user of the medium of television to propagandize, and interminable HUAC hearings were broadcast live. However, the television medium was also to be his undoing when it became a platform for investigative exposure against him by journalists Ed Murrow and Fred Friendly, although the role of the former in McCarthy's downfall has been exaggerated. Television entertainment programmes also communicated the anti-communist menace.

A few films from this period, such as *High Noon*, contained faint suggestions of opposition to the prevalent anti-communist line, and many were well-crafted Hollywood classics, such as *The Inn of the Sixth Happiness*, with Ingrid Bergman, and *The Third Man*, from the Harry Lime novels, but most depicted the Cold War conflict with heavy-handed portrayals of gangster-like, corrupt Soviet bosses who conspired to overturn American freedom and democracy. Domestic culture was portrayed more subtly: the European tour of George Gershwin's popular musical *Porgy and Bess* with an all-black cast, for instance, was funded by 'psychological warfare' as a means of combating Soviet criticism of American racism at a time when legal cases concerning segregation were hitting the headlines.

The Second World War had illustrated that radio was the most effective weapon in the overseas propaganda arsenal, and this continued to be the case during the post-war period. The West invested heavily in powerful transmitters which enabled Voice of America (VOA) and the BBC to be heard in the communist bloc, despite attempts by the authorities to jam the airways – evidence in itself that broadcasting efforts were taken seriously. VOA devoted almost half of its budget to broadcasting behind the Iron Curtain, and transmitted in forty-six languages worldwide. The CIA secretly funded two German-based stations to supplement the services of West Germany's Deutsche Welle: Radio Free Europe for Eastern Europe and Radio Liberation, which became Radio Liberty, for the Soviet Union. In addition the American Forces Network broadcast news, information, popular music and variety via powerful transmitters to the armed forces still stationed in Germany, so Europeans could tune in. The continent was saturated with radio propaganda, which prompted the European Broadcasting Conference to reallocate medium-wave frequencies in 1948 – a restriction that was ignored by the United States, which continued with some unauthorized broadcasting in Germany.

## Clandestine Radio

Secret radio transmissions have also traditionally formed part of both military psychological operations and civilian activist politics during periods of conflict. CIA, press and wire services still monitor the international airways for clandestine broadcasting that can provide intelligence on revolutionary protest. Clandestine stations differ from pirate and foreign broadcasters in a number of ways: they are non-profit-making, they do not have offices and the location of their transmission is often unclear – which often makes them vulnerable to enemy 'black propaganda' or broadcasting which is deliberately misleading in terms of its source. For example, in 1958 the Cuban rebel army in the Sierra Maestra, under the leadership of Che Guevara, established its own station, Radio Rebelde, which commanded such a large audience that it became the target of a black station claiming the same name, frequency and provenance, but broadcasting anti-Castro messages. Revolutionaries decried the black operation as a 'trick used by Batista to deceive the people'. Similar efforts existed in Asia and the Middle East as well as the Eastern bloc. Surprisingly the number of clandestine stations worldwide increased after the collapse of communism.

The BBC's external service continued its international reputation for objectivity and fair reporting, because propaganda was both subtle and credible, notwithstanding formal and informal links with the British Foreign Office. In contrast, VOA's reputation was less elevated because of a cruder and more strident style of broadcasting and a lack of independence from the American government. Even music by outstanding Russian classical composers such as Rimsky-Korsakov was banned. Music was viewed politically as a means of increasing the popularity of the American way of life, with jazz and rock and roll as trump cards, along with blue jeans, Coca-Cola and McDonald's.

Active anti-communist broadcasting encouraged rebellion and expectations of Western intervention against Russia in 1956. As this never materialized, radio was seen as contributing to suffering during the Hungarian uprising, and such criticism led VOA to emulate the BBC's more measured objectivity. Thereafter, aggressive psychological warfare gave way to the longer term, more gradualist approach of cultural diplomacy. Although radio was increasingly viewed as one of many tools for cultural assault, the Cuban missile crisis of 1962 illustrated that the medium was still crucial to international diplomacy. At a time when the nuclear threat was at its most imminent, both sides used it to communicate with each other as well as for disseminating propaganda.

## Television and the Berlin Wall

In 1961 the Berlin Wall was erected between the Russian and Western sectors of the city. At the time the event seemed to increase tension, but in retrospect it allowed a relationship to develop with Russia, facilitating a debate about the future in which the Federal Republic's television played a crucial part. However, the German Democratic Republic allowed no such discourse on the role of media within society: pluralism was constrained by a system of state licensing and a monopolistic news agency. The authorities tried to control the flow of programmes from the FRG while also providing technical excellence to compete with the West. Within East Berlin, the most impressive new building was the television tower, a symbolic landmark immortalized by the movie director Wim Wenders. Within the GDR, one television programme, *Der schwarze Kanal* (The Black Channel), replayed parts of West German programmes, selecting elements that were to the credit of the East, and to the discredit of the West, as a form of counter-propaganda.

Henceforth, however, the rise of television was to play a key role worldwide. In East Germany, for instance, political attitudes were influenced by the credible images portrayed by neighbouring West German television.

Later in the 1980s, satellite transmissions defied physical boundaries such as the Berlin Wall, and the materialism that programmes demonstrated had an impact on the way people viewed the communist system.

As the inter-war period had indicated, for a long time the wider social environment had not been receptive to the diffusion of the television medium, although television had been conceived and patented in the nineteenth century. After the Second World War, the purchase of sets was contingent on rising living standards as countries reconstructed their economies. Meanwhile in Europe and Japan both the concept and structures of public-service broadcasting became institutionalized as a form of national consciousness, a process that had started with radio before the war.

### Television and Radio

At first the growth of television also led to a decline in radio listening: in Britain the number of radio licences was at a peak in 1950, but fell as the number of combined radio and TV licences rose in 1955 to 4.5 million. In Japan radio listening declined from three hours a day in 1950 to thirty minutes in 1965. Yet watching TV never completely replaced listening to the wireless: indeed, in France the amount of time spent listening stayed more or less the same despite the arrival of television viewing. In that country radio still dominated in the 1940s and 1950s. Even in 1961, 80 per cent of the French population had a radio, whereas less than 20 per cent had a television set. In 1960, there were only thirty staff journalists working in television for the state broadcaster RTF, as opposed to 310 who worked in radio. By 1989, 98 per cent of the French population had at least one radio. Again, although the radio licence in Japan was abolished in 1968, within five years there were still fifty-one radio organizations.

The predominant influence of radio on television in countries such as Britain, France, Japan and most other European countries was an organizational and structural one: the monopoly control of radio was extended to TV, with the same management and regulatory system. For instance, in 1950 Japan's radio and broadcasting law revalidated NHK's legal status as well as guaranteeing freedom of expression in broadcasting. Cross-over influence among media industries was evident before the Second World War; yet this period in history was unique in the extent to which a cross-over from radio to television was both possible and likely.

## Radio and Music

Technology saved radio by enabling it to reinvent itself in a more portable and individualized way that ensured its worldwide survival, to the extent that by the mid-1960s almost every household had a radio set. Breakthroughs that improved the quality of transmission and reception, such as FM, were accompanied by changing radio usage within consumer lifestyles. The latter came to be affected by the profusion of transistor radios, hi-fi stereo tuners, car radios, radio alarms, walkmans and other devices that made listening more flexible and adaptable. Radio's response to the new serious competition from television was to concentrate more on the local and the specialized, resulting in a more diverse range of music being played, which in turn affected the record industry.

By the early 1950s sales of discs had outstripped those of sheet music; then radio stimulated demand for rock and roll, which was emerging as more than a passing fad, and for black music styles that had been marginalized by the major record companies. The response of the big four record companies, RCA Victor, Decca, Columbia and Capitol, which in 1948 shared 75 per cent of the market, was to try and follow the successful example of Decca, which had signed up Bill Haley and the Comets from the independent label Essex: *Rock Around the Clock* was the big hit of 1955. Similarly, RCA signed up Elvis Presley from Sun Records for a mere $33,000 plus a cadillac. Although some of Presley's early songs were based on black music, his career soon took on a more anodyne commercial flavour after it came under the control of a major label. In the late 1950s, concentration in the music industry was challenged by increasing numbers of independent record companies supplying the huge range and quantity of music that radio now required. As early as 1951 the American DJ Alan Freed was successfully introducing black 'rhythm and blues' styles to white audiences, but his ability to thrive as an independent operator was later destroyed by litigation, prompted by the majors' attempt via the industry's ASCAP publishing association to eliminate competition. In the volatile market of the time, another means to achieve this same end, according to Peter Martin, was for the majors to resort to illegal methods such as 'payola' to radio DJs to play specific discs.

## The Influence of Radio and Television on Politics and the Public: Some Comparisons

When it came to communication via broadcasting, politicians cut their teeth on radio then, sometimes apprehensively, transferred the skills that they had developed to television. It was radio that first attracted them to broadcasting, but it was television that displayed the performance 'warts and all', making politics less distant, more accessible. In the process boundaries between public and private were further redrawn, promoting a trend that newspapers had started and to which radio had contributed. There was also a movement of personnel and of successful programme formats from the one broadcast medium to the other. Hence, in the case of both Britain and France, the unified nature of the broadcasting systems had a positive impact.

In America, the growth of advertising, public relations and television as a communications weapon for politicians meant that the medium played a crucial part in elections. Kennedy, for instance, would probably not have been elected without it. But, as both Pierre Bourdieu and Daniel Boorstin have noted, the forms and conventions of production dictated the nature of both the viewing experience and the experience for those appearing on television. Politicians in America accepted the existing genres.

Conversely, relentless news coverage of civil disturbances at home and of carnage abroad during the Vietnam War offered no respite for president Lyndon B. Johnson. It produced the impression that he was not in control, making it impossible for him to seek another term of office. His successor, Richard Nixon, put pressure on television stations to be more 'loyal' towards government policy at a time during the late 1960s when the foreign policy of the United States in South-East Asia was the key issue in international affairs. Vietnam was called the first 'television war', provoking debate about the effects of global coverage. Some people believed that daily battle news led to public boredom, others that it encouraged opposition to American intervention. The effects of news coverage have also been hotly debated, with claims that the civil rights movement in America would not have existed without television. Protests involving civil disorder tend to be newsworthy, but were said by some to be given more prominence by virtue of the media attention to them. A similar argument emerged later in relation to terrorism when Mrs Thatcher referred to the 'oxygen of publicity'.

For libertarian media historians, May 1968 was a defining date, when worker and youth protests erupted in Europe. In France they were centred mainly around barricades erected in Paris's Latin Quarter. Radio became part of events as they unfolded and was therefore criticized by some for provoking the trouble, running 'the risk of creating a media event to serve its own appetite for news and sensation'.

During the revolt, the use of radio by student leaders to mobilize support among the student body was strategic. The medium helped to gain the sympathy of the public on the issues of university reform and police violence against protesters as young people became politically important in Germany and France. It was also used as a forum for debate and negotiation between the two main players – the authorities and the student protesters. Finally de Gaulle, choosing not to appear on television, reasserted his authority and that of the Fifth Republic via radio, in a move designed to be reminiscent of 18 June 1944. It had the desired effect: a huge demonstration in support of the Gaullist regime meant that law and order was reimposed.

This was the second occasion that radio became integral to politics in post-Second World War France. The first was during the Algerian War for Independence. As the conflict was drawing to a close in 1961, elements of the professional army staged a revolt in opposition to de Gaulle's policy of independence for the country from colonial rule. De Gaulle immediately went on television to condemn the rebellion categorically, and the speech was heard by hundreds of thousands of French conscripts who listened in on

their transistor radios at the barracks. They were persuaded that their leader was determined to take a firm stand and therefore backed him against the renegades. It was called
a 'transistor victory' against the attempted coup, reminiscent of radio's role in pre-war
Japan during a military rebellion.

## The Relationship between Deregulation and Endangered Species of Programming

In the United States, the Federal Communications Commission spent much of the 1980s
and 1990s abandoning what are called 'behavioural controls' in radio, that is, definitions
of acceptable content in terms of public-service elements. These included requirements
on stations to offer 'community service' items, controls on the amount of air-time
permitted for advertising, and obligations to deal with controversial issues in a fair and
balanced way. The Telecommunications Act of 1996 permitted market-driven growth
among group owners by changing station ownership restrictions. The subsequent
increased concentration did not lead to more listener choice, but did influence higher
advertising rates. A study of radio news in 1995 found that newscasts were not serving
the public interest by offering political voices to the audience and were not providing
relevant information for listeners to evaluate the government.

## Radio

Deregulation has not been confined to Western Europe, or simply to the television
industry. Radio has been subject to deregulation worldwide, yet it continues to be a vital
broadcast medium. In Germany there was a dramatic increase in the number of radio
stations following reunification, and more recently web radio has become popular. In
Britain large numbers of regular listeners to the BBC's up-market talk channel, Radio 4,
protested over proposed changes to the schedules, demonstrating the importance of the
station's broadcasting to daily life in the country.

   In Europe, three types of radio – national, independent and community – developed to meet the diverse needs of listeners. At the beginning of radio, there was a
shortage of programmes, then once more with the introduction of digital radio the
number of channels exceeded the amount of programming available to fill them. By the
1990s there was also more competition for existing audiences because of a fragmentation of the previous mass audience, threatening the traditions of public-service broadcasting. Segmentation of audience and market was just one clear trend that accorded
with the pattern of deregulation and corporate concentration mentioned above. Another,
according to one study, was for a small number of industrial groupings to reflect the
concentration of digital activity. These operators showed a propensity to exploit the
potential of multimedia and interactivity in order to create new sources of revenue,
again highlighting the tendency towards convergence.

   The comparative approach between epochs as well as countries and media branches
raises many questions. For instance, what differentiates Reuters as an instrument of
nineteenth-century British imperialism and the pre-First World War Wolff–Havas–
Reuter news agency cartel from today's global cartel of conglomerates? There are three
new features.

Firstly, there is more extensive cross-ownership, both within media industries, which are now wider and more extensive, and with other trading areas. Reuters' other business was financial information, not construction, garages, electricity or consumer retail. Herein lies a major difference between past and present: for the first time in media history, news is produced by companies outside of journalism, which throws up the possibility that independent news could be replaced by self-interested commercialism posing as news.

Secondly, faster, easier and more instant geographic reach exists today – satellite and the Internet ensure this – although nineteenth-century journalists were pretty enterprising in their intrepid efforts to bring news speedily to the remoter parts of the globe, often facing danger in the process. The *Gold Coast Independent* concentrated on news brought to it from all over West Africa by canoe or by hazardous jungle journeys.

Thirdly, the scale is now different: access to consumers has been enhanced to the point of saturation and to the extent that the degree of media exposure has the effect of obscuring reality. In 1856 W. H. Russell, war correspondent of *The Times*, travelled through the Crimea on horseback, writing his dispatches alone, by hand and by candlelight. He had few competitors. In 2003 the Pentagon opened the battlefields in Iraq to about 600 US and 100 British and other international journalists and embedded them with military units for the duration of this most recent Gulf War. Russell's lone pen caused the downfall of a British prime minister and rocked the empire, while also raising issues of journalistic dilemma and independence. In 2003 the depth of access granted to correspondents, the routine use of videophone and satellite technology, and the resulting speed of contact and exposure of operations were all unprecedented. But the same problems of ethics emerged, and it could be argued that Russell's influence on politics was more instant.

Such differences of scale, speed and reach, in addition to changing patterns of business ownership, do not happen overnight and their development is never an even one; nor is it necessarily a fair one when linked inextricably to the advance and survival of modern capitalism. The starting point for modernity can be clearly linked to the victory of the liberal system of economic organization, which began with the first industrial revolution in Britain, was supported by the ideologies of the Franco-American political revolutions, and was underpinned theoretically by nineteenth-century British political economy and utilitarian philosophy. The first was important because it established the production capacity and system for economic penetration globally; the second was significant because it inspired the leading institutions for bourgeois society.

How do the media slot into this development? Existing structures of authority have sometimes been challenged by the growth of modern communications as the latter have created new centres of power themselves – such as the corporate influence of the media multinational. Sometimes the media have offered channels for communication that bypass existing institutions, but on other occasions technological proximity has meant that new forms of information and expression have been assimilated into the system. The institutionalization of broadcasting illustrates this point, and the Internet looks set to follow as the technologies that use it adapt themselves to the current political culture rather than creating a new one.

In the meantime, the nature of the power has also changed. In 1995 the editor of *Vanity Fair* summed it up: 'The power center of America . . . has moved from its role as military-industrial giant to a new supremacy as the world's entertainment-information superpower.' The present trajectory of almost unrestricted international capital has provoked a strong reaction:

> In the last five years, a small number of the country's largest industrial corporations has acquired more public communications power – including ownership of the news – than any private businesses have ever before possessed in world history. Nothing in earlier history matches this corporate group's power to penetrate the social landscape. Using both old and new technology, by owning each other's shares, engaging in joint ventures as partners, and other forms of cooperation, this handful of giants has created what is, in effect, a new communications cartel within the United States.

The global media cartel appears to be evolving into a global communications cartel, and sadly this process has taken place with very little public debate within the United States.

The never-ending story of unequal global economics continues to run. Although Time Warner experienced a catastrophic loss in 2002 from a write-down of its AOL online arm, net profits were up again by 2003/4 as New Line Cinema benefited from the *Lord of the Rings* franchise and Warner Bros. continued to earn from *Harry Potter* and *The Matrix*. Warner Music was sold for €2 billion and the CD and DVD manufacturing operations were sold for €0.88 billion. Nevertheless, this one example of the scale of numbers should not mask our appreciation of the historical dimension to current trends in order to appraise economic power critically.

# Chapter 6

**ELLIOT KING**

# FREE FOR ALL: THE INTERNET'S TRANSFORMATION OF JOURNALISM

T HE INTERNET HAS CAUSED THE GREATEST DISRUPTION in the gathering and distribution of news at least since the invention of broadcasting and perhaps since the invention of printing. A significant factor in the demise of the urban daily newspaper and magazines of all kinds, the Internet has provided a technology platform that is enabling a complete redefinition of who is a journalist and what is journalism.

As the Internet is still an emerging technology, there is very little scholarship about the impact of the Internet on journalism written from a broad or long-range perspective. *Free for All* intertwines the development of computing as a communications platform with the history of the efforts to deploy computer-based communication as both a delivery medium and a tool for reporting in journalism. The core argument running through the book is that while the available technology does not define the limits of journalism, it does play a large role in shaping it.

A veteran of technology, Elliot King was an early user of the Internet and its precursor technologies. In the mid-1990s, he co-authored one of the first books suggesting how the Internet could be applied to journalism and edited three issues of a scholarly journal that took one of the first academic looks at the impact of the Internet on journalism. The excerpt of *Free for All* here summarizes the role of the Internet in journalism in the first decade of the 21st Century.

## The Acceleration of Change

In 2002, Dave Winer, the creator of RSS (really simple syndication) and EditThisPage PHP blogging technology, made a bet with Martin Nisenholtz, then head of digital operations at the *New York Times*. Winer contended that by 2007 more people would get their news from blogs than from the *New York Times*.[1] Winer clearly did not win the bet, but in early 2009 it was not clear that he had lost either. By 2008, leading politicians routinely attended the annual conference organized by Markos Moulitsas, the founder of Daily Kos, and paid homage to the blogging community in the same way that they might visit the *New York Times* editorial board. Moreover, like the *New York Times*, blogs have demonstrated that they can push stories onto the national agenda.

Blogging has carved out a role in journalism. In January 2008, The Huffington Post was in the top 500 most visited sites on the Web and within the top 120 sites in the United States. However, those numbers pale in comparison to audiences the Web sites of what has come to be called the mainstream media attract. According to Alexa, a Web site that monitors Web traffic, in 2009 the Web site of the *New York Times* was the ninetieth most visited site, with nearly eighty times more traffic than Daily Kos and four times more traffic than The Huffington Post. The most visited news Web site, CNN. com, was the forty-ninth most visited Web site, with nearly twice the traffic of the *New York Times*. In 2008, CNN averaged approximately 485 million visitors a month.[2] Coupled with CNN's broadcast reach and the subscribers to the *New York Times* newspaper, clearly both are more powerful sources of news than bloggers.

But blogging is only one part of the equation for online news. Fifteen years after the *San Jose Mercury News* launched the Mercury Center and the *Raleigh News and Observer* started NandO.Net, the Web is a routine and growing platform to deliver the news. When Barack Obama was sworn in as the forty-fourth president of the United States, it was assumed that tens of millions of people around the world would watch the ceremony via the Web. By 2009, the idea that breaking news drives huge traffic to news Web sites is as unexceptional as cutting between images of the Brooklyn Bridge and the Golden Gate Bridge on television. On election day in 2008, CNN.com recorded 282 million page views, which represents more than 80 million visitors, nearly three times the amount that visited the site on election day in 2004. Officials in Washington, D.C. anticipated that tens of thousands of people would be blogging and sending their own pictures and video from the inaugural events in 2009. Extra cellular telephone network capacity was installed to handle the event, and warnings were issued that there could be delays if too much video was transmitted.[3]

As more people got Internet access and as using the Internet became a more routine part of people's daily activities, accessing news online became increasingly commonplace. The movement online posed a clear threat to newspapers. In 2004, the Carnegie Corporation commissioned a study that found among 18- to 34-year-old adults, while television was the most popular source of news for women and people with lower incomes, the Internet was emerging as the most popular source of news for men and people with higher incomes. Newspapers had no clear pockets of strength among any audiences. Moreover, nearly half of this demographic group reported using portals that also had daily news, such as Yahoo! and MSN.com. More than 40 percent of the respondents indicated that the Internet offered news when they wanted it, which was a very important consideration for them.[4]

Studies conducted by the Pew Charitable Trusts produced similar results. In the summer of 2006, Pew reported that 13 percent of all Americans were accessing online news about the midterm congressional elections, two and a half times more than the number who accessed political news online in the summer before the 2002 midterm elections.[5] At the end of 2008, the Pew Charitable Trusts reported the Internet had surpassed newspapers as a source of news. In a survey conducted by the Pew Research Center for the People and the Press in December 2008, 40 percent of the respondents reported that they get most of their news about national and international issues from the Internet, up from 24 percent in September 2007. Newspapers were a primary source of news for 35 percent of the respondents, while television continued to be the most popular news medium. Seventy percent of the respondents said that television was a main source of national and international news.

For younger people, the results were even more startling. Among people under the age of thirty, 59 percent reported that they got most of their national and international news online, figures that matched those of television. Only 28 percent of the respondents under the age of thirty reported that newspapers were a main source of news. The poll results marked a sharp change from September 2007. By late 2008, the number of young people reporting television as a main source of news had plunged eleven percentage points compared to 2007, while the number of people identifying the Internet as a main source of news had jumped an impressive twenty-five percentage points. In September 2007, twice as many young people said they relied mostly on television for news than mentioned the Internet. To fully understand the growth of the Internet as a primary source of news, in 2002, only 14 percent of the respondents to the Pew survey said that the Internet was a main source of national and international news while 82 percent said television was a main source of news. Forty-two percent relied on newspapers for national and international news.

The pronounced shift toward the Internet as a primary source of news is intertwined with at least three major relatively independent long-term trends. Each of these trends raises serious questions about the future structure and practice of journalism in the United States. The most obvious and immediate trend is that online journalism has placed urban daily newspapers under tremendous pressure, and the days of city newspapers supporting news rooms staffed with hundreds seem to be over. But the need to report local news remains. What kind of structures, if any, will replace city newspapers? Second, the established news media can no longer serve as gatekeepers for the news. News can get onto the Internet from anybody, anywhere, and at anytime. On the one hand, the diminishing role of big media calls into question who is a journalist and what is journalism. On the other hand. mainstream media currently serve as megaphones for online journalism. Although unique stories may break on the Internet, their impact is magnified by the mainstream media. What happens if there is no megaphone? The third major trend is that the rate of technological change is accelerating. While the Web and blogging have already carved out roles within journalism, new technologies are emerging, including Wikis, handheld devices, and other communication technologies like Twitter, which may or may not play a role in journalism over time. The question remains as to which technologies will be suitable for a journalism that supports a rich social, cultural, and political life and which technologies may not? Taken together, the answers to these questions will have an enormous impact on American life.

## Is the Big City Newspaper Dead?

The long-term, steady deterioration of newspaper readership had been well documented. According to the Newspaper Association of America, from 1972 to 1998, the percentage of people age thirty to thirty-nine who read a paper every day dropped from 73 percent to 30 percent. As the Web geared up, the situation got worse. Between 1997 and 2000, the percentage of people age eighteen to twenty-four who say they read yesterday's newspaper dropped by 14 percent. While newspapers created Web sites, many industry observers argued that newspapers never made a full commitment to Web and new product development. Their Web efforts were always seen as supplemental to the print newspaper.[6] For example, it was only in 2007 that the *Atlanta Journal-Constitution* made the commitment to put its digital operation on an equal footing with its print operation. Even then, the fear that the Web effort could hasten the demise of the print product was still evident.

News companies tried to pull off a balancing act between the Web and print. As a part of its reorganization, the *Journal-Constitution* consciously cut back the area in which the newspaper was distributed and reduced home-delivery discounts. The editorial staff was trimmed by 15 percent and coverage was focused more on local events. On the other hand, with the new attention to the Web site, by August 2007, page views climbed 22 percent compared to the prior year.[7]

Even with the nearly generation-long slide in newspaper readership and the clear understanding that online journalism posed a significant challenge to print, most people envisioned a long, and perhaps benign, transition along the lines the *Atlanta Journal-Constitution* was trying to engineer. Traditional newspaper companies may have been slow to fully grapple with both the risks and the rewards of the Web but most news organizations assumed that ultimately many of them would manage the transformation.[8] Moreover, the attrition that newspapers had experienced in the face of competition from television had occurred over two decades or more. Many anticipated a similarly long transition period.

A severe economic recession that started in 2008 dramatically altered the equation. Along with the slide of readership, the advertising base of newspapers had long been eroding. In the 1990s, there had been a sustained consolidation in department store chains and supermarkets, two stalwart advertisers. Classified advertising, particularly help wanted ads, had migrated largely to Web sites like Craigslist, which would post ads for free. The recession of 2008 hit two of the remaining advertising pillars for news-papers the hardest—automobiles and real estate. As the economy contracted, the impact on newspapers was swift and dramatic. In October 2008, the *Christian Science Monitor* announced that it would suspend its print edition and publish only online.[9] In December 2008, the Tribune Company, owner of the *Chicago Tribune*, the *Los Angeles Times*, and ten other newspapers, filed for bankruptcy, weighted down by the debt acquired during a leveraged buyout a year earlier. When the company filed for bankruptcy, it noted that advertising revenues were down 19 percent, the sharpest drop since the recession of 1981.[10] That same month, the *Detroit News* and the *Detroit Free Press* announced that they would stop home delivery of their newspaper four days a week, offering only a slimmer version of the newspaper for newsstand sales and online access. "My theory behind this continues to be, I'm going to invest less in paper, fuel, ink and distribution. It allows me to maintain my journalism," Dave Hunke, chief executive of the partnership and publisher of the *Free Press*, said at the time. The move also entailed laying off nine percent of the newspaper's work force.[11] In January 2009, the *Minneapolis Star Tribune* filed for bankruptcy.[12]

Even the *New York Times* was not immune to the problems. On the day that the Tribune Company filed for bankruptcy, the *New York Times* announced that it received $225 million through a sale and lease back arrangement of its new headquarters on Times Square. In January 2009, the company revealed that Mexican billionaire Carlos Slim had agreed to lend the company $250 million. The net result of the complicated deal would leave Slim owning 17 percent of the *Times*. In comparison, the Sulzberger family, the longtime owners of the *Times*, would hold only 19 percent of the company.[13]

As the winter turned into spring in 2009, the news got worse. In February, the *Rocky Mountain News* was closed after its parent company, E.W. Scripps, failed to find a buyer. Founded in 1859, the newspaper had lost $16 million over the past three years.[14] The same week, the Hearst Company threatened to sell or close the *San Francisco Chronicle* if it could not wring economic concessions from its unions.[15] In March 2009, the *Seattle Post-Intelligencer* stopped printing a newspaper and went to an all-Web delivery of the news. Although with the move the *Post-Intelligencer* became the largest daily to go to an all-Web format, as part of the process it cut its news staff from 165 people to 20. The future of the *Post-Intelligencer*'s competitor, the *Seattle Times*, with whom it had a joint operating agreement, was also in doubt.[16]

The economic difficulties faced by urban newspapers were not completely attributable to the competition from online journalism. From 2005 to 2007, many major newspapers had experienced ownership changes, fueled by the availability of easy credit. When the economic downturn hit and credit dried up, those companies were not in the position to manage their debt load. Nonetheless, with the demise of many urban newspapers apparently imminent, could online journalism fill the void they would leave as the dominant reporters of news in their geographic areas? The economic model of online journalism did not seem likely to be able to support the same kind of news gathering operations that urban newspapers supported. An analysis of the popular Web site of the *New York Times*, for example, suggested that it could only support about 20 percent of the current news staff.[17]

With the future of the city daily newspaper in doubt, many interesting online and hybrid news experiments have been launched. One approach is to create not-for-profit reporting teams whose work can then be used across a wide variety of media. In 2007, former managing editor of the *Wall Street Journal* Paul Steiger and Stephen Engelberg, a former managing editor of the *Oregonian* in Portland, helped to found ProPublica, an independent, nonprofit newsroom that produces investigative journalism in the public interest. Funded primarily by the Sandler Foundation, ProPublica was created to address what its founders felt was the contraction of original reporting. Although the Internet created a proliferation of publishing platforms, many of those sites aggregated material from elsewhere. ProPublica's goal was to be the largest, best-led, and best-funded investigative journalism operation in the United States.[18] In a twist on the same approach, Spot.us solicits contributions from readers to fund projects that can be published anywhere. Some of the stories that received funding addressed the rise of car and tent encampments in San Francisco and why the San Francisco transit authority doesn't run more express buses.[19]

In the spring of 2009, The Huffington Post launched a hybrid initiative to fund investigative journalism. It teamed with American News Project, an independent video journalism project, to create the Huffington Post Investigative Fund. The fund's initial $1.75 million budget was provided by both The Huffington Post and The Atlantic Philanthropies, whose mission is to bring lasting change to disadvantaged people. According to the announcement when the fund was launched, the fund will support long-form investigations as well as short, breaking news stories presented in a variety of media—including text, audio, and video. The stories will be available free for any media outlet to publish simultaneously.[20]

Politico represents yet another innovative approach for journalism. Founded in 2007 by John Harris and Jim VandeHei, two former *Washington Post* reporters, and owned by Allbritton Communications, a mainstream communications company that owns local District of Columbia television stations WJLA-TV and NewsChannel 8, Politico launched a Web site to give extensive coverage to the federal government. While Congress is in session, it also publishes a print edition, but the focus of its efforts is on the Web site. The idea was to cover the federal government extensively.[21] During the 2008 presidential election, this kind of focused coverage proved that it could attract an audience. For example, when Politico sponsored one of the Republican debates in May of that year, some 648,000 people visited its Web site, up 162 percent from April. Even more narrowly targeted Web sites such as Five Thirty Eight, Pollster.com, and Real Clear Politics, which provided comprehensive coverage of all the polling taking place during the elections, also saw spikes in traffic.[22]

Finally, there has been a proliferation of independent citizen-based media efforts. The idea of citizen media was pioneered by the Korean Web site OhmyNews. Launched in the year 2000, by 2003 the site had forty editors posting two hundred stories a day and attracting two million visitors daily. The stories were being generated by 26,000 citizen-journalists. The site was given credit for helping to elect South Korea's progressive president, Roh Moo-hyun, in the early 2000s.[23] In 2007, the Knight Foundation, in conjunction with the Institute for Interactive Journalism, then housed at the University of Maryland, unveiled a Web portal to help citizens and journalists create community news sites.[24] Supporting what was called the Knight Citizen News Network, there were over 800 innovative community-based news efforts around the country.[25]

## Everybody is a Reporter

With the proliferation of citizen media, virtually anybody can post news. Even CNN encourages what it calls Ireporters to submit photos and videos of the events they attend. Within a short period of time, Ireports was receiving 10,000 submissions a month. So, on the one hand, news gathering is proliferating broadly. On the other hand, the distinction between professional news gathering and amateur news gathering is becoming blurred. For example, in 2008, Mayhill Fowler, a blogger for The Huffington Post, attended a closed-door fundraiser on behalf of presidential candidate Barack Obama in San Francisco. While there, using her cell phone, she videotaped Obama commenting that some small-town residents in Pennsylvania were bitter at being passed by in economic terms and therefore clung to religion and guns. She posted the videotape to The Huffington Post. When it was seized on and criticized by Hillary Clinton, Obama's chief rival for the Democratic nomination, it became the subject of heated debate and was seen as a major gaffe on the part of the Obama campaign. At one point, some pundits felt the remark could change the direction of the race. Ironically, Fowler was at the fundraiser because she was an Obama supporter but felt she had to post the video to fulfill her obligations as a journalist. Her responsibilities as a journalist, she said, outweighed her responsibilities as a supporter.[26]

Fowler's contribution to the 2008 presidential campaign would have been impossible prior to the spread of the Internet. Could what she did even be considered journalism? Fowler was part of a project launched by The Huffington Post called OffTheBus, in which it recruited 7,500 citizen journalists to be its eyes and ears during the presidential campaign. The idea was for the OffTheBus correspondents to sweep up information in hope of uncovering overlooked news of importance, establishing trends that might not otherwise be obvious, or simply establishing a strong database of information that could be used to bolster future reporting.[27]

The effectiveness of citizen journalists was an open question. Obviously, no news organization could actually support 7,500 correspondents. But the quality of the materials from 7,500 correspondents would be very uneven. Citizen journalists could perhaps capture and report on a demonstration in Bagdad or terrorist violence in Mumbai that would be beyond the reach of professional news organizations. But could citizen journalists provide accurate coverage of ongoing events consistently enough to keep people accurately informed about what they need to know?[28]

For citizen journalists, credibility and accuracy are major issues. In the OffTheBus project, correspondents had to acknowledge their political affiliations. But the possibility that an individual's personal perspective would color his or her coverage of a specific event is high. While a community developing a software application can be self-correcting, this is not necessarily the case in journalism. Social networks make mistakes.[29]

Since the very beginnings of Usenet, the Internet has been a medium for rumors, urban legends, hoaxes, and falsehoods. Although professional journalism organizations are not immune to making mistakes, there are safeguards in place. In the age of citizen journalism, those safeguards have weakened. For example, an incorrect citizen report on CNN's IReport site that Apple CEO Steve Jobs, whose health had been an open question, was rushed to the emergency room sent Apple stock plunging five percent in one day. In a similar example, false information about United Airlines led to a stock sell-off. When Matt Drudge reported that Oprah Winfrey refused to have Republican vice presidential candidate Sarah Palin on her show, it spread through the Internet and ultimately onto the NBC Nightly News, even though Winfrey denied it. New tools like Digg, a Web site designed to discover and share content on the Web, helped accelerate the rate at which mistakes spread through the Internet.[30]

But the widespread availability of news from all sources works in the other direction as well. In January 2008, MSNBC began to allow Web sites to embed video from the NBC Nightly News, making it easier for other Web sites to use MSNBC content on their sites.[31] This process has set up an echo chamber between the Web and other forms of media. For example, when the comedienne Tina Fey lampooned vice presidential candidate Sarah Palin on the television show *Saturday Night Live*, many more people watched the segment on YouTube than on the original broadcast. As Fey continued offering send-ups of the candidate, *Saturday Night Live*'s ratings soared, with the show ultimately airing a special edition on a Thursday night.[32]

## Accelerating Changes

Online journalism is changing the way that content becomes available for public discussion. Anybody can upload words, images, or video that potentially can be read by the public, however the word *public* is defined. At the same time, professional news organizations are making at least part of their content available for anybody to embed into their own Web sites. These changes are enabled by the development of new technology, which continues to develop rapidly.

It took about two hundred years for all the technology that allowed for the development of the modern newspaper to emerge. By the early 1900s, however, newspapers began to look very much like they looked a hundred years later. It took about fifty years for the technology that enabled the modern television news broadcast to develop. But by the late 1980s, newscasts looked pretty much the same as they did twenty years later. For online journalism, the technology continues to develop at an accelerated clip, and there is no evidence to indicate when the rate of development may slow. It is not yet clear which technologies will shape the ultimate contours of online journalism.

In late 2008, the Israeli army invaded the Gaza Strip, a sliver of land ruled by its bitter enemy, the Palestinian organization Hamas. The invasion sparked protests around the world. To defend its position, the Israeli Consulate in New York conducted a news conference that could be attended by anybody. It used Twitter, a social medium that allows people to send messages of 140 characters or less. "Since the definition of war has changed, the definition of public diplomacy has to change as well," an Israeli diplomat who helped organize the news conference said at the time.[33] Twitter represented the next step in the development of an always-on communication culture that bypasses the traditional media. Celebrities, sports stars, politicians, and even business executives have taken to sending out regular updates regarding their thoughts, views, and whereabouts.[34]

Twitter, in turn, has been enabled by the proliferation of mobile and handheld devices. The release of the Apple iPhone in 2007 led to an explosion in the use of smart phones. Over the next two years, Apple's competitors, such as Research in Motion and Palm, also released devices that provided access to the Internet and a wide array of features found on personal computers. Even before the iPhone was released, text messaging had exploded as a channel of communication for younger people. When Barack Obama, who assiduously courted the youth vote, announced that Senator Joe Biden of Delaware was his choice to run for vice president, he sent a text message directly to supporters rather than holding a press conference. To go from text messaging and e-mail to downloading Web pages and receiving tweets, the name for Twitter messages, is a short leap. Since the release of the Apple iPod, many communities of people have become very used to downloading music and information onto a handheld device. Amazon.com joined the fray with the release of its Kindle reader, on which readers can not only download books but magazines and newspapers as well. Like in the early days of the online services, publishers are making content created for other media available to download on Kindle. These handheld devices have the potential to serve as delivery platforms for original online journalism.

Wiki technology also pushes the envelope of collaboration. Wikis are Web applications that allow multiple authors to add, remove, and edit content in a collaborative process. Wikipedia, the collaborative online encyclopedia, is the primary example of a large-scale wiki project. In 2004, Wikipedia launched Wikinews. The idea was that several authors could collaborate in writing a single article. The only requirements were that all sources of information must be cited and that articles should take a neutral point of view. Several other publications have tried developing articles using wiki technology. In 2005, *Esquire* used Wikipedia itself to develop an article about Wikipedia. It received 224 edits in twenty-four hours and ultimately received 500 edits before the article was closed to be printed. In 2006, *Wired* magazine experimented with an article about wikis. It received 348 edits. With that kind of interaction, some observers have argued the wikis are the next step in participatory journalism.[35]

The potential application of wiki technology to journalism slipped into sight in the aftermath of the sudden death of Tim Russert, the host of NBC's long-running Sunday political talk show *Meet the Press* and a pillar of the Washington, D.C., political media establishment. On June 13, 2008, Russert collapsed in NBC's Washington newsroom. He was rushed to the hospital and pronounced dead at 2:23 P.M. Customarily, television news organizations allow the network with which a journalist is affiliated to announce news of a death first. But about twenty minutes before Tom Brokaw of NBC News informed the world of Russert's death, Russert's page on Wikipedia had been updated with the news. A junior staffer at the Internet Broadcasting Services of St. Paul, Minnesota, which provides Web services to the local NBC affiliate, had seen the news and updated the page.[36]

## What We Know

By 2009, online journalism had fully emerged as a significant platform for news, but it was not yet fully formed. Like newspapers in the 1830s, and television in the 1960s, online journalism already has had significant social impact and serves as an important platform for people to learn about the world around them. But because it is intertwined with computer technology, the technical underpinnings for online journalism are still under development. As with all media, the technological development shapes and conditions both the production and consumption of online journalism.

Media products can be judged on a spectrum ranging from intensive to extensive. Intensive products are fewer in number but those that are produced are used over and over again. The quintessential intensive product is the Bible. People who acquire a Bible tend to read it over and over again. Extensive products are generally shorter and used for a shorter duration of time. The daily newspaper is an extensive product. It is widely circulated but by the next day it is considered fit only to line birdcages. The Internet has generally been used to develop extensive news products. Blog posts are shorter and have a shorter shelf life than newspaper articles. Tweets are shorter and have a shorter shelf life than blog posts. The old joke about the newspaper *USA Today* is that it would never win a Pulitzer Prize because Pulitzer Prizes were not awarded for the best paragraph of the year. A paragraph is a standard length for a blog post and beyond the parameters of a tweet. Some critics claim that television helped to destroy the attention of its viewers through its cut-quick production. But a thirty-minute video is a long-form production on the Web.

On the other hand, with online journalism a lot more people have the opportunity to put what they have seen and what they think in front of the public. One of the fundamental pillars of the philosophy of free speech is that the truth is more likely to emerge from a multitude of tongues; online journalism could put that faith to the test.

But that test of faith has not come yet. Although major stories have been broken online, and online journalism already has the potential to have an impact on the public agenda, to date, generally speaking, the impact of news broken online has been felt through the megaphone of the mainstream media. Only after stories have been picked up by the national media have they become national issues. What will happen to the stories that break online if the megaphone media—large urban newspapers like the *Chicago Tribune*, the *Boston Globe*, or the *Los Angeles Times*, which make up a critical element of the national media—fail is hard to anticipate.

The established media do more than disseminate information. They put items on the agenda for discussion and perhaps entertain their readers and viewers. Both newspapers and national news broadcasts help to define specific communities.[37] By creating a shared sense of the news, national television broadcasts in part help define who is an American. Newspapers play an even greater role in shaping local identities. The urban newspaper has long been the primary engine for local reporting. Reading the *Baltimore Sun*, for example, defined who was a Baltimorean as opposed to people who read the *Washington Post* as their hometown newspaper.

Writing about the online service The WELL in the 1980s, Howard Rheingold, in what is generally considered to be a prescient book, wrote that online computer users have the ability to form communities among themselves.[38] It is true that people can form communities online, feeling a common bond and perhaps a sense of shared identity with people to whom have they no other connection except their online interactions. But can online journalism focused on local issues build the same sense of community for those who live geographically near each other, people who actually have a relationship to each other beyond their online interactions? Over time, perhaps it can, 140 characters at a time.

## Notes

1.   Stephen Levy, "Will the Blogs Kill Old Media?" *Business Week*, May 20, 2002, 54.
2.   Brian Stelter, "Can the Go-to Site Get You to Stay?" *New York Times*, January 17,2009 (accessed online March 31, 2009).
3.   Matt Richtel, "Inauguration Crowd Will Test Cell Phone Networks," *New York Times*, January 18, 2009 (accessed online March 31, 2009).
4.   Merrill Brown, "Abandoning the News," *The Carnegie Reporter* 3, no. 2 (Spring 2005): 2–12.
5.   "Internet Overtakes Newspapers as News Source," Pew Research Center Publications, December 23, 2008, http://pewresearch.org/pubs/1066/internet-overtakes-newspapers-as-news-source (accessed April 1, 2009).
6.   Brown, "Abandoning the News," 5.
7.   Julia M. Klein, "If You Build It . . .," *Columbia Journalism Review*, November/December 2007, 40–45.
8.   Michael Hirschorn, "End Times," *The Atlantic*, January/February 2009, http://www.theatlantic.com/doc/200901/new-york-times (accessed April 1, 2009).
9.   Stephanie Clifford, "Christian Science Paper to End Daily Print Edition," *New York Times*, October 28, 2008 (accessed online April 1, 2009).
10.  Richard Perez Pena, "Tribune Company Seeks Bankruptcy Protection," *New York Times*, December 8, 2008 (accessed online April 1, 2009).
11.  Richard Perez Pena, "Fewer Papers Will Hit the Porch in Detroit," *New York Times*, December 15, 2008 (accessed online April 1, 2009).
12.  Richard Perez Pena, "Bankruptcy Protection Filing at Minneapolis Star Tribune," *New York Times*, January 15, 2008 (accessed online April 1, 2009).
13.  Eric Dash, "Mexican Billionaire Invests in Times Company," *New York Times*, January 19, 2009 (accessed online April 1, 2009).
14.  Richard Perez-Pena, "Rocky Mountain News Fails to Find Buyer and Will Close," *New York Times*, February 26, 2009 (accessed online April 1, 2009).
15.  Richard Perez-Pena, "Hearst Threatens to End San Francisco Paper," *New York Times*, February 24, 2009 (accessed online April 1, 2009).
16.  William Yardley and Richard Perez-Pena, "Seattle Paper Shifts Entirely to the Web," *New York Times*, March 17, 2009 (accessed online April 1, 2009).
17.  Hirschorn, "End Times."
18.  "About Us," Pro Publica, http://www.propublica.org/about (accessed April 1, 2009).

19. "What Is Spot.Us About?" Spot.us, http://spot.us/pages/about (accessed April 1, 2009).

20. "The Huffington Post to Launch Non-Profit Investigative Journalism Venture," http://journalism.nyu.edu/pubzone/weblogs/pressthink/2009/03/26/flying_seminar.html#comment52571 (accessed September 4, 2009).

21. Howard Kurtz, "Politico: Niche Web Site Isn't Yet a Notch Above," *Washington Post*, January 29, 2007, Style, Final Edition, C1.

22. Tom Regan, "Political Websites: Clocks That Never Stop," *Christian Science Monitor*, November 25, 2008, Innovation, 25.

23. Leander Kahney, "Citizen Reporters Make the News," *Wired*, May, 17, 2003, http://www.wired.com/culture/lifestyle/news/2003/05/58856 (accessed April 1, 2009).

24. Institute for Interactive Journalism, http://www.j-lab.org/kcnn_launch_release.shtml (accessed April 1, 2009).

25. "Directory of Citizen Media Sites," Knight Citizen News Network, http://www.kcnn.org/citmedia_sites/ (accessed April 1, 2009).

26. Katharine Q. Seelye, "Blogger Is Surprised by Uproar Over Obama Story, But Not Bitter," *New York Times*, April 14, 2008 (accessed online April 1, 2009).

27. Katharine Q. Seelye, "Citizen Journalism Project Gains a Voice in the Campaign," *New York Times*, July 25, 2008 (accessed online April 1, 2009).

28. Jack Shafer, "Blog Overkill: The Danger of Hyping a Good Thing into the Ground," Slate, January 26, 2005, http://www.slate.com/default.aspx?search_input=Jack+Shafer&search_loc=on&qt=Jack+Shafer&id =3944&x=9&y=5 (accessed April 1, 2009).

29. "A Group Is Its Own Worst Enemy," Clay Shirky's Writing about the Internet, http://www.shirky.com/writings/group_enemy.html (accessed April 1, 2009).

30. Noam Cohen, "Spinning a Web of Lies at Digital Speed," *New York Times*, October 12, 2008 (accessed online April 1, 2009).

31. "Exclusive: NBC Nightly News and Other MSNBC Shows Will Be Sharable via Embed," Beet TV, http://www.beet.tv/2008/01/exclusive-nbc-n-html (accessed April 1, 2009).

32. Bill Carter, "An Election to Laugh About," *New York Times*, October 8, 2008 (accessed online May 27, 2009).

33. Noam Cohen, "The Toughest Q's Answered in the Briefest Tweets," *New York Times*, January 4, 2009 (accessed online April 1, 2009).

34. Noam Cohen, "All a-Twitter About Stars Who Tweet," *New York Times*, January 5, 2008 (accessed online April 1, 2009).

35. Paul Bradshaw, "Wiki Journalism: Are Wikis the New Blogs?" Paper presented at the Future of the Newspaper Conference, September 2007, http://onlinejournalismblog.files.wordpress.com/2007/09/wiki_journalism.pdf (accessed April 1, 2009).

36. Noam Cohen, "Delaying the News in the Era of the Internet," *New York Times*, June 23, 2008 (accessed online April 1, 2009).

37. Benedict Anderson, *Imagined Communities: Reflections on the Origin and Spread of Nationalism*, 2nd ed. (London: Verso, 1991).

38. Howard Rheingold, *The Virtual Community: Finding Connection in a Computerized World*, rev. ed. (Cambridge, Mass.: MIT Press, 2000).

# SECTION II

# Doing Journalism

# INTRODUCTION

JOURNALISM IS FIRST AND FOREMOST a social practice and a craft. People "do" journalism. The excerpts in this section explore how journalists covered the most important issues of the 20th century, such as the war in Viet Nam, the civil rights movement and the Watergate scandal. The social outcomes and impact of this journalism have been profound. These selections examine how journalists have gone about doing their jobs when what they have reported on has changed the world in which we live.

The section starts off with sociologist Herbert Gans' landmark study of the way journalists worked in newsrooms in the 1970s. He demonstrated how organizational routines shaped news products and succinctly described the culture of journalism culti-vated within media companies. This was a landmark study that offered an in-depth look into journalistic practices in major media companies.

Perhaps the most notable demonstration of how the sound practice of jour-nalism can effect great social change is *All the President's Men*, Carl Bernstein and Bob Woodward's account of their reporting on the Watergate scandal that led to the resignation of President Richard Nixon. This was the only time in U.S. history that a president has been forced to resign. If there is one book that every student should have read, many people in and close to professional journalism feel it is *All the President's Men*. Bernstein and Woodward pursued the scandal, ignited by a burglary of the Democratic National Committee headquarters in the Watergate office and apartment complex by people found to be associated with Richard Nixon's re-election campaign committee, by the use of old-fashioned and tenacious reporting. They knocked on doors, identified potential sources in positions high and low, and did not give up until they had the story. Each story they published in *The Washington Post* was confirmed by at least two sources. They also cultivated the person who became the most famous confidential source in history, who Bernstein and Woodward called Deep Throat. Though in retrospect, many scholars no longer give Bernstein and Woodward the credit for forcing the resignation of Richard Nixon, their stories kept Watergate on the front pages of *The Washington Post* and prodded the U.S. Senate and the U.S. District court to pursue the scandal as well.

Along with Watergate, Viet Nam and the civil rights campaign were the big post Second World War issues that commanded the attention of reporters, contributing to what has become known as the "Golden Age" of American journalism. In the excerpt from Gene Roberts and Hank Klibanoff's *The Race Beat*, probably the definitive account of reporting on the civil rights movement in the 1950s and 1960s, the media bandwagon arrives at Little Rock, Arkansas, as the spotlight turns on de-segregation in a single community and one school. In their book, Roberts and Klibanoff argue that the mainstream media's focus on the injustices in the South played a critical role in correcting the injustice of segregation, racism and racial discrimination. As more reporters covered the civil rights movement, civil rights moved up in importance on the national political agenda, leading to its legislative successes in the 1960s.

If civil rights was the dominant political issue in the United States in the mid-to-late 1950s and early 1960s, in the mid-to-late 1960s the war in Viet Nam polarized the nation and took a central position in the political and news agenda. Many leading journalists including David Halberstam, Neil Sheehan, Morley Safer, Michael Herr, Peter Arnett and Seymour Hersh established their reputations through their reporting in Viet Nam. M. Phillip Knightley's account of the reporting on Viet Nam is part of his larger work on war reporting, *The First Casualty*. Within the fog of war, objectivity and accurate reporting are often the first to suffer. Knightley recounts the challenges reporters faced as they reported on Viet Nam.

The practice of journalism, however, is not always benign. Who gets to be a reporter and who has authority in media organizations are of utmost importance in shaping the way news is covered and presented to the public. In *The Girls in the Balcony*—a book title that describes the marginalized physical location at the National Press Club in Washington D.C. where women were forced to stand, as a humiliating form of exclusion from the main action—Nan Robertson chronicles the women's fight for equality in journalism, at the *New York Times* in the 1970s.

The experiences of Nan Robertson and other women reporters at the *Times* stand in sharp contrast to those of Martha Gellhorn in World War II. As World War II approached Gellhorn funded her own trip to Europe, selling articles to pay her way. From that inauspicious start, she ultimately won recognition as one of the greatest war correspondents of the 20th century. Robertson and her colleagues were constrained by the news organization within which they found themselves, even though *The New York Times* was already recognized as the premier news organization of the period. In contrast, Gellhorn launched her journalistic career without accreditation from an established news organization. But her creativity and innovative presentation, which presaged similar journalism by Michael Herr and others reporting on Viet Nam, is a reminder that great journalism is not simply the product of news routines but of individuals dedicated to telling important stories.

Journalism that has impact is often not for the faint hearted. Robertson's campaign for women journalists was brave in defense of equal rights for the job (rights that are often taken for granted today), Woodward and Bernstein confronted ambition and treachery at the highest levels of government. Reporters covering the civil rights movement, particularly in the south, faced real physical danger as did reporters in Viet Nam. Nonetheless, the practices they followed were professional and honest—giving credibility and power to the work they produced.

# Chapter 7

# HERBERT GANS

# DECIDING WHAT'S NEWS

WHEN IT WAS FIRST PUBLISHED IN 1979, *Deciding What's News* represented an effort to understand the organizational routines of leading media companies and how those organizational routines determined and defined the presentation of the news. It is a major work in what has become the "sociology of news," joining works like Gaye Tuchman's *Making News*, and others. Gans, a distinguished sociologist at Columbia University, spent a considerable amount of time observing journalists at work at the CBS Evening News, NBC Nightly News, *Time* and *Newsweek* magazines. He wanted to uncover the "unwritten rules" of journalism—what informs the story selection process and what are the news values underlying that process.

Gans found that without their being fully conscious of it, the work of journalists reflected the ruling ideas of American society, and the assumption that "distorted" news could somehow be replaced by "undistorted" news could not hold up in practice. He called for a "multiperspectival" approach to news, with news being presented from a variety of different frameworks. In these selections from Chapter 6, Gans explores how values in general and the value of objectivity in particular are operationalized in journalists' daily routines.

The world of journalism has changed dramatically in the years since *Deciding What's News* was first published. News organizations have been downsized; the audience has been fragmented; and there are many new, albeit much smaller, competitors. When Gans wrote *Deciding What's News*, only the networks and the news magazines were truly national media. Now, every news blog potentially has a national and international reach. Nonetheless, in the preface to the 25th Anniversary edition, Gans argues that the processes supporting news selection and the values and assumptions that inform news judgments remain largely unchanged, at least in the major news organizations.

## Objectivity, Values, and Ideology

Journalism resembles other empirical disciplines and professions in its aim to be objective: to be free from values and ideology; accordingly, journalists practice value exclusion. Of course, objectivity is itself a value, but journalists try to exclude values in the narrower sense of the term: as preference statements about nation and society.

Editorials, commentary, and at the magazines, the endings of some stories are exempted from value exclusion; the primary task in story selection, however, is, as one top editor put it, "to tell the readers this is what we think is important, and we hope they'll feel the same way, but our aim isn't ideological." Yet, because the importance judgments include national values as well as the enduring values, journalists do make preference statements about nation and society. Value exclusion is therefore accompanied by value inclusion, both through story selection and as opinions expressed in specific stories.

The enduring values are built into news judgment; as a result, most values and opinions enter unconsciously (in a non-Freudian sense). "Every reporter operates with certain assumptions about what constitutes normative behavior, if not the good society," Peter Schrag has written, "and the more 'objective' he tries to be, the more likely those assumptions will remain concealed."[1] Since journalists can no more operate without values than anyone else, the ones concealed in their work make it possible for them to leave their conscious personal values "at home."

## Value Exclusion

Journalists seek to exclude conscious values, and they do so in three ways: through objectivity, the disregard of implications, and the rejection of ideology (as they define it). Value exclusion, however, is not solely a goal but also a practical consideration, for it defends journalists against actual or possible criticism, and protects them against demands by powerful critics for censorship and self-censorship (see Chapter 8 [of the original publication]).

### Objectivity and Detachment

Journalists justify their right to individual autonomy by the pursuit of objectivity and detachment; in a way, they strike an implied bargain, which allows them autonomy in choosing the news in exchange for leaving out their personal values. The outcome restricts the news to facts (or attributed opinions), which, journalists argue, are gathered objectively. This objectivity derives from the use of similar fact-gathering methods; like scientific method, journalistic method is validated by consensus. Equally important, the methods themselves are considered objective because journalists, being detached, do not care how the story comes out.

Most journalists fully realize that objective methods provide no guidelines for the selection either of stories or of which facts go into stories. Nevertheless, in making the selection, journalists strive to be objective, both in intent, by applying personal detachment; and in effect, by disregarding the implications of the news.[2] They do not choose the news on the basis of whom it will help or hurt; and when they cannot ignore implications, they try to be fair.

Objectivity so defined even enables journalists to reach evaluative conclusions and to state opinions. As long as their intent is to exclude conscious personal values, then opinions become "subjective reactions," which follow from objectively gathered facts.[3] Journalistic values are seen as reactions to the news rather than a priori judgments which determine what becomes newsworthy. Investigative reporters, who always end with explicit value judgments, often pick a topic because they smell a good story, not because they have already passed judgment on the target of their investigation. (In addition, the exposé story typically judges the exposed against their own expressed values, and these can be determined empirically by the reporter; as a result, even his or her value judgment is considered objective.[4]) Although journalists may not be aware of it, they are perhaps the strongest remaining bastion of logical positivism in America.

Whether journalists can be truly objective will be discussed in Chapter 10 [of the original publication], but they try hard to live up to their definition of objectivity. Most train themselves, or are trained, to practice value exclusion, and many do not vote in order to preserve their political detachment. I found some exceptions: some older journalists described themselves as anti-Communist liberals worried about the dangers of American fascism, and of the Far Right generally; a few were fervent supporters of racial integration, a couple described themselves as moderate segregationists; there were some Zionists and some anti-Zionists; during the Vietnam War, a handful were hawks, and a somewhat larger number were doves; before elections, some became devotees of one or another candidate.

These journalists expressed their values freely in office discussions and, like the "house radicals" and "house conservatives" to be described later, became known for and by them. If they were unwilling or unable to keep their values out of their work, they asked to be taken off a story or were not assigned to it in the first place. Sometimes, however, editors would assign writers with known personal values to work on a story in which their values were relevant, which would ensure their bending over backwards to remain detached. When their values coincided with an organization's conscious stands, they did not need to be excluded; when their values were at odds with a stand but the story had been assigned to them because of seniority or special expertise, discordant values were "edited out" or "toned down." This happened rarely, since experienced writers are also experienced at value exclusion.

However, journalists with conscious values were in the minority, for the news media I studied seem to attract people who keep their values to themselves. Those unable to do so seldom look for work in these media, especially when their values are discordant; and those who come with discordant values do not remain long. But equally important, the national media, and journalism generally, appear to recruit people who do not hold strong personal values in the first place. They have no prior values about the topics which become news, nor do they always develop them about topics on which they are working. Many of the reporters and writers constantly immersed in American politics did not seem particularly interested in it apart from their work. Even women journalists who felt strongly about sexual equality in their firm and profession, and who pressed male colleagues to choose more stories about women, often indicated that they did not share the values of the feminist movement. The abstention from values extended to story preferences, for when I asked people about their favorite story subjects, hoping in this manner to obtain clues to their values, almost all pointed out that they had no favorites. They were only interested in "getting the story."

Although most of the people I studied discovered their future occupation in high school, they did not become journalists to advocate values or to reform society.[5] Some liked to write, and a few magazine journalists are frustrated or "failed" novelists. Others wanted to be storytellers, enjoying the idea of reporting news to an audience; a few saw themselves as teachers, instructing people in current events. But for the majority, journalism offered the opportunity to be in the midst of exciting activities without having to be involved. Daniel Schorr has written: "Participants took positions, got excited, shaped events for woe or weal, but ended up losing perspective on reality. I remained the untouched observer, seeing the whole picture because I was not in the picture. . . . The notion of being the invisible stranger always appealed to me."[6]

A variety of organizational mechanisms exist to reinforce objectivity and detachment. Journalists are rewarded for getting the story, and personal interests or values can interfere. General reporters move so quickly from story to story that they do not have time to develop attachment, while those covering emotionally charged stories like wars and election campaigns are rotated frequently to preserve detachment. Story selectors, on the other hand, rarely are out of their offices long enough to become involved; they are detached by their duties.

The high salaries and perquisites enjoyed by many, if hardly all, national journalists also foster the feeling of objectivity. A *Time* writer, reporting on his own loss of detachment during the 1976 strike at the magazine, noted that even though he himself had covered many strikes as a reporter, he had never felt the need "to choose between capital and labor. In the print and electronic sweatshops of the Manhattan idea business, there are no class divisions."[7] I doubt that many of his colleagues would agree about the absence of class divisions, and he himself describes the news organization, perhaps unwittingly, as a sweatshop. Still, the income and prestige that go with being a national journalist encourage conscious feelings of being "above" many social and political conflicts. Needless to say, being above them is not equivalent to objectivity, but it may feel that way.

Like social scientists and others, journalists can also feel objective when they assume, rightly or wrongly, that their values are universal or dominant. When values arouse no dissent or when dissent can be explained away as moral disorder, those who hold values can easily forget that they are values. Similarly, the journalists' facts remain facts as long as the unconscious value and reality judgments that go into them are not questioned by trusted critics, or when, as Tuchman points out, they are validated by "common sense."[8]

But above all, objectivity is reinforced by necessity: the need to protect journalistic credibility. If journalists were not viewed as being objective, every story could be criticized as resulting from one or another journalistic bias, and the news would be distrusted by even larger numbers of viewers and readers than is now the case. For this reason, objectivity is also a commercial consideration; indeed, the Associated Press is often credited with having invented objectivity in order to sell uniform wire-service news to a politically and otherwise diverse set of local newspapers.[9]

Nevertheless, most journalists see objectivity in positive terms. Proud that it once helped eliminate the partisan news of party newspapers and of journalists bribed by their sources, they also feel a professional obligation to protect audiences, who cannot gather their own news, from being misled by people who, having "axes to grind," would withhold information contrary to their values. Journalists believe, furthermore, that their role is to supply information that will enable the audience to come to its own conclusions.[10] As a result, they were not in favor of either "personal journalism," which includes personal feelings, or "advocacy journalism," which includes personal values.[11] Television journalists were not even fond of commentary, but mostly because it slowed down the pace of the news programs. Journalists questioned objectivity, however, when it prevented them from reporting what they knew to be lies, although since Watergate, they have been less reluctant either to find sources who will expose liars or to attribute information in such a way that readers and viewers will hopefully realize that the journalists are reporting lies.[12] But much of the time, journalists cannot prove that sources are lying, for they have not been able to do the necessary legwork; this is why investigative reporters, who have done the legwork, are permitted to identify liars more explicitly. Nor do journalists know how to report politicians who are either unaware that they are lying or powerful enough to define honesty to suit their needs.

[. . .]


## Freedom from Implications

Because objectivity is defined as a matter of intent, it includes the freedom to disregard the implications of the news. Indeed, objectivity could not long exist without this freedom, for the moment journalists are required to consider the effects of the news on sources and others they would have to begin assessing their own intent and to relinquish their detachment, especially if they wanted to prevent injury to someone.

Journalists realize, of course, that news has myriad effects, many of which cannot even be anticipated; consequently, they feel that they are entitled to choose stories, and facts, without first considering the possible consequences.[13] Once more, the crucial ingredient is intent for objectivity requires only that journalists avoid intended effects They adopt what Reuven Frank has called an artificial innocence, ". . . the refusal of journalists to alter the story for the purpose of controlling its effects [and] . . . the newsman's necessary deliberate detachment from aiming his work or letting someone else aim it to changing society—even for the noblest motive."[14] But journalists want to be equally free to ignore unintended effects and not to be obligated to consider either the manifest or latent functions (or dysfunctions) of their work.

Freedom from implications exists, like objectivity, to protect journalists from undue criticism, for it makes irrelevant the objections of those who see themselves disadvantaged by the news. As a result, freedom from implications almost becomes an imperative for story selection and production. Story selectors are exempt from the responsibility of worrying whom their choices will help or hurt; and reporters are able to gain access to sources for whom the news might have negative effects, and to ask them any and all questions they regard as newsworthy. Above all, the right to ignore implications eliminates the possibility of paralyzing uncertainty. If journalists had to assess the implications of the stories or facts they choose, and had to determine, much less anticipate, the not immediately obvious implications, they would be incapable of making news judgments—at least, not in time to meet their deadlines.

Objectivity as intent is not difficult to implement at the conscious level, for journalists can know and control their own intentions; however, implications, which are determined by the people affected by the news, are not within their control. Effects cannot be turned on and off by journalists, and they accompany the news regardless of the journalists' intentions or actions. While journalists do not systematically predict story implications, and are therefore less aware of them than nonjournalists think, they also know, from experience, that implications can be expected.

Therefore, in practice, they are not free from implications. The only freedom they have—and it is limited—is the choice of implications (among those expected), which they do take into account. The general consideration has military overtones: to protect the innocent. Accordingly, journalists may sometimes kill or alter stories that can endanger the lives or livelihoods of people who are seen as innocent bystanders at the events that make the news. However, they do not care how the news affects publicity seekers or people whom they consider socially or morally disorderly. Of course, journalists shy away from news that could hurt their own firms, themselves, or their ability to obtain the news; nor do they want, if at all possible, to endanger the national interest or well-being. In wartime, they do not report news that may damage the war effort, and in wartime or peacetime, what may genuinely jeopardize national security; and at all times, they seek to prevent panic among the population.

When implications fall outside these areas or are unpredictable, journalists apply a further consideration, which they call fairness. Fairness, like objectivity, is a matter of intent, and journalists who believe they have acted fairly can ignore charges to the contrary. Generally speaking, fairness is determined in accordance with the enduring values, which is why socially and morally disorderly actors need not be treated fairly. Fairness is also regulated by the libel laws [and] in television, by F. C. C. rules . . .

Producers and editors function as additional enforcers of fairness, for most of their non-stylistic editing is devoted to "softening," the altering of a writer's harsh judgments and/or adjectives thought to be unfair. By softening, reactionary politicians become "conservatives," and lobbyists are sometimes described as "advocates." Conversely, editors rarely "harden" judgments; and if they agree with a writer's critical adjectives, they will not edit them. Unpopular actors and activities may be unfairly described without anyone recognizing, or caring, that the adjectives are pejorative.

The magazines compete against each other and the remaining news media with dramatic writing, and unfair but picturesque adjectives sometimes remain because they liven up a story. Unflattering pictures are chosen for somewhat the same purpose, although *Time* once selected them to put down its political enemies. The safest way to be unfair is to use a cartoon, for it is a reprint; and while cartoons are chosen primarily because they are dramatic, no one can be certain whether or not they represent an editor's opinion.

### The Exclusion of "Ideology"

The exclusion of conscious values implies the exclusion of conscious ideology, but the ways in which journalists reject ideology and deal with it when it appears provide further insight into the workings of objectivity—and an understanding of how unconscious values, and thereby unconscious ideology, enter into news judgment.

Unlike European peers working for party or government news media, American journalists do not formulate conscious and consistent political viewpoints; they are not ideologists. This is true even of columnists and commentators. While they tend to develop a set of viewpoints, they do so because they must write or broadcast on a regular basis, and cannot possibly approach every column or program *de novo*. Moreover, they compete with each other by their points of view, particularly now that newspaper "Op Ed" pages, network radio, and local television feature a "spectrum" approach.

In America, conscious ideological thought is mainly left to intellectuals and political activists. Journalists are neither; nor do they have much contact with ideologists and their publications. As a result, most journalists have only a cursory acquaintance with the ideological debates in which activists and intellectuals engage. Although the news constantly touches on ideological issues of moment, journalists are, for the most part, not even aware of this, as I was surprised to discover when I first began my fieldwork. The few American journalists with ideological concerns either work for journals of opinion, the papers and magazines of political parties that stress ideology, or here and there serve as advocacy journalists.

The dearth of ideologically inclined journalists reflects the general dearth of ideologists in America; as many observers have pointed out, America's economic and political structures have thus far not created conditions to encourage the plethora of ideological thought and politics found in Europe. Nor are the news media, including those I studied, likely to attract people with ideological interests. As far as I could tell, few apply for jobs there either because they do not want to work there, their opinions being too far to the right or left of the opinions expressed in the national media, or because they do not expect to be hired. However, even people with conscious centrist ideologies are absent.

More important, ideologists are not wanted by the news media, for most journalists believe ideology to be an obstacle to story selection and production. They see ideologists, rightly or wrongly, as doctrinaire people with axes to grind, and therefore committed to choosing and reporting stories which would advance their ideological interests. While magazine journalists would have liked them around to enliven office discussions, they and their colleagues in television considered them to be inflexible and incapable of applying the source and suitability considerations, especially balance. They would, it is felt, continually pursue the same kinds of stories and sources, which would, among other things, produce boring news. Such news might attract other ideologists, but they constitute only a tiny part of the audience. In addition, ideologists would impair efficiency in story production. "I wouldn't hire a Goldwaterite," a senior editor explained to me in the 1960s. "It would be too much work to argue with him and edit him." But, of course, ultraconservatives (and socialists) would consume precious time and energy only because their political values diverge from the enduring ones.

The view of ideology as rigid doctrine is complemented by the journalists' definition of ideology which, although hardly unique to the profession, identifies ideology with political values at the extreme ends of the political spectrum. In their view, ideology is to be found among the "extremists" of the Far Right and Left rather than among liberals, conservatives, and moderates. However, liberal and conservative groups which support principles rather than explicit economic or political interests, and are therefore viewed as reluctant to compromise in the pursuit of votes or government funds, are also defined as ideological. . . . [T]he news is suspect about highly principled politicians, and so are journalists.

Nevertheless, ideology is primarily associated with extremism; and while journalists make this association without much deliberation, it also provides a useful defense against outside political pressure, for it automatically excludes political values which, if they entered the news, could generate protest from parts of the audience, management, advertisers, and the government. At the same time, the journalists' definition of ideology is self-serving, if not intentionally so, for it blinds them to the fact that they also have ideologies, even if these are largely unconscious.

[. . .]

## *Reality Judgments*

Values enter the news most pervasively in the form of reality judgments, the assumptions about external reality associated with the concepts which journalists use to grasp it.[15] These are innumerable; and rather than being preference statements, most are assumptions built into the considerations that journalists apply. When journalists must decide what is new, they must also make assumptions about what is old and therefore no longer newsworthy; when they report what is wrong or abnormal, they must also decide what is normal. If they favor the old or the new, and if they believe that what is normal should be normal, reality judgments then become preference statements.

In any case, journalists cannot exercise news judgment without a composite of nation, society, and national and social institutions in their collective heads, and this picture is an aggregate of reality judgments. When journalists perceive California as the fountainhead of bizarre new fads; look at adolescents as exotic; or, at the magazines, universalize the lifestyles of upper-middle-class Americans and project them onto the entire population, they are making reality judgments. In so doing, they cannot leave room for the reality judgments that, for example, poor people have about America; nor do they ask, or even think of asking, the kinds of questions about the country that radicals, ultraconservatives, the religiously orthodox, or social scientists ask as a result of their reality judgments. Many reality judgments are stereotypes, accurate or inaccurate, which journalists borrow from elsewhere because of their availability and familiarity both to the journalists and the audience. As Walter Lippmann pointed out many years ago, the news depends on and reinforces stereotypes. At times it also invents them, although more often than not, the stereotypes journalists create coincide with those invented independently by many other people. The stereotype of adolescents as exotic—and highly libidinous—beings is not, after all, limited to journalists.

Strictly speaking, reality judgments develop apart from preference statements, but even so, they are often interconnected. The inter-dependence of reality judgments and values, and their effect on story selection are perhaps best illustrated by the initial—and continuing—conception of the Vietnam War. From the very beginning, journalists saw the war as a conflict between America and its allies, and a Communist enemy, from which followed the value judgment to support the American side.

It could be argued—and rightly, I think—that the news media should have perceived the American role in the war as a late chapter in a foreign civil war that had been raging for over a generation, but this conceptualization would have required a reality judgment that American journalists—and Americans generally—could not easily make. Civil wars of the kind fought in Vietnam and other developing countries have not been part of the recent American experience from which reality judgments originate. The American Civil War was too distinctive to serve as a model for Vietnam, and the nostalgic image now held of the Revolutionary War ignores the extent to which it was a guerrilla war somewhat similar to that fought in Vietnam.

Prior to American intervention, journalists might have reported Vietnam as a civil war, but even that reality judgment probably would have been accompanied by a value judgment. For at least fifty years now, the first question many Americans have asked about civil wars has been whether Communists were involved in them, and civil wars with Communist participation have rarely been called civil wars either by public officials or journalists. Most often, they have been seen as instances in the Cold War. The reality judgments about Vietnam and the values associated with them however, were accompanied by a substantive consideration: that domestic news is always more important than foreign news. This consideration preceded the reality judgment, for it discouraged journalists from paying attention to Southeast Asia before the American involvement—and later, to the nonmilitary aspects of South and North Vietnamese life. Once American troops arrived, Vietnam was classified as domestic news, a decision that made the resulting reality and value judgments almost mandatory.

## The Journalistic Paraideology

Taken together, the enduring values, conscious and unconscious opinions, and reality judgments constitute what I deem as paraideology—and distinguish from ideology . . . The paraideology that I saw in the news comes, of course, from the journalists, although it expresses the values of the workplace and the profession more than it does the journalists' personal values.

The journalistic paraideology is not inflexible, but then, neither are ideologies, unless they are forcibly imposed party lines. Conformity pressures encourage paraideological homogeneity; but individual autonomy, as well as the organizational divisions of labor and power, makes for diversity. On the whole, top editors and producers adhere to a politically and culturally more conservative conception of the paraideology, just as they take more conservative stands than other journalists, if only because they must keep in mind potential or actual protest from conservative critics and audience members.

When all is said and done, however, the journalistic paraideology is an ideology, an untested and often untestable set of beliefs. That it is an ideology can be illustrated, if not demonstrated, by the fact that those who adhere to it do not conceive of it as ideology. Like other empiricists working within a dominant paradigm, journalists believe themselves to be objective.

## Notes

1. Peter Schrag, "An Earlier Point in Time," *Saturday Review/World*, 23 March 1974, pp. 40–41, quote at p. 41.
2. Here I draw, of course, on Robert K. Merton's distinction between purpose and function. See his *Social Theory and Social Structure* (New York: Free Press of Glencoe, 1949), pp. 25–26.
3. I borrow the phrase, but not his definition, from Peter Braestrop, *Big Story*, 2 vols. (Boulder, Colo.: Westview Press, 1977), 1:708.
4. Michael Schudson, "A Matter of Style," *Working Papers* (Summer 1976): 90–93.
5. Johnstone and his associates found that of a national sample of journalists, over 60 percent had decided to enter their field before the age of 20, the median age being 19. John W. Johnstone, Edward J. Slawski, and William W. Bowman, *The News People* (Urbana: University of Illinois Press, 1976), Table 4–1.
6. Schorr, *Clearing the Air*, p. viii.
7. Morrison, "Bring Back Henry Luce," p. 24.
8. Tuchman, "Objectivity as Strategic Ritual."
9. James Reston, *The Artillery of the Press* (New York: Harper & Row, 1966), pp. 14–15. For a contrary view, see Michael Schudson, *Discovering the News: A Social History of American Newspapers* (New York: Basic Books, 1978), Introduction.
10. Accordingly, Sigelman calls objectivity an "institutional myth," which states and justifies the journalists' "mission in society." Lee Sigelman, "Reporting the News: An Organizational Analysis," *American Journal of Sociology* 79 (July 1973): 132–51, quotes at p. 133.

11.  For data on the attitudes of a national sample of journalists about alternative forms of jour-
     nalism, see Johnstone et al., *The News People*, chapter 7.

12.  Edward R. Murrow has become a journalistic hero in part because he was one of the first to
     call a politician (Senator Joseph McCarthy) a liar. News from Communist sources has,
     however, always been attributed with the qualification that it could be a lie, or at least
     "propaganda."

13.  What Louis Wirth once wrote about logical positivism in the social sciences applies equally
     to journalism; ". . . every assertion, no matter how objective it may be, has ramifications
     extending beyond the limits of science itself. Since every assertion of a 'fact' about the social
     world touches the interest of some individual or group, one cannot even call attention to the
     existence of certain 'facts' without courting the objections of those whose very *raison d'être*
     in society rests upon a divergent interpretation of the 'factual' situation." Louis Wirth,
     Preface to *Ideology and Utopia*, by Karl Mannheim, (New York: Harcourt, Brace and Co.,
     1936), p. xvii.

14.  Reuven Frank, "Address Before the 12th Annual Television Award Dinner," NBC xeroxed
     typescript (January 12, 1970), pp. 16, 20, 33.

15.  Interestingly enough, although journalists develop equivalent terms for many of those used
     by other empirical disciplines, there is no word for "concepts" in the journalistic lexicon.
     One writer once described them as "conceits" but only to indicate their lack of relevance.

# Chapter 8

# MARTHA GELLHORN

# THE FACE OF WAR

MARTHA GELLHORN IS CONSIDERED one of the greatest war correspondents in the 20th century. Born in 1908 in St Louis, Missouri, in 1930 she travelled to Europe to do research and write, paying for her trans-Atlantic passage by composing an article on the shipping line's service. In Paris, she worked for a number of journals, including *Vogue* and the *St. Louis Post-Dispatch* and she published six novels between 1934 and 1967. Gellhorn established herself as a war correspondent by filing reports from the Spanish Civil War during 1937 and 1938 for *Collier's Weekly*. While reporting from Madrid she worked alongside the celebrated novelist Ernest Hemingway whom she married on November 21, 1940.

In 1936 while working in Stuttgart, Germany, on background research for a novel, she read about the beginning of the Spanish Civil War in the German press. Gellhorn was determined to back the Republicans against General Franco's forces, and made her way to Madrid via France carrying a letter from *Collier's* but no formal accreditation. Gellhorn's contribution to the reporting of that time was to describe for the reader the daily life of Madrid citizens living in a city under siege—snapshots of the devastating impact of military conflict.

In Gellhorn's journalism, first person narrative and acute observations of people, their lives and situations, were dominant. She eschewed objective intellectual analysis, giving a voice instead to those who would not otherwise be heard. After Japan bombed Pearl Harbor (on December 7, 1941) front line reporting became more difficult. The U.S. military objected to women correspondents in conflict zones, so Gellhorn went to England—where the war was accessible to her. She was able to file a story on the D-Day landings by joining a hospital ship, and when the Allies felt the war was progressing in their favor and could perhaps be coming to an end, there was a greater relaxation on the control of journalists and Gellhorn was able to join the troops in mainland Europe. She surreptitiously joined up with an American medical team as, in the wake of the flotilla, their hospital ship was sent across the Channel to bring back injured servicemen.

She went on to report on the liberation of the Dachau concentration camp and later reported from Vietnam in 1966 for Britain's *The Guardian*, the 1967 Arab/Israeli Six Day War, with her final war assignment—at the age of 81—the 1989 American invasion of Panama. Collections of Gellhorn's journalism were compiled as *The Face of War* (1959) and *The View From the Ground* (1988). Her sole overtly autobiographical work, and the only piece in which she wrote in the first person, was *Travels With Myself and Another* (1978), that includes the account of a trip to China in 1941, with Hemingway referred to throughout as "UC"—Gellhorn's Unwilling Companion.

Gellhorn wrote emotive journalistic prose—subsequently referred to more generally as the "journalism of attachment"—but her legacy was that she marked a trail for women reporters to follow and was determined that women could tell stories from places where they were traditionally denied access. The two extracts below demonstrate her personal approach. These are "The Besieged City" about Madrid during the Spanish Civil War and "Bomber Boys" about the Second World War.

## The Besieged City, November 1937

At the end of the day the wind swooped down from the mountains into Madrid and blew the broken glass from the windows of the shelled houses. It rained steadily and the streets were mustard-colored with mud. It rained and people talked about the coming offensive, wondering when, when . . . Someone said he knew that food and munitions were being moved; someone else said that Campesino's outfit was in the south or in the north; villages (forty of them, in this direction, in that direction) had been evacuated; the transport unit was ready to go; have you heard? All front passes have been recalled, leaves are cancelled. Who told you, does he know? What, what did you say? So it went, and then the rain would start again. And everyone waited. Waiting is a big part of war and it is hard to do.

Finally it was someone's birthday, or a national holiday (and still cold and nothing happening, only the rain and the rumours), so we decided to have a party. There were two of us who lived in this hotel in Madrid and the third was a visiting friend, an American soldier from the Abraham Lincoln Brigade. A machine-gun bullet had smashed his hip and he had come to the city on his first leave from the brigade hospital. We took the entire hoard of cans from the bottom bureau drawer – canned soup, canned sardines, canned spinach, canned corned beef and two bottles of new red wine – and planned to eat ourselves warm and talk about something else, not the offensive. We would talk about movie stars and pretty places we had seen and have a proper party. It went perfectly until the coffee (one teaspoonful in a cup of hot water and stir). Then the first shell plunged into the building next door, brought down a shower of glass on the inner hotel courtyard and rattled the typewriter on the table.

The boy with the splintered hip moved his heavy plaster-encased leg and said, "Anybody seen my crutches?" He found his crutches and shifted to the place between the windows, and we opened the windows so that we could hear better and so that they wouldn't break, turned off the lights and waited.

We knew this well: the whirling scream of the shells as they came, the huge round roar as they hit, guessing where they went, where they came from, timing them with a stop watch, counting, betting on the size of the shells. The boy was sad. He was used to war at the front where you could do something about it, not to this helpless war in the city; but he would never go to any front again, as his leg would always be too short, and you can't be an infantryman with a cane. There was smoke in the room and the hotel had been hit several times, so we took our wine glasses next door, on the agreeable and traditional theory that if a shell came in the front room it would not bother to come as far as the back room, passing through the bathroom on its way.

We counted six hundred shells and got tired of it, and an hour later it was all over. We said to one another, "Well, that was a nice little shelling." Then we said, "Maybe that means the offensive will start." On the strength of this, we ate up the last bar of chocolate and called it a night.

The next day it rained again, and Madrid picked itself up as it had done before. Streetcars clanked slowly through the streets, collecting the fallen bricks, the broken glass, the odd bits of wood and furniture. People stopped on their way to work, looking at the new shell holes. The front of the hotel gaped a little more. The elevator man, who worked in bronze for his pleasure, hunted for unexploded shells in the rooms, to make lamps from them. His friend, the night concierge, painted warlike scenes on parchment for the lamp shades, and they were both busy all the time. The maid said, "Come and see the room you used to have," and we went merrily in to where nothing remained except the dressing table, with the mirror uncracked, and I found the nosecap of the shell in the broken wood of the bureau. On the fourth floor, lying against the staircase railing, was a long heavy shell that had not exploded. It had only ripped out half a wall and chopped up the furniture of room 409, pulled down the door, and come to rest there in the hall, where everyone admired it because it had a new shape. Some friends telephoned and remarked, "Ah, so you aren't dead." It was just like before. Like the last time and the time before and all the other times. Everybody wondered why the Fascists shelled last night and not some other night; does it mean anything? What do you think?

In Madrid there is not only first-aid service for wounded people, but there is also a first-aid service for wounded houses. The men who manage this are architects and engineers and bricklayers and electricians, and some workers are employed only to dig bodies from the collapsed houses. This staff is always active because when they are not propping up, repairing, plugging holes and cleaning off debris, they make plans for a beautiful new city, which they will build in place of what has been destroyed, when the war is over. So that morning in the rain, I went about with them to see what had happened during the night and what could be done.

In the best residential section, at one street corner, police were telling the people not to crowd and to move on. A shell had burst through the top floor of a fine new apartment house, blown the iron balcony railing onto the roof of a house across the way, and now the top floor stood without support, ready to fall into the street. Farther up, a water main had been cracked by a shell and the street was rapidly flooding. One of the architects had with him, wrapped in a newspaper, his day's ration of bread. He was very careful all morning, climbing through ruins, jumping flooded gutters, not to drop the bread; he had to take it home – there were two small children there, and come death and destruction and anything else, the bread mattered.

We climbed to the top floor, moving gently into a room where half the floor hung in space. We shook hands with all the friends and visitors who had come to see also. Two women lived here, an old woman and her daughter. They had been in the back of the apartment when the front of it blew out. They were picking up what they could save: a cup that had no saucer left, a sofa pillow, two pictures with the glass broken. They were chatty and glad to be alive and they said everything was quite all right – look, the whole back of the apartment could still be lived in, three rooms, not as bright or as nice as the rooms that had been destroyed, but still they were not without a home. If only the front part didn't fall into the street and hurt someone.

A mud road, behind the bull ring on the other side of Madrid, led into a square where there was a trough for the women of that place to wash clothes. There were ten little houses, huddled together, with cloth tacked over the windows and newspaper stuck in the walls to keep the wind out. Women with quiet, pale faces and quiet children stood by the trough and looked at one house, or what was left of it. The men stood a little nearer. A shell had landed directly on one flimsy shack, where five people were keeping warm, talking with one another for comfort and for gaiety, and now there was only a mound of clay and kindling wood, and they had dug out the five dead bodies as soon as it was light. The people standing there knew the dead. A woman reached down suddenly for her child and took it in her arms, and held it close to her.

Disaster had swung like a compass needle, aimlessly, all over the city. Near the station, the architect asked a concierge if everyone was all right in her house. Four shells had come that way. Yes, she said, do you want to see it? Upstairs the family, including the husband's sister and mother, and the wife's niece, and her baby, were standing in their living room, getting used to what had happened. The front wall was gone. The china was broken, and the chairs.

The wife said to me, "What a shame for the sewing machine; it will never work again."

The husband picked a thin, dead canary off the sideboard, showed it to me sadly, shrugged and said nothing.

I asked where they would live now. (The wind coming in, looking down five flights into the street, the broken furniture and all of them crowded into one room and the kitchen. It is bad enough to be cold, never to eat enough, to wait for the sound of the shells, but at least one must have four walls, at least four solid walls, to keep the rain out.)

The woman was surprised. "But we will live here," she said. "Where else shall we go? This is our home, we have always lived here."

The architect said to me, miserably, "No, I cannot patch up the walls; we must save the wood for essentials. The walls are not going to fall out; there is no danger from them."

"But the cold," I said.

"Ah, the cold," he said. "What can we do?" He said to them, Good luck, and they said to him, Thank you, we are all right, and then we walked silently down the steep, unlighted stairs.

It was night now. Streetcars, with people sticking like ivy on the steps and bumpers, burned muffled blue lights. People hurried, with their heads down against the rain, through the dark streets to their homes, where they would cook whatever they had and try to keep warm and wait for tomorrow and be surprised at nothing. A man walked along by himself, singing. Two children sat on a doorstep having a long, serious conversation. A shop window showed a bargain in silk stockings. We were tired, but there was a house near here that the architect had to see. A man brought a candle and we found our way up the stairs. It was hardly worth while going inside the apartment. There was nothing left at all, nothing to save; the walls were gored, and the ceiling and the floor. What had been a place to live was now a collection of old rags and paper, pieces of plaster and broken wood, twisted wires and slivers of glass. The man held the candle above his head so that we could see, and the shadows crawled over chaos.

An old woman had been standing by the door. She came in now. She took my arm and pulled at me to come closer to hear her. She said, very softly, as if she were telling me a secret, "Look at that, look at that, do you see, that is my home, that's where I live, there, what you see there." She looked at me as if I should deny it, with wide, puzzled, frightened eyes. I did not know what to say. "I cannot understand," she said slowly, hoping I would understand and explain; after all I was a foreigner, I was younger than she, I had probably been to school, surely I could explain. "I do not understand," she said. "You see, it is my home."

And all the time it was cold. Madrid flowed with rain, rain everywhere; oh, the cold and, oh, the wet feet, and the thick smell of wet wool overcoats. And we waited for the offensive. The rumors grew each day; they rushed and swayed over the town. People looked wise or sly or happy or worried or anything, and you wondered, What do they know about the offensive? We knew it was to be an important offensive; everyone had confidence in its success whenever it came; everyone was waiting. But there was nothing to do.

And so, to fill the days, we went visiting at the nearest fronts (ten blocks from the hotel, fifteen blocks, a good brisk walk in the rain, something to circulate your blood). There were always funny people in the trenches, new faces, always something to talk about. So we strolled to University City and Usera, to the Parque del Oeste, to those trenches that are a part of the city and that we knew so well. No matter how often you do it, it is surprising just to walk to war, easily, from your own bedroom where you have been reading a detective story or a life of Byron, or listening to the phonograph, or chatting with your friends.

It was as usual cold, and that day we walked through all the trenches in that particular park. In these trenches, in this once fine Madrid park, the mud was like chewing gum. We admired the dug-outs smelling of fresh wood and of wood smoke from the little stoves, the bright blankets over the machine guns, the pictures of movie stars on the walls, the curious serenity — and, after all, there was no news in it. But on the other hand, it was different at night. Every night, clearly, you could hear from the hotel the machine guns hammering, and the echoing thud of mortars, and what was normal in the daytime became a strange business at night.

So the next evening, when the sky turned blue-purple, we presented ourselves at staff headquarters, in a bombed apartment house. It was a homelike spot: there were three women, the wives of officers, shrill as birds. A five-months-old baby slept on the plush sofa and his mother told us all about him breathlessly, with astonishment, as women will. The Major was tired but very courteous. The staff cook wandered in, laughing like Ophelia and a little mad, and asked when they wanted dinner. The soldier who would be our guide was at a dance given by another battalion. They had been making war here for over a year; it was right in the city and the dance was within ten minutes' walk, and a man wants a change now and again. Presently he came, a boy with fantastic eyelashes and an easy laugh, and we walked a block, went down some slippery steps and were in the trenches.

The flashlight was fading, and the mud pulled at our shoes, and we had to walk bent over to avoid hitting the low beams that held up the trench, and it was very cold. In the third line we leaned against the mud walls and looked at the thin, stripped trees of what had once been a city park, and listened. We had come to hear the loud-speakers. At night, one side or the other presents the soldiers in those trenches with a program of propaganda and music. The loud-speakers were hidden near the front line, and you could hear everything, as you can hear a telephone conversation. Tonight the enemy was speaking. A careful, pompous radio voice began: "The chief of Spain, the only chief, is willing to give his blood for you . . . Franco, Franco . . ."

Another soldier had come up and he and our guide lighted cigarettes, and our guide, who was anxious for us to enjoy ourselves, said, "This talking part is very tiresome, but it won't last long; afterward comes music."

Suddenly, blaring across that narrow no man's land, we heard "Kitten on the Keys," played seven times too fast. "Ah," said our guide, "that is very pretty, that is American music."

Then the smooth, careful voice came back: "Your leaders live well in the rear guard while you are given guns to go out and die." There was a burst of irritated machine-gun fire after his remark. "He is too stupid," the soldier guide said, with disgust. "Usually we do not listen to him. Why doesn't he stop talking and play the music? The music is very nice. We all enjoy the music. It helps pass the time."

At this point the music started: *Valencia, deedle-deedle-deedle-dee* . . . It went on for about an hour. We were moving forward with some difficulty because the flashlight had worn out, feeling our way through covered trenches with our hands out, touching both walls, bending beneath the beams of tunnels, slipping on the duckboards when there were any, or stumbling in mud. At one point a mortar exploded, flashing through the trees, and the machine guns clattered an answer. The radio voice said, *"Viva Franco! Arriba España!"*; and we could hear from up ahead in the first line, the jeers of the government troops. Then we heard the voice but not the words of a soldier who was answering that remote radio orator.

The guide explained, "The fight will now start. Now it is mainly a joke, but that loud-speaker used to make us angry. We have heard it so much, and we know it is so silly, and sometimes it announces a great victory right here where we have been all day and seen nothing, and we do not pay attention to it. But it is the custom to answer back."

Very thin and high, through the trees, we could still hear the soldier's voice, shouting.

"He says," the guide said, after listening, "that it is useless to talk to them in Spanish because they are all Moors over there."

We waited but could not make out any other words. The guide went on: "One of our boys usually tells them they are liars and are destroying Spain, and they tell him he is a murderous Red, and later they will get angry and throw mortars at one another. Their loudspeaker is a waste of time, but the music is agreeable."

"You seem very much at home here," I said, because it suddenly struck me that we were as casual as people at an outdoor concert in any peacetime city in the summer. (The stadium in New York with all the stars, that place in a park in St. Louis, with the two great trees growing from the stage, the little brass bands in the little squares in Europe. I thought, it takes something to be so calm about war.)

"These trenches are good," the soldier said. "You can see that for yourself. And we have been here a long time." The machine guns down by the Puente de los Franceses echoed over the black land. "If necessary," the boy said quietly, "we can stay here forever."

I asked where the government loud-speaker was. He said probably up the line some-where, toward the Clinical Hospital; they didn't always work at the same place at the same time.

"You should come and hear ours some night," the guide said. "We have very pretty music, too, but only Spanish songs. You would like it."

We were by this time in a communicating trench, on our way to the first line. A mortar shook the walls of the trench and scattered mud over us, and did not explode, to everyone's delight. The guide said to the other soldier, "It is scarcely worth while to kill foreign journalists for a little music." He told us he could not take us farther and, as we could see, both the music and the speaking were finished, and now there were only mortars. We argued it, bracing ourselves against the walls of the trench, but he said, "No, the Major would be very angry with me and I will get in trouble."

So we went back as we had come.

"Well," the Major said, "how did you enjoy it?"

"Very much."

"How was the music?"

"A little too fast."

"I have here something that will interest you," the Major said. He took a rocket, like a Fourth of July rocket, from the table. "The Facists send these over with propaganda in them, and sometimes I write an answer and we send them back. It is quite a discussion."

He now showed us the propaganda. "It is too much," he said. "It makes you laugh. They think we know nothing. Look at this."

He thumbed through the little booklet quickly, dismissing statements he had seen before and arguments he considered either too boring or too ridiculous. One page started: "What are you fighting for?" The Major smiled and said, "That's something we all know."

He then read us his reply, all very careful, very dull. And we said, "That is fine."

A lieutenant offered me some acorns and the talk turned to America. The guide said he knew a great deal about America because he had read Zane Grey and also James Oliver Curwood, although he realized that was about Canada. Aragon must be very much like Arizona, no? Yes, that's right.

The Major said when the war was over he would like to visit America, but he was a poor man. "I am a worker," he said gently and yet proudly. "Would I ever have enough money to go to America?"

"Certainly," we said. Well, then, how much? Ah, now, that was difficult, in the cities it was more, in the small towns less, travel by bus was not expensive.

"Well, it's hard to say how much it would cost, *Commandante*."

"How about two dollars? Could you do it with two dollars a day?"

"That depends," I said.

"Well, three dollars."

"Oh, surely, with three dollars."

They were all quiet. The Major looked at his adjutant. "*Hombre*," he said, "thirty-six pesetas a day. Something." And then to me, "Ah, well, there is much work to do here and we are all needed. But America must be so beautiful. I would like all the same to see it."

At the end of the cold wet waiting days, Chicote's is the place to go in search of company and conversation and more rumours about the offensive. Chicote's used to be a bar where the elegant young men of Madrid came to drink a few cocktails before dinner. Now it is like a dugout on the Gran Via, that wide rich street where you can hear the shells, even when there is silence. Chicote's is not in a safe locality at all, and every day it is so crowded that you remember, comfortably, the subway at five o'clock, Times Square and the Grand Central Station.

A group of us were sitting in Chicote's wondering whether to drink the sherry, which was tasteless, or the gin, which was frankly fatal. The English girl, who looked like a small, good-humored boy, drove an ambulance for a base hospital. One of the men, a German, wrote for a Spanish newspaper and was now talking rapid French about politics. There were two American soldiers, the two wonderfully funny ones, so young, and so much braver and gayer than people usually are. The smoke from black tobacco was choking, the noise deafening; soldiers at other tables shouted their news; the indomitable girls with dyed hair and amazing high heels waved and smiled; people walked in through the sandbagged door and stared and saw no one they knew or nothing they liked and walked out again. In this crowded din, one could be entirely alone and quiet, and think one's own thoughts about Spain and the war and the people.

How it is going to be possible ever to explain what this is really like? All you can say is, "This happened; that happened; he did this; she did that." But this does not tell how the land looks on the way to the Guadarrama, the smooth brown land, with olive trees and scrub oak growing beside the dry stream beds, and the handsome mountains curving against the sky. Nor does this tell of Sanchez and Ausino, and the others with them, those calm young men who were once photographers or doctors or bank clerks or law students, and who now shape and train their troops so that one day they can be citizens instead of soldiers. And there is no time to write of the school where the children were making little houses of clay, and dolls from cardboard, and learning to recite poetry and missed school only when the shelling was too bad. And what about all the rest, and all the others? How can I explain that you feel safe at this war, knowing that the people around you are good people?

[. . .]


## The Bomber Boys

### November 1943

They were very quiet. There was enough noise going on around them, but they had no part in it. A truck clanked past with a string of bomb trolleys behind it. The ground crew was still loading the thousand-pound high-explosive bombs that look like huge rust-colored sausages. A WAAF's clear high English voice, relaying orders, mixed with the metal noises. A light on the open bomb bay made the darkness around the plane even darker. The moon was skimmed over with cloud, and around the field the great black Lancasters waited, and men finished the final job of getting them ready. But the crews who were going to fly seemed to have nothing to do with this action and haste. Enormous and top-heavy in their Mae Wests or their electrically heated flying suits, these men seemed over-life-size statues. They stood together near their planes.

The Group Captain had been driving fast around the perimeter track of the field in a beetle of a car, checking up. He appeared the way people seem to, suddenly out of the flat black emptiness of the airdrome, and said, "Come and meet the boys." The pilot of this crew was twenty-one and tall and thin, with a face far too sensitive for this business.

He said, "I was in Texas for nine months. Smashing place." This would mean that Texas was wonderful. The others said how do you do. They were polite and kind and far away. Talk was nonsense now. Every man went tight and concentrated into himself, waiting and ready for the job ahead, and the seven of them who were going together made a solid unit, and anyone who had not done what they did and would never go where they were going could not understand and had no right to intrude. One could only stand in the cold darkness and feel how hard we were all waiting.

We drove to the control station, which looks like a trailer painted in yellow and black checks, and though there was no wind the cold ate into you. The motors were warming up, humming and heavy. Now the big black planes wheeled out and one by one rolled around the perimeter and got into position on the runway. A green light blinked and there was a roar of four motors that beat back in an echo from the sky. Then the first plane was gone into the blackness, not seeming to move very fast, and we saw the tail-light lifting, and presently the thirteen planes that were taking off from this field floated against the sky as if the sky were water. Then they changed into distant, slow-moving stars. That was that. The chaps were off. They would be gone all this night. They were going to fly over France, over known and loved cities, cities they would not see and that did not now concern them. They were going south to bomb marshaling yards, to destroy if possible and however briefly one of the two rail connections between France and Italy. If they succeeded, the infantry in southern Italy would have an easier job for a little while.

Several hundreds of planes, thousands of bomber boys, were taking off into the wavering moon from different fields all over this part of England. They were out for the night with the defended coast of France ahead, and the mountain ranges where the peaks go up to ten thousand feet and the winter weather is never a gift; and then of course there would be the target. This trip, however, came under the heading of "a piece of cake," which means in the wonderful RAF language a pushover. If you were taking a pessimistic view of this raid you might have called it "a long stooge," which means simply a dreary, unsatisfactory bore. No one would have given the mission more importance than that. Still they were very quiet and the airdrome felt bleak when they were gone and the waiting had simply changed its shape. First you wait for them to go and then you wait for them to get back.

Perhaps this is a typical bomber station; I do not know. Perhaps every station is different as every man is different. This was an RAF station and the crews flying tonight were English and Canadian, except for one South African and two Australians and an American pilot from Chicago. The youngest pilot was twenty-one and the oldest thirty-two and before the war they had been various things: a commercial artist, a schoolteacher, a detective, a civil servant, a contractor. None of this tells you anything about them. They look tired, and they look older than they are. They fly by night and sleep somewhat during the day and when they are not flying there is work to do and probably it is exhausting to wait to fly, knowing what the flying is. So they look tired and do not speak of this and if you mention it they say they get plenty of rest and everyone feels very well.

The land where they live is as flat as Kansas and cold now and dun-colored. The land seems unused and almost not lived in, but the air is always busy. At sunset you see a squadron of Spitfires flying back to their station against a tan evening sky, looking like little rowboats and flying home, neat and close. In the thin morning, the day bombers roar over toward the Channel. The air is loud and occupied and the airdrome is noisy too. But the home life of the men is quiet.

They say that if you find all the chaps in the mess reading at teatime, you know there are operations scheduled for that night. This afternoon they sat in the big living room of the country house that has become their mess, and they looked like good tidy children doing their homework. If you read hard enough you can get away from yourself and everyone else and from thinking about the night ahead. That morning they would have made a night flying test, taking the planes up to see that everything was okay. Between the test and the afternoon briefing is the rumor period, during which someone finds out how much gasoline is being loaded on the planes and everyone starts guessing about the target, basing guesses on miles per gallon. The briefing (the instructions about the trip and the target) would normally be finished by late afternoon and then there is an operational meal and then the few bad hours to kill before take-off time. It is a routine they all know and have learned to handle; they have taken on this orderly unshaken quietness as a way of living.

Of course there is relaxation in the nearest village on free nights – the village dance hall and the local girls to dance with, the pubs where you can drink weak war beer, and the movies where you can see the old films. At eleven o'clock all such gaieties stop and the village shuts firmly. No one could say this is a flashing romantic existence; it is somewhere between a boarding school and a monastery. They have their job to do and they take this sort of life as it comes and do not think too much about it or about anything. There is only one clear universal thought and that is: finish it. Win the war and get it over with. There's been enough; there's been too much. The thing to do is win now soon, as fast as possible.

The old life that perhaps seemed flat when they had it becomes beautiful and rare when they remember it. No one who flies could make any detailed plans; there is no sense in counting your bridges as well and safely crossed when you know how many tough bridges are ahead. But vaguely each man thinks of that not-so-distant almost incredible past, when no one did anything much, nothing spectacular, nothing fatal, when a day was quite long and there was an amazing number of agreeable ways to spend it. They want that again, though they want a life that has grown lovelier in their memories. They want a future that is as good as they now imagine the past to have been.

It is a long night when you are waiting for the planes from Europe to come back, and it is cold, but it has to end. At four o'clock or around then, the duty officers go to the control tower. The operations officers walk about a certain amount and smoke pipes and say casual things to each other and the waiting gets to be a thing you can touch. Then the first plane calls in to the control tower switchboard. Two WAAFs, who have been up all night and are still looking wide-awake, wonderfully pink-cheeked, perfectly collected and not frozen stiff, begin to direct the planes in. The girls' voices that sound so remarkable to us (it is hard to decide why, perhaps because they seem so poised, so neat) begin: "Hello George pancake over." In the glassed-in room you hear the pilots answer. Then the girl again: "Hello Queen airdrome one thousand over." The night suddenly becomes weird, with the moon still up and the bright stars and the great searchlights like leaning trees over the runway and the wing lights of the plane far off and then nearer, the noise of the motors circling the field, the ambulances rolling out, and the girls' voices going on and on, cool, efficient, unchanging. "Hello Uncle airdrome twelve fifty over." This means that a plane, U for Uncle, is to circle the field at twelve hundred and fifty feet until told to "pancake" or land. The planes come in slowly at first and then there will be four of them circling and landing. The more planes that come in and are marked up on the blackboard, the worse the waiting gets. None of this shows. No voice changes, no one makes a movement that is in any way unusual, the routine proceeds as normally as if people were waiting in line to buy theater tickets. Nothing shows and nothing is said and it is all there.

Finally all the planes were in except P for Peter and J for Jig. They were late. The job was a piece of cake. They should be in. They would of course be in. Obviously. Any minute now. No one mentioned the delay. We started to go down to the interrogation room and the Group Captain remarked without emphasis that he would stay up here for a bit until the chaps got in.

The crews of the eleven planes that had returned were coming into the basement operations room for questioning. They all had mugs of tea, white china shaving mugs filled with a sweetish ghastly lukewarm drink that seems to mean something to them. They looked tireder around their eyelids and mouths, and slanting lines under their eyes were deeply marked. The interrogation again gives the curious impression of being in school. The crews sit on a wooden bench in front of a wooden table, and the intelligence officer, behind the table, asks questions. Both questions and answers are made in such low ordinary voices that the group seems to be discussing something dull and insignificant. No one liked this trip much. It was very long and the weather was terrible; the target was small; there was a lot of smoke; they couldn't see the results well.

The Group Captain in command sat on a table and spoke to the crew members by name, saying, "Have a good trip?" "Fairly good, sir." "Have a good trip?" "Not bad, sir." "Have a good trip?" "Quite good, sir." That was all there was to that. Then he said, "Anyone get angry with you?" "No sir," they said, smiling, "didn't see a thing." This is the way they talk and behave and this is the way it is. When it was known that all the planes were back, and all undamaged and no one hurt, there was a visible added joviality. But everyone was tired, anxious to get through the questioning and back to the mess, back to the famous operational fried egg, and fried potatoes, the margarine and the marmalade and the bread that seems to be partially made of sand, and then to sleep.

The bomber crews were standing at the mess bar, which is a closet in the wall, drinking beer and waiting for breakfast. They were talking a little now, making private jokes and laughing easily at them. It was after seven in the morning, a dark cold unfriendly hour. Some of the men had saved their raid rations, a can of American orange juice and a chocolate bar, to eat now. They value them highly. The orange juice is fine, the chocolate bar is a treat. There are those who drink the orange juice and eat the chocolate early on, not wanting to be done out of them at least, no matter what happens.

The Lancasters looked like enormous deadly black birds going off into the night; somehow they looked different when they came back. The planes carried from this field 117,000 pounds of high explosive and the crews flew all night to drop the load as ordered. Now the trains would not run between France and Italy for a while, not on those bombed tracks anyhow. Here are the men who did it, with mussed hair and weary faces, dirty sweaters under their flying suits, sleep-bright eyes, making humble comradely little jokes, and eating their saved-up chocolate bars.

# Chapter 9

# GENE ROBERTS AND HANK KLIBANOFF

# THE RACE BEAT

F IRST PUBLISHED IN 2006, *The Race Beat* is perhaps the definitive account of reporting on the Civil Rights movement in the 1950s and 1960. An insight from the Swedish sociologist Gunnar Myrdahl in 1940 acts as the starting point: that racial discrimination was the cruel contradiction at the heart of American culture and only massive publicity in the North could overcome segregation in the South. Roberts, who served as the chief Southern correspondent for *The New York Times* in 1965 and later became executive editor at *The Philadelphia Inquirer* and then managing editor of *The New York Times*, and Klibanoff, who reported in the South in the 1970s, chronicle how civil rights developed from an issue only of interest to the black press through until its landing at the top spot on the American political and news agenda. They detail the reporting at all the major episodes of the Civil Rights movement including the critical U.S. Supreme Court case Brown v. The Board of Education of Topeka, KS that outlawed segregation in schools, the Emmitt Till case, the desegregation of Central High School in Little Rock, the desegregation of University of Mississippi, the role of Martin Luther King, and more.

The book chronicles how everyday reporters followed the story where it took them, regardless of the danger it posed to them. There can be no doubt that reporting on civil rights in the mainstream media made a significant contribution to the achievements of the Civil Rights movement itself. Like the reporting on Watergate and the war in Viet Nam, reporting on civil rights exemplifies the work of journalists in the period from the mid-1950s to the mid-1970s, described by some people as the Golden Age of American journalism. This selection reports on the integration of Central High School in Little Rock, Arkansas, one of the most dramatic moments in African Americans' struggle for civil rights in the 1950s.

## Little Rock Showdown

Rumor by rumor, store by store, reporters at the *Arkansas Gazette* spent the first day of school checking Faubus's claims that "caravans" of troublemakers were descending on Little Rock and that stores were experiencing a run on knives and guns. None of it checked out, which the newspaper reported prominently on the front page, alongside an Ashmore editorial, "The Crisis Mr. Faubus Made."

U.S. District Judge Ronald N. Davies ordered that Central High be opened to the Negro students. The governor insisted that it not be. The collision heightened anxiety on the second day of school, the morning of September 4. The schools superintendent had urged that the nine Negro students arrive at Central High without their parents.

Daisy Bates and several ministers decided that white and Negro ministers should accompany the students. Well after midnight on September 3, Bates had phoned the parents to establish a meeting time and place. But she hadn't reached the family of Elizabeth Eckford because they didn't have a telephone; by daybreak, in the hectic efforts to get everyone prepared for school, Bates forgot to send anyone to tell the Eckfords.

Before the eight students arrived at the school together, Elizabeth Eckford arrived alone, aboard a municipal bus. Departing the bus, clutching her books to her chest, her eyes shielded by sunglasses and her expression fixed, the fifteen-year-old began making the block-long walk to a barrier of National Guardsmen.

"They're here! The niggers are coming!" someone in the growing crowd of more than two hundred people shouted. Fine, Chancellor, CBS News television and radio reporter Robert Schakne, and several local reporters and photographers watched as Eckford approached the Guardsmen. To Fine, the young girl looked sweet and in a state of shock. As the Guard turned her away, he saw she was trembling. She crossed the street and kept walking, then turned around and headed back to the Guardsmen. "Don't let her in our school—that nigger," one person shouted. "Go back where you came from," yelled a woman who lunged at her.[1]

Television news cameras raced for position, then focused on Eckford and the hostile crowd around her. But the CBS cameraman had gotten into place too late to catch on film the contorted faces and the yelling and the Confederate flag waving and the "Nigger Go Home" signs. When Schakne realized he didn't have the footage, he did something that revealed the raw immaturity of this relatively new medium of newsgathering: he ordered up an artificial retake. He urged the crowd, which had fallen quieter, to demonstrate its anger again, this time for the cameras. "Yell again!" Schakne implored as his cameraman started filming.[2]

The television reporter had carried journalism across a sacrosanct line. It wasn't the first time a line had been crossed. Photojournalists and photo editors had all sorts of tricks at their disposal, if they wanted them, to change reality; typically, they happened in the darkroom or with touch-up devices, using methods more sophisticated than sending a crowd into a photogenic tizzy. But here, in Little Rock, where a domestic confrontation of unsurpassable importance was unfolding, where journalistic propriety and lack of it were being put on public display, reporters who were inches from the drama found themselves making up rules as they went along and doing it in front of everyone in a volatile situation with a hot, erratic new technology.

Suddenly, the lawn at Central High had become the set, the television reporter had become the director, and the demonstrators had become his actors. It wasn't as bad as creating news, or making it up; but it was recreating the news, with the possibility, even probability, that the re-creation would beget a whole new round of demonstration and gesticulation, which another cameraman might miss, leading to a new re-creation, which would beget even more flamboyant exhibitions of protest until it was no longer clear what was real and spontaneous, what was engineered and manipulated.

If the impact of what was happening, and of the ethical breach, wasn't clear right there at the scene, it would become powerfully clear that night when the images of Eckford, walking the line, approaching the National Guard, were broadcast. A riveted nation could not help but react with awe at the bravery of this teenage girl; anger at the mob jostling to stop her, even if it was take two; and despair at the visual suggestion that even the National Guard could not, or would not, protect or comfort her.

For a second time, Eckford was turned away. Stuck and unable to leave the scene until the next bus arrived, she sat on a bench at the bus stop, her head tilted downward. For minutes that seemed eternal, she absorbed the jeers, epithets, and threats of an angry crowd that seemed to be bouncing out of control all around her. Eckford sat alone, motionless, her arms folded over her lap.

Schakne's cameraman struggled to move his heavy, cumbersome sound camera, tripod, and lens into place to catch the crowd's hostile mood. Schakne leaned in toward her, extended a microphone close to her face. and asked, "Can you tell me your name, please?" Eckford remained statue like, her face unresponsive. "Are you going to go to school here at Central High?" Eckford didn't move a muscle. The sights and sounds of the young girl, frozen in fear and under assault by a boisterous, noisy mob, were sucked into the television camera without filter. Schakne's simple questions came off as a cruel inquisition of an innocent victim. Seeing that she was petrified, Schakne seemed to look for a way out. "You don't care to say anything, is that right?" he asked, turning then to the camera to describe the scene.[3]

Fine saw tears streaming down her cheeks behind her sunglasses and began thinking about his own fifteen-year-old daughter. His emotions carried him beyond the traditional journalistic role of detached observer. He moved toward Eckford and sat beside her. He put his arm around her, gently lifted her chin, and said, "Don't let them see you cry."

A white woman, Grace Lorch, whose husband was a teacher at a local Negro college, joined Fine and Eckford. "What are you doing, you nigger lover?" one protester yelled at Lorch. "You stay away from that girl."

"She's scared," the white woman replied. "She's just a little girl." Then she walked away with Eckford in search of a taxi. "Six months from now," she told another member of the mob, "you'll be ashamed at what you are doing." She and Eckford made their way to a public bus and left together.[4]

Fine's act in giving Eckford comfort that day was seen by many around him as human but completely inappropriate and probably provocative. Schakne's attempt to interview Eckford at least fell within the bounds of journalistic propriety. Fine, on the other hand, had inserted himself into a live story—only to remove himself from it when he wrote about the day's events a few hours later for the *Times*.[5]

Segregationists exploited the behavior of reporters. Schakne's re-creation of the mob's display may have been competitive impulse, and Fine's sheltering of Eckford may have been paternalism, but the segregationists were not discerning. The two were blended as acts of provocation. Even the segregationists, as happy as they may have been to provide a second opportunity for their hostility to be shown on national television, understood that an important line had been crossed. The governor, facing a large number of out-of-state reporters, administered a lecture; "We want you to get the story in its fullest detail as it develops, but don't try to make stories."[6]

Other journalists were also concerned. The news editor of the *Gazette*, Bob Douglas, would laugh while observing how Fine had given his critics the ammunition they needed to allege that he was the center of an anti-South conspiracy: he was from New York, he was Jewish, and he talked too damn much.[7]

Before classes opened on the third day, some sixty reporters were milling around in front of the school, mingling among the five hundred white men and women who came to witness desegregation stopped in its tracks. Fine, his notebook open, tried to interview teenagers. His questions, his manner, or their visceral reaction to any questions posed by outside reporters, provoked them as they gathered in a clot around him. "Let us ask *you* some questions," they insisted.[8]

"Go ahead and ask me," Fine responded.

Why did he seem more interested in the NAACP's point of view than in theirs? Why didn't he talk to local Negroes about their reaction? The crowd around him was no longer just teenagers, and the questions turned to threats. "You better get out unless you want your head broken," one person said.

"Just leave us alone. We'll solve the problem ourselves," said another as Fine tried to interview a teenager. A middle-aged woman, seething at Fine, blurted, "Have you been to Moscow lately?"

A National Guard major stepped into the crowd and waved a club. Then a lieutenant colonel approached Fine. "Come along," the colonel said to Fine. "I don't want you to talk to these people." If Fine wanted to stay there, he said, "act like the rest of us."

"All right, sir," Fine responded as newsmen quickly gathered around him and the colonel. Fine decided to qualify the limits he was willing to accept. "I intend to do my job as I see it for *The New York Times*," he said. "All I've been doing is trying to interview students and get a sampling of their feeling. I have been doing nothing else. I am going to continue to interview the people as a reporter and try not to draw a crowd."

But there was already a crowd around Fine—other newsmen. Some thought he was asking questions, some thought he was merely asking insistent questions, and some thought he was arguing.[9] Gathered around that crowd was another horde, whites who jeered and taunted the newsmen as they were herded toward Major General Sherman Clinger, the governor's appointee as adjutant general in charge of the Guard.

"Gentlemen, this is not a press conference," Clinger said, resting his right foot on a stump. "I will not answer questions. But I do have something to say." By seeking to interview people, he said, reporters were inciting protesters to riot. "Any member of the press will be barred and arrested if it seems in the judgment of the troop commander or myself that he is inciting to violence," Clinger said.

The reporters fired question back. "Are you referring to the incident that Mr. Fine had this morning?" one reporter asked.

"Yes, I am," he said. "Any repetition will bar him from the grounds and get him arrested."

Military or civil arrest? He didn't know. Would the reporter have the right to habeas corpus? Clinger didn't like the implications of the question. "Does that mean," Clinger asked testily, "that if you had that right, you would be ready to incite to violence? I am not going to answer that question."

Fine was escorted to a private half-hour meeting with Clinger, where he was told his limits: No interviews if a crowd gathered. Interviews with single students were permitted, but only inside the school with the principal's clearance. Clinger told Fine that he was on probation, then added, "Any repetition of the incident of this morning and you will be kept out of here. You would likely be arrested, too."

Who would determine the bounds? Fine asked. "We will determine that," Clinger said. Clinger had a final comment that took some of the edge off his tough talk. In a tone that Fine found almost fatherly, Clinger added, "I would advise you to be careful."

Fine had become so much a part of the story that the *Times* had to allow him to do something that was rare indeed for the newspaper in the 1950s. His front-page news story about all the events of the day, written under his byline, included a passing reference to the warning given to "this reporter." On the inside, also under his byline, was Fine's first-person account of his confrontation with protesters and Clinger.[10]

Overnight, an education story had become a civil rights story and Little Rock had become an international symbol of racial discord. Even the words "Little Rock," when uttered by the character Nellie Forbush in the popular Broadway musical *South Pacific* began drawing boos and jeers from a Long Island audience.[11]

Though most national and regional media relied on the wire services for the first few days, editors understood the significance of Little Rock. The story took the lead position in major newspapers, television newscasts, and newsmagazines from the beginning and grew from there. In *The Washington Post* and *The New York Times*, one-column lead stories became two columns, then three. As the confrontation developed over the next month, both papers were stripping their Little Rock headlines across all eight columns at the top of the front page.

The play of the Little Rock story showed no geographic bias. A week after school opened, 67 percent of the newspapers in the North and 68 percent of the newspapers in the South were giving the events in Little Rock front-page headlines of five or more columns, and virtually all were running two or three related sidebars on the front page each day. Many were carrying two photographs on the front, and some devoted an entire part to photos.

For two months, Little Rock would have a firm grip on page one.[12] In *The New York Times*, Little Rock was the lead story on twenty-three of the first twenty-eight days of the crisis; on nine of those days, the *Times* would publish more than fifteen stories about desegregation in Little Rock and other school systems in the South and devote considerable attention to photographs, profiles, and editorials.[13]

There were other school desegregation stories popping up across the South, and news organizations scrambled to get there. In Birmingham, when the prominent Negro pastor Reverend Fred Shuttlesworth was beaten up by fifteen to twenty white men outside a white high school, AP called a reporter off vacation and sent in three staffers with experience in covering Autherine Lucy and the Montgomery bus boycott. One of the AP reporters who went into the high school with police following a bomb scare was quickly recruited to answer phone calls from worried parents. That night in Nashville, hours after a six-year-old girl had integrated a new elementary school, a bomb demolished one of the school's wings.[14]

Some editors and reporters were shocked by the ferocity of the opposition and found it difficult to keep their feelings out of the story. If the segregationists had hoped to win over the mainstream southern out of the story, their tactics backfired. "The unusual aspect of this story was its emotional impact upon the newsman," *The Tennessean's* editor, Coleman A. Harwell, wrote soon after the bombing. "I recall no instance when everyone felt so deeply about an occurrence. . . . There is something so very personal about a school. It involves our children, their happiness, their safety, their dreams, and our dreams for them."[15]

Little Rock was everyone's big story. *Time* and *Newsweek* sent in teams of reporters whose coverage led their national reports. *Time* had a six-year jump on *Newsweek* in establishing a bureau in the South but had used those years not so much to get ahead of the story as to make a point of trying to straighten out this backward, troglodyte region. *Time* devoted two covers to Little Rock in the first five weeks. *Newsweek* signaled that it intended to be competitive: while it made the choice to send its bureau chief to Nashville, it also dispatched a reporter to Little Rock before the school opening. *Life* magazine assigned a team of reporters and photographers, including two of its most prominent shooters, Grey Villet and Francis Miller, whose work would gain a cover and ten inside pages in early October.

The number of reporters grew every day. *The New York Times* moved in four to help Fine, and the *New York Post* and New York *Daily News* sent in some. The Associated Press put sixteen different Staffers there in that first month, International News Service had thirteen, and United Press placed nine. *The Washington Post* and its competitor, *The Washington Star*, sent in top-flight writers, as did *The Wall Street Journal* and papers in Chicago, Denver, Detroit, Saint Louis, Toronto, and Boston. Three separate London papers were represented. At any given time, the number ranged from forty to a hundred reporters on the scene.[16]

Many journalists landed at Adams Field with little preparation for the story and only three names in their notebooks: Harry Ashmore, Daisy Bates, and Sam Peck, which was the name of the hotel where most stayed. For many white reporters, the *Gazette* newsroom became a workplace, and Ashmore's office served as the classroom for tutorials on the South and coverage of race relations. Day after day, visiting journalists would troop into his office, make his acquaintance, absorb his informed and witty take on the story, then secure an invitation for later that evening to Ashmore's house or the Little Rock press club, where the libations and talk flowed freely. Many came to share his sensibilities about the unfolding story, some without even being there.

"Last night I talked twenty minutes on the telephone to Melbourne, Australia," a weary Ashmore told a visiting newsman as the crisis slogged through its first month. "This fellow wasn't sure where Arkansas was—or what it was, a state or a city. I started out telling him it was a thousand miles south of Chicago. Finally, he said, 'I want you to know that the press of Australia is with you.' " Ashmore laughed at the reach of this story in front of him, then added, "Thank God for that. I may have to fall back there."[17]

The Little Rock story also drew the most talented Negro journalists. These reporters and photographers had seen just about every big civil rights story. But this had the markings of becoming the most dramatic of them all. This, it seemed, was when all those years of hiding in the shadows to cover backwater indignities and quiet brutalities would finally pay off for the Negro reporters. This was a direct challenge to a federal court's enforcement of a Supreme Court mandate—and it would be played out in the open, for the entire world to see.

As the black reporters arrived in Little Rock, most skirted past Ashmore and sought a separate indoctrination, and sometimes a room and a bed, at the home of L. C. and Daisy Bates. They gathered at their kitchen table or in their living room, where the picture window that had been cracked by a rock was crisscrossed with masking tape. They gave and received information and became part of the strategic planning.[18] Two of those wrote for mainstream big city papers: Ted Poston of the *New York Post* and Carl Rowan of the *Minneapolis Tribune*.

Ernest Withers, the photographer who had been at the Till trial, the Montgomery boycott, and other stops for the *Tri-State Defender* in Memphis was part of the retinue as was commercial photographer Earl Davy, who frequently shot photos for Bates's *Arkansas State Press*.

Moses Newson was on his first assignment for the *Baltimore Afro-American*, which had just hired him from the *Tri-State Defender*. He, too, had covered the Till trial and other big stories in the South, including a school desegregation battle in the northeast Arkansas town of Hoxie two years earlier.

James L. Hicks, editor of the New York *Amsterdam News*, was there. Hicks was tough—on other Negro leaders. Earlier in the summer, he had pronounced Reverend Martin Luther King, Jr., "the number one leader of sixteen million Negroes in the United States," then accused Roy Wilkins and the NAACP of "dragging their feet" in organizing a Prayer Pilgrimage in Washington in March 1957. Wilkins had fired back, saying that Hicks's article was "an effort to destroy unity by planting suspicion, jealousy and rivalry." Hicks arrived in Little Rock having responded by printing a series of stories criticizing Negro leaders on a new litany of issues.[19]

The most striking of them all was L. Alex Wilson, age forty-nine, editor of the *Tri-State Defender*, which was also covering for its influential parent, *Chicago Defender*. Wilson was a dark-skinned, lanky, towering figure at six feet, four inches. He was serious and fearless, or made himself appear so. His clipped, professorial speech and his stern demeanor provoked uprightness and formality in others, so much that his colleagues, even in their most casual, shorthand conversations, would frequently refer to him not as "Alex" or "Wilson" but as "L. Alex Wilson." He could be so dour that his friends joked about it; they said he didn't smile much because it hurt when he did so.[20]

Wilson had known as a child in Florida that he wanted to be a newspaperman. Most afternoons, he would come home from school and disappear into his bedroom, where his mother would find him writing, writing, writing.[21] He had gotten his bachelor's degree at Florida A&M, studied in the journalism program at Lincoln University in Missouri, and done graduate work at the University of Wisconsin and Roosevelt College in Chicago. He had served as a Marine in World War II and been a high school principal in Florida. Not long after he fulfilled his longtime ambition and got a job on a newspaper, he had made a name for himself. For his first newspaper, the *Norfolk Journal and Guide*, he had covered the Korean War and had won Negro journalism's highest honor, the Wendell Willkie Award, for feature writing.[22]

John Chancellor had a major problem on his hands. As if getting a meaningful story on film were not difficult enough (and doing so in the same clothes day after day, since he had left Chicago without packing), Chancellor faced a mountain of challenges trying to get the film on the air. NBC's affiliate in Little Rock, KARK, did not have the loops, lines, and other technology available to broadcast anything to New York.

The only way Chancellor could get his stories on the air was to fly to Oklahoma City each day at 3 p.m. to have the film edited and transmitted to New York. In an effort to squeeze in an additional hour of reporting lime, Chancellor and Reuven Frank arranged for Chancellor's film to fly by chartered plane to Oklahoma City at 3 p.m., and he'd leave on another plane an hour later to review the processed film and write his scripts before turning around and flying back to Little Rock.

But Frank didn't want to spend the money to bring the Little Rock station into the loop without knowing that the story would last more than four days. AT&T wasn't inclined to install lines for free just to make NBC happy. But after a couple of weeks of Chancellor ping-ponging back and forth to Oklahoma City, running up airplane bills, Frank wrote a few words for Chet Huntley to say on the evening newscast. They were basically a shot across the bow of AT&T: "You may be wondering why John Chancellor is always signing off his Little Rock story from Oklahoma City instead of Little Rock. The reason is, we can't. AT&T hasn't installed the lines making a newscast possible from Little Rock." A few days later, Chancellor was able to broadcast his reports directly from Little Rock.[23]

At the end of the first week, NBC reinforced Chancellor with Frank McGee, whose spectacular reporting on the bus boycott for the network's Montgomery affiliate a year earlier had been his ticket to the big leagues.

McGee was becoming a master of the one-hour, two-hour, sometimes four-hour specials and documentaries that were so much a part of early television journalism. The race specials were unique in one regard: advertising sponsors were much harder to come by and would sometimes find themselves either offered by the networks at unpopular hours or held by local stations for airing at odder hours, if they were aired at all.[24]

McGee's assignment in Little Rock was to focus on how the white students were handling the upheaval. McGee headed first to the *Gazette* newsroom, where Ashmore gave him a desk near the clanging boxes that were spilling out stories from the Associated Press, United Press, and International News Service.

A few desks away sat Ira Lipman, a dutiful high school student who worked Friday and Saturday nights taking high school sports scores from across the state. Lipman had been a student at Central High until this, his senior year, when a new school had opened. Lipman was active in the school newspaper and the yearbook, as well as the national Jewish service organization for young people, the B'nai B'rith Youth Organization. But nothing charged him up like working for the *Gazette*.

Lipman would sit at a metal desk with a Royal typewriter and a phone and compose short stories from shards of information that were phoned in by youthful stringers from noisy stadiums across the state. "The Hot Springs Trojans defeated the Pine Bluff Zebras by a score of 7–6 at Trojan Stadium last night . . ." For a kid who had a keen interest in journalism, being inside the *Arkansas Gazette* was big stuff. It got even bigger when McGee finally spoke to him.

"Kid, where's a good place to get something to eat?" McGee asked. Lipman told him how to get to the Marion Hotel and what to order. McGee returned later with another question: "Kid, where's a good place in town to stay?" Lipman directed him to the Sam Peck Hotel. McGee then popped the big question: Could Lipman round up some kids to participate in a live network show on Sunday? Two days later, for a Sunday-afternoon telecast from the grounds of Central High and the studio of the local NBC affiliate, Lipman and a friend had brought together fifteen teenagers.

The lights went on and they were on the air, speaking their minds to a national audience. Lipman said he felt the law was clear: the Negro students should be allowed into school. Would he mind attending school with Negroes? Absolutely not, he said without hesitation. Less than an hour after the show concluded, Lipman's mother received three phone calls threatening her son's life. The next day, Lipman wrote a letter to Jewish youth leaders across the nation, seeking their support for forcing Faubus to comply with·the law. "Integration is coming," he confidently wrote his young colleagues, "regardless of the mouthings of rabid segregationists." He urged them to stand up and play a role, whatever it might be, in bringing change.[25]

As McGee was leaving town, he did something perfunctory that, unexpectedly, would help establish television news as legitimate, respectable journalism: he passed Lipman's name to Chancellor as someone who could help.[26]

Over the next three weeks, Little Rock was locked in a standoff. The federal court wouldn't modify its order to enroll the Negro students, President Eisenhower would not intervene, the governor wouldn't pull out the National Guard or allow the Negro students in, the Negro students wouldn't withdraw their intention to enroll, and the white protesters wouldn't leave the lawn of Central High.

Reporters were unsparing in their portrayals of the hundreds of sign-toting, chanting white opponents of integration who gathered in front of the school every morning. Many who showed up in protest had no ties to the school system at all. In *Newsweek*, protesters were "shabby" and "ragged," "trash," and "unshaven men and frowsy women." They were "the riffraff," *Newsweek* said, defining them as "truculent street-corner drunks, the viragos of the back-alley tenements, the squatters on near forgotten tobacco Roads." It was not just in Little Rock that writers took such liberties.[27]

*Time* magazine was as demeaning in writing about the Arkansas governor. Describing a reporter's private meeting with Faubus, it portrayed the governor as a backwater slob. It showed him greeting a visitor perfunctorily, collapsing into a contour chair, groaning from eating too much sweet corn and sweet potatoes the night before, and snapping rudely at his wife when she served him stewed chicken and rice. He ordered her to pour milk into the rice, then "wolfed it down, milk dribbling down his chin." He then turned to his guest and "belched gustily."[28]

As crowds gathered outside Central High every morning, reporters routinely came under harassment, finding themselves elbowed, jostled, stepped on, heckled, and, especially in the case of Negro reporters, escorted from the scene by National Guardsmen. Fine, William Hines, a *Washington Star* reporter who asked Faubus tough questions during the ABC television interview, and just about any Negro reporter drew the crowd's wrath as soon as they showed up.

"That's the man who made Faubus look like a fool last night," one man shouted toward Hines, who was then booed. Unable to get any interviews, Hines left, and some in the crowd of five hundred turned their attention to Fine.[29]

A waitress from a Little Rock tavern aimed a steady stream of invective at Fine, asking sharp questions he would not acknowledge. "You got a nigger wife," she bellowed at one point. Fine gave no response. She kept at it. "Are you a Jew?" she asked. This time, Fine answered, "Yes."

Negro reporters faced a more frightening challenge as they tried to get close to the action. "Let him come over here and we'll take care of him," a white protester shouted at Alvin Nall, a young reporter for the New York *Amsterdam News*, when Nall was spotted in front of the school. National Guard leaders and state troopers fell into line next to Nall, but the taunting continued. "Send that New York nigger home," said one demonstrator.[30] As the jeering continued, Nall was stymied. Another reporter asked if he planned to interview people. He looked at the crowd around him, responded, "Not in this area," and left, escorted by Guardsmen.[31]

The limitation on the Negro press's ability to cover the story, and the humiliation that went with it, were evident the next day when Moses Newson arrived for the

*Baltimore Afro-American.* Newson, a camera around his neck, reached the barricades at Central High, where a National Guard colonel told him that no Negroes, including journalists, were being allowed at the scene.

Seeing a white colleague from *The Commercial Appeal*, Newson went to speak with him—not because he had anything to say but because he didn't want to leave the scene and didn't want to be pushed or escorted away. He wanted to show the Guard, the crowd, and whoever else was looking that he was a known and familiar figure to *somebody* there. So Newson made up a conversation about wanting the white reporter's help in getting a photograph from the scene for the *Afro-American*. Then, to the tune of heckles and insults from two white men who walked along with him, he was escorted away by the Guard.[32] Newson would return to the school two weeks later with other Negro reporters—only to face trouble of a more brutal kind.

[. . .]

[S]till advertising with the *Gazette*, Ashmore went so far as to write, "The *Gazette* has never advocated integration. The *Gazette* has never called for the breaking down of our segregation laws. The *Gazette* has consistently supported every legal effort to maintain the social patterns of segregation, and will continue to do so."[33]

Personal threats became quite common for Ashmore. His home phone would ring constantly with warnings that snipers were trailing him, and his mail was filled with vile threats. He and Hugh Patterson would find some relief in telling the story of the subscriber who had written that she was so distraught by the *Gazette*'s editorials that she had lost seven pounds. She urged the paper to keep it up for three more pounds.[34]

While both the *Gazette* and *Democrat* provided better ongoing coverage of the Negro community than many southern dailies during ordinary times, neither newspaper broke through the protective cocoon that Bates, the NAACP, and the students' parents wove around the students. The cocoon allowed the Negro press inside, where it assumed its customary front-row seat at events the mainstream press never saw. Notably absent from the *Gazette* and *Democrat* were authoritative, consistent reports explaining what the students might do or how they, their parents, or the Bateses were reacting to developments. When the papers carried a response from Daisy Bates, rarely were more than two paragraphs printed. Both papers misspelled the names of the students early in the coverage, and neither devoted any time or space in the first days to providing profiles of the courageous students or an explanation of what they and their families were experiencing. When the newspapers did finally carry profiles, the Associated Press typically provided them, and they were short, shallow, and not prominently played.[35]

What Moses Newson, Alvin Nail, and other Negro reporters couldn't get from the high school scene, they more than made up for with their access to the Negro community. They were part of the regular gatherings of the nine students, their parents, and Negro leaders and lawyers. Anyone wanting to know more about the Negro students and how they felt could turn to the stories written by Negro journalists. Encamping at the Bateses' home, the reporters got the story of the fear, travail, and determination that marked the lives of the students and their families. The *New York Post*'s Ted Poston immediately began churning out a series of profiles, "Nine Kids Who Dared." Only through reading this series would one know, for example, that Gloria Ray wanted to be an atomic scientist.[36]

As the situation drew more attention, Faubus's refusal to budge inspired stronger national censure. But the person who had to break the standoff was neither Faubus nor the federal judge handling the case. The break had to come from President Eisenhower, whose own conflicted views about racial integration made him slow to express outrage that a governor was thumbing his nose at federal authority. Eisenhower, against the advice of Vice President Richard Nixon and Attorney General Herbert Brownell, accepted an Arkansas congressman's proposal to invite Faubus to Newport, Rhode Island, where the president was vacationing.[37]

As the president and the governor spoke, Faubus was quite persuasive that all would work out if only the federal government would give the state a couple more weeks. Eisenhower was warm to the idea. Brownell and Eisenhower's chief of staff, Sherman Adams, were not.[38]

In the end, Faubus agreed to issue a statement declaring that *Brown* was "the law of the land and must be obeyed." He then returned to Little Rock and took the opposite position in court. "Just because I said it doesn't make it so," Faubus explained.[39]

Six days later, Judge Davies ordered Faubus to remove the National Guard from the school. By nightfall, the Guard was gone. The question that lingered over the weekend was whether the Negro students would try to enroll the following Monday, September 23, and whether the city police force stood a chance of holding back a mob. This time, Daisy Bates was the one keeping plans under wraps. The students would enroll, she told reporters, but she wouldn't say when.

With the Guard gone, Little Rock lapsed into an uncertain fear over what would happen when the Negro students arrived. News organizations began implementing their coverage plans. The Associated Press had supplemented its already sizable Little Rock bureau with reporters and photographers from Chicago, Dallas, Kansas City, New Orleans, and Memphis.

AP signaled the importance of the story by sending in Relman "Pat" Morin, one of its most respected and tested reporters. Morin, who would spend his fiftieth birthday covering Little Rock, had been collecting far-flung datelines since 1930, when he had covered the meat-cleaver murder and decapitation of ten people in the French Concession of Shanghai. He still recalled his first editor insisting that the story would be strongest if Morin didn't get fancy and just wrote what he saw: the blood running so deep a cop slipped in it and fell. Over the next several years, he went to Tokyo, China, Korea, Manchuria, Mongolia, Indonesia, Malaya, Thailand, and Indochina.[40]

It seemed as though nothing could keep the lanky correspondent from the hottest stories in Asia—until he found himself on temporary assignment in Saigon the day the Japanese attacked Pearl Harbor. An abrupt knock at his door produced four Japanese men, three in military garb. For the next nine months. Pat Morin was a prisoner, confined mostly to his room. He was offered the chance to leave, in exchange for broadcasting propaganda. He refused, then kept his wits by writing a novel. When his release finally came and he was aboard a ship, he opened a porthole and pitched it into the ocean, grateful, he liked to say, that fish can't read.

Postings to London, Africa, Italy, Paris, and Washington followed before he was sent to cover the conflict in Korea. Nothing he saw in war had as much impact on him as something he witnessed in June 1953: the executions of Julius and Ethel Rosenberg. He relieved the tension leading up to the execution the way he had learned to handle stress in war: by furious note taking. Almost mindlessly, he scribbled in his notebook as much as he could, as fast as he could, leaving nothing out, making himself a mechanical device and detaching himself from the emotional scene before him. It was a strategy that would rescue him again in Little Rock.

AP planned to have two or three reporters, sometimes more, at Central High at all times, with one stationed at each end of the high school building. Since the AP reporters would have to dictate most of their stories live, they took note of the three phone booths the telephone company had installed on the perimeter of the school, then made additional arrangements with one of the teachers who lived near the school to use her home phone if necessary.

Bob Ford, sent in from Dallas, would write the leads for the morning papers; Pat Morin would handle them for the afternoon papers. Bureau chief Keith Fuller would take their dictation, help craft their stories, and send them out.

AP assumed, correctly, that Daisy Bates and the NAACP would try to enroll the students at the first opportunity, the following Monday, September 23. On that morning, in his hotel room, Pat Morin's telephone rang with a wake-up call, as it had every morning for weeks. "Seven o'clock," the hotel operator said enthusiastically. "Mustn't be late for school today."[41]

Across town, the Bateses' home was the staging area for the day's drama. Well before eight o'clock, it was crowded with the nine students, their parents, friends, advisers, and reporters. After the white reporters left her house, Daisy Bates told the Negro reporters and photographers that they, too, would have to go to the school on their own, and they'd have to go a different way. She let them know which entrance the students planned to use. Alex Wilson, whose experience and bearing led others to view him as the leader among the Negro editors and reporters, took a last look at the nine students and marveled at how stouthearted they were. Then he jumped into his car with Jimmy Hicks, Moses Newson, and Karl Davy and headed toward ground zero of the confrontation.

When Pat Morin arrived at the school, the two to three hundred people gathered in front struck him as curious, not menacing As Morin was surveying the scene, taking note of the greens and golds of a lovely fall day, Alex Wilson was parking two blocks away. This was not the first time they had covered the same story: both had reported from the Korean War; Morin's articles had won a Pulitzer Prize.

Morin stepped into one of the glass-encased phone booths to update the AP office. To one side, he could see the front of the high school; to the other he could view the street running along the school's south side. At the AP office, Keith Fuller answered. "Do you want to dictate?" he asked Morin.

"Such as it is . . . not much to report," Morin said.

"I'll take it myself," Fuller said. "The boys are busy."

Down the street, the four Negro newsmen were drawing a small and hostile crowd as they started walking apprehensively toward the school. Wilson and Newson walked in front; Hicks and Davy, who had a Graflex camera dangling from his neck, in back. Wilson, so tall and noticeable above the crowd, impeccable with his suit coat fastened at the middle button and wearing a wide-brimmed tan hat, saw that the mass of white people in front of them seemed to be metastasizing as they walked toward it. Behind them, two white men quickly jumped into their traces and trailed them.[42]

"Get out of here!" one segregationist yelled at them, "Go home, you son of a bitch nigger!" bellowed another.

Two other men jumped in front of the newsmen and spread out their arms as if to block them. "You'll not pass," one of them said.

"We are newspapermen," Wilson responded.

"We only want to do our jobs," said Hicks.

"You'll not pass."

Blocked in, Wilson turned the only way he could and headed toward a police officer, "What is your business here?" the officer asked, Wilson showed his press card. The officer reviewed it, slowly. "You better leave" he finally said. "Go on across the sidewalk." As Wilson and the others crossed the street, they could see that the officer had let the whites trailing them keep pace and close in on them.

"Anyone got a rope?" one white man shouted. "We'll hang 'em. I can get one awful quick."

As Morin was finishing dictating what little he had, a shout from the outside penetrated the booth. "The niggers are coming!" Morin could see everyone turn away from the school and start moving in the other direction. "Hang on!" Morin yelled into the phone, "Hang on! There's a helluva fight starting."

"Roll it," Fuller told Morin calmly. Turning to another editor at the office, Fuller said, "Get ready for a bulletin."

Suddenly, two men, one wearing a crash helmet, assaulted Davy and chased after him, terror written all over Davy's face as he looked back. They caught him, muscled him toward some high grass, then slugged and kicked him while others smashed his Graflex onto a concrete sidewalk, destroying his film. Another group of white men sputtered curses as they kicked and hit Newson and Hicks until they could break free and run away.

Morin, with a front-row view inside the phone booth, held his position, opening the door to hear the commotion better and breathlessly dictating everything he saw and heard. Using his war-reporting technique, he didn't feel he was fashioning stories so much as mechanically sucking up the entire scene with his eyes and funneling it into the phone with his voice.[43] At one point, a magical moment for Morin, he took his eyes away from the confrontation to look at the panorama afforded by the booth's glass walls. To his amazement, he saw a station wagon ease up to the south entrance of the school, and he watched—one of the few newsmen who did—as the nine Negro students and two adults emerged. Morin saw that they were not running and not even walking fast. He was able to jot down what they were wearing, how they were carrying their books, and the way they examined the crowd with curiosity but little interest.

Closer to Morin, other white reporters were drawn to the attack on the four Negro newsmen, but they could do nothing to stop it, and policemen did not intervene. Wilson, taunted, pushed, and slapped as he kept walking, was suddenly rushed from behind by a man who planted one foot and swung the other as hard as he could, landing it solidly just below Wilson's back. Another man surged forward with a kick that landed so hard that Wilson's lanky frame looked as though it was folding as he went lurching forward. His hat fell to the ground, so Wilson stopped, then paused to pick it up. In that moment, he had a chance to run. The idea crossed his mind long enough to reject it. Elizabeth Eckford had not run, he told himself. And all that time spent training as a Marine in World War II, then working as a reporter in Korea, then covering the gruesome, demeaning Emmett Till case made him want to stand up and hold his ground. So did an incident years earlier down in Florida, one he had told few people about.

Long before he became a journalist, Wilson had been a teacher in Leesburg, Florida. Just to intimidate local Negro residents, the Ku Klux Klan liked to parade through town every now and then. Wilson had a long, sharp memory of a time when they had rolled through, sending Negro residents including himself, scattering in fear. Wilson never forgot it and never forgave himself for it, and he vowed never to run away again.[44] Now, as the members of the mob darted in and out at him, throwing fists and feet, Wilson picked up his hat, stood erect, and took some time to run his hand along the crease. But they wouldn't let him go. Wilson's refusal to show fear was provoking the mob. "Run, damn you, run," one man said as others started cuffing Wilson around inside a moving scrum.

One man jumped onto Wilson's back and wrapped his left arm around Wilson's neck, locking him in a stranglehold. Two feet away, a burly, muscular man gripping a brick stared at the immobilized Wilson, ready to start swinging. But he couldn't. A man standing beside him had a tight grip on his arm, not allowing him to throw punches with the brick. As the man on Wilson's back drove him to the ground, the man with the brick got close enough to crack Wilson's skull but again was pulled back by the man beside him. Finally, the man with the brick settled for a hard kick into the center of Wilson's chest.

Wilson, still holding his hat even as he fell to the ground, got up, recreased it, and kept walking, taking one last powerful blow to the head before being pushed away by the crowd just as it realized that the nine Negro students had quietly slipped into the high school.[45] As the mob went crazy over the latest information, Wilson walked to his car. He still had not unfastened the middle button of his suit coat.

Amid the hysteria, Morin suddenly felt his phone booth rocking back and forth. Looking out, he saw a boy trying to topple it, with him inside, by bouncing on the cable that connected the booth to the telephone pole. The booth tipped but never fell, and Morin was able to continue as a one-man wire service telling the Little Rock story to the world.[46]

Protesters yelled to their children inside the school, demanding that they come out. They cheered those who did, as well as the police officer who turned in his badge. Chaos reigned, and every rumor caught a tailwind. When protesters surmised that the Negro newspapermen had conspired to be part of a ruse to draw attention from the students, they grew angrier.[47] Benjamin Fine, feeling like a marked man every time he showed up, came in for some bony elbows in the ribs. A reporter for the Pine Bluff newspaper, mistaken for an out-of-stater, was slugged under the chin and knocked down. A United Press photographer from Dallas was manhandled, and a New Orleans television reporter and cameraman were assaulted when they filmed a white girl leaving the school.

When *Life* magazine's three-person team—the photographers Grey Villet and Francis Miller and reporter Paul Welch—tried to take pictures of a white girl who had walked out of the school in protest, whites retaliated. One attacker punched Miller in the mouth and drew blood. Police threw Miller into a police wagon—along with his assailant. Villet and Welch were cornered by toughs and not allowed to move. They were pushed, shoved, and hit in the face, neck, and ribs. *Life* later agreed to help the FBI bring the agitators to heel. It supplied names, photographs, and whatever help agents needed from *Life*'s files.[48]

Almost all of the day's violence had been directed at journalists, but it was sufficient to make school officials worry that they could not contain the crowd and protect students at dismissal time. Three hours and thirteen minutes after the Negro students had entered the building, even as mobs were beating reporters, the students were removed without the demonstrators' even knowing it. The only way they became convinced that the Negro students had departed for the day was to have two members of the mob enter the school and search for them.

The attack on the reporters prompted a new surge of interest among newspapers. *Washington Post* publisher Philip Graham's interest was less in how his paper covered the exploding story than in getting the Eisenhower administration to respond with force. Graham got Ashmore on the phone, then abruptly transferred him to the deputy attorney general, William Rogers. Ashmore told Rogers that the police could no longer control the situation. "I'll give it to you in one sentence. The police have been routed, the mob is in the streets and we're close to a reign of terror." It was a call that Ashmore would spend years explaining, for it appeared he had stepped beyond his role of editor to urge that federal troops be sent in. No, Ashmore would later say, he had not. He had told Rogers only what the *Gazette* would report the next day.[49]

As that newspaper was heading for the presses, President Eisenhower went on national television and told an audience of 100 million people—62 percent of the nation's television sets were tuned to him—that he had decided to intervene. Within hours, 1,000 soldiers from the racially integrated 101st Airborne Division were flooding into town.[50] Nearly 10,000 members of the Arkansas National Guard were federalized, and some were told to return to the school, working this time for the president under orders to protect the students, not block them, as they entered.

On the 101st Airborne's first full day in Little Rock, news directors for the three networks got clearance to break into daytime programming virtually at will. CBS broke in eleven times, NBC eight times. ABC joined later in the day. Far away, in the Pentagon, Army Secretary Wilber M. Brucker was handed an update on the troops in Little Rock. "But what's happening there right now?" he snapped.

"Why not turn on the television set?" an officer suggested. A television was brought into the room, plugged in, and turned on, and images of soldiers at stiff parade rest emerged on the screen.

"They look good, sharp," said Chief of Staff Maxwell D. Taylor, who had previously commanded the 101st. Then he blurted out, "Why, there's one man whose belt is undone!" Looking closer, he concluded that the man was off duty and resting.[51]

That an army secretary and his chief of staff were able to examine their soldiers in action from nine hundred miles away, live, was a powerful sensation, one the American public would share in the coming years.

In the days after the nine students started attending classes, John Chancellor began reporting information that other reporters weren't getting. He seemed to have details from inside the school on how the white students were responding to the Negro students and vice versa, how the teachers were treating the new arrivals, what questions they asked the Negro students, and how the students answered. There was a reason.

Days before, Chancellor had called Ira Lipman, the high schooler Frank McGee had befriended in the *Gazette* newsroom. "I understand you're our contact," the newsman said. From that point, and for weeks to come, Lipman became a critical conduit of valuable information to Chancellor. Though Lipman had transferred to the new high school that year, he made regular visits to Central in his capacity as business manager of the school newspaper, and he knew students throughout the building.

Calling sometimes from a phone inside Central, Lipman would reach Chancellor at the Sam Peck Hotel, the *Gazette*, or KARK or one of the temporary phone booths that the telephone company had installed outside the high school. Speaking in a whisper, he provided Chancellor with interior scenes, action, and insights from the corridors of Central High. The information was pure gold because school officials and the 101st Airborne weren't giving any hint at all about what was going on inside the school.

Lipman himself had a fortuitous link to the Negro students. His parents were members of a Jewish country club outside Little Rock. While swimming there, he had come to know a locker room attendant, a Negro kid his own age. Lipman would sometimes drive the fellow back to his home in Little Rock. The attendant was Ernest Green, the only senior among the Negro students trying to get into Central High.

On the day Faubus was ordered to pull back the National Guard and let the students enter, Lipman placed a call to Green. Would he tell Lipman which entrance the students would be using on Monday? Would he pause on his way in to give John Chancellor an exclusive interview? The next morning, Chancellor and his cameraman, Maurice Levy, were positioned in the right place at the right time to watch the students walk by, then to have a few moments with Green.

In such ways, Chancellor set a standard for television reporting that lifted it, even in the eyes of its cynical competitors on the print side. Night after night, Chancellor's reports from Little Rock, enhanced by dramatic images, became a fixture in the American household. The evening news show ran fifteen minutes, of which twelve minutes and forty seconds were news. Race stories dominated, none so much as those from Little Rock, presented to viewers by the midwestern man with the nice voice, pleasant disposition, and owlish face.

CBS did some serious reporting with Schakne and Bob Allison. Because ABC came in late and gave the story less attention, Faubus provided that network with his first national interview. Watching that live program, New Your Times television critic Jack Gould was impressed by television's immediacy. Now when Faubus chose not to respond to questions, he did so under the critical eyes of an entire nation. "Whatever may be the individual set owner's reaction . . . it still is TV as its best," Gould wrote. But television news owed its viewers a "comprehensive and searching study of the Little Rock story," Gould added. "Television registered a beat in putting the governor on the air, but it has an obligation to dig more deeply into the other side of the story."[52]

The television coverage was provocative and in some ways confusing. There were reporters and commentators, and the line between them wasn't always clear. Night after night, words, phrasings, tones, and inflections became a concern to some television critics and certainly to the segregationists. The networks had pledged earlier in the year to keep opinion out of newscasts. The pledge seemed to dissipate at Little Rock, The Atlanta Constitution's television critic wrote, where "all of the newscasters have become 'analysts' and 'commentators' with a free rein to speak their own minds about what is right and what is wrong in the integration dispute."[53]

On the eastern seaboard, the segregationist editors Tom Waring and Jack Kilpatrick watched the television coverage with disgust. Waring suggested in a letter to Kilpatrick that some sort of media monitoring committee be set up to examine race reporting by news outlets they considered anti-South, Kilpatrick wasn't ready to support any kind of watchdog but shared Waring's reaction. "These past two weeks have seen Faubus absolutely crucified by the television and radio people," Kilpatrick wrote, "and some gesture ought to be made of resistance to the incredible influence on public opinion exerted by these radio and TV people."[54]

Nonetheless, in ways even Gunnar Myrdal could never have anticipated in pretelevision days, the daily visual broadcasts of news as it happened had a profound impact on the nation's understanding of the race drama in the South.

On the print side, the Arkansas Gazette was proving to be exactly the kind of newspaper that Ashmore had hoped for when his concerns about the short-comings of southern papers had led to the creation of *Southern School News*. The *Gazette* demonstrated that local newspapers in the South could provide vigorous, hard-nosed, in-depth and fair coverage of their own communities in the midst of a racial crisis.

The *Gazette* showed that by swarming the story; by becoming the paper of record and carrying the transcripts of every important court ruling, speech, press conference, and interview; by challenging official versions of events and relying on more than official sources; by routinely publishing the editorial views of other newspapers; and by foreseeing the long-term impact of the daily events, it could comprehensively and for a sustained period cover the difficult, breaking, explosive story. It also found it could stay in business in the face of circulation boycotts and advertising cancellations.

Ashmore's courageous editorials and civic leadership, backed by a fearless owner, would show his southern brethren that they could challenge racial and political orthodoxy, survive, and get national praise and prizes. In 1958, the *Gazette* won two Pulitzers, the paper for its news coverage and Ashmore for his editorials.

The lesson at the *Arkansas State Press* would be harder. The *Gazette*, though hurt by the advertising boycott, could endure more pain than L. C. and Daisy Bates could. National advertisers, feeling the heat of wholesale distributors in the state, dropped their advertising in the *State Press*, costing the Negro weekly almost its entire national base. Having aimed editorial wrath at Negro leaders it considered complacent, the newspaper found that the combination of slashed advertising and rapidly diminishing circulation put it on an irreversible death spiral.[55] Its epitaph, said a scholar of the Negro press, should have read: "A survivor of terror, but a victim of boycott."[56]

But the more immediate problem for the Negro press was evident on the streets, where the day's events, the violence, made it impossible for the reporters to do their jobs. The impact was devastating. On the power side of the barricade, the white side, Negro reporters could never go unnoticed and untargeted. Negro journalists, to protect themselves, could pull all the little tricks that white reporters deployed to hide their notebooks, dress low-key, avoid arguments—and still they would be unmistakable in a mob scene. As the civil rights movement reached across the South, and as confrontations at other notorious datelines made Little Rock look like a beginner course in racial violence, the Negro press lost its front-row seat.

## Notes

1. Benjamin Fine, "Arkansas Troops Bar Negro Pupils; Governor Defiant," *NYT*, September 5, 1957, pp. 1, 20; Jerry Dhonau, "Negro Girl Turned Back, Ignores Hooting Crowd," *AG*, September 5, 1957. *Gazette* reporters had not yet established a strong relationship with Daisy Bates or the nine students and misspelled Eckford's name as Echford; in the same story, it also misspelled the last name of the white woman, Grace Lorch, who later comforted Eckford.

2. Robert Schakne, oral history, BUI; Philip N. Schuyler, "Panelists Agree: Journalistic Code Violated at Little Rock," *E&P*, November 2, 1957, pp. 11, 66. Schakne expressed regret that he had encouraged the crowd and said he learned then that it was inappropriate. In the *E&P* account, former CBS correspondent Bob Allison said that he, too, encouraged Little Rock protesters to repeat demonstrations that cameras had missed; see also Charles Quinn, oral history, BUI.

3. Schakne, oral history, BUI; *Eyes on the Prize*, part 2, Blackside Inc., Boston, Mass., Henry Hampton, executive producer. In his oral history, Schakne expressed misgivings about his attempt to interview Eckford that day.

4. Two months later, Senator James Eastland called Mrs. Lorch before the Senate Internal Security Subcommittee to answer charges that she was a member of the Communist Party.

5. Benjamin Fine, "Arkansas Troops Bar Negro Pupils; Governor Defiant," *NYT*, September 5, 1957, pp. 1, 20. Fine told of Lorch's role, but not his own.

6. Ken Parker and Matilda Tuohey, "Eisenhower Asked to Curb U.S. Agents," *AG*, September 5, 1957, p. 2.

7. Bob Douglas, author interview, undated.

8. The scenes that follow come from extensive reports published in the *AG* and *NYT* on September 6, 1957. In a front-page story in the *Times*, Fine wrote about the day's events and referred to threats to arrest newsmen after "this reporter" was told to stop interviewing people. His first-person account of the incident with the Guard and Clinger was published on page 8. The *Times* played up the confrontation with the newsmen, publishing as its lead photograph on page 1 a picture of Clinger talking to reporters and carrying an inside photograph of a National Guardsman using a billy club to separate Fine from people he was trying to interview.

9. Charles Quinn, oral history, BUI.

10. *NYT*, September 6, 1957, p. 8.

11. *Newsweek* reporter William Emerson's file to New York offices, September 27, 1957, located in *Newsweek* archives at EUSC, Atlanta.

12. The AP Log, September 5–11, 1957, provided by Hoyt Hughes Purvis, author of "Little Rock and the Press," master's thesis, University of Texas, 1963, pp. 64–65.

13. *NYT*, September 3–30, 1957; also Purvis conducted an extensive survey of how the story was played in "Little Rock and the Press," master's thesis, University of Texas, 1963, p. 167.

14. The AP Log, September 12–18, 1957.

15. Ibid., September 12–18, 1957.

16. Purvis, "Little Rock and the Press," *passim*.

17. File by *Newsweek* reporter Joe Cumming to editors in New York, September 23, 1957, located in *Newsweek* archives at EUSC, Atlanta.

18. Dorothy Gilliam, oral history, BUI; Gilliam was a rookie reporter for the *T-SD* who went to Little Rock to help L. Alex Wilson, against his advice.

19. James L. Hicks, "King Emerges as Top Negro Leader," "Wilkins Raps Hicks on Pilgrimage Comment," New York *Amsterdam News*, June 1, 1957, June 8, 1957. Reddick, *Crusader Without Violence*, p. 197.

20. Newson, Wilson, Withers, Tisdale, Martin, author interviews; also Enoch P. Waters, *American Diary* (Chicago: Path Press, 1987), p. 109.

21. *T-SD*, October 22–28, 1960, citing an interview with his mother, Mrs. Luetta Patterson.

22. Newson, Wilson, Withers, Tisdale, author interviews. In *Forum for Protest*, Lee Finkle notes that the Wendell Willkie Award, which paid cash prizes, never had universal acclaim in the black press as the highest honor in black journalism because it had been established by southern white liberals such as Virginius Dabney, Mark Ethridge, Ralph McGill, and Douglas Southall Freeman in 1945, when they were accusing the northern black press of being too militant. Other criticisms were that only two of the original board members had been black and that the initial winner, though a black journalist, had publicly lambasted most black newspapers as "nauseating." But there was no other honor as well known.

23. Frank, Chancellor, author interviews.

24. J. Fred MacDonald, *Blacks and Whites on TV: Afro-Americans in Television Since 1948* (Chicago: Nelson Hall Publishers, 1983), p. 91.

25. Letter from Ira A. Lipman to All BBYO leaders, September 9, 1957, provided by Lipman.

26. Ira A. Lipman, author interview.

27. "The Riffraff," *Newsweek*, September 23, 1957, pp. 32–33; William Emerson's undated file from Nashville to *Newsweek* in New York, in *Newsweek* archives at Emory University Library's Special Collections.

28. "What Hath Orval Wrought," *Time*, September 23, 1957, pp. 11–12, 15.

29. AP, "Crowd at School Jeers Newsmen," *NYT*, September 10, 1957; Jerry Dhonau, "Quiet Crowd at Central Grows Spiteful as Rumor Sifts in From North Side," *AG*, September 10, 1957, p. 10.

30. Dhonau, "Quiet Crowd," *AG*, September 10, 1957, p. 10.

31.   AP, "Crowd at School Jeers Newsmen," *NYT,* September 10, 1957; Dhonau, "Quiet Crowd," *AG,* September 10, 1957.

32.   Newson, author interview, April 22, 1996; Dhonau, "Crowd at Central High is Passive as Guard 'Escorts' Negro Newsman," *AG,* September 11, 1957.

33.   *AG* editorial, December 13, 1957, as cited in Purvis, "Little Rock and the Press," pp. 49–50.

34.   Hugh Patterson, oral history, BUI, p. 11.

35.   The *Democrat's* first such story, " 'Didn't Think It Would Go This Far,' Rebuffed Student Asserts," by AP, was published September 5, 1957, p. 3, as cited by Ritz in "The *Arkansas Democrat,* September 1, 1957–September 30, 1957." The *Gazette's* first such story was "Little Rock Negroes Give Views on School Integration Dispute," September 15, 1957, p. 7, as cited by Kevin R. Ogburn in "*Arkansas Gazette* Coverage of the Little Rock School Crisis, September 1–30, 1957," paper done for a journalism class at University of Maryland. The first general insight into the nine students published in the *Gazette* came on September 16, in "Nine Negroes Marking Time Until CHS Dispute Settled." The story was from the AP and published in the *Gazette* on page 15. Perhaps in recognition of these holes in the *Gazette's* coverage and the AP's work in filling them, when Pulitzer Prizes were handed out, the *Gazette's* two went to Ashmore for editorial writing and to the newspaper for public service (not for local reporting), while the national reporting award went to AP's Relman Morin for his Little Rock coverage. The *Gazette* publisher, J. N. Heiskell, also won several prestigious awards.

36.   Ted Poston, "Nine Kids Who Dared: Gloria Ray," *NYP,* October 28, 1957, sec. M, p. 2, as cited in Kathleen A. Hauke, *Ted Poston, Pioneer American Journalist* (Athens: University of Georgia Press, 1998), pp. 147–148. Also, Rowan, *Breaking the Barriers,* pp. 154–155.

37.   Brownell commented on his distrust of Faubus at a conference in Abilene, Kansas, in 1990. Reed, *Faubus,* p. 220.

38.   Faubus would later say the president seemed, halfheartedly, to be taking a position scripted by Brownell and Adams. Faubus, knowing the federal judge in the case had invited suggestions from the Justice Department, felt that Brownell had misinformed Eisenhower by saying the president could not get involved in the case. Faubus attributed Brownell's resignation six weeks later to Eisenhower's belated belief that Brownell had deceived him. Faubus, *Down from the Hills,* pp. 255–258; Reed, *Faubus,* pp. 219–220; Ashmore, *Hearts and Minds,* pp. 262–264; contemporaneous *AGs* and *NYT.*

39.   Reed, *Faubus,* p. 219.

40.   "A Reporter Reports," an April 1960 compilation of a six-part series in *E&P* about Relman "Pat" Morin, provided by Hoyt Hughes Purvis.

41.   Ibid.

42.   This scene is as told by Relman Morin in "A Reporter Reports," L. Alex Wilson in the *T-SD,* James Hicks in *Eyes on the Prize,* Daisy Bates in *The Long Shadow of Little Rock,* and other accounts.

43.   Morin's work that day won him his second Pulitzer Prize. Morin remained modest about his role, saying, "Some other intelligence, if that is the word, and a far deeper one than mine, was in command." AP's in-house newspaper, the *AP Log,* said that Morin "was as close to a one-man show as we ever get in AP. . . . Morin's reporting of the scene at the high school won stature as rare journalistic artistry . . . derived from the cool, dispassionate presentation and the cumulative impact of grim detail."

44.   Newson, author interview.

45.   L. Alex Wilson, "Defender Editor Tells of Attack," *T-SD,* September 28, 1957, pp. 1–2; Jerry Dhonau, "Mobs at Both Ends of School Kick, Beat, Chase and Yell," *AG,* September 24, 1957, pp. 1–2; Benjamin Fine, "President Threatens to Use U.S. Troops, Orders Rioters in Little Rock to Desist; Mob Compels 9 Negroes to Leave School"; Farnsworth Fowle, "Little Rock Police, Deployed at Sunrise, Press Mob Back at School Barricades," *NYT,* September 24, 1957, pp. 1, 18, 19; *Eyes on the Prize,* part 2; Daisy Bates, *The Long Shadow of Little Rock,* pp. 88–93.

46.   This scene is as told by Relman Morin in a letter to Hoyt Purvis, July 17, 1962.

47.   All four of the newsmen and Bates have been convincing in denying that the newsmen were used as decoys. The *T-SD* didn't help matters, however, when a copy editor put the following headline on a story that Wilson dictated to the *Defender* for September 28, 1957: "Ruse Helps

Get 9 into School." Wilson, in several subsequent stories, went to great pains to insist that there was never an arrangement to distract the crowd.

48.  Richard Stolley, Atlanta bureau, *Life* magazine, oral history, BUI; letter from Ben Fine to Hoyt Purvis, July 30, 1962, cited in Purvis master's thesis.

49.  David Halberstam, *The Powers That Be* (New York: Alfred A. Knopf, 1979), pp. 310–311; Ashmore, *Hearts and Minds,* pp. 261–262, 265; Bates, *The Long Shadow of Little Rock,* pp. 93–94.

50.  The 100 million figure comes from "Eyes on Little Rock," *Time,* October 7, 1957, p. 61. *NYT* reported the 62 percent figure at the time, Purvis, p. 114.

51.  "Eyes on Little Rock," *Time,* October 7, 1957, p. 61.

52.  Jack Gould, "Little Rock Speaks," *NYT,* September 9, 1957, as cited by Purvis, "Little Rock and the Press," pp. 71–72.

53.  Paul Jones, "Newscasters Take Sides on Little Rock," *AC,* October 2, 1957, p. 14.

54.  Letter, Kilpatrick to Waring, September 20, 1957. TRWP.

55.  Purvis, "Little Rock and the Press," pp. 56–58, citing Armistead S. Pride, "The Arkansas State Press: Squeezed to Death," *Grassroots Editor,* vol. 2, no. 1, January, 1962, p. 7; also, Suggs, *The Black Press in the South,* p. 82–83.

56.  Purvis, "Little Rock and the Press," pp. 56–58, citing Pride, "The Arkansas State Press," p. 7; also Suggs, *The Black Press in the South,* pp. 82–83.

# Chapter 10

# M. PHILLIP KNIGHTLEY

# THE FIRST CASUALTY

THE SUBTITLE OF THIS NOW SEMINAL HISTORY of war reporting is "The War Correspondent as Hero, Propagandist and Myth–Maker from the Crimea to Iraq," that sums up the main thrust of Knightley's classic study. It is probably the most entertaining but also the most stringent "j'accuse" of war reporting ever written. Knightley, who was an investigative journalist with the *Sunday Times* (London) for 20 years and has won many awards, including the Overseas Press Club of America Award for the best book on foreign affairs, throws down the gauntlet at journalists to examine their role in the encouragement of propaganda and myths, particularly those based on information released by governments.

Nearly 150 years ago, W.H. Russell was sent by *The Times* of London to cover the Crimea War. When he found himself enveloped in a catalogue of disasters, blunders, unnecessary killings and lies, he wrote to his editor Delane, "Am I to tell these things or am I to hold my tongue?" His missives took a week to reach London by horse and steamer, but later the word came back, "Continue to tell as much truth as you can." Both men were accused of treason, until Russell's reporting eventually forced the government to resign.

It is precisely the consistency of theme over the ages in this book that prompted fellow investigative journalist John Pilger to write in his 1999 introduction, "The following pages ought to be read by every young reporter and by those who retain pride in our craft of truth-telling, no matter how unpopular and unpalatable the truth. The rest is not journalism."

Knightley reveals that time and time again truth is concealed behind a cloud of so-called 'objectivity'. Knightley notes the now famous comment by British Prime Minister David Lloyd George to C.P. Scott, editor of the *Manchester Guardian* during the First World War: "If people really knew (the truth) the war would be stopped tomorrow. But of course they don't know and can't know." The excerpt that follows looks at the reporting on the war in Viet Nam, a war in which the press played a very controversial role and television came of age as a medium to report war.

A Gallup poll in mid-1967 revealed that half of all Americans had no idea what the war in Vietnam was about. Just after the Tet offensive in 1968, the chairman of the Appropriations Committee of the House of Representatives, without whose consent there would be no money for the war, genuinely seeking enlightenment, asked the Chief of Staff of the United States Army: "Who would you say is our enemy in this conflict?"[1]

Clearly, those charged with the responsibility of informing the United States public about Vietnam had not fulfilled their task. Given that the issues were complex and the facts unpalatable, this failure has never been satisfactorily explained. True, the whole story did come out in the end, but the feeling of the American reader that he was not getting a satisfactory running story of the war still concerns those correspondents who did their best to provide it. The most likely theory is that the combination of low understanding of the war at home and high drama in Vietnam created a challenge that few correspondents were able to meet. And when such correspondents were present, too often their efforts were frustrated by the attitude of their editors in the United States.

All sorts of correspondents, from all sorts of publications, went to Vietnam. There were specialist writers from technical journals, trainee reporters from college newspapers, counter-insurgency experts from military publishers, religious correspondents, famous authors, small-town editors, old hands from Korea, even older hands from the Second World War, and what Henry Kamm of the *New York Times* called "proto-journalists," men who had never written a professional word or taken a professional photograph in their lives until the war brought them to Saigon. They all wrote stories that were used and presumably read or took photographs that were bought and reproduced. Michael Herr, who went to Vietnam for *Esquire*, estimated that, at a time when there were between 600 and 700 accredited correspondents, "only fifty gave journalism a better name than it deserved, particularly in Vietnam."

Ambition, principally, had brought them all there. The war was the biggest story in the world at the time—"the longest-running front-page story in history," as a United Press man put it; "the best story going on anywhere in the world at the moment," said Peter Arnett—and there was no better place for a young reporter to put a gloss on a new career or an old reporter to revitalise a fading one. Herbert Matthews had made it sound better in the pre-Second World War days: "If you have not seen a battle, your education has been somewhat neglected—for after all, war has ever been one of the primary functions of mankind, and unless you see men fight you miss something fundamental."[2] But what it comes down to is that war provides rich material for a correspondent, and Vietnam was the richest ever. "You see these things, these terrible things," said Charles Mohr, "but in an odd way they're good stories."[3]

The mechanics of becoming accredited were straightforward. The correspondent applied to his nearest South Vietnamese embassy for an entry visa. It was usually granted.[4] In Saigon, the correspondent reported to the U.S. authorities with a letter from his newspaper requesting accreditation and accepting responsibility for him. If he wished to be accredited as a free-lance, he needed letters from two organisations saying that they were prepared to buy his dispatches. The correspondent was then issued an accreditation card identifying him and stating: "*The bearer of this card should be accorded full co-operation and assistance . . . to assure the successful completion of his mission. Bearer is authorised rations and quarters on a reimbursable basis. Upon presentation of this card, bearer is entitled to air, water, and ground transportation under a priority of 3. . . ."*

The correspondent signed an agreement to abide by a set of fifteen ground rules, dealing mainly with preserving military security, and was on his way. Some got a tailor to run up a safari jacket—Saigon tailors called it a "CBS jacket"—with matching trousers, which looked vaguely like a uniform, not, in most cases, out of any sense of commitment, but so as to be less conspicuous in a military situation. On his army fatigues he could sew his official identification, his name and organisation, thus: JOHN SHAW, TIME, or, to the disbelief of most GIs, in his particular case, ALAN WILLIAMS, QUEEN.

The MACV card would admit the correspondent to the daily briefing on the war's progress given at the Joint United States Public Affairs Office (JUSPAO), which had been created to handle press relations and psychological warfare. ("I never met anyone there," claimed one correspondent, "who seemed to realise that there was a difference.") If he was prepared to believe JUSPAO, a correspondent could cover the war simply by attending the briefings each day. Most correspondents considered them a waste of time, but one, Joe Fried of the *New York Daily News*, built up a reputation, during his nine years and eight months in Vietnam—"longer than anyone and without a vacation"—by his daily, persistent, and provocative questioning, sometimes driving the briefing officer into revealing an item of genuine news value.

For the correspondent who preferred to spend more time in the field, the problem was not in finding material, but in the risk of being overwhelmed by it. Murray Sayle wrote to me saying: "I arrived here as everyone else does, hoping to sum it all up in 1,000 crisp words. I wind up in the hotel on Friday nights trying to make some sense out of a great whirl of experience—the ghastly sights you see and your own feelings of fear and loneliness."

Sayle, then working for the *Sunday Times* of London, wrote an article on April 28, 1968, describing a day in his life in Vietnam. It is worth looking at as an example of the "whirl of experience" a correspondent could expect to face as he tried to follow the war. "I begin the day at sea approaching the mouth of the Perfume River aboard the American landing craft Universal No. 70, bound for Hue with 190 tons of reinforcing sheet for runways. I am trying to get to Camp Evans, north of Hue, where it is unofficially reported that a big battle is developing—but it is impossible to fly direct from Da Nang."

Sayle leaves the boat and sets out to walk to Phu Bai, a big American base, seven and a half miles away. Crossing a floating bridge, he is overtaken by an American and two South Vietnamese soldiers escorting four barefoot Vietcong prisoners, three boys and a girl, all about seventeen years old. He is mistaken for part of the escort and finds himself in the interrogation room at the headquarters of the South Vietnamese First Infantry Division, where the proceedings open with the interrogating officer kicking one of the prisoners in the stomach "with his well-polished, heavy military boots."

At this point the American soldier realises that Sayle is a correspondent and asks him to leave. Sayle, feeling shaken, has a cup of coffee at the Cercle Sportif, or what is left of it, and then hitches a ride with a convoy of United States army trucks, "many of which are decorated with little rows of two, three, or four yellow figures wearing conical hats and sandals, each one neatly crossed out."

As he nears Phu Bai, there is a tremendous explosion, followed by leaping sheets of orange flame and billowing smoke—a helicopter has shed a rotor blade and crashed into the base ammunition dump. While he waits for a helicopter to take him to Evans, Sayle watches a Vietnamese engraving mottoes on the soldiers' cigarette lighters. "Favourites are 'Make war, not work' and 'I pass through the Valley of Death unafraid, for I am the meanest bastard in the valley.'" At Evans, Sayle joins the officers' chow line for dinner: deep-frozen shrimps, grilled steak, plum tart, and coffee. Then the colonel whose battalion is to make the first air assault in the morning outlines his plan to fourteen correspondents and photographers, who draw straws for the order in which they will go. Sayle draws the first wave, with a French news agency man and an Italian photographer. He fills two water bottles, collects a C ration, and finds an empty stretcher in the press tent, which turns out to be alongside a battery of two 175-millimetre guns firing two rounds of harassment and interdiction at nothing in particular every half-hour through the night. "Thinking about copy deadline, I suddenly remember the date—tomorrow is Anzac Day and the day after is the fourteenth anniversary of the Geneva agreements which ended the French war in Vietnam."

As well as trying to assess the significance of so varied a day, correspondents faced other major difficulties. Covering the war was highly dangerous, and Vietnam had no respect for reputations. Forty-five war correspondents were killed in Vietnam and eighteen listed as missing. Those killed included such experienced correspondents as Larry Burrows, Dickey Chapelle, Marguerite Higgins (who died in the United States of a tropical disease contracted in Vietnam), François Sully, and the author and historian Bernard Fall. They died in helicopter crashes, from stepping on land-mines, and, in one instance, directly at the hands of the Vietcong. This occurred in May 1968, when five correspondents driving in Cholon were attacked, and, although the one survivor said they had shouted "*Bao chi*" ("press"), they were machine-gunned. The next day, a United Press photographer called Charlie Eggleston took a weapon and announced that he was going out on a mission of revenge. He, too, was shot dead, but, as the story in Saigon went, not before he had first killed three Vietcong.

There, was some argument among correspondents, after the Cholon incident, about the wisdom of carrying arms. The difficulty was that if even one correspondent continued to go armed, this entitled the Vietcong to assume—as perhaps they had in the Cholon case—that all the correspondents were armed, and to react accordingly. Nothing came of the discussions, and many correspondents continued to carry personal weapons, ranging from Sean Flynn's pearl-handled twenty-two-calibre pistol in a shoulder holster to Peter Arnett's old Mauser pistol. Ward Just noted that most of these weapons were seldom fired, "save for one legendary American correspondent who lived in the field with the First Cavalry Division and left Vietnam with three notches in his belt." This was Charlie Black, a correspondent for the *Columbus Inquirer*, of Columbus, Georgia, home of the First Cavalry. Black has not denied the charge. "I'm not really a Wyatt Earp, but if some guy comes after me I answer back."[5]

Another daily difficulty was that not all military authorities welcomed correspondents or understood their function. In fact, some actively hated them. These ranged from officers who felt that correspondents were undermining the war effort—"My Marines are winning this war and you people are losing it for us in your papers"—to GIs who resented the correspondents' freedom to choose whether and when to risk their lives. "Those bastards," one rifleman said, watching a jeepload of correspondents drop Michael Herr and drive away. "I hope they die."[6] This visible enmity and the recurring accusation that they were doing a lousy job of reporting the war—"Why don't you guys tell it like it really is?"—caused considerable introspection among correspondents. What should be their attitude to the war, and how should they report it? Peter Arnett's method was to get out with the units doing the actual fighting.

From the time Arnett arrived in Vietnam in 1962, a tough twenty-seven-year-old New Zealander, until the war's end thirteen years later, he spent more time in the field than any other correspondent. "It's essential that a reporter see for himself those thousands of little battles at the lowest command levels to begin to comprehend what it is all about. With luck, with enough small definitions, he might be able to begin to generalise, but to stand off and take a long-range view has been proved erroneous time and again."[7] In the field, as elsewhere, Arnett determined to "observe with as much professional detachment as possible, to report a scene with accuracy and clarity." Above all, he never became *involved* in what he was reporting or photographing, and that made him, according to the author Marina Warner, "as hardboiled as a Chinese thousand-year-old egg."

Arnett has described his standing one hot noon outside the Saigon market and seeing a Buddhist monk squat on the pavement, squirt gasoline over himself from a rubber bottle, flick a cigarette lighter, and turn himself in a matter of minutes into a blackened corpse. "I could have prevented that immolation by rushing at him and kicking the gasoline away. As a human being I wanted to, as a reporter I couldn't."[8] So Arnett photographed the monk ablaze, beat off the Vietnamese secret police trying to grab his camera, raced back to the Associated Press office, and sent his photograph and story round the world.

Other correspondents, particularly photographers, tended to agree with this view of their rôle. (Television was in a class of its own here and must be dealt with as such.) Even Philip Jones Griffiths, whose portrayal of suffering Vietnamese civilians forms perhaps the best photographic testament of the war, has said, "Your job is to record it all for history. You can't not feel involved, but you have to steel yourself and do you job, take your photographs. That's what you're there for. It's no use crying. You can't focus with tears in your eyes. It's better to do the breaking down later in the darkroom."[9]

Clearly, this emotional detachment came more easily to some correspondents than to others. Clare Hollingworth of the *Daily Telegraph*, who had been reporting wars since 1939, was intrigued by the conflict in Vietnam. "The Americans were fighting a war with fantastic weaponry. I made it my business to know what weapons, planes, etc, were being used there. I love weapons and know a fair amount about them. I daresay I can take a machine-gun apart and put it together again, and as fast as any man. The tactical side appealed to me immensely. My emotions weren't really involved."[10] To remain as detached as this, it was necessary for a correspondent to keep aloof from debate on the origins of the war. As Julian Pettifer of the BBC said, "There is simply no point in arguing whether the war is right or wrong. You're always left with the fact that it is there and it's your job to cover it."[11]

But, while most correspondents saw their rôle in terms as clear and uncomplicated as this, others went through deep and sometimes agonising examination of their motives and began to question whether it was possible to cover the war with an untroubled conscience. Usually, the first serious doubt appeared under pressure. Alec Shimkin of *Newsweek* was on Route 1, near the village of Trang Bang, in 1972, when the Vietnamese air force dropped napalm on their own side and burned two infants to death. Shimkin came back down the roadway towards a group of correspondents, who were hoping to get from him an eye-witness account of what had happened. But Shimkin was temporarily crazed with fury and grief, and he shouted, "Goddamn you! Leave me alone. Get the hell out," at the correspondents who approached him.[12] Whether the incident would have had any lasting effect on Shimkin must remain speculation, because he was reported soon afterwards as missing, presumed dead, at Quang Tri. Marina Warner, reporting at the time for the *Spectator*, recalls the effect on her of her first encounter with civilian casualties. "I saw this old woman coming down the road with a child in her arms. The child's flesh was falling off. I said to myself, 'My God, I've seen this all before.' I had. On television. Somehow seeing it before on television took away some of the reality and I wasn't as shocked as I had expected to be. But later, when the horror sank in, I stood on the roadway exposing myself to fire when I didn't need to. And I stood there longer than I needed to. It was some sort of expiation. I had the feeling that if I could have been wounded it would have taken away the guilt I felt about the burnt child, the guilt I felt about Vietnam."[13]

Murray Sayle went out on the "body detail" that brought back the bodies of the four correspondents killed in the attack in Cholon in 1968. He wrote to me: "There's a strange calm about the dead, they don't feel any pain. You look at them and then look away and when you look back they look exactly the same. When you see people badly hit you feel very healthy and you think, when I get out of here without a scratch I will have beaten the system and nothing can ever be as bad as hearing the shooting and that second or two before you know if it is you or not. Then, when it's not you, you feel like an impostor, an intruder, crouching off to the side, notebook in hand. I sometimes feel I am engaging in some clinical investigation of my own motives at the expense of other people."

Those correspondents sufficiently frank to admit it agree that there are moments in war when the exhilaration compensates for all the horror, all the doubt. Some of them look for historical or psychological justification. Tim Page, who worked for *Life*, says, "War has always been glamorous. And I don't care who he is, if you put a gun into a man's hand, then he feels bigger."[14] Others simply accept it without question. "I can't explain it," says Peter Gill of the *Daily Telegraph*, "but there is something fantastically exhilarating about being terrified out of your wits." Chris Dobson of the *Daily Mail* agrees. "When I'm actually taking part in an action it's always as though I'm three martinis up. I'm in another, a higher, gear, and it's marvellous."[15] And Horst Faas, the Associated Press photographer, for whom war has become a way of life, says, in his urbane German accent, "Vot I like eez boom boom. Oh yes."[16]

This fascination for violence and death, along with the struggle the more sensitive correspondents had in trying to reconcile their hatred of war with their very real enjoyment of it, puzzled and annoyed some observers. "It is impossible to realize how much of Ernest Hemingway still lives in the hearts of men until you spend time with the professional war correspondents," wrote Nora Ephron in *New York* magazine. "Most of the Americans are stuck in the Hemingway bag and they tend to romanticize war, just as he did. Which is not surprising: unlike fighting in the war itself, unlike big-game hunting, working as a war correspondent is almost the only classic male endeavor left that provides physical danger and personal risk without public disapproval and the awful truth is that for correspondents, war is not hell. It is fun."

It would be hard to disagree with Nora Ephron's accusation when applied to most correspondents in most wars. But, just as the First World War marked a turning point in the history of war correspondents—never again could a war be reported so badly—so Vietnam stands out, for it was there that correspondents began seriously to question the ethics of their business. Photographers were particularly troubled, because their craft is by its nature more obviously voyeuristic and intrusive than that of a writer. So in Vietnam, while one found photographers who, like Horst Faas, enjoyed taking hard-news pictures of violent events, and for whom death and atrocity held no horror,[17] there were also men like Larry Burrows, who began to wonder what it was all about.

Burrows, a Londoner, who lived in Hong Kong and worked for *Life*, was described by the former *Picture Post* editor Tom Hopkinson as "the greatest war photographer there has ever been." When he first went to Vietnam, in 1962, he was able to rationalise his attitude: "It's an important time in history and if I can convey a little of what goes on, then it's a good reason to be here." But later he began to shield his readers from the horror of the war. "I was trying to take a shot of this guy who was dying in the helicopter. I never took his face. I don't like making it too real. I've wondered about that point quite a lot. I think if the pictures are too terrible, people quickly turn over the page to avoid looking. So I try to shoot them so that people will look and feel, not revulsion, but an understanding of war." The more Burrows thought about the soldier in the helicopter series—"Yankee Papa 13"—the more it appears to have worried him. "I was torn between being a photographer and the normal human feelings. It is not easy to photo-graph a pilot dying in a friend's arms and later to photograph the breakdown of the friend. I didn't know what to do. Was I simply capitalising on someone else's grief?" He felt the troops' resentment more keenly. "They look up from their dying friends and see me shooting pictures. They feel that I am capitalising on their misery and get very angry." Burrows was killed in a helicopter crash in February 1971, and so we will never know where this self-questioning would have led him. But we have an indication, from an encounter with Burrows described by *Esquire* writer Michael Herr.

Burrows and Herr were on a landing zone when a Chinook helicopter arrived. Burrows ran down and photographed the crew, the soldiers coming down an incline to get on board, three wounded being carefully lifted up, six corpses in closed body bags. Then he took one picture each of the helicopter rearing, settling, and departing. "When it was gone," Herr wrote, "he looked at me and he seemed to be in the most open distress. 'Sometimes one feels like such a bastard,' he said."[18]

Herr said that correspondents discussed the problem often, and in the end "there's no way around it; if you photographed a dead marine with a poncho over his face and got something for it, you were some kind of parasite. But what were you if you pulled the poncho back first to make a better shot, and did that in front of his friends? . . . What were you if you stood there watching it, making a note to remember it later in case you might want to use it?"

If a photographer puzzled over his professional ethics too long, he risked missing a picture. Harri Peccinotti spent weeks in Vietnam, for *Nova*, a London magazine, waiting for one particular photograph—a South Vietnamese woman loading her husband's body into a body bag and onto a helicopter taking the dead and wounded from a place where there had been a battle. Eventually, the circumstances were right photographically, even better than Peccinotti had hoped for: the woman had her child with her. But, at the moment he could have taken the picture, the helicopter crew asked for Peccinotti's help in getting the wounded on board. "I had to make a choice. I went to help the wounded and I never got the photograph."[19]

In 1967, Donald McCullin of the *Sunday Times* said he would like to do war photog-raphy every day of the week. "I used to be a war-a-year man, but now that's not enough. I need two a year now. When it gets to be three or four, then I'll start to be worried." McCullin admitted that he tended to romanticise war, but insisted that "photographically war can be very beautiful." In 1970 he was wounded and was taken from the front, with other casualties, in the back of a truck. "I knew the man next to me had died when his toes next to my face went lifeless and began to move with the jolting . . . it's incredible to see somebody not alive. I don't want to be maimed, but why them and not me?" McCullin recovered and went back to photographing in Vietnam. Now he became less reckless and much more calculating—"I know just what photograph justifies what risk"—and, although he still found danger exhilarating, he noticed that his detachment had gone. "Almost without realising it, I found myself getting involved with helping wounded and carrying stretchers and that sort of thing. And my photography started to suffer. It started to come second."[20]

The most intrusive medium in Vietnam was television, and, as the war went on, the hunger of editors for combat footage increased. "Before they were satisfied with a corpse," Richard Lindley, a British television reporter, said. "Then they had to have people dying in action."[21] Michael Herr described a truck carrying a dying ARVN soldier that stopped near a group of correspondents. The soldier, who was only nineteen or twenty, had been shot in the chest. A television cameraman leaned over the Vietnamese and began filming. The other correspondents watched. "He opened his eyes briefly a few times and looked back at us. The first time he tried to smile . . . then it left him. I'm sure he didn't even see us the last time he looked, but we all knew what it was that he had seen just before that."[22] The Vietnamese had seen the zoom lens of a sixteen-millimetre converted Auricon sound camera capturing his last moments of life on film that, if the flight connections worked and the editors back at the network liked it, would be shown in American living rooms within forty-eight hours.

This little item would not be exceptional. During the Tet offensive, a Vietnamese in a checked shirt appeared on television being walked—that is, dragged—between two soldiers. The soldiers took him over to a man holding a pistol, who held it to the head of the man in the checked shirt and blew his brains out. All of it was seen in full colour on television (and later in a memorable series of photographs taken by Eddie Adams of the AP).

Any viewer in the United States who watched regularly the television reporting from Vietnam—and it was from television that 60 per cent of Americans got most of their war news—would agree that he saw scenes of real-life violence, death, and horror on his screen that would have been unthinkable before Vietnam. The risk and intrusion that such filming involved could, perhaps, be justified if it could be shown that television had been particularly effective in revealing the true nature of the war and thus had been able to change people's attitudes to it. Is there any evidence to this effect?

The director of CBS News in Washington, William Small, wrote: "When television covered its 'first war' in Vietnam it showed a terrible truth of war in a manner new to mass audiences. A case can be made, and certainly should be examined, that this was cardinal to the disillusionment of Americans with this war, the cynicism of many young people towards America, and the destruction of Lyndon Johnson's tenure of office."[23] A *Washington Post* reporter, Don Oberdorfer, amply documents, in his book *Tet*, the number of commentators and editors (including those of Time Inc.) who had to re-examine their attitudes after extensive television—and press—coverage brought home to them the bewildering contradictions of a seemingly unending war.

Television's power seems to have impressed British observers even more than American. The director-general of the Royal United Service Institution, Air Vice-Marshal S. W. B. Menaul, believes that television had "a lot to answer for [in] the collapse of American morale in relation to the Vietnam war." The then editor of the *Economist*, Alistair Burnet, wrote that the television reporting of Vietnam had made it very difficult for two American administrations to continue that war, "which was going on in American homes," irrespective of the merits or demerits of why the United States was actually involved in Vietnam. Robin Day, the BBC commentator, told a seminar of the Royal United Service Institution that the war on colour-television screens in American living rooms had made Americans far more anti-militarist and anti-war than anything else: "One wonders if in future a democracy which has uninhibited television coverage in every home will ever be able to fight a war, however just. . . . The full brutality of the combat will be there in close up and colour, and blood looks very red on the colour television screen." And the Director of Defence Operations, Plans and Supplies at the Ministry of Defence, Brigadier F. G. Caldwell, said that the American experience in Vietnam meant that if Britain were to go to war again, "we would have to start saying to ourselves, are we going to let the television cameras loose on the battlefield?"[24]

All this seems very persuasive, and it would be difficult to believe that the sight, day after day, of American soldiers and Vietnamese civilians dying in a war that seemed to make no progress could not have had *some* effect on the viewer. Yet a survey conducted for *Newsweek* in 1967 suggested a remarkably different conclusion: that television had encouraged a majority of viewers to *support* the war. When faced with deciding whether television coverage had made them feel more like "backing up the boys in Vietnam" or like opposing the war, 64 per cent of viewers replied that they were moved to support the soldiers and only 26 per cent to oppose the war. A prominent American psychiatrist, Fredric Wertham, said, in the same year, that television had the effect of conditioning its audience to accept war, and a further *Newsweek* enquiry, in 1972, suggested that the public was developing a tolerance of horror in the newscasts from Vietnam—"The only way we can possibly tolerate it is by turning off a part of ourselves instead of the television set."

Edward Jay Epstein's survey of television producers and news editors, for his book *News from Nowhere*, showed that more than two-thirds of those he interviewed felt that television had had little effect in changing public opinion on Vietnam. An opinion commonly expressed was that people saw exactly what they wanted to in a news report and that television only served to reinforce existing views. *The New Yorker*'s television critic, Michael J. Arlen, reported, on several occasions, that viewers had a vague, unhappy feeling that they were not getting "the true picture" of Vietnam from the medium.[25] So if it was true that television did not radically change public opinion about the war, could it have been because of the quality of the coverage?

Television is a comparatively new medium. There were 10,000 sets in the United States in 1941; at the time of Korea there were 10 million, and at the peak of the Vietnam War 100 million. There was some television reporting in Korea, a lot of it daring—an American general had to order the BBC cameraman Cyril Page to get down off the front of a tank to which he had tied himself so as to get a grandstand view of the battle as the tank went into action. But, until Vietnam, no one knew what problems the prolonged day-by-day coverage of a war by television would produce. The first was surprising—a lack of reality. It had been believed that when battle scenes were brought into the living room the reality of war would at last be brought home to a civilian audience. But Arlen was quick to point out, in *The New Yorker*, that by the same process battle scenes are made less real, "diminished in part by the physical size of the television screen, which, for all the industry's advances, still shows one a picture of men three inches tall shooting at other men three inches tall."[26] Sandy Gall of ITN found shooting combat footage difficult and dangerous, and the end result very disappointing. "I think you lose one dimension on television's small screen and things look smaller than life; the sound of battle, for example, never coming across. I am always let down when I eventually see my footage and think, Is that all? The sense of danger never comes across on television and you, the correspondent, always look as though you had an easy time of it."[27]

For many Americans in Vietnam, there emerged a strange side to the war that became directly related to television—the fact that the war seemed so unreal that sometimes it became almost possible to believe that everything was taking place on some giant Hollywood set and all the participants were extras playing a remake of *Back to Bataan*. GIs—and even correspondents—brought up on Second World War movies shown on television, used to seeing Errol Flynn sweeping to victory through the jungles of Burma or Brian Donlevy giving the Japanese hell in the Coral Sea, tended to relate their experiences in Vietnam to the Hollywood version of America at war.[28] Michael Herr, making a dash, with David Greenway of *Time*, from one position at Hué to another, caught himself saying to a Marine a line from a hundred Hollywood war films: "We're going to cut out now. Will you cover us?" One should not be surprised, therefore, to find that GIs sometimes behaved, in the presence of television cameras, as if they were making *Dispatch from Da Nang*. Herr describes soldiers running about during a fight because they knew there was a television crew nearby. "They were actually making war movies in their heads, doing little guts and glory Leatherneck tap dances under fire, getting their pimples shot off for the networks."[29]

So it is not difficult to understand how, when seen on a small screen, in the enveloping and cosy atmosphere of the household, sometime between the afternoon soap-box drama and the late-night war movie, the television version of the war in Vietnam could appear as just another drama, in which the hero is the correspondent and everything will come out all right at the end. Jack Laurence of CBS, an experienced war correspondent, who spent a lot of time in Vietnam, had this possibility brought home to him in Israel during the 1973 conflict. He was in a hotel lobby, and a couple who had just arrived from the United States recognised him and said, "We saw you on television and we knew everything was going to be all right because you were there."[30] There is not much a television correspondent can do about such a situation as that; it seems inherent in the nature of the medium. However, correspondents, or, more fairly, their editors, do have something to answer for in their selection of news in Vietnam.

Years of television news of the war have left viewers with a blur of images consisting mainly of helicopters landing in jungle clearings, soldiers charging into undergrowth, wounded being loaded onto helicopters, artillery and mortar fire, air strikes on distant targets, napalm canisters turning slowly in the sky, and a breathless correspondent poking a stick microphone under an army officer's nose and asking, "What's happening up there, Colonel?" (The only honest answer came, in 1972, from a captain on Highway 13. "I wish the hell I knew," he said.) The networks claimed that combat footage was what the public wanted; that concentrating on combat prevented the film's being out of date if it was delayed in transmission; that it was difficult to shoot anything other than combat film when only three or four minutes were available in the average news program for events in Vietnam; and that the illusion of American progress created by combat footage shot from only one side was balanced by what the correspondent had to say.

This is simply not true. To begin with, combat footage fails to convey all aspects of combat. "A cameraman feels so inadequate, being able to record only a minute part of the misery, a minute part of the fighting," said Kurt Volkert, a CBS cameraman. "You have to decide what the most important action is. Is it the woman holding her crying baby? Is it the young girl cringing near her house because of the exploding grenades? Or is it the defiant looking Vietcong with blood on his face just after capture?"[31] When the cameraman's thirty minutes of combat footage are edited down to three minutes—not an unusual editing ratio—the result is a segment of action that bears about as much relation to the reality in Vietnam as a battle scene shot in Hollywood does. In fact, the Hollywood version would probably appear more realistic.

The American viewer who hoped to learn something serious about Vietnam was subjected, instead, to a television course in the techniques of war, and he was not sufficiently exposed either to what the war meant to the people over whose land it was being fought, or to the political complexities of the situation, or even to the considered personal views of reporters who had spent years covering the situation. Yet, even by the networks' own standards, the limited aspects of the war that the viewer was permitted to see could produce excellent television. One of the most dramatic pieces of film on the war was shot by a CBS team on Highway 13 late in April 1972. A South Vietnamese mine, intended to stop advancing enemy tanks, had caught a truck loaded with refugees. The film showed dead children, distressed babies, and a woman weeping over the body of her son. The reporter, Bob Simon, described what had happened and then, with perhaps the best sign-off line from Vietnam, said simply; "There's nothing left to say about this war, nothing at all." "Morley Safer's Vietnam," an hour-long report by the CBS correspondent in Saigon, was Safer's own explicit view, and was hailed by *The New Yorker*'s critic, Michael J. Arlen, as "one of the best pieces of journalism to come out of the Vietnam war in any medium." But film like this was rare.

Competition for combat footage was so intense that it not only forced American television teams to follow each other into what the BBC's correspondent Michael Clayton called "appallingly dangerous situations," but it also made editors reluctant to risk allowing a team the time and the freedom to make its own film of the war. Where were the television equivalents of Martha Gellhorn's series on Vietnamese orphanages and hospitals, or Philip Jones Griffiths' searing book on the nature of the war, *Vietnam Inc.?* True, television was handicapped by its mechanics—a three-man, or even a two-man, team loaded with camera, sound equipment, and film is less mobile and more dependent on military transport, and in a dangerous situation more vulnerable, than a journalist or a photographer. In its presentation, too, television is sometimes handicapped by its commercial associations. The Vietnamese cameraman Vo Suu filmed the brutal shooting of a Vietcong suspect by General Nguyen Ngoc Loan during the Tet offensive. NBC blacked out the screen for three seconds after the dead man hit the ground, so as to provide a buffer before the commercial that followed. (What television *really* wanted was action in which the men died cleanly and not too bloodily. "When they get a film which shows what a mortar does to a man, really shows the flesh torn and the blood flowing, they get squeamish," says Richard Lindley. "They want it to be just so. They want television to be cinema.")[32]

American television executives, showed too little courage in their approach to Vietnam. They followed each other into paths the army had chosen for them. They saw the war as "an American war in Asia—and that's the only story the American audience is interested in," and they let other, equally important, aspects of Vietnam go uncovered.

All this said, attempts to film the war from the other side were even less successful. James Cameron, Romano Cagnoni, and Malcolm Aird went to North Vietnam in 1965.

They went as an independent team—Cameron to report, Cagnoni to take photographs, and Aird to make a film—paying their own expenses. Although the North Vietnamese had given them visas, they were not freely welcomed. "We were treated with considerable suspicion," Aird said, "and it took not just days but weeks to break this down. Even then, we were not able to film all the things we naïvely supposed we would be able to film—stuff like bombs failing and American prisoners.[33] But in 1965 any film at all out of North Vietnam was news." The film Cameron and Aird made, before the North Vietnamese suddenly and without explanation asked them to leave, presented a sympathetic view of the country. "It was interesting to see how quickly you are on the side you are working with," Aird said. "In North Vietnam the Americans to us were the enemy."[34]

The North Vietnamese themselves had no correspondents as we understand the word. They followed the progress of the war as best they could from party newspapers, government broadcasts, and large wall posters. The flavour of the news presentation in the North can best be had by extracts from wall posters appearing in Hanoi on March 21, 1975, as the North Vietnamese army pushed south towards Saigon: "The South attacks and rises. Very big victories. Nearly a million countrymen have risen to be their own masters. Complete liberation of five provinces." Then followed a list of casualties inflicted and equipment captured. The posters ended with "Long live the victory of the soldiers and people of the western region."

Western correspondents were allowed into the North only if the North Vietnamese government could see some advantage to itself from the visit. This is not to say that the North Vietnamese dictated what the correspondents wrote, but it does help to explain why Western correspondents who went to the North were looked upon with suspicion in their own countries. They had to be prepared for attacks on their reliability, their competence, and their professional ability. "The kindest thing anyone could say of me," says Cameron, "was that I was a misguided, gullible Commie tool."[35]

Harrison E. Salisbury of the New York Times, the first correspondent from a major United States newspaper to go to North Vietnam, writing from Hanoi in December 1966, said: "Whatever the explanation, one can see that United States planes are dropping an enormous weight of explosives on purely civilian targets." This forced the administration to concede that American pilots had accidentally struck civilian areas while attempting to bomb military targets, and made Salisbury a much-hated figure in Washington. Secretary of State Dean Rusk asked the New York Times' publisher how long Salisbury planned to stay in Hanoi. The Pentagon called him "Ho Chi Salisbury of the Hanoi Times." The Washington Post alleged that the casualty figures he gave after one raid that he reported were exactly the same as those in Communist propaganda pamphlets, and a Post article said that Salisbury was Ho Chi Minh's new weapon in the war. William Randolph Hearst, Jr., reminded his readers of the treasonable war-time broadcasts by Lord Haw-Haw and Tokyo Rose. The columnist Joseph Alsop wrote: "Whether a United States reporter ought to go to an enemy capital to give the authority of his by-line to enemy propaganda figures is an interesting question." Some of his critics accused Salisbury of being politically naïve, of not giving proper attribution of his sources, and, as in Cameron's case, of being duped by the Communists. The Pulitzer Prize jury recommended him for a prize by a vote of four to one, but the Pulitzer Advisory Board rejected the recommendation by six votes to five. Being a war correspondent on the enemy side was clearly not the easiest way to advance one's career.

Others who went to Hanoi later included Mary McCarthy, Anthony Lewis, Michael MacLear from the Canadian Broadcasting Corporation, and, R. K. Karanjia from India, and Agence France Presse maintained a bureau there throughout the war. But to be a war correspondent with the Vietcong in South Vietnam was a much rarer occurrence.

Wilfred Burchett, the Australian who had sent the first story to the West from Hiroshima and who had reported the Korean peace talks from the North Korean side, began reporting the Vietnam War in 1963, freelancing for the Japanese *Mainichi* group, the British Communist daily *Morning Star*, and the American *National Guardian*, and working from the Vietcong side. Burchett made no pretence about where his sympathies were—"The US puppet regime, no matter what new personalities the puppet masters may push to the top in the endless cycle of coup and counter-coup, is doomed." But his reports on Vietcong schools, arsenals, hospitals, the administrative structure, transport, and commissary made intriguing reading: "Hunting teams attached to every unit ensured that there was always something to go with the rice. The 'something' varied from elephant steaks—the Americans bombed and strafed them from the air as potential 'supply vehicles'—to jungle rats, with monkey, wild pig, porcupine, civets, and other wild creatures in between."[36]

Burchett travelled mainly on foot or by bicycle, occasionally on horseback or by motorised sampan. He was several times within a few miles of Saigon and appeared to have no trouble in traversing at night even the Saigon-controlled areas. But, although he wore the typical native black pyjamas and conical straw hat, his bulk, his colouring, and his features clearly distinguished him as non-Vietnamese, and the United States forces soon heard rumours of a "white man" working with the Vietcong. (Madeleine Riffaud of the French Communist paper *L'Humanité* was travelling with Burchett at this stage, but, being slight and dark, she was able to pass as a Vietnamese.) Burchett has said that the American military authorities' reaction to his presence was to try to kill him. "My size and grey hair probably showed up on reconnaissance photographs, because four planes came over one morning, headed straight for our overnight camp, and bombed it, one after the other. Fortunately, the guards with us had dug shelters immediately on our arrival the previous night and the first blast almost blew us into the holes. The first string landed within two or three hundred yards, but the jungle absorbed most of the blast and the shrapnel."[37]

Madeleine Riffaud was the only woman correspondent with the Vietcong, but there were many with the American forces, either on brief visits or on long-term assignments. Jillian Robertson, of the *London Sunday Express*, went on a bombing mission in South Vietnam in a B-57—"Before, I had just been a spectator of this war, now I was part of it."[38] Patricia Penn wrote in the *New Statesman* about amputees at a Quaker limb centre at Quang Ngai—"Ho Min, who's seven, lost his parents when he lost his leg. He sits crying alone in a corner, soaking his stump in a bucket of antiseptic. Now and then he lifts it out of the liquid, stares at it puzzled, and then—as if for an answer—looks at me."[39] Victoria Brittain, a resident correspondent for *The Times* of London, mixed straight reporting with articles on child victims—"Even a 'relatively good' orphanage is chaotic, filthy, stuffed with children so starved of adult contact that the moment you step inside the courtyard your whole lower body and legs are covered with small exploring hands."[40] Gloria Emerson of the *New York Times* wrote a fine series of articles on refugees, mentioning in one of them Richard Hughes, a former correspondent, who had abandoned journalism in Vietnam to run four orphanages.

Lest this concentration on personal experience and human-interest reporting give the wrong impression, it should be noted that there were also women writers who were interested in the political, cultural, and historical background of the war, Frances FitzGerald probably being the best known. There were also women combat correspondents. Catherine Leroy, a French photographer in her early twenties, was captured at Hué and photographed the Vietcong troops in action before they released her. She had mixed feelings about the war: "I want people who see my pictures to hate war as I do. But although I am afraid, I have to be there when the killing starts."[41] Oriana Fallaci, an Italian correspondent, said she wanted to report a war because "I was a little girl in the Second World War and my father was a partisan. So I went to Vietnam because it was the war of our time." She interviewed General Vo Nguyen Giap, commander-in-chief of the North Vietnamese army, and, in the South, President Thieu—"He was very passionate, and he even cried. They were real tears. I really liked him."[42] Kate Webb, a New Zealander, worked for the United Press and saw more action than most men did. She was among the first correspondents into the compound of the United States Embassy after the Vietcong had occupied it during the Tet offensive in 1968. She described it later: "It was like a butcher shop in Eden, beautiful but ghastly. The green lawns and white ornamental fountains were strewn with bodies."

Kate Webb was captured by North Vietnamese troops in Cambodia in April 1971 and held for twenty-five days before being released—"I was asked, 'If you really are an objective reporter, as you say, you must want to stay with us, having spent so much time with the other side. Do you want to go back to your family or stay with us?' I thought of my own dictum—dead men don't write stories. Then I answered seriously, 'I'd like to stay with you a few weeks and then return home.' " She could describe in graphic terms what it was like being on patrol in Vietnam: "The first time I went out, there was a bit of a fire fight and I was so scared that I wet my pants. I hoped the GIs would think that it was sweat and that no one would notice. Then I saw that some of the GIs had wet pants, too, and it didn't matter any more."[43]

What Henry Kamm of the *New York Times* called proto-journalists were the non-professionals, who "come without real involvement, come with the vocation of being onlookers, of mixing with those, like the press, who have a safe share in the war." Some of these went on to become correspondents or photographers. (One of them, Tim Page, prefers the description "mercenary journalists.") Some correspondents have objected to being bracketed with them, on the grounds that they were not serious professionals, interested in reporting the war, but "thrill seekers," gun-carrying hippies, who smoked pot and used acid and sometimes heroin, and that, although they looked young and harmless, they were really old and deadly. "Tim Page was twenty-three when I first met him," wrote Michael Herr. "And I can remember wishing that I'd known him when he was still young."[44]

But the accreditation system in Vietnam made it possible for anyone calling himself a free-lance journalist to get an MACV card. All he needed were two letters from agencies or newspapers saying that they would be prepared to buy his material. The Associated Press, for one, would lend virtually anyone a camera, complete with film, light metre, and brief instructions on its use, promise to pay a minimum of $15 for any acceptable picture, and provide a letter to help the new man get his accreditation. A local or hometown newspaper would usually be prepared to provide the second letter. After that, the correspondent was on his own. Transport was free, he could live on C rations, and in the field he was not likely to be charged for accommodations. If he was prepared to take risks, he could find himself comparatively rich overnight.

Tim Page was twenty when he first arrived in Vietnam. At the end of a hippie trip across Asia, he found himself in the middle of a battle at Chu Lai. A series of his photographs appeared in *Life* on September 3, 1965, covering six pages, and for these *Life* paid him $6,000. Over the next eighteen months, mostly by taking photographs where other photographers were not prepared to go, Page made $28,000—not a lot by professional standards, but a lot of money for an orphan boy from a London suburb. Page, Eddie Adams, Sean Flynn, Steve Nerthup, John Steinbeck, Jr., and Simon Dring moved around together. Page and Flynn used to ride in and out of some combat areas on Honda motor-cycles. They had a flip, throwaway attitude to the war, but some of it was quite perceptive. "No one wants to admit it," Page says, "but there is a lot of sex appeal and a lot of fun in weapons. Where else but in Vietnam would a man get a chance to play with a supersonic jet, drive a tank, or shoot off a rocket, and even get highly paid for it?"[45]

Page was slightly wounded in the fighting at Chu Lai, and then more seriously during the Buddhist riots in 1966, receiving shrapnel in the head, chest, and arms. In 1967, a B-57 mistook a United States coast guard cutter, in which Page was travelling, for a Vietcong vessel, and in nine strafing and bombing runs it sank the ship, killed three of the crew, and wounded eight. Page received multiple wounds, and needed twelve operations and weeks in hospital to recover. In 1969, he got out of a helicopter near Cu Chi to help pick up two wounded. The sergeant with him stepped on a mine, which blew off the sergeant's legs and sent a two-inch piece of shrapnel through Page's forehead, above the right eye, and deep into the base of his brain. For some time he was close to death; he recovered sufficiently to be moved to a hospital in Japan, then to the Walter Reed Army Hospital, in Washington, D.C., and finally to the Institute of Rehabilitation Medicine, in New York. He was eighteen months recovering. *Time* and *Life* had bought most of his photographs, and they undertook to pay his hospital bills. They came to $136,000. While he was still receiving treatment, he had a letter from a British publisher asking him to write a book to be called *Through with War*, which would "once and for all take the glamour out of war." Page remembers his bewilderment. "Jesus! Take the glamour out of war. How the hell can you do that? You can't take the glamour out of a tank burning or a helicopter blowing up. It's like trying to take the glamour out of sex. War is *good* for you."

The type of war that Page and others found glamorous—the ground war of attrition against the North Vietnamese and the Vietcong—began to wind down from 1969 on. The American public had been aware of the war in Vietnam in proportion to the number of American combat troops involved and the level of casualties they suffered. President Nixon's policy became, therefore, steadily to withdraw these troops, to pass the ground war over to the Vietnamese, to order the remaining GIs to fight as little as possible, and to switch the weight of the American attack to the air. Since the bombing campaign was not very evident to the American public, the war seemed to fade away. Correspondents attuned to battle reporting found fewer battles to report, editors and producers became less willing to devote space and time to a war that the administration assured them was as good as over, and those reporters who went digging for other stories about Vietnam found that the army had suddenly become extremely obstructive and had started "administering the news with an eye-dropper," as *Time* magazine's correspondent Jonathan Larsen wrote.

There were two main reasons for this. The military authorities did not want reported the sad state of the United States Army, and they wanted to encourage public apathy about the war by keeping as secret as possible the escalation of the bombing. They were not successful on the first count. The year 1971 saw a series of stories revealing the massive heroin problem among United States troops (about one in ten was addicted),[46] the "fragging," or blowing up by grenades, of unpopular officers (forty-five killed, 318 wounded in 1971), the staggering desertion rate, the number of combat refusals, and the growing tendency to regard an order simply as a basis for discussion. The *Washington Post* headed its series on the problem ARMY IN ANGUISH, and Colonel Robert Heinl, a military historian, wrote in the *Armed Forces Journal* that conditions in Vietnam among the American forces "have only been exceeded in this century by the French Army's Nivelle mutinies in 1917 and the collapse of the Tsarist armies in 1916 and 1917."[47] GIs were photographed carrying peace symbols, a picture appeared in *Newsweek* of a helicopter with a sign on the side saying "My God! How'd we get into this mess?"[48] and CBS News ran film of GIs smoking pot from a gun barrel.

There was less success in revealing the new emphasis in the war—the intensified bombing of North Vietnam, Laos, and Cambodia. There can be some excuse for the correspondents' failure here, because reporters and photographers were not allowed on air strikes and the official concealment operation was massive—*Newsweek* described it as "the most systematic military cover-up in the history of America's role in the Indo-Chinese war." A former United States Air Force major later revealed—and an embarrassed Pentagon later confirmed—that the United States, over a period of fourteen months in 1969–70, had conducted a clandestine bombing campaign against Cambodia, whose neutrality Washington then professed to respect. Scores of American pilots took part in the cover-up by making fictitious reports, and the Pentagon did its bit by falsifying statistics. What the military was so anxious to conceal was that the bombing of Indo-China was on a scale far greater than anything previously known. During the whole of the Second World War, less than 80,000 tons of bombs fell on Britain. In Indo-China, the United States dropped more than 4 million tons—fifty times as much. Or, put another way, the United States used explosives cumulatively equal to hundreds of the nuclear weapon used at Hiroshima.

The military successfully hid the real extent of this bombing campaign behind a screen of lies, evasions, and "newspeak." The Pentagon insisted that its air operations were announced daily by MACV in Saigon. To see how informative these announcements were, it is necessary to quote only one. On March 10, 1972, MACV's release 70–10 said: "Yesterday U.S. aircraft, including U.S. Air Force B-52s, continued air operations along the Ho Chi Minh trail in Laos. In addition, U.S. aircraft flew combat missions in support of Royal Laotian forces in Laos. Yesterday, U.S. aircraft, including U.S. Air Force B-52s, continued air operations against enemy forces and their lines of supply in Cambodia." How many aircraft? How many tons of bombs? What, exactly, was attacked? Were any of the targets (as revealed in classified American military documents quoted in *Air War in Indo-China*)[49] civilian villages that the air force was ordered to destroy—in the mind-boggling "newspeak" phrase—"so as to deprive the enemy of the population resource"? William Shawcross, writing in the *New Statesman*, quoted a Pentagon spokesman as saying, "We do not hit civilian targets. Correction. We do not target civilian targets." To explain how targets that were clearly civilian came to be hit, the spokesman produced explanations involving terms such as "collateral damage" and "circular error probability."

## Notes

1.  Don Oberdorfer, *Tet* (New York: Doubleday, 1971; Avon edition, 1972), p. 100.
2.  Herbert Matthews, *The Education of a Correspondent* (New York: Harcourt Brace, 1946), p. 44.
3.  Nora Ephron, "The War Followers," *New York Magazine*, November 12, 1973.
4.  Apart from the case of Martha Gellhorn, the only correspondents I know personally who were refused visas were Philip Jones Griffiths, William Shawcross of the *Sunday Times*, whose refusal in 1972 was because his reporting during an earlier visit had been "negative," and John Philby, who was deported from Saigon in 1968, presumably because his father is Kim Philby of the KGB. Other correspondents were denied visas but told to reapply for them later, when whatever offences they had committed would have been forgotten.
5.  Interview with Charlie Black.
6.  *Esquire*, April 1970.
7.  Quoted in H. Mulligan, "Three Years of Reporting in Vietnam," an AP feature on Arnett circulated to editors, 1965.
8.  Address at Pennsylvania Press Conference, May 15, 1971.
9.  Interview with Philip Jones Griffiths.
10. *Daily Telegraph Magazine*, May 31, 1968.
11. *Daily Telegraph Magazine*, May 31, 1968.
12. *Spectator*, July 1, 1972.
13. Interview with Marina Warner.
14. Interview with Tim Page.
15. Quoted in J. Bradshaw, "The Trouble-shooters," *London Daily Telegraph Magazine*, May 31, 1968.
16. *Spectator*, July 1, 1972.
17. On the walls of Faas' office in Saigon were all those photographs that the Associated Press considered too shocking to use. *Town* magazine, in December 1964, listed some of them— severed heads floating in a river, a face with gouged eyes, a hand hanging from a piece of string, a Vietcong suspect being tortured by a soldier who has a comic-strip balloon making him say, "That'll teach you to talk to the press."
18. *Newsweek*, February 22, 1971; *Radio Times*, October 2, 1969; *Sunday Times*, February 14, 1971; *Esquire*, April 1970.
19. Interview with Harri Peccinotti.
20. Interview with Donald McCullin.
21. *Spectator*, July 1, 1972.
22. *Esquire*, April 1970.
23. J. Epstein, *News from Nowhere* (New York: Random House, 1973), p. 9.
24. Royal United Service Institution seminar, London, October 13, 1970; Alistair Burnet quotation from *U.K. Press Gazette*, December 21, 1970.
25. See Michael J. Arlen, *The Living Room War* (New York: Viking, 1966).
26. Arlen, p. 8.
27. *Daily Telegraph Magazine*, May 31, 1968.
28. The arrival in 1965 of Flynn's son, Sean, as a correspondent tended to confirm this feeling.
29. *Esquire*, April 1970.
30. Ephron, "The War Followers."
31. Kurt Volkert, "Combat Cameraman—Vietnam," in *Dateline* (New York: Overseas Press Club, 1968).
32. *Spectator*, July 1, 1972.
33. A Canadian television team was allowed to film an American POW camp in 1970.
34. Interview with Malcolm Aird.
35. Interview with James Cameron.
36. Wilfred Burchett, *Passport* (Australia: Nelson, 1969), p. 257.
37. Interview with Wilfred Burchett. Burchett, who told the author that it is not his style to refuse a proffered hand, must nevertheless have remembered this incident, when, after the banquet at Hangchow during President Nixon's visit to China in February 1972, Chou

En-lai, with a mischievous light in his eye, introduced Nixon to Burchett. "Ah, yes," Nixon said, shaking hands. "You're an Australian correspondent. I've heard of you."

38.  *Sunday Express*, February 13, 1966.
39.  *New Statesman*, May 29, 1970.
40.  *The Times*, June 5, 1972.
41.  *Observer Magazine*, September 3, 1967.
42.  *Newsweek*, January 22, 1973; *U.K. Press Gazette*, February 12, 1973.
43.  Interview with Kate Webb.
44.  *Esquire*, April 1970.
45.  Interview with Tim Page.
46.  Report of U.S. House of Representatives Committee on Foreign Affairs, May 25, 1971.
47.  *The Times*, October 18, 1971.
48.  *Newsweek*, February 22, 1971.
49.  R. Littauer and Cornell University faculty and student groups, *Air War in Indo-China* (Boston: Beacon Press, 1971).

# Chapter 11

# CARL BERNSTEIN AND BOB WOODWARD

## ALL THE PRESIDENT'S MEN

CARL BERNSTEIN AND BOB WOODWARD'S account of how they uncovered and pursed the Watergate scandal that ultimately forced the resignation of President Richard Nixon is one of the central stories in modern journalism. Watergate was a defining political episode of a generation and Bernstein and Woodward's reporting on Watergate reflected the very best journalism had to offer in that period characterized as the age of objectivity. Two young reporters stand up to power, and through diligence and hard work topple the president of the United States. Bernstein and Woodward's work inspired many young people to enter the field of journalism, and investigative reporting entered a new golden age. Told in a lively fashion, the book was made into a major motion picture starring Robert Redford and Dustin Hoffman.

Although memories have faded, Bernstein and Woodward's narrative takes readers from the initial suspicions, onto a trail of secrecy, lies, false leads and high level pressure to curtail their reporting. The reporters then painstakingly pieced together the jigsaw puzzle, writing and publishing in the *Washington Post* the Pulitzer-Prize winning series—arguably with the most political impact of any contemporary journalism. Although some observers commented that while Bernstein and Woodward kept the story alive, it was Judge John J. Sirica, who presided over the trial of the Watergate burglars, and the Senate investigatory committee chaired by Senator Sam Ervin, that uncovered the existence of the White House tapes that actually led to Nixon's resignation, nevertheless, *All the President's Men* represents the pinnacle of reporting in the modern era.

Tellingly, Bernstein and Woodward were not political reporters being fed information from self-interested sources. Instead, they got the story through good old-fashioned, street-level reporting. Woodward went on to become assistant managing editor for *The Washington Post* and the best-selling author of non-fiction books in America with a string of insider accounts of various presidential administrations.

Carl Bernstein had a more speckled career, serving for a time as the Washington bureau chief for ABC News. According to a national survey of journalism educators, *All the President's Men* is the top book all people interested in journalism should read. The excerpts here recount the beginning and the end of the Watergate saga.

June 17, 1972. Nine o'clock Saturday morning. Early for the telephone. Woodward fumbled for the receiver and snapped awake. The city editor of the *Washington Post* was on the line. Five men had been arrested earlier that morning in a burglary at Democratic headquarters, carrying photographic equipment and electronic gear. Could he come in?

Woodward had worked for the *Post* for only nine months and was always looking for a good Saturday assignment, but this didn't sound like one. A burglary at the local Democratic headquarters was too much like most of what he had been doing— investigative pieces on unsanitary restaurants and small-time police corruption. Woodward had hoped he had broken out of that; he had just finished a series of stories on the attempted assassination of Alabama Governor George Wallace. Now, it seemed, he was back in the same old slot.

Woodward left his one-room apartment in downtown Washington and walked the six blocks to the *Post*. The newspaper's mammoth newsroom—over 150 feet square with rows of brightly colored desks set on an acre of sound-absorbing carpet—is usually quiet on Saturday morning. Saturday is a day for long lunches, catching up on work, reading the Sunday supplements. As Woodward stopped to pick up his mail and telephone messages at the front of the newsroom, he noticed unusual activity around the city desk. He checked in with the city editor and learned with surprise that the burglars had not broken into the small local Democratic Party office but the headquarters of the Democratic National Committee in the Watergate office-apartment-hotel complex.

It was an odd place to find the Democrats. The opulent Watergate, on the banks of the Potomac in downtown Washington, was as Republican as the Union League Club. Its tenants included the former Attorney General of the United States John N. Mitchell, now director of the Committee for the Re-election of the President; the former Secretary of Commerce Maurice H. Stans, finance chairman of the President's campaign; the Republican national chairman, Senator Robert Dole of Kansas; President Nixon's secretary, Rose Mary Woods; and Anna Chennault, who was the widow of Flying Tiger ace Claire Chennault and a celebrated Republican hostess; plus many other prominent figures of the Nixon administration.

The futuristic complex, with its serpent's-teeth concrete balustrades and equally menacing prices ($100,000 for many of its two-bedroom cooperative apartments), had become the symbol of the ruling class in Richard Nixon's Washington. Two years earlier, it had been the target of 1000 anti-Nixon demonstrators who had shouted "Pigs," "Fascists" and "*Sieg Heil*" as they tried to storm the citadel of Republican power. They had run into a solid wall of riot-equipped Washington policemen who had pushed them back onto the campus of George Washington University with tear gas and billy clubs. From their balconies, anxious tenants of the Watergate had watched the confrontation, and some had cheered and toasted when the protesters were driven back and the westerly winds off the Potomac chased the tear gas away from the fortress. Among those who had been knocked to the ground was *Washington Post* reporter Carl Bernstein. The policeman who had sent him sprawling had probably not seen the press cards hanging from his neck, and had perhaps focused on his longish hair.

As Woodward began making phone calls, he noticed that Bernstein, one of the paper's two Virginia political reporters, was working on the burglary story, too.

Oh God, not Bernstein, Woodward thought, recalling several office tales about Bernstein's ability to push his way into a good story and get his byline on it.

That morning, Bernstein had Xeroxed copies of notes from reporters at the scene and informed the city editor that he would make some more checks. The city editor had shrugged his acceptance, and Bernstein had begun a series of phone calls to everybody at the Watergate he could reach—desk clerks, bellmen, maids in the housekeeping department, waiters in the restaurant.

Bernstein looked across the newsroom. There was a pillar between his desk and Woodward's, about 25 feet away. He stepped back several paces. It appeared that Woodward was also working on the story. That figured, Bernstein thought. Bob Woodward was a prima donna who played heavily at office politics. Yale. A veteran of the Navy officer corps. Lawns, greensward, staterooms and grass tennis courts, Bernstein guessed, but probably not enough pavement for him to be good at investigative reporting. Bernstein knew that Woodward couldn't write very well. One office rumor had it that English was not Woodward's native language.

Bernstein was a college dropout. He had started as a copy boy at the *Washington Star* when he was 16, become a full-time reporter at 19, and had worked at the *Post* since 1966. He occasionally did investigative series, had covered the courts and city hall, and liked to do long, discursive pieces about the capital's people and neighborhoods.

Woodward knew that Bernstein occasionally wrote about rock music for the *Post*. That figured. When he learned that Bernstein sometimes reviewed classical music, he choked that down with difficulty. Bernstein looked like one of those counterculture journalists that Woodward despised. Bernstein thought that Woodward's rapid rise at the *Post* had less to do with his ability than his Establishment credentials.

They had never worked on a story together. Woodward was 29, Bernstein 28.

The first details of the story had been phoned from inside the Watergate by Alfred E. Lewis, a veteran of 35 years of police reporting for the *Post*. Lewis was something of a legend in Washington journalism—half cop, half reporter, a man who often dressed in a blue regulation Metropolitan Police sweater buttoned at the bottom over a brass Star-of-David buckle. In 35 years, Lewis had never really "written" a story; he phoned the details in to a rewrite man, and for years the *Washington Post* did not even have a type-writer at police headquarters.

The five men arrested at 2:30 A.M. had been dressed in business suits and all had worn Playtex rubber surgical gloves. Police had seized a walkie-talkie, 40 rolls of unexposed film, two 35-millimeter cameras, lock picks, pen-size tear-gas guns, and bugging devices that apparently were capable of picking up both telephone and room conversations.

"One of the men had $814, one $800, one $215, one $234, one $230," Lewis had dictated. "Most of it was in $100 bills, in sequence. . . . They seemed to know their way around; at least one of them must have been familiar with the layout. They had rooms on the second and third floors of the hotel. The men ate lobster in the restaurant there, all at the same table that night. One wore a suit bought in Raleigh's. Somebody got a look at the breast pocket."

Woodward learned from Lewis that the suspects were going to appear in court that afternoon for a preliminary hearing. He decided to go.

Woodward had been to the courthouse before. The hearing procedure was an insti-tutionalized fixture of the local court's turnstile system of justice: A quick appearance before a judge who set bond for accused pimps, prostitutes, muggers—and, on this day, the five men who had been arrested at the Watergate. A group of attorneys—known as the "Fifth Street Lawyers" because of the location of the courthouse and their storefront offices—were hanging around the corridors as usual, waiting for appointments as government-paid counsel to indigent defendants. Two of the regulars—a tall, thin attorney in a frayed sharkskin suit and an obese, middle-aged lawyer who had once been disciplined for soliciting cases in the basement cellblock—were muttering their distress. They had been tentatively appointed to represent the five accused Watergate burglars and had then been informed that the men had retained their own counsel, which is unusual.

Woodward went inside the courtroom. One person stood out. In a middle row sat a young man with fashionably long hair and an expensive suit with slightly flared lapels, his chin high, his eyes searching the room as if he were in unfamiliar surroundings.

Woodward sat down next to him and asked if he was in court because of the Watergate arrests.

"Perhaps," the man said. "I'm not the attorney of record. I'm acting as an individual."

He said his name was Douglas Caddy and he introduced a small, anemic-looking man next to him as the attorney of record, Joseph Rafferty, Jr. Rafferty appeared to have been routed out of bed; he was unshaven and squinted as if the light hurt his eyes. The two lawyers wandered in and out of the courtroom. Woodward finally cornered Rafferty in a hallway and got the names and addresses of the five suspects. Four of them were from Miami, three of them Cuban-Americans.

Caddy didn't want to talk. "Please don't take it personally," he told Woodward. "It would be a mistake to do that. I just don't have anything to say."

Woodward asked Caddy about his clients.

"They are not my clients," he said.

But you are a lawyer? Woodward asked.

"I'm not going to talk to you."

Caddy walked back into the courtroom. Woodward followed.

"Please, I have nothing to say."

Would the five men be able to post bond? Woodward asked.

After politely refusing to answer several more times, Caddy replied quickly that the men were all employed and had families—factors that would be taken into consideration by the judge in setting bond. He walked back into the corridor.

Woodward followed: Just tell me about yourself, how you got into the case.

"I'm not in the case."

Why are you here?

"Look," Caddy said, "I met one of the defendants, Bernard Barker, at a social occasion." Where?

"In D.C. It was cocktails at the Army-Navy Club. We had a sympathetic conversation . . . that's all I'm going to say."

How did you get into the case?

Caddy pivoted and walked back in. After half an hour, he went out again.

Woodward asked how he got into the case.

This time Caddy said he'd gotten a call shortly after 3:00 A.M. from Barker's wife. "She said her husband had told her to call me if he hadn't called her by three, that it might mean he was in trouble."

Caddy said he was probably the only attorney Barker knew in Washington, and brushed off more questions, adding that he had probably said too much.

At 3:30 P.M., the five suspects, still dressed in dark business suits but stripped of their belts and ties, were led into the courtroom by a marshal. They seated themselves silently in a row and stared blankly toward the bench, kneading their hands. They looked nervous, respectful and tough.

Earl Silbert, the government prosecutor, rose as their case was called by the clerk. Slight, intent and owlish with his horn-rimmed glasses, he was known as "Earl the Pearl" to Fifth Streeters familiar with his fondness for dramatic courtroom gestures and flowery speech. He argued that the five men should not be released on bond. They had given false names, had not cooperated with the police, possessed "$2300 in cold cash, and had a tendency to travel abroad." They had been arrested in a "professional burglary" with a "clandestine" purpose. Silbert drew out the word "clandestine."

Judge James A. Belsen asked the men their professions. One spoke up, answering that they were "anti-communists," and the others nodded their agreement. The Judge, accustomed to hearing unconventional job descriptions, nonetheless appeared perplexed. The tallest of the suspects, who had given his name as James W. McCord, Jr., was asked to step forward. He was balding, with a large, flat nose, a square jaw, perfect teeth and a benign expression that seemed incongruous with his hard-edged features.

The Judge asked his occupation.

"Security consultant," he replied.

The Judge asked where.

McCord, in a soft drawl, said that he had recently retired from government service. Woodward moved to the front row and leaned forward.

"Where in government?" asked the Judge.

"CIA," McCord whispered.

The Judge flinched slightly.

Holy shit, Woodward said half aloud, the CIA.

He got a cab back to the office and reported McCord's statement. Eight reporters were involved in putting together the story under the byline of Alfred E. Lewis. As the 6:30 P.M. deadline approached, Howard Simons, the *Post*'s managing editor, came into the city editor's office at the south side of the newsroom. "That's a hell of a story," he told the city editor, Barry Sussman, and ordered it onto Sunday's front page.

The first paragraph of the story read: "Five men, one of whom said he is a former employee of the Central Intelligence Agency, were arrested at 2:30 A.M. yesterday in what authorities described as an elaborate plot to bug the offices of the Democratic National Committee here."

A federal grand jury investigation had already been announced, but even so it was Simons' opinion that there still were too many unknown factors about the break-in to make it the lead story. "It could be crazy Cubans," he said.

Indeed, the thought that the break-in might somehow be the work of the Republicans seemed implausible. On June 17, 1972, less than a month before the Democratic convention, the President stood ahead of all announced Democratic candidates in the polls by no less than 19 points. Richard Nixon's vision of an emerging Republican majority that would dominate the last quarter of the century, much as the Democrats had dominated two previous generations, appeared possible. The Democratic Party was in disarray as a brutal primary season approached its end. Senator George McGovern of South Dakota, considered by the White House and Democratic Party professionals alike to be Nixon's weakest opponent, was emerging as the clear favorite to win the Democrats' nomination for President.

The story noted: "There was no immediate explanation as to why the five suspects would want to bug the Democratic National Committee offices, or whether or not they were working for any other individuals or organizations."

Bernstein had written another story for the Sunday paper on the suspects. Four were from Miami: Bernard L. Barker, Frank A. Sturgis, Virgilio R. Gonzalez and Eugenio R. Martinez. He had called a *Miami Herald* reporter and obtained a long list of Cuban exile leaders. A *Post* reporter had been sent from the President's press party in Key Biscayne to make checks in Miami's Cuban community. All four of the Miami suspects had been involved in anti-Castro activities and were also said to have CIA connections. ("I've never known if he works for the CIA or not," Mrs. Barker told Bernstein. "The men never tell the women anything about that.") Sturgis, an American soldier-of-fortune and the only non-Cuban among them, had been recruiting militant Cubans to demonstrate at the Democratic national convention, according to several persons. One Cuban leader told Bernstein that Sturgis and others whom he described as "former CIA types" intended to use paid provocateurs to fight anti-war demonstrators in the streets during the national political conventions.

Woodward left the office about eight o'clock that Saturday night. He knew he should have stayed later to track down James McCord. He had not even checked the local telephone directory to see if there was a James McCord listed in Washington or its suburbs.

The national staff of the *Washington Post* rarely covers police stories. So, at Sussman's request, both Bernstein and Woodward returned to the office the next morning, a bright Sunday, June 18, to follow up. An item moving on the Associated Press wire made it embarrassingly clear why McCord had deserved further checking. According to campaign spending reports filed with the government, James McCord was the security coordinator of the Committee for the Reelection of the President (CRP).

The two reporters stood in the middle of the newsroom and looked at each other. What the hell do you think it means? Woodward asked. Bernstein didn't know.

In Los Angeles, John Mitchell, the former U.S. Attorney General and the President's campaign manager, issued a statement: "The person involved is the proprietor of a private security agency who was employed by our committee months ago to assist with the installation of our security system. He has, as we understand it, a number of business clients and interests, and we have no knowledge of these relationships. We want to emphasize that this man and the other people involved were not operating on either our behalf or with our consent. There is no place in our campaign or in the electoral process for this type of activity, and we will not permit or condone it."

In Washington, the Democratic national chairman, Lawrence F. O'Brien, said the break-in "raised the ugliest question about the integrity of the political process that I have encountered in a quarter-century of political activity. No mere statement of innocence by Mr. Nixon's campaign manager, John Mitchell, will dispel these questions."

The wire services, which had carried the Mitchell and O'Brien statements, could be relied upon to gather official pronouncements from the national politicians. The reporters turned their attention to the burglars.

The telephone book listed the private security consulting agency run by McCord. There was no answer. They checked the local "criss-cross" directories which list phone numbers by street addresses. There was no answer at either McCord's home or his business. The address of McCord Associates, 414 Hungerford Drive, Rockville, Maryland, is a large office building, and the cross-reference directory for Rockville lists the tenants. The reporters divided the names and began calling them at home. One attorney recalled that a teenage girl who had worked part-time for him the previous summer knew McCord, or perhaps it was the girl's father who knew him. The attorney could only remember vaguely the girl's last name—Westall or something like that. They contacted five persons with similar last names before Woodward finally reached Harlan A. Westrell, who said he knew McCord.

Westrell, who obviously had not read the papers, wondered why Woodward wanted to know about McCord. Woodward said simply that he was seeking information for a possible story. Westrell seemed flattered and provided some information about McCord, his friends and his background. He gave Woodward some other names to call.

Gradually, a spare profile of McCord began to emerge: a native of the Texas Panhandle; deeply religious, active in the First Baptist Church of Washington; father of an Air Force Academy cadet and a retarded daughter; ex-FBI agent; military reservist; former chief of physical security for the CIA; teacher of a security course at Montgomery Junior College; a family man; extremely conscientious; quiet; reliable. John Mitchell's description of McCord notwithstanding, those who knew him agreed that he worked full-time for the President's re-election committee.

Several persons referred to McCord's integrity, his "rocklike" character, but there was something else. Westrell and three others described McCord as the consummate "government man"—reluctant to act on his own initiative, respectful of the chain of command, unquestioning in following orders.

Woodward typed out the first three paragraphs of a story identifying one of the Watergate burglars as a salaried security coordinator of the President's re-election committee and handed it to an editor on the city desk. A minute later, Bernstein was looking over the editor's shoulder, Woodward noticed. Then Bernstein was walking back to his desk with the first page of the story; soon he was typing. Woodward finished the second page and passed it to the editor. Bernstein had soon relieved him of it and was back at his typewriter. Woodward decided to walk over and find out what was happening.

Bernstein was rewriting the story. Woodward read the rewritten version. It was better.

That night, Woodward drove to McCord's home, a large two-story brick house, classically suburban, set in a cul-de-sac not far from Route 70-S, the main highway through Rockville. The lights were on, but no one answered the door.

After midnight, Woodward received a call at home from Eugene Bachinski, the *Post*'s regular night police reporter. The night police beat is generally considered the worst assignment at the paper. The hours are bad—from about 6:30 P.M. to 2:30 A.M. But Bachinski—tall, goateed and quiet—seemed to like his job, or at least he seemed to like the cops. He had come to know many of them quite well, saw a few socially and moved easily on his nightly rounds through the various squads at police headquarters: homicide, vice (grandly called the Morals Division), traffic, intelligence, sex, fraud, robbery—the catalogue of city life as viewed by the policeman.

Bachinski had something from one of his police sources. Two address books, belonging to two of the Miami men arrested inside the Watergate, contained the name and phone number of a Howard E. Hunt, with the small notations "*W. House*" and "*W.H.*" Woodward sat down in a hard chair by his phone and checked the telephone directory. He found a listing for E. Howard Hunt, Jr., in Potomac, Maryland, the affluent horse-country suburb in Montgomery County. No answer.

At the office next morning, Woodward made a list of the leads. One of McCord's neighbors had said that he had seen McCord in an Air Force officer's uniform, and another had said that McCord was a lieutenant colonel in the Air Force Reserve. Half a dozen calls to the Pentagon later, a personnel officer told him that James McCord was a lieutenant colonel in a special Washington-based reserve unit attached to the Office of Emergency Preparedness. The officer read him the unit roster, which contained only 15 names. Woodward started calling. On the fourth try, Philip Jones, an enlisted man, mentioned casually that the unit's assignment was to draw up lists of radicals and to help develop contingency plans for censorship of the news media and U.S. mail in time of war.

Woodward placed a call to a James Grimm, whose name and Miami telephone number Bachinski had said was in the address book of Eugenio Martinez. Mr. Grimm identified himself as a housing officer for the University of Miami, and said that Martinez had contacted him about two weeks earlier to ask if the university could find accommodations for about 3000 Young Republicans during the GOP national convention in August. Woodward called CRP, the Republican National Committee headquarters and several party officials who were working on convention planning in Washington and Miami. All said they had never heard of Martinez or of plans to use the university for housing Young Republicans.

But the first priority on that Monday was Hunt. The Miami suspects' belongings were listed in a confidential police inventory that Bachinski had obtained. There were "two pieces of yellow-lined paper, one addressed to 'Dear Friend Mr. Howard,' and another to 'Dear Mr. H.H.,' " and an unmailed envelope containing Hunt's personal check for $6.36 made out to the Lakewood Country Club in Rockville, along with a bill for the same amount.

Woodward called an old friend and sometimes source who worked for the federal government and did not like to be called at his office. His friend said hurriedly that the break-in case was going to "heat up," but he couldn't explain and hung up.

It was approaching 3:00 P.M., the hour when the *Post*'s editors list in a "news budget" the stories they expect for the next day's paper. Woodward, who had been assigned to write Tuesday's Watergate story, picked up the telephone and dialed 456–1414—the White House. He asked for Howard Hunt. The switchboard operator rang an extension. There was no answer. Woodward was about to hang up when the operator came back on the line. "There is one other place he might be," she said. "In Mr. Colson's office."

"Mr. Hunt is not here now," Colson's secretary told Woodward, and gave him the number of a Washington public-relations firm, Robert R. Mullen and Company, where she said Hunt worked as a writer.

Woodward walked across to the national desk at the east end of the newsroom and asked one of the assistant national editors, J. D. Alexander, who Colson was. Alexander, a heavy-set man in his mid-thirties with a thick beard, laughed. Charles W. Colson, special counsel to the President of the United States, was the White House "hatchet man," he said.

Woodward called the White House back and asked a clerk in the personnel office if Howard Hunt was on the payroll. She said she would check the records. A few moments later, she told Woodward that Howard Hunt was a consultant working for Colson.

Woodward called the Mullen public-relations firm and asked for Howard Hunt.

"Howard Hunt here," the voice said.

Woodward identified himself.

"Yes? What is it?" Hunt sounded impatient.

Woodward asked Hunt why his name and phone number were in the address books of two of the men arrested at the Watergate.

"Good God!" Howard Hunt said. Then he quickly added, "In view that the matter is under adjudication, I have no comment," and slammed down the phone.

Woodward thought he had a story. Still, anyone's name and phone number could be in an address book. The country-club bill seemed to be additional evidence of Hunt's connection with the burglars. But what connection? A story headlined "White House Consultant Linked to Bugging Suspects" could be a grievous mistake, misleading, unfair to Hunt.

Woodward called Ken W. Clawson, the deputy director of White House communications, who had been a *Post* reporter until the previous January. He told Clawson what was in the address books and police inventory, then asked what Hunt's duties at the White House were. Clawson said that he would check. An hour later, Clawson called back to say that Hunt had worked as a White House consultant on declassification of the Pentagon Papers and, more recently, on a narcotics intelligence project. Hunt had last been paid as a consultant on March 29, he said, and had not done any work for the White House since.

"I've looked into the matter very thoroughly, and I am convinced that neither Mr. Colson nor anyone else at the White House had any knowledge of, or participation in, this deplorable incident at the Democratic National Committee," Clawson said.

The comment was unsolicited.

Woodward phoned Robert F. Bennett, president of the Mullen public-relations firm, and asked about Hunt. Bennett, the son of Republican Senator Wallace F. Bennett of Utah, said, "I guess it's no secret that Howard was with the CIA."

It had been a secret to Woodward. He called the CIA, where a spokesman said that Hunt had been with the agency from 1949 to 1970.

Woodward didn't know what to think. He placed another call to his government friend and asked for advice. His friend sounded nervous. On an off-the-record basis he told Woodward that the FBI regarded Hunt as a prime suspect in the Watergate investigation for many reasons aside from the address-book entries and the unmailed check. Woodward was bound not to use the information in a story because it was off the record. But his friend assured him that there would be nothing unfair about a story which reported the address-book and country-club connections. That assurance could not be used in print either.

Barry Sussman, the city editor, was intrigued. He dug into the *Post* library's clippings on Colson and found a February 1971 story in which an anonymous source described Colson as one of the "original back room boys . . . the brokers, the guys who fix things when they break down and do the dirty work when it's necessary." Woodward's story about Hunt, which identified him as a consultant who had worked in the White House for Colson, included the quotation and noted that it came from a profile written by "Ken W. Clawson, a current White House aide who until recently was a [*Washington Post*] reporter."

The story was headlined "White House Consultant Linked to Bugging Suspects."

That morning at the Florida White House in Key Biscayne, presidential press secretary Ronald L. Ziegler briefly answered a question about the break-in at the Watergate by observing: "Certain elements may try to stretch this beyond what it is." Ziegler described the incident as "a third-rate burglary attempt" not worthy of further White House comment.

The next day, Democratic Party chairman O'Brien filed a $1 million civil damage suit against the Committee for the Re-election of the President. Citing the "potential involvement" of Colson in the break-in, O'Brien charged that the facts were "developing a clear line to the White House" and added: "We learned of this bugging attempt only because it was bungled. How many other attempts have there been and just who was involved? I believe we are about to witness the ultimate test of this administration that so piously committed itself to a new era of law and order just four years ago."

[. . .]

On December 28, General Alexander Haig, the White House Chief of Staff, reached Katharine Graham by telephone in a Washington restaurant. He was calling from San Clemente to discuss two of the reporters' stories on the *Post*'s front page that morning. The first said that Operation Candor, the name given the campaign by the President to defend himself, had been shut down, and that two of the President's most trusted advisers, who had steadfastly maintained his innocence, were no longer convinced of it. The second story said that the President's lawyers had been supplying attorneys for H. R. Haldeman and John Ehrlichman with copies of documents and other evidence that the White House was submitting to the special prosecutor's office.

Haig characterized the stories as "scurrilous," accused the *Post* of "disservice" to the nation, and appealed to Mrs. Graham to stop publishing such accounts.

Haig himself, the reporters soon learned, had come to doubt the wisdom of the President's course. For more than six months he and Henry Kissinger had been urging the President to cut his ties with the three former aides who had been the closest to him and were now the primary targets of the special prosecutor's investigation—Haldeman, Ehrlichman and Colson.

Instead, the President had built his legal defense in concert with the three, and had continued to meet with them and talk with them on the telephone. During the summer of 1973, Kissinger had tried to persuade the President to disavow his former aides publicly and to accept a measure of responsibility for Watergate. The suggestion had been angrily rejected by Ron Ziegler. "Contrition is bullshit," he had responded to the presidential speechwriter who brought him Kissinger's recommendation.

[. . .]

By late February 1974, the special Watergate prosecution force had obtained guilty pleas from Jeb Magruder, Bart Porter, Donald Segretti, Herbert Kalmbach, Fred LaRue, Egil Krogh and John Dean. Eight corporations and their officers had pleaded guilty to charges of making illegal contributions to CRP. In Washington, Dwight Chapin was under indictment for perjury. In New York, John Mitchell and Maurice Stans were on trial, charged with obstruction of justice and perjury.

On March 1, the Washington grand jury that had indicted the original conspirators and burglars of the Democratic National Headquarters in 1972 handed up its major indictments in the Watergate cover-up case. It charged seven of the President's former White House and campaign aides with conspiracy to obstruct justice: Haldeman, Ehrlichman, Colson, Mitchell, Strachan, Mardian and lawyer Kenneth Parkinson.

A week later, a second Washington grand jury handed up indictments in the conspiracy to burglarize the office of Daniel Ellsberg's psychiatrist. Those charged were Ehrlichman, Colson, Liddy and three Cuban Americans, including Bernard Barker and Eugenio Martinez, who were among the original Watergate break-in defendants.

Acting for the full House, to which the Constitution gives the "sole power to impeach," the House Judiciary Committee had begun the first investigation in more than one hundred years into such possible action against a President. The chief Watergate grand jury turned over to Judge Sirica, in addition to the seven indictments, a briefcase containing a report and the accompanying evidence of what Deep Throat, and others, assert to be a staggering case against the President. Since the prosecutors had argued strongly that the Constitution precludes the possibility of indicting an incumbent President, the grand jurors recommended that both be turned over to the House committee.

On January 30, the President had delivered his annual State of the Union Message to a joint session of the House and Senate, the justices of the Supreme Court and the members of the Cabinet, as well as to other guests and a national TV audience. "One year of Watergate is enough," he declared at the conclusion, and he implored the country and the Congress to turn to other, more urgent, matters. To those who will decide if he should be tried for "high crimes and misdemeanors"—the House of Representatives—

And to those who would sit in judgment at such a trial if the House impeaches—the Senate—

And to the man who would preside at such an impeachment trial—the Chief Justice of the United States, Warren Burger—

And to the nation . . .

The President said, "I want you to know that I have no intention whatever of ever walking away from the job that the American people elected me to do for the people of the United States."

# Chapter 12

# NAN ROBERTSON

# THE GIRLS IN THE BALCONY

IN JULY 1972, A DOZEN WOMEN on the editorial staff of *The New York Times* representing the newly formed Women's Caucus met in the company's board room with the publisher Arthur Ochs Sulzberger and other senior executives at the newspaper. The meeting had been called in response to a letter the women had sent documenting the sorry status of women at the *Times*. The letter noted that there was not one female executive on the masthead; that there was not one women vice president and no women well positioned to become a vice president; that two of the top three ranking women editors worked in the family/style department, positions traditionally held by women, and 11 reporters in that department were women. Not one national correspondent was a woman and only three of 33 foreign correspondents were women. And perhaps most importantly, the 88 male general assignment reporters averaged $59 more in weekly pay than 26 women in the same position. Women across the country were asserting their rights, the letter said, and it was time to address the position of women at the *Times*. The women ultimately filed a sex discrimination lawsuit against the *Times*, known as "Elizabeth Boylan et al. v. The New York Times"—that was settled in 1978.

*The Girls in the Balcony* chronicles women's fight for equality at the *Times* and in journalism in general in the 1970s. The title refers to the balcony where women stood in the all-male National Press Club in Washington, D.C. before it admitted women as members in 1971. Nan Robertson, a Pulitzer Prize winning reporter for the *Times*, describes the men and women of journalism before and after the "balcony." But the real focus is on the suit and the battle for gender equity in journalism. This selection describes the conditions under which women journalists worked when they were consigned to the balcony at the National Press Club and a short profile of Eileen Shanahan, a pioneering financial journalist at the *Times*.

No woman who was a reporter in Washington during the 1950s and 1960s could forget the balcony at the National Press Club. I remember it well. To this day, Marjorie Hunter and Eileen Shanahan and I, colleagues during those years in *The New York Times*'s Washington bureau, look up and think of that vanished balcony every time we enter the new ballroom of the refurbished press club, which finally allowed women as members in 1971. The men had fought fiercely over the female invasion in vote after vote at the club; finally, the pro-women forces within the membership triumphed. Until then, a time still close to our own, the balcony was one of the ugliest symbols of discrimination against women to be found in the world of journalism. It was a metaphor for what working women everywhere faced.

After World War II, every man of consequence on the globe who wanted to deliver an important speech in the capital preferred to do so at the club. What these leaders said was carried that night on radio and television and the next day on the front pages of newspapers across the country. Prime ministers of Britain and France, presidents of the United States, spoke there. It was almost as prestigious as appearing before a joint session of Congress. Women reporters never covered such speeches. They were not allowed even to set foot inside the press club doors for any reporting events. The women protested that they didn't want to be members, all they wanted was equal access to the news. They were not believed. The State Department colluded in the arrangement. It continued to route foreign chiefs of state and other high government officials to the club.

And then in 1955, after years of pressure from the Women's National Press Club, the men thought of a solution. They would put the women reporters in the balcony of the ballroom. Of course they would get nothing to eat during the speeches, which were usually delivered at lunch. And there would be no place to sit up there—it was too narrow for chairs if there was any kind of crowd. But by God, no woman would be able to say that the club didn't let her in to cover the assignment. The National Press Club's officers congratulated themselves, and the bureau chiefs began sending their women reporters off to speeches and press conferences there. It was humiliating.

During the balcony days, Bonnie Angelo, ninety-eight pounds of pepper out of North Carolina, was chief of the *Newsday* bureau in Washington and then became a star reporter for *Time* magazine. Decades later she could barely contain her outrage as she described the scene:

> "I remember being in that damned balcony crowded up against Pulitzer Prize winners like Miriam Ottenberg of *The Evening Star* and Marguerite Higgins [who won her Pulitzer on the *New York Herald Tribune* during the Korean War], and I was in the middle of it. I stood and looked down at all those lobbyists and patent lawyers and doctors and dentists—the male reporters loved bringing their doctors and dentists to hear the bigwigs, and the patent lawyers had their offices in the building—sitting there on the ballroom floor and luxuriating over their crummy National Press Club apple pie. They were people who had never written a line of a newspaper story in their lives. In professional terms, it couldn't have been meaner, it couldn't have been pettier. God, it was mean.

> "Here were the people in the balcony, distinguished journalists treated like second-class citizens. I *had* to cover the stories there. Some people equated the balcony with the back of the bus, but at least the bus got every-body to the same destinations just as well. We could not ask questions of

the speakers. Most of the questions were written and passed along the tables up to the dais. When the speakers left with their security guards, there was no way to gather around as the men on the floor did to shoot questions at them.

"It was so hot, it was so hot in that balcony. All those bodies up there, jammed under the eaves. There were camera crews up there. Television equipment was much bulkier then, and the TV lights were hotter than they are now. It was hard to hear. It was hard to see. People would come early to try to get to the front of the balcony. All this standing—it was like a cattle car. And all the time you were really boiling inside. You entered and left through a back door, and you'd be glowered at as you went through the club quarters. It was discrimination at its rawest."

Maggie Hunter recalled the day she started a little mutiny at the *New York Times* bureau because of the balcony. Scotty Reston, then the bureau chief, had sent her off to the club to cover a speech by Madame Nhu, the beautiful and sinister female leader of South Vietnam, the wife of Ngo Dinh Nhu.

Now, Maggie, a Southern lady and a thorough professional, was no feminist fire-brand. That day, however, "I stood on a rolled-up carpet in the back of the balcony and I couldn't hear a goddamned word going on down there—I couldn't hear a word." Afterwards, she marched, fuming, into Reston's office. She blurted out, "Scotty, don't you ever send me to that damned National Press Club ever again."

Reston turned to Wallace Carroll, the bureau's news editor, who had befriended Maggie at the Winston-Salem *Journal* in North Carolina and had brought her to the *Times*. "Wally," said Reston slowly, with an air of innocent wonderment, "what's wrong with Maggie?"

"I don't think," she said years later, "that Scotty ever understood why I was so mad."

Eileen Shanahan and I joined her boycott, refusing to cover any event at the club from then on. Reston, the most venerated newspaperman of his time in Washington, was not only baffled by the fuss, he was quietly furious. He dropped any effort to assign us to the National Press Club.

Scotty belonged to the "What Do Women *Want?*" school of thought. There is a story about him and Mary McGrory, one of the most beloved, as well as one of the most literary and intuitive, political journalists, which was widely circulated in the Washington of my day. Gay Talese put it into print: ". . . when one of the best reporters in the country, Mary McGrory, appeared for a job on his Washington staff [Reston] said she could have it if she would work part-time on the telephone switchboard, which she refused to do."

I often wondered if it had really happened as Talese had reported it. In 1990, when I asked Mary point-blank about the anecdote, she answered simply: "It's true." As Mary remembered it, the job interview took place in 1954, following her coverage of the Army-McCarthy hearings that brought about the downfall of the Red-baiting Senator Joseph McCarthy. Eileen Shanahan, who has superb recall, talked to Mary about it much closer to the time of the event, probably in the same year. The way Eileen remembers it, McGrory told her: "Scotty made me feel as though he wanted me to work the tele-phone switchboard part-time." Whichever version is accurate, the story says something important about how Reston's views on professional women were perceived.

McGrory never joined the *Times*. She won a long-deserved Pulitzer Prize in 1975 for her work on the Washington *Evening Star*. When the *Star* folded in 1981 she went to The

*Washington Post.* Now in her early seventies, she is still a columnist on the *Post,* still hitting home runs every week.

When I came to the Washington bureau in 1963, I discovered immediately that Scotty ran it like a men's club. There were only two other women reporters there, along with Nona Brown, for many years the Sunday department representative, and Barbara Dubivsky, her assistant. The reporters were Maggie, who had been hired in 1961, and Eileen, who came in 1962.

The men lunched with the men. The women ate with each other. Every day this went on. Hunter would frequently try to throw a grappling hook over the wall by going down the aisle of the newsroom and asking plaintively, "Anybody for lunch?" The men invariably begged off or bent their heads silently over their work. It was the men Scotty called to his councils in his office, and the men who were invited to lunch or dinner at the Metropolitan Club. The club excluded women.

When Punch Sulzberger, the new publisher in 1963, came down to Washington to meet the staff, off went Scotty and Reston's Rangers, as they were called, to the Metropolitan Club while the women reporters stayed behind, mortified. I figured there was little I could do alone to desegregate the Metropolitan, but there must be some way I could tear down the barrier between the men and women at lunchtime. It was ludicrous. After the easy camaraderie of the city room, I wasn't going to stand for it. So I went around the bureau, asking several men each day, lightly and with assurance, to join me and one or two of the other women for lunch. Maybe by now they were ready. It worked at once. The wall simply melted away. The men obviously liked the new openness. Of course, so did we.

[. . .]

Scotty Reston had hired Hunter because he needed a woman to cover the first lady, although Maggie was by instinct and training a first-class legislative reporter. He had taken on Shanahan as an economics reporter because she was too able and experienced to pass over, and because Richard Mooney and Edwin Dale, both bureau members specializing in economics, had repeatedly assured Scotty that Eileen was the tops—and neither a bitch nor a troublemaker. "We practically had to tie Scotty down to get him to hire her," Mooney recalled. She arrived to take Mooney's place when he was transferred to London.

According to Eileen, I had been the first person in the *Times* city room to make her feel welcome when she was in New York for her month-long training period. She did the same for me when I came down to the Washington bureau.

On my first day in the office, she burst out of the elevator and made straight for my desk with her long, loping stride. Her eyes were ablaze with excitement. "The Federal Reserve is split!" she cried, and paused hopefully for my response. I was stunned speechless and could only reward her with a nervous giggle. She never lost patience with me. Tony Lewis, then in the bureau, used to crack up many a cocktail party with a takeoff on the daily dialogue between Eileen and Ed Dale, another high-decibel enthusiast. One spoof began this way: Eileen, rushing up to Ed: "Did you hear? Did you hear? Australian shorts are long today!" (This had something to do with money, I think.)

Eileen and Ed sat near me in the bureau, and so I, too, was regaled with such fascinating tidbits as this:

> Ed: "Is Joe Schlunk a liberal or a conservative on the Federal Reserve Board?"
> Eileen, snapping her usual wad of gum: "What, on liquidity?"

She made an immediate impact, frequently getting out on page one with such fluffy topics as John Kennedy's tax program, the debt ceiling, the balance of payments, and the trade tariff war. Typical headlines over her stories read: "U.S. TO RETALIATE AGAINST EUROPE WITH TARIFF RISE" and "STUDY FOR S.E.C. CHARGES CONTRACT MUTUAL FUNDS WITH VICTIMIZING BUYERS." In one extraordinary column she discussed the problem of the national debt ceiling in household terms, with the man representing Congress and his wife the Kennedy administration.

Washington and its labyrinthian politics were no mystery to Eileen. She had been born and raised in the capital and had spent her entire working life there. The will to work hard, to be first and best, had been drummed into her from her earliest years.

In her time, and in the poor neighborhoods where she had grown up, "a mixed marriage was when an Irish Catholic girl married an Italian Catholic boy and both the mothers rent their garments at the wedding." Irish-Jewish marriages were almost unheard of. Tom Shanahan, despite his own choice of a Jewish wife, was a bigot. In his eyes, there were few "good Jews" other than Malvena and her family. Eileen ingested her father's biases and became ashamed of being half Jewish.

She came to college "dying to be beautiful and popular and to get into a sorority, where they would show me how to be beautiful and popular and make me better-looking than I knew how to make myself." Boys had avoided this brainy, superenergetic girl in high school. She had had a total of four dates in four years.

At George Washington University, she went through sorority "rush," the screening ritual for social acceptability, and was pledged by "not the nerdiest sorority; it was about third from the bottom." The night of pledge initiation, the chapter president came down a line of the newly anointed with some questions for each. Eileen was standing in the middle. She heard the president ask the first pledge, "Is there any Jewish, Negro, or Oriental blood in your family?" and the girl almost shrieked, "No, of course not!" By the time the president reached Eileen, she had decided to lie. "I wanted so desperately to be in a sorority," she says.

A few months later, a national officer of the sorority came to the campus. By then, some of the group's gloss had rubbed off on Eileen—she had learned a bit about dress and makeup and was enjoying more dates than she had ever dreamed of. The officer summoned Eileen to an appointment. "We understand," she said, "that your mother is Jewish. Is that true?"

"And I knew the jig was up," Shanahan recalls. "And she held out her hand and said, 'I must ask you for your pin,' and I gave her the pin and walked out and I didn't cry until I got out the door. I thought my life was over."

But the incident caused her to think about her own behavior, and about prejudice. It led her to take an interest in her heritage. She began a serious romance with a Jewish boyfriend. They went to temple on Friday nights. She learned about the great culture and history of the Jews. "Nobody had ever told me there was anything to be proud of. Joe Epstein told me," Eileen remembers. She went to a rabbi, a distant relative by marriage, "to learn who I was."

She had joined the student newspaper, *The Hatchet,* in her first week as a freshman, urged on by a new friend. And there she found her first real home at any school, among other students who were accepting, fun to be with, intellectually stimulating, engaged with life. For the first time, she was meeting people her own age who were even brighter than she. She rose through the ranks to become *The Hatchet*'s editor.

When Eileen Shanahan walked into the city room of *The Washington Post* for a summer job in 1942 at the end of her sophomore year, she was eighteen years old and, she says, "so innocent that it is fair to say that I had barely been properly kissed."

It was wartime; all the copyboys had enlisted or been drafted. Eileen was the second copygirl ever hired at *The Washington Post*. When the reporters wanted their copy run up to the city desk, they still yelled "Boy!" "Boy!" "Boy!" "Copy!" "Copy!" "Copy!" and Shanahan leaped from the copyboys' bench at the front of the room. She fetched coffee and cleaned paste pots, she sharpened pencils, she ripped dispatches from the chattering Teletypes. At deadline hour, the din of manual typewriters rose to a pounding crescendo, and Eileen rushed hither and yon, snatching the sheets of paper from urgent outstretched hands. Before the week was out, Shanahan was a goner. She thought the people in the city room were the most interesting, friendly, exciting bunch of people she had ever met, even though there seemed to be quite a few boozehounds and womanizers among them.

By the time she had finished her second summer as a copygirl at *The Washington Post*, she knew a career in journalism was for her. It was 1943; the United States was deep into the war and beginning to win; the news was exciting every day. Even Eileen, compiling college football scores and covering high school football games, with a *Post* byline of "E. J. Shanahan" so readers wouldn't know she was a female, felt part of the larger picture.

One stormy night that summer, Shanahan was sent over to the *Washington Evening Star* to pick up some wirephotos. There was a cloudburst, and Eileen, who is five feet six inches tall, borrowed a raincoat from the *Post's* assistant night city editor, who was six feet four inches tall. Coming back, she bounded up the stairs to the city room, huaraches squelching, dark hair sopping, past a tall, calm young man named John Waits, a clerk in the advertising department, who was attending George Washington University part-time. "I've got to meet this woman," Waits said to himself. He managed an introduction that very night and they began dating. They were married fifteen months later, in September 1944, three months after Shanahan got her college degree.

Eileen applied for her first full-time job at the United Press. Those were the days when hard-bitten newsmen thought the business was going to hell, what with all the women, and even worse, *college graduates*, begging to witness life as it was really lived. But editors were desperate because the men were away in the military; they would take anybody. "Can you spell, college girl?" asked the night wire editor. "Yessir!" said Eileen. She was hired as a telephone dictationist, typing thousands of words night after night as U.P. correspondents dictated their stories to her by phone from all over the nation.

"One time I spelled 'recommend' with two *c*'s and one *m*, and Harry Sharpe, my boss, came over and waggled the copy in front of my nose and said, 'I thought you could spell, college girl—you're fired!' I was concentrating on only one thing—not crying. I walked to my locker at the end of that long room, and Sharpe followed me and clapped me on the shoulder and said, 'Aw, you're not fired, college girl. Come on back.' "

Soon thereafter, Eileen took dictation from a reporter who phoned in two and one-half tedious pages about the wartime Office of Price Administration setting new, increased prices on canned sour pitted cherries. Sharpe said, "Rewrite it for what it's worth." Eileen was scared to death.

This was what she carved out of that two and one-half pages, remembered decades later word-for-word, the way reporters often remember their first real story: "The Office of Price Administration announced today higher prices for sixteen different grades and sizes of canned sour pitted cherries. The increases ranged from one and one-half cents a can on lower grades and smaller can sizes to six cents on higher grades and larger can sizes." Period. The end. It was not poetry, but it was an early example of the clarity with which Shanahan thinks and talks and writes.

"A few minutes later," Eileen recalls, "Sharpe jumped out of his chair and pointed at me and said, 'You'll do, college girl!' and he never called me college girl again."

In the winter of 1946, with the war over and the demobilization of the gigantic American armed forces accelerating, United Press, reflecting what was happening all over the country, fired all but three women in its Washington bureau. The holdovers were Eileen Shanahan; Helen Thomas, who rose over decades of tenacious reporting to become the first woman dean of the White House press corps; and Charlotte Moulton, who covered the Supreme Court and humiliated generations of her news competitors by always getting it right. She was so good that, according to Eileen, U.P. "was afraid to fire her." As for Thomas and Shanahan, "one might think, given our successful subsequent careers, that we, too, were kept on because of our perceived excellence," she says. "Not so. Helen and I were kept on because nobody else wanted those crummy jobs rewriting the news from the local papers for the radio wire."

A year later, Shanahan left United Press to have her first child. After eighteen months at home alone with Mary Beth, however, she went through a frightening emotional deterioration, becoming so depressed she would leave dishes in the sink for days. Finally her husband said, "Go get a job. You've got to get out of here. You've got to go back to work."

"Well," she recalls, "it was pariah city out there." She heard the same lines that women would hear into the 1960s: "Your husband has a good job and you're leaving your baby at home?" The man at CBS radio said, "What on earth makes you think I'd hire a woman?" The man at ABC said he already had one woman on the staff. She worked her way down from the top floor of the National Press Building, where the Washington bureaus of almost every news organization in the nation were then located. On the eighth floor, she rapped on yet another frosted-glass door. Inside sat Walter Cronkite, aged thirty-two. He had covered the war for United Press and was then the Washington correspondent for a string of midwestern radio stations. It was February 28, 1949, Eileen's twenty-fifth birthday. Cronkite hired her that very day. In less than two years, he taught her as much about the news business as any mentor ever did. To her distress, he then moved on to CBS and fame.

Eileen's second child, Kathleen, was born. Soon there was war again—this time in Korea. Eileen joined the Research Institute of America, a newsletter publisher. There were full-scale wage and price controls during the Korean War and many industrial materials were rationed. She found that covering price controls was a way to understand the anatomy and physiology of the economy and how industries worked. When the war in Korea was over, she started covering bills in Congress and Supreme Court decisions that affected business. Her course was already set. She would be an economics reporter.

The most prestigious business newsletter of the era was the *Kiplinger Letter*. She wangled an appointment with its founder, Willard Kiplinger. Her friends told her it was hopeless. Kiplinger opened the interview by saying, "You wanted to see me?" and then said not another word, Eileen recounts. "I talk of my qualifications and interests. He says nothing. I talk some more. Still nothing. Finally, desperately, I ask, 'Do you have some questions that I'm not answering?'

"He replied that he wanted to see what kind of woman would apply for a job doing the kind of reporting the *Kiplinger Letter* required—inside information. 'A respectable woman, the only kind of woman we would want here, just couldn't do it,' he said. I didn't ask him what kind of favors his male colleagues gave in return for the inside information *they* got."

A *Washington Post* editor told her that he liked her work, but that an economics story under a woman's byline would not have any credibility. Eileen kept looking. The stodgy but widely respected *Journal of Commerce* hired her in 1956.

In 1961, the *Journal* printed her ten-part, ten-thousand-word series, "The Kennedy Administration and Business." Secretary of the Treasury Douglas Dillon called it "the only accurate interpretation of the whole economic policy of the Kennedy administration." Dillon asked her to become his spokesman for the tax side of the Treasury. She decided to stay only a year. She stayed a year and three days, and then she joined the Washington bureau of the *Times*. She was thirty-nine years old. It had taken her twenty-one years to rise from her copygirl's job on *The Washington Post* to star economics reporter at *The New York Times*.

# Biography

# INTRODUCTION

**T**HE EXACT ROLE INDIVIDUALS PLAY in the development and practice of a profession is often up for dispute. Historians have long debunked the "Great Man" theory of history, the idea that individual genius shaped events. Instead, history is seen as the result of a complex interplay of economic, cultural and political factors.

Nevertheless, people often can serve as focal points and a kind of shorthand for a specific historical period or approach to a particular activity or problem. For example, in 1872, Horace Greeley, the editor of the *New York Tribune* was a major candidate for the presidency. Though he served as a member of Congress in the 1840s, Greeley lost many other attempts to hold public office. He was nominated as a candidate for the presidency while he was solely the editor of the *Tribune*. Greeley was but one of the editors in his generation deeply involved in politics. In fact, most editors were. But Greeley can serve as a exemplar of the political involvement of journalists in the middle of the 19th century.

Furthermore, the study of individual journalists does more than use a person to represent an era in journalism. Prominent journalists can be role models for those entering the profession. In the 1970s, journalism was flooded with young people who wanted to be the next Robert Woodward or Carl Bernstein, the triumphant star reporters of Watergate fame. Unfortunately, many people who aspire to careers in journalism today cannot name a single journalist, either contemporary or historical. They are entering the field without guides to help them imagine the road they may want to travel. Consequently, resurrecting and keeping the focus on leading figures in journalism is an important task. Finally, people are at the heart of great stories and the development and practice of journalism is a great story. The understanding of journalism would be incomplete without an understanding of some of the people who were in the limelight when they practiced journalism.

The excerpts from biographies, autobiographies and memoirs in this section are intended to provide an alternative avenue to understanding the history of journalism, as well as to offer role models to young journalists. The people selected played different roles in journalism, lived in different time periods and took different avenues into journalism. Yet all can be seen to represent something important in and about journalism.

So what can be learned from Joseph Pulitzer, the publisher of *The New York World*, who recreated the mass newspaper in the 1880s making it the most important newspaper of its age? This excerpt from James McGrath Morris's new biography of Pultizer, who is now known to many more for the prizes he endowed than the newspapers he published, concentrates on the episode when the great proprietor first purchased *The World* and made it the most widely read newspaper in American history. He embarked on this task in a modest way at first: the priority was to influence his staff on how to write—for content, he felt, was king. The headline was the lure, the copy the hook to catch the readers. Simplicity and colorful details were everything, but above all, accuracy came first.

Lincoln Steffens is probably the best remembered of the muckraking journalists of the late 1800s and early 1900s. Today we would call them investigative reporters. In the first extract from his autobiography, he recounts how he broke into the profession and paints a picture far different than breaking into the profession now. His words will resonate with many who have embarked on a new challenge, thinking it will be simple, only to face failure and rejection. Journalists need to be tenacious, and Steffens kept going, undeterred, until he succeeded—both in his first job, then in the second excerpt in his aim to expose corruption.

The achievements of Margaret Bourke were of a different order. She developed the essay style of photojournalism as a new democratic art (with a collaborative effort). She was a perfectionist who always managed to find the symbolic moment or expression, and these according to biographer Vicki Goldberg "amount to opinions that had been compressed to the size of an aphorism to be instantly grasped by the viewer." Bourke was a pioneer in two senses. First, she helped create the field of photojournalism as one of its first practitioners. Secondly, she helped carve out a role for women in journalism, not on the women's pages or covering society news, but at the front lines of the most important issues of the day.

Arguably, Edward Murrow may still be the most famous name in broadcast news. His famous confrontation with Senator Joseph McCarthy was made into a major motion picture by the actor George Clooney in 2005. Biographer A.M. Sperber calls Murrow's talent for finding the succinct, key expression his "editorial punch." Fred Friendly, Murrow's producer for the hard-hitting documentary and exposé of the conditions of farmers in the United States, *Harvest of Shame*, that aired on CBS in 1960, referred to Murrow's talent as a "question of identification. People believed the shows; people could identify." However, when Murrow spoke out in criticism of McCarthy, he "stepped out of the role of newsman, into the leadership vacuum."

Journalism, like all professional fields, exhibited the racism prevalent in the United States for most of its history. One of the first journalists to overcome that racism was Carl Rowan. In this excerpt from his memoir *Breaking Barriers* Rowan describes an episode when he confronted President Reagan face to face about what he saw as Reagan's discriminatory policies.

The final excerpt comes from Katherine Graham's memoir *Personal History*. Graham's story is also the story of the entry of women into the workforce in the period from the 1930s through the 1990s. Though she worked for a time as a reporter, when her father Eugene Mayer wanted to pass *The Washington Post* onto the next generation, he named Katherine's husband, Philip Graham, as the publisher. It was only after Philip Graham's suicide that Katherine Graham assumed the leadership of the *Post*. Over time, however, she came to be seen as the most powerful woman in journalism in the contemporary period.

The excerpt contained here recounts one of Grahams' most glorious moments, when she made history by deciding to publish The Pentagon Papers in the *Post*, in the face of enormous establishment opposition from the U.S. government and the real possibility that she could do serious financial damage to the newspaper. Making a tough decision at a very tense moment, Graham kept faith with her readers and the citizens of the United States—and also stayed true to her principles of journalism.

All of these people left their marks on the history of journalism and most of them displayed principled professional courage at key moments. They were all leaders in different ways, and served as examples for their colleagues and those who followed them. Of course, other journalists have manifested these honorable human qualities, and there were many candidates who could have been included in this section. The selection here is intended to be as inclusive as possible. Its goal is to focus on exemplars representing the possibility and promise of journalism to inspire those entering the profession, and to comfort those already practicing journalism.

# Chapter 13

## JAMES MCGRATH MORRIS

# PULITZER: A LIFE IN POLITICS, PRINT AND POWER

N OW KNOWN PRIMARILY FOR THE PRIZES that bear his name, Joseph
Pulitzer revolutionized journalism in the 1880s, creating the modern American
mass circulation newspaper. A Hungarian immigrant, Pulitzer arrived in the United
States in 1864 and served briefly with the Union army during the Civil War. He got his
start in journalism in 1868, when he took a job as a reporter with the German-language
*Westliche Post* newspaper in St. Louis, a city with a large German-speaking population. He found that journalism was his calling and in 1878 he bought the *St. Louis
Dispatch* that he merged with the *St. Louis Post* to form *the St. Louis Post-Dispatch*,
still the dominant newspaper in the city.

Pulitzer's major impact on journalism, however, began after he purchased the
*New York World* in 1883 for $346,000. Pulitzer slashed the price of the newspaper
and ramped up the circulation and the amount of news each edition contained. He filled
the newspaper with human interest stories. The front page sported huge headlines
designed to catch the public interest. Pulitzer also used the newspaper to push for the
political positions he favored.

William Randolph Hearst's purchase of the *New York Journal* in 1896 set off a
fierce circulation war with the *World*. By this time Pulitzer had begun to withdraw
from active management of his newspapers due to poor health. The sensationalism and
outlandish claims designed to attract readers has come to be called "yellow journalism," describing a journalism that was less interested in the facts than the drama
that could be generated.

As his health declined, Pulitzer largely ceded the operation of the *World* to others.
He left $2 million in his will to Columbia, providing the financial foundation for the
Graduate School of Journalism that opened in 1914. The first Pulitzer Prizes recognizing outstanding achievements in journalism were awarded in 1917. The selection
below describes Pulitzer's purchase of the *World* and the energy he brought to the
operation.

## The Great Theater

On April 7, 1883, Jay Gould took his family and friends by private railcar to Philadelphia for the launching of his new yacht, *Atalanta*, named after the huntress of Greek mythology. Built at a cost of $140,000, the yacht was a floating palace with gold-edged curtains, oriental rugs, and a built-in piano. But as Gould participated in the festivities of the day, he was beset with worries. The country was in the midst of a business downturn, his nerves were frayed, and the constant public attacks on him had begun to hit home. For the first time, he was considering retirement. At the very least, it was time to lighten his load.

He decided to rid himself of the burdensome *New York World*. It was a Democratic paper and he was a Republican. But perhaps an even greater sin in the eyes of a railroad and industrial baron was that it had never made a dime since he acquired it four years earlier. "I never cared anything about the *World*," Gould said. The *World* had an anemic circulation of 15,000 and was losing money every week.

In January, Gould had come close to disposing of the paper to John McLean, the publisher of the *Cincinnati Enquirer*, but McLean had been unwilling to meet the $385,000 price. There was only one man trolling for a New York paper for whom price did not seem to be a consideration. "As Joseph has more stamps than the rest of us, I might say the only one with stamps," said McLean when his bid failed, "I suspect he will get it ultimately."

On the day Gould watched his new yacht slip into the water, Pulitzer was riding a train to New York. The Pulitzer family had just concluded the stay of several months in the South, undertaken out of concern for Ralph's asthma. Joseph and Kate had given up on St. Louis and were looking for a place to buy or rent in New York City. The *Post-Dispatch* practically ran itself: But to be sure that it remained on track, Pulitzer received daily preprinted one-page reports that showed him at a glance all the essential information, such as circulation, advertising, expenses, and the times when the presses started and ended their runs. He was forever asking the men who managed the business side of his operations to be brief in responding to his ceaseless queries. In his words, he wanted the information in "a nutshell."

On the way north, Joseph dropped Kate and the children off in Washington for a stay with her family. He pushed on to New York. If the intelligence he had learned from his friend William H. Smith, director of the Associated Press, was sound and if he played his hand deftly, the *World* could be his. The press was reporting that Gould would leave any day for the West in the company of tycoon Russell Sage. Pulitzer would have to work fast.

He obtained a meeting with Gould at his Western Union office, a few blocks from Park Row. As the two sat facing each other, it was clear there wasn't much to negotiate. For Gould, who had once stacked $53 million in stock certificates on his desk and who lived in a forty-room Gothic mansion, selling the *World* was a Lilliputian deal. True, owning the paper had become an irritation, and Pulitzer was a willing purchaser. But Gould could have easily closed the *World* without making a dent in his petty cash. He wasn't going to grant any favors to a man who made a sport of pillorying him; from a negotiating perspective, Gould's uninterest trumped Pulitzer's desire.

This purchase, unlike that of the *Staats-Zeitung* or the *Dispatch*, was no fire sale. The negotiations dragged on for a couple of weeks over two issues. Gould wanted to retain a small ownership share for his son and wanted the current editor to keep his job. In the end, Gould conceded on both points and Pulitzer met his price of $346,000. The sum, according to Gould, represented the amount he had paid for the paper and the losses incurred during his four years of ownership.

Pulitzer did not have that much cash. If he sold the *Post-Dispatch*, he would be trading a moneymaker for, in his own words, a "mummified corpse of the once bright and lively New York *World*." His craving for the *World* was so intense that he would take a loan from Gould, a man whom he deemed "one of the most sinister figures that have ever flitted bat-like across the vision of the American people."

On April 28, Pulitzer drew up the sales contract in his own hand, with the advice and counsel of the former U.S. senator Roscoe Conkling, whom Pulitzer had befriended since Conkling had fallen out of favor with the Republican Party and opened a law practice. To take possession of the *World*, Pulitzer would give Gould a down payment of $34,600, and Gould would finance the remainder at a 5 percent interest rate. Under the terms of the loan, Pulitzer would pay $79,200 in 1884; $121,100 in 1885; and $121,100 in 1886, as well as the interest on the outstanding balance, which could amount to $33,730. In addition, Pulitzer promised to rent for a decade the Park Row building housing the *World*, for $13,560 a year. Signing the contract put Pulitzer nearly $500,000 in debt. Less than five years after spending his last few thousand dollars to buy the bankrupt *Dispatch*, he was betting he could repeat his success on a far grander scale.

The stakes were high. The *Post-Dispatch*, which had recovered from its slump after Slayback's murder, looked as though it would generate profits of $120,000 to $150,000 in 1883. But the *World* was losing thousands of dollars each month. If New York didn't take to his so-called western journalism, Pulitzer would be ruined.

He confessed his anxiety to Kate, who had installed herself and the children in the Fifth Avenue Hotel. Five years with Joseph had convinced her that it was no use trying to restrain his ambition. He was, as he had promised in his wedding-eve letters, driven by an insatiable need to be occupied, to have meaningful work, to keep moving. On the other hand, Kate had witnessed his talent. She had, after all, accompanied him to St. Louis to spend their last dime on a bankrupt paper. She believed in him and urged him on, even if it meant risking everything they had.

Word of the pending sale began to leak out. It was hard to keep it a secret, with Cockerill shuttling between New York and St. Louis and the *Post-Dispatch* business manager joining Pulitzer in New York. On May 6, the rival *Globe-Democrat* confirmed that Pulitzer had concluded the deal.

On May 9, the day before Gould transferred the *World* to him, Pulitzer proposed to his brother that they consolidate their papers into a new one, to be called the *World-Journal*. Albert's seven-month-old *Journal* had three times the circulation of the *World* and was acquiring thousands of new subscribers each month. If Albert agreed to the merger, Joseph promised him a profit of no less than $100,000 a year.

"That is a good deal of money," Albert said. "I shall be perfectly satisfied if I can even make a fifth of that out of the *Journal*."

"You needn't come to the office at all, if you like you can stay at home in bed all day long," continued Joseph, who could never brook an equal in the office.

In hoping to combine the papers, Joseph was following the game plan he had used in St. Louis when he had merged his new paper there with Dillon's *Post*. But this situation was different: Albert was making money on his own, lots of it, and his paper was not threatened by Joseph. He declined the invitation.

"Don't be so cock-sure of your success," Joseph snapped. "It is the men you have got and who get the paper out every night for you that are making it what it is. When they are gone what will you do?"

That night, Albert confronted this question. He discovered that his managing editor, E. C. Hancock, had resigned, his lead columnist had vanished, and his editorial writer had called in sick. "I did not lose a moment, jumped into a car as I was determined to get at the truth, rode to his house, obtained admission after some difficulty and soon learned that my surmise was true—my whole staff, my three most valuable men whom I had trained with such pains since the first issue of the *Morning Journal*, had gone over in the dead of night to a rival newspaper! This blow was intended to kill me."

Of course, the rival paper was the *World*. In a city teeming with editorial talent, Joseph had chosen to raid his brother's shop. He was seeking more than editors. Driven by jealousy, he wanted to put his kid brother in his place.

At the Fifth Avenue Hotel, a reporter caught up with Pulitzer, eager to learn his plans for the *World*. "I intend to make it a thorough American newspaper—to un-Anglicize it, so to speak," Pulitzer said. He promised that no immediate personnel changes were in the works. "I have no intention to bring any new men to the city for the purpose of placing them on the editorial staff of the paper," he said. Once again Pulitzer was resorting to his old habit of lying when talking to a reporter. He preferred to keep it quiet that Cockerill, with a reputation as an editor who shot complaining readers, was on his way to New York to run the *World*. "In the news sense and in other ways," Pulitzer promised, "I shall, of course, in time make considerable changes in the paper."

In the company of his newly purloined editor from Albert's paper, Pulitzer went to inspect his new property on the evening of May 10. The paper was housed in a fire-damaged building at the lower end of Park Row. The fabled block housed a dozen or more daily papers. This was the newspapers' golden age, and Park Row was the richest vein. But in New York, unlike St. Louis, Pulitzer faced competition from sophisticated, well-funded, worldly publications. Aside from Albert's *Morning Journal*, there were the immensely profitable *New York Herald*, run by James Gordon Bennett Jr.; Charles Dana's *Sun*, still attracting more than 100,000 readers each day with its compact four-page format; the late Horace Greeley's *New York Tribune*, now ruled by Whitelaw Reid, a conservative Republican sheet serving the prosperous. If there was a turtle among these hares, it was the sober *New York Times*, slowly winning a loyal following.

Pulitzer and Hancock entered the *World* newsroom just as the staff was putting the finishing touches on the next day's edition. Although Pulitzer's arrival had been preceded by a memo telling the employees that the new owner wished to retain them in their positions at their current salaries, the nearly 100 reporters, editors, compositors, and printers were anxious to catch a glimpse of this thirty-six-year-old outsider who held their future in his hands. The departure of the existing senior management, fleeing like ship rats, forecast great changes.

Escorting Pulitzer around the newsroom, Hancock urged him to write some sort of pronouncement for the next day's edition. Taking a pen, Pulitzer hurriedly began. While a newspaper must be independent, he wrote for his first editorial in the paper, "it must not be indifferent or neutral on any question involving public interest." Then, collating phrases from his stump speeches and from five years of editorial struggles against entrenched interests in St. Louis, Pulitzer pledged that the *World* would fight against monopolies, organized privilege, corrupt officials, and other threats to democracy. "Its rock of faith must be true Democracy," he wrote. "Not the Democracy of a political machine. Not the Democracy which seeks to win the spoils of office from a political rival, but the Democracy which guards with jealous care the rights of all alike, and perpetuates the free institutions it first established.

"Performance is better than promises. Exuberant assurances are cheap," Pulitzer continued, adding a signed announcement of the change of ownership that he had drafted to accompany his editorial. Simply watch the paper and see for yourself, he said. "There is room in this great and growing city for a journal that is not only cheap but bright, not only bright but large, not only large but truly Democratic—dedicated to the cause of the people rather than that of purse-potentates—devoted more to the news of the New than the Old World—that will expose all fraud and sham, fight all public evils and abuses—that will serve and battle for the people with earnest sincerity." Done, Pulitzer handed the sheets to an eighteen-year-old compositor, who would later become one of his editors, and his words were rapidly set into type in time for the press run.

Before leaving for the night, Pulitzer made one alteration to the look of the paper that hinted at his ambitions. He dropped "New York" from the name and restored the nameplate that had been used when the *World* began in 1860. At its center, framed by the words "The World," was a printing press with rays of light emanating from it like the sun flanked by the two hemispheres of the globe.

While Joseph made plans for his newspaper, Albert made repairs to his. He had managed to locate a new editor. In fact, the replacement turned out to be an improvement, and the stolen Hancock lasted only a few days under Joseph. Still fuming over the raid, Albert ran into Joseph at Madison Square Garden.

"I congratulate you on your new recruits," Albert said. "Perhaps you would now like to offer me a stated sum annually for the sole purpose of looking up and supplying your paper with bright writers?"

Joseph dismissed the sarcastic remark with a wave. "I'll admit that you have a wonderful nose for ferreting out talent," he said. "I have read your paper today and it is really not half bad."

There may have been enough room for two Pulitzer papers in New York, but not enough for two Pulitzers. Although Albert was willing to share the stage, Joseph wasn't. Stung by the malevolent actions of his only living sibling, Albert took an angry swipe at Joseph's handiwork. He told the *Herald* that the success of the *Journal* showed that for a newspaper to find readers "it is not necessary to make it slanderous, vituperative, or nasty."

A few weeks after their encounter, Joseph made an attempt to be civil. He stopped in at Albert's office for fifteen minutes. "He made a closer study of us and took in more during that time than another less observing man would have done in a whole day," Albert wrote, describing the visit to a friend. "After Joe left someone asked, 'I wonder what he dropped in for?' My officious office-boy quickly replied, 'I guess he dropped in to see if there was anyone else he could coax away!' "

After the visit, the two brothers would forever remain estranged. The only two remaining members of Fülöp and Elize Pulitzer's children left in the world found they could not get along.

For those who had watched Pulitzer climb from being a lawyer's errand boy to being a newspaper publisher, his purchase of the *World* held great promise. "You have entered, upon the stage of a great theater and stand as if it were before the footlights in presence of the nation," one of his oldest friends from St. Louis wrote. Another compared him to a previous newspaper giant: "The present situation is not unlike that which the elder

Bennett found when he moved to attack the established dailies. You are in a magnificent field and you ought to move all of America."

But unless Pulitzer could spark a spectacular increase in circulation he would not ascend a pinnacle of political power. Instead, he would be crushed under an avalanche of debt. Every tactic, device, scheme, plan, and method that he employed in St. Louis would have to work in New York, and he also needed to think up new ones. But before introducing his ideas, he decided to create the appearance of change.

Taking from his bag a trick he had used in St. Louis, Pulitzer sent reporters out to interview leading Democrats about the "new *World*," even though it still looked like the old one. Flattered by the attention and the promise of free publicity, the party figures immediately studied the paper. Typical was the response of one party official. "I guess we are going to have a real Democratic paper at last," he said. "The paper in its new dress is an immense improvement and the short distinct paragraphs, instead of running everything together, make the paper very readable."

Then—also as he had done in St. Louis—Pulitzer took to reprinting all the press comments on the *World*'s change in ownership. He sought to project a sense of dramatic change. "He took every occasion to blow his horn and tell the public what a good newspaper he was making," remarked the owner of a stationery and newspaper store on the West Side. "This was unusual in New York and by many people it was considered very bad taste on his part to be continually boasting and bragging about the merits of his publication." However distasteful it might have seemed to some, it worked. Within the first few days, circulation had a modest increase. New Yorkers were curious about the *World*.

What they found when they picked up a copy was not all that different from before. Except for Pulitzer's tinkering with the masthead, the layout of the paper remained unchanged. He filled in the empty spaces on each side of the top of the front page with a circle or square containing promotional copy such as "Only 8-Page Newspaper in the United States Sold for 2 Cents." (This little innovation, which he may have stolen from Albert, became known in the business as "ears" and eventually was adopted by most papers.) The front page was divided into six or seven narrow columns, just as in other newspapers. The headlines remained small because convention bound them to the limits of the column width.

But if the new *World* looked like the old, life inside its building certainly didn't. James B. Townsend, a reporter who had been absent at a funeral in Vermont when Pulitzer took over, was startled by what he found upon his return. "It seemed as if a cyclone had entered the building, completely disarranged everything, and had passed away leaving confusion." Avoiding collisions with messenger boys exiting with urgent deliveries, Townsend made his way to the city room and found his colleagues running around excitedly. He asked the general manager what was the cause of all the commotion.

"You will know soon enough, young man," the manager replied. "The new boss will see you in five minutes." He then glanced up at Townsend and added. "After us the deluge—prepare to meet your fate."

Indeed, Townsend was soon summoned to Pulitzer's office. As he entered, Townsend made his first examination of his new boss, and Pulitzer of him. Dressed in a frock coat and gray trousers, Pulitzer stared back through his glasses. "So, this is Mr. T," he said. "Well, Sir, you've heard that I am the new chief of this newspaper, I have already introduced new methods—new ways I proposed to galvanize this force: are you willing to aid me?"

Almost as if the breath had been sucked from him by Pulitzer's vigor, Townsend stammered that he would like to remain on the staff. "Good, I like you," replied Pulitzer. "Get to work."

During the following days, editors and reporters arriving in the early morning found Pulitzer already in his office, often toiling in his shirtsleeves. When the door was open and he was dictating an editorial, recalled one man, "his speech was so interlarded with sulphurous and searing phrases that the whole staff shuddered. He was the first man I ever heard who split a word to insert an oath. He did it often. His favorite was 'indegoddampendent.' "

As the staff settled in for the day's work, they couldn't escape Pulitzer. One moment he would be in the city room arguing with a reporter about some aspect of a story. No detail was too small. In one case, he was overheard discussing the estimated number of cattle that an editor had expected to arrive in New York from the West the previous day. He loved debating with his staff, usually provoking the arguments himself. "It is by argument," he told Townsend, "that I measure a man, his shortcomings, his possession or lack of logic, and, above all, whether he has the courage of his convictions, for no man can long work for me with satisfaction to himself or myself unless he has this courage."

Finished with the city room, Pulitzer would bark out orders in the composing room or dash into the counting room to get a report on revenues. It wasn't long before the old-timers couldn't take it anymore, and new faces, often younger, appeared in the editorial quarters. The men in the composing and printing rooms were content with their new manager, though Pulitzer had one dustup with them. On May 24, he and Cockerill returned from the dedication of the Brooklyn Bridge brimming with ideas about how to cover the momentous occasion, only to discover that forty-three of the fifty-one men had walked off the job in a wage dispute. It took Pulitzer only three hours to capitulate and agree to recognize the men's union. "The whole difficulty has been amicably settled, and the men have returned happy," Pulitzer said as he headed out with the union president and others for a glass of beer at a neighboring bar.

There was a sense that Pulitzer was pushing the *World* forward. "We in the office felt from the first that this remarkable personality, which has so impressed us upon its arrival inside the building, would soon make its impress felt on the great cosmopolitan public of New York," Townsend said, "and in time the country."

Pulitzer launched his journalistic revolution modestly. The dramatic changes for which he would eventually become known were still years away. At this point, he sought solely to condition his editorial staff to his principles of how a paper should be written and edited. This effort, however modest it may seem, is how the *World* began on its path to becoming the most widely read newspaper in American history. In an era when the printed word ruled supreme and 1,028 newspapers competed for readers, content was the means of competition. The medium was not the message; the message was. This was where Pulitzer started.

The paper abandoned its old, dull headlines. In place of BENCH SHOW OF DOGS: PRIZES AWARDED ON THE SECOND DAY OF THE MEETING IN MADISON SQUARE GARDEN on May 10 came SCREAMING FOR MERCY: HOW THE CRAVEN CORNETTI MOUNTED THE SCAFFOLD on May 12. Two weeks later the *World*'s readers were greeted with BAPTIZED IN BLOOD, on top of a story, complete with a diagram, on how eleven people were crushed to death in a human stampede when panic broke out in a large crowd enjoying a Sunday stroll on the newly opened Brooklyn Bridge. In a city where half a dozen newspapers offered dull, similar fare to readers each morning, Pulitzer's dramatic head-lines made the *World* stand out like a racehorse among draft horses.

If the headline was the lure, the copy was the hook. Pulitzer could write all the catchy headlines he wanted, but it was up to the reporters to win over readers. He pushed his staff to give him simplicity and color. He admonished them to write in a buoyant, colloquial style comprising simple nouns, bright verbs, and short, punchy sentences. If there was a "Pulitzer formula," it was a story written so simply that anyone could read it and so colorfully that no one would forget it. The question "Did you see that in the *World*?" Pulitzer instructed his staff, "should be asked every day and something should be designed to cause this."

Pulitzer had an uncanny ability to recognize news in what others ignored. He sent out his reporters to mine the urban dramas that other papers confined to their back pages. They returned with stories that could leave no reader unmoved. Typical, for instance, was the *World*'s front-page tale, which ran soon after Pulitzer took over, of the destitute and widowed Margaret Graham. She had been seen by dockworkers as she walked on the edge of a pier in the East River with an infant in her arms and a two-year-old girl clutching her skirt. "All at once the famished mother clasped the feeble little girl round her waist and, tottering to the brink of the wharf, hurled both her starving young into the river as it whirled by. She stood for a moment on the edge of the stream. The children were too weak and spent to struggle or to cry. Their little helpless heads dotted the brown tide for an instant, then they sank out of sight. The men who looked on stood spellbound." Graham followed her children into the river but was saved by the onlookers and was taken to jail to face murder charges. For Pulitzer a news story was always a *story*. He pushed his writers to think like Dickens, who wove fiction from the sad tales of urban Victorian London, to create compelling entertainment from the drama of the modern city. To the upper classes, it was sensationalism. To the lower and working classes, it was their life. When they looked at the *World*, they found stories about their world. In the Lower East Side's notorious bars, known as black and tans, or at dinner in their cramped tenements, men and women did not discuss society news, cultural events, or happenings in the investment houses. Rather, the talk was about the baby who fell to his death from a rooftop, the brutal beating that police officers dispensed to an unfortunate waif, or the rising cost of streetcar fares to the upper reaches of Fifth Avenue and the mansions needing servants. The clear, simple prose of the *World* drew in these readers, many of whom were immigrants struggling to master their first words of English. Writing about the events that mattered in their lives in a way they could understand, Pulitzer's *World* gave these New Yorkers a sense of belonging and a sense of value. In one stroke, he simultaneously elevated the common man and took his spare change to fuel the *World*'s profits.

The moneyed class learned to pick up the *World* with trepidation. Each day brought a fresh assault on privilege and another revelation of the squalor and oppression under which the new members of the laboring class toiled. Pulitzer found readers where other newspaper publishers saw a threat. Immigrants were pouring into New York at a rate never before seen. By the end of the decade, 80 percent of the city's population was either foreign-born or of foreign parentage. Only the *World* seemed to consider the stories of this human tide as deserving news coverage. The other papers wrote about it; the *World* wrote for it.

The *World*'s stories were animated not just by the facts the reporters dug up but by the voices of the city they recorded. Pulitzer drove his staff to aggressively seek out interviews, a relatively new technique in journalism pioneered by his brother, among others. Leading figures of the day were used to a considerable wall of privacy and were affronted by what Pulitzer proudly called "the insolence and impertinence of the reporters for the *World*."

Not only did he have the temerity to dispatch his men to pester politicians, manufacturers, bankers, society figures and others for answers to endless questions, but he instructed them to return with specific personal details that would illustrate the resulting articles. Pulitzer was obsessed with details. A tall man was six feet two inches tall. A beautiful woman had auburn hair, hazel eyes, and demure lips that occasionally turned upward in a coy smile. Vagueness was a sin.

As was inaccuracy. A disciple of the independent press movement, Pulitzer was convinced that accuracy built circulation, credibility, and editorial power. Words could paint brides as blushing, murderers as heinous, politicians as venal, but the facts had to be right. "When you go to New York, ask any of the men in the dome to show you my instructions to them, my letters written from day to day, my cables," Pulitzer told an associate late in life. "You will see that accuracy, accuracy, accuracy, is the first and the most urgent, the most constant demand I have made on them."

Pulitzer practically lived at his cramped headquarters on Park Row. Kate and the children hardly ever saw him. His day began with editorial conferences—an editor who came unprepared never repeated the mistake—and ended under the harsh white gaslight as he read and reread proofs for the next morning's edition. When not writing or editing, Pulitzer studied all the New York papers as well as more than a dozen British, German, and French ones. He demanded a great deal from his staff but even more from himself. When he had been in St. Louis, if the paper was dull he would steal home feeling sick. If it met his standard, he would be elated. As spring turned into summer in New York, Pulitzer was feeling elated.

In his first weeks at the *World*, the paper's circulation soared by 35 percent. "Increasing in circulation? You can just bet it is," said a newsstand operator on the corner of Cortland and Greenwich streets. "I used to sell fourteen *Worlds* a day. I now sell thirty-four. If that ain't an increase I don't know what is."

[. . .]

Despite his best efforts the rumors persisted. The *Brooklyn Eagle*, for instance, remarked, Pulitzer "claims that Mr. Gould has nothing to do with the paper, but the claim is simply the rankest sort of nonsense, Mr. Gould still owns the paper."

The rumors were only a nuisance. When he returned from the West, Pulitzer was greeted by proof positive of his success. His competitors had flinched and were cutting their price. The *Tribune* went from four to three cents, the *Times* from four to two, and the *Herald* from three to two. Gloating, Pulitzer proclaimed, "Another victory for the *World*."

As the *World*'s circulation rose each week, Pulitzer sought to use his newfound political leverage to help bring Democrats back to power. From the start he made no pretenses about his plans. "I want to talk to a nation, not to a select committee," he said. Within days of buying the paper, Pulitzer had made his political aims clear and so specific that they formed a ten-point list consisting of only thirty-five words. The first five goals were to tax luxuries, inheritances, large incomes, monopolies, and corporations. The remaining goals were to eliminate protective tariffs, reform the civil service, and punish corrupt government officials and those who bought votes, as well as employers who coerced their employees during elections.

When he returned from his western junket, Pulitzer worked to unite New York's Democrats. In 1880, the party had failed to win the White House when it lost the state by a few thousand votes. Then, Pulitzer had been a bystander. Now that he was in a position of influence in the state, he was determined that 1884 would be different. On September 24, he joined Dana at a rally of Democrats at Cooper Union. With a display of fireworks and a brass band, the Democrats pledged themselves to unity in hopes of ending their quarter-century exile from the White House. Dana, age sixty-four, who was the dean of New York editors, did not object to sharing a stage with his young rival. In May, he had been one of the few publishers in New York to comment favorably on the sale of the *World*, reminding readers that Pulitzer had once been his protégé.

Weeks later, as the Democrats began their usual intra-party bickering, Pulitzer met with the leaders. It seemed to him as if all Democrats in New York were intent on losing the election: he was astonished by the fractious debate on the eve of the voting. One of the veteran party members asked Pulitzer if he knew anything about New York politics. Pulitzer conceded that his experience was limited to Missouri and other midwestern states but added sarcastically that the longer he lived in New York the less able he was to divine the objectives of the city's politicians.

Pulitzer had shed none of his animus toward the Republican Party, which he was convinced was completely under the thumb of robber barons, monopolies, and corporate interests. "These people seem to have an idea that they are superior people—a sort of upper ruling class, and have a right through the power of their money to rule in this country as the upper classes rule in Europe," he said. "But the millions are more powerful than the millionaires."

In November, Pulitzer was so confident of his paper's success that he taunted his rivals by publishing notarized statements of its circulation. The *World*'s average circulation was now 45,000 copies a day. In six months, he had tripled the circulation and forced his rivals to cut their prices. If he continued at this rate, the previously moribund *World* would be the equal of any newspaper on Park Row within the next six months. If not stopped, it would eclipse them all.

At Albert's *Morning Journal*, there was also cause to celebrate. The circulation of his paper had hit 80,000. One year earlier, most New Yorkers had never heard the name Pulitzer. Now the two most talked-about newspapers belonged to the brothers. For Albert, every upward tick in circulation meant more money. For Joseph, it brought money and political power.

# Chapter 14

## LINCOLN STEFFENS

# THE AUTOBIOGRAPHY OF LINCOLN STEFFENS

L INCOLN STEFFENS CAN BE CONSIDERED to be one of America's first "celebrity" reporters. He also set the model for the muckrakers at the turn of the 20th century and is in many ways the epitome of the sophisticated reporter and editor of the period.

After studying at the University of California, Berkeley and then traveling in Europe, Steffens worked at newspapers in New York City and eventually for *McClure's* magazine, where his investigations into urban corruption were part of the movement in journalism that included Ida B. Tarbell and Ray Stannard Baker, prompting President Theodore Roosevelt to coin the term "muckrakers" in a speech he delivered in 1906. The term came from a character in John Bunyan's classic work *Pilgrim's Progress*, "the Man with the Muck-rake" who could look no way but down and was therefore unable to exchange his muck rake for a celestial crown, because he kept his eyes fixed on the filth. The collection of Steffens' articles, *The Shame of the Cities*, published in 1904, became a best seller, and is still a prime exemplar of enterprise journalism.

Published in 1931, *The Autobiography of Lincoln Steffens* traces Steffens' journey from budding intellectual to social reformer who used journalism as his weapon to right wrongs and expose injustice. In the first selection, Steffens recalls his entry into the profession. It offers a colorful look into journalism at the time. The second section tells about his exposé of corruption in St. Louis, the second in what would become "The Shame of the Cities" series. This section is quintessential Steffens, a relatively self-mocking look at his effort. Steffens wrote that he wanted to develop a theory of urban corruption and how to solve it. His editor S.S. McClure, who also owned *McClure's*, the magazine for which Steffens was writing, wanted to sell more magazines.

## I Became a Reporter

When my ship sailed into New York Harbor, my father's agent brought down to quarantine a letter which I still remember, word-perfect, I think.

"My dear son: When you finished school you wanted to go to college. I sent you to Berkeley. When you got through there, you did not care to go into my business; so I sold out. You preferred to continue your studies in Berlin. I let you. After Berlin it was Heidelberg; after that Leipzig. And after the German universities you wanted to study at the French universities in Paris. I consented, and after a year with the French, you had to have half a year of the British Museum in London. All right. You had that too.

"By now you must know about all there is to know of the theory of life, but there's a practical side as well. It's worth knowing. I suggest that you learn it, and the way to study it, I think, is to stay in New York and hustle.

"Enclosed please find one hundred dollars, which should keep you till you can find a job and support yourself."

This letter made me feel as if the ship were sinking under me; I had to swim. I did not know how, not in those waters, but it was not fear that hit me so hard. Nor disappointment. I had no plans to be disturbed. My vague idea was to go home to California and "see" what chance there was, say, at some college, to teach or lecture on the theories of ethics while making a study of morals: the professional ethics and the actual conduct of men in business, politics, and the professions. I could get no academic position in the east, where I was not known, but I might carry on my research as an insider in business just as well as I could as an observer. My wife asked me how I was going to go about getting a job in business and how meanwhile we were to live. For the first time, I think, I realized that I was expected to support my wife and that meanwhile my wife expected my father to help us. And my father would have done it. He said afterward that if he had known that I was married, he would not have thrown me off as he did—for my good, "just to see what you could do for yourself," he said. My wife was for telling him then and there, but I could not. I declared that I would never ask my father for another cent, and I didn't. The next money transaction between us was a loan I made to him.

No, my father was putting me to a test, I said, and I would show him. And my mother-in-law, Mrs. Bontecou, backed me up. She said she would see us through with her little money. Josephine was angry, and, in brief, ours was a gloomy landing-party. I alone was cheerful, secretly; I had an idea. I would write.

At the small hotel Josephine knew, I took pencil and paper and I wrote a short story, "Sweet Punch." That was a Saturday. I did it that day and rewrote and finished it on Sunday. Louis Loeb called that night. He was illustrating for *Harper's Magazine*, and he said he would offer them my story the next day. He sold it to them for fifty dollars. I sat me down to calculate. That story was done and sold in three days. Call it a week. I could make fifty dollars a week, which multiplied by fifty-two was, say, $2500 a year. Enough to live on. But I didn't do another story that week nor the next. Too busy looking for a job, I excused; but the fact was that I couldn't do another for a month, and then the second story was rejected. It was years before I got into the magazines again.

It was weeks before I found a job. I was amazed at the difficulty. There I was, all dressed up in my beautiful morning coat with top hat, answering ads, any ads for anything, from an editorship to errand boy. Literally. The juvenile literature I had read as a boy, about lads who began at the bottom and worked up, had stuck. Here I was, what I had once grieved that I was not, a poor but willing young fellow, without parents, friends, or money, seeking a start in life, just a foothold on the first rung of the ladder: I would, like my boy heroes, attend to the rest. And I couldn't get the chance! I couldn't understand it.

The most urgent ads came from the water front, and I would go into one of those shabby little dirty, dark shops, where they dealt in ship furnishings or produce—dressed like a dude, remember; especially careful to be in my best to make a good first impression—and showing the clipping from the paper, ask for an opening. The shopkeeper would throw himself back in his chair and stare at me and splutter, "But—but do you think you can do the work? It's hard work and—and—are you—qualified? What has been your experience?" And I answered that I had studied at Berkeley, Berlin, Heidelberg, the Sorbonne! And for some reason that seemed to end it.

Those were the days when businessmen were prejudiced against a college education. My father's partners had the prejudice. They warned him that his course with me would ruin me, and I think that it was they who advised him to drop me in New York and see who was right, he or they. Business men have learned since that college does not unfit average young men for anything but an intellectual career; they take them on and will tell you that the colleges are the best source in the world for cheap labor. But in my day, next to my clothes and general beautifulness, the heaviest handicap I had was my claim to a college education, and not only one college, but—five. Some employers dropped their hands and jaw and stared me silently out of their sight; others pushed me out, and others again—two I remember vividly—called in all hands to "see this college graduate that wants to clean the windows and run errands."

My father was right. As I went home to my wife and mother-in-law to describe life as I found it and business men as they found me, I had to confess that I was learning something, that life wasn't what I had expected from my reading. My money was all gone, all the one hundred and also the fifty dollars, and I was paying for myself alone. Mrs. Bontecou paid for her daughter, and soon she was paying for her son-in-law too. I became desperate. My father had given me a letter from the supervising editor of all the Southern Pacific Railroad publications, the monthly magazines, weeklies, and daily newspapers that "the Road" owned or subsidized, to an editor of the *Century Magazine*. I had not used it, because I preferred not to apply "pull." I was for getting my start in life on merit alone. Mrs. Bontecou was with me on that; Josephine was impatient and practical. She pressed me to deliver the letter of introduction, and I did. I asked Mr. Robert Underwood Johnson to give me an editorial position on the *Century*.

He read the letter, pondered, asked me questions, and sized me up. Seeing through my clothes and my story, I guess, he very cautiously asked me if I would be willing to start—just for the practice—to begin my editorial career as—a—reporter. Would I? I certainly would; I would have laid off my top hat to be a copy boy. That cleared the air for him; maybe it stripped off my English clothes. Anyway he offered to get me on either the *Tribune* or the *Evening Post*, and I went home, happy and proud, to discuss with my family the choice I had between those two New York papers.

I can't recall what decided us, but I think it was only that the *Evening Post* was an evening paper; I could be home at night and so have time to do some literary work. However it was, I took a note from Mr. Johnson to Joseph B. Bishop, an editorial writer on the *Post*. Bishop frowned, but he led me out to the city room and introduced me to Henry J. Wright, the city editor, who looked helplessly at me and, I thought, resentfully at Bishop.

"I don't need any more reporters," he said to Bishop, "but," to me, "you can come in next Monday and sit down out there with the reporters, and as I get a chance, I'll try you out—on space."

I didn't know what that meant, but I didn't care. I had a job. As I described it to my wife and her mother, Josephine was not elated as her mother was, and the next Monday when I sat out there in the city room, ignored, while all the world seemed to be in a whirl, I was not elated either. The next day I saw "Larry" Godkin, the editor who wrote the leaders I read and re-read, admiring; he passed by the city door. Bishop nodded to me once, but neither Wright nor the other reporters looked my way. Interesting fellows they seemed to be; they must know all the mysteries of a great city. They did not talk much, but I overheard enough to infer that they were familiar and bored with sport, politics, finance, and society. I was awed by the way they would, upon a few words from the city editor, dart or loaf out of the room, be gone an hour or so, come in, report briefly, and then sit down, write, turn in their copy carelessly, and lie back and read, idly read, newspapers.

One afternoon about one o'clock Mr. Wright came into the room, and seeing no one there but me, exclaimed impatiently and went out. A moment later he came back and right up to me.

"See here," he said, "there's a member of a stock brokerage firm missing. Disappeared utterly. Something wrong. Go and see his partner and find out why the man is gone, whether there's funds missing, too."

He handed me a memorandum giving the firm name and address in Wall Street. An assignment! I was to report. I darted out of the office into the elevator, and asking anybody for directions, found my way to Wall Street—Wall Street!—and the office of the lost broker. His partner rebuffed me. "No, I don't know why he skipped. No idea. No, nothing missing. How should there be?" But I wasn't going to fail on my first chance; so I persisted, asking questions, all about the missing man, his character, antecedents, habits, and when that caused only irritation, I asked about Wall Street. The broker soon was talking; we moved into his private office, sat down, and I told him the story of my life; he told me his, and I was thinking all the time how I could write something inter- esting about the ethics of a stock broker; I had long since been convinced that the missing broker was innocent of anything more than a drink or an escapade with a woman, when all of a sudden the partner sprang up and said: "Well, you are the most persistent son of a gun I ever met in all my life, and you win. I'll give you what you seem so damn sure of anyhow. My — — partner has not only skipped, I don't know where; he has taken every cent there was in the office, in the banks, and—then some." He named the amount, and I, astonished by the revelation, but satisfied that I had a front-page sensation, ran back to the office, where I astonished my city editor.

"Really?" he said. "You are sure? It's libel, you know, if it's wrong. He told you himself, the partner did? Sure? Umh—Well, write it, and we'll see."

I had pencils all sharpened—sharpened every day—ready for this moment, and I went to work. It was easy enough to report the facts, but I felt I must write this big news as the news was written. That I had studied in my idle hours, the newspaper style, and that was not easy. I labored till the city editor darted out to see what I was doing; he saw; he read over my shoulder the writes and re-writes of my first paragraph, and picking up one, said, "This is enough." And away he went with it. All I had to do was to lie back in a chair and wait to read my stuff in print, a long wait, perhaps half an hour, till three o'clock, when the last edition went to press, and then twenty minutes before the paper came down. And then when it came down, the damp, smelly paper, my paragraph wasn't in it! I searched again and again, with anxiety, hope, dread. I did not care for the money; the space was too short to count, but I felt that my standing as a reporter was at stake, and so, when I was at last convinced that my "story" was left out, I got up and dragged home, defeated and in despair. I told Mrs. Bontecou about it, not my wife, and was comforted some. If I failed at journalism, the old lady argued, there still was literature.

The facts of my story appeared in the morning newspapers, but they were better, more neatly, briefly stated, than I had put them; perhaps I had failed, not as a reporter, but as a writer. And this conclusion was confirmed at the office, where the city editor said "Good morning" to me and, after all the other reporters were gone out, gave me an assignment to ask the Superintendent of Schools something. One more chance.

Braced to make the most of it, I gave that official a bad hour. He had to answer, not only the question the city editor asked, but others, many others. He found himself telling me all about the schools, education and its problems, and his policy. I had some ideas on that subject, and he got them; and he had to accept or refute them. He became so interested that, when he had to break off, I was invited to come back another day to "continue our conversation." Good. I returned to the office and wrote a column interview, beginning with the city editor's question and the answer. This time, when the paper came out it had my story, but cut down to the first question and answer, rewritten as an authoritative statement of fact. My reporting was all right; my writing was not. The next day, a Friday, I had to go out, confirm a reported suicide, and telephone the news, which another reporter took down and wrote.

That afternoon I saw reporters clipping from the cut files of the *Post*. I asked what it was for, and one of them said he was making up his bill. He cut out his own stories, stuck them together in a long strip, and measuring them with a foot-rule, reckoned up the amount of space and charged for it so much a column. I did the same, and my poor little bill of earnings for my first week of practical life was something like two dollars and ten cents. And I was not ashamed of it; I was reassured, if not proud.

Nor was that all. As I was finishing this task the city editor called me up to his desk and bade me rewrite as a separate story for the Saturday paper the interview I had had with the Superintendent of Schools during the week. He suggested the idea or theme to write it around, and I, elated, stayed there in the office till closing-time, grinding out my first long "story." And the next day I had the deep gratification of reading it at full length, the whole thing as I had written it. I measured it, secretly, and it came to four dollars plus—a fine start for my next week.

That Sunday was a bore; I could hardly wait for Monday to go on with my reporting, and talking with my wife and her mother, I developed ideas and plans. There were several promising questions to put to the Superintendent of Schools; the news suggested other men to see and talk to, and no doubt now the city editor himself would ask me to do more. When I walked into the office on Monday morning, eager and confident, I was dashed by the way I was ignored. No greetings from anybody, and as the morning wore on and the other reporters were sent off on assignments, I realized heavily that I was not to be used. I took my hat and told the city editor I would like to go out on a quest of my own. He nodded consent, and I went and had with the Superintendent of Schools a long interview which I wrote and handed in. It did not appear in the paper, and for two days I was ignored and got nothing out of my own assignments. The men I tried to see were not in or would not see me. I had the experience so common for reporters of being defeated, and in an obscure way, too. Toward the end of the week I was sent out to see a Rapid Transit Commissioner and got some news which pleased the city editor: a formal, printed statement, which was printed. That was all. My space bill was about six dollars. But on Saturday, too late to be included, appeared my interview with the Superintendent of Schools.

With this to start with again, I could live over Sunday and was ready to dive on Monday into my journalism. I had to be my own city editor, but I could be, now. I got another school story, which was printed; it was news; and another which was held, I knew now, for Saturday. I called again on the Rapid Transit Commissioner, and he gave me a brief interview which I used to tempt the other Commissioners to answer. That was news and appeared right away. So was a statement by the Mayor which I went for all by myself. Somebody had said something in print that was critical in a small way of some department, and his office being open to the public, I walked in and talked to him about it. My bill that week was something like fifteen dollars.

My system was working, and, I learned afterward, was amusing the staff and interesting the city editor, who described it as I could not have described it. It was a follow-up system, well known in journalism but unknown to me as a method. Every time I was sent to or met a man in a position to furnish news, I cultivated him as a source and went back repeatedly to him for more news or more general views on the news. If there was a news story in the papers, and not too big, I would read it through for some angle overlooked and slip out to the persons involved and ask some questions. My contribution often appeared as a part of some other reporter's story, usually at the end, but several times as the lead. And always there were school news articles from my Superintendent, who was talking policy to me weekly and letting me visit and write about schools. These articles brought letters to the editor, which showed that we were tapping a field of interest. I had a free hand here till, later, there was an education department which included the universities and private schools, and so brought in advertising. But there was the Art Museum, too, to "cover" and report; Rapid Transit with its plans, not only for transportation in the city, but for real estate, park, and street development. Every time the city editor sent me into a field for a bit of news I got what he wanted and went back for more general reports. He used me very little, however, leaving me to my own devices; and his reason came out when, after a few months, my bills were running up to fifty, sixty, and more dollars a week, and the other reporters were taking rather unfriendly notice of me.

One Friday, as I was making out my bill, William G. Sirrene, a fine southern boy who was one of the star reporters, looked over my shoulder and exclaimed, "What's that? Seventy-two dollars! Why, that's nearly three times what I'm getting on salary."

He called out to the others the amount of my bill, and when they also exclaimed, he explained: "Why, you are the best-paid man on the staff!"

I felt like exclaiming myself. It was news to me. I had no knowledge of salaries or earnings on the paper; all I knew was that I was supporting myself and my wife at last, saving a little each week, and driving on for more, and more. And I would have given it all to be a regular reporter like Sirrene or the others, and that is what I was asked to do. I think now that some of the reporters, not Sirrene, "kicked" to the city editor that I, a new man, was being paid more than they were, the veterans. Anyway he sent for me, and explaining that my bills were running too high, asked me if I would be changed from space to a salary, the best salary they paid the ordinary reporter, $35 a week.

"Then," he said, "I can use you more myself on more important news."

I not only consented, I was dazed with the implication of my triumph. All became clear in that short talk with my chief. I had not been sent off on assignments because I was making too much money on my own and I had "made good." Even my first disappointment, the failure to print my news of the defalcation of the missing broker, was to my credit. The city editor did not dare print the report, by a new and untried man, of a piece of libelous news; he had sent an old reporter down to confirm it, and the broker who had talked to me not only repeated what he told me; he had spoken well of me; but by the time the confirmation was delivered, it was too late. The paper was gone to press. I was "reliable, quick, and resourceful," the city editor said, as he made me a regular reporter.

In a word I was a success, and though I have never since had such a victory and have come to have some doubt of the success of success, I have never since failed to understand successful men; I know, as I see them, how they feel inside.

[. . .]


# V

## The Shamelessness of St. Louis

When Circuit Attorney Folk confirmed my theory that there was organized police corruption in St. Louis as well as boodling business, I was eager to go on to another city to see if the same system of graft existed there—Chicago, for example. Enough was known of Chicago and Philadelphia to indicate that they would come up to standard, but it would not be scientific, sportsmanlike, or convincing to choose such sure things.

"Did I hear you say you were going to walk to the station?" a downtown hotel clerk asked me in Chicago one night. "Don't do it. It isn't safe. Take a cab."

Chicago was very tempting. Mr. McClure urged me to do it next, for editorial reasons. My article on Minneapolis had succeeded beyond all expectations. The newsstand sales had exhausted the printed supply; subscriptions were coming in; and the mail was bringing letters of praise, appreciation, and suggestion. "Come here to this place," they wrote from many cities, towns, and even villages; "you will find scandals that will make Minneapolis and St. Louis look like models of good government."

"Evidently," I argued with the editor-in-chief, "you could shoot me out of a gun fired at random and, wherever I lighted, there would be a story, the same way."

My mind was on my theory, but Mr. McClure's was on our business; we must increase the sensationalism of our articles if we were to hold and reap our advantage. We must find some city, like Chicago or Philadelphia, that was worse than St. Louis and Minneapolis. The disagreement became acute; it divided the office and might have caused trouble had not Miss Ida M. Tarbell made peace, as she so often did thereafter. Sensible, capable, and very affectionate, she knew each one of us and all our idiosyncrasies and troubles. She had none of her own so far as we ever heard. When we were deadlocked we might each of us send for her, and down she would come to the office, smiling, like a tall, good-looking young mother, to say, "Hush, children." She would pick out the sense in each of our contentions, and putting them together with her own good sense, give me a victory over S.S., him a triumph over Phillips, and take away from all of us only the privilege of gloating. The interest of the magazine was pointed out, and we and she went back to work. In this case she saw and reminded us that there was plenty of time to decide on the next place to choose. Meanwhile St. Louis was to be done again and more thoroughly. I wanted to trace and comprehend for myself the ramifications of this typical, invisible government of the American city; the magazine wanted to publish the further revelations of Mr. Folk's later inquiries and, by the way, to help elect this man governor of Missouri. We made a vague compromise, therefore. I was to write little or nothing of my theory, stick to facts, and then, St. Louis done, we would choose almost any place I liked for our fourth city.

This was good journalism. S. S. McClure was a good journalist, one of the best I ever knew, and he knew it, and he knew why. One day when I returned to him a manuscript he had asked me to read and pass upon, he picked up, glanced at, and dropped unread into the waste-basket a long memorandum I had written. "What's this?" he demanded. "A review? I don't want your literary criticism of a manuscript. All I ask of you is whether you like it or not." Seeing that I was miffed, he explained.

"Look," he said. "I want to know if you enjoy a story, because, if you do, then I know that, say, ten thousand readers will like it. If Miss Tarbell likes a thing, it means that fifty thousand will like it. That's something to go by. But I go most by myself. For if I like a thing, then I know that millions will like it. My mind and my taste are so common that I'm the best editor." He paused, smiled, and slowly, reluctantly added, "There's only one better editor than I am, and that's Frank Munsey. If he likes a thing, then everybody will like it."

Mr. McClure was interested in facts, startling facts, not in philosophical generalizations. He hated, he feared, my dawning theory. He had his own theories, like his readers. They differed among themselves, but they were sure, every one of them. I alone did not know. I alone was not to give my theory. That was our agreement. When I entered into it, however, I made a mental reservation that while I would indeed load my new article on St. Louis with the libelous, dangerous, explosive facts in Folk's possession, I would aim them and the whole story, like a gun, at the current popular theories (including Mr. McClure's); and, I hoped, blow them out of the way for a statement later of my own diagnosis, when I was ready to frame one. I was a good shot in those days. I could write to the understanding and hit the convictions of the public because I shared or had so recently shared them.

I have told how, as the boy chum of a page in the Legislature of California, I had seen from below the machinery and bribery of politics; as a New York reporter I had seen police, political, legislative, and judicial corruption; but I did with these observations what other people do with such disturbing knowledge: I put them off in a separate compartment of the brain. I did not let them alter my conception of life. My picture of the world as it seemed to be was much the same as my readers'. It was this that made me a pretty good journalist; it is this that makes good journalism. The reporter and the editor must sincerely share the cultural ignorance, the superstitions, the beliefs, of their readers, and keep no more than one edition ahead of them. You may beat the public to the news, not to the truth.

The leading question raised in my second article on St. Louis was, "Is democracy a failure?" A trick, a political trick! I had no doubt that the people could and would govern themselves, and Folk had none. The question was put only to appeal to the pride and the loyalty of the voters. Folk had shown, and I wrote, how they were herded into parties—the majority of them; how they were led to transfer to the party machines the loyalty they owed to their city, State, and the United States; how they were fooled thus, into voting straight for the nominees of a bi-partisan or a non-partisan gang of known grafters, who controlled both machines and won elections by swinging the purchasable votes of the minority of worst citizens to the worst ticket; and how these leading grafters used their power to sell out franchises, permissions, and other valuable grants and public properties to the highest bidders, sometimes "good" local business men, sometimes "bad" New York and other "foreign" financiers. Folk had learned, and I reported, that these crooked politicians had intended to sell the Union Market, the old Court House, and the water works. Nor had they given up these plans. The water works—the water supply of the city—was estimated to be worth forty millions by the boodlers, who proposed to let it go for fifteen millions and so make a million each for the fifteen members of the ring.

## The Shamelessness of St. Louis

*Something New in the History of American Municipal Democracy*

## By Lincoln Steffens

*Author of "The Shame of Minneapolis"*

Tweed's classic question, "What are you going to do about it?" is the most humiliating challenge ever delivered by the One Man to the Many. But it was pertinent. It was the question then; it is the question now. Will the people rule? That is what it means. Is democracy possible? The recent accounts in this magazine, of financial corruption in St. Louis and of police corruption in Minneapolis raised the same question. They were inquiries into American municipal democracy, and, so far as they went, they were pretty complete. I have organized to keep it safe, and make the memory of "Doc" Ames a civic treasure, and Minneapolis a city without reproach.

### What St. Louis "Did About It"

Minneapolis may fail, as New York has failed; but at least these two cities could be moved by shame. Not so St. Louis. Joseph W. Folk, the circuit attorney, who began alone is going right on alone, indicting, trying, convicting boodlers, high and low, following the workings of the combine through all of its startling

> *McClure's Magazine*, March, 1903
> "The scheme was to do it and skip," said one of the gang to me, "and if you could mix it all up with some filtering scheme, it could be done. . . . It will be done some day."

This we printed, and the facts that these very men, confessing, indicted, some of them on trial, still sat in the municipal council; that they were going on with their grafting there and fighting Folk step by step; that they were organizing the next political campaign to beat him and keep their places, their power, and carry out their piratical plans. *McClure's Magazine* "told the world" all this that St. Louis knew better and in more detail than "we" did, in the hope and in the faith that the citizens of St. Louis would rise up and vindicate the democracy which the American people, Folk, and I believed in. Yes, I too believed in political democracy even while I was observing that all political signs indicated that the boodle gang would defeat Folk if he ran for reelection as circuit attorney in St. Louis, and therefore was advising him to appeal over the heads of the people of St. Louis to the people of Missouri by running for governor! What about the mind of man that can see and think that way? My mind, for example. My brain is at least human. What sort of organ is it that can face all the facts against a belief and still stick to its belief?

Folk had his case against Ed Butler, the boss, transferred from the courts of St. Louis to Columbia, the university town of Missouri. I went there to see that trial, and I felt the sentiment for Folk. It was expressed in chiseled words over the old court house: "Oh, Justice, when driven from other habitations, make this thy dwelling-place." Folk did not attack Butler; he handled his case as if democracy and Missouri were on trial, not the boss, and his final plea, almost whispered, was for "Missouri, Missouri." The boss was convicted. The people were all right—in Missouri. But back in St. Louis they were not right. The first comment I heard there when we all returned was the obstinate declaration, everywhere repeated, that "Butler would never wear the stripes." The boss himself behaved wisely. He stayed indoors for a few weeks—till a committee of citizens from the best residence section called upon him to come out and put through the House of Delegates a bill for the improvement of a street in their neighborhood. And Butler had this done. One of the first greetings to Folk was a warning from a high source that now at length he had gone far enough. He paid no heed to this. He proceeded to the trial of other cases. One of them was of Henry Nicolaus, a rich brewer, for bribery. Mr. Nicolaus pleaded that he did not know what was to be the use of a note for $140,000 which he had endorsed. Pretty bad? The judge immediately took the case from the jury and directed a verdict of not guilty. This was the first case Folk had lost; he won the next eight, making his record fourteen won to one lost. But the Supreme Court took up the fight. Slowly, one by one, then by wholesale, this highest court of appeal reversed the boodle cases. The machinery of justice broke down under the strain of boodle pull. And the political machinery did not break down. The bi-partisan gang, with reformers and business men for backers, united on a boodle ticket, elected it, and—Boss Butler reorganized the "new" House of Delegates with his man for speaker and the superintendent of his garbage plant (in the interest of which he offered the bribe for which he was convicted) for chairman of the Sanitary Committee!

What was the matter? Folk and I asked that question many a time, without finding or framing an answer to it. And all that time we were acting upon the answer, which we must have had in our nervous system somewhere; it simply did not take the form of words in our brains. Our talks were all in the course of making up speeches for his campaign in Missouri for governor of the State, things for him to say to the people of Missouri to persuade them to save him from defeat at the hands of the people of St. Louis. We knew in our bones, and those addresses of Joe Folk to Missouri will show that we knew, that the voters of the State were in that stage of mental innocence which the voters of St. Louis were in when the disclosures of corruption began there. They thought they were innocent; they thought that bad men were deceiving and misleading them; they did not know that they themselves were involved and interested in the corruption. St. Louis found out. Missouri would find out some day, too. When that day came, as it did, then the people of the State would unite with the citizens of St. Louis to stop Folk and his interference with their business.

The people of St. Louis, like the people of Minneapolis and New York, were against bribery in the abstract, and against the corruption that involved the police, vice, and petty politicians. They backed reformers who attacked these petty evils. When Folk went on to discover that not only Ed Butler's garbage business but the franchises of public service corporations were linked up with garbage and gambling and prostitution, some of the people turned against Folk. They had stock or friends who held stock in these companies and so could see that they did not belong with what they called the honest citizenry. Therefore Folk had to appeal to the people of Missouri. And they elected him governor before he had gone so far that they saw that they were in it. Then Folk had the people of the United States behind him. He was a possibility for president at one time after he was governor of Missouri, when he could not have been reëlected governor of Missouri.

What did this all mean? What was this system? Folk and I could not answer this question either. Like the other question, we knew the answer, but we didn't want to face it—not clearly. I'm sure Folk didn't. One day I saw a book on his living-room table, *Social Problems* by Henry George. He saw me see it; we had just been wondering together about the nature and the cure of political corruption.

"That book explains the whole thing," Folk said.

"Have you read it?" I asked.

"No," he said: "I read into it enough to see that that man has it all sized up, and—I dropped it, as I did another book a socialist brought me."

"Why?" I demanded, astonished.

"Oh," said Folk, "if I once got socialism or any other cut-and-dried solution into my head, I'd be ruined—politically. Couldn't get anywhere. But you are not in politics. Why don't you read them?"

I gave him my reason, which was different from his, much better, I thought. My reason was that I had not only read, I had studied those books under a regular professor of political economy at college, and so knew that there was nothing in them. As Folk was to go on blundering to a career, so I was to go on "scientifically" to trace the system and see if it was the same in other cities as in St. Louis, Minneapolis, and New York.

# Chapter 15

## VICKI GOLDBERG

# MARGARET BOURKE WHITE: A BIOGRAPHY

MARGARET BOURKE WHITE was a pioneering photojournalist. The first staff photographer for *Fortune* magazine, Bourke White was also the first staff photographer for *Life* magazine when it was launched in 1936. Her image of the Fort Peck Dam in Montana was on the cover of *Life*'s first issue. *Life* quickly emerged as the most significant outlet for photojournalism in the country and Bourke White played a significant role in shaping the look of the magazine and the contours of photojournalism generally. Born in 1904, Bourke White first demonstrated her talent for photography while she was a student at Cornell University, where she would sell photos of the campus and its scenic surroundings to other students. After her graduation, she opened a studio in Cleveland, Ohio, where she specialized in architectural photography. Her image of the Otis Steel factory caught the eye of Henry Luce, the founder of *Life, Fortune, Time* and eventually other major magazines. Luce invited her to join the staff of *Fortune* magazine, a new publication devoted to reporting on the "glamour" of business. Through her experiences on *Fortune* and then *Life*, which popularized the photoessay as a genre, Bourke White came to see photography not just as an artistic activity but a vital medium to inform the public. She was the first Western photographer to document the industrial rise of the Soviet Union (that was made up of Russia and a number of other now-independent countries) with her photos appearing in the book *Eyes on Russia*. In 1936, in conjunction with the best-selling author Erskine Caldwell, she created a photo essay about the social conditions in the South. The work was published in the book *You Have Seen Their Faces* in 1937.

During World War II, Bourke White served as a war correspondent for *Life* and the U.S. Air Force. She was with General George Patton when he opened the gates to the Buchenwald concentration camp, revealing the horrors to the world. After the war, she traveled to South Africa and exposed the cruelty of apartheid and later photographed the Korean War. She died of Parkinson's disease in 1971. These selections recount the founding of *Life* magazine and her influence on its development.

## *Life* Begins

*The great revolutions of journalism are not revolutions in public opinion, but revolutions in the way in which public opinion is formed. The greatest of these, a revolution greater even than the revolution of the printing press . . . is the revolution of the camera.*

*. . . But it is also a revolution which has not been brought to use. Magazines and newspapers have made use of photographs, but not in their own terms. Photographs have been used as illustrations, but the camera no longer illustrates. The camera tells. . . . The camera shall take its place as the greatest and by all measurements the most convincing reporter of contemporary life.*

Archibald MacLeish, telegram to Henry Luce, June 29, 1936

The advent of the picture magazine amounted to a triumph for photography as an instrument of communication. It happened in the late twenties in Europe, in 1936 in America. Before *Life*, none of the illustrated periodicals in this country gave the news (or any other kind of story) principally and coherently in photographs. From 1914 on, the *New York Times* published a magazine called *Midweek Pictorial* that relayed events in pictures as the Sunday rotogravure sections did, but the photographs had little relation to each other and virtually no narrative thrust. In the late twenties and early thirties, several picture publications were launched without adequate planning or technology; they failed to fly. *Eyes on the World: A Photographic Record of History in the Making*, published in 1935 (with a frontispiece and numerous pictures by Margaret Bourke-White), was meant to inaugurate an annual photographic history of the world. There never was a second issue.

For some years photographs had been gaining a steadily stronger hold on the public imagination and playing a more crucial role in the communication of news. In 1919, the *New York Daily News*, then called the *Illustrated Daily News*, published its first issue, with a front page full of pictures; its logo was a winged camera. Within two years the *News* had the biggest circulation in New York; within five, the biggest of any daily paper in America.

In 1925, the Cowles brothers, using a new polling technique developed by a young man named George Gallup, discovered that the reader of the *Des Moines Register and Tribune* had a high level of interest in pictures and an even higher interest in groups of related pictures. When the poll results were applied to the rotogravure section, circulation increased by 50 percent. In 1937, a mere two months after *Life* appeared, the Cowleses brought out *Look* magazine.

As usual, technological advances had contributed to the changing appetites and attitudes of the culture: the small camera, faster emulsions, improved presses and engraving methods, a wire service to transmit the new photographs everywhere. By 1924, halftones were being sent by wire from Cleveland to New York; by 1935, the Associated Press Wire Service had networked the newspapers of the country.

Picture agencies arose in the twenties to ride the swelling tide of photographs. Ralph Ingersoll, who played a large role in shaping *Life*, wrote in May of 1936 that each week in New York, five thousand original photographs were offered for sale. Most, he said, were cheesecake, publicity shots, or bodies rudely interrupted by bullets, for "the only two members of the Fourth Estate to recognize the potency of the picture today are the press agent and the tabloid editor."

In the thirties, newsreels grew astonishingly popular. Time Inc. itself gave them a vital boost. Beginning in 1931, the radio version of *The March of Time* recreated current events, with actors impersonating the major figures, then in early '35, *The March of Time* came to the screen as a monthly newsreel, combining actual newsreel footage with reenactments of those few scenes no movie photographer had had the foresight to sneak into. *The March of Time* tackled critical issues the industry had previously neglected: Germany's rearmament, Nazi persecution of the Jews, Wendell Willkie arguing against the new TVA.

Within fourteen months, *The March of Time* was playing monthly to an estimated international audience of fifteen million. In 1936, Time Inc. touted its newsreels in a book called *Four Hours a Year*. Essentially photographic and designed to show advertisers how successfully the company had experimented with photojournalism, *Four Hours a Year* was also intended as a kind of preparation for *Life*.

By 1938, an observer could write that "it was safe to say that the average citizen acquired most of his news through the medium of pictures. Over twenty million Americans go to the movies each day of the week and the newsreel is a regular part of every motion picture program." Theaters that showed newsreels exclusively increased in number throughout the decade. The newsreel mania prefigured one aspect of our present camera-dominated society: a historian remarked that "Finally, by the late 1930's and the early 1940's, many scheduled events, such as political appearances, conventions, and campaigns were staged by their protagonists in such a manner as to conform to the requirements of newsreel coverage."

The world's new and crying hunger for photographs was so evident that everyone wanted to start a picture magazine. Ralph Ingersoll says that while he was working on plans for *Life*, he discovered that every ad agency in New York had a blueprint for just such a magazine in the top desk drawer. When Henry Luce first met Clare Boothe Brokaw at a dinner party in 1934, she told him that in 1931 when she was at *Vanity Fair* she'd prepared a dummy of a picture magazine and called it "Life."

Luce himself tested the limits of magazine photography long before he was certain that picture magazines were feasible. *Fortune*, as *Four Hours a Year* claimed, had given the camera "a greater opportunity than it had ever had before." *Time*, which in the twenties had relied on head shots alone, began to experiment (on Luce's orders) with multiple pictures of events as early as 1933, expanded its picture coverage in '34, and in February of '35 published the first candid photographs of FDR.

Luce established the first experimental department to plot a picture magazine in 1933 but disbanded it seven months later. At the end of '35, the second and final department swung into action. It was powered by a technical breakthrough.

R. R. Donnelley & Sons Company, printers for *Time*, had developed a fast-drying ink that could print on coated paper run through rotary presses. That meant that photographs could be better reproduced in quantity on better paper and at less cost than had ever been possible before. The printers were still uncertain the process would work; the innovation was such a closely held secret that company policemen guarded the plant until the day the first issue of the new magazine hit the stands.

Luce had decided the world needed a picture magazine. In May of '36, in the first draft of a prospectus for *Life*, he wrote: "We have got to educate people to take pictures seriously, and to respect pictures as they do not now do. . . . While people love pictures, they do not respect them." The final prospectus, written one month later, began with these words:

> To see life; to see the world; to eyewitness great events; to see strange things—machines, armies, multitudes, shadows in the jungle and on the moon, to see man's work—his paintings, towers and discoveries; to see things thousands of miles away, things hidden behind walls and within

rooms, things dangerous to come to; the women that men love and many children; to see and to take pleasure in seeing; to see and be amazed; to see and be instructed.

Thus to see, and to be shown, is now the will and new expectancy of half mankind

Margaret went to work for *Life* a mere two months before it began publication. The last notes from her southern trip were made on August 12, 1936. On August 13, NEA terminated its contract with her—a calamity from which fate immediately plucked for her a new and yet more brilliant career.

"I think the best thing in the world was that fiasco over Earl Browder," Peggy Sargent says. "If it hadn't happened she'd have been tied up with a year's contract with NEA and couldn't have got out of it to work for *Life*." On September 4, a bare two weeks later, Margaret signed a contract to work exclusively for Time Inc. ten months a year for twelve thousand dollars per annum, with two months free to do any work that did not compete with the company's publications. By then, *Life* had a name but little else, Luce having just bought a faltering humor magazine called *Life* for its title.

It was something of a miracle that the first issue of the magazine came out at all. On October 23, Luce removed the editor who had been overseeing the creation of *Life*, summoned John Shaw Billings into his office, and asked him to step in as managing editor. Billings, then managing editor of *Time*, had had virtually no experience with pictures and was perhaps the only editor in all of Time Inc. who had not yet worked on the new magazine. Seventeen days before the first issue was to go to press, he took over.

Proper, austere, and impassive at work, Billings never removed his suit jacket and almost never said hello—"on an average, a new employee did not get spoken to for about a year," according to Edward K. Thompson, who would later be managing editor himself. Billings commanded enormous respect. He was by turns remote and paternal; for either side of him, his staff performed prodigies of work. Some found him terrifying, but Margaret admired him greatly and feared him not at all; she was impressed with his "cloak of Olympian calm."

John Shaw Billings cared more about news and more about visual impact than he did about aesthetics. He is said to have made no sharp distinction between news and features, so that the early years of *Life* (he was managing editor from '36 to '44) were a vigorous, sometimes raucous, and often visually unsophisticated mix. As it happened, he turned out to have a genius for pictures; he could pick the best photographs with the speed and decisiveness of a photographer snapping candids. *Life* was Billings's magazine, cobbled together on deadline each week by his authority, his tough-mindedness, his tastes, and his intuitions. He is thought by many to be the greatest editor the magazine ever had.

His picture editor was Dan Longwell, a breezy, fidgety Nebraskan "with the wind blowing through his armpits" and an aristocratic face, Longwell cared about fashion, art, society, theater, aesthetics—all the areas Billings did not cover. Newspaper clippings on the latest trends overflowed from his every pocket. Longwell had a new idea every minute, and if for one minute he did not, he borrowed one from someone with a deeper mind. "Longwell's mind was essentially that of an entertainer, not a thinker," according to *Life*'s Maitland Edey; he sounds like the ideal man for a mass-circulation magazine.

Early on, Longwell had recognized the significance of the 35 mm camera. Luce hired him in '34 to increase *Time*'s picture coverage, which he did promptly. Margaret was as devoted to Longwell as to Billings, and she had reason, for he later recalled that he had hired her, as well as the photographer Alfred Eisenstaedt, a recent émigré from Germany with extensive experience with 35 mm, at salaries higher than his own. *Life* had four photographers on the masthead of the first issue, and three of them were 35 mm men: Eisenstaedt, Tom McAvoy, and Peter Stackpole. Margaret was the only woman as well as the only big-camera photographer. *Life* needed to balance the small camera's journalistic spontaneity with the art and monumentality of Bourke-White's studied compositions.

Henry Luce himself gave Margaret her first assignment. He wanted photographs of the great chain of dams that the Public Works Administration (PWA) was constructing in the Columbia River Basin to control flooding. Longwell fished a clipping about the revival of frontier life in New Deal, Montana, out of one of his capacious pockets and suggested she stop off there. Fort Peck, the world's largest earth-filled dam, was rising at New Deal, a boom town that had sprung up around the construction.

Margaret went west in late October, about two weeks before the deadline for the new magazine. Her schedule was not impossibly tight, for her assignment was simply to bring back pictures for the magazine's inventory. Accustomed to the magniloquence of dams, she nonetheless discovered that New Deal had certain unique advantages. On October 27 she cabled Longwell: "SWELL SUBJECTS, ESPECIALLY SHANTY TOWNS GETTING GOOD NIGHT LIFE NOBODY CAMERA SHY EXCEPT LADIES OF EVENING BUT HOPE CONQUER THEM ALSO STOP TAKING AIR SHOTS TODAY EXPECT FINISH TOMORROW." (The ladies of the evening were shy because some of them had told their families they'd gone west to take jobs as typists. Their customers were equally shy, and once, after Margaret had photographed some taxi dancers and their partners, a full-scale brawl backed into a corner; she was rescued by a flying wedge of construction workers.)

In New York, where Billings had been at the helm less than a week, the magazine was in magnificent disarray. There was no cover, no lead story, nothing for the section called "*Life* Goes to a Party." Longwell cabled her on the thirtieth: "HAVE YOU GOT GOOD FORT PECK NIGHT LIFE PICS SEND DETAILED INFORMATION ON WHAT YOU HAVE UP AGAINST IT FOR PARTY DEPARTMENT FIRST ISSUE FORT PECK MIGHT BE SWELL IF NECESSARY GO BACK THERE AND TAKE MORE."

Margaret wired back the next day: "THINK FORT PECK NIGHT LIFE WILL BE VERY GOOD OF SEVERAL BAR SCENES CROWDS WATCHING BOWLING BILLIARDS TAXI DANCERS AT WORK TWO OR THREE HARD SNAPS OF PROSTITUTES ALSO EXTERIORS THEIR ESTABLISHMENTS ALSO FAMOUS RUBY SMITH WITH HER BOY FRIENDS ALSO TYPICAL SHANTY TOWN ORCHESTRA ALSO ASSORTED DRUNKS." Longwell was pleased: "GOOD WORK NIGHT LIFE. . . . WANT TO USE AS PARTY IF YOU HAVE ANY EXTRA ONES SHOOT THEM TO ME." That was November 3. *Life* now had a party story, but still no lead and no cover.

On the fifth of November, twenty-four hours before the final deadline, the rest of Margaret's film packs arrived in the office. Ralph Ingersoll took one look at them, carried them straight to Luce's office, spread the photographs out on the floor, and said to Luce, "There's your lead story." Ingersoll and Luce themselves pasted it up, Ingersoll drafted Archibald MacLeish to write the captions in a hurry, and the first lead story of the first true picture magazine in America squeaked past deadline onto the presses.

The staff was astonished to see Margaret's pictures. Turbines and pylons were her forte; no one expected human interest from her. Yet there were the dime-a-dance girls, their eager suitors, and the drinking crew at the Bar X, where the waitress's four-year-old daughter spent the evening sitting on the bar.

The editors were unaware of the extent of Margaret's preparation for a journalistic career. On the introductory page of the issue, opposite a picture of a newborn baby that was captioned "LIFE BEGINS," they wrote:

> If any Charter Subscriber is surprised by what turned out to be the first story in this first issue of LIFE, he is not nearly so surprised as the Editors were. Photographer Margaret Bourke-White had been dispatched to the Northwest to photograph the multi-million dollar projects of the Columbia River Basin. What the Editors expected—for use in some later issue— were construction pictures as only Bourke-White can take them. What the Editors got was a human document of American frontier life which, to them at least, was a revelation.

The lead was settled on November 5. On November 6, Luce picked the photograph to go on the first cover. What he chose was Margaret's picture of Fort Peck Dam. Typically, she had placed two tiny figures of workmen in the foreground to give the scene scale; the dam looked as big as eternity itself. The original photograph was a horizontal shot with a lot of unfinished construction on the left-hand side; the editors cut the image in half so that the cover would show only the mighty repeating forms of an engineering marvel.

Margaret was still out West working on what she thought was "*Life* Goes to a Party" while these decisions were being made. She had gone to the little town of Corvallis, Oregon, to stay for a couple of days with Gil, her first boyfriend. He was married, with three rambunctious children under the age of six, but Margaret brought a new level of turmoil into the house. She was dressed beyond the ambitions of Corvallis; people turned and stared at her on the street. She wore a gray Paris suit with red accessories; when *Life* came out a fortnight later, with Margaret's black-and-white photograph of the dam on the cover, bracketed by wide red bands, Gil's wife decided that Margaret had looked like a walking *Life* magazine.

Cables sped continuously into the Gilfillan household. One told Margaret she had the lead, another that she had the cover. A cable from Longwell on November 13 establishes that *Life*'s perennial emphasis on American success was in the program from the beginning: "FRANKLIN ROOSEVELT'S WILD WEST AT WHEELER MONTANA RAN AWAY WITH THE FIRST ISSUE STOP ITS MAGNIFICENT BUT CANT MAINTAIN PROLETARIAN STRAIN THROUGHOUT YOUR SERIES NEED SIGNS OF PROSPERITY INDUSTRY BOOM ETCETERA NEED INDUSTRIAL BIG ACTIVITY ASPECTS NOW STOP."

Still the cables winged over the wires to Corvallis. "Mother," said the Gilfillans' six-year-old-daughter, awed by the excitement Margaret created, "will she have a flag on her grave when she dies?" The office wanted facts about all the pictures for the captions. Margaret wrote down everything: the amount of concrete in the piers, the amount of steel in the dam, the number of men at work on the job. But New York wanted to know only one detail: "STATE SEX OF BABY SEATED ON BAR IN BEER PARLOR."

The baby eventually caused an uproar. Readers were outraged to think a four-year-old girl would have to spend her evenings in a bar among the rowdies. *Life* had, on its first try, electrified its family audience and ignited a controversy that would set its circulation on a rapid upward course. The principal of schools in New Deal was moved at length to write the magazine that the child was not neglected, that only *Life*'s editors were exploiting her, that the night life of his town had been vastly overplayed, and that he wanted them to send a more objective photographer—this time a man, please, and one who sleeps nights.

Margaret's photographs ran away with the first issue because they encoded all the messages *Life* meant to send. The image of Fort Peck Dam on the cover spoke of power, which Margaret was superbly qualified to summarize, and not merely power but American power, American know-how, the long-lived hope that in technology lay the promise of a better future. In November of 1936, that proposition belonged to Franklin Roosevelt. Later, Henry Luce would grow to hate FDR, and sometimes the magazine would make that quite clear, but this first story was essentially a congratulatory note to the President.

Fort Peck was a PWA project, meant to restore order to the land and work to its people. Between 1933 and 1939, PWA spent over six billion dollars in the process of constructing nearly 70 percent of new buildings for education in America, 65 percent of the city halls, courthouses, and sewage disposal plants, 35 percent of public health facilities and hospitals, and 10 percent of all the roads, subways, and bridges built in the land. Few communities were untouched. America was trying to build its way out of the Depression. Fort Peck Dam was a work-relief project, with a town that called itself New Deal.

The story about "Roosevelt's Wild West" opened with Margaret's picture of taxi dancers, one happy, one blank, one sad, and their eager swains of every age, an image of the necessity of pleasure and profit. The headline read: "1,000 MONTANA RELIEF WORKERS MAKE WHOOPEE ON SATURDAY NIGHT." The next pages presented an aerial view of a shack town: pictures of main streets papered with the store signs and ads that some times seem to be the true American landscape, lots of chummy bar scenes, a huge pipe for the dam's tunnel (to satisfy Longwell's plea for "industrial big activity aspects"), and the baby on the bar, dramatically appearing twice on facing pages. All of this fit under the rubric of human interest, but it also proposed a kind of roisterous, ramshackle, up-by-the bootstraps new pioneer America that suited the magazine and the country just fine.

Although *Life* was a newsmagazine and even the first issue had its share of murder and death, the lead story was about normal, decent, useful, and pleasant (if admittedly rambunctious) behavior out West. Other stories were about Chinese schoolchildren in San Francisco, John Stewart Curry ("the greatest painter Kansas has produced"), Helen Hayes's childhood, a report on Brazil, one on Fort Knox, the black widow spider, golf in Gooneyville. The magazine was a vegetable stew of picture journalism, a mix of fresh ingredients, leftovers, pepper, and a dash of dishwater.

Margaret's lead story was a historic document, not only because the boom town would disappear by the fifties and then would exist only in her photographs, but because it was the first true photographic essay in America. She wrote in her notes: "One of the things I really care about is being given credit for having developed this essay style." She had prepared her own way with her story on hogs in the first issue of *Fortune*, then made the real breakthrough in *Life*.

The picture essay would immediately become a prime mode of communication, and so it would remain, at least until the big photographic magazines bowed out, some thirty-odd years later. For over three decades, a mass audience acquired much of its information and pieces of its education via the form that Margaret had given it first. Not just a picture story, which might be merely a simple chronological account, the essay had wider ramifications and sometimes less neatly drawn perimeters. Strictly speaking, it was not solely Margaret's invention. She provided a wide range of material, then

Ingersoll and Luce laid out a kind of road map of the western boom towns from her photographs. The essay has always been a collaborative effort.

Still, in November of 1936 no one at *Life* had much of an idea what a photo essay was. They were making up the history of photographic magazines as they went along. The form did not even acquire a title until March of 1937, when Henry Luce named it. "Fifteen or twenty years ago," he wrote, "people used to write 'essays' for magazines. . . . The essay is no longer a vital means of communication. But what is vital is *the photographic essay*." The genre that Margaret had pioneered was supposed to fill a vacuum in the literary world with photographs.

The first issue of *Life,* dated November 23, 1936, reached the news-stands on Thursday the nineteenth. That day, a score of Okies drifted into California out of the dust, General Motors hired yet another Pinkerton man to spy on union organizers, a dozen youngsters signed on for the Civilian Conservation Corps, and President Roosevelt, flush from a handy victory over Alf Landon and the highest stock market since 1931, went fishing for the day. Thousands were reading the newly published *Gone with the Wind*, Social Security was gearing up to begin its first payments at the start of the new year, and Eugene O'Neill had been informed one week earlier that he had won the Nobel Prize for literature.

Across the Atlantic, Edward VIII still occupied the throne of England; he would abdicate in two weeks to marry Mrs. Simpson. Rebel troops threatened Madrid. Adolf Hitler was not newsworthy enough that week to appear in *Life*'s first issue, but the magazine did find some room for Winston Churchill fingering a sore tooth. Luce said once, "Today I may not be in a mood nor feel the need to read the finest article about the Prime Minister. But I will stop to watch him take off his shoe."

Time Inc. delivered two hundred thousand copies of the new magazine to the news-stands that day. They sold out within hours. Cities all over the country cabled for more copies of *Life,* sold those out, cabled for still more. The last order went unfilled; the complete press run of 466,000 had been sold. The home office was cautiously optimistic. The country was obviously curious about the magazine, but curiosity is quickly satisfied. Still, the second week sold out. And the third. And fourth. The presses could not print enough copies to meet the demand. An issue of *Life* became such a rare object that people gave cocktail parties on the pretext of having a copy.

*Life*'s success was so brilliant that it had the unprecedented effect of running up staggering losses. No one had been certain a picture magazine would do well in the marketplace. *Life*'s guarantee to advertisers was 250,000 copies, and prepublication contract holders had the right to take additional ads later at the original rate. They took them in early '37, when *Life* was selling a million copies of each issue; the magazine took a loss with every order. By that spring, it was calculated that readers wanted five to six million copies of *Life* each week. The magazine could not be produced in such quantities; the new presses could barely handle a million a week, and coated paper could not always be turned out fast enough to print even that million.

The more copies *Life* sold, the more advertising it attracted, the greater were its losses. The new picture magazine's popularity was so stunning and so unanticipated that it was soon losing $50,000 a week and by the end of 1937 had lost $3,000,000. Time Inc. canceled its year-end dividend. Although *Life*'s circulation, reach, and influence grew at breakneck speed, the magazine did not turn a profit until January 1939.

The runaway demand for *Life* prompted a horde of imitators. *Look*, a monthly that had long been in the planning stages, came out in January 1937 and was an immediate success, although not on the order of *Life*. *Look* was soon followed by *Click, Pic, Photo History, See, Peek, Focus*. (Good names were scarce. A charter subscriber to *Life* had once suggested it be called *Fast and Luce*.) The new magazines vanished one by one in the twinkling of a shutter. *Life* and *Look* remained.

The explosive success of the picture magazine owed a good deal to the fact that it took so little of the subscriber's time. World War I seems to have marked the end of true leisure in America. In the twenties, everything speeded up. Assembly lines turned out cars in record time, the cars they turned out drove at record speed. Airplane travel and airmail changed the way distance was regarded. So did subways. The Automat and the drugstore counter even speeded up the lunch hour.

Life began to be lived in a hurry, and people who wanted to know more wanted to take in their knowledge fast. The *Daily News* succeeded because of shorter stories and more photographs, *Reader's Digest* by digesting its articles. In 1922, the prospectus for *Time* declared that "People are uninformed because no publication has adapted itself to the time which busy men are able to spend on simply keeping informed." *Time* promised to save time. But by 1936 Luce was writing that some people just didn't have the leisure to read *Time* cover to cover; the picture magazine would be for them. Some said later that *Time* was for people who didn't want to read and *Life* for those who didn't want to think.

When Henry Luce wrote the prospectus for *Life,* he claimed to have divined a change in the world's visual culture: "Thus to see, and to be shown, is now the will and new expectancy of half mankind." He was right. Masses of people did indeed unconsciously begin to expect photographs in their daily papers, their magazines, books, and of course films. Photography was incorporated into people's lives.

In 1936, photography was not a new language; it only seemed to be one. It is difficult today to realize what a sense of discovery inhered in photography at the time. In 1934, when *Time* published candid photographs of Roosevelt in his office, no one had ever seen such unposed pictures of the President. In '38, *Life*'s publication of the first photographs ever printed of the U.S. Senate in session amounted to a national epiphany.

An editor who was with *Life* from the beginning says photography seemed so new then that even the staff had to be taught to read pictures, and that captions at first were written to help teach the public how to read the evidence. Some thought the picture magazine would kill off reading of the old-fashioned variety altogether. A 1938 *New Yorker* cartoon had one editor asking another if it was O.K. to refer to their subscribers as *readers*. But in fact *Life*, for all its claims to be a picture magazine, depended heavily on captions to carry the story.

The first half of the thirties had witnessed an enormous increase in amateur photography in this country. By 1932, Americans were exposing eighty-three million rolls of six-shot amateur film a year. As more and more people acquired the habit of photographic vision, the camera became nearly ubiquitous. In 1938, a journalist assigned to photograph Man o' War lamented that he could not get "unposed" pictures because the horse was so used to being photographed that he insisted on looking at the camera every time. *Life* and the picture magazine set the seal on the trend to a photographic perception of the world.

The mass media vastly extended their reach and vastly changed their means in the 1930s. The decade was a turning point in the history of communications, when radio and photography began to supplant the printed word. An electronic revolution was in the making. Only a world war would slow the commercial release of television, which was already well along in the experimental stages. The ground was being prepared for society's ultimate dependence on photographically generated images transmitted in a flash to every home.

To Margaret, *Life* seemed like the perfect means to put her work into alignment with her new social awareness. She wrote Gil shortly after going south and just before *Life* began: "People don't realize how serious conditions in this country are. . . . The new job [*Life*] will give me more opportunity to work with creative things like this. . . . I am delighted to be able to turn my back on all advertising agencies and go on to life as it really is."

In the thirties, the idea grew that a new democratic art was being created. The proletarian novel was supposedly for the worker and sometimes *by* the worker. Painters sponsored by the WPA, putting murals up in post offices and airports, painting canvases about strikers and men on relief, felt that a new art was developing for the people. They may have been right, but the true honors for a new popular art belonged to photography. Photography, ideally suited to social documentary as well as to mass reproduction, reached an enormous audience. Many who pored over images taken for the Farm Security Administration or for *Life* did not consider themselves art lovers, but then, photography was not generally considered an art.

Time Inc. understood the democratic appeal of photographs, which was one key to vast circulation. An ad for *Life* in the December 1936 issue of *Fortune* sought to reassure the wealthy who might find their servants reading the same publication they were:

> The appeal of pictures is universal. Pictures answer the Great Inquisitiveness which is born in a living animal, part of its lust for life. . . . The Great Inquisitiveness makes you and your banker react to pictures much as your cook does, or your taxi-driver. The cook and taxi-driver, then, may find something in LIFE as interesting as you do. That will be as it should be. A magazine called LIFE would be a sorry thing if it turned out to be a snob.

Snobbish or not, *Life*, with its picture format, cut across social boundaries. Margaret's career itself illustrates the breadth of this revolution in journalism; her fame, which spread ever wider as *Life* grew, dramatized the power of the new photographer, a figure who was rapidly becoming the prime witness of the world.

### "Life Likes Life"

> *The very rush around the magazine was food and drink to me. . . . The breathless excitement of it. Holding five pages for the lead. They have to be good—the best there is. Often thought I would die rather than not bring back what* Life *needs and this I really meant.*
>
> (Margaret Bourke-White, Notes)

When Margaret signed the contract with *Life*, she agreed to give up her studio and Time Inc. agreed to supply her with an office, a secretary of her own choosing (she chose Peggy Sargent), a darkroom, and a salary for Oscar Graubner and two assistants. The contract did not mention her animals, but the alligators were adopted by an experimental school, and Peggy Sargent, who Margaret said had a "personal friendship" with the turtles, scouted the city's fountains for a decent home. Loew's Lexington theater, one of the old-time movie palaces, looked sufficiently grand for turtles who had lived in a distinguished penthouse. Sargent loitered in the lobby with a package of turtles until a moment came when she could sneak them into their new home undetected.

Margaret had the only darkroom and the only printer at *Life*. Most of the photographers prided themselves on doing their own printing, yet when editors sent them out on assignment after assignment in quick order, they began to realize that Margaret had a distinct advantage. She stayed out in the field shooting pictures while Graubner developed her film; meanwhile, they were laboring in the darkroom pulling prints.

*Life* soon hired more printers, photographers soon gave them their film. Oscar Graubner became head of the *Life* labs and printed for everyone, but most thought he gave his first allegiance to Margaret and never wavered. The opulent beauty of his prints had to be sacrificed to meet the magazine's weekly deadlines. On November 10, 1936, Peggy Sargent wrote her boss: "I can see that our attitude to your photographs will have to change. They don't seem to care so much for the beautiful workmanship that always had to go out from the Bourke-White studio but are just interested in having a good story told." *Life* was about communication, and the aesthetics of the print and sometimes of the composition tended to take second place.

Yet Margaret still insisted on the best prints the darkroom, with its new limitations, could turn out. *Life* photographer Carl Mydans wrote:

> Maggie established a new measurement of expectation for the art of the photographer. Her influence on all of us is incalculable. It was from her that I learned to worship the quality of a photographic print. Day after day I watched her mark up pictures and send them back for reprinting until they met her standards. She was a perfectionist. Little that she ever did really satisfied her. "It's when my prints come out of the darkroom that I finally judge what I have done," she told me. "Sometimes I find something that gives me a thrill. More often I see what I failed to do, or what I did that wasn't right."

John Szarkowski, director of the photography department at New York's Museum of Modern Art, speculates that Bourke-White strongly influenced the *Life* photograph in the early years. "Her description of surfaces," he says, "was very luxurious, not just precise. Everything in her pictures looked like it was made out of some kind of polished synthetic, even the skins of the people. . . . My guess would be that even if only by example, that kind of luxurious technical quality, really an aesthetic, probably had a large influence on the magazine's standards."

In effect, Margaret set up the *Life* labs, practices, and standards. She was even responsible for one peculiarity of *Life*'s printing. Having made infinitesimal adjustments to the composition while she was photographing, she insisted her negative be printed in full, not permitting them to be cropped so much as an eighth of an inch along the edges by the negative holder. Cornell Capa, who worked in the lab in the late thirties, recalls hours of struggle with her negatives sandwiched between glass plates that made them the very devil to print. In time the lab printed the full negative for everyone, a practice know as "printing black"; a black area is allowed to show around the edges of the print as proof that the image has been printed to its edges. Margaret's demand became the custom.

(Although she insisted on preserving every fraction of her initial vision in the first print, Margaret was herself adept at cropping her photographs for a more dramatic image. *Life*'s editors also cropped for better layouts and visual impact; they began by slicing her cover photograph of Fort Peck Dam in half. Although she would not stand for any subtraction in the darkroom, she never once complained about losing half a photograph in the service of the magazine.)

Margaret also brought *Life* its first film editor: Peggy Sargent. In Bourke-White studio days, Margaret had taught her secretary how to select the best negatives when film came back to the office from out of town. At *Life*, Sargent took over the editing of all the photographers' film, gleaning from the hundreds of pictures on the rolls a manageable group of images to be submitted to the editors; her choices were rarely faulted by photographers. The Bourke-White staff put an indelible stamp on *Life*.

Margaret needed excitement as musicians need practice, to keep her at top form. Because she treated every assignment as if it were the most important challenge in the world, her work paid her back with a high level of intensity. The rush, the pressure of spot news was itself enough to make the blood dance. In January of '37, the Ohio River swelled over its banks in one of the worst floods in American history, pouring into Louisville, Kentucky, at an unprecedented height and killing or injuring nine hundred people. Billings gave Margaret one hour's notice on the story, and she caught the last plane that landed in Louisville before the airfield was flooded out.

Muddy water surged across the highway into town. Margaret hitch-hiked on rowboats that were delivering food packages and searching for survivors marooned on high spots. Once she hauled her cameras aboard a large raft to take pictures of the water roiling across three-quarters of the city. Another time she chanced upon an undertaker who had hauled in a body floating past the door of his funeral parlor, only to discover the corpse was a neighbor. He insisted on showing Margaret how young he had made the corpse look; it was the last service he could perform for a friend.

*Life* ran the story as its lead. The first page was a picture of black men and women lined up with baskets and pails at a relief center, before a billboard of a smiling white family with the headline: "World's Highest Standard of Living—There's no way like the American way." The irony was tailor-made for her camera.

The same issue carried Margaret's four-page spread on the Supreme Court, which Roosevelt was trying to pack. The way one *Life* staffer recalls the Washington trip, she set up her tripod on the perfect spot from which to photograph the Capitol and began to shoot—in the middle of the busiest street in Washington. Streetcars stopped on the tracks; cars lined up behind her for blocks, honking and carrying on. The Washington office repeatedly telephoned and sent memos to New York: "Who is this crazy woman you sent down here, wrecking the town?"

*Life*'s subject matter, aimed at the largest possible audience, ranged from spectacular to urgent to solemn, from silly to domestic to cute—war, race prejudice, cancer, debutantes, horses that wore hats. In the same issue as the tragic flood and the portentous packing of the court was a humorous and fairly explicit picture story on how to undress for your husband. Undress was a staple part of the *Life* mix; the editors ran pictures of young women in their bathing suits or their undies on almost any pretext. In a family magazine in 1937, certain proprieties did have to be observed, and the airbrush man was fondly referred to as "the nipple obliterator." One commentator in 1938 said

*Life* consisted of "equal parts of the decapitated Chinaman, the flogged Negro, the surgically explored peritoneum, and the rapidly slipping chemise."

Through the mix there always ran a strain of optimism that was a potent element of *Life*'s success. The Fort Peck cover sang the dream of recovery through technology; the flood story told of survivors. The underlying current of optimism in the American character, stilled by the dark years of the Depression, had resurfaced in the nation at least as early as Roosevelt's first election. Writers who went forth to explore the homeland found a sturdiness out there that gave them unanticipated hope. Photographers for the Farm Security Administration saw courage writ large in the face of frightful odds. Luce built optimism into *Life* from the start. In a confidential memo of March 1937, he said: "*Life* has a bias. *Life* is in favor of the human race, and it is hopeful. *Life* likes life. *Life* is quicker to point with pride than to view with alarm."

Henry Luce saw photography as a kind of remedy for the disheartening effects of the news. He wanted to feature normalcy, itself a corrective for the reporter's emphasis on disaster and crime. "While journalism accents the abnormal, the hopeful fact is that the photograph can make normal, decent, useful and pleasant behavior far more interesting than word journalism." In 1952, *Life* reminded its readers that "Back in 1937 . . . Henry R. Luce . . . predicted that photography could be useful in correcting that really inherent evil of journalism which is its imbalance between the good news and the bad."

Luce had already built the love of America into his magazines; *Life* was to be its celebration. Tex McCrary, reporter and radio interviewer, says that Clare Boothe Luce (she became Mrs. Luce one year before *Life* began) told him that in *Time* Harry was trying to say "Gosh" about America, in *Fortune* "My God," and in *Life* "Gee whiz." One *Life* writer says that "for a great many people *Life* discovered America. There was no TV, movies were never-never land, illustrated magazines were few. Everybody had seen pictures of the scenic wonders of America but the American people had not been photographed in the ordinary occassions of life, or the extraordinary. Bourke-White helped define *Life* as a discoverer of America. All those pictures of farmlands, the contoured fields"—*Life* made good use of her skill at aerial photography—"the hand of man on the land . . ."

In '42, when American interests had become more international, *Life* was still explaining America to Americans. An ad for *Life* in the magazine proclaimed: "One of LIFE's functions is introducing the Vermonter and the Californian to each other. . . . Thus LIFE serves as a force for creating understanding between widely separated, variously occupied people."

In early 1937, the sociologists Helen and Robert Lynd returned to the town of Muncie, Indiana, which they had studied in the twenties as *Middletown*, and studied it once more. *Middletown in Transition* revealed that good times were returning to the town, that federal aid had contributed to visible improvements, and that Muncie, which had never before voted Democratic, had gone for FDR in '36. *Life* decided to put the news about America into pictures and sent Margaret to Indiana.

She took a series of portraits of townspeople that had the variety of a collection of "types": a prissy-mouthed schoolteacher, a fat city father sporting a big grin and a bigger cigar. Most telling were the set pieces of families and clubs, which began with the richest manufacturer in town, who had introduced "the first pink-coated fox hunt ever to astonish an Indiana landscape," and ran all the way down the economic scale to two poor hillbillies in a one-room shack.

Margaret had become expert at making poses look natural and adept at keeping her subjects at it long enough to wear down their camera shyness and catch them off guard. As she had known how to simplify industrial subjects and present the detail that summed up a process, so she knew how to simplify her human subjects and present a moment that would instantly telegraph a message on the page. On occasion she flirted with stereotype or caricature, but it worked remarkably well in a mass medium and she knew it.

The Muncie story got the lead once more. *Life* called the story an essay, "the Erst picture essay of what [Middletown] looks like," thus calling attention to the camera's admirable power to bring to life the words of sociologists. In smaller print, the magazine declared these photographs "an important American document," something *Life* meant to specialize in.

Wilson Hicks, the former picture editor of the Associated Press, who had been hired by *Life* in March to direct the photographic staff, wrote her about the photographs: "You did a swell job. . . . I haven't seen all the pictures you have taken in your career, but in my opinion these have something that none of the others which I have seen have had."

After Billings and Longwell, Hicks was the most important shaping force on the new magazine. A connoisseur of talent who could instantly recognize a photographer in the making, he kept the magazine supplied with top photographers for thirteen years. "I trust in God and Wilson Hicks for pictures," John Billings said. Carefully dressed, his "black patent leather hair" parted in the middle and slicked down, Hicks sat with his feet upon his desk and his cigar jammed into his mouth and surveyed the photographic world with an icy stare. He knew how to encourage a photographer. Philippe Halsman, who took more *Life* covers than anyone else, recalled Hicks's reactions to an unusual picture: "He'd laugh; his eyes would light up; his hands would tremble; and he would look like a man who had discovered treasure! . . . We all tried to produce this excitement in Wilson Hicks, for his excitement was one of the great influences on our work."

But Hicks could also rage. He would sweep photographs off his desk in a fury. He had the Machiavellian notion that photographers would do better work if he pitted them against one another; sometimes he assigned two men to the same story. He inspired fear and chronic anger in most of his staff—"a fantastic genius when it came to photography, but the biggest bastard when it came to handling people," one of them said. Those he favored were devoted to him. Margaret once wrote that when she took a particularly dangerous risk to get a photograph, in the back of her mind she thought, "I'm doing this for Wilson Hicks."

Hicks once told an interviewer that the Muncie story marked Margaret's final transition into journalism and made everyone in the business sit up and take notice. He was right. Beaumont Newhall, who wrote America's first history of photography, wrote her to say that Muncie was the "finest piece of documentary photography" he had seen. Hicks, however, also thought Margaret had definite limitations. He said she remained "a photographer of things" long after leaving the industrial scene, and that the women in the Muncie story were little more than dummies.

Both the photographer Alfred Eisenstaedt and Richard Pollard, who later became director of photography at *Life*, also regard Bourke-White as primarily a photographer of objects, even of people as objects, and there is an element of truth in this estimate. She was as good at photographing people as most, and among the pictures of sharecroppers made down South can be found a moving account of humanity in decay. But at least before the second half of the forties, most of Margaret's photographs were more concerned with reporting than with emotion and psychology.

This concentration on the more public aspects of both public and private lives was fairly typical of photojournalism in the thirties. Intimate details were still considered too personal for a family publication. Photojournalists were always eager to record the large and readily identifiable emotions, such as grief, fear, and joy, but psychological nuance was not considered the crux of their stories until after the Second World War. Margaret's working methods and sense of irony would have tended to distance her somewhat from her subjects, and her accustomed way of working, with a big camera, a battery of lights, and firm control over the direction, was less conducive to intimacy than the small camera was.

But the relative lack of psychological depth in many of her pictures of people can also be seen as one result of a continuing strength in her work: the ability to find the symbolic detail. "I made a picture of plow blades," she once said, "plow handles which symbolized the whole plow factory." In photojournalism she found the symbolic moment or the symbolic expression—and the symbolic moment, in an era when self-confession was not yet the order of the day, did not necessarily have a weighty emotional cast. The fat man grins around his cigar; the women of Muncie's Conversation Club wear their most ladylike hats and manners: such pictures symbolize city fathers and women's clubs as effectively as plow blades symbolized a factory. They amount to opinions that have been compressed to the size of an aphorism to be instantly grasped by the viewer.

Like *Life* itself, these pictures often tend to repeat a stereotype in a more visually compelling form than it usually commands. Margaret could produce with surety and apparent ease the summaries that made good journalism in the thirties and still constitute a major part of it today. However much she longed to find greater insight with her camera, much of her work was clearly intended to be the most efficient and pointed reporting of surfaces.

The up-and-coming trend in photography when *Life* began was 35 mm work. Eisenstaedt, McAvoy, Stackpole, Mydans, William Vandivert—the first men at *Life* took pride in the very idea of natural, spontaneous photography. There were always photographers around who used large cameras for portrait work and studio pictures, but still they regarded the 35 mm camera as the real challenge, the instrument of the future. In a sense, Margaret Bourke-White represented the old order, with its tripods, floodlights, and poses, and the younger men represented the new.

Yet if Margaret's equipment might have seemed old-fashioned and cumbersome to some, most photographers took up the large camera at some point, hoping that if they brought back negatives of as high quality as hers, they would have as high a percentage of their stories in the magazine. She was on her way to perfecting the posed candid picture, and nearly everyone used a method like Margaret's at one time or another.

Margaret and Erskine went south again in the spring of '37 to round out their book. Caldwell wrote the text, but they wrote the captions together, each making notations privately, then together choosing one caption or combination. Margaret was especially proud that the book was such a true collaboration. *You Have Seen Their Faces*, both a report on sharecropping and an indictment, came out in November.

It is odd that years later she would write with such pride of their captions. These were inventions, Margaret and Erskine's ideas of what might have been said or what best expressed the photograph's message. Critics complained that such fictions meant that the evidence had not been gathered scrupulously enough and the book was not truthful. In 1940, when the photographer Dorothea Lange and her husband, Paul Schuster Taylor, published An *American Exodus*, a book similarly dedicated to the nation's social problems, the text took a quiet swipe at Margaret and Erskine: "Quotations which accompany the photographs report what the persons photographed said, not what we think might be their unspoken thoughts."

Yet Erskine did the book expressly to present convincing evidence, and truth was the credo that underlay Margaret's photographic career. Caldwell was a fiction writer to whom truth meant the deepest dramatic expression, sometimes expressed by the most convincing myth. Margaret had believed since the early days of her career that the most dramatic and most symbolic views embodied the truest expressions. And so they chose drama above unembellished fact.

Still, the book was a publishing milestone, a force for social good, and a great popular success. The most important work of its day on sharecroppers and related social problems, it would soon influence the country's legislation. Its reviews ran from the *Southern Review's* "as a student of farm tenancy in the South Mr. Caldwell would make a splendid curator of a Soviet Park of Recreation and Culture" to "a stirring and painful document, magnificently produced. It should provoke something of the effect that Swift's 'A Modest Proposal' . . . was calculated to make."

No one could be indifferent to this document. Erskine's anger was evident on every page; too evident, some said. The prose was strong but the message relentless and repetitive. Margaret's photographs were almost as theoretical and at least as forceful. The consequences of deprivation are unavoidable in these pictures, not only in the tight, downturned mouths and the skin mapped with lines but in the camera's unblinking stare at pellagra, goiter, shrunken limbs, retardation. Few of her contemporaries would so unsparingly document physical and mental disabilities. In the early pictures she recorded a few smiles and only at the end gave way to unremitting despair, but throughout the book, her photographs are filled with anger and passion.

It was this theatricality that subjected them to the most serious criticism. Photographic documents of the social ills of America were not a new phenomenon—Jacob Riis's late-nineteenth-century pictures of New York slums and Lewis Hine's subsequent record of child labor are early examples—but the genre was being reformulated under the pressure of the Depression and the new regard for the camera's power, and the search was on for a new kind of factual and impartial truth. The chief instruments of the new social reporting were documentary films such as Pare Lorentz's *The Plow That Broke the Plains*, newsreels at their most serious, the Farm Security Administration, and, after the birth of *Life*, the picture magazine.

The FSA's photographic arm, founded in 1935 and headed by Roy Stryker, sent photographers far afield to document America in crisis: the dust bowl, migrant camps, sharecroppers, small-town life. Stryker believed his photographers' reports should be objective and unbiased. Arthur Rothstein, the first photographer hired by Stryker, said that his boss greatly respected Bourke-White's work but thought her style a little theatrical for an essay on southern tenant farmers.

But the FSA had paved the way for her. Photographers like Rothstein, Walker Evans, Dorothea Lange, Russell Lee, Carl Mydans, Ben Shahn, in '35 and '36, were establishing a style of reporting that gave photography a credibility beyond the printed word's. As their pictures were made for the government, they were free, and were soon reprinted in newspapers and magazines and brought back to the *Fortune* offices for study. In '37, when Margaret and Erskine were in the South, *Life* wrote her to promise they would wait for her sharecropper pictures. "The only thing we may do," her editor said, "is use a few of the Resettlement Administration's [the FSA's earlier name] pictures in a general take-out on the use of photography by the Roosevelt Administration.

They have been extremely modern." Margaret took the FSA's general approach and added to it a more journalistic emphasis and a drama that came from her own love of spectacle, the depth of her new commitment, and the influence of Caldwell's crusading spirit.

In the summer of '36, Walker Evans photographed in the South with the critic James Agee. A publisher was prepared to bring out their book, but *You Have Seen Their Faces* scored such an enormous success that the competition killed it; the book finally appeared in 1941 but lost money. Called *Let Us Now Praise Famous Men*, it is recognized today as one of the signal documents of the thirties. Evans reportedly felt that Caldwell and Bourke-White's book exploited people who were already exploited, but it was probably Agee who included in *Famous Men* a newspaper article in which Bourke-White burbled about her "superior red coat" and related how she and Erskine had bribed one couple with snuff to take their picture.

Yet Margaret had also expressed Agee and Evans's own philosophy of photography in that article: "Whatever facts a person writes," she said, "have to be colored by his prejudice and bias. With a camera, the shutter opens and closes and the only rays that come in to be registered come directly from the object in front of you." Agee himself wrote that photography's pure objectivity "is why the camera seems to me, next to unassisted and weaponless consciousness, the central instrument of our time."

The documentary camera was a different instrument in Evans's hands than it was in Bourke-White's. Walker Evans's complex but clear-eyed, dispassionate, seemingly uninflected and uninterpreted view of the world is recognized now as one of the great achievements of the time. His style exerted a major influence on subsequent photography and set a standard by which to measure documentary. If Bourke-White's imagery today occasionally seems excessive, that is precisely because Evans's apparently impersonal style has replaced in our estimation the more engaged and overt attitudes, highly valued at the time, that made Margaret's book so influential.

The influence of *You Have Seen Their Faces* extended far beyond its time to photographers whose styles were entirely different from Bourke-White's. Gordon Parks, a photographer for the FSA and later for *Life*, says, "I was very much in search of some way to express my own feelings about the situation in America as concerned race, discrimination, and minority groups, especially black people, since I was black. *You Have Seen Their Faces,* along with some of the FSA photos, opened my eyes to the possibility of using my camera as an instrument or a weapon against this sort of thing. For me, that book was a pretty important step."

Robert Frank, the Swiss-born photographer whose grainy, shot-from-the-hip, disaffected view of America in the fifties is still influencing photographers today, also credits Bourke-White's inspiration. Frank admired her book greatly when he came to America early in his career, finding it "rather straight and unpretentious and unartistic, purely documentary photography"—an attitude, although certainly not a style, that matched the one he adopted himself. "I thought she had a lot of feeling for the people," Frank says.

*You Have Seen Their Faces* established a new genre: the book in which photographs and text have equal weight. Although photographically illustrated books had long existed, the photographs themselves had always been secondary to the text. This began to change in the twenties in Europe, in the thirties in America. *You Have Seen Their Faces* welded photographs and literature together in a new balance. Several reviewers thought it the beginning of a new art, and some thought the photographs had stepped up to a level of greater power than the words. The *New York Times* reviewer wrote that "The pictures produce such an effect, indeed, that it is no exaggeration to say that the text serves principally to illustrate them." Margaret had yet again pioneered new territory.

Time Inc. believed in anonymous journalism. Photographers sometimes got more recognition than writers, as when Margaret's name was duly inscribed beneath her *Fortune* photographs. The new *Life*, a picture magazine after all, felt it owed its photographers their names, although not with their pictures. An index to pictures ran in each issue, one narrow column with page numbers and names, usually in the back, often hard to find. Margaret said instantly this was not enough.

Two months after *Life* was founded, she was already fighting for her name and fully prepared to take the matter up with Luce himself if there was trouble. Margaret was generally regarded as Luce's protégée, and although no one at *Life* believes she got special treatment because of her relation to him, she did command a certain amount of awe. She was not above using her connection. In Washington in '37, shortly before she single-handedly fouled up the city's traffic, the reporter on the story said to her, "Peggy, I will do anything in the world for you except carry your damned bags." To this she coyly replied, "Sometimes Mr. Luce carries my bags for me."

Whoever got to Luce on the question of credits, Margaret won her point. By March, photographers were guaranteed their names on the story itself when it ran four pages or more. The stage was set for the appearance of photographers as stars. They were already the major players of the *Life* staff, and it stood to reason that if *Life* was putting photographs on center stage, the photographers would become stars in the eyes of the world, but it took most of a decade for the world to see it that way. Margaret Bourke-White was still the only name a large public knew.

She appeared in the Museum of Modern Art's 1937 exhibition, an honor not given other *Life* photographers. She published with Erskine Caldwell. A woman in her business still amounted to an unaccountable oddity; in 1940, *U.S. Camera* marveled at the strange fate that had made a woman "the most famous on-the-spot reporter the world over."

Once again Margaret endorsed products for advertisers. In '38 it was Camel cigarettes. (The cigarette companies enlisted many distinguished women in their campaigns; Alice Roosevelt Longworth appeared on the back of *Life* in 1937 for Lucky Strike. But the federal government soon began to crack down on truth in advertising, and in 1944 Margaret was called before the Federal Trade Commission. She who often claimed to be devoted to truth and honesty had to testify that she had never been a regular smoker of Camels.) In 1939 she endorsed air travel and telephones, even endorsed wine in a full-page ad in *Life* magazine itself, where other photographers were lucky to get the photographs they had taken reproduced, much less pictures of themselves.

*Life* hired other women photographers, but the public did not know it. "Quite often when I arrived at a job destination," says Hansel Mieth, "people would ask me, 'Are you Miss Bourke-White?' I shook my head 'No' and gave my name. They would look puzzled. 'But Miss Bourke-White is the photographer for LIFE,' they would say. 'Yes,' I'd say, 'yes, but I'm not she. LIFE has a few other photographers.' This was always an awkward beginning, and I had to work doubly hard and yet make it appear so easy, to still their anxiety and mine."

But if the public lionized only Bourke-White, *Life* at least set it the proper example by bowing down to all its staff photographers. "When we went on a job and had a researcher or writer to go with us," the photographer Cornell Capa says, "they were privileged to carry our equipment. The photographer was in charge. We were kings and princes." The reporters acted as researchers, travel agents, assistants, lackies, and, with luck, diplomats. The photographer was the genius of the operation, but the reporter was its motor—and carried the cameras. Sean Callahan, who worked at *Life* and was working with Margaret on a book about her when she died, thinks she may have had a hand in establishing the tradition of "the reporter as sherpa." Not only did she have the requisite glamour before *Life* even began, she was also a woman, with heavy equipment, who would have needed and expected assistance.

Margaret Bourke-White became a prime instrument of *Life's* promotion. On the page with the photography index, *Life* printed a small picture of a photographer each week and a few words about the assignment. In the July 5, 1937, issue, when the magazine printed Margaret's elegant story of paper manufacturing, with its startlingly abstract aerial photograph of logs heading downriver to the mill, the editors breathlessly recounted how she had put on her flying suit, knelt in the open doorway of a four-passenger plane with its side door removed, and fastened herself in with a belt. "The plane banks, Miss Bourke-White leans far out away from the plane holding her twenty pound camera against the tremendous force of the wind . . ." Her derring-do was better copy than the story itself, and *Life* knew it.

# Chapter 16

## A. M. SPERBER

## MURROW: HIS LIFE AND TIMES

E DWARD R. MURROW IS CONSIDERED BY MANY to be the "father" of broadcast journalism, even though he never anchored a nightly news broadcast. In fact, Murrow basically backed into a career in journalism. After being active in campus politics and serving as president of the National Student Federation of America, starting in 1932 Murrow worked for the Institute for International Education, an organization that included among its tasks, help to German (often Jewish) academics who had been dismissed from their university positions in Nazi Germany.

In 1935, Murrow became director of talks for CBS, where his job was to recruit people to be interviewed by CBS radio. In 1937, he was named director of European operations for CBS and began to recruit a news team to compete with NBC radio.

Certainly, Murrow was there at the beginning of network news. His opening "This is London," become the iconic phrase for radio reporting from Europe during World War II. His *See it Now* broadcast focusing on the actions of Senator Joseph McCarthy has captured the historical memory as one of the first examples of the potential power of news on television. His documentary *Harvest of Shame* was a searing indictment of the working conditions for migrant workers in the United States.

Murrow was eventually forced out from CBS News and ended his career as the director of the United States Information Agency, where, in an ironic twist, he worked to prevent the airing of *Harvest of Shame* in the United Kingdom. These extracts that demonstrate the importance of *Harvest of Shame* give an insight into the anxieties that Murrow and his production team experienced over the McCarthy exposé.

### . . . To Love the News

"Harvest of Shame"—the title was Friendly's—had begun as an idea back in 1959. Edward P. Morgan had been handling the migrant problem on radio; Murrow and

Friendly wanted to do it on TV. The matter was still open when Murrow left on sabbatical, the stumbling block, grower cooperation.

Enter David Lowe, a plump teddy bear of a man with an open, ingenuous manner that belied his legal training, master of the naïve opening,[1] a filmmaker with little or no documentary experience, who appeared once a week at CBS, looking for work. No way, said Friendly, they were knee-deep in producers.

## Just One Project Then?

Friendly put him on the migrant story, with a small retainer—"maybe $1,000"[2]—and a month's time, then went ahead when, four weeks later, Lowe informed him he had gotten the growers to cooperate. "Harvest of Shame" was first and foremost the creation of David Lowe and Marty Barnett, a labor of love emerging out of months of following the migrants up and down the eastern seaboard with car and camera. Murrow had come on the scene only after months of shooting.

His emotional involvement was evident, however, from the time of his return. Schultz, editing the film, got used to the sight of Murrow in the screening room, day after day, "looking just rapt at the footage."[3] (Someone years before had asked him, Why was he so invariably pro-union? "Because I hoed corn in a blazing sun," he shot back.)[4]

He wanted to see the camps for himself. Lowe took him down, two or three times, to the Okeechobee labor camp, a dust-blown shantytown not far from Palm Beach, where he talked with agricultural workers and the missionaries who worked among them in the camps.

Friendly, troubled by Murrow's worsening cough, had had misgivings about his going, but "he wanted to. . . . The subject was exceedingly close to him. [These were] people who worked with their hands; he identified with them. Don't forget, Ed had been poorer than anyone who worked on that program."[5]

Almost anyone. Johnny Schultz had come to realize that at least some of Murrow's quiet was a sort of "inwardness," a sense of understanding growing in the cutting room between the logging engineer's son who had hoed corn and seen his parents go hungry, and the migrant logger's son, with his childhood memories of picking potatoes.

[. . .]

"Harvest-of-Shame" was in final editing. A compilation at the outset of filmed interviews, it was being hammered into shape, the draft narrative roughed out by Friendly and the producer in Lowe's first stab at "Murrow copy"—then reworked repeatedly, said Friendly later, by Murrow himself.

(The copy was always turned out first, said Schultz, in what he called "the *CBS Reports* Murrow-Friendly dogma," text and editing tailored till they fitted each other like a glove, involving close work by all concerned, in contrast with a unit like *Twentieth Century*, where "there was very little communication between people: The researcher got up a research packet; gave it to the director; the director would go out and shoot; the film and research packet would go to a writer; then Cronkite would be brought in to narrate.")

A show like "Harvest," on the other hand, was more of a cooperative venture. "David would appear with the copy he had written; Murrow wrote the tailpiece; all the rest was close consultation between Murrow and Friendly."[6]

The tailpiece had been Friendly's idea. "Ed, you've got to do an ending just like the McCarthy program," he told him one day. Murrow wrote it out one Tuesday morning, with perhaps a rewrite.[7]

Lowe had gotten his subjects to open up, the interviews following one another in a drumfire momentum, the pace of the cutting quickening under Friendly's constant admonition to "Tighten it up! Keep it going!"—a filmed continuum of American faces crossing the screen: black members of picking crews; rural whites straight out of Dorothea Lange's Depression photographs. Murrow's people. They screened a clip from Waycross, Georgia, a stranded picker down to his last $1.45. "Say, looks like your father, doesn't he, Ed?" Friendly boomed out.[8]

To Schultz, Murrow, hunched over, saying little, seemed to exude "a sixth sense about human beings—these kind of human beings." At one point, with most of the end copy in hand, Schultz had decided on the final sequence: a girl singing a plaintive song, the camera panning all those faces. The screening room was awash in tears and compliments. Murrow told him, "You don't need it."

Schultz was in shock. But he threw it out.

"He was right," said the editor. "He wanted anger, indignation, not this sort of 'tsk, tsk, those poor people'"; no release in a good cry.[9]

It was clear-cut advocacy journalism, and Murrow's skillful narration, ranging from understated irony to flaming anger, carried along Lowe and Barnett's portrait gallery of pickers, farmers, lobbyists, missionaries, and politicians, from the introductory voice-over juxtaposed against the early-morning "shape-up" for the hired help ("This . . . has nothing to do with Johannesburg or Capetown. . . . This is Florida. . . . These are citizens of the United States") to the closing appeal for action in the muckraking tradition of Ida Tarbell and Lincoln Steffens. It was a new, impassioned style for Murrow, contrasting with the coolly committed, Olympian TV persona of the fifties, marking him as a man of the new decade.

[. . .]

In fact, Jack Gould, praising the first raft of *CBS Reports*, including a Peabody winner and Howard Smith's classic interviews with Walter Lippmann, had taken to wondering: With all the emphasis on corporate entity, not individuals with whom the viewer felt rapport, wasn't some of the "excitement and distinctive character of C.B.S. News" being slightly blurred?[10]

Said Friendly in recent years: "It didn't seem to me to be fair to Murrow or the public. And documentaries haven't had that impact since. Because of that one personality. When people think of them today, they think of "Harvest of Shame," "McCarthy," "Indianapolis," "Radulovich." Even "The Selling of the Pentagon" is remembered mostly because of the criticism against it.

"Now, I may understand this better than anybody, and I haven't said this before, but I think it's important: The question of identification. People believed the shows; people could identify. This was the great lesson of my life. And if we fought for the principle of identification, it was because we knew this—not because Murrow wanted to be the big cheese."[11]

But the network, it seemed, didn't want its biggest drawing card out front.

Friendly's point had seemed proved in late November, as "Harvest of Shame" burst upon the public, an updated *Grapes of Wrath*; a black-and-white document of protest ushering in the sixties on TV, combining Lowe's vision, Barnett's camera eye, Friendly's overall whip hand, and the editorial punch of Murrow—standing among the crop rows, tieless and in shirt sleeves, a lavaliere microphone around his neck, looking like a combination of Henry Fonda and Woody Guthrie.

For Murrow, despite other programs in the works, it was effectively the last hurrah—the final round of *Times* editorials, the praises and damnation in the press and Congress, the anger of the interest groups, the squirming by the sponsors (two executives dispatched to Florida had virtually apologized),[12] as well as the public calls to action that would probably fizzle.

But TV, he always said, could only hold the mirror; the idea was to hold it until something happened: a seven-day-a-week job, defending the Republic and pointing up the warts.

The program also, as things turned out, laid a time bomb.

In company terms he had by now become the extra thumb. Moreover, it was getting crowded at the top. The relationship with Cronkite, the man who had made it in CBS on his own, had never been a good one, a subtle vying for power noticeable even when the balance was in Murrow's favor. It was the classic problem, as a CBS friend observed, of the front-runner: "There's Eric Sevareid in London, sitting in the wings; there's Smith, you had three stars, you had four stars, *you had a whole goddamn galaxy out there!* All sort of champing at the bit."[13]

Why was he staying? The counterquestion was: Where would he go—having never worked for a newspaper, rarely written for print; leaving a department which was in part his creation and the associates of twenty-five years, breaking the semi-incestuous, many-layered ties of the long-term employee and company man.

His recklessness had always coexisted with a strong security drive—the milltown-bred dread of being jobless, the ethic that you didn't quit a job unless you had a job to go to; the hard proletarian conditioning which, his large back salary notwithstanding, had him visualizing income—even the six-figure variety—in terms of a pay envelope.

Bill Downs had thought of quitting CBS to write a book, asked Murrow's advice: How did he think Roz would bear up? "She'll bear up," he answered, "until the second paycheck doesn't come in."[14]

Above all, leaving CBS, still the only place for him, in an industry and time without alternatives, meant leaving broadcasting and therefore journalism. Professional upheaval. At fifty-two, he looked around for a way to spend the rest of his life.

[. . .]

The atmosphere in the screening room on Sunday, March 7, was unusually grim and thoughtful, the flexibility of the past days and weeks freezing into the hard, final decisions of a Sunday night, any bandwagon effect dissipated. Quite the reverse. The signals coming out of the administration seemed to be switching again in an evident backoff, an anticipated strong presidential statement emerging as watered-down sweet reason at Wednesday's press conference, leaving a disappointed, angry press, columnist Joe Alsop overheard commenting audibly, "The yellow son of a bitch!"

"Isn't the White House going to do something about McCarthy?" asked Bonsignori at one point in the screening.

"The White House," said Murrow evenly, "is not going to do, and not going to say, one goddamned thing."[15] His face was red.

That long Sunday session would often be depicted in later accounts by those who were there. The informality, everyone in work clothes, Murrow in blue jeans and suspenders, wearing the red hunting shirt that staffers thought singularly appropriate. The tugs over cuts, shifts of sequences—some of the best clips came from the older shows—and the comments on the film itself: thin stuff; just Joe doing his thing; what was the point? Murrow, indicating the darkened screen, saying, "The terror is right here in this room," that it was *their* fears they were projecting, that the film was neutral; that the context—i.e., the narration—would make the difference.

Asked what he would say, he replied, "No one man can terrorize a whole nation unless we are all his accomplices," elaborating somewhat.

"Mr. Murrow, it's been a privilege to have worked for you," a voice piped up.

"What do you mean—to *have* worked?" roared Friendly.

Nervous laughter. "We were really tense," one man recalled.[16]

It was on what happened afterward that accounts would differ, in what would be a lingering source of controversy.

One of the many ironies of the time was the fact that the McCarthy program ended the insulation of those on *See It Now.* Attacking McCarthy, they became themselves fair game, with Murrow, a buffer in the past, soon to turn target, no longer inviolable, therefore unable to vouch. (The one fear among the staffers, Scott recalled, was, Is Ed too vulnerable?) Which meant ultimately, under the doctrine of guilt by association: everyone under the microscope.

Bonsignori remembered Murrow's meeting with the film editors earlier that week. None of them, he said, could have lived to this age in this atmosphere without the possibility of *something* in their backgrounds. If there was anything they thought worrisome— "Don't tell me; I don't want to know. But if your credits appear on this show, you might be investigated."

He gave them the choice of bowing out, if they wanted, and starting in on next week's show.[17] No one took him up, doubts notwithstanding ("I wanted to do the show"), and there the matter stayed. "Murrow had a great sense of personal privacy," was Bonsignori's recollection; "he didn't want to go into our backgrounds."[18]

But that Sunday evening, recalled Friendly, the staff in fact was encouraged to speak up. Was there any reason, he had asked, why they should not do the broadcast?

"I said, 'Look, this program is going to have impact beyond anything ever done. And the one who's gonna be attacked is gonna be Murrow. . . . Is there anyone in this room who, in their past, has done anything that could be used to hurt Ed?' "[19]

That being said, he later wrote, they took turns unbosoming, resulting in only minor reservations, no one taking himself or herself out of the line of fire, an action criticized in later, admittedly safer times.[20] There was no question, Friendly insisted later, of jobs threatened or of not going ahead, just a matter of knowing what they could be hit with: "*Nothing was going to keep that program off the air.*"[21]

Said Jack Beck: "He didn't imply that anyone would be fired; it was just so we'd know what's coming—better know now than later."[22]

Others, however—Palmer Williams, Mili Bonsignori—had no such recollection of inquiry or collective self-examination in the cutting room that night. Wershba recalled Friendly bringing up the question of past associations, then quickly cutting off response— i.e., "And if anybody tells me, I'll break his head," or words to that effect. To the newsman it seemed clear that Friendly didn't want to compromise the broadcast. When twice after that, said Wershba, some seemed to feel the need to talk, he cut them off. CBS had had it with the blacklist mentality, he said, and Paley was agreed: They weren't going to play these games anymore.[23]

Monday, March 8, Joe McCarthy came roaring into town, demanding airtime now that the Republicans had designated Nixon, not McCarthy, to reply to Stevenson. The networks would grant him time, he threatened, "or know what the law is." An opening attack was scheduled for Tuesday with an address before the Dutch Treat Club, some of whose members had resigned in protest.

At Forty-fifth Street and Fifth Avenue, the cutting room was alive with activity, Murrow openly in charge, working directly with the staff, Friendly at his side, no intermediary, no "Ed wants." Rarely seen in the cutting room two days in a row, this time he kept on top of things, giving the orders. Bonsignori later remembered his constant, restless presence—"looking at this, looking at that."

"He kept saying, 'This is *mine*'; he wanted it to be exactly right, exactly *his* way, *his* concept; said he wanted McCarthy to convict himself out of his own mouth."[24]

The same held true for the narration, heretofore Friendly's in the first draft, dictated this time, word after word, by Murrow, taking over "completely," then working through the script with the producer, Wershba recalled, in an atmosphere "incredibly tense," the communal atmosphere of Sunday night replaced by a professional absorption, the public man in action:

> . . . cold, reserved, seemingly even bored as he methodically reached for the relentless words that would hammer nails into McCarthy's political coffin. At one point he directed me to excerpt key lines from the editorials of the nation's newspapers. . . . "Give me the short, active words," he ordered. . . .[25]

It might have helped account for the McCarthy program's special quality, although dramatically it was not up to the others. More than any other, it was a "Murrow" program. But there was another aspect to the matter, one that disturbed Murrow deeply.

The title notwithstanding, "A Report on Senator Joseph R. McCarthy" was no report; it was a virtual half-hour editorial ending in a call to action,[26] the final step from TV news purveyor to TV activist, with all that that implied.

It was a paradox that the very memories of the thirties that impelled the broadcast—memories sharpened by McCarthy's lavish funding by the corporate right wing, his sub rosa ties with the hate groups of the radical right, his use of anti-Bolshevism as a steppingstone[27]—also caused Murrow to have second thoughts, based on his own experience of the media manipulation of Fascism in its heyday; the concerns he himself had raised at Chatham House in 1937, concerns subsequently proved so painfully valid; above all, his recollections of the Austrian ex-corporal whose rise, oratory, and skillful use of the airwaves reminded him of the man some still persisted, somehow, in seeing as a clown (or would do so later, with the benefit of hindsight).

"He felt," as an associate put it, "that we were in the presence of a man who could turn America around, who had so much power just in terms of being a destroyer. He feared the beginning of a Nazi-like mass movement."[28]

Nonetheless, he questioned his own use, or possible abuse, of the mass media, the power of TV and his proved ability to sway the masses. Colleagues said he was wary of it; Bill Downs later claimed he feared it. Certainly it was the one quality which, run amok, he recognized and hated in a Joe McCarthy.

He was too experienced a newsman not to be aware of the consequence of throwing out the rulebook after sixteen years to mount, openly, a thirty-minute attack on another individual. He worried about the possible example set: Was it a question of two wrongs making a right?

To Ed Scott over drinks, he confessed he'd been walking the streets until all hours, trying to sort it out. "Eddy," he asked, "do you think I'm doing the right thing?"[29]

Of course McCarthy, it could be argued, had amply had his day in court (still did, in fact, via televised subcommittee hearings weekdays at 11:00 A.M.), with little such consideration given to his victims.

"Ed would never hurt anyone," said Janet Murrow with conviction, "but he felt McCarthy was hurting the country."[30] She had left that week unwillingly for Jamaica, fulfilling a long-standing invitation, Murrow adamant that the McCarthy business have no bearing *whatsoever* on family plans. Better to leave than argue, she figured. The Brewsters moved in from Middletown to look after Casey. Jenny Brewster, waking nights, could hear her son-in-law pacing the living room.

"The McCarthy program bothered the *hell* out of him," said a friend from CBS. "The question was, Did he or anyone else have the right to use this tremendous power to attack one man?"

The question never was completely answered. Despite the program's overwhelming success, Murrow was always uneasy about it, almost anxious at times to disown it. When, in 1955, the producers published a hardcover *See It Now* collection with the New York firm of Simon & Schuster, "A Report on Senator Joseph R. McCarthy" was not included.

If the choice of that week—March 8—was astute, the convergence of events March 9 was near-uncanny. In midtown at the Park Lane Hotel, Joe McCarthy, before the Dutch Treat Club and a record audience, parried the barbed queries of Hans Kaltenborn, a onetime supporter turned opponent, and renewed his demands for air. Dick Nixon was an excellent choice to answer for the party, he told reporters, "but Stevenson's main attack was against me." The Senator appeared ruffled for one of the few times in his career.

In Washington another former backer, Ralph Flanders of Vermont, accused McCarthy on the Senate floor of setting out to wreck the GOP and set up a one-man party. At 485 Madison, Murrow, working on his script, worked in Flanders' description, hot off the wires, of the Junior Senator ("He dons his war paint. He goes into his war dance. . . . He goes forth to battle and proudly returns with the scalp of a pink Army dentist").

In the morning there had been a call from Paley: He'd be with Ed tonight and tomorrow as well—a personal gesture for which Murrow was understandably grateful.

Paley also urged Murrow to offer McCarthy reply time on the air. "Beat him to the punch," he said.

"Of course McCarthy would have insisted on it anyway," he recalled later, "but it put Murrow in a much better position. Put *us* in a much better position, for having invited him to."[31]

The program was "an exceptional case," said Paley after three decades, a one-time suspension of the company dicta. "We gave him carte blanche . . . to develop an editorial opinion. . . . We changed our policies in connection with certain matters that we thought were of vital importance to the future and health and security of the country."

How much carte blanche? No one, evidently, cared to know, beginning with the Chairman, who declined to see the film. "I said no, I'd rather not. I'll look at it tonight." And so it went, right down the line.

Thirty years later it would be almost impossible to find a CBS executive who, knowing of the program—fair knowledge following the vetoed ad request—would admit to even the slightest trepidation (a typical comment: "Oh, I was all for it, thought it was great"). Yet Friendly recalled having a hard time finding a middle-management exec willing to discuss the show either before or after airing.

Rumors which circulated of Murrow's being called upstairs for urgent last-minute conferences, were discounted afterward by Friendly: "I think Ed was maybe up there once." But then, he added, he himself was at the cutting room, not 485. The actual extent of the backing would remain a matter of debate. "Paley felt he had a tiger by the tail," said a personal friend to both men, who declined to be identified. "No one stood up to McCarthy like Murrow did. Bill was in the corner going oh, gee, oh, gee. [He] would be calling up, raising hell. . . . no one will talk on that subject. They were all busy climbing up the ladder themselves."

Nonetheless, the bottom line, when all was said and done, was that CBS aired the show, where the rest of the TV industry was silent.

"Murrow," said Dorothy Paley Hirshon, the knowledgeable outsider, "obviously deserved the fullest credit—because I'm sure he carried the day against people who were far more timid than he would ever be. But just from knowing how it operates . . . he couldn't have done it alone. Because you've got to have the final authority."[32]

That being so, the program, its explosive implications notwithstanding, was virtually slipped out the side door—carried over network facilities, unpromoted, unseen by a single member of the working management, released under a set of bet-hedging priorities that refused to alert the viewing public, yet made sure to alert the FBI.

At 7:45 P.M. Murrow read the evening news as usual: a tax bill pigeonholed, McCarthy labeling the networks "dishonest and arrogant," GM record sales, Flanders in the Senate. The French commander in Indochina said his forces would soon take the offensive; in Washington Defense Secretary Charles Wilson refused to comment when asked about possible U.S. troop commitments.

At Vanderbilt Avenue last-minute snags caused the run-through to run late. During a break Wershba saw Murrow standing outside the control room, wiping his face: "It's awful hot in there."

"Gonna be a lot hotter in the country when this goes on the air."[33]

Security guards stood by the elevators, posted in response to crank calls coming in since the morning's *Times* ad. In the newsroom at 485 editors found their attention divided between readying copy for the late news; and awaiting the scuttlebutt from Grand Central, "the tension palpable," as one said later, "as though someone close to you were on the operating table,"[34] a devastating comment on industry morale.

The makeup went on and ran almost immediately; it always did under the lights, pointing up again the qualitative difference between what Murrow was about to do and comparable efforts in print or even over radio. It was a reminder that impact depended not only on program content but on voice and demeanor, the lifting of an eyebrow or the angle of a tie, on sustaining tension and interest over almost thirty minutes; that in going after McCarthy over live TV—no room for fluffs or retakes—he was giving the performance of his life.

Ten-thirty. The titles came on, opening announcements, opening commercial. Murrow looked into the camera—"Good evening."

> *Tonight* See It Now *devotes its entire half hour to a report on Senator Joseph R. McCarthy, told mainly in his own words and pictures. Because a report on Senator McCarthy is by definition controversial, we want to say exactly what we mean to say;*

*and I request your permission to read from script whatever remarks Murrow and Friendly may make. If the Senator feels that we have done violence to his words or pictures, and desires, so to speak, to answer himself, an opportunity will be afforded him on this program.*

Every now and then they had typed in "LOOK UP," but he kept his eyes fixed on the pages, his total absorption more convincing than any pitch to the camera.

Essentially, the program followed the technique of their first McCarthy feature: catching the Senator in his own contradictions, on film, or audiotape when film was unavailable, followed by Murrow as corrective, live or on the voice-over.

There was McCarthy on film, warning statesmanlike that if "this fight against Communism" became a fight between America's two parties, one party would be destroyed—"and the Republic cannot endure very long under a one-party system."

"*But on February 4, 1954, the Senator spoke of one party's treason.*" Murrow, back on camera, flicked a tape switch, and out came McCarthy's voice charging "those who wear the label 'Democrat' "with "the stain of a historic betrayal."

There was McCarthy brandishing alleged secret evidence, "never supposed to have seen the light of day." Murrow coldly identified it as a committee hearing transcript, readily available: "Anyone can buy it for two dollars."

There was McCarthy questioning a witness—"You know the Civil Liberties Union has been listed as a front for . . . the Communist Party?"—with Murrow right behind him: "*The Attorney General's List does not and never has listed the A.C.L.U. as subversive. Nor does the F.B.I. or any other federal government agency.*"

It was the first time McCarthy's allegations had been systematically dissected in the full glare of the mass media.

They re-ran the Milwaukee banquet of December 1951, a choked McCarthy sniffling of being "smeared and bullwhipped," playing on audience sympathies ("My cup and my heart are so full, I can't *talk* to you").

"*But in Philadelphia . . . his heart was so full, he could* talk. . . ." The footage rolled on the Senator's gleeful Washington's Birthday reenactment of his bullwhipping of General Zwicker, to gales of laughter and applause.

They showed McCarthy putting down his press opposition as "extreme left wing," then cut to Murrow reading from a stack of papers, beginning with the Chicago *Tribune*, infuriated by the attack on the Army (though no less furious, it would turn out, at its inclusion on the program), reading off the "active words" he had asked for: "*The unwarranted interference of a demagogue . . .*"; "*The line must be drawn or McCarthy will become the Government. . . .*"

They showed McCarthy defying the administration, vowing to call the shots as he saw them "regardless of who happens to be President," quoting Shakespeare as he mocked the battered Army Secretary, "Upon what meat does this our Caesar feed?"

"*And upon what meat does Senator McCarthy feed?*" In quick response Murrow pointed up "two staples of his diet . . . the investigations, protected by immunity, and the half-truth," and ran the Reed Harris footage of the year before-but still effective: "I resent the tone of this inquiry, Mr. Chairman. . . ." (*See It Now* never did come up with the Wheeling speech, location efforts all dead-ended; a station said to have a tape told them it had been "accidentally" wiped.)

Despite the fear of bugs or breakdown, it went smoothly, the bits and pieces coalescing through the teamwork of the sweating men in the control room, as though the last two and a half years had been a practice drill for this half hour. An effort so successful that in the easier times of film and videotape it would be hard to remember that the so-called McCarthy program was actually a kinescope of what was in large measure a live show.

Some of the specifics later seemed remote, dealing as they did with day-to-day events, aimed at a newspaper-reading public not yet dependent on TV as a primary news source, therefore expected to bring its own context to the viewing. But even when the names and headlines had receded in the public consciousness, two overriding elements would still emerge from the old kinescopes, as powerful as ever: the damning portrait, for better or worse, of Joe McCarthy, and Ed Murrow as electronic adversary.

The program rounded off with a brief update, including the latest on McCarthy versus Benton. Then, reading from the script again, Murrow doubled back to McCarthy's sneering "Upon what meat does this our Caesar feed?" and began the windup on the Senator:

> "Had he looked three lines earlier in Shakespeare's *Caesar,* he would have found this line, which is not altogether inappropriate: 'The fault, dear Brutus, is not in our stars, but in ourselves.' "

His eyes glued to the paper, he attacked not, as McCarthy was to claim, the Senate's investigative power, but its abuse, to the effect that "the line between investigation and persecuting is a very fine one, and the Junior Senator from Wisconsin has stepped over it repeatedly." (Indeed, memories of the crossing of the line would come back to haunt the Senate decades later in the Watergate investigation, as charges of "McCarthyism" emanated from the Senator's former associate, now in the White House.)

But the true virtue of the Murrow sum-up would be that it put McCarthy in his place, treating him as a symptom rather than a cause, picking up on Kennan's earlier challenge to the society that had produced McCarthyism and the witch-hunts ("What causes us to huddle, herdlike. . . .")

Looking straight into the camera—no Teleprompter, direct eye contact—Murrow stepped out of the role of newsman, into the leadership vacuum:

> We will not walk in fear, one of another. We will not be driven by fear into an age of unreason, if we dig deep in our history and our doctrine; and remember that we are not descended from fearful men. Not from men who feared to write, to speak, to associate, and to defend causes that were for the moment unpopular.
>
> This is no time for men who oppose Senator McCarthy's methods to keep silent—or for those who approve. We *can* deny our heritage and our history but we cannot escape responsibility for the result. There is no way for a citizen of a republic to abdicate his responsibility. . . .
>
> The actions of the Junior Senator from Wisconsin have caused alarm and dismay amongst our allies abroad and given considerable comfort to our enemies. And whose fault is that? Not really his. He didn't create this situation of fear, he merely exploited it; and rather successfully.
>
> Cassius was right. "The fault, dear Brutus, is not in our stars, but in ourselves."
>
> Good night, and good luck.

The announcer came on with the incongruous commercial; the credits went up; the tension snapped. Friendly saw Murrow slump in his seat.

Looking at the monitors, they saw Don Hollenbeck on with the eleven o'clock news, his gaunt, harrowed features aglow, announcing his total agreement with "what Ed Murrow has just said." The calls were pouring in at a rate that made the Radulovich response look stillborn.

Down the hall, the See It Now staff, friends, and dependents spilled out of the studio where they'd been following on the monitors. Shirley Wershba, herself a former news staff member, taking time out for a family and nine months pregnant, was among the viewers, later recalling the sober group that filed toward them put of the control room—descending the iron steps to the floor of the narrow corridor, Murrow as usual surrounded by the others, a camel hair overcoat slung about his shoulders.

She ran up and grabbed his hand. "Ed, if it's a boy, I'm gonna name him after you!"

Murrow, usually shy and constrained, held on, unsmiling. "Do you think it was worth it?"

He seemed like a man, she said, "facing his complete defeat.

"He was tense, still living it. And I knew what he meant—were we just whistling in the dark?"[35]

They were not. By 1:30 that morning, CBS, New York had received more than 1,000 telegrams, almost all of them approving, with Western Union reporting a huge backlog of the same. More than 2,000 calls had made it past the overloaded switchboards, hundreds more backed up, with similar responses reported by the CBS stations and affiliates throughout the country—the first surge of a tidal wave reaction running between two- and ten-to-one against McCarthy in the greatest mass response ever generated by a network TV program (the highest figures since the Checkers Speech, said KPIX in San Francisco). CBS in New York reported the switchboard swamped with calls, nineteen hours after See It Now had gone off the air.[36]

Whatever was out there, waiting, the show had touched it off—more than the politicians' speeches of the past week, however headlined in the press, or the rumored maneuvers of a party coping with a former asset turned embarrassment. For the general public one thing alone was tangible: A nationally known figure, nonpartisan and no polemicist, with a high factor of trust, had spoken up on national TV to say he didn't like McCarthy. And tens of thousands were suddenly replying, in letters, calls, and cables, that they didn't like him either.

It might have explained, the theme running through most of the letters—i.e., "Thank God somebody said something," cold comfort to the legions that had fought the good fight in the wilderness years and stark proof that for many, even in 1954, what didn't happen on television wasn't happening.

What the program had done, of course, was provide a flash point. It had served as a catalytic agent, mobilizing and coalescing opinion, hitherto fragmented, into a nationwide expression of popular sentiment, a fact not lost on the White House, itself the recipient of anti-McCarthy telegrams, more than a few reading "LISTEN TO MURROW TOMORROW," the sign-off of the 7:45 radio show. The usual unnamed sources indicated considerable interest in the statistics coming out of CBS.

More than that, there was a palpable relief in the communications, now totaling well over 100,000, complete with names and addresses, predicated for the most part on one supposition: If a big-time commentator could say it out loud on television, it must be okay.

The major liberal TV critics were ecstatic. Jack Gould called the program "crusading journalism of high responsibility and genuine courage." True, it was "strongly one-sided," conceded the *Times* writer, "But the alternative to not handling the story in this manner was not to do the story at all, by far the greater danger. The Senator seldom has shown relish for letting others do the cross-examination."[37]

"He [Murrow] put his finger squarely on the root of the true evil of McCarthyism," wrote John Crosby in the New York *Herald Tribune*, "which is its corrosive effect on the souls of hitherto honest men. . . .

"Now it takes great courage to attack Sen. McCarthy in the first place (though why every one is so afraid of that bumbler I can't imagine), but it takes far greater courage to look you and me in the face and say it's our fault."[38]

But strangely, it was the New York City pro-McCarthy press that gave the program its first headlines, in one case by mistake. The giant *Daily News*, thinking it a backhanded CBS response to McCarthy's roar for airtime, gave the show next morning's front page in the three-star late edition (MCCARTHY GETS TV TIME OFFER. MURROW BLASTS SENATOR, MAKES BID). The afternoon *Journal-American*, solid-gold Hearst, whose peppery critic, Jack O'Brian, had detested the show, more accurately and simply ran a massive head: TELECAST RIP AS MCCARTHY STIRS STORM.

The program had indeed set off a press reaction, from the New York *Post* to the San Francisco *Chronicle*, though upstaged temporarily by the Flanders speech; a Senator outweighed a mere news show by the press standards of 1954 (also as an A.M. story, in contrast with the late-closing *See It Now*), an outlook that was to change radically in the next forty-eight hours.

In the meantime, all was euphoria, especially on 17; "like V-J day," said a staffer, "the war was over." Murrow, walking back from lunch the day after the broadcast, found himself mobbed on the street as word of his presence got around, the crush of pedestrians jamming traffic on Fifth Avenue. "We had to get a taxi to get Ed out of it," remembered Frank Gillard, then visiting from the BBC. *Variety* was calling Murrow "practically . . . a national hero."[39]

At the Waldorf that month 1,500 men and women attending the annual OPC dinner rose in a spontaneous standing ovation as Murrow entered the room. Wershba, returned to Washington, felt the atmosphere there as though a boil had been lanced (also the occasional dig: "Hey, Joe, Ed gonna run for President?").[40]

Alistair Cooke, writing for the British *Guardian Weekly*, called the overall response "a stunning endorsement of Murrow's courage.

"Hence the surprising rally of candour in public men who have stayed astutely silent for 5 years. Hence President Eisenhower's relieved approval of Senator Flanders. Hence a morning chorus of . . . newspaper columnists praising Murrow for 'laying it on the line.' Hence the confident laughter in yesterday's [McCarthy] subcommittee hearing. . . .

"Mr. Murrow may yet make bravery fashionable."[41]

The praise was not unqualified. *Variety* on one page dubbed March 9 " 'Good Tuesday' . . . when 'See It Now' took its stand for television, the networks and the people," and on another, called the program "an expedient of great interest, and some belated courage, but basically . . . a footnote to history rather than a definitive answer to McCarthyism." The distinguished critic Gilbert Seldes, once of CBS; an avid fan and personal friend—in a roasting disputed by his colleagues on the *Saturday Review*—accused Murrow of stacking the deck and setting a dangerous example, best not to have done the show; reflecting Murrow's concerns, if not his conclusions. Dorothy Schiff, whose New York *Post* had been in the forefront from the start:

> "This is no time for men who oppose Senator McCarthy's methods to keep silent, said Ed as he leaped gracefully aboard the crowded bandwagon."

(A few days later, Murrow, coming on Seldes at the Century Club, fixed him with a glare: "You sonuvabitch! You've made me think about a lot of things I thought I'd settled—but God bless you.")[42]

Yet overall, the highest praise came generally from those who had been in the fight the longest, from *I. F. Stone's Weekly* ("Hats off to Ed Murrow") to the editorial writers of the St. Louis *Post-Dispatch*, to cartoonist Walt Kelly, to Joe Alsop, who had immediately sent a cable (ONE OF THE GREAT ACTS OF POLITICAL COURAGE OF OUR TIME).

The reaction abroad, after word of the program hit the news wires, was "phenomenal," as a correspondent put it. "The European newspapers went crazy, they were delighted; it was like America coming into its own again."

The BBC ran a kinescope. In Rome Bill Downs, now bureau chief for CBS, ran nightly screenings at his home to packed houses and standing ovations, mostly from Americans in Rome. (His own reaction: "About time!") Said Roz Downs: "We were getting calls from the embassy, from the USIA, saying, 'We are desperate, we want to *see* this thing.' The State Department was overjoyed; they were terrified of what was going on. And the military attachés—after all, the Army was being attacked.

"The effect was sudden—overnight. Murrow was a hero in Europe. CBS could do no wrong. But it was more than that. Everybody suddenly felt as if there was a chance that the country would start thinking again, instead of this terror, this being frightened of each other. Because that's what it really came down to."[43]

"I can tell you—you were unquestionably the man of the hour," Lauren Bacall wrote him from Europe, where the Bogarts had heard about the program. "Thanks for starting the ball rolling. God knows we're all affected by what's been going on."[44]

At the office, add-on staff coped with the snowstorm of mail while Murrow told Joan Walker of *Newsweek* magazine that he hadn't said anything about McCarthy over TV that he hadn't said on radio and denied that the program marked, as so many claimed, TV's coming of age: "No single show can change the whole medium."[45]

*Variety* reported the industry virtually galvanized into a chorus of praise for Murrow and for CBS, led by NBC in what the trade paper called "the biggest Macy's Loves Gimbel's Week in the history of the medium." Sarnoff himself—the grand old man of RCA—appeared over *Person to Person* (or rather, being scheduled, didn't cancel out), interviewed back to back with Secretary of the Treasury George Humphry: a double imprimatur, proving the usefulness of the mass appeal show.

Telegrams and letters were still pouring in: from Chief Justice Earl Warren, from Clark Clifford, from Fred Bate; a hand-delivered note from Albert Einstein, asking to see him again, in the modest, courtly tone Murrow knew so well from 1934; messages from Adam Clayton Powell, Jr., and Hazel Scott, the artist William Walton, Walter White of the NAACP; from Sig and Maybelle Mickelson; and from his old adversary Burton Wheeler. John Gunther, who had criticized him in the Shirer matter, cabled him on Friday: "BROTHER BROTHER AM PROUD TO CALL YOU FRIEND."

More revealing, however, were the many messages from colleagues in broadcasting and the press. John Scali at the AP cabled as "a fellow reporter," thanking Murrow outright for the show: "It speaks for scores of us who must stifle our opinion even when it hurts."

"When you sailed into McCarthy," wrote the newsroom personnel at an affiliate, "we in this business who are arbitrarily confined to straight reporting must as a man have raised our voices to shout, 'at last.' "

From the various departments at CBS, and the other networks, came an outpouring of sentiment: mass signings and individual notes of gratitude from secretaries, makeup artists, reporters, publicists, producers; from the mail room to programming, across the board. At the other end were fervent thanks from small-town editors, writing of years of isolation.

In fact, far from being an East Coast or liberal-elitist phenomenon, as often later claimed, the show's success was based in large part on strong grass-roots support ("We midwesterners look to you for leadership," wrote the mayor of Chillicothe, Ohio), proving once again that Murrow knew his audience and the trap, to be avoided, of preaching to the converted. Indeed, some of the strongest reactions were to come from that undefined entity later known as Middle America, where the Walter Lippmanns didn't penetrate but many still remembered "this . . . is London" and where, in a rare salute from one medium to another, a cartoonist for the Cleveland *Plain Dealer* depicted a jowly McCarthy staggering in defeat, an object labeled "Murrow's mike" wrapped lethally around his neck.

As press praise turned to hyperbole, however, he grew restive and embarrassed, especially when talking with a bloodied veteran of the McCarthy wars: "I ain't exactly a pioneer in this thing, you know."[46]

Thursday evening, March 11, after a puzzling two-day silence, McCarthy struck back, appearing on the Fulton Lewis, Jr., program over Mutual, the wire services alerted, photographers snapping the Senator with Roy Cohn, waiting for the elevator in the corridor outside the studio. It was billed as a partial reply to Stevenson, but as the AP reported next day, "some of McCarthy's strongest words were devoted to Murrow."

## Notes

1. Schultz, interview.
2. Friendly, interviews.
3. Schultz, interviews.
4. Bliss, interviews.
5. Friendly, interviews.
6. Schultz, interview.
7. Friendly, interviews.
8. Schultz, interview.
9. Ibid.
10. New York *Times*, July 17, 1960.
11. Friendly, interviews.
12. The Tampa [FL] *Tribune*, clipping, no date.
13. Downs, interviews.
14. Ibid.
15. Handwritten notation, October 10, 1956.
16. AIR TEL, Bureau, NY, NY, April 7, 1954, from Kelly, 3-Bureau (101–5828) (Regular).
17. "Memorandum, Mr. A. H. Belmont to Mr. V. P. Keay, Subject: Edward R. Murrow, CBS Commentator," April 14, 1954.
18. Ibid.

19.   ERM to Rex Budd (draft), April 18, 1950.
20.   "From L. N. Conroy to Mr. A Rosen, Subject: Edward R. Murrow/Name Check Request" June 7, 1956.
21.   "Memorandum: from Mr. A. Jones to Mr. Nichols," June 22, 1951.
22.   Note to Miami SAC, April 16, 1956; also limited file check for Presidential Press Secretary Hagerty, July 8, 1955.
23.   File check for Hagerty, ibid.
24.   Friendly, interviews.
25.   Casey Murrow, interviews.
26.   ERM to Seward, February 2,1960.
27.   Casey Murrow, interviews.
28.   ERM to Seward, February 16, 1960.
29.   ERM to Seward, February 2, 1960.
30.   ERM to Seward, February 21, 1960.
31.   ERM to Seward, February 2, 1960.
32.   ERM to Seward, March 1, 1960.
33.   Murphy, interview.
34.   Ibid.
35.   ERM to Seward, March 20, 1960.
36.   Ibid.
37.   Ibid.
38.   ERM to Seward, undated.
39.   Janet Murrow, interviews.
40.   Memo, unsigned, possibly Chester Williams, "Things to Be Done."
41.   As an example, his old logging supervisor, Ken Merredith, was called in Washington State and asked to wire a deposition to the effect that Murrow had never been a member of the IWW plus general character references from 1925 on.
42.   Chester Williams, notes for Adrian Fisher and W. T. Stone, March 26–29, 1954.
43.   *Matter of "M" File*; memorandum for the files, "Conference March 22, 1954, with ERM," March 23, 1954.
44.   Palmer Williams, interviews.
45.   Ibid.
46.   *"M" File*; memo to ERM, undated.

# Chapter 17

# CARL ROWAN

# BREAKING BARRIERS

**C**ARL ROWAN WAS A COMMENTATOR and nationally syndicated newspaper columnist who was once labeled by the *Washington Post* as America's "most visible Black journalist." During Rowan's long career, the issue of race was a reoccurring theme in his work. Rowan made frequent appearances on public affairs radio and television programs, and served in the presidential administrations of John F. Kennedy and Lyndon B. Johnson. He also was one of the first African Americans to serve as a commissioned officer in the U.S. Navy during World War II.

A graduate of Oberlin College after attending Tennessee State University and Washburn University prior to World War II, Rowan earned a master's degree in journalism from the University of Minnesota. He started his career writing for the African American newspapers *Minneapolis Spokesman* and *St. Paul Recorder*. He became a general assignment reporter for the *Minneapolis Tribune* in 1950, and reported extensively on race relations in the South. The articles became the basis of his first book, *South of Freedom*, which was published in 1952. He spent 1954 reporting in India, Pakistan and Southeast Asia, and published the book *The Pitiful and the Proud* based on his travels there in 1956. In this period, Rowan became the first journalist to win the Society of Professional Journalists' award for best newspaper reporting three years in a row. After a stint in government service, he wrote a column for the *Chicago Sun-Times* and the Field Syndicate for 32 years. At one point, his column reached about half of all the households in America.

This memoir is a feisty account of his rise to prominence and an insider's view of journalism and government from Rowan's perch as a nationally syndicated columnist. This section tells of Rowan's interactions with President Ronald Reagan when Rowan was serving as president of the Gridiron Club that hosts an annual dinner in which the president of the United States is humorously roasted and then, in turn, roasts the press. It gives insight into Rowan and President Reagan as well as the routine interaction between a distinguished columnist and politicians of the highest rank.

## The Reagan Years

If I am lucky enough to get old and sit around in a rocking chair telling my grandchildren and great-grandchildren about my career as a journalist, I shall tell them that I was never prouder than in those days of 1981 and 1982 when I kept sticking it to a riches-seeking president who was making already-miserable circumstances almost intolerable for America's poor people.

I know that my grandchildren will not remember, or even understand, that as the lines of hungry people grew longer in city after city, Reagan was moving to wipe out 340,000 public-service jobs, claiming that they were "dead-end jobs" and thus not worthy of the people who were desperate to feed and shelter their families within some reasonable parameters of self-esteem. They will have no way of recalling that Reagan was, in the first months of a terrible recession, forcing a million poor people off the food stamp rolls, reducing medical-care funds for the poor and for impoverished pregnant women and newborn babies, and trying to cut the federal contribution to the education of youngsters in public schools.

But I shall tell my grandchildren that I was one of the few journalists in the land to write bluntly that Reagan's agenda "is neither fair nor humane, but cruelty covered up by glib cliches."

As unemployment grew dramatically, so did the length of the lines at the soup kitchens. The steel mills were operating at less than 60 percent of capacity. Assembly lines of the great American auto factories were shutting down. Farmers were facing foreclosures. Americans were losing their homes. The housing industry was in acute distress. So by March of 1982 I would write:

> Almost everybody in America seems to know that the country is in an economic mess that borders on a great depression—except Reagan.
>
> The President dismisses as "sob sisters" those Americans of every political stripe who see calamity in his budget proposals which would add perhaps half a *trillion* dollars to the national debt in just four years. It is difficult to determine whether Mr. Reagan is absurdly stubborn, a slow learner who has landed a job that is above his level of competency, or just an ideologue imprisoned in a maze of right-wing cliches.

I was fuming when the president talked about how the newspapers were loaded with want ads for jobs for people who really wanted to work — a suggestion that anybody on unemployment rolls was just a lazy bum. I asked the White House to tell that to the 4,508 people who had lined up in Hempstead, New York, to apply for 296 jobs ranging from dishwasher to desk clerk at a new hotel. I asked him to tell that to the 11 million Americans who were jobless and were desperately eager to find work, or to the 700,000-plus families that had been thrown into poverty since Reagan took office.

But I was learning that there were perils to the business of criticizing a president of the United States who had been elected by a landslide.

I knew when the election returns were in that it would not be any fun being a columnist in America, except for those conservatives who suddenly had become the darlings of the nation's editors and publishers. Reagan had been in office less than four months when I realized that things might be more difficult than I had expected.

In one situation the editor was honest enough to tell his readers that he was canceling my column because of my criticism of Reagan. Richard Sept, the managing editor of the *Daily Tidings* in Ashland, Oregon, wrote Kenneth Reiley, the sales manager of Field Newspaper Syndicate, announcing that he was canceling my column and that of Erma Bombeck. Sept first cited the poor economy as the reason to cancel Bombeck. But in explaining the cancellation of my column, he wrote: "The economy played a minor role in this decision. Our primary reason for canceling is a sense that Rowan has recently lost touch with reality since Reagan's election."

Remember, now, that there can't be a handful of black people among the readers of the *Daily Tidings*. But the readers of that newspaper came to my defense. Every now and then, when the critical mail gets heavy because of something I've written, I pick up that file relating to Ashland, Oregon, and chuckle. For example:

> And so it was that on the very day that Reagan first entered the White House normally sharp-eyed and keen-witted Rowan suddenly became a columnist wearing blinders.

A remarkable transformation indeed.

And another subscriber:

> Perhaps we should lend an ear to Mr. Rowan, who speaks to and for all of us when he brings warning that hope is dying at the same time that drugs and weapons are proliferating among large segments of the U.S. population.

And another:

> Is Rowan upsetting because he does not go into the soft shoe yassuh boss routine? If he'd tone down his writing and "behave himself like a good nigger" would you reconsider?

The thing that came through to me from all those letters was that the American people want to read and hear differences of viewpoint, as expressed extremely well by a man named William Ashworth:

> You ask for comments on your decision to drop columnist Carl Rowan from the paper because of his strident anti-Reagan stance. Very well, here is a comment.
>
> I think the decision is abominable . . . .
>
> It is the duty of the journalistic community to present both sides of any issue — the seamy underside as well as the glittering surface. Rowan has been a remarkably consistent and efficient voice pointing out the seamy underside of Reaganomics. At times he has been the only voice. You should not punish him for his consistency and courage; you should not deprive us of a chance to agree or disagree with him, as is our wont.
>
> Somebody once accused Mark Twain of "preaching." His response was, "I only do it because the rest of the clergy seems to be on vacation." Carl

Rowan must not be deprived of his voice because the rest of the clergy is
on vacation.

I am proud to say that in 1990 the *Daily Tidings* is still running the Rowan column.
   [. . .]

This may strike you as terribly anti-intellectual, or a Rowan version of voodoo, but it is
a reality that discerning black people can smell a racist a mile away. Those who have
gone through decades of suffering the slings and barbs of bigotry have a sixth sense that
tells them who in white America is a friend, and who a foe. Black people know that
sometimes their greatest enemy is not an Orval Faubus who throws little black schoolchildren to an Arkansas mob, or a George Wallace who stands in the doorway of the
University of Alabama, trying to keep blacks out, but white people of power who would
never utter a racist sentence in public, yet who quietly and privately will do everything
they can to keep black people as the slave class in this society.

Anger over moral issues is the mother and father of self-righteousness. I did not
have to look far to find anger. Reagan and his Justice Department and other appointees
found ways to keep me outraged. There was Reagan's reluctance to extend the Voting
Rights Act of 1965, which guaranteed a measure of political power for millions of blacks.
There was his attempt to give tax-exempt status to Bob Jones University and the
Goldsboro Christian Schools, institutions that practiced racial discrimination. And then
the restoring of tax-exempt status to the Prince Edward Academy in Farmville, Virginia
— an academy that was created to educate white children after all public schools were
closed to avoid desegregation. "How," I asked myself, "could any president ignore the
fact that he was giving a tax subsidy to whites who had left black children bereft of education for years?" Then Reagan tried to wipe out Legal Services for the poor.

One of my most memorable periods of the Reagan years was the time of celebration
of the two hundredth anniversary of the U.S. Constitution in 1987. The Gannett
Corporation people at the flagship station, WUSA-TV, asked me to host and help
produce a one-hour special that would help Americans to understand what the
Constitution really means. With a marvelous producer, Jeanne Bowers, we developed a
program called "Searching for Justice: Three American Stories." Stories about a woman
in Ohio who had been on death row; about Norma McCorvey, the real-life Texas woman
who had made the history books as "Jane Roe" in the landmark abortion case; and about
the legal struggle to desegregate colleges in the South and Southwest.

The program became a sensation. On the night that it was to be broadcast it
produced the two lead stories on "CBS Evening News with Dan Rather." First, there was
the interview that I had done with Supreme Court Justice Thurgood Marshall in which
he rated American presidents, calling Reagan "the worst." The White House, the Justice
Department, some other justices, and a lot of editors were stunned, because no sitting
justice had ever before spoken so frankly, publicly, about a sitting president. Second,
there was the incredibly emotional scene in which McCorvey told me that contrary to
the story spread wide over the years, she had not become pregnant as the result of
being raped. "Jane Roe" had become pregnant in a liaison of passion, and she had said
rape only because she thought that might work better to establish a woman's right to an
abortion.

Reagan tried to dismiss Marshall's rating of him with humor. He suggested that
Marshall was too old to know what he was saying.

I then did a one-hour TV documentary called "Thurgood Marshall: The Man," which won the Alfred I. duPont-Columbia University Silver Baton, one of the two most coveted awards in American television.

The impact of those two shows made 1987 one of the most glorious years a reporter could ever have.

\*   \*   \*

It was Saturday noon, December 5, 1987, and I had just been elected president of the Gridiron Club, that once call-male, lily-white bastion of journalism.

My colleagues were having fun with the fact that the Gridiron Club was passing a racial milestone—its first black president in its 103 years. We exchanged many jokes, but no one was gauche enough to write about it.

I learned early in my membership, after getting about five hundred elbows in my ribs from more senior members rushing to the front of the chorus at the celebrated spring dinner, that it means something to journalists to be able to speak lines, sing songs, try to dance, make fools of themselves in any Thespian manner, when their editors and publishers are in the audience.

More important, perhaps, was the opportunity for journalists to solidify relationships with talk show hosts and sponsors, to "pay off" their sources of leaks, by inviting corporate leaders, movie stars, cabinet members, to the only dinner I know of where no amount of money can buy you a ticket. You have to be *invited* to the Gridiron dinner.

But the active journalists in the Gridiron Club know that the ultimate payoff is becoming president, showcasing your newspaper, sitting for hours beside the president of the United States, giving the traditional "Speech in the Dark" in which you can display your wit and your disdain for the buffoons who are wasting the public's money or violating the people's trust.

I, who had written at least a hundred columns excoriating Ronald Reagan, was going to have the "privilege" of sitting beside him during a long, long night.

"Dear God, what can I talk about with this man?" I asked myself as I was driving home after my election.

I recalled, that cold December Saturday, that Reagan had been to seven straight Gridiron dinners, making him one of the few national leaders who had not bugged out. Lyndon Johnson had concocted any number of excuses to avoid the satire, the sometimes cutting criticisms, that are in the songs, dialogue, and even dances of a Gridiron affair.

I had my previously expressed hostilities toward the Reagans, but I also had my responsibilities as Gridiron president. I knew that no matter what gripes I had, the spring dinner audience would want to give a warm good-bye to the Reagans, who promptly notified me that they would be delighted to attend.

I asked Mrs. Reagan to sing a farewell song, but after we Gridironers had sung a good-bye song loaded with political bite. This woman, who had once offended me with that remark about "all these beautiful white people," was warm and friendly as she met me and other Gridironers at the Capital Hilton for a rehearsal of what we all knew would be a showstopper. I watched her with rapidly vanishing uneasiness.

She rehearsed her number four times over for about forty-five minutes, kissed pianist Les Karr, and gave me a glowing good-bye.

On Saturday, March 26, 1988, the Reagans arrived at 7:04 P.M. in a driving rain. They got out of the White House limousine wrapless, he in the traditional white tie and tails, she wearing a trademark red gown.

As we walked up the steps and took the trek toward the head table, the president began to tell me a story of the Secret Service, and "shooting from the hip," but he got interrupted quickly.

Suddenly the orchestra was playing "Hail to the Chief," the guests were standing to give rousing applause, and Reagan was taking a place on my right while, across the lectern, Mrs. Reagan stood on Viv's left. Stood because, in more than a century of Gridiron tradition, no one had been able to sit down until a Gridiron quartet sang "There's music in the air," and the Gridiron president gave his "Speech in the Dark."

"You see, these FBI agents, cops, and others drop to their knees to fire at criminals," Reagan continued his story, "but the Secret Service guys stand up so their bodies can protect a president or other target of assassination. They shoot from their hips . . ."

Many Gridiron presidents have had humorists, even writers for Johnny Carson and Bob Hope, conjure up funny lines. But I had written my own speech, choosing to ridicule the "first black in history" obsession of white journalists and to deal in light sarcasm with my serious concerns and outrages regarding the Reagan years.

I broke all the Gridiron traditions by letting Reagan and the other guests sit and listen to my "Speech in the Dark" in the light, a bow to one of my teacher's warnings that smart guys should be "seen as well as heard."

I told the Reagans and others that I was pleased to have them present "to help the Gridiron Club make history. For the first time in one hundred and three years, this club has a president who is . . . from McMinnville, Tennessee."

I turned to Reagan and told him that my Gridiron presidency was exactly like his. Every time I took a nap, some young whippersnapper tried to stage a coup.

"That, Mr. President," I said, "is why I'm going to double the support I've given you in my columns over the last seven years."

I noted that Reagan guffawed above the laughter of the audience.

Charlie McDowell of the *Richmond Times-Dispatch* had only told me that "Reagan is a talker." He didn't warn me that Reagan would talk to me during the other closely scheduled chores that I had to do.

"Mr. President!" boomed the voice of Emory.

I was supposed to stand and say, as Gridiron history decreed: "Mr. Alan S. Emory of the *Watertown* [New York] *Daily Times*, the music chairman of the Gridiron Club!" But as Emory was giving his cue, Reagan had me by the arm and was saying, "Now, about this business of me calling Ollie North and Admiral John Poindexter heroes . . . ."

As politely as I could, I silenced the president for the moments it took me to turn the audience over to Emory. When I sat down, Reagan was still in midsentence: ". . . I meant that they had been military heroes, but not necessarily heroes in their handling of this weapons-to-Iran matter."

"Well, that's quite a difference, Mr. President, and I'm not sure Americans understand it," I said.

"I want you to know that I never thought I was exchanging arms to Iran for American hostages," Reagan said, "and some people did some things without my authority."

"Isn't it true that Mrs. Reagan thinks North and Poindexter and perhaps Bill Casey [the late CIA director and the leader of the 1984 campaign in which Reagan won the presidency] co-opted, or took over, your presidency?"

"She's not happy with any of them," Reagan said.

I kept glancing at the table filled with my guests, Lee Iacocca from Chrysler Corporation, my editor Fredrica Friedman from Little, Brown and Company, my sons

Carl and Jeff, and daughter Barbara, and I could see that they were wondering what Reagan and I were talking about. Then the tone of the conversation eased.

"Carl, I need to take a leak. Do I have to go to that toilet that's a mile away?"

"Mr. President," I said, "there's a bathroom just outside the door."

"Let's go," he said, and as we got up there was a shifting of security agents that I thought could only be noticed by someone who had been in government and spent years dealing with the Secret Service. Some thirty White House aides slithered toward that room.

Reagan and I walked into "my reception room" and I found that it had been transformed into a bastion of technology that could launch World War III in seconds.

"You all know Ambassador Rowan," Reagan said, revealing that he remembered parts of his briefing.

He went into the john, came out, and said: "It took me years to learn that you Gridironers call this 'the piss break.' "

We then returned to the dining room, and Reagan, sipping his wine, began telling me that "You never really understood me on this business of racism."

"Mr. President," I said, "I have never written a column criticizing you that was based on personal or political opposition. I have written every column out of a profound belief that you didn't understand America's racial problems, and that you rejected the black Americans who could help you in favor of the blacks who would become sellouts, quislings, traitors."

Reagan replied: "I tried hard to win friendship among blacks, but I couldn't do it. I talked to black leaders after my election in 1980, and they went out and criticized me in horrible ways."

"And that's why you went almost eight years refusing to talk to the acknowledged black leaders of America?" I asked.

"They attacked me at the outset, so I said to hell with 'em," Reagan replied.

"Sir," I said, "I've criticized you in my columns because I believe that any president of all the people must talk to all the people and their leaders."

"You know something?" Reagan said, with a long pause. "I should have talked to *you* seven years ago."

Reagan seemed to sip his wine a little faster and to talk less. As Mrs. Reagan left the head table to go onstage, he said, "She seems nervous as hell," and in the damnedest segue I can recall, said, "She wanted me to tell you that we are not the enemies of poor and black people."

I had been drinking my wine a little faster, too, and was emboldened to say what I really felt.

"Mr. President," I said, "I know that you and she want to believe that. But the people you have named to the Supreme Court, the appeals courts, the district courts, are not the friends of black people, or my children, or poor black pregnant women, or anyone who is needy in America. That is the rap against your presidency."

Reagan reddened, then he pointed to our left down the head table to where his then national security adviser Colin Powell was sitting.

"Now there," Reagan said, "is one of the smartest black men I ever knew."

I got the message. Reagan was saying that as the first president to put a black man in so critical a job, he didn't have to argue about his commitment to racial equality. I knew that, for this Gridiron dinner, Reagan was ready to end our serious discussions.

*And banishing Al Haig*
*And bloodying up*

*Don Regan's nose . . .*
*Oh, thank you, so much.*

Mrs. Reagan came onstage to great applause and gave a fetching response:

*Thanks for the memories*
*Of all the times we had,*
*The happy and the sad.*
*Looking back Don Regan*
*Doesn't even seem so bad.*
*Oh, thank you, so much.*
*Thanks for the memories*
*Of all the whole press corps.*
*At times I cursed and swore.*
*You sometimes were a headache*
*But you never were a bore.*
*I thank you. Bye-bye.*

As the dinner guests gave roaring applause, she stepped to the mike for this encore:

*So, thanks for the memories.*
*It's time to say good-bye.*
*Oh, how the time does fly.*
*Ronnie's loved these past eight years*
*And so I confess have I.*
*So thank you. Bye-bye!*

[. . .]

A few days after the dinner I reported a bit of my conversation with Reagan to Charlie McDowell and Allan Cromley of the *Daily Oklahoman.*

"It's not over," said Cromley. "You'll surely get a private invitation from Reagan."

A few weeks went by before I got a call from the White House asking if I would have lunch privately with the president on May 9.

It was an extraordinary occasion during which I saw the many facets, mind twists, and vulnerabilities of a president whose views and actions dominated American life in the 1980s. A president whose appointments and policies will affect the American mind-set, and legal posture, on issues like abortion and civil liberties well into the next century.

When I was taken to Reagan, he said: "I hear you and Howard Baker [brand-new White House chief of staff] were bunkmates in midshipman school in World War Two."

"Platoon mates, sir — two of the luckiest guys ever to come out of Tennessee."

"I don't have any press people watching over this luncheon, which is just between you and me, but I know Howard would like to join us."

"I can't think of anyone I'd rather have join us than my old Navy buddy," I replied.

Baker walked up with a big smile on his face, and we sat down to a bowl of corn soup, some raw carrots, and a few balls of melon.

"This Reagan sure knows how to get even," I thought, as I surveyed the victuals at hand.

Then, out of nowhere, he hit me with a punch that reminded me that presidents watched the television show "Agronsky and Company cum Inside Washington," which I had been on for nineteen years, but they never remembered who said what.

Reagan started to scold me gently for saying on TV that his wife had consulted an astrologer and decided that he would be sworn in as governor of California at precisely one minute after midnight.

"I was not the one who mentioned the midnight swearing in," I replied. "I didn't even know that you were sworn in at a minute past midnight. You've got me confused with someone else."

Reagan sniffled, blinked his eyes several times, and said: "Well, then, I'm sorry. I got it wrong."

Reagan was "bleeding" over "revelations" by his ousted chief of staff, Donald Regan, that Mrs. Reagan used an astrologer to decide the time of important presidential events and had kept him virtually inactive after his prostate surgery because the stars weren't in the proper alignment.

"Dammit," said Reagan, "most of these things are absolutely untrue. And, dammit, I'm not going to stand by and let anybody railroad my wife.

"She didn't fire Don Regan. He wasn't fired, as a matter of fact. He had said several months before that he just had to get back to private life. Then, when this Iran-Contra thing came on, he said, 'You know, I don't think I should jump ship now.'

"Regan set the date of his resignation, so I had to find someone to replace him. When the story leaked that Baker would replace him, he became incensed. He thought Nancy was the leaker. Wrong. I telephoned him to apologize for the leak, but he wouldn't take my call."

Reagan's outrage over Regan's remarks just rolled out, like mud from a gully washer. Asked about Regan's claim that Nancy pressured him to fire the late CIA director William Casey, Reagan scrunched up his nose, fought to get air up it, and replied: 'Never happened." Knowing that Casey could never again function as the nation's top spy, Reagan said, "We went to him [in the hospital] with the proposal that he resign as CIA director, but with an assurance that when he was able to resume work there'd be a post for him here in the White House. Mrs. Casey was happy with that."

He sipped soup, talked about the benefits of eating raw carrots, then eased into the real reason for inviting me to lunch.

"Carl, I suggested this [meeting] when we were together [at the Gridiron dinner] because I had a feeling often that you didn't have the straight thing on me and racism and so forth . . . Carl, I was on the side of civil rights years before anyone ever used the term 'civil rights.' "

I said I knew it couldn't be pleasing to have black leaders describe his administration as "eight years of disaster for the civil rights movement."

Reagan didn't eat another bite as he went through a long speech about how his administration had prosecuted successfully more job, housing, and other discrimination cases "than all the other administrations put together." This was so erroneous as to be laughable, but it was obvious that the president believed the figures put before him by Justice Department and other sycophants.

I listened to him tell me how, as governor of California, he had been the best friend minorities ever had. I heard about how his Catholic father was the victim of "extreme prejudice." I listened to his story of a hotel refusing to let a black member of his football team stay there, and how he took the black to spend the night at his home. I just sipped soup as he went on and on about how Meese and Reynolds and their Justice Department were powerful foes of racial discrimination.

My soup gone, I said: "Well, you know I told you at that [Gridiron] dinner that there was not one iota of personal malice in any column that I wrote. But . . . you went down to kick off your presidential campaign in Philadelphia, Mississippi, where the three civil rights workers had been killed [in 1964]. In the view of a lot of people . . . that was an affront."

"I don't even remember that I did that," Reagan replied.

As I left the White House I told myself that that single sentence exposed the essence of Ronald Wilson Reagan. He often didn't know what he was doing, and he rarely remembered what he had done.

# Chapter 18

# KATHERINE GRAHAM

## PERSONAL HISTORY

**W**HEN SHE TOOK OVER AS THE PUBLISHER of *The Washington Post* after the death of her husband Philip Graham, Katherine Graham became perhaps the most powerful woman in journalism. Under her leadership, the *Post* emerged as the primary rival of *The New York Times* for influence in Washington and in the country at large.

In what came to be her most notable and courageous decision, in 1971, against the advice of her lawyers, she decided that the *Post* should follow the lead of the *New York Times* and print the Pentagon Papers, secret documents detailing the policy deliberations associated with the U.S. entry into the Vietnam War and the prosecution of the war itself. The following year Graham said she would go to jail, if necessary, to uphold the right to publish disclosures of wrongdoing by the Nixon administration in the Watergate scandal and she resolutely backed the relentless pursuit of the Watergate story even though other news media paid little attention and Nixon administration officials actively worked to silence the newspaper. When revelations of Nixon's misconduct vindicated the *Post* coverage, the *Post* soared in prestige and received the Pulitzer Prize for public service in 1973.

*Personal History*, which won the Pulitzer Prize for biography in 1998, tells of Graham's transformation from a meek housewife dominated by her husband into a towering figure in media circles as well as her struggle to develop self-confidence and exercise authority in a male-dominated world. Her personal story runs parallel to the rise of the *Post* from an also-ran in Washington journalism to one of the most powerful newspapers in the world. This selection paints the breakout moment for the *Post*, when Graham decides to risk the company by defying the government and printing the Pentagon Papers.

Don, Mary, and I had gone down to Glen Welby for the weekend to attend the country wedding of Scotty and Sally Reston's middle son, Jimmy. The wedding was a casual event, and while we were talking to Scotty, he told Don and me that the *Times* would be publishing, starting the next day, articles about a super-secret history of the decision-making that led us into and through Vietnam, labeled the "Pentagon Papers," but more formally titled "History of the United States Decision-Making Process on Vietnam Policy."

Unbeknownst to President Johnson, the review had been commissioned by Secretary of Defense Robert McNamara sometime in the middle of 1967, before he left the Pentagon. McNamara later said he had started the study "to bequeath to scholars the raw material from which they could re-examine the events of the time."

Don and I were unclear what it was the *Times* had, but we knew that, whatever it was, it was important, and that editors and reporters there had been working on it for some time. And, important for us, whatever it was, *The New York Times* had it exclusively. When we got back to Glen Welby, I called the *Post's* editors, who immediately started calling around, to no effect. Ben had heard rumors, starting in the early spring, that the *Times* was working on some kind of "blockbuster," but was not able to find out anything about it until he read it in the paper himself.

On Sunday morning, I sent to Warrenton for ten copies of the *Times*, since there was a sizable group staying at the house over the weekend. Most of us spent much of the day poring over the six pages of news stories and articles in the *Times* that were based on the Pentagon Papers, and in discussing their content and their possible impact.

What emerged was that the Pentagon Papers had turned out to be in large part just what McNamara had envisioned—a massive history of the role of the United States in Indochina, which he had intended to be "encyclopedic and objective." We learned of a year-and-a-half-long study that had resulted in a three-thousand-page narrative history with a four-thousand-page appendix of documents—forty-seven volumes in all, covering American involvement in Indochina from the Second World War to May of 1968, when peace talks on the Vietnam War began in Paris.

Later we understood that there had been a bitter fight at the *Times* over whether or not to publish these so-called top-secret documents, with Scotty and other editors arguing for publication. Scotty believed always that this was a question not merely of legality but of a higher morality: a vast deception had been perpetrated on the American people, and the paper must publish. The lawyers for the *Times*—Lord, Day and Lord—felt so strongly against publishing that they ultimately refused to handle the case. But the *Times* went ahead and delivered their bombshell on that Sunday morning in mid-June.

Ben Bradlee anguished over being scooped. He had worked so hard to build up the paper, not just to be competitive with the *Times* but to be taken as seriously, to be "out there" with them, to be mentioned in the same sentence. Now the *Times* had landed this big one on us, and Ben, mortified but unbowed, set to work to try to get the Papers for the *Post*. Meanwhile, he swallowed his pride and rewrote the stories that appeared in the *Times*, crediting the competition with their original publication.

The next day, Monday, I was in New York and ended up having dinner with some friends, including Abe Rosenthal, managing editor of the *Times*. When we had settled down with a predinner glass of wine, I congratulated Abe on the publication of the Papers. Soon afterwards, before we had been served dinner, he got word that the government was asking the *Times* to suspend publication. In fact, Attorney General John

Mitchell and Robert Mardian, assistant attorney general in charge of the Justice Department's internal-security division, had dispatched the message, with the president's approval, that if the *Times* did not comply the government would seek an injunction. Abe left immediately, and I used the head-waiter's telephone to phone Ben and tell him what was going on.

Meanwhile, the *Times* "respectfully" declined to cease publication of the series, sending the paper on its path through the courts. By an odd coincidence, when Scotty heard about the government's reaction he and Sally were dining alone with Bob McNamara, whose wife was in the hospital. Scotty asked McNamara what he thought of the *Times*'s defying the government, and McNamara considered the issues in his usual objective way and, despite his distaste for the early publication of these documents, nevertheless encouraged the *Times* to go ahead. He even went over with Scotty the message that the *Times* proposed to send back to the government, responding to Mitchell's message. It was Bob who suggested altering the proposed sentence that the *Times* would abide by the "decisions of the Courts" to read "the highest Court." In fact, a compromise was reached by which the *Times* agreed to abide by "the final decision of the Court." Scotty later recalled that, had it not been for McNamara's intervention, the *Times* would have been committed to stop printing by the adverse decision of *any* court. So, half an hour before its deadline, the *Times* recovered from a careless and potentially harmful mistake, courtesy of the former secretary of defense.

Deciding to continue publishing the Papers also meant that the *Times* had to scurry to find new lawyers after seventy-five years with one firm. They were lucky to get Alexander Bickel, a Yale law professor, and a young lawyer, Floyd Abrams, to work with him as litigator. On Tuesday morning, the *Times* carried the third part of the series, as well as the story of the government's effort to stop the paper from publishing. Also on Tuesday morning, after an all-night stint by the lawyers, the *Times* went before Judge Murray Gurfein, who was only in his second day on the bench. Gurfein asked the paper to suspend publishing voluntarily, which the *Times* refused to do. He then issued a temporary restraining order, setting a hearing for Friday of that week. This was America's first-ever order for prior restraint of the press.

The last story rewritten from the *Times* ran in the *Post* on June 16, my birthday, which I celebrated at dinner with Polly Wisner and Bob McNamara at Joe Alsop's. That day was also the last on which the *Times* was free to publish, and the day we received the Papers—a tremendous day for the *Post*, and for me as well.

Our editors and reporters had been trying desperately to get their hands on the Papers. Ben Bagdikian, the national editor, had guessed that Daniel Ellsberg was the source for them at the *Times*, and he had been frantically calling Ellsberg. Finally, on the 16th, a friend of Ellsberg's phoned Bagdikian and asked him to call back from a pay phone. Bagdikian spoke to Ellsberg, who said he would give him the Papers that night. He then returned to the paper and consulted with Gene Patterson—Ben Bradlee was away—asking for assurances that if we got the Papers we would start printing them on Friday morning. Gene said we would but felt Bagdikian should check with Bradlee, which Bagdikian did from the airport. Bradlee's response, which may be apocryphal but certainly sounds like something Ben would say, was: "If we don't publish, there's going to be a new executive editor of *The Washington Post*."

Bagdikian then departed for Boston with an empty suitcase, as per instructions. He returned to Washington the next morning with what has been described as "a disorganized mass of photocopied sheets completely out of sequence and with very few page numbers." The suitcase he'd brought was too small for what he was given, so he loaded the Papers into a big cardboard box and flew back to Washington on a first-class seat, with the box occupying the seat beside him—an additional expense the *Post* didn't mind paying.

Bagdikian went straight to Ben Bradlee's house, rushing past, as Ben later reported, "Marina Bradlee, age ten, tending her lemonade stand outside." Ben Bradlee had already gathered there several reporters—Chalmers Roberts, Murrey Marder, and Don Oberdorfer among them—and two secretaries to help sort out the mess, as well as Phil Geyelin and Meg Greenfield from the editorial page, and Howard Simons. Chal was two weeks short of retirement, but he and Murrey knew the most about the story, and Chal was the fastest writer on the paper. They were joined at Ben's house by Roger Clark and Tony Essaye, our principal lawyers since Bill Rogers had left his firm to become secretary of state.

Sorting out the forty-four hundred pages that we had and deciding what to write was more than a day's chore in itself, and we were also working under the added pressure of knowing that the *Times* had been enjoined from further publication and that The Washington Post Company was about to go public, with all that that entailed.

I was pleased that we had found the Papers and had them in hand, but I spent the day of June 17 in a rather routine way. I had planned a large party to be held that afternoon at my house for Harry Gladstein, a lovely man who was leaving the *Post*. He had come to the paper as circulation director but was vice-president and business manager at the time. The whole business staff of the *Post* was gathered for the party, including Fritz, who had come down to Washington for it but had gone over to Ben's house to check on things there. As it turned out, a fierce legal battle was being waged.

What Ben experienced as he rushed back and forth between the rooms where the reporters were working and the living room, where the lawyers were conferring, was that the lawyers seemed to be pushing strongly for not publishing, or at least for waiting until there was a decision on the injunction against the *Times*. Our situation, however, was very different from that of the *Times*. The court order against them meant that, if we were to publish, our action might be viewed as defying the law and disrespecting the court. Even more difficult than that was the delicacy of our business position. In going public, a company negotiates with its underwriters—in this case a group led by Lazard Frères—and on the day of the offering, everyone agrees on a price and signs an agreement. Our agreement said that in a week the underwriters would buy all the stock from the company and then turn around and resell it to those they'd offered it to in the intervening week. There was a standard stipulation that if any one of a variety of crises—such as a war or national emergency or, more to the point in our case, the company's being subjected to criminal action—were to intervene, the underwriter would be let out of the contract. We were exposing ourselves to just such a possibility if we published while the *Times* was enjoined.

In addition, Fritz had written into the original prospectus a paragraph stating that we would publish a newspaper dedicated to the community and national welfare. He now worried that the underwriters could make a case—as indeed the administration was trying to do—that what we were doing was contrary to the national welfare. Fritz had an extraordinary sensitivity to editorial issues and to the editors themselves, both at the *Post* and at *Newsweek*, but in this case, as a lawyer, he had to worry about the future of the company. Furthermore, he worried that we could be in trouble under the Espionage

Act. He thought the government would be most likely to prosecute the corporation or the company, and if the corporation acquired the status of a felon, we would be stripped of our licenses to own and operate our television stations, adding a huge financial issue to the already high stakes.

So, while in one room at Ben's house Chal was banging out his story for publication the next day, Murrey was slowly reading through the material, and Don Oberdorfer was working on installments on the late Johnson years, in another room the lawyers, with Fritz and the editors, were locked in tough and tense arguments. Clark and Essaye argued against publication and in favor of letting the *Times* handle the freedom-of-the-press issue. Fritz seemed to be siding with the lawyers.

Ben was beginning to feel squeezed between the editors and the reporters, who were solidly lined up for publishing and supporting the *Times* on the issue of freedom of the press, and the lawyers, who at one point suggested a compromise whereby the *Post* would not publish the Papers on Friday but would notify the attorney general of its intention to publish on Sunday. Howard Simons, who was 100 percent for publishing, summoned the reporters to talk directly with the lawyers. Oberdorfer said the compromise was "the shittiest idea I've ever heard." Roberts said the *Post* would be "crawling on its belly" to the attorney general; if the *Post* didn't publish, he would move his retirement up two weeks, make it a resignation, and publicly accuse the *Post* of cowardice. Murrey Marder recalled saying, "If the *Post* doesn't publish, it will be in much worse shape as an institution than if it does," since the paper's "credibility would be destroyed journalistically for being gutless." Bagdikian reminded the lawyers of the commitment to Ellsberg to publish the Papers and declared, "The only way to assert the right to publish is to publish."

In the midst of the bedlam, Ben left the room to call his closest friend, Ed Williams, who by now was also a good friend of mine. Ed was in Chicago trying a divorce case, and Ben reached the editor of the *Chicago Sun-Times* and asked him to send a copy boy down to the court with a message saying he needed to talk to Ed immediately, conveying the idea that this was, as Ben later said, "as serious as anything I've ever faced."

Ed was a great lawyer with a lot of political as well as common sense. The two men talked for perhaps ten minutes, according to Ben, during which Ben, as objectively as he could, told Ed everything that had happened to that point and then waited for a response. Ed finally said, "Well, Benjy, you've got to go with it."

Gene Patterson's job that day was to run the newsroom as though nothing were happening. But the people in the newsroom are as good at sniffing out something happening right in their midst as they are at following stories outside. No one could help noticing the absence of Chal, Murrey, and Don Oberdorfer as well as Bagdikian, Howard, and Ben. Certainly something was up. Gene stopped by Ben's house on his way to my party, and then walked up the hill to my house. As I was receiving guests, he pulled me aside and gave me the first warning of what was to come, saying that he believed the decision on whether to print was going to be checked with me and that he "knew I fully recognized that the soul of the newspaper was at stake."

"God, do you think it's coming to that?" I asked. Yes, Gene said, he did.

By now, crucial time was passing. The deadline for the second edition was fast approaching. Jim Daly had come up to me twice at Gladstein's party, worrying about when we'd get the story and be able to put it into print, and asking if I had yet heard from the other house. I was strangely unconcerned and said I was sure they were just finishing and we would get it in time.

It was a lovely June day, and the party for Harry spilled out of the house onto the terrace and the lawn. I was making a toast to him and going full-blast about how much he had meant to the paper and to me personally when someone tugged at my sleeve and said with some urgency, "You're wanted on the phone."

I protested that I had to finish the toast, but the response was, "They want you now." I finally got the idea that it was really important, wound up the toast quickly, and took the call in a corner of the library. I was sitting on a small sofa near the open door, and Paul Ignatius stood near me. Fritz was on the other end of the line. He told me about the argument between the lawyers and the editors over whether to publish the next day, outlined the reasoning on both sides, and concluded by saying, "I'm afraid you are going to have to decide."

I asked Fritz for his own view; since he was so editorial-minded and so decent, I knew I could trust his response. I was astonished when he said, "I guess I wouldn't." I then asked for time to think it over, saying, "Can't we talk about this? Why do we have to make up our minds in such haste when the *Times* took three months to decide?"

At this point, Ben and the editors got on various extensions at Ben's house. I asked them what the big rush was, suggesting we at least think about this for a day. No, Ben said, it was important to keep up the momentum of publication and not to let a day intervene after getting the story. He also stressed that by this time the grapevine knew we had the Papers. Journalists inside and outside were watching us.

I could tell from the passion of the editors' views that we were in for big trouble on the editorial floor if we didn't publish. I well remember Phil Geyelin's response when I said that deciding to publish could destroy the paper. "Yes," he agreed, "but there's more than one way to destroy a newspaper."

At the same time that the editors were saying, seriatim, "You've got to do it," Paul Ignatius was standing beside me, repeating—each time more insistently—"Wait a day, wait a day."

I was extremely torn by Fritz's saying that he wouldn't publish. I knew him so well, and we had never differed on any important issue; and, after all, he was the lawyer, not I. But I also heard *how* he said it: he didn't hammer at me, he didn't stress the issues related to going public, and he didn't say the obvious thing—that I would be risking the whole company on this decision. He simply said he guessed he wouldn't. I felt that, despite his stated opinion, he had somehow left the door open for me to decide on a different course. Frightened and tense, I took a big gulp and said, "Go ahead, go ahead, go ahead. Let's go. Let's publish." And I hung up.

So the decision was made. But later that evening Fritz came over to my house. Roger Clark, still worried, had thought of a new problem: he feared an extra charge of collusion with the *Times* and wanted to know the source of our obtaining the Papers. Bagdikian by this time had gone to the paper, carrying the last of Chal's story to set in type. At first Bagdikian maintained that the source was confidential, but when Clark insisted, he identified Ellsberg, the presumed source for the *Times*, which only increased Clark's concern about collusion. This time Fritz really helped. I had no idea whether collusion made our situation more vulnerable or not, but Fritz said that we'd made up our minds and should go ahead. I was relieved, and agreed.

Our lawyers by then were behind us and very supportive. In addition, Fritz had Roswell Gilpatric of the Cravath firm down from New York, with whom he was informally consulting, as Ben was with Edward Bennett Williams. The two young lawyers in the Washington branch of our law firm—Royall, Koegel & Wells—sent to New York for a litigator, William Glendon, whom we didn't know and who was relatively inexperienced with cases like this.

At about 3:00 p.m. Friday, while I happened to be sitting in Ben's office, a call came from William Rehnquist, then the assistant attorney general for the Department of Justice's Office of Legal Counsel. Rehnquist read the same message to Ben that he had sent to the *Times*. Ben told Rehnquist, "I'm sure you will understand that I must respectfully decline." He also refused to delay the rest of the series pending resolution of the *Times*'s case in New York. The government promptly filed suit against the *Post*, a suit that matched the one lodged against the *Times*, and named as defendants everyone on the masthead of the paper, plus the author of the first article (the one that had appeared on June 18), Chalmers Roberts.

The case was routinely assigned to Judge Gerhard Gesell, a distinguished jurist of a liberal mind. He had helped in the 1954 acquisition of the *Times-Herald*, at a time when he worked for Covington & Burling and had also been a friend of Phil's and mine when we were all young, but our paths had gone different ways and I no longer saw him and his wife, Peggy. In fact, Phil had fired him during one of his bad years, which was what enabled Gerry to take the case.

At 8:05 p.m. on June 18, Gesell ruled for the *Post*, refusing to grant an order restraining the paper from further publication of the series and saying, "The court has before it no precise information suggesting in what respects, if any, the publication of this information will injure" the nation. The court of appeals, to which the government instantly went, ruled for the government at about 1:20 a.m., reversing Gesell's decision. Fritz was at the court with the lawyers arguing that we had several thousand papers on the street and the plates on the presses. So, at 2:10 a.m., the court agreed with us that the injunction didn't apply to that night's paper, and we finished the press run.

Gerry Gesell confided to me after his retirement, "If anybody ever carves anything on my tombstone, they might say I was the only judge out of twenty-nine judges who heard the Pentagon Papers case who never stopped the presses for a minute. The only one. I've always taken a little pride in that." In staying Gesell's order, the appeals court had also told him to hold a fuller, more detailed hearing on Monday, June 21. Over the weekend, he tried to get a handle on what was behind the case, to get it into some kind of shape to be heard. Because the courthouse was undergoing construction, Gesell held a meeting at his house with some Justice Department officials, telling them to select the ten most damaging things in the Papers and that he would limit the Monday hearing to that list. At some point, a Justice Department lawyer told Gesell that, of course, the defendants—meaning all of us connected with the *Post* who'd been named in the suit—wouldn't be present at the hearing; it had to be held in secret. Gesell told him firmly, "We don't do things that way," adding, "If that's the way it's going to go, I'll dismiss the case. I won't even hold a hearing." He suggested the lawyer call the White House—or, as Gesell put it, "wherever or whoever it was that gave you those instructions"—and tell them he would dismiss the case if that was the condition. The lawyer did call someone and returned to say it would be all right to have the defendants present. Finally, the Justice Department lawyers left, leaving the Papers behind. As Gesell later recounted:

> They hadn't been gone but two or three minutes when there was a knock on the door and here were two fellows all in uniform, great big white sashes, or whatever it is, across their uniform, and guns and all this and said, "We've come for the Papers." I said, "I don't have to give you the

Papers. I want to read them." Well, they said, "You don't have any security out here; we can't let you have these Papers." I said, "I've got the best security in the world. I put them under my sofa pillow and you're not going to have them. You can stay here all night if you want to guard the place, but I'm going to have the Papers." They disappeared after that.

On Monday, Fritz, Ben, Don and Mary Graham, and I, among others, went into court for the hearing. There was a swarm of press people outside. All the windows of the courtroom were blacked out. At one point as the case proceeded, the government put on the stand an ex-CIA man who had been working in the Pentagon who testified how serious the situation was and that publication of some of these papers would reveal certain war plans of the United States. Gesell didn't believe this man and called for the general in charge of the war plans to be sent over to testify. He was duly brought in—the quintessential general, bedecked with medals—and as Gesell remembers it, after taking the oath to tell the truth, he stated, "Judge, if anybody thinks these are our war plans, I sure hope they do, because these are entirely out of date."

The government then tried to hit another of its points on the list, claiming that there was a Canadian diplomat who had infiltrated Vietnam and was passing information to the Americans, which was a violation of Canadian treason laws. The government's point was that, if the information got out, this was a capital offense and the man would be executed. Here is where the skill of our reporters helped us. Not only did they write depositions, but they came up with citations proving that the alleged top-secret items had already been published. Chal Roberts promptly supplied several published books to our lawyers, in each of which the Canadian diplomat was mentioned by name along with a description of what he was doing. So much for that argument.

In the end, Gesell refused to grant the government an injunction against the *Post*, allowing the series to resume. Later that day, however, the U.S. Court of Appeals for the District of Columbia continued the temporary restraining order and ordered a hearing before the full nine-judge appellate court, which heard the case on June 22. I attended the proceedings that day also. The court affirmed Gesell's decision, upholding the *Post*'s constitutional right to continue the series based on the Papers. At the same time, however, the court continued the restraining order to allow for an appeal.

The day *The New York Times* had published its first story, Erwin Griswold, solicitor general of the United States, and his wife were in Florida sunning themselves at a hotel pool and resting after he had made a speech to the Florida State Bar Association the night before. When he read the *Times*'s story on the Pentagon Papers, he immediately turned to his wife and said, "Well, it looks as though I'm going to have a case in the Supreme Court one of these days." Much later he told me that he assumed November would be the earliest conceivable moment the case would be brought to the Court. When he got back from Florida, there was a note for him to call the attorney general. Griswold—who had been a Johnson appointee but was still serving under Nixon—said that, at meetings with Mitchell and other Justice Department officials, he consistently "counseled against going ahead with the case. I said, 'The trouble is you don't have any ground to stand on.' But nobody except me ever had any thought of not going ahead."

On Friday, June 25, the Supreme Court granted the petitions for certiorari from both the *Times* and the *Post*. At the same time, since the *Times*, because of its separate route through the courts, was still prohibited from publishing, and the *Post* was not, the Court—at least until a final decision could be handed down—put both newspapers under equal restraints, marking the first time the Supreme Court had restricted publication of a newspaper article. What the Court's decision to accept the cases meant for Griswold was that he had only twenty-four hours to prepare his brief, still not having seen the Papers themselves. He began to focus on them at once, arranging to see three government people, and asking each of them to tell him what problems might arise if the Papers were published in full. Even after talking with these people, he realized he didn't have a very strong case.

Griswold was back in his office early Saturday morning to finish preparing his brief. With no help in the Justice Department on Saturday, he and his secretary ran it off on the mimeograph machine. They then assembled the pages, stamped them "Top Secret," and went off to court. Griswold had two extra copies of his brief, one for the *Times*'s counsel and one for the *Post*'s. He recalled being taken aback when the guard for the Papers asked him what he intended doing with those copies and when he was told said, "Well, that's treason; that's giving them to the enemy." Griswold nearly had a set-to with the security man, insisting it was his professional responsibility to furnish copies of the brief to the other side. So bizarre were the security and secrecy surrounding the case that officials from the government had taken away our own brief, impounding it as top secret!

On Saturday, June 26, the two cases—that of *The New York Times* and that of the *Post*—met for the first time, in that they were being heard together at the Supreme Court. None of us fully understood the nuances of what was being acted out in court after court—national security, prior restraint, the right to know—until we actually got to the Supreme Court. I went to the Court with Fritz and several others from the *Post* for this unusual special session. The government's case was argued by Griswold, and the newspapers' case was argued by Alexander Bickel for the *Times* and William Glendon for the *Post*.

I was in the *Post*'s newsroom around midday on Wednesday, June 30, when we received word that the Court would convene at two-thirty. Everyone in the newsroom was deadly quiet, waiting for the news. Right on time, Chief Justice Warren Burger announced the decision. Simultaneously, Deputy National Editor Mary Lou Beatty heard the news on an open phone line to the Supreme Court and Gene Patterson heard it in the wire room, then jumped on a desk and called out, "We win and so does *The New York Times*." The newspapers were free to publish.

By a six-to-three vote, the Supreme Court ruled that the government had not met "the heavy burden of showing justification" for restraining further publication of the Pentagon Papers as endangering national security. At the *Post*, having regarded ourselves as doing the public's business, we were gratified by the results and felt that the principle of no prior restraint of the press had been vindicated.

We were also proud of the *Post* and its people. In a memo to the staff I said, "I know I speak for all of us when I say what a great moment this is for *The Washington Post*." Ben Bradlee was equally proud. He told the staff, "The guts and energy and responsibility of everyone involved in this fight, and the sense that you all were involved, has impressed me more than anything in my life. You are beautiful."

We had prevailed, but ours was an incomplete "victory." Basically, we were challenging the right of the executive branch to prevent a newspaper from publishing material we believed should be available to the public. In court, we had challenged the government's contention that the material in the Papers was too sensitive for the public eye. We had strongly argued the case against prior restraint, but we had in fact been restrained. We were disappointed that the Court's decree was both limited and ambiguous. Though the decision was in favor of allowing the newspapers to publish, there was, as I later said, "no ringing reaffirmation of First Amendment guarantees that all publishers yearn to hear."

The Supreme Court's decision had caused enormous rejoicing in the press at large and at the *Post* and *Times* in particular, but hidden away in the details of the separate opinions were some views that were of great concern to us, having to do with possible criminal prosecution after the fact. It was clear to us that Attorney General Mitchell felt avenues of criminal prosecution remained open, and that the Department of Justice was continuing its investigation and would prosecute those who in any way violated federal criminal laws in connection with the Papers. Aspects of this threat were made even clearer to me by two strange messages received over the fence. One came from Ken Clawson, then still a *Post* reporter.

A few days after the Supreme Court decision was handed down, Clawson told me he had had a message from Richard Kleindienst, then deputy attorney general. At one point, we had independently, and in an effort to act responsibly, decided we wouldn't publish those items that had been specified in the solicitor general's secret brief as being those most threatening to the national interest. We didn't even have some of the volumes of the Papers that the government found most objectionable; others we felt had no news value. Kleindienst, however, wanted me to know that it would not be enough to agree not to publish the portions of the Papers that the government felt endangered national security; rather, the *Post* would have to *relinquish* the parts of the Papers it held relating to this kind of information.

[. . .]

The Pentagon Papers may or may not have been the compelling case we all thought it was, but it set in motion certain trends. Although the case came and went, unbelievably, in only two and a half weeks, its ripple effect was great. And publishing the Papers went a long way toward advancing the interests of the *Post*. As Ben later said, "That was a key moment in the life of this paper. It was just sort of the graduation of the *Post* into the highest ranks. One of our unspoken goals was to get the world to refer to the *Post* and *New York Times* in the same breath, which they previously hadn't done. After the Pentagon Papers, they did."

From my point of view, the *Post* and I had been hurled onto the national scene almost unwittingly. For the first time in my professional life, we became major players. Eyes were on us; what we did mattered to the press and to the country. To some degree, I gained a measure of self-assurance. This was my first serious visibility on the national scene. I was very publicly exposed, written about, photographed, and interviewed, which both seared me and to some extent fed my ego. The pressure, the intensity, and the rapidly unfolding developments were another extraordinary learning experience for me.

The whole affair also bound many of us at the *Post* even more closely together, especially Ben, Howard Simons, Phil Geyelin, Meg Greenfield, and me. The editors had been wonderful. From the late 1960s, these people had worked so well together, having a great deal of fun at the same time. There was trust and affection among them, as well as between them and me. Our group was one of the great strengths that kept me going and lightened my life.

I gained even more confidence in Ben. He and I had already created a true understanding between us, as well as a respect and admiration for each other, but until the

Pentagon Papers we had never been tested publicly in any way. Ben later said that not publishing the Papers could have been a real disaster for the *Post*, with many people quitting the paper. He reflected that he himself probably wouldn't have quit, "but I would have been beaten and the goals, the aspirations that we were just beginning to see would have been lost."

What Ben and I told each other at the time says a lot about the point to which our relationship had evolved and how much we depended on and appreciated each other. Ben had started a tradition of writing me a letter at Christmastime in lieu of flowers. I always responded in kind, but I wrote him now in the middle of the year, on the very day the Supreme Court announced its decision:

> We always write each other love letters at Christmas—but the paper over the last 2+ weeks is better than Christmas and it's earlier too. There never was such a show—it was incredible. And it was only possible because of that extra 10% of the 110% that you and those under you put into it. . . . It was beautiful and fun too. And it was a trip—a pleasure to do business with you as ever.

Ben wrote me right back:

> Doing business with you is so much more than a pleasure—it's a cause, it's an honor, and such a rewarding challenge.
>
> I'm not sure I could handle another one of these tomorrow, but it is so great to know that this whole newspaper will handle the next one with courage and commitment and style.

Indeed, publishing the Pentagon Papers made future decisions easier, even possible. Most of all it prepared us—and I suspect, unfortunately, Nixon as well—for Watergate.

SECTION IV

# Classic Reporting

# INTRODUCTION

**F**OR MOST OF ITS HISTORY, the route into professional journalism was through an apprenticeship-like system. Aspiring reporters would secure a position on a newspaper and then learn to report and write on the job, usually under the tutelage of a no-nonsense editor. Even today, many people think that the way to learn to write as a journalist is to read good journalism and then to write.

Ironically, however, daily newspaper reporting often does not stand the test of time. As the cliché has it, the daily newspaper is the first draft of history. First drafts, unfortunately, are routinely discarded. Another cliché is that no matter how compelling a newspaper may be one day, the next day it is fit mainly to line the bottom of a bird cage or to wrap fish. Written under deadline, after a while, daily journalism often seems stale and uninspired. What is retained is the second, third and fourth efforts to capture that which must be understood in order to make sense of the world.

Nevertheless, on many levels, it is great reporting that changes the world—and the excerpts here are powerful and moving. Ida Wells-Barnett's reports on lynching helped prick a nation's conscience. Her reporting stirred the consciousness of a nation and the world. Lynching was a form of terrorism commonly practiced from the end of the Civil War until the early decades of the twentieth century. Primarily though not exclusively committed in the American south, it was ignored in the north; but Wells Barnett's reporting and writing made the problem and horror of lynching impossible to ignore.

Every war, it seems, generates its own style of reporting and Ernie Pyle may be the best known correspondent from World War II. Primary a columnist, he followed and covered the ordinary soldier rather than wartime leaders. Pyle's columns during World War II captured the experience of the common G.I. and it is the human, simple detail of his description in the now famous *Death of Captain Waskow* that makes the piece so moving—and all the more because throughout the piece Pyle retains a calm dignity of style.

Of all the excerpts in this section, the one from Ida Tarbell and *Silent Spring* by Rachel Carson, probably had the most impact historically. *The History of Standard Oil Company* demonstrates how well-reported information told in a non-emotional, even-handed fashion can address the most important issues and confront powerful people and industries. Tarbell's book paved the way for legislation that broke the monopoly control Standard Oil had on the oil industry. Tarbell took on the richest person in the world at that time and won, through meticulous reporting and a fact-based narrative.

The selection from Truman Capote's *In Cold Blood* is not exactly journalism, although the account of a grisly murder in Kansas is based on six years of research. Capote argued that he had invented a new form—the non-fiction novel. The techniques he used in writing *In Cold Blood* were more associated with writing fiction than writing journalism, including direct dialogue and vivid descriptions of scenes at which he was not present. *In Cold Blood* was harshly criticized for violating many of the basic rules of journalism. Moreover, critics said that Capote made many minor and major errors including the way he portrayed the confession of one of the murderers. Nevertheless, the techniques Capote pioneered were used by Tom Wolfe, Gay Talese and other leaders of what came to be called New Journalism in the 1960s. New Journalism was extremely influential in redeeming the tradition of literary journalism that preceded and followed it.

In fact, one of the best examples of the New Journalism is Timothy Crouse's *The Boys on the Bus*. Writing for the Rolling Stone magazine, Crouse pulled the curtain back on the reporters covering the presidential campaigns of 1972. Not really an exposé, the book painted pictures of reporters and the politicians whom they covered: warts, foibles and all. Political reporting would never really be the same.

Taking this section as a whole, the key elements of great journalism become apparent. Great journalism consists of aggressive, comprehensive reporting, an attention to significant detail, and compelling and appropriate storytelling. When those ingredients are applied to issues of profound social importance, journalism can change the public's perceptions, the political agenda and, indeed, the world.

# Chapter 19

## IDA WELLS-BARNETT

# SOUTHERN HORRORS: LYNCH LAW IN ALL ITS PHASES

IDA B. WELLS-BARNETT MAY BE BEST KNOWN for the anti-lynching campaign she waged between 1892 and 1900 in the United States and during two trips to the United Kingdom. Born in Holly Springs, Mississippi, in 1862, she attended Rust College and then moved to Memphis, Tennessee, where she joined a lyceum that met weekly to recite essays, hold debates, and present dramatic scenes. She discovered her calling as a journalist and activist while in Memphis and when, in 1884 she refused to give up her seat in the "ladies car" to move to the "smoker" of the Chesapeake, Ohio and Southwestern Railroad it was widely reported in both white and black newspapers. She sued the railroad for assault and discrimination, initially winning in the lower court. However, the ruling was overturned by the Tennessee State Supreme Court, who upheld a state law that authorized "separate but equal" accommodations on railroads.

In 1889, Wells purchased an interest in the Memphis *Free Speech and Headlight*, becoming the editor. Then in May 1892 she published a provocative editorial about the recent lynching of three men, including a good friend, who owned a Memphis grocery store and also detailed her investigations of the latest hangings in Mississippi and Tennessee. She eloquently demonstrated that mob violence was not to punish African American men for raping white women but a result of white fears of interracial relations and post-Reconstruction resentment of black progress.

One week later, while Wells was in New York City visiting *New York Age* editor T. Thomas Fortune, she learned that a white mob had destroyed her office and run the business manager out of town. She joined the *New York Age* and in 1892 she wrote *Southern Horrors: Lynch Law in All Its Phases*, the first of three lengthy pamphlets documenting the number and causes of lynchings in the United States, and outlining remedies. This was followed by *A Red Record* in 1895 and *Mob Rule in New Orleans* in 1900. Her efforts led to invitations to give dozens of public lectures on the subject, both in the United States and in the British Isles in 1893 and 1894, which were commented on in both the black and white press. The two selections here include her editorial detailing the lynching of the owners of The People's Grocery store, whose publication forced her to leave Memphis, and an account of an innocent black man being lynched.

## The Malicious and Untruthful White Press

The "Daily Commercial" and "Evening Scimitar" of Memphis, Tenn., are owned by leading business men of that city, and yet, in spite of the fact that there had been no white woman in Memphis outraged by an Afro-American, and that Memphis possessed a thrifty law-abiding, property owning class of Afro-Americans the "Commercial" of May 17th, under the head of "More Rapes, More Lynchings" gave utterance to the following:

> The lynching of three Negro scoundrels reported in our dispatches from Anniston, Ala., for a brutal outrage committed upon a white woman will be a text for much comment on "Southern barbarism" by Northern newspapers; but we fancy it will hardly prove effective for campaign purposes among intelligent people. The frequency of these lynchings calls attention to the frequency of the crimes which causes lynching. The "Southern barbarism" which deserves the serious attention of all people North and South, is the barbarism which preys upon weak and defenseless women. Nothing but the most prompt, speedy and extreme punishment can hold in check the horrible and bestial propensities of the Negro race. There is a strange similarity about a number of cases of this character which have lately occurred.
>
> In each case the crime was deliberately planned and perpetrated by several Negroes. They watched for an opportunity when the women were left without a protector. It was not a sudden yielding to a fit of passion, but the consummation of a devilish purpose which has been seeking and waiting for the opportunity. This feature of the crime not only makes it the most fiendishly brutal, but it adds to the terror of the situation in the thinly settled country communities. No man can leave his family at night without the dread that some roving Negro ruffian is watching and waiting for this opportunity. The swift punishment which invariably follows these horrible crimes doubtless acts as a deterring effect upon the Negroes in that immediate neighborhood for a short time. But the lesson is not widely learned nor long remembered. Then such crimes, equally atrocious, have happened in quick succession, one in Tennessee, one in Arkansas, and one in Alabama. The facts of the crime appear to appeal more to the Negro's lustful imagination than the facts of the punishment do to his fears. He sets aside all fear of death in any form when opportunity is found for the gratification of his bestial desires.
>
> There is small reason to hope for any change for the better. The commission of this crime grows more frequent every year. The generation of Negroes which have grown up since the war have lost in large measure the traditional and wholesome awe of the white race which kept the Negroes in subjection, even when their masters were in the army, and their families left unprotected except by the slaves themselves. There is no longer a restraint upon the brute passion of the Negro.

What is to be done? The crime of rape is always horrible, but to the Southern man there is nothing which so fills the soul with horror, loathing and fury as the outraging of a white woman by a Negro. It is the race question in the ugliest, vilest, most dangerous aspect. The Negro as a political factor can be controlled. But neither laws nor lynchings can subdue his lusts. Sooner or later it will force a crisis. We do not know in what form it will come.

In its issue of June 4th, the Memphis "Evening Scimitar" gives the following excuse for lynch law:

Aside from the violation of white women by Negroes, which is the out-cropping of a bestial perversion of instinct, the chief cause of trouble between the races in the South is the Negro's lack of manners. In the the state of slavery he learned politeness from association with white people, who took pains to teach him. Since the emancipation came and the tie of mutual interest and regard between master and servant was broken, the Negro has drifted away into a state which is neither freedom nor bondage. Lacking the proper inspiration of the one and the restraining force of the other he has taken up the idea that boorish insolence is independence, and the exercise of a decent degree of breeding toward white people is identical with servile submission. In consequence of the prevalence of this notion there are many Negroes who use every opportunity to make themselves offensive, particularly when they think it can be done with impunity.

We have had too many instances right here in Memphis to doubt this, and our experience is not exceptional. *The white people won't stand this sort of thing, and whether they be insulted as individuals or as a race, the response will be prompt and effectual.* The bloody riot of 1866, in which so many Negroes perished, was brought on principally by the outrageous conduct of the blacks toward the whites on the streets. It is also a remarkable and discouraging fact that the majority of such scoundrels are Negroes who have received educational advantages at the hands of the white taxpayers. They have got just enough of learning to make them realize how hopelessly their race is behind the other in everything that makes a great people, and they attempt to "get even" by insolence, which is ever the resentment of inferiors. There are well-bred Negroes among us, and it is truly unfortunate that they should have to pay, even in part, the penalty of the offenses committed by the baser sort, but this is the way of the world. The innocent must suffer for the guilty. If the Negroes as a people possessed a hundredth part of the self-respect which is evidenced by the courteous bearing of some that the "Scimitar" could name, the friction between the races would be reduced to a minimum. It will not do to beg the question by pleading that many white men are also stirring up strife. The Caucasian blackguard simply obeys the promptings of a depraved disposition, and he is seldom deliberately rough or offensive toward strnagers or unprotected women.

The Negro tough, on the contrary, is given to just that kind of offending, and he almost invariably singles out white people as his victims.

On March 9th, 1892, there were lynched in this same city three of the best specimens of young since-the-war Afro-American manhood. They were peaceful, law-abiding citizens and energetic business men.

They believed the problem was to be solved by eschewing politics and putting money in the purse. They owned a flourishing grocery business in a thickly populated suburb of Memphis, and a white man named Barrett had one on the opposite corner. After a personal difficulty which Barrett sought by going into the "People's Grocery" drawing a pistol and was thrashed by Calvin McDowell, he (Barrett) threatened to "clean them out." These men were a mile beyond the city limits and police protection; hearing that Barrett's crowd was coming to attack them Saturday night, they mustered forces and prepared to defend themselves against the attack.

When Barrett came he led a *posse* of officers, twelve in number, who afterward claimed to be hunting a man for whom they had a warrant. That twelve men in citizen's clothes should think it necessary to go in the night to hunt one man who had never before been arrested, or made any record as a criminal has never been explained. When they entered the back door the young men thought the threatened attack was on, and fired into them. Three of the officers were wounded, and when the *defending* party found it was officers of the law upon whom they had fired, they ceased and got away.

Thirty-one men were arrested and thrown in jail as "conspirators," although they all declared more than once they did not know they were firing on officers. Excitement was at fever heat until the morning papers, two days after, announced that the wounded deputy sheriffs were out of danger. This hindered rather than helped the plans of the whites. There was no law on the statute books which would execute an Afro-American for wounding a white man, but the "unwritten law" did. Three of these men, the president, the manager and clerk of the grocery—"the leaders of the conspiracy"—were secretly taken from jail and lynched in a shockingly brutal manner. "The Negroes are getting too independent," they say, "we must teach them a lesson."

What lesson? The lesson of subordination. "Kill the leaders and it will cow the Negro who dares to shoot a white man, even in self-defense."

Although the race was wild over the outrage, the mockery of law and justice which disarmed men and locked them up in jails where they could be easily and safely reached by the mob—the Afro-American ministers, newspapers and leaders counselled obedience to the law which did not protect them.

Their counsel was heeded and not a hand was uplifted to resent the outrage; following the advice of the "Free Speech," people left the city in great numbers.

The dailies and associated press reports heralded these men to the country as "toughs," and "Negro desperadoes who kept a low dive." This same press service printed that the Negro who was lynched at Indianola, Miss., in May, had outraged the sheriff's eight-year-old daughter. The girl was more than eighteen years old, and was found by her father in this man's room, who was a servant on the place.

Not content with misrepresenting the race, the mob-spirit was not to be satisfied until the paper which was doing all it could to counteract this impression was silenced. The colored people were resenting their bad treatment in a way to make itself felt, yet gave the mob no excuse for further murder, until the appearance of the editorial which is construed as a reflection on the "honor" of the Southern white women. It is not half so libelous as that of the "Commercial" which appeared four days before, and which has been given in these pages. They would have lynched the manager of the

"Free Speech" for exercising the right of free speech if they had found him as quickly as they would have hung a rapist, and glad of the excuse to do so. The owners were ordered not to return, "The Free Speech" was suspended with as little compunction as the business of the "People's Grocery" broken up and the proprietors murdered.

[. . .]

## Lynched as a Scapegoat

Wednesday, July 5th, about 10 o'clock in the morning, a terrible crime was committed within four miles of Wickliffe, Ky. Two girls, Mary and Ruby Ray, were found murdered a short distance from their home. The news of this terrible cowardly murder of two helpless young girls spread like wild fire, and searching parties scoured the territory surrounding Wickliffe and Bardwell. Two of the searching party, the Clark brothers, saw a man enter the Dupoyster cornfield; they got their guns and fired at the fleeing figure, but without effect; he got away, but they said he was a white man or nearly so. The search continued all day without effect, save the arrest of two or three strange Negroes. A bloodhound was brought from the penitentiary and put on the trail which he followed from the scene of the murder to the river and into the boat of a fisherman named Gordon. Gordon stated that he had ferried one man and only one across the river about half past six the evening of July 5th; that his passenger sat in front of him, and he was a white man or a very bright mulatto, who could not be told from a white man. The bloodhound was put across the river in the boat, and he struck a trail again at Bird's Point on the Missouri side, ran about three hundred yards to the cottage of a white farmer named Grant and there lay down refusing to go further.

Thursday morning a brakesman on a freight train going out of Sikeston, Mo., discovered a Negro stealing a ride; he ordered him off and had hot words which terminated in a fight. The brakesman had the Negro arrested. When arrested, between 11 and 12 o'clock, he had on a dark woolen shirt, light pants and coat, and no vest. He had twelve dollars in paper, two silver dollars and ninety-five cents in change; he had also four rings in his pockets, a knife and a razor which were rusted and stained. The Sikeston authorities immediately jumped to the conclusion that this man was the murderer for whom the Kentuckians across the river were searching. They telegraphed to Bardwell that their prisoner had on no coat, but wore a blue vest and pants which would perhaps correspond with the coat found at the scene of the murder, and that the names of the murdered girls were in the rings found in his possession.

As soon as this news was received, the sheriffs of Ballard and Carlisle counties and a posse of thirty well armed and determined Kentuckians, who had pledged their word the prisoner should be taken back to the scene of the supposed crime, to be executed there if proved to be the guilty man, chartered a train and at nine o'clock Thursday night started for Sikeston. Arriving there two hours later, the sheriff at Sikeston, who had no warrant for the prisoner's arrest and detention, delivered him into the hands of the mob without authority for so doing, and accompanied them to Bird's Point. The prisoner gave his name as Miller, his home at Springfield, and said he had never been in Kentucky in his life, but the sheriff turned him over to the mob to be taken to Wickliffe, that Frank Gordon, the fisherman, who had put a man across the river might identify him.

In other words, the protection of the law was withdrawn from C. J. Miller, and he was given to a mob by this sheriff at Sikeston, who knew that the prisoner's life depended on one man's word. After an altercation with the train men, who wanted another $50 for taking the train back to Bird's Point, the crowd arrived there at three o'clock, Friday morning. Here was anchored "The Three States," a ferry boat plying between Wickliffe, Ky., Cairo, Ill., and Bird's Point, Mo. This boat left Cairo at twelve o'clock, Thursday, with nearly three hundred of Cairo's best citizens and thirty kegs of beer on board. This was consumed while the crowd and the bloodhound waited for the prisoner.

When the prisoner was on board "The Three States" the dog was turned loose, and after moving aimlessly around, followed the crowd to where Miller sat handcuffed and there stopped. The crowd closed in on the pair and insisted that the brute had identified him because of that action. When the boat reached Wickliffe, Gordon, the fisherman, was called on to say whether the prisoner was the man he ferried over the river the day of the murder.

The sheriff of Ballard county informed him, sternly that if the prisoner was not the man, he (the fisherman) would be held responsible as knowing who the guilty man was. Gordon stated before, that the man he ferried across was a white man or a bright colored man; Miller was a dark brown skinned man, with kinky hair, "neither yellow nor black," says the Cairo Evening Telegram of Friday, July 7th. The fisherman went up to Miller from behind, looked at him without speaking for fully five minutes, then slowly said, "Yes, that's the man I crossed over." This was about six o'clock, Friday morning, and the crowd wished to hang Miller then and there. But Mr. Ray, the father of the girls, insisted that he be taken to Bardwell, the county seat of Ballard, and twelve miles inland. He said he thought a white man committed the crime, and that he was not satisfied that was the man. They took him to Bardwell and at ten o'clock, this same excited, unauthorized mob undertook to determine Miller's guilt. One of the Clark brothers who shot at a fleeing man in the Dupoyster cornfield, said the prisoner was the same man; the other said he was not, but the testimony of the first was accepted. A colored woman who had said she gave breakfast to a colored man clad in a blue flannel suit the morning of the murder, said positively that she had never seen Miller before. The gold rings found in his possession had no names in them, as had been asserted, and Mr. Ray said they did not belong to his daughters. Meantime a funeral pyre for the purpose of burning Miller to death had been erected in the center of the village. While the crowd swayed by passion was clamoring that he be burnt, Miller stepped forward and made the following statement: "My name is C. J. Miller. I am from Springfield, Ill.; my wife lives at 716 N. 2d street. I am here among you today, looked upon as one of the most brutal men before the people. I stand here surrounded by men who are excited, men who are not willing to let the law take its course, and as far as the crime is concerned, I have committed no crime, and certainly no crime gross enough to deprive me of my life and liberty to walk upon the green earth."

A telegram was sent to the chief of the police at Springfield, Ill., asking if one C. J. Miller lived there. An answer in the negative was returned. A few hours after, it was ascertained that a man named Miller, and his wife, did live at the number the prisoner gave in his speech, but the information came to Bardwell too late to do the prisoner any good. Miller was taken to jail, every stitch of clothing literally torn from his body and examined again. On the lower left side of the bosom of his shirt was found a dark reddish spot about the size of a dime. Miller said it was paint which he had gotten on him at Jefferson Barracks. This spot was only on the right side, and could not be seen from the under side at all, thus showing it had not gone through the cloth as blood or any liquid substance would do.

Chief-of-Police Mahaney, of Cairo, Ill., was with the prisoner, and he took his knife and scraped at the spot, particles of which came off in his hand. Miller told them to take his clothes to any expert, and if the spot was shown to be blood, they might do anything they wished with him. They took his clothes away and were gone some time. After a while they were brought back and thrown into the cell without a word. It is needless to say that if the spot had been found to be blood, that fact would have been announced, and the shirt retained as evidence. Meanwhile numbers of rough, drunken men crowded into the cell and tried to force a confession of the deed from the prisoner's lips. He refused to talk save to reiterate his innocence. To Mr. Mahaney, who talked seriously and kindly to him, telling him the mob meant to burn and torture him at three o'clock, Miller said: "Burning and torture here lasts but a little while, but if I die with a lie on my soul, I shall be tortured forever. I am innocent." For more than three hours, all sorts of pressure in the way of threats, abuse and urging, was brought to bear to force him to confess to the murder and thus justify the mob in its deed of murder. Miller remained firm; but as the hour drew near, and the crowd became more impatient, he asked for a priest. As none could be procured, he then asked for a Methodist minister, who came, prayed with the doomed man, baptized him and exhorted Miller to confess. To keep up the flagging spirits of the dense crowd around the jail, the rumor went out more than once, that Miller had confessed. But the solemn assurance of the minister, chief-of-police, and leading editor—who were with Miller all along—is that this rumor is absolutely false.

At three o'clock the mob rushed to the jail to secure the prisoner. Mr. Ray had changed his mind about the promised burning; he was still in doubt as to the prisoner's guilt. He again addressed the crowd to that effect, urging them not to burn Miller, and the mob heeded him so far, that they compromised on hanging instead of burning, which was agreed to by Mr. Ray. There was a loud yell, and a rush was made for the prisoner. He was stripped naked, his clothing literally torn from his body, and his shirt was tied around his loins. Some one declared the rope was a "white man's death," and a log-chain, nearly a hundred feet in length, weighing over one hundred pounds, was placed round Miller's neck and body, and he was led and dragged through the streets of the village in that condition followed by thousands of people. He fainted from exhaustion several times, but was supported to the platform where they first intended burning him.

The chain was hooked around his neck, a man climbed the telegraph pole and the other end of the chain was passed up to him and made fast to the cross-arm. Others brought a long forked stick which Miller was made to straddle. By this means he was raised several feet from the ground and then let fall. The first fall broke his neck, but he was raised in this way and let fall a second time. Numberless shots were fired into the dangling body, for most of that crowd were heavily armed, and had been drinking all day.

Miller's body hung thus exposed from three to five o'clock, during which time, several photographs of him as he hung dangling at the end of the chain were taken, and his toes and fingers were cut off. His body was taken down, placed on the platform, the torch applied, and in a few moments there was nothing left of C. J. Miller save a few bones and ashes. Thus perished another of the many victims of Lynch Law, but it is the honest and sober belief of many who witnessed the scene that an innocent man has been barbarously and shockingly put to death in the glare of the 19th century civilization, by those who profess to believe in Christianity, law and order.

# Chapter 20

# IDA TARBELL

# A HISTORY OF STANDARD OIL COMPANY

IDA TARBELL'S NINETEEN-PART EXPOSÉ of Standard Oil for *McClure's Magazine* in 1904 set a new benchmark in investigative reporting and was one the central pieces of journalism produced by the muckrakers of the early twentieth century. It was an extraordinary achievement: in effect she single-handedly tangled with John D. Rockefeller, reputedly the world's richest man and the most powerful corporate leader around the turn of the century, and fueled an outcry that helped force the break up Standard Oil in 1911, requiring Rockefeller and other "titans of industry" to change their routine business practices.

Tarbell had first-hand knowledge of the oil industry—her father was a small independent oil operator who was driven into bankruptcy by Standard Oil's monopolistic practices. But it was her research that made her indictment of Standard Oil so compelling. After trawling magazine and newspaper articles on Standard Oil, she immersed herself in copious court records relating to civil suits against the company. She carried out a series of interviews with a Standard Oil executive introduced to her by Samuel Clemens (Mark Twain). This executive gave her chapter and verse on the benefits of monopoly and provided reams of statistics attesting to the company's benign influence that she then proceeded to use against the corporation. Standard Oil had been under federal and state government scrutiny from its formation in 1870 for allegedly receiving rebates from the railroads and engaging in the restraint of trade.

The corporation launched a vigorous national campaign to try to discredit the book and its conclusions. Rockefeller donated huge sums to charity in a bid for public support and Standard Oil distributed five million copies of an essay extolling the benefits of monopolies. Ultimately his campaign failed and the U.S. Congress passed the Hepburn Act in 1906 that effectively abolished oil company rebates, one of Standard Oil's primary anti-competitive tools. That same year a Bureau of Corporations was formed in the newly created U.S. Department of Commerce and Labor and charged with investigating the oil industry. It concluded that Standard Oil had been getting preferential treatment from railroad companies for some time. The corporation was fined $29 million and broken up into 38 separate companies—some still trading today as Chevron-Mobil and Exxon. The sections here include the formation of the South Improvement Company, which served as Rockefeller's tool to implement the consolidation of the oil business through collusion with the railroads and the conclusion of the book in which she dissects the size and scope of Standard Oil and summarizes how Rockefeller's schemes worked.

In the fall of 1871, while Mr. Rockefeller and his friends were occupied with all these questions, certain Pennsylvania refiners, it is not too certain who, brought to them a remarkable scheme, the gist of which was to bring together secretly a large enough body of refiners and shippers to persuade all the railroads handling oil to give the company formed special rebates on its oil, and drawbacks on that of other people. If they could get such rates it was evident that those outside of their combination could not compete with them long and that they would become eventually the only refiners. They could then limit their output to actual demand, and so keep up prices. This done, they could easily persuade the railroads to transport no crude for exportation, so that the foreigners would be forced to buy American refined. They believed that the price of oil thus exported could easily be advanced fifty per cent. The control of the refining interests would also enable them to fix their own price on crude. As they would be the only buyers and sellers, the speculative character of the business would be done away with. In short, the scheme they worked out put the entire oil business in their hands. . . .

The first thing was to get a charter—quietly. At a meeting held in Philadelphia late in the fall of 1871 a friend of one of the gentlemen interested mentioned to him that a certain estate then in liquidation had a charter for sale which gave its owners the right to carry on any kind of business in any country and in any way; that it could be bought for what it would cost to get a charter under the general laws of the state, and that it would be a favour to the heirs to buy it. The opportunity was promptly taken. The name of the charter bought was the "South (often written Southern) Improvement Company." For a beginning it was as good a name as another, since it said nothing. . . .

Mr. Watson was elected president and W. G. Warden of Philadelphia secretary of the new association. . . . The company most heavily interested in the South Improvement Company was the Standard Oil of Cleveland. . . .

It has frequently been stated that the South Improvement Company represented the bulk of the oil-refining interests in the country. The incorporators of the company in approaching the railroads assured them that this was so. As a matter of fact . . . the thirteen gentlemen . . . who were the only ones ever holding stock in the concern, did not control over one-tenth of the refining business of the United States in 1872. That business in the aggregate amounted to a daily capacity of about 45,000 barrels . . . and the stockholders of the South Improvement Company owned a combined capacity of not over 4,600 barrels. In assuring the railroads that they controlled the business, they were dealing with their hopes rather than with facts.

The organisation complete, there remained contracts to be made with the railroads. Three systems were to be interested: The Central, which, by its connection with the Lake Shore and Michigan Southern, ran directly into the Oil Regions; the Erie, allied with the Atlantic and Great Western, with a short line likewise tapping the heart of the region; and the Pennsylvania, with the connections known as the Allegheny Valley and Oil Creek Railroad. The persons to be won over were: W. H. Vanderbilt, of the Central;

H. F. Clark, president of the Lake Shore and Michigan Southern; Jay Gould, of the Erie; General G. B. McClellan, president of the Atlantic and Great Western; and Tom Scott, of the Pennsylvania. There seems to have been little difficulty in persuading any of these persons to go into the scheme after they had been assured by the leaders that all of the refiners were to be taken in. This was a verbal condition, however; not found in the contracts they signed. . . .

A second objection to making a contract with the company came from Mr. Scott of the Pennsylvania road and Mr. Potts of the Empire Transportation Company. The substance of this objection was that the plan took no account of the oil producer—the man to whom the world owed the business. Mr. Scott was strong in his assertion that they could never succeed unless they took care of the producers. . . . So strongly did Mr. Scott argue . . . that finally the members of the South Improvement Company yielded, and a draft of an agreement, to be proposed to the producers, was drawn up in lead-pencil; it was never presented. It seems to have been used principally to quiet Mr. Scott.

The work of persuasion went on swiftly. By the 18th of January the president of the Pennsylvania road, J. Edgar Thompson, had put his signature to the contract, and soon after Mr. Vanderbilt and Mr. Clark signed for the Central system, and Jay Gould and General McClellan for the Erie. The contracts to which these gentlemen put their names fixed gross rates of freight from all *common points*, as the leading shipping points within the Oil Regions were called, to all the great refining and shipping centres—New York, Philadelphia, Baltimore, Pittsburg and Cleveland. For example, the open rate on crude to New York was put at $2.56. On this price the South Improvement Company was allowed a rebate of $1.06 for its shipments; but it got not only this rebate, it was given in cash a like amount on each barrel of crude shipped by parties outside the combination.

The open rate from Cleveland to New York was two dollars, and fifty cents of this was turned over to the South Improvement Company, which at the same time received a rebate enabling it to ship for $1.50. Again, an independent refiner in Cleveland paid eighty cents a barrel to get his crude from the Oil Regions to his works, and the railroad sent forty cents of this money to the South Improvement Company. At the same time it cost the Cleveland refiner in the combination but forty cents to get his crude oil. Like drawbacks and rebates were given for all points—Pittsburg, Philadelphia, Boston and Baltimore.

An interesting provision in the contracts was that full waybills of all petroleum shipped over the roads should each day be sent to the South Improvement Company. This, of course, gave them knowledge of just who was doing business outside of their company—of how much business he was doing, and with whom he was doing it. Not only were they to have full knowledge of the business of all shippers—they were to have access to all books of the railroads.

The parties to the contracts agreed that if anybody appeared in the business offering an equal amount of transportation, and having equal facilities for doing business with the South Improvement Company, the railroads might give them equal advantages in drawbacks and rebates, but to make such a miscarriage of the scheme doubly improbable each railroad was bound to co-operate as "far as it legally might to maintain the business of the South Improvement Company against injury by competition, and lower or raise the gross rates of transportation for such times and to such extent as might be necessary to overcome the competition. The rebates and drawbacks to be varied *pari passu* with the gross rates."

The reason given by the railroads in the contract for granting these extraordinary privileges was that the "magnitude and extent of the business and operations" purposed to be carried on by the South Improvement Company would greatly promote the interest of the railroads and make it desirable for them to encourage their undertaking. The evident advantages received by the railroad were a regular amount of freight—the Pennsylvania was to have forty-five per cent of the East-bound shipments, the Erie and Central each 27½ per cent, while West-bound freight was to be divided equally between them—fixed rates, and freedom from the system of cutting which they had all found so harassing and disastrous. That is, the South Improvement Company, which was to include the entire refining capacity of the company, was to act as the evener of the oil business.

It was on the second of January, 1872, that the organisation of the South Improvement Company was completed. . . . There were at that time some twenty-six refineries in the town—some of them very large plants. All of them were feeling more or less the discouraging effects of the last three or four years of railroad discriminations in favour of the Standard Oil Company. To the owners of these refineries Mr. Rockefeller now went one by one, and explained the South Improvement Company. "You see," he told them, "this scheme is bound to work. It means an absolute control by us of the oil business. There is no chance for anyone outside. But we are going to give everybody a chance to come in. You are to turn over your refinery to my appraisers, and I will give you Standard Oil Company stock or cash, as you prefer, for the value we put upon it. I advise you to take the stock. It will be for your good." Certain refiners objected. They did not want to sell. They did want to keep and manage their business. Mr. Rockefeller was regretful, but firm. It was useless to resist, he told the hesitating; they would certainly be crushed if they did not accept his offer, and he pointed out in detail, and with gentleness, how beneficent the scheme really was—preventing the creek refiners from destroying Cleveland, ending competition, keeping up the price of refined oil, and eliminating speculation. Really a wonderful contrivance for the good of the oil business. . . .

A few of the refiners contested before surrendering. Among these was Robert Hanna, an uncle of Mark Hanna, of the firm of Hanna, Baslington and Company. Mr. Hanna had been refining since July, 1869. According to his own sworn statement he had made money, fully sixty per cent, on his investment the first year, and after that thirty per cent. Some time in February, 1872, the Standard Oil Company asked an interview with him and his associates. They wanted to buy his works, they said. "But we don't want to sell," objected Mr. Hanna. "You can never make any more money, in my judgment," said Mr. Rockefeller. "You can't compete with the Standard. We have all the large refineries now. If you refuse to sell, it will end in your being crushed." Hanna and Baslington were not satisfied. They went to see Mr. Watson, president of the South Improvement Company and an officer of the Lake Shore, and General Devereux, manager of the Lake Shore road. They were told that the Standard had special rates; that it was useless to try to compete with them. General Devereux explained to the gentlemen that the privileges granted the Standard were the legitimate and necessary advantage of the larger shipper over the smaller, and that if Hanna, Baslington and Company could give the road as large a quantity of oil as the Standard did, with the same regularity, they could have the same rate. General Devereux says they "recognised the propriety" of his excuse. They certainly recognised its authority. They say that they were satisfied they could no longer get rates to and from Cleveland which would enable them to live, and "reluctantly" sold out. It must have been reluctantly, for they had paid $75,000 for their works, and had made thirty per cent, a year on an average on their investment, and the Standard appraiser allowed them $45,000. "Truly and really less than one-half of what they were absolutely worth, with a fair and honest competition in the lines of transportation," said Mr. Hanna, eight years later, in an affidavit.

Under the combined threat and persuasion of the Standard, armed with the South Improvement Company scheme, almost the entire independent oil interest of Cleveland, collapsed in three months' time. Of the twenty-six refineries, at least twenty-one sold out. From a capacity of probably not over 1,500 barrels of crude a day, the Standard Oil Company rose in three months' time to one of 10,000 barrels. By this manœuvre it became master of over one-fifth of the refining capacity of the United States. . . .

[. . .]

The profits of the present Standard Oil Company are enormous. For five years the dividends have been averaging about forty-five million dollars a year, or nearly fifty per cent, on its capitalisation, a sum which capitalised at five per cent, would give $900,000,000. Of course this is not all that the combination makes in a year. It allows an annual average of 5.77 per cent for deficit, and it carries always an ample reserve fund. When we remember that probably one-third of this immense annual revenue goes into the hands of John D. Rockefeller, that probably ninety per cent, of it goes to the few men who make up the "Standard Oil family," and that it must every year be invested, the Standard Oil Company becomes a much more serious public matter than it was in 1872, when it stamped itself as willing to enter into a conspiracy to raid the oil business—as a much more serious concern than in the years when it openly made warfare of business, and drove from the oil industry by any means it could invent all who had the hardihood to enter it. For, consider what must be done with the greater part of this $45,000,000. It must be invested. The oil business does not demand it. There is plenty of reserve for all of its ventures. It must go into other industries. Naturally, the interests sought will be allied to oil. They will be gas, and we have the Standard Oil crowd steadily acquiring the gas interests of the country. They will be railroads, for on transportation all industries depend, and, besides, railroads are one of the great consumers of oil products and must be kept in line as buyers. And we have the directors of the Standard Oil Company acting as directors on nearly all of the great railways of the country, the New York Central, New York, New Haven and Hartford, Chicago, Milwaukee and St. Paul, Union Pacific, Northern Pacific, Delaware, Lackawanna and Western, Missouri Pacific, Missouri, Kansas and Texas, Boston and Maine, and other lesser roads. They will go into copper, and we have the Amalgamated scheme. They will go into steel, and we have Mr. Rockefeller's enormous holdings in the Steel Trust. They will go into banking, and we have the National City Bank and its allied institutions in New York City and Boston, as well as a long chain running over the country. . . . The result is that the Standard Oil Company is probably in the strongest financial position of any aggregation in the world. And every year its position grows stronger, for every year there is pouring in another $45,000,000 to be used in wiping up the property most essential to preserving and broadening its power. . . .

So much for present organisation, and now as to how far through this organisation the Standard Oil Company is able to realise the purpose for which it was organised—the control of the output, and, through that, the price, of refined oil. That is, what per cent, of the whole oil business does Mr. Rockefeller's concern control. First as to oil production. In 1898 the Standard Oil Company reported to the Industrial Commission that it produced 35.58 per cent, of Eastern crude—the production that year was about

52,000,000 barrels. . . . But while Mr. Rockefeller produces only about a third of the entire production, he controls all but about ten per cent, of it; that is, all but about ten per cent, goes immediately into his custody on coming from the wells. It passes entirely out of the hands of the producers when the Standard pipe-line takes it. The oil is in Mr. Rockefeller's hands, and he, not the producer, can decide who is to have it. The greater portion of it he takes himself, of course, for he is the chief refiner of the country. In 1898 there were about twenty-four million barrels of petroleum products made in this country. Of this amount about twenty million were made by the Standard Oil Company; fully a third of the balance was produced by the Tidewater Company, of which the Standard holds a large minority stock, and which for twenty years has had a running arrangement with the Standard. Reckoning out of the Tidewater's probable output, and we have an independent output of about 2,500,000 in twenty-four million. It is obvious that this great percentage of the business gives the Standard the control of prices. This control can be kept in the domestic markets so long as the Standard can keep under competition as successfully as it has in the past. It can be kept in the foreign market as long as American oils can be made and sold in quantity cheaper than foreign oils. Until a decade ago the foreign market of American oils was not seriously threatened. Since 1895, however, Russia, whose annual output of petroleum had been for a number of years about equal in volume to the American output, learned to make a fairly decent product; more dangerous, she had learned to market. She first appeared in Europe in 1885. It took ten years to make her a formidable rival, but she is so to-day, and, in spite of temporary alliances and combinations, it is very doubtful whether the Standard will ever permanently control Russian oil. . . .

In the East the oil market belonged practically to the Standard Oil Company until recently. Last year (1903), however, Sumatra imported more oil into China than America, and Russia imported nearly half as much. About 91,500,000 gallons of kerosene went into Calcutta last year, and of this only about six million gallons came from America. In Singapore representatives of Sumatra oil claim that they have two-thirds of the trade.

Combinations for offensive and defensive trade campaigns have also gone on energetically among these various companies in the last few years. One of the largest and most powerful of these aggregations now at work is in connection with an English shipping concern, the Shell Transport and Trading Company, the head of which is Sir Marcus Samuel, formerly Lord Mayor of London. This company, which formerly traded almost entirely in Russian oil, undertook a few years ago to develop the oil fields in Borneo, and they built up a large Oriental trade. They soon came into hot competition with the Royal Dutch Company, handling Sumatra oil, and a war of prices ensued which lasted nearly two years. In 1903, however, the two competitors, in connection with four other strong Sumatra and European companies, drew up an agreement in regard to markets which has put an end to their war. The "Shell" people have not only these allies, but they have a contract with Guffey Petroleum Company, the largest Texas producing concern, to handle its output, and they have gone into a German oil company, the Petroleum Produkten Aktien Gesellschaft. Having thus provided themselves with a supply they have begun developing a European trade on the same lines as their Oriental trade, and they are making serious inroads on the Standard's market.

The naphthas made from the Borneo oil have largely taken the place of American naphtha in many parts of Europe. One load of Borneo benzine even made its appearance in the American market in 1904. It is a sign of what well may happen in the future with an intelligent development of these Russian and Oriental oils—the Standard's domestic market invaded. It will be interesting to see to what further extent the American government will protect the Standard Oil Company by tariff on foreign oils if such a time does come. It has done very well already. The aggressive marketing of the "Shell" and its allies in Europe has led to a recent Oil War of great magnitude. For several months in 1904 American export oil was sold at a lower price in New York than the crude oil it takes to make it costs there. For instance, on August 13, 1904, the New York export price was 4.80 cents per gallon for Standard-white in bulk. Crude sold at the well for $1.50 a barrel of forty-two gallons, and it costs sixty cents to get it to seaboard by pipe-line; that is, forty-two gallons of crude oil costs $2.10, or five cents a gallon in New York— twenty points loss on a gallon of the raw material! But this low price for export affects the local market little or none. The tank-wagon price keeps up to ten and eleven cents in New York. Of course crude is depressed as much as possible to help carry this competition. For many months now there has been the abnormal situation of a declining crude price in face of declining stocks. The truth is the Standard Oil Company is trying to meet the competition of the low-grade Oriental and Russian oils with high-grade American oil—the crude being kept as low as possible, and the domestic market being made to pay for the foreign cutting. It seems a lack of foresight surprising in the Standard to have allowed itself to be found in such a dilemma. Certainly, for over two years the company has been making every effort to escape by getting hold of a supply of low-grade oil which would enable it to meet the competition of the foreigner. There have been more or less short-lived arrangements in Russia. An oil territory in Galicia was secured not long ago by them, and an expert refiner with a full refining plant was sent over. Various hindrances have been met in the undertaking, and the works are not yet in operation. Two years ago the Standard attempted to get hold of the rich Burma oil fields. The press of India fought them out of the country, and their weapon was the Standard Oil Company's own record for hard dealings! The Burma fields are in the hands of a monopoly of the closest sort which has never properly developed the territory, but the people and government prefer their own monopoly to one of the American type!

Altogether the most important question concerning the Standard Oil Company today is how far it is sustaining its power by the employment of the peculiar methods of the South Improvement Company. It should never be forgotten that Mr. Rockefeller never depended on these methods alone for securing power in the oil trade. From the beginning the Standard Oil Company has studied thoroughly everything connected with the oil business. It has known, not guessed at conditions. It has had a keen authoritative sight. It has applied itself to its tasks with indefatigable zeal. It has been as courageous as it has been cautious. Nothing has been too big to undertake, as nothing has been too small to neglect. These facts have been repeatedly pointed out in this narrative. But these are the American industrial qualities. They are common enough in all sorts of business. They have made our railroads, built up our great department stores, opened our mines. The Standard Oil Company has no monopoly in business ability. It is the thing for which American men are distinguished to-day in the world.

These qualities alone would have made a great business, and unquestionably it would have been along the line of combination, for when Mr. Rockefeller undertook to work out the good of the oil business the tendency to combination was marked throughout the industry, but it would not have been the combination whose history we have traced. To the help of these qualities Mr. Rockefeller proposed to bring the peculiar aids of the South Improvement Company. He secured an alliance with the railroads to drive out rivals. For fifteen years he received rebates of varying amounts on at least the greater part of his shipments, and for at least a portion of that time he collected drawbacks of the oil other people shipped; at the same time he worked with the railroads to prevent other people getting oil to manufacture, or if they got it he worked with the railroads to prevent the shipment of the product. If it reached a dealer, he did his utmost to bully or wheedle him to countermand his order. If he failed in that, he undersold until the dealer, losing on his purchase, was glad enough to buy thereafter of Mr. Rockefeller. How much of this system remains in force to-day? The spying on independent shipments, the effort to have orders countermanded, the predatory competition prevailing, are well enough known. . . . As for the rebates and drawbacks, if they do not exist in the forms practised up to 1887, as the Standard officials have repeatedly declared, it is not saying that the Standard enjoys no special transportation privileges. As has been pointed out, it controls the great pipe-line handling all but perhaps ten per cent, of the oil produced in the Eastern fields. This system is fully 35,000 miles long. It goes to the wells of every producer, gathers his oil into its storage tanks, and from there transports it to Philadelphia, Baltimore, New York, Chicago, Buffalo, Cleveland, or any other refining point where it is needed. This pipe-line is a common carrier by virtue of its use of the right of eminent domain, and, as a common carrier, is theoretically obliged to carry and deliver the oil of all comers, but in practice this does not always work. It has happened more than once in the history of the Standard pipes that they have refused to gather or deliver oil. Pipes have been taken up from wells belonging to individuals running or working with independent refiners. Oil has been refused delivery at points practical for independent refiners. For many years the supply of oil has been so great that the Standard could not refuse oil to the independent refiner on the ground of scarcity. However, a shortage in Pennsylvania oil occurred in 1903. A very interesting situation arose as a result. There are in Ohio and Pennsylvania several independent refiners who, for a number of years, have depended on the Standard lines (the National Transit Company) for their supply of crude. In the fall of 1903 these refiners were informed that thereafter the Standard could furnish them with only fifty per cent, of their refining capacity. It was a serious matter to the independents, who had their own markets, and some of whom were increasing their plants. . . . The independent refiners decided to compromise, and an agreement terminable by either party at short notice was made between them and the Standard, by which the members of the former were each to have eighty per cent. of their capacity of crude oil, and were to give to the Standard all of their export oil to market. As a matter of fact, the Standard's ability to cut off crude supplies from the outside refiners is much greater than in the days before the Interstate Commerce Bill, when it depended on its alliance with the railroads to prevent its rival getting oil. It goes without saying that this is an absurd power to allow in the hands of any manufacturer of a great necessity of life. It is exactly as if one corporation aiming at manufacturing all the flour of the country owned all but ten per cent of the entire railroad system collecting and transporting wheat. They could, of course, in time of shortage, prevent any would-be competitor from getting grain to grind, and they could and would make it difficult and expensive at all times for him to get it.

It is not only in the power of the Standard to cut off outsiders from it, it is able to keep up transportation prices. Mr. Rockefeller owns the pipe system—a common carrier—and the refineries of the Standard Oil Company pay in the final accounting cost for transporting their oil, while outsiders pay just what they paid twenty-five years ago. There are lawyers who believe that if this condition were tested in the courts, the

National Transit Company would be obliged to give the same rates to others as the Standard refineries ultimately pay. It would be interesting to see the attempt made.

Not only are outside refiners at just as great disadvantage in securing crude supply today as before the Interstate Commerce Commission was formed; they still suffer severe is-crimination on the railroads in marketing their product. . . .

There is no independent refiner or jobber who tries to ship oil freight that does not meet incessant discouragement and discrimination. Not only are rates made to favour the Standard refining points and to protect their markets, but switching charges and dock charges are multiplied. Loading and unloading facilities are refused, payment of freights on small quantities are demanded in advance, a score of different ways are found to make hard the way of the outsider. "If I get a barrel of oil out of Buffalo," an independent dealer told the writer not long ago, "I have to *sneak* it out. There are no public docks; the railroads control most of them, and they won't let me out if they can help it. If I want to ship a carload they won't take it if they can help it. They are all afraid of offending the Standard Oil Company."

This may be a rather sweeping statement, but there is too much truth in it. There is no doubt that to-day, as before the Interstate Commerce Commission, a community of interests exists between railroads and the Standard Oil Company sufficiently strong for the latter to get any help it wants in making it hard for rivals to do business. The Standard owns stock in most of the great systems. It is represented on the board of directors of nearly all the great systems, and it has an immense freight not only in oil products, but in timber, iron, acids, and all of the necessities of its factories. It is allied with many other industries, iron, steel, and copper, and can swing freight away from a road which does not oblige it. It has great influence in the money market and can help or hinder a road in securing money. It has great influence in the stock market and can depress or inflate a stock if it sets about it. Little wonder that the railroads, being what they are, are afraid to "disturb their relations with the Standard Oil Company," or that they keep alive a system of discriminations the same in effect as those which existed before 1887.

Of course such cases as those cited above are fit for the Interstate Commerce Commission, but the oil men as a body have no faith in the effectiveness of an appeal to the Commission, and in this feeling they do not reflect on the Commission, but rather on the ignorance and timidity of the Congress which, after creating a body which the people demanded, made it helpless. The case on which the Oil Regions rests its reason for its opinion has already been referred to in the chapter on the co-operative independent movement which finally resulted in the Pure Oil Company. The case first came before the Commission in 1888. . . . The hearing took place in Titusville in May, 1889 . . . and in December, 1892, it gave its decision. . . . It ordered that the railroads make the rates the same on oil in both tanks and barrels, and that they furnish shippers tanks whenever reasonable notice was given. As the amounts wrongfully collected by the railroads from the refiners could not be ascertained from the evidence already taken, the Commission decided to hold another hearing and fix the amounts. This was not done until May, 1894, five years after the first hearing. Reparation was ordered to at least eleven different firms, some of the sums amounting to several thousand dollars; the entire award ordered amounted to nearly $100,000.

In case the railroads failed to adjust the claims the refiners were ordered to proceed to enforce them in the courts. The Commission found at this hearing that none of their orders of 1892 had been followed by the roads and they were all repeated. As was to be expected, the roads refused to recognise the claims allowed by the Commission, and the case was taken by the refiners into court. It has been heard three times. Twice they have won, but each time an appeal of the roads has forced them to appear again. The case was last heard at Philadelphia in February, 1904, in the United States Circuit Court of Appeals. No decision had been rendered at this writing. . . .

See the helplessness of the Commission. It takes full testimony in 1889, digests it carefully, gives its orders in 1892, and they are not obeyed. More hearings follow, and in 1895 the orders are repeated and reparation is allowed to the injured refiners. From that time to this the case passes from court to court, the railroad seeking to escape the Commission's orders. The Interstate Commerce Commission was instituted to facilitate justice in this matter of transportation, and yet here we have still unsettled a case on which they gave their judgment twelve years ago. The lawyer who took the first appeal to the Commission . . . has been continually engaged in the case for sixteen years!

In spite of the Interstate Commerce Commission, the crucial question is still a transportation question. Until the people of the United States have solved the question of free and equal transportation it is idle to suppose that they will not have a trust question. So long as it is possible for a company to own the exclusive carrier on which a great natural product depends for transportation, and to use this carrier to limit a competitor's supply or to cut off that supply entirely if the rival is offensive, and always to make him pay a higher rate than it costs the owner, it is ignorance and folly to talk about constitutional amendments limiting trusts. So long as the great manufacturing centres of a monopolistic trust can get better rates than the centres of independent effort, it is idle to talk about laws making it a crime to undersell for the purpose of driving a competitor from a market. You must get into markets before you can compete. So long as railroads can be persuaded to interfere with independent pipelines, to refuse oil freight, to refuse loading facilities, lest they disturb their relations with the Standard Oil Company, it is idle to talk about investigations or anti-trust legislation or application of the Sherman law. So long as the Standard Oil Company can control transportation as it does today, it will remain master of the oil industry, and the people of the United States will pay for their indifference and folly in regard to transportation a good sound tax on oil, and they will yearly see an increasing concentration of natural resources and transportation systems in the Standard Oil crowd.

If all the country had suffered from these raids on competition, had been the limiting of the business opportunity of a few hundred men and a constant higher price for refined oil, the case would be serious enough, but there is a more serious side to it. The ethical cost of all this is the deep concern. We are a commercial people. We cannot boast of our arts, our crafts, our cultivation; our boast is in the wealth we produce. As a consequence business success is sanctified, and, practically, any methods which achieve it are justified by a larger and larger class. All sorts of subterfuges and sophistries and slurring over of facts are employed to explain aggregations of capital whose determining factor has been like that of the Standard Oil Company, special privileges obtained by persistent secret effort in opposition to the spirit of the law, the efforts of legislators, and the most outspoken public opinion. How often does one hear it argued, the Standard Oil Company is simply an inevitable result of economic conditions; that is, given the practices of the oil-bearing railroads in 1872 and the elements of speculation and the over-refining in the oil business, there was nothing for Mr. Rockefeller to do but secure special privileges if he wished to save his business.

[. . .]

Now in 1872 Mr. Rockefeller owned a successful refinery in Cleveland. He had the advantage of water transportation a part of the year, access to two great trunk lines the year around. Under such able management as he could give it his concern was bound to go on, given the demand for refined oil. It was bound to draw other firms to it. When he went into the South Improvement Company it was not to save his own business, but to destroy others. When he worked so persistently to secure rebates after the breaking up of the South Improvement Company, it was in the face of an industry united against them. It was not to save his business that he compelled the Empire Transportation Company to go out of the oil business in 1877. Nothing but grave mismanagement could have destroyed his business at that moment; it was to get every refinery in the country but his own out of the way. It was not the necessity to save his business which compelled Mr. Rockefeller to make war on the Tidewater. He and the Tidewater could both have lived. It was to prevent prices of transportation and of refined oil going down under competition. What necessity was there for Mr. Rockefeller trying to prevent the United States Pipe Line doing business?—only the greed of power and money. Every great campaign against rival interests which the Standard Oil Company has carried on has been inaugurated, not to save its life, but to build up and sustain a monopoly in the oil industry. These are not mere affirmations of a hostile critic; they are facts proved by documents and figures.

Certain defenders go further and say that if some such combination had not been formed the oil industry would have failed for lack of brains and capital. Such a statement is puerile. Here was an industry for whose output the whole world was crying. Petroleum came at the moment when the value and necessity of a new, cheap light was recognised everywhere. Before Mr. Rockefeller had ventured outside of Cleveland kerosene was going in quantities to every civilised country. Nothing could stop it, nothing check it, but the discovery of some cheaper light or the putting up of its price. The real "good of the oil business" in 1872 lay in making oil cheaper. It would flow all over the world on its own merit if cheap enough.

The claim that only by some such aggregation as Mr. Rockefeller formed could enough capital have been obtained to develop the business falls utterly in face of fact. Look at the enormous amounts of capital, large amount of it speculative, to be sure, which the oil men claim went into their business in the first ten years. It was estimated that Philadelphia alone put over $168,000,000 into the development of the Oil Regions, and New York $134,000,000, in their first decade of the business. . . . Indeed, there has always been plenty of money for oil investment. It did not require Mr. Rockefeller's capital to develop the Bradford oil fields, build the first seaboard pipe-line, open West Virginia, Texas, or Kansas. The oil business would no more have suffered for lack of capital without the Standard combination than the iron or wheat or railroad or cotton business. The claim is idle, given the wealth and energy of the country in the forty-five years since the discovery of oil.

Equally well does both the history and the present condition of the oil business show that it has not needed any such aggregation to give us cheap oil. The margin between crude and refined was made low by competition. It has rarely been as low as it would have been had there been free competition. For five years even the small independent refineries outside of the Pure Oil Company have been able to make a profit on the prices set by the Standard, and this in spite of the higher transportation they have paid on both crude and refined, and the wall of seclusion the railroads build around domestic markets.

Very often people who admit the facts, who are willing to see that Mr. Rockefeller has employed force and fraud to secure his ends, justify him by declaring, "It's business." That is, "it's business" has to come to be a legitimate excuse for hard dealing, sly tricks, special privileges. It is a common enough thing to hear men arguing that the ordinary laws of morality do not apply in business. Now, if the Standard Oil Company were the only concern in the country guilty of the practices which have given it monopolistic power, this story never would have been written. Were it alone in these methods, public scorn would long ago have made short work of the Standard Oil Company. But it is simply the most conspicuous type of what can be done by these practices. The methods it employs with such acumen, persistency, and secrecy are employed by all sorts of business men, from corner grocers up to bankers. If exposed, they are excused on the ground that this is business. If the point is pushed, frequently the defender of the practice falls back on the Christian doctrine of charity, and points that we are erring mortals and must allow for each other's weaknesses!—an excuse, which, if carried to its legitimate conclusion, would leave our business men weeping on one another's shoulders over human frailty, while they picked one another's pockets.

One of the most depressing features of the ethical side of the matter is that instead of such methods arousing contempt they are more or less openly admired. And this is logical. Canonise "business success," and men who make a success like that of the Standard Oil Trust become national heroes! The history of its organisation is studied as a practical lesson in money-making. It is the most startling feature of the case to one who would like to feel that it is possible to be a commercial people and yet a race of gentlemen. . . .

The effects on the very men who fight these methods on the ground that they are ethically wrong are deplorable. Brought into competition with the trust, badgered, foiled, spied upon, they come to feel as if anything is fair when the Standard is the opponent. The bitterness against the Standard Oil Company in many parts of Pennsylvania and Ohio is such that a verdict from a jury on the merits of the evidence is almost impossible! A case in point occurred a few years ago in the Bradford field. An oil producer was discovered stealing oil from the National Transit Company. He had tapped the main line and for at least two years had run a small but steady stream of Standard oil into his private tank. Finally the thieving pipe was discovered, and the owner of it, after acknowledging his guilt, was brought to trial. The jury gave a verdict of Not guilty! They seemed to feel that though the guilt was acknowledged, there probably was a Standard trick concealed somewhere. Anyway it was the Standard Oil Company and it deserved to be stolen from! The writer has frequently heard men, whose own business was conducted with scrupulous fairness, say in cases of similar stealing that they would never condemn a man who stole from the Standard! Of course such a state of feeling undermines the whole moral nature of a community.

The blackmailing cases of which the Standard Oil Company complain are a natural result of its own practices. Men going into an independent refining business have for years been accustomed to say: "well, if they won't let us alone, we'll make them pay a good price." The Standard complains that such men build simply to sell out. There may be cases of this. Probably there are, though the writer has no absolute proof of any such. Certainly there is no satisfactory proof that the refinery in the famous Buffalo case was built to sell, though that it was offered for sale when the opposition of the Everests, the managers of the Standard concern, had become so serious as later to be stamped as criminal by judge and jury, there is no doubt. Certainly nothing was shown to have been done or said by Mr. Matthews, the owner of the concern which the Standard was fighting, which might not have been expected from a man who had met the kind of opposition he had from the time he went into business.

The truth is, blackmail and every other business vice is the natural result of the peculiar business practices of the Standard. If business is to be treated as warfare and not as a peaceful pursuit, as they have persisted in treating it, they cannot expect the men they are fighting to lie down and die without a struggle. If they get special privileges they must expect their competitors to struggle to get them. If they will find it more profitable to buy out a refinery than to let it live, they must expect the owner to get an extortionate price if he can. And when they complain of these practices and call them blackmail, they show thin sporting blood. They must not expect to monopolise hard dealings, if they do oil.

These are considerations of the ethical effect of such business practices on those outside and in competition. As for those within the organisation there is one obvious effect worth noting. The Standard men as a body have nothing to do with public affairs, except as it is necessary to manipulate them for the "good of the oil business." The notion that the business man must not appear in politics and religion save as a "stand-patter"— not even as a thinking, aggressive force—is demoralising, intellectually and morally. Ever since 1872 the organisation has appeared in politics only to oppose legislation obviously for the public good. At that time the oil industry was young, only twelve years old, and it was suffering from too rapid growth, from speculation, from rapacity of railroads, but it was struggling manfully with all these questions. The question of railroad discriminations and extortions was one of the "live questions" of the country. The oil men as a mass were allied against it. The theory that the railroad was a public servant bound by the spirit of its charter to treat all shippers alike, that fair play demanded open equal rates to all, was generally held in the oil country at the time Mr. Rockeller and his friends sprung the South Improvement Company. One has only to read the oil journals at the time of the Oil War of 1872 to see how seriously all phases of the transportation question were considered. The country was a unit against the rebate system. Agreements were signed with the railroads that all rates henceforth should be equal. The signatures were not on before Mr. Rockefeller had a rebate, and gradually others got them until the Standard had won the advantages it expected the South Improvement Company to give it. From that time to this Mr. Rockefeller has had to fight the best sentiment of the oil country and of the country at large as to what is for the public good. He and his colleagues kept a strong alliance in Washington fighting the Interstate Commerce Bill from the time the first one was introduced in 1876 until the final passage in 1887. Every measure looking to the freedom and equalisation of transportation has met his opposition, as have bills for giving greater publicity to the operations of corporations. In many of the great state Legislatures one of the first persons to be pointed out to a visitor is the Standard Oil lobbyist. Now, no one can dispute the right of the Standard Oil Company to express its opinions on proposed legislation. It has the same right to do this as all the rest of the world. It is only the character of its opposition which is open to criticism, the fact that it is always fighting measures which equalise privileges and which make it more necessary for men to start fair and play fair in doing business.

Of course the effect of directly practising many of their methods is obvious. For example, take the whole system of keeping track of independent business. There are practices required which corrupt every man who has a hand in them. One of the most deplorable things about it is that most of the work is done by youngsters. The freight clerk who reports the independent oil shipments for a fee of five or ten dollars a month is probably a young man, learning his first lessons in corporate morality. If he happens to sit in Mr. Rockefeller's church on Sundays, through what sort of a haze will he receive the teachings? There is something alarming to those who believe that commerce should be a peaceful pursuit, and who believe that the moral law holds good throughout the entire range of human relations, in knowing that so large a body of young men in this country are consciously or unconsciously growing up with the idea that business is war and that morals have nothing to do with its practice.

And what are we going to do about it? for it is *our* business. We, the people of the United States, and nobody else, must cure whatever is wrong in the industrial situation, typified by this narrative of the growth of the Standard Oil Company. That our first task is to secure free and equal transportation privileges by rail, pipe and waterway is evident. It is not an easy matter. It is one which may require operations which will seem severe; but the whole system of discrimination has been nothing but violence, and those who have profited by it cannot complain if the curing of the evils they have wrought bring hardship in turn on them. At all events, until the transportation matter is settled, and settled right, the monopolistic trust will be with us, a leech on our pockets, a barrier to our free efforts.

As for the ethical side, there is no cure but in an increasing scorn of unfair play—an increasing sense that a thing won by breaking the rules of the game is not worth the winning. When the business man who fights to secure special privileges, to crowd his competitor off the track by other than fair competitive methods, receives the same summary disdainful ostracism by his fellows that the doctor or lawyer who is "unprofessional," the athlete who abuses the rules, receives, we shall have gone a long way toward making commerce a fit pursuit for our young men.

# Chapter 21

# DAVID NICHOLS

# ERNIE'S WAR

ERNIE PYLE IS PERHAPS AMERICA'S most famous war correspondent. Traveling with the troops in North Africa and then Europe during World War II, Pyle captured the voice of the quintessential American soldier, the proverbial G.I. Joe.

Born in 1900, Pyle attended Indiana University, leaving one semester short of graduation, and after a short stint at a newspaper in Indiana joined the staff of *The Washington Daily News*, a relatively new tabloid newspaper. He quickly rose to become managing editor, but he always wanted to return to writing. In 1935, on the strength of columns he had written in place of another columnist who was on vacation, Pyle began to write an "on-the-road" column for the Scripps-Howard Alliance group. At one point, his column was carried in around 300 newspapers.

With the U.S entry into World War II, Pyle became a war correspondent. He did not write about the movement of troops or record the words of generals. Most often he wrote from the perspective of the common foot soldier. In 1944, his work won a Pulitzer Prize. In 1945, Pyle died after being hit by machine gun fire on an island near to Okinawa.

Four of Pyle's columns are included here including "The Death of Captain Waskow," perhaps his best known piece.

### A Dreadful Masterpiece

LONDON, December 30, 1940—Someday when peace has returned to this odd world I want to come to London again and stand on a certain balcony on a moonlit night and look down upon the peaceful silver curve of the Thames with its dark bridges.

And standing there, I want to tell somebody who has never seen it how London looked on a certain night in the holiday season of the year 1940.

For on that night this old, old city—even though I must bite my tongue in shame for saying it—was the most beautiful sight I have ever seen.

It was a night when London was ringed and stabbed with fire.

They came just after dark, and somehow I could sense from the quick, bitter firing of the guns that there was to be no monkey business this night.

Shortly after the sirens wailed I could hear the Germans grinding overhead. In my room, with its black curtains drawn across the windows, you could feel the shake from the guns. You could hear the boom, crump, crump, crump, of heavy bombs at their work of tearing buildings apart. They were not too far away.

Half an hour after the firing started I gathered a couple of friends and went to a high, darkened balcony that gave us a view of one-third of the entire circle of London.

As we stepped out onto the balcony a vast inner excitement came over all of us—an excitement that had neither fear nor horror in it, because it was too full of awe.

You have all seen big fires, but I doubt if you have ever seen the whole horizon of a city lined with great fires—scores of them, perhaps hundreds.

The closest fires were near enough for us to hear the crackling flames and the yells of firemen. Little fires grew into big ones even as we watched. Big ones died down under the firemen's valor only to break out again later.

About every two minutes a new wave of planes would be over. The motors seemed to grind rather than roar, and to have an angry pulsation like a bee buzzing in blind fury.

The bombs did not make a constant overwhelming din as in those terrible days of last September. They were intermittent—sometimes a few seconds apart, sometimes a minute or more.

Their sound was sharp, when nearby, and soft and muffled, far away.

Into the dark, shadowed spaces below us, as we watched, whole batches of incendiary bombs fell. We saw two dozen go off in two seconds. They flashed terrifically, then quickly simmered down to pinpoints of dazzling white, burning ferociously.

These white pinpoints would go out one by one as the unseen heroes of the moment smothered them with sand. But also, as we watched, other pinpoints would burn on and pretty soon a yellow flame would leap up from the white center. They had done their work—another building was on fire.

The greatest of all the fires was directly in front of us. Flames seemed to whip hundreds of feet into the air. Pinkish-white smoke ballooned upward in a great cloud, and out of this cloud there gradually took shape—so faintly at first that we weren't sure we saw correctly—the gigantic dome and spires of St. Paul's Cathedral.

St. Paul's was surrounded by fire, but it came through. It stood there in its enormous proportions—growing slowly clearer and clearer, the way objects take shape at dawn. It was like a picture of some miraculous figure that appears before peace-hungry soldiers on a battlefield.

The streets below us were semi-illuminated from the glow.

Immediately above the fires the sky was red and angry, and overhead, making a ceiling in the vast heavens, there was a cloud of smoke all in pink. Up in that pink shrouding there were tiny, brilliant specks of flashing light—anti-aircraft shells bursting. After the flash you could hear the sound.

Up there, too, the barrage balloons were standing out as clearly as if it were daytime, but now they were pink instead of silver. And now and then through a hole in that pink shroud there twinkled incongruously a permanent, genuine star—the old-fashioned kind that has always been there.

Below us the Thames grew lighter, and all around below were the shadows—the dark shadows of buildings and bridges that formed the base of this dreadful masterpiece.

Later on I borrowed a tin hat and went out among the fires. That was exciting too, but the thing I shall always remember above all the other things in my life is the monstrous loveliness of that one single view of London on a holiday night—London stabbed with great fires, shaken by explosions, its dark regions along the Thames sparkling with the pinpoints of white-hot bombs, all of it roofed over with a ceiling of pink that held bursting shells, balloons, flares and the grind of vicious engines. And in yourself the excitement and anticipation and wonder in your soul that this could be happening at all.

These things all went together to make the most hateful, most beautiful single scene I have ever known.

[. . .]

## Digging and Grousing

ON THE NORTH AFRICAN DESERT, March 23, 1943—When our Sahara salvage expedition finally found the wrecked airplanes far out on the endless desert, the mechanics went to work taking off usable parts, and four others of us appointed ourselves the official ditchdiggers of the day.

We were all afraid of being strafed if the Germans came over and saw men working around the planes, and we wanted a nice ditch handy for diving into. The way to have a nice ditch is to dig one. We wasted no time.

Would that all slit trenches could be dug in soil like that. The sand was soft and moist; just the kind children like to play in. The four of us dug a winding ditch forty feet long and three feet deep in about an hour and a half.

The day got hot, and we took off our shirts. One sweating soldier said: "Five years ago you couldn't a got me to dig a ditch for five dollars an hour. Now look at me.

"You can't stop me digging ditches. I don't even want pay for it; I just dig for love. And I sure do hope this digging today is all wasted effort; I never wanted to do useless work so bad in my life.

"Any time I get fifty feet from my home ditch you'll find me digging a new ditch, and brother I ain't joking. I love to dig ditches."

Digging out here in the soft desert sand was paradise compared with the claylike digging back at our base. The ditch went forward like a prairie fire. We measured it with our eyes to see if it would hold everybody.

"Throw up some more right here," one of the boys said, indicating a low spot in the bank on either side. "Do you think we've got it deep enough?"

"It don't have to be so deep," another one said. "A bullet won't go through more than three inches of sand. Sand is the best thing there is for stopping bullets."

A growth of sagebrush hung over the ditch on one side. "Let's leave it right there," one of the boys said. "It's good for the imagination. Makes you think you're covered up even when you ain't."

That's the new outlook, the new type of conversation, among thousands of American boys today. It's hard for you to realize, but there are certain moments when a plain old ditch can be dearer to you than any possession on earth. For all bombs, no matter where they may land eventually, do all their falling right straight at your head. Only those of you who know about that can ever know all about ditches.

While we were digging, one of the boys brought up for the thousandth time the question of that letter in Time magazine. What letter, you ask? Why, it's a letter you probably don't remember, but it has became famous around these parts.

It was in the November 23 [1942] issue, which eventually found its way over here. Somebody read it, spoke to a few friends, and pretty soon thousands of men were commenting on this letter in terms which the fire department won't permit me to set to paper.

To get to the point, it was written by a soldier, and it said: "The greatest Christmas present that can be given to us this year is not smoking jackets, ties, pipes or games. If people will only take the money and buy war bonds . . . they will be helping themselves and helping us to be home next Christmas. Being home next Christmas is something which would be appreciated by all of us boys in service!"

The letter was all right with the soldiers over here until they got down to the address of the writer and discovered he was still in camp in the States. For a soldier back home to open his trap about anything concerning the war is like waving a red flag at the troops over here. They say they can do whatever talking is necessary.

"Them poor dogfaces back home," said one of the ditch-diggers with fine soldier sarcasm, "they've really got it rugged. Nothing to eat but them old greasy pork chops and them three-inch steaks all the time. I wouldn't be surprised if they don't have to eat eggs several times a week."

"And they're so lonely," said another. "No entertainment except to rassle them old dames around the dance floor. The USO closes at ten o'clock and the nightclubs at three. It's mighty tough on them. No wonder they want to get home."

"And they probably don't get no sleep," said another, "sleeping on them old cots with springs and everything, and scalding themselves in hot baths all the time."

"And nothing to drink but that nasty old ten-cent beer and that awful Canadian Club whiskey," chimed in another philosopher with a shovel.

"And when they put a nickel in the box nothing comes out but Glenn Miller and Artie Shaw and such trash as that. My heart just bleeds for them poor guys."

"And did you see where he was?" asked another. "At the Albuquerque Air Base. And he wants to be home by next Christmas. Hell, if I could just see the Albuquerque Air Base again I'd think I was in heaven."

That's the way it goes. The boys feel a soldier isn't qualified to comment unless he's on the wrong side of the ocean. They're gay and full of their own wit when they get started that way, but just the same they mean it. It's a new form of the age-old soldier pastime of grousing. It helps take your mind off things.

Pyle took a vacation in late February and early March, during which he toured the Belgian Congo. When he returned, Montgomery's British 8th Army had chased the Afrika Korps well into Tunisia, and the Allies were taking German and Italian prisoners. Pyle, like most Americans, was curious about the Germans. What were they like, these members of a supposedly superior race who had ruthlessly subjugated so many? The following was the first of a series of reports Pyle filed on Germans captured in the Tunisian campaign.

[. . .]

## The God-Damned Infantry

IN THE FRONT LINES BEFORE MATEUR, NORTHERN TUNISIA, May 2, 1943—We're now with an infantry outfit that has battled ceaselessly for four days and nights.

This northern warfare has been in the mountains. You don't ride much anymore. It is walking and climbing and crawling country. The mountains aren't big, but they are constant. They are largely treeless. They are easy to defend and bitter to take. But we are taking them.

The Germans lie on the back slope of every ridge, deeply dug into foxholes. In front of them the fields and pastures are hideous with thousands of hidden mines. The forward slopes are left open, untenanted, and if the Americans tried to scale these slopes they would be murdered wholesale in an inferno of machine-gun crossfire plus mortars and grenades.

Consequently we don't do it that way. We have fallen back to the old warfare of first pulverizing the enemy with artillery, then sweeping around the ends of the hill with infantry and taking them from the sides and behind.

I've written before how the big guns crack and roar almost constantly throughout the day and night. They lay a screen ahead of our troops. By magnificent shooting they drop shells on the back slopes. By means of shells timed to burst in the air a few feet from the ground, they get the Germans even in their foxholes. Our troops have found that the Germans dig foxholes down and then under, trying to get cover from the shell bursts that shower death from above.

Our artillery has really been sensational. For once we have enough of something and at the right time. Officers tell me they actually have more guns than they know what to do with.

All the guns in any one sector can be centered to shoot at one spot. And when we lay the whole business on a German hill the whole slope seems to erupt. It becomes an unbelievable cauldron of fire and smoke and dirt. Veteran German soldiers say they have never been through anything like it.

Now to the infantry—the God-damned infantry, as they like to call themselves.

I love the infantry because they are the underdogs. They are the mud-rain-frost-and-wind boys. They have no comforts, and they even learn to live without the necessities, And in the end they are the guys that wars can't be won without.

I wish you could see just one of the ineradicable pictures I have in my mind today. In this particular picture I am sitting among clumps of sword-grass on a steep and rocky hillside that we have just taken. We are looking out over a vast rolling country to the rear.

A narrow path comes like a ribbon over a hill miles away, down a long slope, across a creek, up a slope and over another hill.

All along the length of this ribbon there is now a thin line of men. For four days and nights they have fought hard, eaten little, washed none, and slept hardly at all. Their nights have been violent with attack, fright, butchery, and their days sleepless and miserable with the crash of artillery.

The men are walking. They are fifty feet apart, for dispersal. Their walk is slow, for they are dead weary, as you can tell even when looking at them from behind. Every line and sag of their bodies speaks their inhuman exhaustion.

On their shoulders and backs they carry heavy steel tripods, machine-gun barrels, leaden boxes of ammunition. Their feet seem to sink into the ground from the overload they are bearing.

They don't slouch. It is the terrible deliberation of each step that spells out their appalling tiredness. Their faces are black and unshaven. They are young men, but the grime and whiskers and exhaustion make them look middle-aged.

In their eyes as they pass is not hatred, not excitement, not despair, not the tonic of their victory—there is just the simple expression of being here as though they had been here doing this forever, and nothing else.

The line moves on, but it never ends. All afternoon men keep coming round the hill and vanishing eventually over the horizon. It is one long tired line of antlike men.

There is an agony in your heart and you almost feel ashamed to look at them. They are just guys from Broadway and Main Street, but you wouldn't remember them. They are too far away now. They are too tired. Their world can never be known to you, but if you could see them just once, just for an instant, you would know that no matter how hard people work back home they are not keeping pace with these infantrymen in Tunisia.

[. . .]

## The Death of Captain Waskow

AT THE FRONT LINES IN ITALY, January 10, 1944—In this war I have known a lot of officers who were loved and respected by the soldiers under them. But never have I crossed the trail of any man as beloved as Capt. Henry T. Waskow of Belton, Texas.

Capt. Waskow was a company commander in the 36th Division. He had led his company since long before it left the States. He was very young, only in his middle twenties, but he carried in him a sincerity and gentleness that made people want to be guided by him.

"After my own father, he came next," a sergeant told me.

"He always looked after us," a soldier said. "He'd go to bat for us every time."

"I've never knowed him to do anything unfair," another one said.

I was at the foot of the mule trail the night they brought Capt. Waskow's body down. The moon was nearly full at the time, and you could see far up the trail, and even part way across the valley below. Soldiers made shadows in the moonlight as they walked.

Dead men had been coming down the mountain all evening, lashed onto the backs of mules. They came lying belly-down across the wooden pack-saddles, their heads hanging down on the left side of the mule, their stiffened legs sticking out awkwardly from the·other side, bobbing up and down as the mule walked.

The Italian mule-skinners were afraid to walk beside dead men, so Americans had to lead the mules down that night. Even the Americans were reluctant to unlash and lift off the bodies at the bottom, so an officer had to do it himself, and ask others to help.

The first one came early in the morning. They slid him down from the mule and stood him on his feet for a moment, while they got a new grip. In the half light he might have been merely a sick man standing there, leaning on the others. Then they laid him on the ground in the shadow of the low stone wall alongside the road.

I don't know who that first one was. You feel small in the presence of dead men, and ashamed at being alive, and you don't ask silly questions.

We left him there beside the road, that first one, and we all went back into the cowshed and sat on water cans or lay on the straw, waiting for the next batch of mules.

Somebody said the dead soldier had been dead for four days, and then nobody said anything more about it. We talked soldier talk for an hour or more. The dead man lay all alone outside in the shadow of the low stone wall.

Then a soldier came into the cowshed and said there were some more bodies outside. We went out into the road. Four mules stood there, in the moonlight, in the road where the trail came down off the mountain. The soldiers who led them stood there waiting. "This one is Captain Waskow," one of them said quietly.

Two men unlashed his body from the mule and lifted it off and laid it in the shadow beside the low stone wall. Other men took the other bodies off. Finally there were five lying end to end in a long row, alongside the road. You don't cover up dead men in the combat zone. They just lie there in the shadows until somebody else comes after them.

The unburdened mules moved off to their olive orchard. The men in the road seemed reluctant to leave. They stood around, and gradually one by one I could sense them moving close to Capt. Waskow's body. Not so much to look, I think, as to say something in finality to him, and to themselves. I stood close by and I could hear.

One soldier came and looked down, and he said out loud, "God damn it." That's all he said, and then he walked away. Another one came. He said, 'God damn it to hell anyway." He looked down for a few last moments, and then he turned and left.

Another man came; I think he was an officer. It was hard to tell officers from men in the half light, for all were bearded and grimy dirty. The man looked down into the dead captain's face, and then he spoke directly to him, as though he were alive. He said: "I'm sorry, old man."

Then a soldier came and stood beside the officer, and bent over, and he too spoke to his dead captain, not in a whisper but awfully tenderly, and he said:

"I sure am sorry, sir."

Then the first man squatted down, and he reached down and took the dead hand, and he sat there for a full five minutes, holding, the dead hand in his own and looking intently into the dead face, and he never uttered a sound all the time he sat there.

And finally he put the hand down, and then reached up and gently straightened the points of the captain's shirt collar, and he sort of rearranged the tattered edges of his uniform around the wound. And then he got up and walked away down the road in the moonlight, all alone.

After that the rest of us went back into the cowshed, leaving the five dead men lying in a line, end to end, in the shadow of the low stone wall. We lay down on the straw in the cowshed, and pretty soon we were all asleep.

[. . .]

## A Pure Miracle

NORMANDY BEACHHEAD, June 12, 1944—Due to a last-minute alteration in the arrangements, I didn't arrive on the beachhead until the morning after D-day, after our first wave of assault troops had hit the shore.

By the time we got here the beaches had been taken and the fighting had moved a couple of miles inland. All that remained on the beach was some sniping and artillery fire, and the occasional startling blast of a mine geysering brown sand into the air. That plus a gigantic and pitiful litter of wreckage along miles of shoreline.

Submerged tanks and overturned boats and burned trucks and shell-shattered jeeps and sad little personal belongings were strewn all over these bitter sands. That plus the bodies of soldiers lying in rows covered with blankets, the toes of their shoes sticking up in a line as though on drill. And other bodies, uncollected, still sprawling grotesquely in the sand or half hidden by the high grass beyond the beach.

That plus an intense, grim determination of work-weary men to get this chaotic beach organized and get all the vital supplies and the reinforcements moving more rapidly over it from the stacked-up ships standing in droves out to sea.

Now that it is over it seems to me a pure miracle that we ever took the beach at all. For some of our units it was easy, but in this special sector where I am now our troops faced such odds that our getting ashore was like my whipping Joe Louis down to a pulp.

In this column I want to tell you what the opening of the second front in this one sector entailed, so that you can know and appreciate and forever be humbly grateful to those both dead and alive who did it for you.

Ashore, facing us, were more enemy troops than we had in our assault waves. The advantages were all theirs, the disadvantages all ours. The Germans were dug into positions that they had been working on for months, although these were not yet all complete. A one-hundred-foot bluff a couple of hundred yards back from the beach had great concrete gun emplacements built right into the hilltop. These opened to the sides instead of to the front, thus making it very hard for naval fire from the sea to reach them. They could shoot parallel with the beach and cover every foot of it for miles with artillery fire.

Then they had hidden machine-gun nests on the forward slopes, with crossfire taking in every inch of the beach. These nests were connected by networks of trenches, so that the German gunners could move about without exposing themselves.

Throughout the length of the beach, running zigzag a couple of hundred yards back from the shoreline, was an immmense V-shaped ditch fifteen feet deep. Nothing could cross it, not even men on foot, until fills had been made. And in other places at the far end of the beach, where the ground is flatter, they had great concrete walls. These were blasted by our naval gunfire or by explosives set by hand after we got ashore.

Our only exits from the beach were several swales or valleys, each about one hundred yards wide. The Germans made the most of these funnel-like traps, sowing them with buried mines. They contained, also, barbed-wire entanglements with mines attached, hidden ditches, and machine guns firing from the slopes.

This is what was on the shore. But our men had to go through a maze nearly as deadly as this before they even got ashore. Underwater obstacles were terrific. The Germans had whole fields of evil devices under the water to catch our boats. Even now, several days after the landing, we have cleared only channels through them and cannot yet approach the whole length of the beach with our ships. Even now some ship or boat hits one of these mines every day and is knocked out of commission.

The Germans had masses of those great six-pronged spiders, made of railroad iron and standing shoulder-high, just beneath the surface of the water for our landing craft to run into. They also had huge logs buried in the sand, pointing upward and outward, their tops just below the water. Attached to these logs were mines.

In addition to these obstacles they had floating mines offshore, land mines buried in the sand of the beach, and more mines in checkerboard rows in the tall grass beyond the sand. And the enemy had four men on shore for every three men we had approaching the shore.

And yet we got on.

Beach landings are planned to a schedule that is set far ahead of time. They all have to be timed, in order for everything to mesh and for the following waves of troops to be standing off the beach and ready to land at the right moment.

As the landings are planned, some elements of the assault force are to break through quickly, push on inland, and attack the most obvious enemy strong points. It is usually the plan for units to be inland, attacking gun positions from behind, within a matter of minutes after the first men hit the beach.

I have always been amazed at the speed called for in these plans. You'll have schedules calling for engineers to land at H-hour plus two minutes, and service troops at H-hour plus thirty minutes, and even for press censors to land at H-hour plus seventy-five minutes. But in the attack on this special portion of the beach where I am—the worst we had, incidentally—the schedule didn't hold.

Our men simply could not get past the beach. They were pinned down right on the water's edge by an inhuman wall of fire from the bluff. Our first waves were on that beach for hours, instead of a few minutes, before they could begin working inland.

You can still see the foxholes they dug at the very edge of the water, in the sand and the small, jumbled rocks that form parts of the beach.

Medical corpsmen attended the wounded as best they could. Men were killed as they stepped out of landing craft. An officer whom I knew got a bullet through the head just as the door of his landing craft was let down. Some men were drowned.

The first crack in the beach defenses was finally accomplished by terrific and wonderful naval gunfire, which knocked out the big emplacements. They tell epic stories of destroyers that ran right up into shallow water and had it out point-blank with the big guns in those concrete emplacements ashore.

When the heavy fire stopped, our men were organized by their officers and pushed on inland, circling machine-gun nests and taking them from the rear.

As one officer said, the only way to take a beach is to face it and keep going. It is costly at first, but it's the only way. If the men are pinned down on the beach, dug in and out of action, they might as well not be there at all. They hold up the waves behind them, and nothing is being gained.

Our men were pinned down for a while, but finally they stood up and went through, and so we took that beach and accomplished our landing. We did it with every advantage on the enemy's side and every disadvantage on ours. In the light of a couple of days of retrospection, we sit and talk and call it a miracle that our men ever got on at all or were able to stay on.

Before long it will be permitted to name the units that did it. Then you will know to whom this glory should go. They suffered casualties. And yet if you take the entire beachhead assault, including other units that had a much easier time, our total casualties in driving this wedge into the continent of Europe were remarkably low—only a fraction, in fact, of what our commanders had been prepared to accept.

And these units that were so battered and went through such hell are still, right at this moment, pushing on inland without rest, their spirits high, their egotism in victory almost reaching the smart-alecky stage.

Their tails are up. "We've done it again," they say. They figure that the rest of the army isn't needed at all. Which proves that, while their judgment in this regard is bad, they certainly have the spirit that wins battles and eventually wars.

# Chapter 22

# RACHEL CARSON

# SILENT SPRING

RACHEL CARSON WAS NOT A JOURNALIST. She had received an MA in zoology from The Johns Hopkins University in 1932 and was hired to write radio scripts for the U.S. Department of Fisheries. She eventually became the editor-in-chief for the U.S. Fish and Wildlife Service. Her book *The Sea Around Us*, published in 1952, established her as a major nature writer.

Carson had become concerned about the damage being done to the environment by pesticides while still working at the U.S. Fish and Wildlife Service. That concern deepened after the introduction of DDT in 1945. In 1958, Carson received a letter from a friend in Massachusetts bemoaning the deaths of large birds on Cape Cod caused by the use of DDT. Having already accumulated a large amount of material about DDT, she decided to write a book on the subject, having been unable to get a magazine assignment to write about the topic. The book took four years to complete. Her conclusion was that DDT had harmed birds and other wildlife irrevocably and had contaminated the world's food supply.

The book was serialized in *The New Yorker* in 1962 and the reaction was immediate and furious, with the chemical industry striking back vigorously. *Silent Spring* changed the public debate and the response of the chemical industry helped focus public opinion on the issues Carson raised. Shortly after *Silent Spring*'s publication, the use of DDT came under much stricter government regulation and the debate shifted from whether pesticides were safe to which pesticides were not safe. Today, *Silent Spring* is credited with launching the modern environmental movement. It radically reshaped public attitudes about nature, the environment and about technological advances in general. In this section, Carson calmly, almost clinically, describes how DDT and malathion are poisoning the environment and ourselves.

## Elixirs of Death

Substitute chlorine atoms for all of the hydrogen atoms and the result is carbon tetra-chloride, the familiar cleaning fluid.

In the simplest possible terms, these changes rung upon the basic molecule of methane illustrate what a chlorinated hydrocarbon is. But this illustration gives little hint of the true complexity of the chemical world of the hydrocarbons, or of the manipulations by which the organic chemist creates his infinitely varied materials. For instead of the simple methane molecule with its single carbon atom, he may work with hydro-carbon molecules consisting of many carbon atoms, arranged in rings or chains, with side chains or branches, holding to themselves with chemical bonds not merely simple atoms of hydrogen or chlorine but also a wide variety of chemical groups. By seemingly slight changes the whole character of the substance is changed; for example, not only what is attached but the place of attachment to the carbon atom is highly important. Such ingenious manipulations have produced a battery of poisons of truly extraordinary power.

DDT (short for dichloro-diphenyl-trichloro-ethane) was first synthesized by a German chemist in 1874, but its properties as an insecticide were not discovered until 1939. Almost immediately DDT was hailed as a means of stamping out insect-borne disease and winning the farmers' war against crop destroyers overnight. The discoverer, Paul Müller of Switzerland, won the Nobel Prize.

DDT is now so universally used that in most minds the product takes on the harm-less aspect of the familiar. Perhaps the myth of the harmlessness of DDT rests on the fact that one of its first uses was the wartime dusting of many thousands of soldiers, refugees, and prisoners, to combat lice. It is widely believed that since so many people came into extremely intimate contact with DDT and suffered no immediate ill effects the chemical must certainly be innocent of harm. This understandable misconception arises from the fact that — unlike other chlorinated hydrocarbons — DDT *in powder form* is not readily absorbed through the skin. Dissolved in oil, as it usually is, DDT is definitely toxic. If swallowed, it is absorbed slowly through the digestive tract; it may also be absorbed through the lungs. Once it has entered the body it is stored largely in organs rich in fatty substances (because DDT itself is fat-soluble) such as the adrenals, testes, or thyroid. Relatively large amounts are deposited in the liver, kidneys, and the fat of the large, protective mesenteries that enfold the intestines.

This storage of DDT begins with the smallest conceivable intake of the chemical (which is present as residues on most foodstuffs) and continues until quite high levels are reached. The fatty storage depots act as biological magnifiers, so that an intake of as little as 1/10 of 1 part per million in the diet results in storage of about 10 to 15 parts per million, an increase of one hundredfold or more. These terms of reference, so common-place to the chemist or the pharmacologist, are unfamiliar to most of us. One part in a million sounds like a very small amount — and so it is. But such substances are so potent that a minute quantity can bring about vast changes in the body. In animal experiments, 3 parts per million has been found to inhibit an essential enzyme in heart muscle; only 5 parts per million has brought about necrosis or disintegration of liver cells; only 2.5 parts per million of the closely related chemicals dieldrin and chlordane did the same.

This is really not surprising. In the normal chemistry of the human body there is just such a disparity between cause and effect. For example, a quantity of iodine as small as two ten-thousandths of a gram spells the difference between health and disease. Because these small amounts of pesticides are cumulatively stored and only slowly excreted, the threat of chronic poisoning and degenerative changes of the liver and other organs is very real.

Scientists do not agree upon how much DDT can be stored in the human body. Dr. Arnold Lehman, who is the chief pharmacologist of the Food and Drug Administration, says there is neither a floor below which DDT is not absorbed nor a ceiling beyond which absorption and storage ceases. On the other hand, Dr. Wayland Hayes of the United States Public Health Service contends that in every individual a point of equilibrium is reached, and that DDT in excess of this amount is excreted. For practical purposes it is not particularly important which of these men is right. Storage in human beings has been well investigated, and we know that the average person is storing potentially harmful amounts. According to various studies, individuals with no known exposure (except the inevitable dietary one) store an average of 5.3 parts per million to 7.4 parts per million; agricultural workers 17.1 parts per million; and workers in insecticide plants as high as 648 parts per million! So the range of proven storage is quite wide and, what is even more to the point, the minimum figures are above the level at which damage to the liver and other organs or tissues may begin.

One of the most sinister features of DDT and related chemicals is the way they are passed on from one organism to another through all the links of the food chains. For example, fields of alfalfa are dusted with DDT; meal is later prepared from the alfalfa and fed to hens; the hens lay eggs which contain DDT. Or the hay, containing residues of 7 to 8 parts per million, may be fed to cows. The DDT will turn up in the milk in the amount of about 3 parts per million, but in butter made from this milk the concentration may run to 65 parts per million. Through such a process of transfer, what started out as a very small amount of DDT may end as a heavy concentration. Farmers nowadays find it difficult to obtain uncontaminated fodder for their milk cows, though the Food and Drug Administration forbids the presence of insecticide residues in milk shipped in interstate commerce.

The poison may also be passed on from mother to offspring. Insecticide residues have been recovered from human milk in samples tested by Food and Drug Administration scientists. This means that the breast-fed human infant is receiving small but regular additions to the load of toxic chemicals building up in his body. It is by no means his first exposure, however: there is good reason to believe this begins while he is still in the womb. In experimental animals the chlorinated hydrocarbon insecticides freely cross the barrier of the placenta, the traditional protective shield between the embryo and harmful substances in the mother's body. While the quantities so received by human infants would normally be small, they are not unimportant because children are more susceptible to poisoning than adults. This situation also means that today the average individual almost certainly starts life with the first deposit of the growing load of chemicals his body will be required to carry thenceforth.

All these facts — storage at even low levels, subsequent accumulation, and occurrence of liver damage at levels that may easily occur in normal diets, caused Food and Drug Administration scientists to declare as early as 1950 that it is "extremely likely the potential hazard of DDT has been underestimated." There has been no such parallel situation in medical history. No one yet knows what the ultimate consequences may be.

Chlordane, another chlorinated hydrocarbon, has all the unpleasant attributes of DDT plus a few that are peculiarly its own. Its residues are long persistent in soil, on foodstuffs, or on surfaces to which it may be applied, yet it is also quite volatile and poisoning by inhalation is a definite risk to anyone handling or exposed to it. Chlordane makes use of all available portals to enter the body. It penetrates the skin easily, is breathed in as vapor, and of course is absorbed from the digestive tract if residues are swallowed. Like all other chlorinated hydrocarbons, its deposits build up in the body in cumulative fashion. A diet containing such a small amount of chlordane as 2.5 parts per million may eventually lead to storage of 75 parts per million in the fat of experimental animals.

So experienced a pharmacologist as Dr. Lehman has described chlordane as "one of the most toxic of insecticides — anyone handling it could be poisoned." Judging by the carefree liberality with which dusts for lawn treatments by suburbanites are laced with chlordane, this warning has not been taken to heart. The fact that the suburbanite is not instantly stricken has little meaning, for the toxins may sleep long in his body, to become manifest months or years later in an obscure disorder almost impossible to trace to its origins. On the other hand, death may strike quickly. One victim who accidentally spilled a 25 per cent solution on his skin developed symptoms of poisoning within 40 minutes and died before medical help could be obtained. No reliance can be placed on receiving advance warning which might allow treatment to be had in time.

Heptachlor, one of the constituents of chlordane, is marketed as a separate formulation. It has a particularly high capacity for storage in fat. If the diet contains as little as 1/10 of 1 part per million there will be measurable amounts of heptachlor in the body. It also has the curious ability to undergo change into a chemically distinct substance known as heptachlor epoxide. It does this in soil and in the tissues of both plants and animals. Tests on birds indicate that the epoxide that results from this change is about four times as toxic as the original chemical, which in turn is four times as toxic as chlordane.

As long ago as the mid-1930s a special group of hydrocarbons, the chlorinated naphthalenes, was found to cause hepatitis, and also a rare and almost invariably fatal liver disease in persons subjected to occupational exposure. They have led to illness and death of workers in electrical industries; and more recently, in agriculture, they have been considered a cause of a mysterious and usually fatal disease of cattle. In view of these antecedents, it is not surprising that three of the insecticides that belong to this group are among the most violently poisonous of all the hydrocarbons. These are dieldrin, aldrin, and endrin.

Dieldrin, named for a German chemist, Diels, is about 5 times as toxic as DDT when swallowed but 40 times as toxic when absorbed through the skin in solution. It is notorious for striking quickly and with terrible effect at the nervous system, sending the victims into convulsions. Persons thus poisoned recover so slowly as to indicate chronic effects. As with other chlorinated hydrocarbons, these long-term effects include severe damage to the liver. The long duration of its residues and the effective insecticidal action make dieldrin one of the most used insecticides today, despite the appalling destruction of wildlife that has followed its use. As tested on quail and pheasants, it has proved to be about 40 to 50 times as toxic as DDT.

There are vast gaps in our knowledge of how dieldrin is stored or distributed in the body, or excreted, for the chemists' ingenuity in devising insecticides has long ago outrun biological knowledge of the way these poisons affect the living organism. However, there is every indication of long storage in the human body, where deposits may lie dormant like a slumbering volcano, only to flare up in periods of physiological stress when the body draws upon its fat reserves. Much of what we do know has been learned through hard experience in the antimalarial campaigns carried out by the World Health Organization. As soon as dieldrin was substituted for DDT in malaria-control work (because the malaria mosquitoes had become resistant to DDT), cases of poisoning among the spraymen began to occur. The seizures were severe — from half to all (varying in the different programs) of the men affected went into convulsions and several died. Some had convulsions as long as *four months* after the last exposure.

Aldrin is a somewhat mysterious substance, for although it exists as a separate entity it bears the relation of alter ego to dieldrin. When carrots are taken from a bed treated with aldrin they are found to contain residues of dieldrin. This change occurs in living tissues and also in soil. Such alchemistic transformations have led to many erroneous reports, for if a chemist, knowing aldrin has been applied, tests for it he will be deceived into thinking all residues have been dissipated. The residues are there, but they are dieldrin and this requires a different test.

Like dieldrin, aldrin is extremely toxic. It produces degenerative changes in the liver and kidneys. A quantity the size of an aspirin tablet is enough to kill more than 400 quail. Many cases of human poisonings are on record, most of them in connection with industrial handling.

Aldrin, like most of this group of insecticides, projects a menacing shadow into the future, the shadow of sterility. Pheasants fed quantities too small to kill them nevertheless laid few eggs, and the chicks that hatched soon died. The effect is not confined to birds. Rats exposed to aldrin had fewer pregnancies and their young were sickly and short-lived. Puppies born of treated mothers died within three days. By one means or another, the new generations suffer for the poisoning of their parents. No one knows whether the same effect will be seen in human beings, yet this chemical has been sprayed from airplanes over suburban areas and farmlands.

Endrin is the most toxic of all the chlorinated hydrocarbons. Although chemically rather closely related to dieldrin, a little twist in its molecular structure makes it 5 times as poisonous. It makes the progenitor of all this group of insecticides, DDT, seem by comparison almost harmless. It is 15 times as poisonous as DDT to mammals, 30 times as poisonous to fish, and about 300 times as poisonous to some birds.

In the decade of its use, endrin has killed enormous numbers of fish, has fatally poisoned cattle that have wandered into sprayed orchards, has poisoned wells, and has drawn a sharp warning from at least one state health department that its careless use is endangering human lives.

In one of the most tragic cases of endrin poisoning there was no apparent carelessness; efforts had been made to take precautions apparently considered adequate. A year-old child had been taken by his American parents to live in Venezuela. There were cockroaches in the house to which they moved, and after a few days a spray containing endrin was used. The baby and the small family dog were taken out of the house before the spraying was done about nine o'clock one morning. After the spraying the floors were washed. The baby and dog were returned to the house in midafternoon. An hour or so later the dog vomited, went into convulsions, and died. At 10 P.M. on the evening of the same day the baby also vomited, went into convulsions, and lost consciousness. After that fateful contact with endrin, this normal, healthy child became little more than a vegetable — unable to see or hear, subject to frequent muscular spasms, apparently completely cut off from contact with his surroundings. Several months of treatment in a New York hospital failed to change his condition or bring hope of change. "It is extremely doubtful," reported the attending physicians, "that any useful degree of recovery will occur."

The second major group of insecticides, the alkyl or organic phosphates, are among the most poisonous chemicals in the world. The chief and most obvious hazard attending their use is that of acute poisoning of people applying the sprays or accidentally coming in contact with drifting spray, with vegetation coated by it, or with a discarded container. In Florida, two children found an empty bag and used it to repair a swing. Shortly thereafter both of them died and three of their playmates became ill. The bag had once contained an insecticide called parathion, one of the organic phosphates; tests established death by parathion poisoning. On another occasion two small boys in Wisconsin, cousins, died on the same night. One had been playing in his yard when spray drifted in from an adjoining field where his father was spraying potatoes with parathion; the other had run playfully into the barn after his father and had put his hand on the nozzle of the spray equipment.

The origin of these insecticides has a certain ironic significance. Although some of the chemicals themselves — organic esters of phosphoric acid — had been known for many years, their insecticidal properties remained to be discovered by a German chemist, Gerhard Schrader, in the late 1930's. Almost immediately the German government recognized the value of these same chemicals as new and devastating weapons in man's war against his own kind, and the work on them was declared secret. Some became the deadly nerve gases. Others, of closely allied structure, became insecticides.

The organic phosphorus insecticides act on the living organism in a peculiar way. They have the ability to destroy enzymes — enzymes that perform necessary functions in the body. Their target is the nervous system, whether the victim is an insect or a warm-blooded animal. Under normal conditions, an impulse passes from nerve to nerve with the aid of a "chemical transmitter" called acetylcholine, a substance that performs an essential function and then disappears. Indeed, its existence is so ephemeral that medical researchers are unable, without special procedures, to sample it before the body has destroyed it. This transient nature of the transmitting chemical is necessary to the normal functioning of the body. If the acetylcholine is not destroyed as soon as a nerve impulse has passed, impulses continue to flash across the bridge from nerve to nerve, as the chemical exerts its effects in an ever more intensified manner. The movements of the whole body become uncoordinated: tremors, muscular spasms, convulsions, and death quickly result.

This contingency has been provided for by the body. A protective enzyme called cholinesterase is at hand to destroy the transmitting chemical once it is no longer needed. By this means a precise balance is struck and the body never builds up a dangerous amount of acetylcholine. But on contact with the organic phosphorus insecticides, the protective enzyme is destroyed, and as the quantity of the enzyme is reduced that of the transmitting chemical builds up. In this effect, the organic phosphorus compounds resemble the alkaloid poison muscarine, found in a poisonous mushroom, the fly amanita.

Repeated exposures may lower the cholinesterase level until an individual reaches the brink of acute poisoning, a brink over which he may be pushed by a very small additional exposure. For this reason it is considered important to make periodic examinations of the blood of spray operators and others regularly exposed.

Parathion is one of the most widely used of the organic phosphates. It is also one of the most powerful and dangerous. Honeybees become "wildly agitated and bellicose" on contact with it, perform frantic cleaning movements, and are near death within half an hour. A chemist, thinking to learn by the most direct possible means the dose acutely toxic to human beings, swallowed a minute amount, equivalent to about .00424 ounce.

Paralysis followed so instantaneously that he could not reach the antidotes he had prepared at hand, and so he died. Parathion is now said to be a favorite instrument of suicide in Finland. In recent years the State of California has reported an average of more than 200 cases of accidental parathion poisoning annually. In many parts of the world the fatality rate from parathion is startling: 100 fatal cases in India and 67 in Syria in 1958, and an average of 336 deaths per year in Japan.

Yet some 7,000,000 pounds of parathion are now applied to fields and orchards of the United States — by hand sprayers, motorized blowers and dusters, and by airplane. The amount used on California farms alone could, according to one medical authority, "provide a lethal dose for 5 to 10 times the whole world's population."

One of the few circumstances that save us from extinction by this means is the fact that parathion and other chemicals of this group are decomposed rather rapidly. Their residues on the crops to which they are applied are therefore relatively short-lived compared with the chlorinated hydrocarbons. However, they last long enough to create hazards and produce consequences that range from the merely serious to the fatal. In Riverside, California, eleven out of thirty men picking oranges became violently ill and all but one had to be hospitalized. Their symptoms were typical of parathion poisoning. The grove had been sprayed with parathion some two and a half weeks earlier; the residues that reduced them to retching, half-blind, semi-conscious misery were sixteen to nineteen days old. And this is not by any means a record for persistence. Similar mishaps have occurred in groves sprayed a month earlier, and residues have been found in the peel of oranges six months after treatment with standard dosages.

The danger to all workers applying the organic phosphorus insecticides in fields, orchards, and vineyards, is so extreme that some states using these chemicals have established laboratories where physicians may obtain aid in diagnosis and treatment. Even the physicians themselves may be in some danger, unless they wear rubber gloves in handling the victims of poisoning. So may a laundress washing the clothing of such victims, which may have absorbed enough parathion to affect her.

Malathion, another of the organic phosphates, is almost as familiar to the public as DDT, being widely used by gardeners, in household insecticides, in mosquito spraying, and in such blanket attacks on insects as the spraying of nearly a million acres of Florida communities for the Mediterranean fruit fly. It is considered the least toxic of this group of chemicals and many people assume they may use it freely and without fear of harm. Commercial advertising encourages this comfortable attitude.

The alleged "safety" of malathion rests on rather precarious ground, although — as often happens — this was not discovered until the chemical had been in use for several years. Malathion is "safe" only because the mammalian liver, an organ with extraordinary protective powers, renders it relatively harmless. The detoxification is accomplished by one of the enzymes of the liver. If, however, something destroys this enzyme or interferes with its action, the person exposed to malathion receives the full force of the poison.

Unfortunately for all of us, opportunities for this sort of thing to happen are legion. A few years ago a team of Food and Drug Administration scientists discovered that when malathion and certain other organic phosphates are administered simultaneously a massive poisoning results — up to 50 times as severe as would be predicted on the basis of adding together the toxicities of the two. In other words, 1 / 100 of the lethal dose of each compound may be fatal when the two are combined.

This discovery led to the testing of other combinations. It is now known that many pairs of organic phosphate insecticides are highly dangerous, the toxicity being stepped up or "potentiated" through the combined action. Potentiation seems to take place when one compound destroys the liver enzyme responsible for detoxifying the other. The two need not be given simultaneously. The hazard exists not only for the man who may spray this week with one insecticide and next week with another; it exists also for the consumer of sprayed products. The common salad bowl may easily present a combination of organic phosphate insecticides. Residues well within the legally permissible limits may interact.

The full scope of the dangerous interaction of chemicals is as yet little known, but disturbing findings now come regularly from scientific laboratories. Among these is the discovery that the toxicity of an organic phosphate can be increased by a second agent that is not necessarily an insecticide. For example, one of the plasticizing agents may act even more strongly than another insecticide to make malathion more dangerous. Again, this is because it inhibits the liver enzyme that normally would "draw the teeth" of the poisonous insecticide.

[. . .]

What of other chemicals in the normal human environment? What, in particular, of drugs? A bare beginning has been made on this subject, but already it is known that some organic phosphates (parathion and malathion) increase the toxicity of some drugs used as muscle relaxants, and that several others (again including malathion) markedly increase the sleeping time of barbiturates.

So far in this chapter we have been discussing the deadly chemicals that are being used in our war against the insects. What of our simultaneous war against the weeds?

The desire for a quick and easy method of killing unwanted plants has given rise to a large and growing array of chemicals that are known as herbicides, or, less formally, as weed killers. . . . [T]he question that concerns us here is whether the weed killers are poisons and whether their use is contributing to the poisoning of the environment.

The legend that the herbicides are toxic only to plants and so pose no threat to animal life has been widely disseminated, but unfortunately it is not true. The plant killers include a large variety of chemicals that act on animal tissue as well as on vegetation. They vary greatly in their action on the organism. Some are general poisons, some are powerful stimulants of metabolism, causing a fatal rise in body temperature, some induce malignant tumors either alone or in partnership with other chemicals, some strike at the genetic material of the race by causing gene mutations. The herbicides, then, like the insecticides, include some very dangerous chemicals, and their careless use in the belief that they are "safe" can have disastrous results.

Despite the competition of a constant stream of new chemicals issuing from the laboratories, arsenic compounds are still liberally used, both as insecticides (as mentioned above) and as weed killers, where they usually take the chemical form of sodium arsenite. The history of their use is not reassuring. As roadside sprays, they have cost many a farmer his cow and killed uncounted numbers of wild creatures. As aquatic weed killers in lakes and reservoirs they have made public waters unsuitable for drinking or even for swimming. As a spray applied to potato fields to destroy the vines they have taken a toll of human and nonhuman life.

In England this latter practice developed about 1951 as a result of a shortage of sulfuric acid, formerly used to burn off the potato vines. The Ministry of Agriculture considered it necessary to give warning of the hazard of going into the arsenic-sprayed fields, but the warning was not understood by the cattle (nor, we must assume, by the wild animals and birds) and reports of cattle poisoned by the arsenic sprays came with monotonous regularity. When death came also to a farmer's wife through arsenic-contaminated water, one of the major English chemical companies (in 1959) stopped production of arsenical sprays and called in supplies already in the hands of dealers, and shortly thereafter the Ministry of Agriculture announced that because of high risks to people and cattle restrictions on the use of arsenites would be imposed. In 1961, the Australian government announced a similar ban. No such restrictions impede the use of these poisons in the United States, however.

Some of the "dinitro" compounds are also used as herbicides. They are rated as among the most dangerous materials of this type in use in the United States. Dinitrophenol is a strong metabolic stimulant. For this reason it was at one time used as a reducing drug, but the margin between the slimming dose and that required to poison or kill was slight—so slight that several patients died and many suffered permanent injury before use of the drug was finally halted.

A related chemical, pentachlorophenol, sometimes known as "penta," is used as a weed killer as well as an insecticide, often being sprayed along railroad tracks and in waste areas. Penta is extremely toxic to a wide variety of organisms from bacteria to man. Like the dinitros, it interferes, often fatally, with the body's source of energy, so that the affected organism almost literally burns itself up. Its fearful power is illustrated in a fatal accident recently reported by the California Department of Health. A tank truck driver was preparing a cotton defoliant by mixing diesel oil with pentachlorophenol. As he was drawing the concentrated chemical out of a drum, the spigot accidentally toppled back. He reached in with his bare hand to regain the spigot. Although he washed immediately, he became acutely ill and died the next day.

While the results of weed killers such as sodium arsenite or the phenols are grossly obvious, some other herbicides are more insidious in their effects. For example, the now famous cranberry-weed-killer aminotriazole, or amitrol, is rated as having relatively low toxicity. But in the long run its tendency to cause malignant tumors of the thyroid may be far more significant for wildlife and perhaps also for man.

Among the herbicides are some that are classified as "mutagens," or agents capable of modifying the genes, the materials of heredity. We are rightly appalled by the genetic effects of radiation; how then, can we be indifferent to the same effect in chemicals that we disseminate widely in our environment?

# Chapter 23

# TRUMAN CAPOTE

# IN COLD BLOOD

*IN COLD BLOOD* IS NOT STANDARD JOURNALISM at all in the usual sense of the term. In 1959, Truman Capote, an already celebrated author and writer for *The New Yorker* magazine, read a short article about a grisly murder in the small town of Holcomb, Kansas. A wealthy wheat farmer, his wife and two children had been bound, gagged and killed by shot gun blasts from close range. There was no sign of struggle at the house and nothing had been stolen. The telephone line, however, had been cut.

Capote set out initially to find out how the small Kansas town was coping with the murders. At one point he even told Alvin Dewey, supervising investigator for the Kansas Bureau of Investigation: "It really doesn't make any difference to me if the case is ever solved or not". What Capote wanted to discover was the effect of the killings on such an isolated community, its inhabitants and the family itself. The *New Yorker* commissioned a relatively short piece from him on this basis. But within a couple of weeks of Capote's arrival in Kansas, two suspects had been arrested in Las Vegas. The two men, Dick Hickock and Perry Smith, subsequently confessed to the murders. Capote then wanted to understand why they did it.

Capote spent six years doing research and when *In Cold Blood* was published it was an immediate sensation. The first print run quickly sold out. Capote claimed that he had invented a new literary form—the non-fiction novel that combined the meticulous research and reporting associated with journalism with the literary techniques and conventions associated with fiction. Tom Wolfe, a leading practitioner of what was called New Journalism at the time, asserted that *In Cold Blood* was one of the pioneering works of that genre.

Sometimes blurring the line between fact and fiction, New Journalism has always held a controversial place in the field. Many people object to including dialogue between several people at scenes at which the author could not have actually been present or known precisely what was said. Other critics object to the writers of New Journalism injecting themselves into the story. Capote claimed that everything he wrote from the beginning to the end of *In Cold Blood* was true. In 1966, Philip Tompkins wrote a devastating critique of *In Cold Blood* in *Esquire* magazine. Tompkins pointed out both minor errors that Capote made and challenged Capote's reporting on key moments in the affair, including the confession of one of the murderers. This selection provides an excellent representation of Capote's non-fiction novel. It describes the arrest and interrogation of Hitchcock and Smith.

## Answer

The evening of Wednesday, December 30, was a memorable one in the household of Agent A. A. Dewey. Remembering it later, his wife said, "Alvin was singing in the bath. 'The Yellow Rose of Texas.' The kids were watching TV. And I was setting the diningroom table. For a buffet. I'm from New Orleans; I love to cook and entertain, and my mother had just sent us a crate of avocados and black-eyed peas, and—oh, a heap of real nice things. So I decided: We're going to have a buffet, invite some friends over—the Murrays, and Cliff and Dodie Hope. Alvin didn't want to, but I was determined. My goodness! The case could go on forever, and he hadn't taken hardly a minute off since it began. Well, I was setting the table, so when I heard the phone I asked one of the boys to answer it—Paul. Paul said it was for Daddy, and I said, 'You tell them he's in the bath,' but Paul said he wondered if he ought to do that, because it was Mr. Sanford calling from Topeka. Alvin's boss. Alvin took the call with just a towel around him. Made me so mad—dripping puddles everywhere. But when I went to get a mop I saw something worse—that cat, that fool Pete, up on the kitchen table gorging crabmeat salad. My avocado stuffing.

"The next thing was, suddenly Alvin had hold of me, he was hugging me, and I said, 'Alvin Dewey, have you lost your mind?' Fun's fun, but the man was wet as a pond, he was ruining my dress, and I was already dressed for company. Of course, when I understood why he was hugging me I hugged him right back. You can imagine what it meant to Alvin to know those men had been arrested. Out in Las Vegas. He said he had to leave for Las Vegas straightaway, and I asked him hadn't he ought to put on some clothes first, and Alvin, he was so excited, he said, 'Gosh, honey, I guess I've spoiled your party!' I couldn't think of a happier way of having it spoiled—not if this meant that maybe one day soon we'd be back living an ordinary life. Alvin laughed—it was just beautiful to hear him. I mean, the past two weeks had been the worst of all. Because the week before Christmas those men turned up in Kansas City—came and went without getting caught—and I never saw Alvin more depressed, except once when young Alvin was in the hospital, had encephalitis, we thought we might lose him. But I don't want to talk about that.

"Anyway, I made coffee for him and took it to the bedroom, where he was supposed to be getting dressed. But he wasn't. He was sitting on the edge of our bed holding his head, as if he had a headache. Hadn't put on even a sock. So I said, 'What do you want to do, get pneumonia?' And he looked at me and said, 'Marie, listen, it's got to be these guys, has to, that's the only logical solution.' Alvin's funny. Like the first time he ran for Finney County Sheriff. Election Night, when practically every vote had been counted and it was plain as plain he'd won, he said—I could have strangled him—said over and over, 'Well, we won't know till the last return.'

"I told him, 'Now, Alvin, don't start that. Of course they did it.' He said, 'Where's our proof? We can't prove either of them ever set foot inside the Clutter house!' But that seemed to me exactly what he could prove: footprints—weren't footprints the one thing those animals left behind? Alvin said, 'Yes, and a big lot of good they are—unless those boys still happen to be wearing the boots that made them. Just footprints by themselves aren't worth a Dixie dollar.' I said, 'All right, honey, drink your coffee and I'll help you pack.' Sometimes you can't reason with Alvin. The way he kept on, he had me almost convinced Hickock and Smith were innocent, and if they weren't innocent they would never confess, and if they didn't confess they could never be convicted—the evidence was too circumstantial. What bothered him most, though—he was afraid that the story would leak, that the men would learn the truth before the K.B.I. could question them. As it was, they thought they'd been picked up for parole violation. Passing bad checks. And Alvin felt it was very important they keep thinking that. He said, 'The name Clutter has to hit them like a hammer, a blow they never knew was coming.'

"Paul—I'd sent him out to the washline for some of Alvin's socks—Paul came back and stood around watching me pack. He wanted to know where Alvin was going. Alvin lifted him up in his arms. He said, 'Can you keep a secret, Pauly?' Not that he needed to ask. Both boys know they mustn't talk about Alvin's work—the bits and pieces they hear around the house. So he said, 'Pauly, you remember those two fellows we've been looking for? Well, now we know where they are, and Daddy's going to go get them and bring them here to Garden City.' But Paul begged him, 'Don't do that, Daddy, don't bring them here.' He was frightened—any nine-year-old might've been. Alvin kissed him. He said, 'Now that's O.K., Pauly, we won't let them hurt anybody. They're not going to hurt anybody ever again.' "

At five that afternoon, some twenty minutes after the stolen Chevrolet rolled off the Nevada desert into Las Vegas, the long ride came to an end. But not before Perry had visited the Las Vegas post office, where he claimed a package addressed to himself in care of General Delivery—the large cardboard box he had mailed from Mexico, and had insured for a hundred dollars, a sum exceeding to an impertinent extent the value of the contents, which were suntans and denim pants, worn shirts, underwear, and two pairs of steel-buckled boots. Waiting for Perry outside the post office, Dick was in excellent spirits; he had reached a decision that he was certain would eradicate his current difficulties and start him on a new road, with a new rainbow in view. The decision involved impersonating an Air Force officer. It was a project that had long fascinated him, and Las Vegas was the ideal place to try it out. He'd already selected the officer's rank and name, the latter borrowed from a former acquaintance, the then warden of Kansas State Penitentiary: Tracy Hand. As Captain Tracy Hand, smartly clothed in a made-to-order uniform, Dick intended to "crawl the strip," Las Vegas's street of never-closed casinos. Small-time, big-time, the Sands, the Stardust—he meant to hit them all, distributing en route "a bundle of confetti." By writing worthless checks right around the clock, he expected to haul in three, maybe four thousand dollars within a twenty-four-hour period. That was half the plot; the second half was: Goodbye, Perry. Dick was sick of him—his harmonica, his aches and ills, his superstitions, the weepy, womanly eyes, the nagging, whispering voice. Suspicious, self-righteous, spiteful, he was like a wife that must be got rid of. And there was but one way to do it: Say nothing—just go.

Absorbed in his plans, Dick did not notice a patrol car pass him, slow down, reconnoiter. Nor did Perry, descending the post-office steps with the Mexican box balanced on a shoulder, observe the prowling car and the policemen in it.

Officers Ocie Pigford and Francis Macauley carried in their heads pages of memorized data, including a description of a black-and-white 1956 Chevrolet bearing Kansas license plate No. Jo 16212. Neither Perry nor Dick was aware of the police vehicle trailing them as they pulled away from the post office, and with Dick driving and Perry directing, they traveled five blocks north, turned left, then right, drove a quarter mile more, and stopped in front of a dying palm tree and a weather-wrecked sign from which all calligraphy had faded except the word "OOM."

"This it?" Dick asked.

Perry, as the patrol car drew alongside, nodded.

The Detective Division of the Las Vegas City Jail contains two interrogation rooms—fluorescent-lighted chambers measuring ten by twelve, with walls and ceilings of celotex. In each room, in addition to an electric fan, a metal table, and folding metal chairs, there are camouflaged microphones, concealed tape recorders, and, set into the door, a mirrored one-way observation window. On Saturday, the second day of 1960, both rooms were booked for 2:00 P.M.—the hour that four detectives from Kansas had selected for their first confrontation of Hickock and Smith.

Shortly before the appointed moment, the quartet of K.B.I. agents—Harold Nye, Roy Church, Alvin Dewey, and Clarence Duntz—gathered in a corridor outside the interrogation rooms. Nye was running a temperature. "Part flu. But mostly sheer excitement," he subsequently informed a journalist. "By then I'd already been waiting in Las Vegas two days—took the next plane out after news of the arrest reached our headquarters in Topeka. The rest of the team, Al and Roy and Clarence, came on by car—had a lousy trip, too. Lousy weather. Spent New Year's Eve snowed up in a motel in Albuquerque. Boy, when they finally hit Vegas, they needed good whiskey and good news. I was ready with both. Our young men had signed waivers of extradition. Better yet: We had the boots, both pairs, and the soles—the Cat's Paw and the diamond pattern—matched perfectly life-size photographs of the footprints found in the Clutter house. The boots were in a box of stuff the boys picked up at the post office just before the curtain fell. Like I told Al Dewey, suppose the squeeze had come five minutes sooner!

"Even so, our case was very shaky—nothing that couldn't be pulled apart. But I remember, while we were waiting in the corridor—I remember being feverish and nervous as hell, but *confident*. We all were; we felt we were on the edge of the truth. My job, mine and Church's, was to pressure it out of Hickock. Smith belonged to Al and Old Man Duntz. At that time I hadn't seen the suspects—just examined their possessions and arranged the extradition waivers. I'd never laid eyes on Hickock until he was brought down to the interrogation room. I'd imagined a bigger guy. Brawnier. Not some skinny kid. He was twenty-eight, but he looked like a kid. Hungry—right down to the bone. He was wearing a blue shirt and suntans and white socks and black shoes. We shook hands; his hand was drier than mine. Clean, polite, nice voice, good diction, a pretty decent-looking fellow, with a very disarming smile—and in the beginning he smiled quite a lot.

"I said, 'Mr. Hickock, my name is Harold Nye, and this other gentleman is Mr. Roy Church. We're Special Agents of the Kansas Bureau of Investigation, and we've come here to discuss your parole violation. Of course, you're under no obligation to answer our questions, and anything you say may be used against you in evidence. You're entitled to a lawyer at all times. We'll use no force, no threats, and we'll make you no promises.' He was calm as could be."

"I KNOW the form," Dick said. "I've been questioned before."

"Now, Mr. Hickock—"

"Dick."

"Dick, we want to talk to you about your activities since your parole. To our knowledge, you've gone on at least two big check sprees in the Kansas City area."

"Uh-huh. Hung out quite a few."

"Could you give us a list?"

The prisoner, evidently proud of his one authentic gift, a brilliant memory, recited the names and addresses of twenty Kansas City stores, cafés, and garages, and recalled, accurately, the "purchase" made at each and the amount of the check passed.

"I'm curious, Dick. Why do these people accept your checks? I'd like to know the secret."

"The secret is: People are dumb."

Roy Church said, "Fine, Dick. Very funny. But just for the moment let's forget these checks." Though he sounds as if his throat were lined with hog bristle, and has hands so hardened that he can punch stone walls (his favorite stunt, in fact), persons have been known to mistake Church for a kindly little man, somebody's bald-headed, pink-cheeked uncle. "Dick," he said, "suppose you tell us something about your family background."

The prisoner reminisced. Once, when he was nine or ten, his father had fallen ill. "It was rabbit fever," and the illness lasted many months, during which the family had depended upon church assistance and the charity of neighbors—"otherwise we would've starved." That episode aside, his childhood had been O.K. "We never had much money, but we were never really down-and-out," Hickock said. "We always had clean clothes and something to eat. My dad was strict, though. He wasn't happy unless he had me doing chores. But we got along O.K.—no serious arguments. My parents never argued, either. I can't recall a single quarrel. She's wonderful, my mother. Dad's a good guy, too. I'd say they did the best for me they could." School? Well, he felt he might have been more than an average student if he had contributed to books a fraction of the time he'd "wasted" on sports. "Baseball. Football. I made all the teams. After high school I could have gone to college on a football scholarship. I wanted to study engineering, but even with a scholarship, deals like that cost plenty. I don't know, it seemed safer to get a job."

Before his twenty-first birthday Hickock had worked as a railway trackman, an ambulance driver, a car painter, and a garage mechanic; he'd also married a girl sixteen years old. "Carol. Her father was a minister. He was dead against me. Said I was a full-time nobody. He made all the trouble he could. But I was nuts about Carol. Still am. There's a real princess. Only—see, we had three kids. Boys. And we were too young to have three kids. Maybe if we hadn't got so deep into debt. If I could've earned extra money. I tried."

He tried gambling, and started forging checks and experimenting with other forms of theft. In 1958 he was convicted of house burglary in a Johnson County court and sentenced to five years in Kansas State Penitentiary. But by then Carol had departed and he'd taken as a bride another girl aged sixteen. "Mean as hell. Her and her whole family.

She divorced me while I was inside. I'm not complaining. Last August, when I left The Walls, I figured I had every chance to start new. I got a job in Olathe, lived with my family, and stayed home nights. I was doing swell—"

"Until November twentieth," said Nye, and Hickock seemed not to understand him. "The day you stopped doing swell and started hanging paper. Why?"

Hickock sighed, and said, "That would make a book." Then, smoking a cigarette borrowed from Nye and lighted by the courteous Church, he said, "Perry—my buddy Perry Smith—was paroled in the spring. Later on, when I came out, he sent me a letter. Postmarked Idaho. He wrote reminding me of this deal we used to talk over. About Mexico. The idea was we would go to Acapulco, one of them places, buy a fishing boat, and run it ourselves—take tourists deep-sea fishing."

Nye said, "This boat. How did you plan to pay for it?"

"I'm coming to that," Hickock said. "See, Perry wrote me he had a sister living in Fort Scott. And she was holding some heavy change for him. Several thousand dollars. Money his dad owed him from the sale of some property up in Alaska. He said he was coming to Kansas to get the dough."

"And the two of you would use it to buy a boat."

"Correct."

"But it didn't work out that way."

"What happened was, Perry showed up maybe a month later. I met him at the bus station in Kansas City—"

"When?" said Church. "The day of the week."

"A Thursday."

"And when did you go to Fort Scott?"

"Saturday."

"November fourteenth."

Hickock's eyes flashed with surprise. One could see that he was asking himself why Church should be so certain of the date; and hurriedly—for it was too soon to stir suspicions—the detective said, "What time did you leave for Fort Scott?"

"That afternoon. We did some work on my car, and had a bowl of chili at the West Side Café. It must have been around three."

"Around three. Was Perry Smith's sister expecting you?"

"No. Because, see, Perry lost her address. And she didn't have a telephone."

"Then how did you expect to find her?"

"By inquiring at the post office."

"Did you?"

"Perry did. They said she'd moved away. To Oregon, they thought. But she hadn't left any forwarding address."

"Must have been quite a blow. After you'd been counting on a big piece of money like that."

Hickock agreed. "Because—well, we'd definitely decided to go to Mexico. Otherwise, I never would've cashed them checks. But I hoped . . . Now listen to me; I'm telling the truth. I thought once we got to Mexico and began making money, then I'd be able to pay them off. The checks."

Nye took over. "One minute, Dick." Nye is a short, short-tempered man who has difficulty moderating his aggressive vigor, his talent for language both sharp and outspoken. "I'd like to hear a little more about the trip to Fort Scott," he said, soft-pedaling. "When you found Smith's sister no longer there, what did you do then?"

"Walked around. Had a beer. Drove back."

"You mean you went home?"

"No. To Kansas City. We stopped at the Zesto Drive-In. Ate hamburgers. We tried Cherry Row."

Neither Nye nor Church was familiar with Cherry Row.

Hickock said, "You kiddin'? Every cop in Kansas knows it." When the detectives again pleaded ignorance, he explained that it was a stretch of park where one encountered "hustlers mostly," adding, "but plenty of amateurs, too. Nurses. Secretaries. I've had a lot of luck there."

"And this particular evening. Have any luck?"

"The bad kind. We ended up with a pair of rollers."

"Named?"

"Mildred. The other one, Perry's girl, I think she was called Joan."

"Describe them."

"Maybe they were sisters. Both blond. Plump. I'm not too clear about it. See, we'd bought a bottle of ready-mix Orange Blossoms—that's orange pop and vodka—and I was getting stiff. We gave the girls a few drinks and drove them out to Fun Haven. I imagine you gentlemen never heard of Fun Haven?"

They hadn't.

Hickock grinned and shrugged. "It's on the Blue Ridge Road. Eight miles south of Kansas City. A combination night-club-motel. You pay ten bucks for the key to a cabin."

Continuing, he described the cabin in which he claimed that the foursome had stayed the night: twin beds, an old Coca-Cola calendar, a radio that wouldn't play unless the customer deposited a quarter. His poise, his explicitness, the assured presentation of verifiable detail impressed Nye—though, of course, the boy was lying. Well, wasn't he? Whether because of flu and fever or an abrupt lessening in the warmth of his confidence, Nye exuded an icy sweat.

"Next morning we woke up to find they'd rolled us and beat it," said Hickock. "Didn't get much off me. But Perry lost his wallet, with forty or fifty dollars."

"What did you do about it?"

"There wasn't nothing to do."

"You could've notified the police."

"Aw, come on. Quit it. *Notify* the police. For your information, a guy on parole's not allowed to booze. Or associate with another Old Grad—"

"All right, Dick. It's Sunday. The fifteenth of November. Tell us what you did that day from the moment you checked out of Fun Haven."

"Well we ate breakfast at a truck stop near Happy Hill. Then we drove to Olathe, and I dropped Perry off at the hotel where he was living. I'd say that was around eleven. Afterward, I went home and had dinner with the family. Same as every Sunday. Watched TV—a basketball game, or maybe it was football. I was pretty tired."

"When did you next see Perry Smith?"

"Monday. He came by where I worked. Bob Sands' Body Shop."

"And what did you talk about? Mexico?"

"Well, we still liked the idea, even if we hadn't got hold of the money to do all we had in mind—put ourselves in business down there. But we wanted to go, and it seemed worth the risk."

"Worth another stretch in Lansing?"

"That didn't figure. See, we never intended coming Stateside again."

Nye, who had been jotting notes in a notebook, said, "On the day following the check spree—that would be the twenty-first—you and your friend Smith disappeared. Now, Dick, please outline your movements between then and the time of your arrest here in Las Vegas. Just a rough idea."

Hickock whistled and rolled his eyes. "Wow!" he said, and then, summoning his talent for something very like total recall, he began an account of the long ride—the approximately ten thousand miles he and Smith had covered in the past six weeks. He talked for an hour and twenty-five minutes—from two-fifty to four-fifteen—and told, while Nye attempted to list them, of highways and hotels, motels, rivers, towns, and cities, a chorus of entwining names: Apache, El Paso, Corpus Christi, Santillo, San Luis Potosí, Acapulco, San Diego, Dallas, Omaha, Sweetwater, Stillwater, Tenville Junction, Tallahassee, Needles, Miami, Hotel Nuevo Waldorf, Somerset Hotel, Hotel Simone, Arrowhead Motel, Cherokee Motel, and many, many more. He gave them the name of the man in Mexico to whom he'd sold his own old 1949 Chevrolet, and confessed that he had stolen a newer model in Iowa. He described persons he and his partner had met: a Mexican widow, rich and sexy; Otto, a German "millionaire"; a "swish" pair of Negro prizefighters driving a "swish" lavender Cadillac; the blind proprietor of a Florida rattlesnake farm; a dying old man and his grandson; and others. And when he had finished he sat with folded arms and a pleased smile, as though waiting to be commended for the humor, the clarity, and the candor of his traveler's tale.

But Nye, in pursuit of the narrative, raced his pen, and Church, lazily slamming a shut hand against an open palm, said nothing—until suddenly he said. "I guess you know why we're here."

Hickock's mouth straightened—his posture, too.

"I guess you realize we wouldn't have come all the way to Nevada just to chat with a couple of two-bit check chiselers."

Nye had closed the notebook. He, too, stared at the prisoner, and observed that a cluster of veins had appeared in his left temple.

"Would we, Dick?"

"What?"

"Come this far to talk about a bunch of checks."

"I can't think of any other reason."

Nye drew a dagger on the cover of his notebook. While doing so, he said, "Tell me, Dick. Have you ever heard of the Clutter murder case?" Whereupon, he later wrote in a formal report of the interview, "Suspect underwent an intense visible reaction. He turned gray. His eyes twitched."

Hickock said, "Whoa, now. Hold on here. I'm no goddam killer."

"The question asked," Church reminded him, "was whether you'd *heard* of the Clutter murders."

"I may have read something," Hickock said.

"A vicious crime. Vicious. Cowardly."

"And almost perfect," Nye said. "But you made two mistakes, Dick. One was, you left a witness. A living witness. Who'll testify in court. Who'll stand in the witness box and tell a jury how Richard Hickock and Perry Smith bound and gagged and slaughtered four helpless people."

Hickock's face reddened with returning color. "Living witness! There can't be!"

"Because you thought you'd got rid of everyone?"

"I said whoa! There ain't anybody can connect me with any goddam murder. Checks. A little petty thievery. But I'm no goddam killer."

"Then why," Nye asked hotly, "have you been lying to us?"

"I've been telling you the goddam truth."

"Now and then. Not always. For instance, what about Saturday afternoon, November fourteenth? You say you drove to Fort Scott."

"Yes."

"And when you got there you went to the post office."

"Yes."

"To obtain the address of Perry Smith's sister."

"That's right."

Nye rose. He walked around to the rear of Hickock's chair, and placing his hands on the back of the chair, leaned down as though to whisper in the prisoner's ear. "Perry Smith has no sister living in Fort Scott," he said. "He never has had. And on Saturday afternoons the Fort Scott post office happens to be closed." Then he said, "Think it over, Dick. That's all for now. We'll talk to you later."

After Hickock's dismissal, Nye and Church crossed the corridor, and looking through the one-way observation window set in the door of the interrogation room, watched the questioning of Perry Smith—a scene visible though not audible. Nye, who was seeing Smith for the first time, was fascinated by his feet—by the fact that his legs were so short that his feet, as small as a child's, couldn't quite make the floor. Smith's head—the stiff Indian hair, the Irish-Indian blending of dark skin and pert, impish features—reminded him of the suspect's pretty sister, the nice Mrs. Johnson. But this chunky, misshapen child-man was not pretty; the pink end of his tongue darted forth, flickering like the tongue of a lizard. He was smoking a cigarette, and from the evenness of his exhalations Nye deduced that he was still a "virgin"—that is, still uninformed about the real purpose of the interview.

Nye was right. For Dewey and Duntz, patient professionals, had gradually narrowed the prisoner's life story to the events of the last seven weeks, then reduced those to a concentrated recapitulation of the crucial weekend—Saturday noon to Sunday noon, November 14 to 15. Now, having spent three hours preparing the way, they were not far from coming to the point.

Dewey said, "Perry, let's review our position. Now, when you received parole, it was on condition that you never return to Kansas."

"The Sunflower State. I cried my eyes out."

"Feeling that way, why did you go back? You must have had some very strong reason."

"I told you. To see my sister. To get the money she was holding for me."

"Oh, yes. The sister you and Hickock tried to find in Fort Scott. Perry, how far is Fort Scott from Kansas City?"

Smith shook his head. He didn't know.

"Well, how long did it take you to drive there?"

No response.

"One hour? Two? Three? Four?"

The prisoner said he couldn't remember.

"Of course you can't. Because you've never in your life been to Fort Scott."

Until then, neither of the detectives had challenged any part of Smith's statement. He shifted in his chair; with the tip of his tongue he wet his lips.

"The fact is, nothing you've told us is true. You never set foot in Fort Scott. You never picked up any two girls and never took them to any motel—"

"We did. No kidding."

"What were their names?"

"I never asked."

"You and Hickock spent the night with these women and never asked their names?"

"They were just prostitutes."

"Tell us the name of the motel."

"Ask Dick. He'll know. I never remember junk like that."

Dewey addressed his colleague. "Clarence, I think it's time we straightened Perry out."

Duntz hunched forward. He is a heavyweight with a welterweight's spontaneous agility, but his eyes are hooded and lazy. He drawls; each word, formed reluctantly and framed in a cattle-country accent, lasts awhile. "Yes, sir," he said. " 'Bout time."

"Listen good, Perry. Because Mr. Duntz is going to tell you where you really were that Saturday night. Where you were and what you were doing."

Duntz said, "You were killing the Clutter family."

Smith swallowed. He began to rub his knees.

"You were out in Holcomb, Kansas. In the home of Mr. Herbert W. Clutter. And before you left that house you killed all the people in it."

"Never. I never."

"Never what?"

"Knew anybody by that name. Clutter."

Dewey called him a liar, and then, conjuring a card that in prior consultation the four detectives had agreed to play face down, told him, "We have a living witness, Perry. Somebody you boys overlooked."

A full minute elapsed, and Dewey exulted in Smith's silence, for an innocent man would ask who was this witness, and who were these Clutters, and why did they think he'd murdered them—would, at any rate, say *something*. But Smith sat quiet, squeezing his knees.

"Well, Perry?"

"You got an aspirin? They took away my aspirin."

"Feeling bad?"

"My legs do."

It was five-thirty. Dewey, intentionally abrupt, terminated the interview. "We'll take this up again tomorrow," he said. "By the way, do you know what tomorrow is? Nancy Clutter's birthday. She would have been seventeen."

"She would have been seventeen." Perry, sleepless in the dawn hours, wondered (he later recalled) if it was true that today was the girl's birthday, and decided no, that it was just another way of getting under his skin, like that phony business about a witness—"a living witness." There couldn't be. Or did they mean— if only he could talk to Dick! But he and Dick were being kept apart; Dick was locked in a cell on another floor. "Listen good, Perry. Because Mr. Duntz is going to tell you where you really were . . ." Midway in the questioning, after he'd begun to notice the number of allusions to a particular November weekend, he'd nerved himself for what he knew was coming, yet when it did, when the big cowboy with the sleepy voice said, "You were killing the Clutter family"—well, he'd damn near died, that's all. He must have lost ten pounds in two seconds. Thank God he hadn't let them see it. Or hoped he hadn't. And Dick? Presumably they'd pulled the same stunt on him. Dick was smart, a convincing performer, but his "guts" were unreliable, he panicked too easily. Even so, and however much they pressured him, Perry was sure Dick would hold out. Unless he wanted to hang. "And before you left that house you killed all the people in it." It wouldn't amaze him if every Old Grad in Kansas had heard that line. They must have questioned hundreds of men, and no doubt accused dozens; he and Dick were merely two more. On the *other* hand—well, *would* Kansas send four Special Agents a thousand miles to pick up a small-time pair of parole violators? Maybe somehow they *had* stumbled on something, somebody—"a living witness." But that was impossible. Except— he'd give an arm, a leg to talk to Dick for just five minutes.

And Dick, awake in a cell on the floor below, was (he later recalled) equally eager to converse with Perry—find out what the punk had told them. Christ, you couldn't trust him to remember even the outline of the Fun Haven alibi—though they had discussed it often enough. And when those bastards threatened him with a witness! Ten to one the little spook had thought they meant an *eye*witness. Whereas he, Dick, had known at once who the so-called witness must be: Floyd Wells, his old friend and former cellmate. While serving the last weeks of his sentence, Dick had plotted to knife Floyd—stab him through the heart with a handmade "shiv"—and what a fool he was not to have done it. Except for Perry, Floyd Wells was the one human being who could link the names Hickock and Clutter. Floyd, with his sloping shoulders and inclining chin—Dick had thought he'd be too afraid. The sonofabitch was probably expecting some fancy reward—a parole or money, or both. But hell would freeze before he got it. Because a convict's tattle wasn't proof. Proof is footprints, fingerprints, witnesses, a confession. Hell, if all those cowboys had to go on was some story Floyd Wells had told, then there wasn't a lot to worry about. Come right down to it, Floyd wasn't half as dangerous as Perry. Perry, if he lost his nerve and let fly, could put them both in The Corner. And suddenly he saw the truth: It was *Perry* he ought to have silenced. On a mountain road in Mexico. Or while walking across the Mojave. Why had it never occurred to him until now? For now, now was much too late.

Ultimately, at five minutes past three that afternoon, Smith admitted the falsity of the Fort Scott tale. "That was only something Dick told his family. So he could stay out overnight. Do some drinking. See, Dick's dad watched him pretty close—afraid he'd break parole. So we made up an excuse about my sister. It was just to pacify Mr. Hickock." Otherwise, he repeated the same story again and again, and Duntz and Dewey, regardless of how often they corrected him and accused him of lying, could not make him change it—except to add fresh details. The names of the prostitutes, he recalled today, were Mildred and Jane (or Joan). "They rolled us," he now remembered. "Walked off with all our dough while we were asleep." And though even Duntz had forfeited his composure—had shed, along with tie and coat, his enigmatic drowsy dignity—the suspect seemed content and serene; he refused to budge. He'd never heard of the Clutters or Holcomb, or even Garden City.

Across the hall, in the smoke-choked room where Hickock was undergoing his second interrogation, Church and Nye were methodically applying a more roundabout strategy. Not once during this interview, now almost three hours old, had either of them mentioned murder—an omission that kept the prisoner edgy, expectant. They talked of everything else: Hickock's religious philosophy ("I know about hell. I been there. Maybe there's a heaven, too. Lots of rich people think so"); his sexual history ("I've always behaved like a one-hundred-percent normal"); and, once more, the history of his recent cross-country hegira ("Why we kept going like that, the only reason was we were looking for jobs. Couldn't find anything decent, though. I worked one day digging a ditch . . ."). But things unspoken were the center of interest—the cause, the detectives were convinced, of Hickock's escalating distress. Presently, he shut his eyes and touched the lids with trembling fingertips. And Church said, "Something wrong?"

"A headache. I get real bastards."

Then Nye said, "Look at me, Dick." Hickock obeyed, with an expression that the detective interpreted as a pleading with him to speak, to accuse, and let the prisoner escape into the sanctuary of steadfast denial. "When we discussed the matter yesterday, you may recall my saying that the Clutter murders were almost a perfect crime. The killers made only two mistakes. The first one was they left a witness. The second—well, I'll show you." Rising, he retrieved from a corner a box and a briefcase, both of which he'd brought into the room at the start of the interview. Out of the briefcase came a large photograph. "This," he said, leaving it on the table, "is a one-to-one reproduction of certain footprints found near Mr. Clutter's body. And here"—he opened the box— "are the boots that made them. Your boots, Dick." Hickock looked, and looked away. He rested his elbows on his knees and cradled his head in his hands. "Smith," said Nye, "was even more careless. We have his boots, too, and they exactly fit another set of prints. Bloody ones."

Church closed in. "Here's what's going to happen to you, Hickock," he said. "You'll be taken back to Kansas. You'll be charged on four counts of first-degree murder. Count One: That on or about the fifteenth day of November, 1959, one Richard Eugene Hickock did unlawfully, feloniously, willfully and with deliberation and premeditation, and while being engaged in the perpetration of a felony, kill and take the life of Herbert W. Clutter. Count Two: That on or about the fifteenth day of November, 1959, the same Richard Eugene Hickock did unlawfully—"

Hickock said, "Perry Smith killed the Clutters." He lifted his head, and slowly straightened up in the chair, like a fighter staggering to his feet. "It was Perry. I couldn't stop him. He killed them all."

# Chapter 24

# TIMOTHY CROUSE

# THE BOYS ON THE BUS

IN 1960 WITH THE PUBLICATION of *The Making of the President,* Theodore White reinvented campaign journalism. He took readers behind the scenes of the major presidential campaigns and presented the race for the presidency as a human drama. In 1972, Timothy Crouse followed in the same tradition but his focus was not on the campaign itself but on the press corps traveling with the candidates.

*The Boys on the Bus* grew out of several articles Crouse wrote for *Rolling Stone* magazine, arguably the premier magazine for music and popular culture and a show-case for the New Journalism that had blossomed in the 1960s. Crouse salutes, critiques and lampoons many reporters who turned out to be the most significant journalists in the last quarter of the 20th century, including David Broder of *The Washington Post,* R.W. Apple of *The New York Times,* and Hunter S. Thompson, considered the "father" of "gonzo" journalism, who also wrote for *Rolling Stone.* The politicians the reporters were covering—including the eventual candidates Richard M. Nixon and George McGovern—did not escape his acute and wry observations.

*The Boys on the Bus* marked the emergence of the media itself as a subject worthy of reporting about in political campaigns. It was one of the first examples of press coverage of press coverage and its ironic, self-reflective and raucous approach resulted in it becoming an instant best seller and a New Journalism classic. The following excerpt comes from Chapter 1 of the book where Crouse explains the concept of pack journalism and the reasons journalists on campaigns often reported almost exactly the same things their colleagues reported.

## On the Bus

June 1—five days before the California primary. A grey dawn was fighting its way through the orange curtains in the Wilshire Hyatt House Hotel in Los Angeles, where George McGovern was encamped with his wife, his staff, and the press assigned to cover his snowballing campaign.

While reporters still snored like Hessians in a hundred beds throughout the hotel, the McGovern munchkins were at work, plying the halls, slipping the long legal-sized handouts through the cracks under the door of each room. According to one of these handouts, the Baptist Ministers' Union of Oakland had decided after "prayerful and careful deliberation" to endorse Senator McGovern. And there was a detailed profile of Alameda County (". . . agricultural products include sweet corn, cucumbers, and lettuce"), across which the press would be dragged today—or was it tomorrow? Finally, there was the mimeographed schedule, the orders of the day.

At 6:45 the phone on the bed table rang, and a sweet, chipper voice announced: "Good Morning, Mr. Crouse. It's six forty-five. The press bus leaves in forty-five minutes from the front of the hotel." She was up there in Room 819, the Press Suite, calling up the dozens of names on the press manifest, awaking the agents of every great newspaper, wire service and network not only of America but of the world. In response to her calls, she was getting a shocking series of startled grunts, snarls and obscenities.

The media heavies were rolling over, stumbling to the bathroom, and tripping over the handouts. Stooping to pick up the schedule, they read: "*8:00—8:15, Arrive Roger Young Center, Breakfast with Ministers.*" Suddenly, desperately, they thought: "Maybe I can pick McGovern up in Burbank at nine fifty-five and sleep for another hour." Then, probably at almost the same instant, several score minds flashed the same guilty thought: "But maybe he will get shot at the ministers' breakfast," and then each mind branched off into its own private nightmare recollections of the correspondent who was taking a piss at Laurel when they shot Wallace, of the ABC cameraman who couldn't get his Bolex to start as Bremer emptied his revolver. A hundred hands groped for the toothbrush.

It was lonely on these early mornings and often excruciatingly painful to tear oneself away from a brief, sodden spell of sleep. More painful for some than others. The press was consuming two hundred dollars a night worth of free cheap booze up there in the Press Suite, and some were consuming the lion's share. Last night it had taken six reporters to subdue a prominent radio correspondent who kept upsetting the portable bar, knocking bottles and ice on the floor. The radioman had the resiliency of a Rasputin—each time he was put to bed, he would reappear to cause yet more bedlam.

And yet, at 7:15 Rasputin was there for the baggage call, milling in the hall outside the Press Suite with fifty-odd reporters. The first glance at all these fellow sufferers was deeply reassuring—they all felt the same pressures you felt, their problems were your problems. Together, they seemed to have the cohesiveness of an ant colony, but when you examined the scene more closely, each reporter appeared to be jitterbugging around in quest of the answer that would quell some private anxiety.

They were three deep at the main table in the Press Suite, badgering the McGovern people for a variety of assurances. "Will I have a room in San Francisco tonight?" "Are you sure I'm booked on the whistle-stop train?" "Have you seen my partner?"

The feverish atmosphere was halfway between a high school bus trip to Washington and a gambler's jet junket to Las Vegas, where small-time Mafiosi were lured into betting away their restaurants. There was giddy camaraderie mixed with fear and low-grade hysteria. To file a story late, or to make one glaring factual error, was to chance losing everything—one's job, one's expense account, one's drinking buddies, one's mad-dash existence, and the methedrine buzz that comes from knowing stories that the public would not know for hours and secrets that the public would never know. Therefore reporters channeled their gambling instincts into late-night poker games and private bets on the outcome of the elections. When it came to writing a story, they were as cautious as diamond-cutters.

It being Thursday, many reporters were knotting their stomachs over their Sunday pieces, which had to be filed that afternoon at the latest. They were inhaling their cigarettes with more of a vengeance, and patting themselves more distractedly to make sure they had their pens and notebooks. In the hall, a Secret Service agent was dispensing press tags for the baggage, along with string and scissors to attach them. From time to time, in the best Baden-Powell tradition, he courteously stepped forward to assist a drink-palsied journalist in the process of threading a tag.

The reporters often consulted their watches or asked for the time of departure. Among this crew, there was one great phobia—the fear of getting left behind. Fresh troops had arrived today from the Humphrey Bus, which was the Russian Front of the California primary, and they had come bearing tales of horror. The Humphrey Bus had left half the press corps at the Biltmore Hotel on Tuesday night; in Santa Barbara, the bus had deserted Richard Bergholz of the Los Angeles *Times*, and it had twice stranded George Shelton, the UPI man.

"Jesus, am I glad I'm off the Humphrey Bus," said one reporter, as he siphoned some coffee out of the McGovern samovar and helped himself to a McGovern sweet roll. "Shelton asked Humphrey's press officer, Hackel, if there was time to file. Hackel said, 'Sure, the candidate's gonna mingle and shake some hands.' Well, old Hubie couldn't find but six hands to shake, so they got in the bus and took off and left the poor bastard in a phone booth right in the middle of Watts."

To the men whom duty had called to slog along at the side of the Hump, the switch to the McGovern Bus brought miraculous relief. "You gotta go see the Hump's pressroom, just to see what disaster looks like," a reporter urged me. The Humphrey pressroom, a bunker-like affair in the bowels of the Beverly Hilton, contained three tables covered with white tablecloths, no typewriters, no chairs, no bar, no food, one phone (with outside lines available only to registered guests), and no reporters. The McGovern press suite, on the other hand, contained twelve typewriters, eight phones, a Xerox Telecopier, a free bar, free cigarettes, free munchies, and a skeleton crew of three staffers. It was not only Rumor Central, but also a miniature road version of Thomas Cook and Son. As the new arrivals to the McGovern Bus quickly found out, the McGovern staff ran the kind of guided tour that people pay great sums of money to get carted around on. They booked reservations on planes, trains and hotels; gave and received messages; and handled Secret Service accreditation with a fierce, Teutonic efficiency. And handed out reams of free information. On any given day, the table in the middle of the Press Suite was laden with at least a dozen fat piles of handouts, and the door was papered with pool reports.[1]

It was just these womblike conditions that gave rise to the notorious phenomenon called "pack journalism" (also known as "herd journalism" and "fuselage journalism"). A group of reporters were assigned to follow a single candidate for weeks or months at a time, like a pack of hounds sicked on a fox. Trapped on the same bus or plane, they ate, drank, gambled, and compared notes with the same bunch of colleagues week after week.

Actually, this group was as hierarchical as a chess set. The pack was divided into cliques—the national political reporters, who were constantly coming and going; the campaign reporters from the big, prestige papers and the ones from the small papers; the wire-service men; the network correspondents; and other configurations that formed according to age and old Washington friendships. The most experienced national political reporters, wire men, and big-paper reporters, who were at the top of the pecking order, often did not know the names of the men from the smaller papers, who were at the bottom. But they all fed off the same pool report, the same daily handout, the same speech by the candidate; the whole pack was isolated in the same mobile village. After a while, they began to believe the same rumors, subscribe to the same theories, and write the same stories.

Everybody denounces pack journalism, including the men who form the pack. Any self-respecting journalist would sooner endorse incest than come out in favor of pack journalism. It is the classic villain of every campaign year. Many reporters and journalism professors blame it for everything that is shallow, obvious, meretricious, misleading, or dull in American campaign coverage.

On a muggy afternoon during the California primary campaign, I went to consult with Karl Fleming, a former political reporter and Los Angeles bureau chief for *Newsweek*, who was rumored to be a formidable critic of pack journalism. Fleming was beginning a whole new gig as editor of a fledgling semi-underground paper called *LA;* I found him in dungarees and shirtsleeves, sitting behind a desk that was covered with the makings of *LA*'s pilot issue.[2] He was a ruggedly built North Carolinian with the looks and accent to play Davy Crockett in a Disney remake. He was very busy putting his magazine together, taking phone calls, and giving instructions to one long-haired writer after another, but he seemed to enjoy letting off steam about political journalism. One of the reasons he quit *Newsweek* was that he got fed up riding around on campaign extravaganzas.

"I got so frustrated during the Nixon campaign in 1968," he grinned, "that I went to Ron Ziegler one day—we were flying some-goddam-where—and said, 'Ron, I come to you as a representative of the press corps to ask you this question.' I said, 'The question is, What does Nixon do upon the occasion of his semiannual erection?' Ziegler never cracked a goddam smile. Then I said, 'The consensus is that he smuggles it to Tijuana.' "

Fleming leaned back in his chair and laughed hard.

"Gee," I said, "you must have been fucked after that."

"It doesn't make any difference if you're fucked or you're not fucked," said Fleming. "You delude yourself into thinking, 'Well, if I get on the bad side of these guys, then I'm not gonna get all that good stuff.' But pretty soon the realization hits that there *isn't* any good stuff, and there isn't gonna *be* any good stuff. Nobody's getting anything that you're not getting, and if they are it's just more of the same bullshit."

I told Fleming that I was puzzled as to why so many newspapers felt they needed to have correspondents aboard the press bus; a couple of wire-service guys and a camera crew should be able to cover a candidate's comings, goings, and official statements more than thoroughly.

"Papers that have enough money are not content to have merely the AP reports," said Fleming. "They want to have their own person in Washington because it means prestige for the paper and because in a curious way, it gives the editors a feeling of belonging to the club, too. I'll guarantee you that three fourths of the goddam stuff—the good stuff—that the Washington press corps reporters turn up never gets into print at all. The reason it's collected is because it's transmitted back to the editor, to the publisher, to the 'in' executive cliques on these newspapers and networks and newsmagazines. It's sent in confidential FYI memos or just over the phone. You give the publisher information that his business associates or his friends at the country club don't have; you're performing a very valuable function for him, and that, by God, is why you get paid.

"But while these papers want to have a guy there getting all the inside stuff, they don't want reporters who are ballsy enough and different enough to make any kind of trouble. It would worry the shit out of them if their Washington reporter happened to come up with a page-one story that was different from what the other guys were getting. And the first goddam thing that happens is they pick up the phone and call this guy and say, 'Hey, if this is such a hot story, how come AP or the Washington *Post* doesn't have it?' And the reporter's in big fuckin' trouble. The editors don't want scoops. Their abiding interest is making sure that nobody else had got anything that they don't have, not getting something that nobody else has.

"So eventually a very subtle kind of thing takes over and the reporter says to himself. 'All I gotta do to satisfy my editor and publisher is just get what the other guys are getting, so why should I bust my ass?' And over a period of a few years he joins the club. Now, most of these guys are honest, decent reporters who do the best job they can in this kind of atmosphere. The best reporters are the ones who sit around and talk about what assholes their editors and publishers are, and that still happens, thank God, with a great amount of frequency, even at the high levels of the Washington press corps.

"All the same, any troublemaking reporter who walks into a press conference and asks a really mean snotty question which is going to make the candidate and his people really angry is going to be treated like a goddam pariah. 'Cause these guys in this club, they don't want any troublemakers stirring up the waters, which means they might have to dig for something that's not coming down out of the daily handout, or coming in from the daily pool report about what went on. They'd rather sit around the pressroom at the hotel every night, drinking booze and playing poker."

Fleming said that in June, and as I followed the press through the next five months of the campaign, I discovered that some of his accusations checked out, but others did not. Almost everything he said held true for the White House press corps,[3] but his charges did not always apply to the men who covered the Democratic candidates in 1972. It was true that some editors were still reluctant to run a story by their own man until the wire services had confirmed it. It was true that newsmagazine reporters and network correspondents occasionally leaked part of a hot story to *The New York Times* or *The Wall Street Journal;* after the story had gained respectability by appearing in one of these major establishment organs, the correspondent would write the whole story for his own organization. And it was impossible to tell how often the reporters censored themselves in anticipation of some imaginary showdown with a cautious editor, preferring to play it safe and go along with whatever the rest of the pack was writing.

But things had also begun to change since Fleming's campaign stories in 1968. The men on the bus had more authority and independence than ever before, and many of them were searching for new ways to report on the freakish, insular existence of the press bus, and for ways to break away from the pack. Very few of them filed any confidential memos to their superiors, or phoned in any inside information, except to suggest that such information might be worked up into a story.

Take, for example, the case of Curtis Wilkie, a young reporter for the Wilmington, Delaware *News-Journal* whom I met for the first time on the morning of June 1. I walked out of the lobby of the Wilshire Hyatt House, past all the black Nauga-hide furniture, and stepped into the first of the two silver buses that were waiting at the curb. It was the kind of bus to which most bus-fanciers would give three stars—the windows were tinted and there was a toilet in the rear, but the seats did not recline. The time was 7:30 A.M. and two-thirds of the seats were already filled with silent and bleary-eyed reporters who looked as cheerful as a Georgia chain gang on its way to a new roadbed. Most of them were sending out powerful "No Trespassing" vibes. My company was in no great demand, word having gotten around that I was researching an article on the press. Reporters snapped their notebooks shut when I drew near. The night before, Harry Kelly, a tall, hard-eyed Irishman from the Hearst papers, had looked at me over his shoulder and muttered, "Goddam gossip columnist."

I finally sat down next to a thirtyish dark-haired reporter wearing a Palm Beach suit and a drooping moustache, who looked too hungover to object to my presence. After a long silence, he spoke up in a twangy Southern accent and introduced himself as Curtis Wilkie. He was from Mississippi and had been a senior at Ole Miss in 1964 when General Walker led his famous charge on the administration building. After graduating, Wilkie had put in seven years as a reporter on the Clarksdale, Mississippi *Register* (circ. 7,000), and, as I later found out, had won a slew of journalism prizes. In 1968, he had gone to the Chicago Convention as a member of the "loyalist" Mississippi delegation and had cast his vote for Eugene McCarthy. Soon after that he won a Congressional fellowship and worked for Walter Mondale in the Senate and John Brademas in the House. In 1971, the Wilmington paper hired him as its main political writer; they got their money's worth, for he wrote two separate 750-word articles every day, a "hard" news story for the morning *News* and a "soft" feature story for the afternoon *Journal*.

"Last night, I filed a story unconditionally predicting that the Hump's gonna get rubbed out in the primary," he said. Now he was worried that his editors might object to so firm a stand, or that Humphrey, through some terrible accident, might win. As if to reassure himself, Wilkie kept telling funny, mordant stories about the last-ditch hysterics of the Humphrey campaign.

Wilkie had experienced a few bad moments over a Humphrey story once before. During the Pennsylvania primary, Humphrey unwisely decided to hold a student rally at the University of Pennsylvania. The students booed and heckled, calling Humphrey "America's Number 2 War Criminal," until Humphrey, close to tears, was forced to retreat from the stage. Wilkie filed a long story describing the incident and concluding that Humphrey was so unpopular with students that he could no longer speak on a college campus.

There were no TV cameramen at the rally, and of the fifteen reporters who covered the speech, only one beside Wilkie filed a detailed account of the heckling. The next day, when Wilkie went into the office, the managing editor was laughing about the story. "We've kind of started wondering," he teased Wilkie. "Several people have called and said that they didn't see anything about Humphrey on Channel Six, and they seem to think you made it up. And we're beginning to wonder ourselves, because none of the wire services mentioned it." Wilkie began to sweat; he nearly convinced himself that he had grossly exaggerated the incident. Late that afternoon, Wilkie came across a piece by Phil Potter, a veteran reporter for the Baltimore *Sun*. Potter's version of the incident agreed with Wilkie's. With great relief, Curt clipped the article and showed it to the managing editor.

For months afterward, Wilkie felt slightly qualmish whenever he thought about the Humphrey story. "They sort of put me on notice that somebody was carefully reading my stuff, that time," he said after the election. "It may have inhibited me, I don't know."

But it didn't drive him back to the safety of the pack. He continued to trust his own judgment and write about whatever he himself thought was important. In October, when he was one of the few reporters to file a full account of an ugly Nixon rally where the President smiled at the sight of demonstrators being beaten up, the paper printed his articles without questioning them. "After a while," he said, "the guys on my desk began to have enough faith in me that they would accept anything I gave them regardless of what their wire services were telling them. They may have wondered a couple of times, but that didn't prevent them from running it."

What made this all the more remarkable was that the *News-Journal* was owned by the arch-conservative DuPont family,[4] and had long been famous for resisting news stories that gave any comfort to liberals. Ben Bagdikian, in his book *The Effete Conspiracy*, had used the *News-Journal* as a case study in biased journalism. According to Bagdikian, one of the owners had once even "complained bitterly to the editors that the paper's reporter had written a conventional news account of a Democratic rally when he should have turned it into a pro-Republican essay."[5] In the late sixties, however, stronger editors had taken over, and in the fall of 1972 they decided not to endorse either Nixon or McGovern, much to the displeasure of the DuPonts. The DuPonts' dissenting editorial, which exhorted readers to vote for every Republican on the ballot, was relegated to the letters column under the coy heading "A View from the Top." Wilkie was assigned to write a story about the rift. Interviewing the DuPonts, he asked whether a proposed merger pending before the SEC had anything to do with their endorsement of Nixon. Only a few years before, such impertinence would have been unthinkable.[6]

But one should not make too much of Curt Wilkie and the *News-Journal*. There were still lazy men on the bus, and men with large families to feed or powerful ambitions to nurture, who feared losing their jobs and thus played it safe by sticking with the pack. And there were still editors whose suspicions of any unusual story made pack journalism look cozy and inviting to their reporters. Campaign journalism is, by definition, pack journalism; to follow a candidate, you must join a pack of other reporters; even the most independent journalist cannot completely escape the pressures of the pack.

Around 8:15 A.M. ON June 1 the buses rolled past the stucco housefronts of lower-middle-class Los Angeles and pulled up in front of a plain brick building that looked like a school. The press trooped down a little alley and into the back of the Grand Ballroom of the Roger Young Center. The scene resembled Bingo Night in a South Dakota parish hall—hundreds of middle-aged people sitting at long rectangular tables. They were watching George McGovern, who was speaking from the stage. The press, at the back of the room, started filling up on free Danish pastry, orange juice and coffee. Automatically, they pulled out their notebooks and wrote something down, even though McGovern was saying nothing new. They leaned sloppily against the wall or slumped in folding chairs.

McGovern ended his speech and the Secret Service men began to wedge him through the crush of ministers and old ladies who wanted to shake his hand. By the time he had made it to the little alley which was the only route of escape from the building, three cameras had set up an ambush. This was the only "photo opportunity," as it is called, that the TV people would have ah morning. Except in dire emergencies, all TV film has to be taken before noon, so that it can be processed and transmitted to New York. Consequently, the TV people are the only reporters who are not asleep on their feet in the morning. Few TV correspondents ever join the wee-hour poker games or drinking.

Connie Chung, the pretty Chinese CBS correspondent, occupied the room next to mine at the Hyatt House and she was always back by midnight, reciting a final sixty-second radio spot into her Sony or absorbing one last press release before getting a good night's sleep. So here she was this morning, bright and alert, sticking a mike into McGovern's face and asking him something about black ministers. The print reporters stood around and watched, just in case McGovern should say something interesting. Finally McGovern excused himself and everybody ran for the bus.

> 8:20–8:50 A.M. *En Route / Motorcade*
> 8:50–9:30 A.M. *Taping—"Newsmakers"*
>     *CBS-TV 6121 Sunset Boulevard, Hollywood*
> 9:30–9:55 A.M. *En Route / Motorcade*
> 9:55–10:30 A.M. *Taping—"News Conference"*
>     *NBC-TV 3000 West Alameda Ave., Burbank*
> 10:30–10:50 A.M. *Press filing*
> 10:50–Noon *En Route / Motorcade*
> Noon–1:00 P.M. *Senior Citizens Lunch and Rally*
>     *Bixby Park—Band Shell*
>     *Long Beach*
> 1:00–1:15 P.M. *Press filing*

The reporters began to wake up as they walked into the chilly Studio 22 at CBS. There was a bank of telephones, hastily hooked up on a large work table in the middle of the studio, and six or seven reporters made credit card calls to bureau chiefs and home offices. Dick Stout of *Newsweek* found out he had to file a long story and couldn't go to San Francisco later in the day. Steve Gerstel phoned in his day's schedule to UPI. Connie Chung dictated a few salient quotes from McGovern's breakfast speech to CBS Radio.

A loudspeaker announced that the interview was about to begin, so the reporters sat down on the folding chairs that were clustered around a monitor. They didn't like having to get their news secondhand from TV, but they did enjoy being able to talk back to McGovern without his hearing them. As the program started, several reporters turned on cassette recorders. A local newscaster led off by accusing McGovern of using a slick media campaign.

"Well, I think the documentary on my life is very well done," McGovern answered ingenuously. The press roared with laughter. Suddenly the screen of the monitor went blank—the video tape had broken. The press started to grumble.

"Are they gonna change that first question and make it a toughie?" asked Martin Nolan, the Boston *Globe*'s national political reporter. "If not, I'm gonna wait on the bus." Nolan, a witty man in his middle thirties, had the unshaven, slack-jawed, nuts-to-you-too look of a bartender in a sailors' café. He grew up in Dorchester, a poor section of Boston, and he asked his first tough political question at the age of twelve. "Sister, how do you *know* Dean Acheson's a Communist?" he had challenged a reactionary nun in his parochial school, and the reprimand he received hadn't daunted him from asking wise-acre questions ever since.

The video tape was repaired and the program began again. The interviewer asked McGovern the same first question, but Nolan stayed anyway. Like the others, Nolan had sat through hundreds of press conferences holding in an irrepressible desire to heckle. Now was the big chance and everyone took it.

"Who are your heroes?" the newscaster asked McGovern.

"General Patton!" shouted Jim Naughton of the *Times*.

"Thomas Jefferson and Abraham Lincoln," said McGovern.

"What do you think of the death penalty?" asked the newscaster.

"I'm against the death penalty." There was a long pause. "That is my judgment," McGovern said, and lapsed into a heavy, terminal silence. The press laughed at McGovern's discomfiture.

By the time the interview was over, the press was in a good mood. As they filed back onto the buses, the normal configurations began to form: wire service reporters and TV cameramen in the front, where they could get out fast; small-town daily and big-city daily reporters in the middle seats, hard at work; McGovern staffers in the rear seats, going over plans and chatting. Dick Stout and Jim Naughton held their tape recorders to their ears, like transistor junkies, and culled the best quotes from the TV interview to write in their notebooks. Lou Dombrowski of the Chicago *Tribune*, who looked like a hulking Mafia padrone, typed his Sunday story on the portable Olympia in his lap. The reporters working for morning newspapers would have to begin to write soon, and they were looking over the handouts and their notes for something to write about.

So it went. They went on to another interview in another chilly studio, at NBC. This time the reporters sat in the same studio as McGovern and the interviewer, so there was no laughter, only silent note-taking. After the interview there were phones and typewriters in another room, courtesy of the network. Only a few men used them. Then to Bixby Park for a dull speech to old people and a McGovern-provided box lunch of tiny, rubbery chicken parts. Another filing facility, this one in a dank little dressing room in back of the Bixby Park band shell. While McGovern droned on about senior citizens, about fifteen reporters used the bank of twelve phones that the McGovern press people had ordered Pacific Telephone to install.

At every stop there was a phone bank, but the reporters never rushed for the phones and fought over them as they do in the movies. Most of them worked for morning papers and didn't have to worry about dictating their stories over the phone until around 6 P.M. (Eastern Standard Time).[7] Earlier in the day they just called their editors to map out a story, or called a source to check a fact, or sometimes they called in part of a story, with the first paragraph (the "lead") to follow at the last moment. There was only one type of reporter who dashed for the phones at almost every stop and called in bulletins about almost everything that happened on the schedule. That was the wire service reporter.

## Notes

1. Every day, a "pool" of one or two reporters was delegated to stay close to the candidate at those times (i.e., during motorcades, small dinners, fund-raising parties) when the entire press corps could not follow him. The regular reporters on the bus took turns filling the pool assignments. After each event, the pool wrote a report which was posted in the pressroom, and was usually also Xeroxed by the candidate's press staff and distributed on the bus. According to the rules, the pool reporters were not supposed to include in their own articles any information which they had not put in the pool report. The reports usually dealt in trivia—what the candidate ate, what he said, whose hands he had shaken. Pool reports varied in length. Jim Naughton of the *Times*, the most meticulous pooler on the bus, once turned in a report that went on for eight double-spaced pages. Dick Stout of *Newsweek* wrote the year's shortest report: "Oct. 30, 1972. 5 P.M. to bed. Nothing happened untoward. Details on request."

2. *LA* folded several months later.

3. It applied best to the White House reporters in the Johnson years, many of whom knew all about Johnson's growing isolation and loosening grip on reality, but wrote nothing about it. In 1967, David Halberstam met a China expert in Hong Kong who recounted several fascinating anecdotes about Johnson's increasing lack of control. When Halberstam asked about the source of the stories, the China expert said that he had heard the anecdotes from three top White House correspondents who had recently been in Hong Kong during one of Johnson's trips to Asia. "The White House guys were talking about these things and they were concerned, but they weren't writing about them," says Halberstam. "Because that's a hell of a story to have to write, saying the President of the United States is isolated from reality. They'd have a goddam crazy, angry President the next day."
   They were, however, passing on these anecdotes to the executives on their papers.

4. Most American newspapers—at least 85 percent—are owned by conservative Republicans and regularly endorse Republican candidates. The greatest cross that these owners have to bear is that most reporters are Democrats.

5. *The Effete Conspiracy* by Ben H. Bagdikian (New York, Harper & Row, 1972) p. 75.

6. On the other hand, take the case of Hamilton Davis, the political reporter and Washington Bureau chief of the Providence *Journal*, who was also on the McGovern bus that day. In January 1972 Davis was given a weekly column. As the year went on the column got increasingly ballsy. Davis took well-aimed shots at both the national candidates and the Rhode Island candidates. He was equally critical of both of Rhode Island's Senatorial candidates, Sen. Claiborne Pell and the Republican challenger, John H. Chafee. Only one problem. The Chafee family owned a hunk of the paper. Davis was abruptly informed that the paper's policy was that no reporter should write a column. Davis thought it very strange that the owners had taken eleven months to remember this policy.

7. The reporters who worked for afternoon papers, such as the Washington *Star*, the Philadelphia *Bulletin*, or the Boston *Evening Globe*, had a much rougher schedule. Their deadline was between six and eight in the morning, and they usually wrote their stories late at night, when everyone else was having supper or drinking. Having gone to bed late, they then had to be up to inspect the first handouts and to cover the first event, just in case there was something important to file in the last few minutes before their papers went to bed. If a reporter from a morning paper missed an early morning event, he had the rest of the day to catch up on it.

SECTION V

# Journalism and Society

# INTRODUCTION

**T**HE REASON WHY PEOPLE SHOULD study journalism—its development, its practices, its performance, its people, its institutions and its critics—is because journalism matters. The way news is reported and distributed has a profound effect on shaping society and the way people live together. Since the 1830s, when the Frenchman Alexis de Tocqueville toured America and marveled at the role newspapers played in American civic life, the influence of the media on American society—and similarly with other societies elsewhere—has clearly been the subject of serious and consequential debate.

This section includes selections that explore both the potential and the short-comings of the media's ability to play a vital and constructive role in shaping western society. Most critics, of course, focus on its shortcomings. But when something falls short, it falls short of an aspiration or a goal, and an understanding of the important aims and objectives as originally articulated is critical to conducting an informed discussion. This section includes selections that explore these themes.

In the 1830, Alexis de Tocqueville, a conservative supporter of republicanism in France, toured the United States, ostensibly to study the prison system in a demo-cratic country. Instead, in his report he went into detailed investigation of the primary institutions and cultured habits that served as the foundations for American democ-racy. Interestingly de Tocqueville is upbeat about the potential for newspapers to foster the democratic process. He draws a contrast between the relatively extensive knowledge even the rural population in the United States had about political and civil life compared to the stultifying public life in Europe at the time.

Less than 100 years later Walter Lippmann, who many observers pinpoint as the first great contemporary commentator on the impact of press performance on society, is far less sanguine. He outlines the limitations of journalism and tries to reduce our expectations about the role the press can play in democracy. In his analysis, part of the problem lies with the press itself and part of the problem is with the public.

According to Lippman, a leading writer, editor and columnist (whose career in journalism went from 1913 when he helped found *The New Republic*, a journal of politics and ideas, until the 1960s when he retired as the leading columnist in the United States), the public cannot sustain its attention to the critical issues of the day. When it came to politics, he likened the public to an audience at the theater who arrives late and leaves before the end. Although the press provides the "pictures" that people have in their minds about public affairs, those pictures are incomplete and faulty.

Lippman represents a technocratic vision of a politics that relies heavily on experts to resolve social issues. In this view, many so-called political problems have technical solutions. Writing at the same time, Upton Sinclair's critique of the press takes the opposite point of view. Based on his own experience and the experience of others, he excoriates the mainstream media for slavishly supporting the elite while abandoning its commitment to defending the people and promoting social justice. Sinclair, a socialist, accuses the press of corruption and excluding many voices from the public debate. *The Brass Check* itself served as evidence for his argument. When he could not find a publisher for the book, he published it himself and sold more than 150,000 copies in the first decade.

In the 1960s, Sinclair's critique of the press was echoed and elaborated on by critics such as Edward S. Herman and Noam Chomsky, who argue that given the ownership structure, profit motive, size, dependence on official sources, its vulnerability to organized "propaganda" by lobbying groups, and political pre-disposition towards anti-communism, the news media do little but reinforce the current political structure, that they believe is oppressive. Though *Manufacturing Consent: The Political Economy of the Mass Media*, Herman and Chomsky's best known book, has been vigorously contested in America, it is very popular among critics of the United States around the world.

Judgments on press performance come from all parts of the political spectrum, for they act as a reflection of the central role the press plays in political and social life. The Hutchins Commission, convened after World War II, was one of the more unusual assessments of journalistic performance. Conceptualized by Henry Luce, the founder and owner of Time, Inc., the commission, whose formal name was Commission on the Freedom of the Press, was headed by Robert Hutchins, the president of the University of Chicago, and denigrated by journalists at the time for its failure to include working journalists. Nevertheless, its report has served as an articulate statement of the underlying values of the press in the post World War II era. In many ways, the Hutchins Commission report mirrors de Tocqueville's belief in the potential of journalism as facilitator of social and political discourse.

The post-World War II period also saw the emergence of A. J. Liebling as perhaps the most elegant writer who served as a media critic. A staff writer for *The New Yorker* magazine from 1935 to 1963, Liebling's monthly "The Wayward Press" column was a running commentary on the foibles of primarily the New York based media, frequently skewering the high and mighty with carefully crafted characterizations. His columns combine great insight with fine writing.

American newspapers are not the only target for the analysis of media performance. The French sociologist Pierre Bourdieu's essay *On Television* set off a firestorm when it was first published in 1996. He accuses the media of not living up to its responsibilities to a democratic society by devoting too much attention to spectacles, disasters and human interest stories at the expense of the careful examination of critical issues. Politics is presented as a cynical game with no real acknowledgement of the actual impact it has on the lives of people. According to Bourdieu, television imposes a covert censorship limiting not only public discourse but the public's very vision of reality.

In many ways, since the establishment of democracy in America, one of the fundamental ideals of the press is that it must play a central role in democratic government. The first responsibility of the press is to provide the information and intelligence the public needs to be self-governing. Clearly most critics believe that the media and not just newspapers, fall far short of that goal, but the debate itself demonstrates that the aspiration is still vibrant.

# Chapter 25

# ALEXIS DE TOCQUEVILLE

# DEMOCRACY IN AMERICA

*D*EMOCRACY IN AMERICA IS Alexis de Tocqueville's classic account of the culture of the early Republic. In 1831, de Tocqueville and a colleague, Gustave de Beaumont, were sent by the French government to study the American prison system. They toured the United States for nine months, taking notes on all that they observed about America's culture, its economy, its political systems and its social mores. They included reflections on the role of newspapers in the lives of Americans as well.

De Tocqueville was shocked by the number of periodicals he found. Virtually every community in America had its own periodicals, he noted, and while politically oriented journals either supported or attacked the administration in power, since there were so many of them, the arguments presented both in favor and in opposition to the party in power were diverse and robust. Moreover, de Tocqueville observed, the sheer number of periodicals diffused the power of any single journal.

Nonetheless, according to de Tocqueville, the power of the press was enormous, not only on politics but on taste and morality as well. The power of the press in aggregate, he said, was subordinate only to the power of the people. De Tocqueville's sections on newspapers establish a clear baseline for understanding the relationship of the press to society.

In fact, de Tocqueville's classic is still widely acknowledged to be a meaningful and inspiring interpretative study of a socio-historical phenomenon with modern day relevance. His defense of freedom of the press is particularly important for the understanding of basic principles underwriting the extracts that follow. He asserted that, "I love it more from considering the evils it prevents than on account of the good it does."

He argues that freedom of the press is a necessary consequence of the sovereignty of the people as understood in America. He talks of the difficulty in restricting press freedom, for censorship and sovereignty of the people are incompatible. He stresses the need for pluralistic debate in a similar way to James Carey's argument for "conversation" presented almost 150 years later, "When each man is given a right to rule society, clearly one must recognise his capacity to choose between the different opinions debated among his contemporaries and to appreciate the various facts which may guide his judgement." The sections here look at de Tocqueville's insight into the mechanism of American democracy and the links between voluntary associations, the press and the idea of enlightened self-interest, which de Tocquville saw as the foundation of American political life.

## Origin of the Anglo-Americans, and its Importance in Relation to their Future Condition

After the birth of a human being his early years are obscurely spent in the toils or pleasures of childhood. As he grows up the world receives him, when his manhood begins, and he enters into contact with his fellows. He is then studied for the first time, and it is imagined that the germ of the vices and the virtues of his maturer years is then formed. This, if I am not mistaken, is a great error. We must begin higher up; we must watch the infant in its mother's arms; we must see the first images which the external world casts upon the dark mirror of his mind; the first occurrences which he witnesses; we must hear the first words which awaken the sleeping powers of thought, and stand by his earliest efforts, if we would understand the prejudices, the habits, and the passions which will rule his life. The entire man is, so to speak, to be seen in the cradle of the child.

The growth of nations presents something analogous to this: they all bear some marks of their origin; and the circumstances which accompanied their birth and contributed to their rise affect the whole term of their being. If we were able to go back to the elements of states, and to examine the oldest monuments of their history, I doubt not that we should discover the primal cause of the prejudices, the habits, the ruling passions, and, in short, of all that constitutes what is called the national character; we should then find the explanation of certain customs which now seem at variance with the prevailing manners; of such laws as conflict with established principles; and of such incoherent opinions as are here and there to be met with in society, like those fragments of broken chains which we sometimes see hanging from the vault of an edifice, and supporting nothing. This might explain the destinies of certain nations, which seem borne on by an unknown force to ends of which they themselves are ignorant. But hitherto facts have been wanting to researches of this kind: the spirit of inquiry has only come upon communities in their latter days; and when they at length contemplated their origin, time had already obscured it, or ignorance and pride adorned it with truth-concealing fables.

America is the only country in which it has been possible to witness the natural and tranquil growth of society, and where the influence exercised on the future condition of states by their origin is clearly distinguishable. At the period when the peoples of Europe landed in the New World their national characteristics were already completely formed; each of them had a physiognomy of its own; and as they had already attained that stage of civilization at which men are led to study themselves, they have transmitted to us a faithful picture of their opinions, their manners, and their laws. The men of the sixteenth century are almost as well known to us as our contemporaries. America, consequently, exhibits in the broad light of day the phenomena which the ignorance or rudeness of earlier ages conceal from our researches. Near enough to the time when the states of America were founded, to be accurately acquainted with their elements, and sufficiently removed from that period to judge of some of their results, the men of our own day seem destined to see further than their predecessors into the series of human events. Providence has given us a torch which our forefathers did not possess, and has allowed us to discern fundamental causes in the history of the world which the obscurity of the past concealed from them. If we carefully examine the social and political state of America, after having studied its history, we shall remain perfectly convinced that not an opinion, not a custom, not a law, I may even say not an event, is upon record which the origin of that people will not explain. The readers of this book will find the germ of all that is to follow in the present chapter, and the key to almost the whole work.

The emigrants who came, at different periods to occupy the territory now covered by the American Union differed from each other in many respects; their aim was not the same, and they governed themselves on different principles. These men had, however, certain features in common, and they were all placed in an analogous situation. The tie of language is perhaps the strongest and the most durable that can unite mankind. All the emigrants spoke the same tongue; they were all offsets from the same people. Born in a country which had been agitated for centuries by the struggles of faction, and in which all parties had been obliged in their turn to place themselves under the protection of the laws, their political education had been perfected in this rude school, and they were more conversant with the notions of right and the principles of true freedom than the greater part of their European contemporaries. At the period of their first emigrations the parish system, that fruitful germ of free institutions, was deeply rooted in the habits of the English; and with it the doctrine of the sovereignty of the people had been introduced into the bosom of the monarchy of the House of Tudor.

[. . .]

The remarks I have made will suffice to display the character of Anglo-American civilization in its true light. It is the result (and this should be constantly present to the mind of two distinct elements), which in other places have been in frequent hostility, but which in America have been admirably incorporated and combined with one another. I allude to the spirit of Religion and the spirit of Liberty.

The settlers of New England were at the same time ardent sectarians and daring innovators. Narrow as the limits of some of their religious opinions were, they were entirely free from political prejudices. Hence arose two tendencies, distinct but not opposite, which are constantly discernible in the manners as well as in the laws of the country.

It might be imagined that men who sacrificed their friends, their family, and their native land to a religious conviction were absorbed in the pursuit of the intellectual advantages which they purchased at so dear a rate. The energy, however, with which they strove for the acquirement of wealth, moral enjoyment, and the comforts as well as liberties of the world, is scarcely inferior to that with which they devoted themselves to Heaven.

Political principles and all human laws and institutions were moulded and altered at their pleasure; the barriers of the society in which they were born were broken down before them; the old principles which had governed the world for ages were no more; a path without a turn and a field without an horizon were opened to the exploring and ardent curiosity of man: but at the limits of the political world he checks his researches, he discreetly lays aside the use of his most formidable faculties, he no longer consents to doubt or to innovate, but carefully abstaining from raising the curtain of the sanctuary, he yields with submissive respect to truths which he will not discuss. Thus, in the moral world everything is classed, adapted, decided, and foreseen; in the political world everything is agitated, uncertain, and disputed: in the one is a passive, though a voluntary, obedience; in the other an independence scornful of experience and jealous of authority.

These two tendencies, apparently so discrepant, are far from conflicting; they advance together, and mutually support each other.

[. . .]

## The Principle of the Sovereignty of the People in America

Whenever the political laws of the United States are to be discussed, it is with the doctrine of the sovereignty of the people that we must begin. The principle of the sovereignty of the people, which is to be found, more or less, at the bottom of almost all human institutions, generally remains concealed from view. It is obeyed without being recognized, or if for a moment it be brought to light, it is hastily cast back into the gloom of the sanctuary. "The will of the nation" is one of those expressions which have been most profusely abused by the wily and the despotic of every age. To the eyes of some it has been represented by the venal suffrages of a few of the satellites of power; to others by the votes of a timid or an interested minority; and some have even discovered it in the silence of a people, on the supposition that the fact of submission established the right of command.

In America the principle of the sovereignty of the people is not either barren or concealed, as it is with some other nations; it is recognized by the customs and proclaimed by the laws; it spreads freely, and arrives without impediment at its most remote consequences. If there be a country in the world where the doctrine of the sovereignty of the people can be fairly appreciated, where it can be studied in its application to the affairs of society, and where its dangers and its advantages may be foreseen, that country is assuredly America.

I have already observed that, from their origin, the sovereignty of the people was the fundamental principle of the greater number of British colonies in America. It was far, however, from then exercising as much influence on the government of society as it now does. Two obstacles, the one external, the other internal, checked its invasive progress. It could not ostensibly disclose itself in the laws of colonies which were still constrained to obey the mother-country: it was therefore obliged to spread secretly, and to gain ground in the provincial assemblies, and especially in the townships.

American society was not yet prepared to adopt it with all its consequences. The intelligence of New England, and the wealth of the country to the south of the Hudson (as I have shown in the preceding chapter), long exercised a sort of aristocratic influence, which tended to retain the exercise of social authority in the hands of a few. The public functionaries were not universally elected, and the citizens were not all of them electors. The electoral franchise was everywhere placed within certain limits, and made dependent on a certain qualification, which was exceedingly low in the North and more considerable in the South.

The American revolution broke out, and the doctrine of the sovereignty of the people, which had been nurtured in the townships and municipalities, took possession of the State: every class was enlisted in its cause; battles were fought, and victories obtained for it, until it became the law of laws.

A no less rapid change was effected in the interior of society, where the law of descent completed the abolition of local influences.

At the very time when this consequence of the laws and of the revolution was apparent to every eye, victory was irrevocably pronounced in favor of the democratic cause. All power was, in fact, in its hands, and resistance was no longer possible. The higher orders submitted without a murmur and without a struggle to an evil which was thenceforth inevitable. The ordinary fate of falling powers awaited them; each of their several members followed his own interests; and as it was impossible to wring the power from the hands of a people which they did not detest sufficiently to brave, their only aim was to secure its good-will at any price. The most democratic laws were consequently voted by the very men whose interests they impaired; and thus, although the higher classes did not excite the passions of the people against their order, they accelerated the triumph of the new state of things; so that by a singular change the democratic impulse was found to be most irresistible in the very States where the aristocracy had the firmest hold. The State of Maryland, which had been founded by men of rank, was the first to proclaim universal suffrage, and to introduce the most democratic forms into the conduct of its government.

When a nation modifies the elective qualification, it may easily be foreseen that sooner or later that qualification will be entirely abolished. There is no more invariable rule in the history of society: the further electoral rights are extended, the greater is the need of extending them; for after each concession the strength of the democracy increases, and its demands increase with its strength. The ambition of those who are below the appointed rate is irritated in exact proportion to the great number of those who are above it. The exception at last becomes the rule, concession follows concession, and no stop can be made short of universal suffrage.

At the present day the principle of the sovereignty of the people has acquired, in the United States, all the practical development which the imagination can conceive. It is unencumbered by those fictions which have been thrown over it in other countries, and it appears in every possible form according to the exigency of the occasion. Sometimes the laws are made by the people in a body, as at Athens; and sometimes its representatives, chosen by universal suffrage, transact business in its name, and almost under its immediate control.

In some countries a power exists which, though it is in a degree foreign to the social body, directs it, and forces it to pursue a certain track. In others the ruling force is divided, being partly within and partly without the ranks of the people. But nothing of the kind is to be seen in the United States; there society governs itself for itself. All power centres in its bosom; and scarcely an individual is to be met with who would venture to conceive, or, still less, to express, the idea of seeking it elsewhere. The nation participates in the making of its laws by the choice of its legislators, and in the execution of them by the choice of the agents of the executive government; it may almost be said to govern itself, so feeble and so restricted is the share left to the administration, so little do the authorities forget their popular origin and the power from which they emanate.

[. . .]

## Of the Relation between Public Associations and Newspapers

When men are no longer united amongst themselves by firm and lasting ties, it is impossible to obtain the cooperation of any great number of them, unless you can persuade every man whose concurrence you require that this private interest obliges him voluntarily to unite his exertions to the exertions of all the rest. This can only be habitually and conveniently effected by means of a newspaper; nothing but a newspaper can drop the same thought into a thousand minds at the same moment. A newspaper is an adviser who does not require to be sought, but who comes of his own accord, and talks to you briefly every day of the common weal, without distracting you from your private affairs.

Newspapers therefore become more necessary in proportion as men become more equal, and individualism more to be feared. To suppose that they only serve to protect freedom would be to diminish their importance: they maintain civilization. I shall not deny that in democratic countries newspapers frequently lead the citizens to launch together in very ill-digested schemes; but if there were no newspapers there would be no common activity. The evil which they produce is therefore much less than that which they cure.

The effect of a newspaper is not only to suggest the same purpose to a great number of persons, but also to furnish means for executing in common the designs which they may have singly conceived. The principal citizens who inhabit an aristocratic country discern each other from afar; and if they wish to unite their forces, they move towards each other, drawing a multitude of men after them. It frequently happens, on the contrary, in democratic countries, that a great number of men who wish or who want to combine cannot accomplish it, because as they are very insignificant and lost amidst the crowd, they cannot see, and know not where to find, one another. A newspaper then takes up the notion or the feeling which had occurred simultaneously, but singly, to each of them. All are then immediately guided towards this beacon; and these wandering minds, which had long sought each other in darkness, at length meet and unite.

The newspaper brought them together, and the newspaper is still necessary to keep them united. In order that an association amongst a democratic people should have any power, it must be a numerous body. The persons of whom it is composed are therefore scattered over a wide extent, and each of them is detained in the place of his domicile by the narrowness of his income, or by the small unremitting exertions by which he earns it. Means then must be found to converse every day without seeing each other, and to take steps in common without having met. Thus hardly any democratic association can do without newspapers. There is consequently a necessary connection between public associations and newspapers: newspapers make associations, and associations make newspapers; and if it has been correctly advanced that associations will increase in number as the conditions of men become more equal, it is not less certain that the number of newspapers increases in proportion to that of associations. Thus it is in America that we find at the same time the greatest number of associations and of newspapers.

This connection between the number of newspapers and that of associations leads us to the discovery of a further connection between the state of the periodical press and the form of the administration in a country; and shows that the number of newspapers must diminish or increase amongst a democratic people, in proportion as its administration is more or less centralized. For amongst democratic nations the exercise of local powers cannot be entrusted to the principal members of the community as in aristocracies. Those powers must either be abolished, or placed in the hands of very large numbers of men, who then in fact constitute an association permanently established by law for the purpose of administering the affairs of a certain extent of territory; and they require a journal, to bring to them every day, in the midst of their own minor concerns, some intelligence of the state of their public weal. The more numerous local powers are, the greater is the number of men in whom they are vested by law; and as this want is hourly felt, the more profusely do newspapers abound.

The extraordinary subdivision of administrative power has much more to do with the enormous number of American newspapers than the great political freedom of the country and the absolute liberty of the press. If all the inhabitants of the Union had the suffrage—but a suffrage which should only extend to the choice of their legislators in Congress—they would require but few newspapers, because they would only have to act together on a few very important but very rare occasions. But within the pale of the great association of the nation, lesser associations have been established by law in every country, every city, and indeed in every village, for the purposes of local administration. The laws of the country thus compel every American to co-operate every day of his life with some of his fellow-citizens for a common purpose, and each one of them requires a newspaper to inform him what all the others are doing.

I am of opinion that a democratic people, without any national representative assemblies, but with a great number of small local powers, would have in the end more newspapers than another people governed by a centralized administration and an elective legislation. What best explains to me the enormous circulation of the daily press in the United States, is that amongst the Americans I find the utmost national freedom combined with local freedom of every kind. There is a prevailing opinion in France and England that the circulation of newspapers would be indefinitely increased by removing the taxes which have been laid upon the press. This is a very exaggerated estimate of the effects of such a reform. Newspapers increase in numbers, not according to their cheapness, but according to the more or less frequent want which a great number of men may feel for intercommunication and combination.

[. . .]

## Connection of Civil and Political Associations

There is only one country on the face of the earth where the citizens enjoy unlimited freedom of association for political purposes. This same country is the only one in the world where the continual exercise of the right of association has been introduced into civil life, and where all the advantages which civilization can confer are procured by means of it. In all the countries where political associations are prohibited, civil associations are rare. It is hardly probable that this is the result of accident; but the inference should rather be, that there is a natural, and perhaps a necessary, connection between these two kinds of associations. Certain men happen to have a common interest in some concern—either a commercial undertaking is to be managed, or some speculation in manufactures to be tried; they meet, they combine, and thus by degrees they become familiar with the principle of association. The greater is the multiplicity of small affairs, the more do men, even without knowing it, acquire facility in prosecuting great undertakings in common. Civil associations, therefore, facilitate political association: but, on the other hand, political association singularly strengthens and improves associations for civil purposes. In civil life every man may, strictly speaking, fancy that he can provide for his own wants; in politics, he can fancy no such thing. When a people, then, have any knowledge of public life, the notion of association, and the wish to coalesce, present themselves every day to the minds of the whole community: whatever natural repugnance may restrain men from acting in concert, they will always be ready to combine for the sake of a party. Thus political life makes the love and practice of association more general; it imparts a desire of union, and teaches the means of combination to numbers of men who would have always lived apart.

Politics not only give birth to numerous associations, but to associations of great extent. In civil life it seldom happens that any one interest draws a very large number of men to act in concert; much skill is required to bring such an interest into existence: but in politics opportunities present themselves every day. Now it is solely in great associations that the general value of the principle of association is displayed. Citizens who are individually powerless, do not very clearly anticipate the strength which they may acquire by uniting together; it must be shown to them in order to be understood. Hence it is often easier to collect a multitude for a public purpose than a few persons; a thousand citizens do not see what interest they have in combining together—ten thousand will be perfectly aware of it. In politics men combine for great undertakings; and the use they make of the principle of association in important affairs practically teaches them that it is their interest to help each other in those of less moment. A political association draws a number of individuals at the same time out of their own circle: however they may be naturally kept asunder by age, mind, and fortune, it places them nearer together and brings them into contact. Once met, they can always meet again.

Men can embark in few civil partnerships without risking a portion of their possessions; this is the case with all manufacturing and trading companies. When men are as yet but little versed in the art of association, and are unacquainted with its principal rules, they are afraid, when first they combine in this manner, of buying their experience dear. They therefore prefer depriving themselves of a powerful instrument of success to running the risks which attend the use of it. They are, however, less reluctant to join political associations, which appear to them to be without danger, because they adventure no money in them. But they cannot belong to these associations for any length of time without finding out how order is maintained amongst a large number of men, and by what contrivance they are made to advance, harmoniously and methodically, to the same object. Thus they learn to surrender their own will to that of all the rest, and to make their own exertions subordinate to the common impulse—things which it is not less necessary to know in civil than in political associations. Political associations may therefore be considered as large free schools, where all the members of the community go to learn the general theory of association.

But even if political association did not directly contribute to the progress of civil association, to destroy the former would be to impair the latter. When citizens can only meet in public for certain purposes, they regard such meetings as a strange proceeding of rare occurrence, and they rarely think at all about it. When they are allowed to meet freely for all purposes, they ultimately look upon public association as the universal, or in a manner the sole means, which men can employ to accomplish the different purposes they may have in view. Every new want instantly revives the notion. The art of association then becomes, as I have said before, the mother of action, studied and applied by all.

When some kinds of associations are prohibited and others allowed, it is difficult to distinguish the former from the latter, beforehand. In this state of doubt men abstain from them altogether, and a sort of public opinion passes current which tends to cause any association whatsoever to be regarded as a bold and almost an illicit enterprise.

It is therefore chimerical to suppose that the spirit of association, when it is repressed on some one point, will nevertheless display the same vigor on all others; and that if men be allowed to prosecute certain undertakings in common, that is quite enough for them eagerly to set about them. When the members of a community are allowed and accustomed to combine for all purposes, they will combine as readily for the lesser as for the more important ones; but if they are only allowed to combine for small affairs, they will be neither inclined nor able to effect it. It is in vain that you will leave them entirely free to prosecute their business on joint-stock account: they will hardly care to avail themselves of the rights you have granted to them; and, after having exhausted your strength in vain efforts to put down prohibited associations, you will be surprised that you cannot persuade men to form the associations you encourage.

I do not say that there can be no civil associations in a country where political association is prohibited; for men can never live in society without embarking in some common undertakings: but I maintain that in such a country civil associations will always be few in number, feebly planned, unskillfully managed, that they will never form any vast designs, or that they will fail in the execution of them.

This naturally leads me to think that freedom of association in political matters is not so dangerous to public tranquillity as is supposed; and that possibly, after having agitated society for some time, it may strengthen the State in the end. In democratic countries political associations are, so to speak, the only powerful persons who aspire to rule the State. Accordingly, the governments of our time look upon associations of this kind just as sovereigns in the Middle Ages regarded the great vassals of the Crown: they entertain a sort of instinctive abhorrence of them, and they combat them on all occasions. They bear, on the contrary, a natural goodwill to civil associations, because they readily discover that, instead of directing the minds of the community to public affairs, these institutions serve to divert them from such reflections; and that, by engaging them more and more in the pursuit of objects which cannot be attained without public tranquillity, they deter them from revolutions. But these governments do not attend to the fact that political associations tend amazingly to multiply and facilitate those of a civil character, and that in avoiding a dangerous evil they deprive themselves of an efficacious remedy.

When you see the Americans freely and constantly forming associations for the purpose of promoting some political principle, of raising one man to the head of affairs, or of wresting power from another, you have some difficulty in understanding that men so independent do not constantly fall into the abuse of freedom. If, on the other hand, you survey the infinite number of trading companies which are in operation in the United States, and perceive that the Americans are on every side unceasingly engaged in the execution of important and difficult plans, which the slightest revolution would throw into confusion, you will readily comprehend why people so well employed are by no means tempted to perturb the State, nor to destroy that public tranquillity by which they all profit.

Is it enough to observe these things separately, or should we not discover the hidden tie which connects them? In their political associations, the Americans of all conditions, minds, and ages, daily acquire a general taste for association, and grow accustomed to the use of it. There they meet together in large numbers, they converse, they listen to each other, and they are mutually stimulated to all sorts of undertakings. They afterwards transfer to civil life the notions they have thus acquired, and make them subservient to a thousand purposes. Thus it is by the enjoyment of a dangerous freedom that the Americans learn the art of rendering the dangers of freedom less formidable.

If a certain moment in the existence of a nation be selected, it is easy to prove that political associations perturb the State, and paralyze productive industry; but take the whole life of a people, and it may perhaps be easy to demonstrate that freedom of association in political matters is favorable to the prosperity and even to the tranquillity of the community.

I said in the former part of this work, "The unrestrained liberty of political association cannot be entirely assimilated to the liberty of the press. The one is at the same time less necessary and more dangerous than the other. A nation may confine it within certain limits without ceasing to be mistress of itself; and it may sometimes be obliged to do so in order to maintain its own authority." And further on I added: "It cannot be denied that the unrestrained liberty of association for political purposes is the last degree of liberty which a people is fit for. If it does not throw them into anarchy, it perpetually brings them, as it were, to the verge of it." Thus I do not think that a nation is always at liberty to invest its citizens with an absolute right of association for political purposes; and I doubt whether, in any country or in any age, it be wise to set no limits to freedom of association. A certain nation, it is said, could not maintain tranquillity in the community, cause the laws to be respected, or establish a lasting government, if the right of association were not confined within narrow limits. These blessings are doubtless invaluable, and I can imagine that, to acquire or to preserve them, a nation may impose upon itself severe temporary restrictions: but still it is well that the nation should know at what price these blessings are purchased. I can understand that it may be advisable to cut off a man's arm in order to save his life; but it would be ridiculous to assert that he will be as dexterous as he was before he lost it.

## The Americans Combat Individualism by the Principle of Interest Rightly Understood

When the world was managed by a few rich and powerful individuals, these persons loved to entertain a lofty idea of the duties of man. They were fond of professing that it is praiseworthy to forget one's self, and that good should be done without hope of reward, as it is by the Deity himself. Such were the standard opinions of that time in morals. I doubt whether men were more virtuous in aristocratic ages than in others; but they were incessantly talking of the beauties of virtue, and its utility was only studied in secret. But since the imagination takes less lofty flights and every man's thoughts are centred in himself, moralists are alarmed by this idea of self-sacrifice, and they no longer venture to present it to the human mind. They therefore content themselves with inquiring whether the personal advantage of each member of the community does not consist in working for the good of all; and when they have hit upon some point on which private interest and public interest meet and amalgamate, they are eager to bring it into notice. Observations of this kind are gradually multiplied: what was only a single remark becomes a general principle; and it is held as a truth that man serves himself in serving his fellow-creatures, and that his private interest is to do good.

I have already shown, in several parts of this work, by what means the inhabitants of the United States almost always manage to combine their own advantage with that of their fellow-citizens: my present purpose is to point out the general rule which enables them to do so. In the United States hardly anybody talks of the beauty of virtue; but they maintain that virtue is useful, and prove it every day. The American moralists do not profess that men ought to sacrifice themselves for their fellow-creatures because it is noble to make such sacrifices; but they boldly aver that such sacrifices are as necessary to him who imposes them upon himself as to him for whose sake they are made. They have found out that in their country and their age man is brought home to himself by an irresistible force; and losing all hope of stopping that force, they turn all their thoughts to the direction of it. They therefore do not deny that every man may follow his own interest; but they endeavor to prove that it is the interest of every man to be virtuous. I shall not here enter into the reasons they allege, which would divert me from my subject: suffice it to say that they have convinced their fellow-countrymen.

Montaigne said long ago: "Were I not to follow the straight road for its straightness, I should follow it for having found by experience that in the end it is commonly the happiest and most useful track." The doctrine of interest rightly understood is not, then, new, but amongst the Americans of our time it finds universal acceptance: it has become popular there; you may trace it at the bottom of all their actions, you will remark it in all they say. It is as often to be met with on the lips of the poor man as of the rich. In Europe the principle of interest is much grosser than it is in America, but at the same time it is less common, and especially it is less avowed; amongst us, men still constantly feign great abnegation which they no longer feel. The Americans, on the contrary, are fond of explaining almost all the actions of their lives by the principle of interest rightly understood; they show with complacency how an enlightened regard for themselves constantly prompts them to assist each other, and inclines them willingly to sacrifice a portion of their time and property to the welfare of the State. In this respect I think they frequently fail to do themselves justice; for in the United States, as well as elsewhere, people are sometimes seen to give way to those disinterested and spontaneous impulses which are natural to man; but the Americans seldom allow that they yield to emotions of this kind; they are more anxious to do honor to their philosophy than to themselves.

I might here pause, without attempting to pass a judgment on what I have described. The extreme difficulty of the subject would be my excuse, but I shall not avail myself of it; and I had rather that my readers, clearly perceiving my object, should refuse to follow me than that I should leave them in suspense. The principle of interest rightly understood is not a lofty one, but it is clear and sure. It does not aim at mighty objects, but it attains without excessive exertion all those at which it aims. As it lies within the reach of all capacities, everyone can without difficulty apprehend and retain it. By its admirable conformity to human weaknesses, it easily obtains great dominion; nor is that dominion precarious, since the principle checks one personal interest by another, and uses, to direct the passions, the very same instrument which excites them. The principle of interest rightly understood produces no great acts of self-sacrifice, but it suggests daily small acts of self-denial. By itself it cannot suffice to make a man virtuous, but it disciplines a number of citizens in habits of regularity, temperance, moderation, foresight, self-command; and, if it does not lead men straight to virtue by the will, it gradually draws them in that direction by their habits. If the principle of interest rightly understood were to sway the whole moral world, extraordinary virtues would doubtless be more rare; but I think that gross depravity would then also be less common. The principle of interest rightly understood perhaps prevents some men from rising far above the level of mankind; but a great number of other men, who were falling far below it, are caught and restrained by it. Observe some few individuals, they are lowered by it; survey mankind, it is raised. I am not afraid to say that the principle of interest, rightly understood, appears to me the best suited of all philosophical theories to the wants of the men of our time, and that I regard it as their chief remaining security against themselves. Towards it, therefore, the minds of the moralists of our age should turn; even should they judge it to be incomplete, it must nevertheless be adopted as necessary.

I do not think upon the whole that there is more egotism amongst us than in America; the only difference is, that there it is enlightened—here it is not. Every American will sacrifice a portion of his private interests to preserve the rest; we would fain preserve the whole, and oftentimes the whole is lost. Everybody I see about me seems bent on teaching his contemporaries, by precept and example, that what is useful is never wrong. Will nobody undertake to make them understand how what is right may be useful? No power upon earth can prevent the increasing equality of conditions from inclining the human mind to seek out what is useful, or from leading every member of the community to be wrapped up in himself. It must therefore be expected that personal interest will become more than ever the principal, if not the sole, spring of men's actions; but it remains to be seen how each man will understand his personal interest. If the members of a community, as they become more equal, become more ignorant and coarse, it is difficult to foresee to what pitch of stupid excesses their egotism may lead them; and no one can foretell into what disgrace and wretchedness they would plunge themselves, lest they should have to sacrifice something of their own well-being to the prosperity of their fellow-creatures. I do not think that the system of interest, as it is professed in America, is, in all its parts, self-evident; but it contains a great number of truths so evident that men, if they are but educated, cannot fail to see them. Educate, then, at any rate; for the age of implicit self-sacrifice and instinctive virtues is already flitting far away from us, and the time is fast approaching when freedom, public peace, and social order itself will not be able to exist without education.

# Chapter 26

# WALTER LIPPMANN

# PUBLIC OPINION

WALTER LIPPMANN WAS THE QUINTESSENTIAL public intellectual of his age as well as a leading journalist in the 1920s through the 1960s. He was a co-founder of *The New Republic* and then an editorial writer and editor of *The New York World*, the newspaper brought to prominence by Joseph Pulitzer in the 1880s. When the *World* folded, he moved to the *New York Herald Tribune*, where his syndicated column "Today and Tomorrow" appeared for the next 30 years.

Lippmann wrote *Public Opinion* in 1922. In it, he noted that people no longer experience the world directly but have images in their minds created in part by the mass media. Since their political decisions are based on those images, how can people be sure that those images have not been distorted by special interests? And if those images have been distorted, how can the "common will" or "public opinion" needed to govern in a democracy be formed?

Of course, in countries with democratic forms of government, the press is supposed to inform the people about what they need to know to make sound political judgments. Yet Lippmann saw several major problems with the actual, as opposed to the theoretical, role of the press in democracy. First, people are primarily interested in themselves and the press is more than willing to feed into that self-interest. Secondly, people do not follow politics very closely, coming into political debates well after they have started and often leaving before they are resolved. Third, newspapers, that were the dominant mass medium of the time, were also businesses doing what was necessary to protect their bottom lines. At the end of the day, most people were easily misled and followed a herd mentality. In short, in *Public Opinion*, Lippmann expressed little faith in journalism as a potential agent of democracy.

In this selection, Lippmann describes the role and limitations of the press in public life.

## The Nature of News

**1**

All the reporters in the world working all the hours of the day could not witness all the happenings in the world. There are not a great many reporters. And none of them has the power to be in more than one place at a time. Reporters are not clairvoyant, they do not gaze into a crystal ball and see the world at will, they are not assisted by thought-transference. Yet the range of subjects these comparatively few men manage to cover would be a miracle indeed, if it were not a standardized routine.

Newspapers do not try to keep an eye on all mankind.[1] They have watchers stationed at certain places, like Police Headquarters, the Coroner's Office, the County Clerk's Office, City Hall, the White House, the Senate, House of Representatives, and so forth. They watch, or rather in the majority of cases they belong to associations which employ men who watch "a comparatively small number of places where it is made known when the life of anyone . . . departs from ordinary paths, or when events worth telling about occur. For example, John Smith, let it be supposed, becomes a broker. For ten years he pursues the even tenor of his way and except for his customers and his friends no one gives him a thought. To the newspapers he is as if he were not. But in the eleventh year he suffers heavy losses and, at last, his resources all gone, summons his lawyer and arranges for the making of an assignment. The lawyer posts off to the County Clerk's office, and a clerk there makes the necessary entries in the official docket. Here in step the newspapers. While the clerk is writing Smith's business obituary a reporter glances over his shoulder and a few minutes later the reporters know Smith's troubles and are as well informed concerning his business status as they would be had they kept a reporter at his door every day for over ten years."[2]

When Mr. Given says that the newspapers know "Smith's troubles" and "his business status," he does not mean that they know them as Smith knows them, or as Mr. Arnold Bennett would know them if he had made Smith the hero of a three volume novel. The newspapers know only "in a few minutes" the bald facts which are recorded in the County Clerk's Office. That overt act "uncovers" the news about Smith. Whether the news will be followed up or not is another matter. The point is that before a series of events become news they have usually to make themselves noticeable in some more or less overt act. Generally too, in a crudely overt act. Smith's friends may have known for years that he was taking risks, rumors may even have reached the financial editor if Smith's friends were talkative. But apart from the fact that none of this could be published because it would be libel, there is in these rumors nothing definite on which to peg a story. Something definite must occur that has unmistakable form. It may be the act of going into bankruptcy, it may be a fire, a collision, an assault, a riot, an arrest, a denunciation, the introduction of a bill, a speech, a vote, a meeting, the expressed opinion of a well known citizen, an editorial in a newspaper, a sale, a wage-schedule, a price change, the proposal to build a bridge. . . . There must be a manifestation. The course of events must assume a certain definable shape, and until it is in a phase where some aspect is an accomplished fact, news does not separate itself from the ocean of possible truth.

**2**

Naturally there is room for wide difference of opinion as to when events have a shape that can be reported. A good journalist will find news oftener than a hack. If he sees a building with a dangerous list, he does not have to wait until it falls into the street in order to recognize news. It was a great reporter who guessed the name of the next Indian Viceroy when he heard that Lord So-and-So was inquiring about climates. There are lucky shots but the number of men who can make them is small. Usually it is the stereotyped shape assumed by an event at an obvious place that uncovers the run of the news. The most obvious place is where people's affairs touch public authority. De minimis non curat lex. It is at these places that marriages, births, deaths, contracts, failures, arrivals, departures, lawsuits, disorders, epidemics and calamities are made known.

In the first instance, therefore, the news is not a minor of social conditions, but the report of an aspect that has obtruded itself. The news does not tell you how the seed is germinating in the ground, but it may tell you when the first sprout breaks through the surface. It may even tell you what somebody says is happening to the seed under ground. It may tell you that the sprout did not come up at the time it was expected. The more points, then, at which any happening can be fixed, objectified, measured, named, the more points there are at which news can occur.

So, if some day a legislature, having exhausted all other ways of improving mankind, should forbid the scoring of baseball games, it might still be possible to play some sort of game in which the umpire decided according to his own sense of fair play how long the game should last, when each team should go to bat, and who should be regarded as the winner. If that game were reported in the newspapers it would consist of a record of the umpire's decisions, plus the reporter's impression of the hoots and cheers of the crowd, plus at best a vague account of how certain men, who had no specified position on the field moved around for a few hours on an unmarked piece of sod. The more you try to imagine the logic of so absurd a predicament, the more clear it becomes that for the purposes of newsgathering, (let alone the purposes of playing the game) it is impossible to do much without an apparatus and rules for naming, scoring, recording. Because that machinery is far from perfect, the umpire's life is often a distracted one. Many crucial plays he has to judge by eye. The last vestige of dispute could be taken out of the game, as it has been taken out of chess when people obey the rules, if somebody thought it worth his while to photograph every play. It was the moving pictures which finally settled a real doubt in many reporters' minds, owing to the slowness of the human eye, as to just what blow of Dempsey's knocked out Carpentier.

Wherever there is a good machinery of record, the modern news service works with great precision. There is one on the stock exchange, and the news of price movements is flashed over tickers with dependable accuracy. There is a machinery for election returns, and when the counting and tabulating are well done, the result of a national election is usually known on the night of the election. In civilized communities deaths, births, marriages and divorces are recorded, and are known accurately except where there is concealment or neglect. The machinery exists for some, and only some, aspects of industry and government, in varying degrees of precision for securities, money and staples, bank clearances, realty transactions, wage scales. It exists for imports and exports because they pass through a custom house and can be directly recorded. It exists in nothing like the same degree for internal trade, and especially for trade over the counter.

It will be found, I think, that there is a very direct relation between the certainty of news and the system of record. If you call to mind the topics which form the principal indictment by reformers against the press, you find they are subjects in which the newspaper occupies the position of the umpire in the unscored baseball game. All news about states of mind is of this character: so are all descriptions of personalities, of sincerity, aspiration, motive, intention, of mass feeling, of national feeling, of public opinion, the policies of foreign governments. So is much news about what is going to happen. So are questions turning on private profit, private income, wages, working conditions, the efficiency of labor, educational opportunity, unemployment,[3] monotony, health, discrimination, unfairness, restraint of trade, waste, "backward peoples," conservatism, imperialism, radicalism, liberty, honor, righteousness. All involve data that are at best spasmodically recorded. The data may be hidden because of a censorship or a tradition of privacy, they may not exist because nobody thinks record important, because he thinks it red tape, or because nobody has yet invented an objective system of measurement. Then the news on these subjects is bound to be debatable, when it is not wholly neglected. The events which are not scored are reported either as personal and conventional opinions, or they are not news. They do not take shape until somebody protests, or somebody investigates, or somebody publicly, in the etymological meaning of the word, makes an *issue* of them.

This is the underlying reason for the existence of the press agent. The enormous discretion as to what facts and what impressions shall be reported is steadily convincing every organized group of people that whether it wishes to secure publicity or to avoid it, the exercise of discretion cannot be left to the reporter. It is safer to hire a press agent who stands between the group and the newspapers. Having hired him, the temptation to exploit his strategic position is very great. "Shortly before the war," says Mr. Frank Cobb, "the newspapers of New York took a census of the press agents who were regularly employed and regularly accredited and found that there were about twelve hundred of them. How many there are now (1919) I do not pretend to know, but what I do know is that many of the direct channels to news have been closed and the information for the public is first filtered through publicity agents. The great corporations have them, the banks have them, the railroads have them, all the organizations of business and of social and political activity have them, and they are the media through which news comes. Even statesmen have them."[4]

Were reporting the simple recovery of obvious facts, the press agent would be little more than a clerk. But since, in respect to most of the big topics of news, the facts are not simple, and not at all obvious, but subject to choice and opinion, it is natural that everyone should wish to make his own choice of facts for the newspapers to print. The publicity man does that. And in doing it, he certainly saves the reporter much trouble, by presenting him a clear picture of a situation out of which he might otherwise make neither head nor tail. But it follows that the picture which the publicity man makes for the reporter is the one he wishes the public to see. He is censor and propagandist, responsible only to his employers, and to the whole truth responsible only as it accords with the employers' conception of his own interests.

The development of the publicity man is a clear sign that the facts of modern life do not spontaneously take a shape in which they can be known. They must be given a shape by somebody, and since in the daily routine reporters cannot give a shape to facts, and since there is little disinterested organization of intelligence, the need for some formulation is being met by the interested parties.

## 3

The good press agent understands that the virtues of his cause are not news, unless they are such strange virtues that they jut right out of the routine of life. This is not because the newspapers do not like virtue, but because it is not worthwhile to say that nothing has happened when nobody expected anything to happen. So if the publicity man wishes free publicity he has, speaking quite accurately, to start something. He arranges a stunt: obstructs the traffic, teases the police, somehow manages to entangle his client or his cause with an event that is already news. The suffragists knew this, did not particularly enjoy the knowledge but acted on it, and kept suffrage in the news long after the arguments pro and con were straw in their mouths, and people were about to settle down to thinking of the suffrage movement as one of the established institutions of American life.[5]

Fortunately the suffragists, as distinct from the feminists, had a perfectly concrete objective, and a very simple one. What the vote symbolizes is not simple, as the ablest advocates and the ablest opponents knew. But the right to vote is a simple and familiar right. Now in labor disputes, which are probably the chief item in the charges against newspapers, the right to strike, like the right to vote, is simple enough. But the causes and objects of a particular strike are like the causes and objects of the woman's movement, extremely subtle.

Let us suppose the conditions leading up to a strike are bad. What is the measure of evil? A certain conception of a proper standard of living, hygiene, economic security, and human dignity. The industry may be far below the theoretical standard of the community, and the workers may be too wretched to protest. Conditions may be above the standard, and the workers may protest violently. The standard is at best a vague measure. However, we shall assume that the conditions are below par, as par is understood by the editor. Occasionally without waiting for the workers to threaten, but prompted say by a social worker, he will send reporters to investigate, and will call attention to bad conditions. Necessarily he cannot do that often. For these investigations cost time, money, special talent, and a lot of space. To make plausible a report that conditions are bad, you need a good many columns of print. In order to tell the truth about the steel worker in the Pittsburgh district, there was needed a staff of investigators, a great deal of time, and several fat volumes of print. It is impossible to suppose that any daily newspaper could normally regard the making of Pittsburgh Surveys, or even Interchurch Steel Reports, as one of its tasks. News which requires so much trouble as that to obtain is beyond the resources of a daily press.[6]

The bad conditions as such are not news, because in all but exceptional cases, journalism is not a first hand report of the raw material. It is a report of that material after it has been stylized. Thus bad conditions might become news if the Board of Health reported an unusually high death rate in an industrial area. Failing an intervention of this sort, the facts do not become news, until the workers organize and make a demand upon their employers. Even then, if an easy settlement is certain the news value is low, whether or not the conditions themselves are remedied in the settlement, But if industrial relations collapse into a strike or lockout the news value increases. If the stoppage involves a service on which the readers of the newspapers immediately depend, or if it involves a breach of order, the news value is still greater.

The underlying trouble appears in the news through certain easily recognizable symptoms, a demand, a strike, disorder. From the point of view of the worker, or of the disinterested seeker of justice, the demand, the strike, and the disorder, are merely incidents in a process that for them is richly complicated. But since all the immediate realities lie outside the direct experience both of the reporter, and of the special public by which most newspapers are supported, they have normally to wait for a signal in the shape of an overt act. When that signal comes, say through a walkout of the men or a summons for the police, it calls into play the stereotypes people have about strikes and disorders. The unseen struggle has none of its own flavor. It is noted abstractly, and that abstraction is then animated by the immediate experience of the reader and reporter. Obviously this is a very different experience from that which the strikers have. They feel, let us say, the temper of the foreman, the nerve-racking monotony of the machine, the depressingly bad air, the drudgery of their wives, the stunting of their children, the dinginess of their tenements. The slogans of the strike are invested with these feelings. But the reporter and reader see at first only a strike and some catchwords. They invest these with their feelings. Their feelings may be that their jobs are insecure because the strikers are stopping goods they need in their work, that there will be shortage and higher prices, that it is all devilishly inconvenient. These, too, are realities, And when they give color to the abstract news that a strike has been called, it is in the nature of things that the workers are at a disadvantage. It is in the nature, that is to say, of the existing system of industrial relations that news arising from grievances or hopes by workers should almost invariably be uncovered by an overt attack on production.

You have, therefore, the circumstances in all their sprawling complexity, the overt act which signalizes them, the stereotyped bulletin which publishes the signal, and the meaning that the reader himself injects, after he has derived that meaning from the experience which directly affects him. Now the reader's experience of a strike may be very important indeed, but from the point of view of the central trouble which caused the strike, it is eccentric. Yet this eccentric meaning is automatically the most interesting.[7] To enter imaginatively into the central issues is for the reader to step out of himself, and into very different lives.

It follows that in the reporting of strikes, the easiest way is to let the news be uncovered by the overt act, and to describe the event as the story of interference with the reader's life. That is where his attention is first aroused, and his interest most easily enlisted. A great deal, I think myself the crucial part, of what looks to the worker and the reformer as deliberate misrepresentation on the part of newspapers, is the direct outcome of a practical difficulty in uncovering the news, and the emotional difficulty of making distant facts interesting unless, as Emerson says, we can "perceive (them) to be only a new version of our familiar experience" and can "set about translating (them) at once into our parallel facts."[8]

If you study the way many a strike is reported in the press, you will find, very often, that the issues are rarely in the headlines, barely in the paragraphs, and sometimes not even mentioned anywhere. A labor dispute in another city has to be very important before the news account contains any definite information as to what is in dispute. The routine of the news works that way, with modifications it works that way in regard to political issues and international news as well. The news is an account of the overt phases that are interesting, and the pressure on the newspaper to adhere to this routine comes from many sides. It comes from the economy of noting only the stereotyped phase of a situation. It comes from the difficulty of finding journalists who can see what they have not learned to see. It comes from the almost unavoidable difficulty of finding sufficient space in which even the best journalist can make plausible an unconventional view. It comes from the economic necessity of interesting the reader quickly, and the economic risk involved in not interesting him at all, or of offending him by unexpected news insufficiently or clumsily described. All these difficulties combined make for uncertainty in the editor when there are dangerous issues at stake, and cause him naturally to prefer the indisputable fact and a treatment more readily adapted to the reader's interest.

The indisputable fact and the easy interest, are the strike itself and the reader's inconvenience.

All the subtler and deeper truths are in the present organization of industry very unreliable truths. They involve judgments about standards of living, productivity, human rights that are endlessly debatable in the absence of exact record and quantitative analysis. And as long as these do not exist in industry, the run of news about it will tend, as Emerson said, quoting from Isocrates, "to make of moles mountains, and of mountains moles."[9] Where there is no constitutional procedure in industry, and no expert sifting of evidence and the claims, the fact that is sensational to the reader is the fact that almost every journalist will seek. Given the industrial relations that so largely prevail, even where there is conference or arbitration, but no independent filtering of the facts for decision, the issue for the newspaper public will tend not to be the issue for the industry. And so to try disputes by an appeal through the newspapers puts a burden upon news-papers and readers which they cannot and ought not to carry. As long as real law and order do not exist, the bulk of the news will, unless consciously and courageously corrected, work against those who have no lawful and orderly method of asserting them-selves. The bulletins from the scene of action will note the trouble that arose from the assertion, rather than the reasons which led to it. The reasons are intangible.

4

The editor deals with these bulletins. He sits in his office, reads them, rarely does he see any large portion of the events themselves. He must, as we have seen, woo at least a section of his readers every day, because they will leave him without mercy if a rival paper happens to hit their fancy. He works under enormous pressure, for the competi-tion of newspapers is often a matter of minutes. Every bulletin requires a swift but complicated judgment. It must be understood, put in relation to other bulletins also understood, and played up or played down according to its probable interest for the public, as the editor conceives it. Without standardization, without stereotypes, without routine judgments, without a fairly ruthless disregard of subtlety, the editor would soon die of excitement. The final page is of a definite size, must be ready at a precise moment; there can be only a certain number of captions on the items, and in each caption there must be a definite number of letters. Always there is the precarious urgency of the buying public, the law of libel, and the possibility of endless trouble. The thing could not be managed at all without systematization, for in a standardized product there is economy of time and effort, as well as a partial guarantee against failure.

It is here that newspapers influence each other most deeply. Thus when the war broke out, the American newspapers were confronted with a subject about which they had no previous experience. Certain dailies, rich enough to pay cable tolls, took the lead in securing news, and the way that news was presented became a model for the whole press. But where did that model come from? It came from the English press, not because Northcliffe owned American newspapers, but because at first it was easier to buy English correspondence, and because, later, it was easier for American journalists to read English newspapers than it was for them to read any others. London was the cable and news center, and it was there that a certain technic for reporting the war was evolved. Something similar occurred in the reporting of the Russian Revolution. In that instance, access to Russia was closed by military censorsip, both Russian and Allied, and closed still more effectively by the difficulties of the Russian language. But above all it was closed to effective news reporting by the fact that the hardest thing to report is chaos, even though it is an evolving chaos. This put the formulating of Russian news at its source in Helsingfors, Stockholm, Geneva, Paris and London, into the hands of censors and propagandists. They were for a long time subject to no check of any kind. Until they had made themselves ridiculous they created, let us admit, out of some genuine aspects of the huge Russian maelstrom, a set of stereotypes so evocative of hate and fear, that the very best instinct of journalism, its desire to go and see and tell, was for a long time crushed.[10]

## 5

Every newspaper when it reaches the reader is the result of a whole series of selections as to what items shall be printed, in what position they shall be printed, how much space each shall occupy, what emphasis each shall have. There are no objective standards here. There are conventions. Take two newspapers published in the same city on the same morning. The headline of one reads: "Britain pledges aid to Berlin against French aggression; France openly backs Poles." The headline of the second is "Mrs. Stillman's Other Love." Which you prefer is a matter of taste, but not entirely a matter of the editor's taste. It is a matter of his judgment as to what will absorb the half hour's attention a certain set of readers will give to his newspaper. Now the problem of securing attention is by no means equivalent to displaying the news in the perspective laid down by religious teaching or by some form of ethical culture. It is a problem of provoking feeling in the reader, of inducing him to feel a sense of personal identification with the stories he is reading. News which does not offer this opportunity to introduce oneself into the struggle which it depicts cannot appeal to a wide audience. The audience must participate in the news, much as it participates in the drama, by personal identification. Just as everyone holds his breath when the heroine is in danger, as he helps Babe Ruth swing his bat, so in subtler form the reader enters into the news. In order that he shall enter he must find a familiar foothold in the story, and this is supplied to him by the use of stereotypes. They tell him that if an association of plumbers is called a "combine" it is appropriate to develop his hostility; if it is called a "group of leading business men" the cue is for a favorable reaction.

It is in a combination of these elements that the power to create opinion resides. Editorials reinforce. Sometimes in a situation that on the news pages is too confusing to permit of identification, they give the reader a clue by means of which he engages himself. A clue he must have if, as most of us must, he is to seize the news in a hurry. A suggestion of some sort he demands, which tells him, so to speak, where he, a man conceiving himself to be such and such a person, shall integrate his feelings with the news he reads.

"It has been said" writes Walter Bagehot,[11] "that if you can only get a middle class Englishman to think whether there are 'snails in Sirius,' he will soon have an opinion on it. It will be difficult to make him think, but if he does think, he cannot rest in a negative, he will come to some decision. And on any ordinary topic, of course, it is so. A grocer has a full creed as to foreign policy, a young lady a complete theory of the sacraments, as to which neither has any doubt whatever."

Yet that same grocer will have many doubts about his groceries, and that young lady, marvelously certain about the sacraments, may have all kinds of doubts as to whether to marry the grocer, and if not whether it is proper to accept his attentions. The ability to rest in the negative implies either a lack of interest in the result, or a vivid sense of competing alternatives. In the case of foreign policy or the sacraments, the interest in the results is intense, while means for checking the opinion are poor. This is the plight of the reader of the general news. If he is to read it at all he must be interested, that is to say, he must enter into the situation and care about the outcome. But if he does that he cannot rest in a negative, and unless independent means of checking the lead given him by his newspaper exists, the very fact that he is interested may make it difficult to arrive at that balance of opinions which may most nearly approximate the truth. The more passionately involved he becomes, the more he will tend to resent not only a different view, but a disturbing bit of news. That is why many a newspaper finds that, having honestly evoked the partisanship of its readers, it can not easily, supposing the editor believes the facts warrant it, change position. If a change is necessary, the transition has to be managed with the utmost skill and delicacy. Usually a newspaper will not attempt so hazardous a performance. It is easier and safer to have the news of that subject taper off and disappear, thus putting out the fire by starving it.

## News, Truth, and a Conclusion

As we begin to make more and more exact studies of the press, much will depend upon the hypothesis we hold. If we assume with Mr. Sinclair, and most of his opponents, that news and truth are two words for the same thing, we shall, I believe, arrive nowhere. We shall prove that on this point the newspaper lied. We shall prove that on that point Mr. Sinclair's account lied. We shall demonstrate that Mr. Sinclair lied when he said that somebody lied, and that somebody lied when he said Mr. Sinclair lied. We shall vent our feelings, but we shall vent them into air.

The hypothesis, which seems to me the most fertile, is that news and truth are not the same thing, and must be clearly distinguished.[12] The function of news is to signalize an event, the function of truth is to bring to light the hidden facts, to set them into relation with each other, and make a picture of reality on which men can act. Only at those points, where social conditions take recognizable and measurable shape, do the body of truth and the body of news coincide. That is a comparatively small part of the whole field of human interest. In this sector, and only in this sector, the tests of the news are sufficiently exact to make the charges of perversion or suppression more than a partisan judgment. There is no defense, no extenuation, no excuse whatever, for stating six times that Lenin is dead, when the only information the paper possesses is a report that he is dead from a source repeatedly shown to be unreliable. The news, in that instance, is not "Lenin Dead" but "Helsingfors Says Lenin is Dead." And a newspaper that can be asked to take the responsibility of not making Lenin more dead than the source of the news, is reliable; if there is one subject on which editors are most responsible it is in their judgment of the reliability of the source. But when it comes to dealing, for example, with stories of what the Russian people want, no such test exists.

The absence of these exact tests accounts, I think, for the character of the profession, as no other explanation does. There is a very small body of exact knowledge, which it requires no outstanding ability or training to deal with. The rest is in the journalist's own discretion. Once he departs from the region where it is definitely recorded at the County Clerk's office that John Smith has gone into bankruptcy, all fixed standards disappear. The story of why John Smith failed, his human frailties, the analysis of the economic conditions on which he was shipwrecked, all of this can be told in a hundred different ways. There is no discipline in applied psychology, as there is a discipline in medicine, engineering, or even law, which has authority to direct the journalist's mind when he passes from the news to the vague realm of truth. There are no canons to direct his own mind, and no canons that coerce the reader's judgment or the publisher's. His version of the truth is only his version. How can he demonstrate the truth as he sees it? He cannot demonstrate it, any more than Mr. Sinclair Lewis can demonstrate that he has told the whole truth about Main Street. And the more he understands his own weaknesses, the more ready he is to admit that where there is no objective test, his own opinion is in some vital measure constructed out of his own stereotypes, according to his own code, and by the urgency of his own interest. He knows that he is seeing the world through subjective lenses. He cannot deny that he too is, as Shelley remarked, a dome of many-colored glass which stains the white radiance of eternity.

And by this knowledge his assurance is tempered. He may have all kinds of moral courage, and sometimes has, but he lacks that sustaining conviction of a certain technic which finally freed the physical sciences from theological control. It was the gradual development of an irrefragable method that gave the physicist his intellectual freedom as against all the powers of the world. His proofs were so clear, his evidence so sharply superior to tradition, that he broke away finally from all control. But the journalist has no such support in his own conscience or in fact. The control exercised over him by the opinions of his employers and his readers, is not the control of truth by prejudice, but of one opinion by another opinion that it is not demonstrably less true. Between Judge Gary's assertion that the unions will destroy American institutions, and Mr. Gompers' assertion that they are agencies of the rights of man, the choice has, in large measure, to be governed by the will to believe.

The task of deflating these controversies, and reducing them to a point where they can be reported as news, is not a task which the reporter can perform. It is possible and necessary for journalists to bring home to people the uncertain character of the truth on which their opinions are founded, and by criticism and agitation to prod social science into making more usable formulations of social facts, and to prod statesmen into establishing more visible institutions. The press, in other words, can fight for the extension of reportable truth. But as social truth is organized to-day, the press is not constituted to furnish from one edition to the next the amount of knowledge which the democratic theory of public opinion demands. This is not due to the Brass Check, as the quality of news in radical papers shows, but to the fact that the press deals with a society in which the governing forces are so imperfectly recorded. The theory that the press can itself record those forces is false. It can normally record only what has been recorded for it by the working of institutions. Everything else is argument and opinion, and fluctuates with the vicissitudes, the self-consciousness, and the courage of the human mind.

If the press is not so universally wicked, nor so deeply conspiring, as Mr. Sinclair would have us believe, it is very much more frail than the democratic theory has as yet admitted. It is too frail to carry the whole burden of popular sovereignty, to supply spontaneously the truth which democrats hoped was inborn. And when we expect it to supply such a body of truth we employ a misleading standard of judgment. We misunderstand the limited nature of news, the illimitable complexity of society; we overestimate our own endurance, public spirit, and all-round competence. We suppose an appetite for uninteresting truths which is not discovered by any honest analysis of our own tastes.

If the newspapers, then, are to be charged with the duty of translating the whole public life of mankind, so that every adult can arrive at an opinion on every moot topic, they fail, they are bound to fail, in any future one can conceive they will continue to fail. It is not possible to assume that a world, carried on by division of labor and distribution of authority, can be governed by universal opinions in the whole population. Unconsciously the theory sets up the single reader as theoretically omnicompetent, and puts upon the press the burden of accomplishing whatever representative government, industrial organization, and diplomacy have failed to accomplish

Acting upon everybody for thirty minutes in twenty-four hours, the press is asked to create a mystical force called Public Opinion that will take up the slack in public institutions. The press has often mistakenly pretended that it could do just that. It has at great moral cost to itself, encouraged a democracy, still bound to its original premises, to expect newspapers to supply spontaneously for every organ of government, for every social problem, the machinery of information which these do not normally supply themselves. Institutions, having failed to furnish themselves with instruments of knowledge, have become a bundle of "problems," which the population as a whole, reading the press as a whole, is supposed to solve.

The press, in other words, has come to be regarded as an organ of direct democracy, charged on a much wider scale, and from day to day, with the function often attributed to the initiative, referendum, and recall. The Court of Public Opinion, open day and night, is to lay down the law for everything all the time. It is not workable. And when you consider the nature of news, it is not even thinkable. For the news, as we have seen, is precise in proportion to the precision with which the event is recorded. Unless the event is capable of being named, measured, given shape, made specific, it either fails to take on the character of news, or it is subject to the accidents and prejudices of observation.

Therefore, on the whole, the quality of the news about modern society is an index of its social organization. The better the institutions, the more all interests concerned are formally represented, the more issues are disentangled, the more objective criteria are introduced, the more perfectly an affair can be presented as news. At its best the press is a servant and guardian of institutions; at its worst it is a means by which a few exploit social disorganization to their own ends. In the degree to which institutions fail to function, the unscrupulous journalist can fish in troubled waters, and the conscientious one must gamble with uncertainties.

The press is no substitute for institutions. It is like the beam of a searchlight that moves restlessly about, bringing one episode and then another out of darkness into vision. Men cannot do the work of the world by this light alone. They cannot govern society by episodes, incidents, and eruptions. It is only when they work by a steady light of their own, that the press, when it is turned upon them, reveals a situation intelligible enough for a popular decision. The trouble lies deeper than the press, and so does the remedy. It lies in social organization based on a system of analysis and record, and in all the corollaries of that principle; in the abandonment of the theory of the omnicompetent citizen, in the decentralization of decision, in the coördination of decision by comparable record and analysis. If at the centers of management there is a running audit, which makes work intelligible to those who do it, and those who superintend it, issues when they arise are not the mere collisions of the blind. Then, too, the news is uncovered for the press by a system of intelligence that is also a check upon the press.

That is the radical way. For the troubles of the press, like the troubles of representative government, be it territorial or functional, like the troubles of industry, be it capitalist, coöperative, or communist, go back to a common source: to the failure of self-governing people to transcend their casual experience and their prejudice, by inventing, creating, and organizing a machinery of knowledge. It is because they are compelled to act without a reliable picture of the world, that governments, schools, newspapers and churches make such small headway against the more obvious failings of democracy, against violent prejudice, apathy, preference for the curious trivial as against the dull important, and the hunger for sideshows and three legged calves. This is the primary defect of popular government, a defect inherent in its traditions, and all its other defects can, I believe, be traced to this one.

## Notes

1. See the illuminating chapter in Mr. John L. Given's book, already cited, on "Uncovering the News," Ch. V.
2. *Op. cit.*, p. 57.
3. Think of what guess work went into the Reports of Unemployment in 1921.
4. Address before the Women's City Club of New York, Dec. 11, 1919. Reprinted, *New Republic*, Dec. 31, 1919, p. 44.
5. *Cf.* Inez Haynes Irwin, *The Story of the Woman's Party.* It is not only a good account of a vital part of a great agitation, but a reservoir of material on successful, non-revolutionary, non-conspiring agitation under modern conditions of public attention, public interest, and political habit.
6. Not long ago Babe Ruth was jailed for speeding. Released from jail just before the afternoon game started, he rushed into his waiting automobile, and made up for time lost in jail by breaking the speed laws on his way to the ball grounds. No policeman stopped him, but a reporter timed him, and published his speed the next morning. Babe Ruth is an exceptional man. Newspapers cannot time all motorists. They have to take their news about speeding from the police.
7. *Cf.* Ch. 11, "The Enlisting of Interest."
8. From his essay entitled *Art and Criticism.* The quotation occurs in a passage cited on page 87 of Professor R. W. Brown's, *The Writer's Art.*
9. *Id., supra.*
10. *Cf. A Test of the News*, by Walter Lippmann and Charles Merz, assisted by Faye Lippmann, *New Republic*, August 4, 1920.
11. On the Emotion of Conviction, *Literary Studies*, Vol. III, p. 172.
12. When I wrote *Liberty and the News*, I did not understand this distinction clearly enough to state it, but *cf.* p. 89 ff.

# Chapter 27

# UPTON SINCLAIR

# THE BRASS CHECK

WHEN UPTON SINCLAIR PUBLISHED *The Jungle* in 1906, it changed his career. Not only did the book turn him into a national figure at age 28, but also by the end of 1906 the book had earned him $30,000, a very large sum of money in those days. In addition it helped fuel the momentum that led to passage by the U.S. Congress of the Pure Food and Drugs Act of 1906 and the Meat Inspection Act of 1906. For journalism, *The Jungle* demonstrated the impact publications can have on changing laws for the better. Though a novel, *The Jungle* is seen as a bellwether of investigative reporting.

In *The Brass Check*, Sinclair, a socialist, turned his eye on what today would be called the "mainstream press." His fundamental observation was that newspapers were controlled by powerful interests who shut out any voices who might challenge them—a critique that foreshadowed the arguments of Herman and Chomsky more than a half century later. *The Brass Check* (1919) provided an extensive critique of the constraints commercial control of the media placed on journalism and the implications of those constraints for democracy. The title of the book, that Sinclair self-published, refers to the chit issued to patrons of brothels—an analogy to American journalism as prostitute, "a class institution, serving the rich and spurning the poor".

Sinclair presents his own experiences with the press and his difficulties in getting publicity for what he saw as the pressing issues of the day from a socialist perspective. He documented how the press misreported, distorted and suppressed news and worked to discredit those who challenged the system. In this excerpt, Sinclair rails against the influence of advertisers on newspapers. He calls advertising "legitimate graft." Sinclair's critique of advertising is an element of his broader belief that "Politics, Journalism, and Big Business work hand in hand for the hoodwinking of the public and the plundering of labor."

Not surprisingly, *The Brass Check* was met with enormous hostility including threats of libel (although these did not materialize, with Sinclair offering this as proof that his evidence was watertight). Newspapers refused to review the book and the *New York Times* would not even accept paid advertisements for it. Ironically, then, the very conditions Sinclair sought to expose, critique, and remedy—namely, the suppression of a diversity of voices in the news media, structural inequality in the press industry, and the negative social consequences of plutocratic agenda-setting—were the prime factors that led to the virtual disappearance of *The Brass Check* by the middle of the century. A new edition was published in 2003 and it is now available free on the Internet.

## The Owner and His Advertisers

The third method by which the "kept" press is kept is the method of the advertising subsidy. This is the "legitimate" graft of newspapers and magazines, the main pipeline whereby Big Business feeds its journalistic parasites. Financially speaking, our big newspapers and popular magazines are today more dependent upon their advertisers than they are upon their readers; it is not a cynicism, but the statement of a business fact, that a newspaper or popular magazine is a device for submitting competitive advertising to the public, the reading-matter being bait to bring the public to the hook.

And of course the old saying holds, that "he who pays the piper calls the tune." The extent to which the bait used in the game of journalistic angling is selected and treated by the business fishermen, is a subject which might occupy a volume by itself. Not merely is there general control of the spirit and tone of the paper; there is control in minute details, sometimes grotesque. For example, Arthur Brisbane wrote an article on dietetics, deploring the use of package cereals. The advertising men of the "Evening Journal" came to him, tearing their hair; he had knocked off a hundred thousand dollars a year from the "Journal's" income! Brisbane wrote an editorial pointing out that stiff hats caused baldness, and the "Journal" office was besieged by the hat-dealers who advertised in the paper. Brisbane went to Europe and wrote editorials supporting a municipal subway. Said the advertising man; "Don't you know that Mr.—— at Wanamaker's is dead against that sort of thing?"

Max Sherover, in his excellent little pamphlet, "Fakes in American Journalism," writes:

> The editor of a New York paper wrote an instructive editorial on the right kind of shoes to wear. The editorial was not inspired by any advertiser. It was simply the result of the editor's study and investigation of the problem of footwear. He advised against the wearing of the shoe with the curved point and urged in favor of the square-toed shoe. One of the big advertisers somehow got wind of the shoe-editorial that was intended to appear on the following day. It so happened that this storekeeper had a shoe-sale scheduled for the following week. He called up the business manager of the newspaper on the 'phone. After five minutes of conversation the editorial went to the waste-basket.

And if the advertisers censor the general ideas, needless to say they censor news about themselves. Henry Siegel owned a department-store in New York; his wife divorced him, and nothing about it appeared in the New York papers—that is, not until after the department-store failed! Our great metropolitan dailies are, as you know, strong protectors of the sanctity of the home; you saw how they treated Upton Sinclair, when he got tied up in the divorce-courts; you saw how they treated Gorky and Herron. But how about the late C. W. Post, of "Postum" fame, when he decided to divorce his wife and marry his stenographer? Hardly a line in the newspapers throughout the country!

I have told how the Philadelphia newspapers suppressed the suicide of one of the Gimbel brothers. This same firm has a store in Milwaukee, and I have before me a letter from the District Attorney of Milwaukee County, setting forth what happened when the vice-president of this firm was indicted for bribing an alderman:

> Representatives of Gimbel Brothers requested, as I am credibly informed, the newspapers in which their commercial advertisements appeared to suppress the facts connected with the proceedings of Mr. Hamburger's trial. With two exceptions, so insignificant as to justify their being entirely ignored, the English press did so. The five daily English newspapers published no account whatever of the trial, which occupied about one week and disclosed sensational matter which would have undoubtedly been published broadcast in an ordinary case. Some of these papers printed a very brief notice at the time the case was called, stating this fact, but not all of them did even this much. . . . It was shown that all the books of account of the Gimbel Brothers, together with their correspondence and legal documents pertaining to the transaction in connection with which the bribery was alleged were burned under the direction of the defendant immediately after it was brought to his attention that the grand jury which indicted him was in session and about to investigate this case. This destruction of the books and documents occurred within the period of the statute of limitation, and less than three years after some of the entries had been made in them. The only explanation for this singular proceeding given by defendant or his business associates was that they lacked room in their vault and found it necessary to do away with papers, books and documents which they felt they could dispense with. I mention this particular line of evidence because I am satisfied that if such a showing had been made in an ordinary case or bribery the facts disclosed would have been given the widest publicity by the daily press. That the proceedings of this trial were suppressed by the English papers of this city for commercial reasons which appealed to their advertising department is unquestioned. Every newspaper man of my acquaintance to whom I have mentioned the matter has admitted the fact and deplored it.

In the same way, when Wanamaker's was detected violating the customs laws, only one Philadelphia newspaper reported the circumstances. There was organized a league for honest advertising, and you might have thought that such a league would have appealed to our highly moral newspapers; but when this league prosecuted a merchant in New York for selling furs under false names, not one newspaper mentioned the circumstances. This merchant was convicted, and again not one New York newspaper mentioned it. In Chicago various firms were prosecuted for misbranding goods, and the local papers suppressed the news. In Milwaukee four firms were prosecuted for selling a potted cheese doped with chemicals, and the newspapers withheld the names of the firms. Says Will Irwin: "I have never seen a story of a shop-lifting case in which the name of the store was mentioned." Also he makes the following statement concerning the most august of the Brahmin newspapers of New England:

> The "Boston Evening Transcript" published in its issue of April 8th the fact that a workman had fallen from a tree, that an aged pauper had been found dead in bed, that the Harvard Shooting Club was about to hold a meet, but not the fact that "Harvard Beer," known to every consumer of malt liquors in Massachusetts, was in peril of the law for adulteration. Neither was the fact noted on Monday, April 10. But on Tuesday, April 11, "Harvard Beer—1,000 pure" appeared in the pages of the "Transcript"—as a half-page advertisement!

Every newspaper editor feels this pressure—even though he feels it only in his imagination. A horse that travels in harness does so, not because he likes to travel, but because he carries in his subconsciousness the memory of the whip and the bit which "broke" him in the days of his wild youth. And if, by any chance, he forgets this whip and bit, he is quickly reminded. William Winter, a dramatic critic who had served the "New York Tribune" for forty-four years, was forced to resign because his reviews of plays injured the advertising business of the "Tribune." Certain managers were making money out of producing indecent plays; Mr. Winter rebuked these plays, the advertisers protested to the "Tribune," and the managing editor of the "Tribune" censored Mr. Winter's reviews. During the controversy, Mr. Winter wrote to the managing editor that he had desired to injure the business of the producers of indecent plays; to which the managing editor replied: "My instructions with regard to that page are that the articles are not to be framed with any such purpose."

The same thing happened to Walter Pritchard Eaton, dramatic critic of the "New York Sun." I learned of it just as my book was going to press, and wired Mr. Eaton for the facts. Here is his answer:

> Syndicate withdrew ads from "Sun" after my review of Soul Kiss, demanding my discharge. Six months later I was fired, no cause given. Next Sunday all ads back in paper. No actual proof but conclusion pretty plain.

Everywhere in the world of Journalism, high and low, you see this power of the advertiser. I live in the beautiful millionaire city of Pasadena, and every afternoon I get my news of the world from a local paper, which is in some ways among the best. It publishes no scare headlines, and practically no scandal; but in its attitude toward its big commercial advertisers, the attitude of this newspaper is abject. There is a page of moving-picture advertisements, and side by side are columns of "write-ups" of these plays. Nine out of ten of these plays are unspeakable trash, but from the notices you would think that a new era of art was dawning upon Pasadena. All this is "dope," sent out by the moving-picture exploiters; such a thing as an independent and educative review of a moving-picture is not conceivable in my local newspaper. And it is the same with "write-ups" of bargain-sales, and new openings of department-stores. It is the same with the chain of leisure-class hotels; the man who manages and finances these hotels is a local god, and everything he does and says takes the top of the column.

This system of publicity in return for advertising is a fundamentally dishonest one, but it is inseparable from the business of publishing news for profit, and the legitimate and the illegitimate shade into one another so gradually that it would be hard for an honest editor to know where to draw the line. The rule will differ with every newspaper; it may differ with every editor and every mood of every editor. I have made a little study of it with my local newspaper, and had some amusing experiences. Belonging to the Socialist local in Pasadena, I several times had occasion to solicit publicity for Socialist meetings. Being a naturally polite person, I did not go to the editor and say, "I'll buy ten dollars worth of advertising space, if you'll publish a quarter of a column of news about my radical venture." What I did was to insert the advertisement, and then send to the editor the matter I wanted published, and it was published. So I thought this was a regular rule; but some time later, when the labor-men of Pasadena started a co-operative store, and I became vice-president of the enterprise, I inserted an advertisement of the store, and again presented my "copy" to the newspaper, and I did not get so much space. The advertising manager of the newspaper explained to the manager of the store that his paper could not boost a co-operative store, because the local merchants which supplied the bulk of its advertising were hostile to such an enterprise!

At the last election the people of California had to decide upon a social insurance measure, and a friend of mine wrote an article in favor of this measure, and could not get it published. I suggested that she publish it as an advertisement, but the "Pasadena Star-News" refused it, even in that form, and explained to me the reason—that the lady had referred to Christian Science as "a foolish belief"! The partisans of Christian Science are accustomed to rent a page in this paper every now and then, and to have their foolishness published without question.

A still stranger experience befell a gentleman in Boston, Sinclair Kennedy by name. In April, 1918, Mr. Kennedy learned that his state was falling far behind in the purchase of war savings and thrift stamps, and by way of helping his government in its thrift campaign, he prepared an advertisement consisting of three quotations, the first from a speech by President Wilson, the second from a speech by the Secretary of the Treasury, and the third from a speech by the Chairman of the National War Savings Committee: all three of the quotations urging that people should purchase only necessities, so that the energies of the country might go to war-production. The "Boston Herald and Journal" contracted to publish this advertisement in four issues; it published it in two issues, and then refused to publish it again, and paid to Mr. Kennedy the sum of five hundred dollars damages for breach of contract. The "Boston Post" refused to publish the advertisement at all, its manager giving the reason that it was "contrary to public policy"! I have read of many Socialists being sent to jail upon a charge of interfering with the government's war activities, but if the manager of the "Boston Post" was sent to jail, the other newspapers did not report it!

What this amounts to is a censorship of the small and occasional advertisers by the large and permanent ones; this censorship is common, and sometimes it is made to wear the aspect of virtue. The best-paying advertisements are those of automobiles and other leisure-class luxuries; as such advertisers will not publish alongside cheap patent medicine fakes, publications like "Collier's" and the "Outlook" make a boast of censoring their advertisements. But when it comes to protecting their high-priced advertisers, these publications are, as I have shown, every bit as unscrupulous as the sellers of cancer-cures and headache-powders. I, who wish to attack these high-priced advertisers, am forced to publish what I have to say in a paper which can only exist by publishing the advertisements of cancer-cures and headache-powders. This is very humiliating, but what can I do? Stop writing? If I could have my way, of course, I would write for a publication having a large circulation and publishing honest reading matter and honest advertising matter. But no such publication exists; and I have to decide the question, which does the least harm, a publication with honest advertising matter and dishonest reading matter, or a publication with honest reading matter and dishonest advertising matter.

Also, of course, there will be censorship of advertisements containing news. If the newspaper is suppressing certain facts, it will not permit you to make known these facts, even for money. The "Los Angeles Times," although it bitterly opposed single tax, was willing to take my money for an advertisement in favor of single tax; but the "Times" would not take my money for an advertisement reporting a meeting at which the truth about Russia was told. The "Times" would not sell me space to make known that the Socialists of the city had challenged the Superintendent of Schools to debate the truth of certain false statements which he had made about Russia.

In Louisville is the "People's Church," conducted by an independent clergyman in a theatre, and attended by one or two thousand people every Sunday. The "Louisville Courier-Journal" and its evening edition, the "Times," have not contented themselves with suppressing all news about these meetings for several years; they have also refused all advertisements of this "People's Church." (Since this was written they have put the "People's Church" out of business!)

Some fifteen years ago the most important news being put before the American people was in the form of paid advertisements signed by Thomas W. Lawson. The "New York Times" refused to publish these advertisements, and tens of thousands of New Yorkers, myself among them, were obliged to buy other newspapers in consequence. It cost the "Times" large sums of money to refuse these Lawson broad-sides, but the "Times" made a virtue of it, because the broad-sides threatened the entire profit system, without which the "Times" could not exist. In the same way the newspapers of Baltimore and Boston refused advertisements of a magazine run by Thomas E. Watson in Georgia, on the ground that he was publishing in his magazine articles attacking foreign missions. If you do not believe that interests like this exercise pressure upon newspapers, just try to publish in any capitalist newspaper an advertisement of a book or pamphlet attacking the Roman Catholic Church!

Here in Los Angeles I know a man who set himself up in business as a land-appraiser, and interfered with the leading industry of our community, which is selling real estate to "come ons" from the East. He advised one client that some land in Imperial Valley was worthless, because it contained nearly three per cent of alkali; and this judgment was later vindicated by a report of the U. S. Bureau of Soils, which I have read. But it happened that this land lay perilously near to the tracts of a great land company, in which the heads of Los Angeles newspapers are interested. The three leading newspapers of Los Angeles broke their contracts with this land-appraiser, threw out his "copy" and ruined his business, and now he is working as a cowboy in the "movies." And if you think that the power of the real estate sharks is confined to the places where they prey, consider the experience of Rob Wagner, who wrote two articles about the Southern California land-sharks for the "Saturday Evening Post." The first article, being full of fun, a farce-comedy, was accepted and paid for at once; the second, giving the real story, and being full of meat, was turned down.

# Chapter 28

## ROBERT D. LEIGH (EDITOR)

## A FREE AND RESPONSIBLE PRESS: THE HUTCHINS COMMITTEE RESPONSE

AS THE STORY GOES, AT A MEETING of the board of the Encyclopedia Britannica in the early 1940s, Henry Luce, the co-founder and editor-in-chief of *Time* magazine, asked Robert Hutchins, the president of the University of Chicago, where he could find out about freedom of the press and what his obligations regarding the freedom of the press might be. Hutchins replied that he didn't know. As a result of this exchange, Luce agreed to fund a commission to explore the parameters of a free press and Hutchins agreed to organize and ultimately to chair it.

The 12-person commission consisted of four social scientists including Harold Lasswell, an expert on propaganda, the law professor Zechariah Chafee, one of the country's leading First Amendment scholars, the theologian Reinhold Niebuhr, the poet and Librarian of Congress Archibald MacLeish and the historian Arthur Schlesinger, Sr. There were no working journalists from any news medium on the commission.

At the outset of the project, Hutchins announced that the commission would examine where the press was succeeding and where it was failing. Already, long term trends that would be bemoaned for the next 60 years were in place. The number of daily newspapers was dropping and the number of cities with only one newspaper was rising. Reporting was slanted and citizens were not well informed about the pressing issues of the day.

The commission considered and rejected a series of policy options, including Federal regulation of newspapers along the same way that radio communication was regulated. In the end, however, it was its description of the characteristics of a free press required by a self-governing democracy that was the most memorable aspect of the commission's effort. Its report stated that the press must provide, "first, a truthful, comprehensive, and intelligent account of the day's events in a context which gives them meaning; second, a forum for the exchange of comment and criticism; third, a means of projecting the opinions and attitudes of the groups in the society to one another; fourth, a method of presenting and clarifying the goals and values of the society; and, fifth, a way of reaching every member of the society by the currents of information, thought, and feeling which the press supplies." The commission stated that it did not believe new regulations were required but if press performance did not improve, new regulations were inevitable.

The report stated that freedom of the press was 'in serious danger because of failures, abuses and derelictions on the part of its most powerful owners' who commanded their empires with little concern for the general public or its opinions. The report received mixed reviews from the press. Walter Lippmann described it as an "effort to elucidate the axioms, to define the principles, and to mark out the field, for serious and continuing criticism of the press."

Although freedom of expression has several classic exponents such as John Milton, John Stuart Mill and others, the extract below is one of the best expositions of the principles of press freedom in the English language and became seen as the central values of journalism—at least theoretically—throughout the second half of the twentieth century.

## I. The Parties Directly at Interest

When we use the phrase "freedom of the press," we mention but one party at interest; the term "press" indicates an *issuer* of news, opinions, etc., through the media which reach mass audiences. But since no one cares to utter news or opinions into the void, there must be at least one other party at interest, the reader or listener as *consumer* of news, opinions, etc.; we shall refer to him collectively as the *audience*.

The interest of the issuer is, typically, to express his mind without external constraint or restraint—his ideas and reports of events, also his feelings, judgments, protests, business proposals, appeals, visions, prophecies. . . . . To the press, the implied audience is seldom visibly present or personally known; it is an imagined audience, and it is hopefully considered a representative audience. For, while it is commonly called "the public," it is at most a fair sample of the actual public. From this fragment, given freedom of speech, the message will spread to others and, with good luck, find the listeners to whom it belongs.

The interest of the consumer is, in detail, highly variable and personal. Yet, in any mentally alert society, there is a fairly universal desire for access to a world of experience, thought, and feeling beyond the range of private observation. And also beyond the range of private concern, for it is the genius of the human animal to "take an interest" in what does not immediately concern him. It may be a random and marginal curiosity; it may amount to an insistent hunger. In any case, since the nature of the appetite is such that it exceeds any actual satisfaction, the issuer can usually count on a latent demand; he may develop a demand where none pre-exists.

Wherever there are two parties, within a community, there is always a third party, the community itself. As a social totality including all pairs of (domestic) issuers and consumers, the community has a stake in the impact of all conversation, but especially in that of speech addressed to a mass audience. For all communication, apart from its direct meaning, has an effect on the communicators, on the social fabric, and on the common standards which measure the free cohesion of the group.

## II.  Freedom of the Parties at Interest

Though the issuer's interest cannot be realized without an audience, his interest carries with it no claim whatever to compel the existence of an audience but only to invite an audience from men free not to listen. Freedom of the press must imply freedom of the consumer *not to consume* any particular press product; otherwise, the issuer's freedom could be at the expense of the consumer's freedom.

As the issuer cannot compel an audience, so the consumer cannot compel the existence of a speaker. Nor does it usually occur to him that he has a claim upon anyone for more light and leading than is spontaneously offered. The expresser is offering a gift. Nevertheless, the consumer is not a passive receptacle. Since the issuer cannot survive without his free attention, the consumer has power to encourage or discourage his advances. Through the consumer's willingness to pay for the successful divination of his appetites, he lures out the yield of thought-products; it is his free suffrage that builds up the great press and sustains a mass production in which thought and pseudo-thought devised for the market mix in varying proportions. He may go to the extent of setting up, with a like-minded group, a press organ to meet special group needs, interests, or prejudices; here the consumer controls, or perhaps becomes, the issuer. But the birth of opinion the consumer cannot control; the genesis of thought is incurably free and individual. For its abundance and pertinence he must take his chances as with the fertility of his native soil. He is necessarily interested in the freedom of the sources of opinion, because if they are unchecked and unwarped, even by himself, he will have, other things being equal, the widest and most honest offering to select from or to piece together or to mix with his own thought. His interest here coincides with that of the issuer, actual or potential.

Hence it is that, although there are these two direct interests, *only one of them, in simple conditions, needs protection.* To protect the freedom of the issuer is to protect the interest of the consumer and in general that of the community also. Hitherto in our history it has been sufficient to protect the "freedom of the press" as the freedom of issuers.

But, as this analysis is intended to indicate, under changed conditions the consumer's freedom might also require protection. If his need became more imperative, and if at the same time the variety of sources available to him were limited, as by concentration of the press industry, his freedom not to consume particular products of the existing press might vanish. It would then be no longer sufficient to protect the issuer alone. This theme is resumed in Section XI below. Meantime we trace the theory in terms of the issuer's freedom.

## III.  Freedom of the Issuer Requires Protection

The utterance of opinion is not merely the announcement of an "I think. . . ." It is a social force and is intended to be such.

Since civilized society is a working system of ideas, it lives and changes by the consumption of ideas. It is vulnerable to every shock to the fortunes of the ideas it embodies. And since there is usually less motive for uttering ideas with which everybody and every institution is in accord than for uttering those destined to change men's minds, a significant new idea in the social field is likely to arouse resistance. The issuer will have need of protection. But of what protection?

Freedom of expression can never be made a costless immunity by shackling hostile response, for response is also expression. Free expression is destined not to repress social conflict but to liberate it. But its intention is that the *level of social conflict shall be lifted from the plane of violence to the plane of discussion.* It should mean to the issuer that he is protected, not from anger, contempt, suffering, the loss of his clientele, for in this case his critic would be unfree, but from types of harm not an integral part of the argument or relevant to the argument (wrecking the issuer's shop, threatening his employees, intimidating his patrons . . .).

There are those who would define freedom of expression as meaning no pain and no opprobrium to the issuer, no matter what he proposes. This ideal, if it is such, could be realized only in a society to which all ideas had become either impotent or indifferent. In any actual society free speech will require courage. And the first danger to free expression will always be the danger at the source, the timidity of the issuer, or his purchasability.

## IV. The Effective Agencies for Protecting Free Expression are the Community and the Government

The community acts, by routing social conflict through the ballot box, encouraging the method of discussion by making it a preliminary to action, and, then, by such traditions of self-restraint and toleration as may exist.

But, in the steadiest of communities, the struggle among ideas tends to become physical as it becomes prolonged; there is an incessant downtrend of debate toward the irrelevant exchange of punishments—malicious pressures, threats and bribes, broken windows and broken heads. Government is the only agency which, through its monopoly of physical force, can measurably insure that argument in speech and press will continue to be argument and not competitive injury. The elementary function of government in simply maintaining public order and the rights of person and property must be noted as the cornerstone of free expression, inasmuch as the cruder menaces to freedom are always from within the community.

Wherever in society there is an institution, a body of belief or interest, an organized power—good, bad, or mixed—there is a potential (we do not say actual) foe of the free critic—good, bad, or mixed. This potential hostility to the challenger is due not simply to the fact that it is easier and more natural for the obstinate vein in human nature to discourage or repress the critic than to meet his arguments. It is due also to irrational elements commonly present in the critic and the critic's audience. Freedom of the press to appeal to reason is liable to be taken as freedom to appeal to public passion, ignorance, prejudice, and mental inertia. We must not burke the fact that freedom of the press is dangerous. But there is no cure for bad argument either in refusing to argue or in substituting irrelevant pressures upon, or repression of, the free critic for the patient attempt to reach the elements of reasonableness in the mass mind, as long as the belief persists that such elements are there. The only hope for democracy lies in the validity of this belief and in the resolute maintenance, in that faith, of the critic's freedom.

The first line of defense for press freedom is government, as maintaining order and personal security and as exercising in behalf of press freedom the available sanctions against sabotage, blackmail, and corruption.

## V. Government as Protecting Freedom against Government

Any power capable of protecting freedom is also capable of infringing freedom. This is true both of the community and of government. In modern society the policy of government vis-à-vis the free expression of its citizens is in peculiar need of definition.

For every modern government, liberal or otherwise, has a specific position in the field of ideas; its stability is vulnerable to critics in proportion to their ability and persuasiveness. To this rule, a government resting on popular suffrage is no exception. On the contrary, just to the extent that public opinion is a factor in the tenure and livelihood of officials and parties, such a government has its own peculiar form of temptation to manage the ideas and images entering public debate.

If, then, freedom of the press is to achieve reality, government must set limits upon its capacity to interfere with, regulate, control, or suppress the voices of the press or to manipulate the data on which public judgment is formed.

What we mean by a free society is chiefly one in which government does thus expressly limit its scope of action in respect to certain human liberties, namely, those liberties which belong to the normal development of mature men. Here belong free thought, free conscience, free worship, free speech, freedom of the person, free assembly. Freedom of the press takes its place with these. And all of them, together with some stipulations regarding property, constitute the burden of our bills of rights.

## VI. Free Expression as a Right

If government accepts a limitation of its range of action in view of such interests, the reason is that they are not only important interests but also moral rights. And they are moral rights because their exercise, besides being valuable to both the citizen and the community, has an aspect of duty about it.

The motives of expression are certainly not all dutiful; they are and should be as multiform as human emotion itself, grave and gay, casual and purposeful, artful and idle. In a modern state all social activity, including the conduct of business, requires use of the press as well as of speech and assumes its natural freedom. But there is a vein of expression which has the added impulsion of duty, namely, the expression of thought and belief. If a man is burdened with an idea, he not only desires to express it, he ought to express it. The socially indispensable functions of criticism and appeal may be as abhorrent to the diffident as they are attractive to the pugnacious, but for neither is the issue one of wish. It is one of obligation—to the community and also to something beyond the community, let us say, to truth.[1] It is the duty of the scientist to his result and of Socrates to his oracle; but it is equally the duty of every man to his own belief. Because of this duty to what is beyond the state, freedom of speech and press are moral rights which the state must not infringe.

While dutiful utterance bears the burden of the claim of right as against the state, that right extends its coverage over all legitimate expression.

This self-limitation of the state cannot in the long run be contrary to the public interest. For, whatever its judgment of the opinions expressed, no nation can have a net interest in repressing the conscience of its citizens. On the contrary, the modern state recognizes that the citizen's conscience is a source of its own continued vitality. And, wherever the citizen has a duty of conscience, there the sovereign state has also a duty, namely, to that conscience of its citizen. Thus both its interest and its duty require the state to give the moral right a legal status.

This consideration is logically prior to the traditional ground of a free press, namely, that the unhampered publication of opinion promotes the "victory of truth over false-hood" in the public arena. Public discussion is indeed a necessary condition of a free society, and freedom of expression is a necessary condition of an amply furnished public discussion. It is not a sufficient condition, for the co-presence of a variety of opinions is not equivalent to debate; it may well be questioned whether the actual process we now call public discussion is functioning as the health of a democracy requires. In any case, it is a process which elicits mental power and breadth in those consumers whom it does not baffle or confuse; it is essential to building a mentally robust public; and, without something of the kind, no self-governing society could operate. But the original source of supply for this very process is the duty of the individual thinker to his thought; here is the primary ground of his right.

While it is not, like the right of speech, a universal right that every citizen should own a press or be an editor or have access to the clientele of any existing press, it is the whole point of a free press that ideas deserving a public hearing shall get a public hearing and that the decision of what ideas deserve that hearing shall rest in part with the public, not solely with the particular biases of editors and owners. In any populous community a vigorous trimming-out process among ideas presenting themselves for wide public hearing is obviously essential; but freedom of the press becomes a mockery unless this selective process is free also. This means that free speech, with its informal emphases, is the natural vestibule to a free press and that the circumstance of ownership of press instruments confers no privilege of deafness toward ideas which the normal selective processes of the community promote to general attention.[2]

## VII. The Moral Right of Freedom of Expression is not Unconditional

If reasons can be given for a claim of right—and there are reasons for all of them—those reasons constitute the condition on which the right can be claimed. The absence of that condition, therefore, automatically removes the basis for the claim.

By this logic, since the claim of the right of free expression is based on the duty of a man to his thought, then when this duty is ignored or rejected—as when the issuer is a liar, an editorial prostitute whose political judgments can be bought, a malicious inflamer of unjust hatred—the ground for his claim of right is nonexistent. In the absence of accepted moral duties there are no moral rights.

It may reasonably be doubted whether any man is capable of a thoroughgoing repu-diation of duty. His experiments in the rejection of good faith are likely to be sporadic; a single lie does not make a man a liar nor a single acceptance of bribe a prostitute. Further, if a man is stung into reckless or inflammatory speech by a genuine grievance which ought to be made known, his bedeviled utterance may contain an important piece of truth. Still, if we define a liar as a man who habitually tells the truth except when it suits his policy to deviate, the press liar is not a mythical person. His ultimate humanity and freedom he cannot alienate; but he has used his freedom to undermine his freedom. His claim of right as an issuer of opinion has by his own choice become groundless.

Since all rights, moral or legal, make assumptions regarding the will of the claim-ants, there are no unconditional rights. The notion of rights, costless, unconditional, conferred by the Creator at birth, was a marvelous fighting principle against arbitrary governments and had its historical work to do. But in the context of an achieved political freedom the need of limitation becomes evident. The unworkable and invalid conception of birthrights, wholly divorced from the condition of duty, has tended to beget an arrogant type of individualism which makes a mockery of every free institution, including the press. This conception has concealed the sound basis of our liberal polity, the one natural right, the right to do one's human task. From this one right, the others can be derived so far as they are valid; and into this right the ingredient of duty is inseparably built.

## VIII.  A Right of Liberty Includes a Right to be in Error

Liberty is experimental, and experiment implies trial and error. Debate itself could not exist unless wrong opinions could be rightfully offered by those who suppose them to be right. For social purposes, the cutting edge of the right of free expression is its demand for what is called "toleration" on the part of those who see, or think they see, error in others. What is required is something more positive than toleration—respect for the process of self-correction as against any authoritatively imposed correctness.

The assumption of this respect is that the man in error is actually trying for the truth; and this effort on his part is of the essence of his claim to freedom. What the moral right does not cover is a right to be deliberately or irresponsibly in error.

## IX.  The Abuse of a Right Does Not Ipso Facto Forfeit the Protection of the Legal Right

Legal protection cannot vary with the inner fluctuations of moral direction in individual wills; it does not cease whenever the moral ground of right has been personally abandoned. It is not even desirable that the whole area of the responsible use of freedom should be made legally compulsory, even if such a thing were possible, for in that case free self-control, necessary ingredient of any free state, would be superseded by mechanism.

The attempt to correct abuses of freedom, including press freedom, by resort to legal penalties and controls is the first spontaneous impulse of reform. But the dangers of the cure must be weighed against the dangers of the disease; every definition of an abuse invites abuse of the definition. The law might well be justified in acting against malicious public criticism; but if courts were called on to determine the inner corruptions of intention, honest and necessary criticism would proceed under an added peril and the "courage of disclosure" incur a new cost.

Hence many a lying, venal, and scoundrelly public expression must continue to find shelter under a "freedom of the press" built for widely different ends. There is a practical presumption against the use of legal action to curb press abuse.

## X.  There Are, However, Limits to the Legal Toleration of Abuse of the Liberty of Expression

The already recognized areas of legal correction of misused liberty in this field—libel, misbranding, obscenity, incitement to riot, sedition in case of clear and present danger—

have a common principle, namely, that an utterance or publication invades in a serious, overt, and demonstrable manner recognized private rights or vital social interests. If new categories of abuse come within this definition, the extension of legal remedies is justified. In view of the general presumption against legal action above stated, the burden of proof will rest upon those who would extend these categories; but the presumption is not intended to render society supine in the face of all new types of misuse, actual or possible, of the immense powers of the contemporary press.

Today a further question of public responsibility in the use of freedom is raised in view of the extent to which the function of the press is affected by a public interest. Not only positive misdeeds but omissions and inadequacies of press performance have now a bearing on general welfare. Freedom to express has hitherto included freedom to refrain from expressing; for the press this liberty is no longer perfect.

## XI.  The Work of the Press as Clothed with a Public Interest

As observed at the beginning (Sec. I), the work of the press always involves the interest of the consumer; but, as long as the consumer is free, his interest is protected in the protection of the freedom of the issuer. Today, however, the conditions affecting the consumer's freedom have radically altered. Through concentration of ownership the flow of news and opinion is shaped at the sources; its variety is limited; and at the same time the insistence of the consumer's need has increased. He is dependent on the quality, proportion, and extent of his news supply not alone for his personal access to the world of thought and feeling but also for the materials of his business as a citizen in judging public affairs. With this situation any community in which public opinion is a factor in policy, domestic and international, must be deeply concerned.

Clearly a qualitatively new era of public responsibility for the press has arrived; and it becomes an imperative question whether press performance can any longer be left to the unregulated initiative of the issuers. The moral and legal right of thinkers to utter their opinions must in any case remain intact; this right stands for the kernel of individualism at the heart of all free social life. But the element of duty involved in the right requires a new scrutiny. And the service of news, as distinct from the utterance of opinion, acquires an added importance. The need of the consumer to have adequate and uncontaminated mental food is such that he is under a duty to get it; and, because of this duty, his interest acquires the stature of a *right*. It becomes legitimate to speak of the moral right of men to the news they can use.

Since the consumer is no longer free not to consume, and can get what he requires only through existing press organs, protection of the freedom of the issuer is no longer sufficient to protect automatically either the consumer or the community. The general policy of laissez faire in this field must be reconsidered.

## XII.  The Accountable Press and the Responsible Community

The press today, as the Supreme Court has recently recognized in the case of news services, has responsibilities to the general spread of information which present analogies to those of a common carrier or of a trustee, though the likeness in either of these cases is limited. The analogy is closer to an educational enterprise in which private schools, enjoying the advantages and risks of experimental initiative, are yet performing a necessary public function for which a measure of social accountability would be appropriate. Do these analogies suggest that for the press also some degree of public oversight and co-operation and possibly of regulation must be the way of the future?

An over-all social responsibility for the quality of press service to the citizen cannot be escaped; the community cannot wholly delegate to any other agency the ultimate responsibility for a function in which its own existence as a free society may be at stake.

At the same time, the main positive energy for the improvement of press achievement must come from the issuers. Although the standards of press performance arise as much from the public situation and need as from the conscious goals of the press, these standards must be administered by the press itself. This means that *the press must now take on the community's press objectives as its own objectives.* And for the correction of abuses the maxim holds good that self-correction is better than outside correction, so long as self-correction holds out a reasonable and realistic hope, as distinct from lip service to piously framed paper codes.

How shall this realism be implemented? And how shall the objectives of the press be held to identity with the necessary objectives of the community? By a recognition on the part of the press that, while its enterprise is and should remain a private business, its efforts to define and realize its standards are also a community concern and should be systematically associated with corresponding efforts of community, consumers, and government.

— With those of consumers and community, acting through specialized organs, as responsible critic, gadfly, and source of incentive.
— With those of government in various ways whose principles we may indicate as follows:

1. Without intruding on press activities, government may act to improve the conditions under which they take place so that the public interest is better served—as by making distribution more universal and equable, removing hindrances to the free flow of ideas, reducing confusion and promoting the reality of public' debate.[3]

2. New legal remedies and preventions are not to be excluded as aids to checking the more patent abuses of the press, under the precautions we have emphasized. Such legal measures are not in their nature subtractions from freedom but, like laws which help to clear the highways of drunken drivers, are means of increasing freedom, through removing impediments to the practice and repute of the honest press.

3. Government may and should enter the field of press comment and news supply, not as displacing private enterprise, but as a supplementary source. In so doing, it may present standards for private emulation. While in our experience a democratic government is one in which government itself is one of the main objects of public discussion and can therefore never be allowed to control or to regulate the debate, it is not inconceivable that a government by the people should also be a powerful instrument for the people, in respect to educational and other noncommercial possibilities of the developing press.

## XIII.  Resulting Conception of Freedom of the Press

The emerging conception of freedom of the press may be summarized as follows:

> As with all freedom, press freedom means freedom from and also freedom for.

A free press is free from compulsions from whatever source, governmental or social, external or internal. From compulsions, not from pressures; for no press can be free from pressures except in a moribund society empty of contending forces and beliefs. These pressures, however, if they are persistent and distorting—as financial, clerical, popular, institutional pressures may become—approach compulsions; and something is then lost from effective freedom which the press and its public must unite to restore.

A free press is free for the expression of opinion in all its phases. It is free for the achievement of those goals of press service on which its own ideals and the requirements of the community combine and which existing techniques make possible. For these ends it must have full command of technical resources, financial strength, reasonable access to sources of information at home and abroad, and the necessary facilities for bringing information to the national market. The press must grow to the measure of this market.

For the press there is a third aspect of freedom. The free press must be free to all who have something worth saying to the public, since the essential object for which a free press is valued is that ideas deserving a public hearing shall have a public hearing.

## XIV.  Contemporary Problems of Principle

1.   These several factors of an ideal press freedom are to some extent incompatible with one another.

   A press which has grown to the measure of the national market and to the full use of technical resources can hardly be free from internal compulsions. The major part of the nation's press is large-scale enterprise, closely interlocked with the system of finance and industry; it will not without effort escape the natural bias of what it is. Yet, if freedom is to remain secure, this bias must be known and overcome.

   Again, the growth of the press acts together with the growth of the nation to make more remote the ideal that every voice shall have the hearing it deserves. Concentration of power substitutes one controlling policy for many independent policies, lessens the number of major competitors, and renders less operative the claims of potential issuers who have no press. For this clash there is no perfect remedy. There is relief, to the extent that the wider press, somewhat as a common carrier, assumes responsibility for representing variant facets of opinion. But no listening devices of the human mind have yet secured us from a certain wastage of human genius as the scale of a nation's thinking enlarges; and the contemporary arts of what is called publicity can hardly be acquitted of aiming rather at further lens distortion than at just and proportionate recognition of worth. As commercial arts it is hard to see how they can make justice their supreme object.

2.   There is an antithesis between the current conception of the freedom of the press and the accountability of the press.

Accountability, like subjection to law, is not necessarily a net subtraction from liberty; the affirmative factor of freedom, freedom for, may be enhanced. But the liberty to be carefree is gone. Charles Beard could say with accuracy that "in its origin, freedom of the press had little or nothing to do with truth telling . . . . most of the early newspapers were partisan sheets devoted to savage attacks on party opponents. . . . . Freedom of the press means the right to be just or unjust, partisan or non-partisan, true or false, in news column or editorial column."[4] Today, this former legal privilege wears the aspect of social irresponsibility. The press must know that its faults and errors have ceased to be private vagaries and have become public dangers. Its inadequacies menace the balance of public opinion. It has lost the common and ancient human liberty to be deficient in its function or to offer half-truth for the whole.

The situation approaches a dilemma. The press must remain private and free, *ergo* human and fallible; but the press dare no longer indulge in fallibility—it must supply the public need. Here, again, there is no perfect solution. But the important thing is that the press accept the public standard and try for it. The legal right will stand if the moral right is realized or tolerably approximated. There is a point beyond which failure to realize the moral right will entail encroachment by the state upon the existing legal right.

## Notes

1. For brevity, we shall use the concern for "truth" as token of a group of interests having a similar claim on expression, such as belief regarding "right," or justice of feeling, or public policy, or the advocacy of a legitimate personal interest. To make "truth" the symbol of all this will bring our discussion into close relation with the classical argument for freedom of expression, which has been chiefly concerned with the contest of opinions in respect to truth and falsehood. "Truth" is beyond the state and may symbolize whatever is, in similar fashion, obligatory on individual and state alike.

2. It is worth noting that the Soviet Constitution, while limiting publishable ideas within a fixed orthodoxy, undertakes within these limits to implement press expression for a wide segment of the people who own no presses. It provides (Art. 125) that "printing presses, stocks of paper . . . . communications facilities, and other material requisites" shall be put at the disposal of working people and their organizations.

3. Further illustrations under this head may be found in Hocking, *Freedom of the Press: A Framework of Principle* (University of Chicago Press).

4. *St. Louis Post-Dispatch Symposium on Freedom of the Press, 1938*, p. 13.

# Chapter 29

# A. J. LIEBLING

# THE PRESS

A. J. LIEBLING'S 40-YEAR JOURNALISM career took him from the boroughs of New York to the high life of Paris, from revered columnist to sardonic memoirist, from ring-side boxing reporter to World War II war correspondent, from reporting on politics to reporting on French delicacies, and from championing of the common man to serving as the most perceptive critic of the press during his era—the role for which he is most well known. Some of Liebling's most influential works came during the 18 years he was the press critic for *The New Yorker* magazine, where he wrote the column the *Wayward Press*. It was during his tenure at *The New Yorker*, ending just prior to his death, that Liebling chided newspapers for manipulating and homogenizing the news by eliminating the bipartisan, heterogeneous views of the nation's vast array of newspapers.

Liebling is generally considered America's best press critic. As Jack Shafer wrote in *Slate* magazine in 2004, Liebling "portrayed the press as a comic circus populated with evil clowns, union-busting lions, and crookeder than usual carnies performing inside a tent that could go up in flames at any moment." He was less tendentious than other press critics. He wrote with flair and with humor and through humor opened his readers' minds up to his ideas. Like other critics, Liebling worried about corporate control of the media and growing media concentration; he excoriated the press for being the mouthpieces for "press lords" and corporate interests; and he deplored bad writing. But unlike many other critics, he was willing to turn a jaundiced eye on the liberal press as well as the conservative press. Liebling was also the master of the quip—the most famous one perhaps is, "Freedom of the press is only guaranteed to those who own one."

Two columns are contained here. The first offers an overview of the state of the press. Surprisingly, Liebling looks forward to a day in which an "endowed" press might emerge. In the second, Liebling deplores the attrition taking place in the ranks of newspapers, a trend already in place by the late 1940s.

Here is how I summarized the basic situation, as I thought it existed then, for the *Dartmouth Alumni Magazine* in 1947. There was a symposium. Two other alumni, an editor and an Associated Press man, also took part. As one would expect, they were completely wrong about everything.

## A Free Press?

I think almost everybody will grant that if candidates for the United States Senate were required to possess ten million dollars, and for the House one million, the year-in-year-out level of conservation of those two bodies might be expected to rise sharply. We could still be said to have a freely elected Congress: anybody with ten million dollars (or one, if he tailored his ambition to fit his means) would be free to try to get himself nominated, and the rest of us would be free to vote for our favorite millionaires or even to abstain from voting. (This last right would mark our continued superiority over states where people are compelled to vote for the government slate.)

In the same sense, we have a free press today. (I am thinking of big-city and middling-city publishers as members of an upper and lower house of American opinion.) Anybody in the ten-million-dollar category is free to buy or found a paper in a great city like New York or Chicago, and anybody with around a million (plus a lot of sporting blood) is free to try it in a place of mediocre size like Worcester, Mass. As to us, we are free to buy a paper or not, as we wish.[1]

I am delighted that I do not have to insinuate that they consciously allow their output to be shaped by their personal interests. Psychoanalytical after-dinner talk has furnished us with a lovely word for what they do: they rationalize. And once a man has convinced himself that what is good for him is good for the herd of his inferiors, he enjoys the best of two worlds simultaneously, and can shake hands with Bertie McCormick, the owner of the Chicago *Tribune*.[2]

The profit system, while it insures the predominant conservative coloration of our press, also guarantees that there will always be a certain amount of dissidence. The American press has never been monolithic, like that of an authoritarian state. One reason is that there is always important money to be made in journalism by standing up for the underdog (demagogically or honestly, so long as the technique is good). The underdog is numerous and prolific—another name for him is circulation. His wife buys girdles and baking powder and Literary Guild selections, and the advertiser has to reach her. Newspapers, as they become successful and more to the right, leave room for newcomers to the left. Marshall Field's Chicago *Sun*, for example, has acquired 400,000 readers in five years, simply because the *Tribune*, formerly alone in the Chicago morning field, had gone so far to the right.[3] The fact that the *Tribune*'s circulation has not been much affected indicates that the 400,000 had previous to 1941 been availing themselves of their freedom not to buy a newspaper. (Field himself illustrates another, less dependable, but nevertheless appreciable, factor in the history of the American press—the occasional occurrence of that economic sport, the maverick millionaire.) E. W. Scripps was the outstanding practitioner of the trade of founding newspapers to stand up for the common man. He made a tremendous success of it, owning about twenty of them when he died. The first, James Gordon Bennett's *Herald* and Joseph Pulitzer's *World*, in the eighties and nineties, to say nothing of the Scripps-Howard *World-Telegram* in 1927, won their niche in New York as left-of-center newspapers and then bogged down in profits.

Another factor favorable to freedom of the press, in a minor way, is the circumstance that publishers sometimes allow a certain latitude to employees in departments in which they have no direct interest—movies, for instance, if the publisher is not keeping a movie actress; or horse shows, if his wife does not own a horse. Musical and theatrical criticism is less rigorously controlled than it is in Russia.[4]

The process by which the American press is pretty steadily revivified, and as steadily dies (newspapers are like cells in the body, some dying as others develop), was well described in 1911 by a young man named Joseph Medill Patterson, then an officer of the Chicago *Tribune*, who was destined himself to found an enormously successful paper, the *Daily News* of New York, and then within his own lifetime pilot it over the course he had foreshadowed. The quotation is from a play, *The Fourth Estate*, which Patterson wrote in his young discontent.

"Newspapers start when their owners are poor, and take the part of the people, and so they build up a large circulation, and, as a result, advertising. That makes them rich, and they begin most naturally, to associate with other rich men—they play golf with one, and drink whisky with another, and their son marries the daughter of a third. They forget all about the people, and then their circulation dries up, then their advertising, and then their paper becomes decadent."

Patterson was not "poor" when he came to New York eight years later to start the *News;* he had the McCormick-Patterson *Tribune* fortune behind him, and at his side Max Annenberg, a high-priced journalist condottiere who had already helped the *Tribune* win a pitched battle with Hearst in its own territory. But he was starting his paper from scratch, and he did it in the old dependable way, by taking up for the Common Man— and sticking with him until 1942, by which time the successful-man contagion got him and he threw his arms around unregenerated Cousin Bertie's neck. The *Tribune* in Chicago and the *News* in New York have formed a solid front ever since. Patterson was uninfluenced by golf, whiskey, or social ambitions (he was a parsimonious, unsociable man who cherished an illusion that he had already hit the social peak). I think it is rather the complex of age, great wealth, a swelled head, and the necessity to believe in the Heaven-decreed righteousness of a system which has permitted one to possess such power that turns a publisher's head. The whiskey, weddings, yachts, horse shows, and the rest (golf no longer sounds so imposing as it did in 1911)[5] are symptoms rather than causes.

Unfortunately, circulations do not "dry up" quickly, nor advertising fall away overnight. Reading a newspaper is a habit which holds on for a considerable time. So the erstwhile for-the-people newspaper continues to make money for a while after it changes its course. With the New York *Herald* this phase lasted half a century. It would, moreover, be difficult to fix the exact hour or day at which the change takes place: it is usually gradual, and perceptible to those working on the paper before it becomes apparent to the outside public. At any given moment there are more profitable newspapers in being than new ones trying to come up, so the general tone of the press is predominantly, and I fear increasingly, reactionary. The difference between newspaper publishers' opinions and those of the public is so frequently expressed at the polls that it is unnecessary to insist on it here.

Don't get me wrong, though. I don't think that the battle is futile. I remember when I was a freshman, in 1920, listening to a lecture by Professor Mecklin in a survey course called, I think, Citizenship, in which he told how most of the newspapers had misrepresented the great steel strike of 1919. The only one that had told the truth, he said, as I remember it, was the old *World*. (I have heard since that the St. Louis *Post-Dispatch* was good, too, but he didn't mention it.) It was the first time that I really believed that newspapers lied about that sort of thing. I had heard of Upton Sinclair's book *The Brass Check*, but I hadn't wanted to read it because I had heard he was a "Bolshevik." I came up to college when I was just under sixteen, and the family environment was not exactly radical. But my reaction was that I wanted someday to work for the *World*, or for some other paper that *would* tell the truth. The *World* did a damned good job, on the strikes and on the Ku Klux Klan and on prohibition and prison camps (in Florida, not Silesia), and even though the second-generation Pulitzers let it grow namby-pamby and then dropped it in terror when they had had a losing year and were down to their last sixteen million, it had not lived in vain.

I think that anybody who talks often with people about newspapers nowadays must be impressed by the growing distrust of the information they contain. There is less a disposition to accept what they say than to try to estimate the probable truth on the basis of what they say, like aiming a rifle that you know has a deviation to the right. Even a report in a Hearst newspaper can be of considerable aid in arriving at a deduction if you know enough about (*a*) Hearst policy and (*b*) the degree of abjectness of the correspondent signing the report.[6]

Every now and then I write a piece for *The New Yorker* under the heading of "The Wayward Press" (a title for the department invented by the late Robert Benchley when he started it early in *The New Yorker*'s history). In this I concern myself not with big general thoughts about Trends (my boss wouldn't stand for such), but with the treatment of specific stories by the daily (chiefly New York) press. I am a damned sight kinder about newspapers than Wolcott Gibbs[7] is about the theater, but while nobody accuses him of sedition when he raps a play, I get letters calling me a little pal of Stalin when I sneer at the New York *Sun*. This reflects a pitch that newspaper publishers make to the effect that they are part of the great American heritage with a right to travel wrapped in the folds of the flag like a boll weevil in a cotton boll. Neither theatrical producers nor book publishers, apparently, partake of this sacred character. I get a lot more letters from people who are under the delusion that I can Do Something About It All. These reflect a general malaise on the part of the newspaper-reading public, which I do think will have some effect, though not, God knows, through me.

I believe that labor unions, citizens' organizations, and possibly political parties yet unborn are going to back daily papers. These will represent definite, undisguised points of view, and will serve as controls on the large profit-making papers expressing definite, ill-disguised points of view. The Labor Party's *Daily Herald*, in England, has been of inestimable value in checking the blather of the Beaverbrook-Kemsley-Rothermere newspapers of huge circulation. When one cannot get the truth from any one paper (and I do not say that it is an easy thing, even with the best will in the world, for any one paper to tell all the truth), it is valuable to read two with opposite policies to get an idea of what is really happening. I cannot believe that labor leaders are so stupid they will let the other side monopolize the press indefinitely.[8]

I also hope that we will live to see the endowed newspaper, devoted to the pursuit of daily truth as Dartmouth is to that of knowledge. I do not suppose that any reader of the *Magazine* believes that the test of a college is the ability to earn a profit on operations (with the corollary that making the profit would soon become the chief preoccupation of its officers). I think that a good newspaper is as truly an educational institution as a college, so I don't see why it should have to stake its survival on attracting advertisers of ballpoint pens and tickets to Hollywood peep shows. And I think that private endowment would offer greater possibilities for a free press than state ownership (this is based on the chauvinistic idea that a place like Dartmouth can do a better job than a state university under the thumb of a Huey Long or Gene Talmadge). The hardest trick, of course, would be getting the chief donor of the endowment (perhaps a repentant tabloid publisher) to (a) croak, or (b) sign a legally binding agreement never to stick his face in the editorial rooms. The best kind of an endowment for a newspaper would be one made up of several large and many small or medium-sized gifts (the Dartmouth pattern again). Personally, I would rather leave my money for a newspaper than for a cathedral, a gymnasium, or even a home for streetwalkers with fallen arches, but I have seldom been able to assemble more than $4.17 at one time.[9]

The above piece, written 14 years ago, was in manner laboriously offhand, but represented my serious thought. I erred badly on the side of optimism. The postwar euphoria that lingered in the air like fallout must have trapped me. There has been no new competition in any large American city since the piece was written, and now it seems infinitely less likely that there ever will be.

The period between the two wars, while it marked a great diminution in the number of newspapers in New York, had brought at least one tremendously successful newcomer, the *Daily News*, which changed the whole physiognomy of Metropolitan journalism. When I wrote in 1947, the two Marshall Field entries, *PM* in New York and the *Sun* (the *Sun-Times* to be) in Chicago, were both still in there battling. *PM*, which was destined to fail, had been founded in 1940, and the *Sun*, fated to succeed financially, had begun in 1942. It did not seem to me, therefore, that the times already precluded new starts, although, as I noted, they were harder than before.

The suggestions I made about where new papers might find sponsors now sound infantile, but at the time I thought, wrongly, that labor retained some of the intelligence and coherence of the Roosevelt days, and it seemed to me not inconceivable that some financial Megabelodon might fancy a good newspaper as a more distinctive memorial than the habitual foundation for research into some disease that had annoyed the testator during life. (These bequests always seem to me to mark a vengeful nature, and the viruses they are aimed at profit by them almost as much as the doctors. They eat tons of cultures, play with white rats, and develop resistance by constant practice, as slum children learn to get out of the way of automobiles.) Megabelodon, however, although a huge creature, had a brain cavity about as big as the dime slot on a telephone coin box, and most men who could afford to endow a newspaper seem to be rigged the same way.

Silliest of all, as I read back now, is the line about the profit system guaranteeing a certain amount of dissidence. This shows, on my part, an incurable weakness for judging the future by the past, like the French generals who so charmed me in 1939. I still believe that "there is always important money to be made by standing up for the underdog," but the profit system implies a pursuit of *maximum* profit—for the shareholders' sake, distasteful though it may be. That it is theoretically possible to make money by competition in the newspaper field is therefore immaterial, since there is a great deal more money to be made by (a) selling out and pocketing a capital gain, and (b) buying the other fellow out and then sweating the serfs.

The *Guild Reporter*, organ of the American Newspaper Guild, C.I.O., which includes all editorial workers, recently announced that the guild had achieved a record membership despite "a contracting industry"—a reference that will be clarified by the next item, from The Wayward Press.

[. . .]

## Toward a One-Paper Town

### *February 18, 1949*

"I wouldn't weep about a shoe factory or a branch-line railroad shutting down," Heywood Broun wrote in the newly named *World-Telegram* after the *World* and *Evening World* expired, nearly eighteen years ago. "But newspapers are different."

Little of the emotional writing that followed the passing of the *World* was evident in the recent news stories on the disappearance of the *Star*, the short-lived epilogue to *PM*, which ran out of money on Thursday, January 27. The Pulitzer papers were glorious has-beens in 1931, and could have made a comeback, I still think. Poor *PM* and its continuation, the *Star*, never quite got there. The *World* story was bigger in a physical sense, too. The shutdown in 1931 put twenty-eight hundred men and women on the street, while the *Star*'s end threw out only four hundred and eight. Still, to the people on the *Star* it was tragic, especially because they had tried to put out a memorable newspaper.

The *Star* didn't carry any real news story of its end at all; merely stated the fact in a bleak, page-one announcement, phrased like an office memorandum and signed by Bartley C. Crum, the publisher, and Joseph Barnes, the editor. An old-time newspaperman called this to my attention a little sadly. "When you looked at the last copy of the *World*, you saw a detailed story of the final disposition of the paper all over the right-hand side of the first page," he said. "But *PM* and the *Star* were never strong on reporting." The end result, of course, was the same. It seems more and more to be the rule that the Democrats lose the newspapers and the Republicans the elections.

The *Herald Tribune* was the only New York newspaper to give a full story of the *Star*'s death front-page play. The story was a column and a quarter long and unobtrusively sympathetic. The reporter, Don Ross, had evidently been at the meeting of *Star* editorial employees on the afternoon of January 27, when Crum announced his bad news. "Mr. Crum, who looked drawn and pale, hoisted himself to a desk and said that today's three editions would be the last the *Star* would publish," Ross wrote. "Mr. Barnes, looking equally fatigued, also attended the meeting. The staff was stunned. They had heard reports that the paper needed money, but most of them apparently believed that Mr. Crum and Mr. Barnes would pull them through." Ross might have added that people on *PM* had got used to such scares, having experienced recurrent ones almost since the founding of the paper, in the summer of 1940, when it soon became touch and go whether Marshall Field would take over from his fellow-investors in the original scheme, who had no more to invest.

The *Times*, second only to the *Tribune* in the amount of space devoted to the story, gave it a full column on the first page of the second edition. Five of the six other surviving New York dailies of general circulation apparently took a calm view of the disappearance of their contemporary. The exception was the *Journal-American*, to which I shall refer later. The *News* and *Mirror*, in fact, polished off the *Star* with a well-buried paragraph apiece on the morning after the *Star* suspended publication. The *Mirror*, to be sure, did get word of the occurrence onto its front page a couple of days later, in the form of an announcement that it had taken over the *Star*'s comic strip "Barnaby," and that, beginning Monday, January 31, former *Star* readers would be able to follow their favorite cartoon characters in the pages of the *Mirror*. The *Post* and *Sun* stories, on the day of suspension, were brief but decent. The *World-Telegram* story said that the announcement "brought to an end today a weird and costly chapter in the history of contemporary journalism in which a Chicago millionaire, who inherited a vast department store and real-estate fortune, attempted to establish himself as a New York publisher." Over the weekend, the *Times, Herald Tribune*, and *Post* followed up with kindly editorials.

None of the obituary articles mentioned the fact that *PM*, of which the *Star* was a sequel, was the only new daily started in New York since 1924, a vintage year that produced the *Mirror* and the *Evening Graphic*. Five papers have gone out of business since: the *World* and *Evening World*, in February, 1931; the *Graphic* in July, 1932 (even *PM*, under its own name, lasted a couple of months longer); Mr. Hearst's pet, the *American* ("A Paper for People Who Think"), in June, 1937; and finally *PM* and the *Star*, which I here count as one. This leaves the city with three fewer papers than it had 24 years ago, although the population has increased by at least two million and indicates how quickly the consolidation of control over the sale of news has advanced. I think this was the most important aspect of the *Star* story. The record does not indicate that only papers that try to be liberal or literate, or both, are doomed in New York. The *Graphic* was an atrocious job and the *American* was beneath contempt, but they died just as dead as if they had been meritorious. Someday, a towering genius of the publishing business will get Lil' Abner and Steve Canyon and Dick Tracy and Moon Mullins *and* Barnaby under one tent with Walter Winchell and the Harvest Moon Dance Festival, and some other towering genius—or maybe the same one, using a different corporate name—will get Walter Lippmann and Arthur Krock and the Fresh Air Fund and the Hundred Neediest Cases under the same management, and the number of morning papers will be halved. It is so hard to tell the *World-Telegram* and the *Sun* apart now, except typographically, that a merger would be hardly noticeable. If the trend continues, New York will be a one- or two-paper town by 1975.

One of the good things about *PM* was that it was different from any other New York paper, and the differences were irreconcilable. You couldn't imagine it, or the *Star*, merging with any other paper. Also, it was pure in heart. It sometimes seemed to me to make virtue unnecessarily repulsive by publishing pictures of buck-toothed ballad singers and knobby-kneed rhythmic dancers and interior shots of neglected mental wards in distant states, and it occasionally occurred to me that the space thus employed could have been used for news stories. The injustices it whacked away at were genuine enough, but an awful lot of whacks seemed to fall on the same injustices. A girl to whom I gave a subscription to *PM* in 1946 asked me after a time, "Doesn't *anybody* have any trouble except the Jews and the colored people?" When you read it steadily for a while, you got the impression that you were reading the publication of some such large order as the Lonely Hearts or the American Treehound Association, whose members shared a lot of interests that you didn't. Two articles of *PM*'s faith seemed to be salvation through psychotherapy[10] and damnation through a frivolous approach to amusements. Still, while other papers were inventing anecdotes to discredit price control or lamenting the hard lot of large corporations, *PM* kept the facts of the case available to anybody who would bother to read them.

*PM*'s editors were not humorous men, but they realized that the paper lacked gaiety, and every now and then they brought in professional funnymen to run columns. It never did any good. The humorists look to reading Max Lerner and became ashamed of themselves. They reminded me of the cocker spaniels belonging to the father of Henri Cartier-Bresson, the photographer. "My father was a great fancier of cockers," Cartier-Bresson *fils* once told me. (He pronounced cocker in the French fashion, "co-kare.") "He had a dear friend in Paris who was the director of the morgue. The morgue is a large place quite near the Gare de Montparnasse, where my father would arrive from the country with his dogs when he was going to exhibit them at the National Dog Show, Rather than put them in a boarding kennel, he would keep them in the morgue until the show opened, thus saving expense. But the atmosphere depressed the dogs so much that they never won any prizes."

One trouble with *PM* in its early years, I have heard (I did not see it regularly then), was that it was completely unpredictable, with the result that the reader who had got to like it one week would find it quite different the next. By 1945, when I did begin to see it every day, it had fallen into the antithesis of this difficulty; it always seemed the same. Also, it had gathered about a hundred thousand readers, who loved it exactly as it was. One hundred thousand was an awkward number, because it was half of what *PM* needed to pay its way. It was too many to throw away but not enough to make the paper go. *PM* couldn't get the second hundred thousand unless it changed; it couldn't change without losing a substantial number of the first hundred thousand. Once, in a gesture toward popular appeal, the sports department picked an all-scholastic Greater New York football team. The paper received a flock of letters from old readers reproaching it for exalting brutality and asking why it didn't pick an all-scholastic *scholastic* team.

I think the *Star* was making progress toward a successful changeover, although the process resembled changing clothes under water. The *Star* could—and, tactically, should—have claimed credit for bringing down the price of milk in New York City. Probably the price would have come down eventually without the investigation that the *Star* fostered, but it would have taken a longer time doing it. It seemed to me that a young *Star* cartoonist named Walt Kelly,[11] who used to be a Walt Disney draftsman, did a wonderful job during the presidential campaign. The only bit of caricature that I remember from that period is Kelly's mechanized Mr. Dewey, with a torso that might have been either a cash register or a slot machine. Kelly had an advantage enjoyed by few of his competitors in that he was turned loose on Mr. Dewey. The *Star* took the winning political line, although it shocked half its old customers when it did it; the circulation manager grew melancholy when he heard the paper was going to come out against Wallace. The new management got the circulation up by thirty-five thousand before the *Star* folded, and that meant it must have gained at least fifty thousand new readers, for during the campaign it surely lost many of the old ones to the *Post*, which, as far as I could see, made Zionism the chief issue of the election. The *Post* supported Dewey and Wallace, in equal portions.

I shall always be saddened by the thought that I saw Mr. Crum miss a signal that, had he heeded it, might have sent the *Star*'s circulation up to a quarter of a million almost overnight. I am not in a position to blame him, because I missed it, too. I was in the Biltmore bar with a couple of *Star* men on the evening of the Thursday before the election, when President Truman was making his last campaign tour of the city. The President, of course, was staying at the Biltmore, which houses Democratic National Headquarters. Crum came down from the presidential suite and said, "The old boy is crazy. He thinks he's going to win. He's standing there under the shower telling everybody that he'll sweep the country." I laughed with the others. If, guided by some mystic light, Crum had believed and ordered the *Star* to headline the flat, unique prediction that the President would win, he would have sold more, rather than fewer, papers during the days remaining before election. And after Election Day the *Star* would have been famous from coast to coast. Crum was rooting for Truman. But he didn't believe the feedbox tip. It's a wonderful example of how you get to believe what you read in the opposition newspapers.

The *Journal-American* began its story about the end of the *Star* in this manner: "The New York *Star* wrote its own obituary today, ceasing publication seven months after it succeeded the newspaper *PM*, from which it inherited its leftist line. . . . Demise of the *Star* threw 408 employees out of jobs. Most of them consistently followed the leftist line." This comes under the head of shooting at lifeboats. "The *Star* was the only New York paper to support President Truman, but it also subtly backed Henry Wallace. It also supported pro-Communist Representative Vito Marcantonio and leftist former Rep. Leo Isaacson of the Bronx in his losing bid for reelection. Left-wingers and the Moscow-line faithful said they expected some of the *Star*'s circulation will be picked up by the Communist *Daily Worker*."

Twenty-four hours later, the *Mirror*, which is the *Journal-American*'s sister-in-Hearst, was soliciting circulation from among *Star* readers who liked Barnaby, without insisting upon a loyalty test for anybody possessed of three cents.

The follow-up on this performance was a column in the Monday *Journal-American* by Frank Conniff, one of a large squad of apprentice Peglers. (Pegler himself, as I write this, has not yet got around to the subject of the *Star*'s finish. I presume he is waiting for it to get dead enough for him to light into, like most of the objects of his spleen.) "Many and varied will be the reasons for its demise," Conniff wrote, in part, "but all autopsies must agree on one salient point. The deceased was never a good newspaper. The *Star* consumed its energies poking derision at its betters without bothering to observe the fundamentals of our craft. . . . [Readers] want lively news, intelligent features, good pictures, comics, and departments. And it was in just these categories that the *Star* lagged behind the newspapers it sought to deride."

Eager to observe the fundamentals of Mr. Conniff's craft, I looked through the copy of the *Journal-American* in which his little gem appeared. Not counting the sports and financial pages, it carried eighteen columns of what might be called news—ALI TO SUE WIFE TODAY, EX-COP AND WOMAN DIE IN AUTO CRASH, RED TRIAL POLICE SCAN SPECTATORS, and DOWDY GALS BACK UP DAPPER REDS AT TRIAL are sample headlines. Eight columns—two on the first page and six on the second—were consecrated to the memoirs of Robert Stripling, recently resigned investigator for the House Un-American Activities Committee. ("I want to tell in detail the price that men must pay for the dubious privilege of being reviled in print and on the air. I want to tell how remarkably difficult it is to direct the people's attention to a sleepless conspiracy being waged against them.") There were also 34 columns of space occupied by the output of 26 columnists, including Bob Hope, Major General David P. Barrows (retired president of the University of California), Cholly Knickerbocker (who suggested that the Republicans run Tyrone Power for President, because "President Tyrone Power could do just as well as President Truman"), Mary Haworth, Betty Betz Bets (The Teen Set); Dorothy Kilgallen, Louella Parsons, Paul Gallico, Louis Sobol ("*perdrix aux choux*, that's matzoh balls with a French accent"), Bob Considine, and Conniff himself. Considine, by the way, appeared to be the busiest man in the paper. He was listed as the editor of

Mr. Stripling's autobiography as well as the author of his own column, which means that he filled six columns, or a third as much as the paper's total of straight news. In addition to all this writing, he posed for a picture on page 2, in which he was shown receiving the Golden Book Award of the Catholic Writers' Guild for being the author of a biography of Babe Ruth.

In this copy of the *Journal-American*, I was particularly impressed by a lively bit of news headed, FAITH IN AMERICA SHATTERED ABROAD, by Karl H. von Wiegand, billed by the paper as Dean of Foreign Correspondents. Without Mr. Conniff's guidance, I might have suspected the swatch of rhetoric that followed of having some editorial content. "Germany, Austria, Italy, and Japan, which for a long time have held back expansion of Soviet Russia and its communism in Europe and Asia, were utterly destroyed and their leaders hanged," Dean Von Wiegand had written regretfully. ". . . While trying to 'sell' or impose 'Americanism' in Europe, America imported far greater 'Europeanism' and its socialism, as reflected to the election of Truman and the State of the Union message to Congress."

The most "intelligent feature" in that day's *Journal-American*, I thought, was an Office Orchid contest, in which one girl in each of a number of office buildings is being selected as prettiest by the elevator starter. Elimination beauty contests are being held between the building winners, and there is to be a ten-girl semifinal at the Stork Club, where the contestants will meet Harry M. Popkin, producer of the gay celluloid comedy *My Dear Secretary*. Then there will be a five-girl final, to be decided during a week of voting at the theater where *My Dear Secretary* is playing, and where all the voters will have to pay their way in. I thought right up until I came on the name of the picture that it would be "For Whom the Elevator Bell Tolls." The layout and the story take up slightly less than a half page, and the two Office Orchids *du jour* look even prettier than Mr. Considine.

## Notes

1. *A Free and Responsible Press*, the published report of a committee headed by Robert Maynard Hutchins in 1947, says, "Although there is no such thing as a going price for a great city newspaper, it is safe to assume that it would cost somewhere between five and ten million dollars to build a new 150,000 employees. The press is connected with other big businesses through the advertising of these businesses, upon which it depends for the major part of its revenue. The owners of the press, like the owners of other big businesses, are bank directors, bank borrowers, and heavy taxpayers in the upper brackets.
   "As William Allen White put it: 'Too often the publisher of an American newspaper has made his money in some other calling than journalism. He is a rich man seeking power and prestige. . . . And they all get the unconscious arrogance of conscious wealth.'
   "Another highly respected editor, Erwin D. Canham of the *Christian Science Monitor*, thinks upper-bracket ownership and its big-business character important enough to stand at the head of his list of the 'shortcomings of today's American newspapers.' "
   *A Free and Responsible Press* was published after the appearance of my article.
2. McCormick died in 1955. If he is not in Heaven he is eternally astonished.
3. The *Sun-Times*, having become almost equally prosperous, has by now, 1961, gone almost equally as far. Poor Mr. Field is dead and his son is a Republican. Mavericks seldom breed true.
4. There is, however, no theater to write about, except in New York, and provincial critics of music lean over backward to be kind, because it is hard enough to get people to subscribe for concerts without underlining their deficiencies.

5. There has been a revival since the first Eisenhower inaugural. I attribute it to the invention of the electric go-cart, in which, I am informed, the golfers now circulate, obviating ambulation. It sounds like the most fun since the goat-wagon.

6. Albert Camus, the brilliant and versatile young French novelist, playwright, and critic, who was also editor of *Combat*, a Paris daily, once had an idea for establishing a "control newspaper" that would come out one hour after the others with estimates of the percentage of truth in each of their stories, and with interpretations of how the stories were slanted. The way he explained it, it sounded possible. He said, "We'd have complete dossiers on the interests, policies, and idiosyncrasies of the owners. Then we'd have a dossier on every journalist in the world. The interest, prejudices, and quirks of the owner would equal Z. The prejudices, quirks, and private interests of the journalist, Y. Z times Y would give you X, the probable amount of truth in the story." He was going to make up dossiers on reporters by getting journalists he trusted to appraise men they had worked with. "I would have a card-index system," he said. "Very simple. We would keep the dossiers up to date as best we could, of course. But do people really want to know how much truth there is in what they read? Would they buy the control paper? That's the most difficult problem." Camus died without ever learning the answer to this question. His energies were dissipated in creative writing and we lost a great journalist.

7. Gibbs is dead too. Shortly after his funeral I got a letter from a *New Yorker* reader in Hico, Texas, previously unknown to me, that began: "Well, Gibbs is dead and soon the whole damn lot of you will be."

8. To reread this paragraph makes me glum. Mergerism has hit Britain with a sudden rush; the *News-Chronicle* is gone and the *Herald* looks to be for it.

9. Professor Michael E. Choukas, of the Dartmouth faculty, summing up after the last article of the Public Opinion in a Democracy series, commented: "Mr. Liebling's 'endowed newspaper' would probably be free from direct pressure, but it would be unable to avoid the indirect efforts of the propagandists." I think that Professor Choukas, a sociologist who has specialized in the study of propaganda, has developed an exaggerated respect for the opposition. Albert Camus's plan for the "control newspaper," which I have briefly described in another footnote, is an example of the ingenuity a good newspaperman can bring to bear, and men like Vic Bernstein, Paul Sifton, and Edmund Taylor in this country (to cite only a few—there are hundreds of others) would certainly bring into the ring with them more perspicacity than anybody the National Association of Manufacturers could hire. A man who thinks he can fool other men is always a little a fool himself. His assumption that he can do it presupposes a foolish vanity—like that of the recidivist con man who spends most of his life in jail. His contempt for the truth marks him as a bit subhuman. Professor Choukas did not mention my hopes for strong labor papers.
The professor's own remedy for the dilemma, however, is worthy of citation. I hope somebody makes a good hard try at it.
I frankly do not believe that any indirect assault would have much effect as a check against those who deliberately set out to mislead us," he wrote. "A direct attack could be launched against them by a privately endowed, independent agency whose main task would consist of compiling a list of all the propaganda groups in the country, analyzing their techniques, discovering their goals, and releasing the available information to government officials, to men responsible for our channels of communication, to men who measure public opinion, to colleges and universities, and to those pathetically few groups in the country who have undertaken to fight the battle of accountability in a positive manner.
"This I feel should be done before our crisis reaches unmanageable proportions—before the next depression."

10. The *Post* has picked up this approach and learned to make it pay. It permits a longer, droolier, treatment of sex and crime stories, with more specific details, than the old tabloid method, which was comparatively reticent, being based on hints of the too-awful-to-mention and headlines hard to comprehend: ORGY, MAD, HORROR, FIEND. If you work up on a story of prostitution or murder from an enlightened direction you can say *what kind* of orgy, madness, fiendishness. The reader gets his drool and is at the same time filled with a sense of superiority because he is participating in the progress of science. The call girl feels a need of approval, the murderer has been caught masturbating by his pa. Nobody does anything for

the hell of it. In the frivolous department, though, the *Post* has *not* followed the *PM* formula. It runs endless wordage on movie stars, whom it habitually calls by their first names, and on some days reads like a cross between the *Psychoanalytical Journal* and *Silver Screen*, all clotted around an intelligent editorial page, a couple of superior Washington columns, Herblock's frequently inspired cartoons, and a number of soliloquists with overflowing hearts. The total effect is that of a daily visit to the first act of a play by Clifford Odets.

11.    Mr. Pogo-to-be.

# Chapter 30

# EDWARD S. HERMAN AND NOAM CHOMSKY

# MANUFACTURING CONSENT: THE POLITICAL ECONOMY OF THE MASS MEDIA

EDWARD S. HERMAN WAS A PROFESSOR of finance at the University of Pennsylvania and Noam Chomsky was a world-renowned linguist at the Massachusetts Institute of Technology when they published *Manufacturing Consent* in 1988. Their distinguished academic positions helped to generate worldwide attention for their sustained attack on the American media. The title draws on the notion that far from informing citizens about what they need to know in order to decide where they stand on the great political issues of the day, the mass media "manufacture consent" for the government in power.

This idea that the media can be used to manufacture consent circulated widely in the 1920s and 1930s, as observers became increasingly concerned with the potential influence of propaganda. The notion that governments and ruling elites can engineer the acquiescence of the lower classes to their own domination figures prominently in the Italian revolutionary Antonio Gramsci's concept of hegemony. Herman and Chomsky argue that the American mass media is, in essence, little more than a propaganda arm of the American government. Because the major media are largely owned by large corporations who face the same competitive pressures as other corporations, that is, to generate profit growth, the selection process for news as well as the way news is presented is distorted.

The authors present five case studies to prove their point including comparing the coverage of events in Central America in the 1980s, where tens of thousands of people were killed in civil wars, to the coverage of dissidents in the Soviet Union. In short, despite the popular notion that the press is a check on power, Herman and Chomsky argue that the press panders to the interests of the privileged class.

Many observers believe that *Manufacturing Consent* is little more than a strident left-wing attack on the American media. Nevertheless, the book, which was written by two distinguished academics and has 100 pages of footnotes to support its arguments, has found a widespread following in Europe, which is why it is included in this collection. In this selection, the authors lay out their basic arguments and describe the five "filters" on the media that support their idea of a propaganda model of the press.

## A Propaganda Model

The mass media serve as a system for communicating messages and symbols to the general populace. It is their function to amuse, entertain, and inform, and to inculcate individuals with the values, beliefs, and codes of behavior that will integrate them into the institutional structures of the larger society. In a world of concentrated wealth and major conflicts of class interest, to fulfil this role requires systematic propaganda.

In countries where the levers of power are in the hands of a state bureaucracy, the monopolistic control over the media, often supplemented by official censorship, makes it clear that the media serve the ends of a dominant elite. It is much more difficult to see a propaganda system at work where the media are private and formal censorship is absent. This is especially true where the media actively compete, periodically attack and expose corporate and governmental malfeasance, and aggressively portray themselves as spokesmen for free speech and the general community interest. What is not evident (and remains undiscussed in the media) is the limited nature of such critiques, as well as the huge inequality in command of resources, and its effect both on access to a private media system and on its behavior and performance.

A propaganda model focuses on this inequality of wealth and power and its multi-level effects on mass-media interests and choices. It traces the routes by which money and power are able to filter out the news fit to print, marginalize dissent, and allow the government and dominant private interests to get their messages across to the public. The essential ingredients of our propaganda model, or set of news "filters," fall under the following headings: (1) the size, concentrated ownership, owner wealth, and profit orientation of the dominant mass-media firms; (2) advertising as the primary income source of the mass media; (3) the reliance of the media on information provided by government, business, and "experts" funded and approved by these primary sources and agents of power; (4) "flak" as a means of disciplining the media; and (5) "anticommunism" as a national religion and control mechanism. These elements interact with and reinforce one another. The raw material of news must pass through successive filters, leaving only the cleansed residue fit to print. They fix the premises of discourse and interpretation, and the definition of what is newsworthy in the first place, and they explain the basis and operations of what amount to propaganda campaigns.

The elite domination of the media and marginalization of dissidents that results from the operation of these filters occurs so naturally that media news people, frequently operating with complete integrity and goodwill, are able to convince themselves that they choose and interpret the news "objectively" and on the basis of professional news values. Within the limits of the filter constraints they often are objective; the constraints are so powerful, and are built into the system in such a fundamental way, that alternative bases of news choices are hardly imaginable. In assessing the newsworthiness of the U.S. government's urgent claims of a shipment of MIGs to Nicaragua on November 5, 1984, the media do not stop to ponder the bias that is inherent in the priority assigned to government-supplied raw material, or the possibility that the government might be manipulating the news,[1] imposing its own agenda, and deliberately diverting attention from other material. It requires a macro, alongside a micro- (story-by-story), view of media operations, to see the pattern of manipulation and systematic bias.

Let us turn now to a more detailed examination of the main constituents of the propaganda model, which will be applied and tested in the chapters that follow.

## 1.1. Size, Ownership, and Profit Orientation of the Mass Media: the First Filter

In their analysis of the evolution of the media in Great Britain, James Curran and Jean Seaton describe how, in the first half of the nineteenth century, a radical press emerged that reached a national working-class audience. This alternative press was effective in reinforcing class consciousness: it unified the workers because it fostered an alternative value system and framework for looking at the world, and because it "promoted a greater collective confidence by repeatedly emphasizing the potential power of working people to effect social change through the force of 'combination' and organized action."[2] This was deemed a major threat by the ruling elites. One MP asserted that the working-class newspapers "inflame passions and awaken their selfishness, contrasting their current condition with what they contend to be their future condition—a condition incompatible with human nature, and those immutable laws which Providence has established for the regulation of civil society."[3] The result was an attempt to squelch the working-class media by libel laws and prosecutions, by requiring an expensive security bond as a condition for publication, and by imposing various taxes designed to drive out radical media by raising their costs. These coercive efforts were not effective, and by mid-century they had been abandoned in favor of the liberal view that the market would enforce responsibility.

Curran and Seaton show that the market *did* successfully accomplish what state intervention failed to do. Following the repeal of the punitive taxes on newspapers between 1853 and 1869, a new daily local press came into existence, but not one new local working-class daily was established through the rest of the nineteenth century. Curran and Seaton note that indeed, the eclipse of the national radical press was so total that when the Labour Party developed out of the working-class movement in the first decade of the twentieth century, it did not obtain the exclusive backing of a single national daily or Sunday paper.[4]

One important reason for this was the rise in scale of newspaper enterprise and the associated increase in capital costs from the mid-nineteenth century onward, which was based on technological improvements along with the owners' increased stress on reaching large audiences. The expansion of the free market was accompanied by an "industrialization of the press." The total cost of establishing a national weekly on a profitable basis in 1837 was under a thousand pounds, with a break-even circulation of 6,200 copies. By 1867, the estimated start-up cost of a new London daily was 50,000 pounds. The *Sunday Express*, launched in 1918, spent over two million pounds before it broke even with a circulation of over 250,000.[5]

Similar processes were at work in the United States, where the start-up cost of a new paper in New York City in 1851 was $69,000; the public sale of the *St. Louis Democrat* in 1872 yielded $456,000; and city newspapers were selling at from $6 to $18 million in the 1920s.[6] The cost of machinery alone, of even very small newspapers, has for many decades run into the hundreds of thousands of dollars; in 1945 it could be said that "Even small-newspaper publishing is big business . . . [and] is no longer a trade one takes up lightly even if he has substantial cash—or takes up at all if he doesn't."[7]

Thus the first filter—the limitation on ownership of media with any substantial outreach by the requisite large size of investment—was applicable a century or more ago, and it has become increasingly effective over time.[8] In 1986 there were some 1,500 daily newspapers, 11,000 magazines, 9,000 radio and 1,500 TV stations, 2,400 book publishers, and seven movie studios in the United States—over 25,000 media entities in all. But a large proportion of those among this set who were news dispensers were very small and local, dependent on the large national companies and wire services for all but local news. Many more were subject to common ownership, sometimes extending through virtually the entire set of media variants.[9]

Ben Bagdikian stresses the fact that despite the large media numbers, the twenty-nine largest media systems account for over half of the output of newspapers, and most of the sales and audiences in magazines, broadcasting, books, and movies. He contends that these "constitute a new Private Ministry of Information and Culture" that can set the national agenda.[10]

Actually, while suggesting a media autonomy from corporate and government power that we believe to be incompatible with structural facts (as we describe below), Bagdikian also may be understanding the degree of effective concentration in news manufacture. It has long been noted that the media are tiered, with the top tier—as measured by prestige, resources, and outreach—comprising somewhere between ten and twenty-four systems.[11] It is this top tier, along with the government and wire services, that defines the news agenda and supplies much of the national and international news to the lower tiers of the media, and thus for the general public.[12] Centralization within the top tier was substantially increased by the post-World War II rise of television and the national networking of this important medium. Pre-television news markets were local, even if heavily dependent on the higher tiers and a narrow set of sources for national and international news; the networks provide national and international news from three national sources, and television is now the principal source of news for the public.[13] The maturing of cable, however, has resulted in a fragmentation of television audiences and a slow erosion of the market share and power of the networks.

[. . .]

## 1.2.  The Advertising License to do Business: The Second Filter

In arguing for the benefits of the free market as a means of controlling dissident opinion in the mid-nineteenth century, the Liberal chancellor of the British exchequer, Sir George Lewis, noted that the market would promote those papers "enjoying the preference of the advertising public."[14] Advertising did, in fact, serve as a powerful mechanism weakening the working-class press. Curran and Seaton give the growth of advertising a status comparable with the increase in capital costs as a factor allowing the market to accomplish what state taxes and harassment failed to do, noting that these "advertisers thus acquired a de facto licensing authority since, without their support, newspapers ceased to be economically viable."[15]

Before advertising became prominent, the price of a newspaper had to cover the costs of doing business. With the growth of advertising, papers that attracted ads could afford a copy price well below production costs. This put papers lacking in advertising at a serious disadvantage: their prices would tend to be higher, curtailing sales, and they would have less surplus to invest in improving the salability of the paper (features, attractive format, promotion, etc.). For this reason, an advertising-based system will tend to drive out of existence or into marginality the media companies and types that depend on revenue from sales alone. With advertising, the free market does not yield a neutral system in which final buyer choice decides. The *advertisers'* choices influence media prosperity and survival.[16] The ad-based media receive an advertising subsidy that gives them a price-marketing-quality edge, which allows them to encroach on and further weaken their ad-free (or ad-disadvantaged) rivals.[17] Even if ad-based media cater to an affluent ("upscale") audience, they easily pick up a large part of the "downscale" audience, and their rivals lose market share and are eventually driven out or marginalized.

In fact, advertising has played a potent role in increasing concentration even among rivals that focus with equal energy on seeking advertising revenue. A market share and advertising edge on the part of one paper or television station will give it additional revenue to compete more effectively—promote more aggressively, buy more salable features and programs—and the disadvantaged rival must add expenses it cannot afford to try to stem the cumulative process of dwindling market (and revenue) share. The crunch is often fatal, and it helps explain the death of many large-circulation papers and magazines and the attrition in the number of newspapers.[18]

From the time of the introduction of press advertising, therefore, working-class and radical papers have been at a serious disadvantage. Their readers have tended to be of modest means, a factor that has always affected advertiser interest. One advertising executive stated in 1856 that some journals are poor vehicles because "their readers are not purchasers, and any money thrown upon them is so much thrown away."[19] The same force took a heavy toll of the post–World War II social-democratic press in Great Britain, with the *Daily Herald, News Chronicle,* and *Sunday Citizen* failing or absorbed into establishment systems between 1960 and 1967, despite a collective average daily readership of 9.3 million. As James Curran points out, with 4.7 million readers in its last year, "the *Daily Herald* actually had almost double the readership of *The Times,* the *Financial Times* and the *Guardian* combined." What is more, surveys showed that its readers "thought more highly of their paper than the regular readers of any other popular newspaper," and "they also read more in their paper than the readers of other popular papers despite being overwhelmingly working class. . . ."[20] The death of the *Herald,* as well as of the *News Chronicle* and *Sunday Citizen,* was in large measure a result of progressive strangulation by lack of advertising support. The *Herald,* with 8.1 percent of national daily circulation, got 3.5 percent of net advertising revenue; the *Sunday Citizen* got one-tenth of the net advertising revenue of the *Sunday Times* and one-seventh that of the *Observer* (on a per-thousand-copies basis). Curran argues persuasively that the loss of these three papers was an important contribution to the declining fortunes of the Labor party, in the case of the *Herald* specifically removing a mass-circulation institution that provided "an alternative framework of analysis and understanding that contested the dominant systems of representation in both broadcasting and the mainstream press."[21] A mass movement without any major media support, and subject to a great deal of active press hostility, suffers a serious disability, and struggles against grave odds. The successful media today are fully attuned to the crucial importance of audience "quality": CBS proudly tells its shareholders that while it "continuously seeks to maximize audience delivery," it has developed a new "sales tool" with which it approaches advertisers:

"Client Audience Profile, or CAP, will help advertisers optimize the effectiveness of their network television schedules by evaluating audience segments in proportion to usage levels of advertisers' products and services."[22] In short, the mass media are interested in attracting audiences with buying power, not audiences per se; it is affluent audiences that spark advertiser interest today, as in the nineteenth century. The idea that the drive for large audiences makes the mass media "democratic" thus suffers from the initial weakness that its political analogue is a voting system weighted by income!

The power of advertisers over television programming stems from the simple fact that they buy and pay for the programs—they are the "patrons" who provide the media subsidy. As such, the media compete for their patronage, developing specialized staff to solicit advertisers and necessarily having to explain how their programs serve advertisers' needs. The choices of these patrons greatly affect the welfare of the media, and the patrons become what William Evan calls "normative reference organizations,"[23] whose requirements and demands the media must accommodate if they are to succeed.[24]

For a television network, an audience gain or loss of one percentage point in the Nielsen ratings translates into a change in advertising revenue of from $80 to $100 million a year, with some variation depending on measures of audience "quality." The stakes in audience size and affluence are thus extremely large, and in a market system there is a strong tendency for such considerations to affect policy profoundly. This is partly a matter of institutional pressures to focus on the bottom line, partly a matter of the continuous interaction of the media organization with patrons who supply the revenue dollars. As Grant Tinker, then head of NBC-TV, observed, television "is an advertising-supported medium, and to the extent that support falls out, programming will change."[25]

Working-class and radical media also suffer from the political discrimination of advertisers. Political discrimination is structured into advertising allocations by the stress on people with money to buy. But many firms will always refuse to patronize ideological enemies and those whom they perceive as damaging their interests, and cases of overt discrimination add to the force of the voting system weighted by income. Public-television station WNET lost its corporate funding from Gulf + Western in 1985 after the station showed the documentary "Hungry for Profit," which contains material critical of multinational corporate activities in the Third World. Even before the program was shown, in anticipation of negative corporate reaction, station officials "did all we could to get the program sanitized" (according to one station source).[26] The chief executive of Gulf + Western complained to the station that the program was "virulently anti-business if not anti-American," and that the station's carrying the program was not the behavior "of a friend" of the corporation. The London *Economist* says that "Most people believe that WNET would not make the same mistake again."[27]

In addition to discrimination against unfriendly media institutions, advertisers also choose selectively among programs on the basis of their own principles. With rare exceptions these are culturally and politically conservative.[28] Large corporate advertisers on television will rarely sponsor programs that engage in serious criticisms of corporate activities, such as the problem of environmental degradation, the workings of the military-industrial complex, or corporate support of and benefits from Third World tyrannies. Erik Barnouw recounts the history of a proposed documentary series on environmental problems by NBC at a time of great interest in these issues. Barnouw notes that although at that time a great many large companies were spending money on commercials and other publicity regarding environmental problems, the documentary series failed for want of sponsors. The problem was one of excessive objectivity in the series, which included suggestions of corporate or systemic failure, whereas the corporate message "was one of reassurance."[29]

Television networks learn over time that such programs will not sell and would have to be carried at a financial sacrifice, and that, in addition, they may offend powerful advertisers.[30] With the rise in the price of advertising spots, the forgone revenue increases; and with increasing market pressure for financial performance and the diminishing constraints from regulation, an advertising-based media system will gradually increase advertising time and marginalize or eliminate altogether programming that has significant public-affairs content.[31] Advertisers will want, more generally, to avoid programs with serious complexities and disturbing controversies that interfere with the "buying mood." They seek programs that will lightly entertain and thus fit in with the spirit of the primary purpose of program purchases—the dissemination of a selling message. Thus over time, instead of programs like "The Selling of the Pentagon," it is a natural evolution of a market seeking sponsor dollars to offer programs such as "A Bird's-Eye View of Scotland," "Barry Goldwater's Arizona," "An Essay on Hotels," and "Mr. Rooney Goes to Dinner"—a CBS program on "how Americans eat when they dine out, where they go and why."[32] There are exceptional cases of companies willing to sponsor serious programs, sometimes a result of recent embarrassments that call for a public-relations offset.[33] But even in these cases the companies will usually not want to sponsor close examination of sensitive and divisive issues—they prefer programs on Greek antiquities, the ballet, and items of cultural and national history and nostalgia. Barnouw points out an interesting contrast: commercial-television drama "deals almost wholly with the here and now, as processed via advertising budgets," but on public television, culture "has come to mean 'other cultures.' . . . American civilization, here and now, is excluded from consideration."[34]

Television stations and networks are also concerned to maintain audience "flow" levels, i.e., to keep people watching from program to program, in order to sustain advertising ratings and revenue. Airing program interludes of documentary-cultural matter that cause station switching is costly, and over time a "free" (i.e., ad-based) commercial system will tend to excise it. Such documentary-cultural-critical materials will be driven out of secondary media vehicles as well, as these companies strive to qualify for advertiser interest, although there will always be some cultural-political programming trying to come into being or surviving on the periphery of the mainstream media.

## 1.3. Sourcing Mass-Media News: The Third Filter

The mass media are drawn into a symbiotic relationship with powerful sources of information by economic necessity and reciprocity of interest. The media need a steady, reliable flow of the raw material of news. They have daily news demands and imperative news schedules that they must meet. They cannot afford to have reporters and cameras at all places where important stories may break. Economics dictates that they concentrate their resources where significant news often occurs, where important rumors and leaks abound, and where regular press conferences are held. The White House, the Pentagon, and the State Department, in Washington, D.C., are central nodes of such news activity. On a local basis, city hall and the police department are the subject of regular news "beats" for reporters. Business corporations and trade groups are also regular and credible purveyors of stories deemed newsworthy. These bureaucracies turn out a large volume of material that meets the demands of news organizations for reliable, scheduled flows. Mark Fishman calls this "the principle of bureaucratic affinity: only other bureaucracies can satisfy the input needs of a news bureaucracy."[35]

Government and corporate sources also have the great merit of being recognizable and credible by their status and prestige. This is important to the mass media. As Fishman notes, Newsworkers are predisposed to treat bureaucratic accounts as factual because news personnel participate in upholding a normative order of authorized knowers in the society. Reporters operate with the attitude that officials ought to know what it is their job to know. . . . In particular, a newsworker will recognize an official's claim to knowledge not merely as a claim, but as a credible, competent piece of knowledge. This amounts to a moral division of labor: officials have and give the facts; reporters merely get them.[36]

Another reason for the heavy weight given to official sources is that the mass media claim to be "objective" dispensers of the news. Partly to maintain the image of objectivity, but also to protect themselves from criticisms of bias and the threat of libel suits, they need material that can be portrayed as presumptively accurate.[37] This is also partly a matter of cost: taking information from sources that may be presumed credible reduces investigative expense, whereas material from sources that are not prima facie credible, or that will elicit criticism and threats, requires careful checking and costly research.

The magnitude of the public-information operations of large government and corporate bureaucracies that constitute the primary news sources is vast and ensures special access to the media. The Pentagon, for example, has a public-information service that involves many thousands of employees, spending hundreds of millions of dollars every year and dwarfing not only the public-information resources of any dissenting individual or group but the *aggregate* of such groups. In 1979 and 1980, during a brief interlude of relative openness (since closed down), the U.S. Air Force revealed that its public-information outreach included the following:

140 newspapers, 690,000 copies per week
*Airman* magazine, monthly circulation 125,000
34 radio and 17 TV stations, primarily overseas
45,000 headquarters and unit news releases
615,000 hometown news releases
6,600 interviews with news media
3,200 news conferences
500 news media orientation flights
50 meetings with editorial boards
11,000 speeches[38]

This excludes vast areas of the air force's public-information effort. Writing back in 1970, Senator J. W. Fulbright had found that the air force public-relations effort in 1968 involved 1,305 full-time employees, exclusive of additional thousands that "have public functions collateral to other duties."[39] The air force at that time offered a weekly film-clip service for TV and a taped features program for use three times a week, sent to 1,139 radio stations; it also produced 148 motion pictures, of which 24 were released for public consumption.[40] There is no reason to believe that the air force public-relations effort has diminished since the 1960s.[41]

Note that this is just the air force. There are three other branches with massive programs, and there is a separate, overall public-information program under an assistant secretary of defense for public affairs in the Pentagon. In 1971, an *Armed Forces Journal* survey revealed that the Pentagon was publishing a total of 371 magazines at an annual cost of some $57 million, an operation sixteen times larger than the nation's biggest publisher. In an update in 1982, the *Air Force Journal International* indicated that the Pentagon was publishing 1,203 periodicals.[42] To put this into perspective, we may note the scope of public-information operations of the American Friends Service Committee (AFSC) and the National Council of the Churches of Christ (NCC), two of the largest of the nonprofit organizations that offer a consistently challenging voice to the views of the Pentagon. The AFSC's main office information-services budget in 1984–85 was under $500,000, with eleven staff people.[43] Its institution-wide press releases run at about two hundred per year, its press conferences thirty a year, and it produces about one film and two or three slide shows a year. It does not offer film clips, photos, or taped radio programs to the media. The NCC Office of Information has an annual budget of some $350,000, issues about a hundred news releases per year, and holds four press conferences annually.[44] The ratio of air force news releases and press conferences to those of the AFSC and NCC taken together are 150 to 1 (or 2,200 to 1 if we count hometown news releases of the air force), and 94 to 1 respectively. Aggregating the other services would increase the differential by a large factor. Only the corporate sector has the resources to produce public information and propaganda on the scale of the Pentagon and other government bodies. The AFSC and NCC cannot duplicate the Mobil Oil company's multimillion-dollar purchase of newspaper space and other corporate investments to get its viewpoint across.[45] The number of individual corporations with budgets for public information and lobbying in excess of those of the AFSC and NCC runs into the hundreds, perhaps even the thousands. A corporate *collective* like the U.S. Chamber of Commerce had a 1983 budget for research, communications, and political activities of $65 million.[46] By 1980, the chamber was publishing a business magazine (*Nation's Business*) with a circulation of 1.3 million and a weekly newspaper with 740,000 subscribers, and it was producing a weekly panel show distributed to 400 radio stations, as well as its own weekly panel-discussion programs carried by 128 commercial television stations.[47]

Besides the U.S. Chamber, there are thousands of state and local chambers of commerce and trade associations also engaged in public-relations and lobbying activities. The corporate and trade-association lobbying network community is "a network of well over 150,000 professionals,"[48] and its resources are related to corporate income, profits, and the protective value of public-relations and lobbying outlays. Corporate profits before taxes in 1985 were $295.5 billion. When the corporate community gets agitated about the political environment, as it did in the 1970s, it obviously has the wherewithal to meet the perceived threat. Corporate and trade-association image and issues advertising increased from $305 million in 1975 to $650 million in 1980.[49] So did direct-mail campaigns through dividend and other mail stuffers, the distribution of educational films, booklets and pamphlets, and outlays on initiatives and referendums, lobbying, and political and think-tank contributions. Aggregate corporate and trade-association political advertising and grass-roots outlays were estimated to have reached the billion-dollar-a-year level by 1978, and to have grown to $1.6 billion by 1984.[50]

To consolidate their preeminent position as sources, government and business-news promoters go to great pains to make things easy for news organizations. They provide the media organizations with facilities in which to gather; they give journalists advance copies of speeches and forthcoming reports; they schedule press conferences at hours well-geared to news deadlines;[51] they write press releases in usable language; and they carefully organize their press conferences and "photo opportunity" sessions.[52] It is the job of news officers "to meet the journalist's scheduled needs with material that their beat agency has generated at its own pace."[53]

In effect, the large bureaucracies of the powerful *subsidize* the mass media, and gain special access by their contribution to reducing the media's costs of acquiring the raw materials of, and producing, news. The large entities that provide this subsidy become "routine" news sources and have privileged access to the gates. Non-routine sources must struggle for access, and may be ignored by the arbitrary decision of the gatekeepers. It should also be noted that in the case of the largesse of the Pentagon and the State Department's Office of Public Diplomacy,[54] the subsidy is at the taxpayers' expense, so that, in effect, the citizenry pays to be propagandized in the interest of powerful groups such as military contractors and other sponsors of state terrorism.

Because of their services, continuous contact on the beat, and mutual dependency, the powerful can use personal relationships, threats, and rewards to further influence and coerce the media. The media may feel obligated to carry extremely dubious stories and mute criticism in order not to offend their sources and disturb a close relationship.[55] It is very difficult to call authorities on whom one depends for daily news liars, even if they tell whoppers. Critical sources may be avoided not only because of their lesser availability and higher cost of establishing credibility, but also because the primary sources may be offended and may even threaten the media using them.

Powerful sources may also use their prestige and importance to the media as a lever to deny critics access to the media: the Defense Department, for example, refused to participate in National Public Radio discussions of defense issues if experts from the Center for Defense Information were on the program; Elliott Abrams refused to appear on a program on human rights in Central America at the Kennedy School of Government, at Harvard University, unless the former ambassador, Robert White, was excluded as a participant;[56] Claire Sterling refused to participate in television-network shows on the Bulgarian Connection where her critics would appear.[57] In the last two of these cases, the authorities and brand-name experts were successful in monopolizing access by coercive threats.

Perhaps more important, powerful sources regularly take advantage of media routines and dependency to "manage" the media, to manipulate them into following a special agenda and framework (as we will show in detail in the chapters that follow).[58] Part of this management process consists of inundating the media with stories, which serve sometimes to foist a particular line and frame on the media (e.g., Nicaragua as illicitly supplying arms to the Salvadoran rebels), and at other times to help chase unwanted stories off the front page or out of the media altogether (the alleged delivery of MIGs to Nicaragua during the week of the 1984 Nicaraguan election). This strategy can be traced back at least as far as the Committee on Public Information, established to coordinate propaganda during World War I, which "discovered in 1917–18 that one of the best means of controlling news was flooding news channels with 'facts,' or what amounted to official information."[59]

The relation between power and sourcing extends beyond official and corporate provision of day-to-day news to shaping the supply of "experts." The dominance of official sources is weakened by the existence of highly respectable unofficial sources that give dissident views with great authority. This problem is alleviated by "co-opting the experts"[60]—i.e., putting them on the payroll as consultants, funding their research, and organizing think tanks that will hire them directly and help disseminate their messages. In this way bias may be structured, and the supply of experts may be skewed in the direction desired by the government and "the market."[61] As Henry Kissinger has pointed out, in this "age of the expert," the "constituency" of the expert is "those who have a vested interest in commonly held opinions; elaborating and defining its consensus at a high level has, after all, made him an expert."[62] It is therefore appropriate that this restructuring has taken place to allow the commonly held opinions (meaning those that are functional for elite interests) to continue to prevail.

[. . .]

## 1.4. Flak and the Enforcers: The Fourth Filter

"Flak" refers to negative responses to a media statement or program. It may take the form of letters, telegrams, phone calls, petitions, law-suits, speeches and bills before Congress, and other modes of complaint, threat, and punitive action. It may be organized centrally or locally, or it may consist of the entirely independent actions of individuals.

If flak is produced on a large scale, or by individuals or groups with substantial resources, it can be both uncomfortable and costly to the media. Positions have to be defended within the organization and without, sometimes before legislatures and possibly even in courts. Advertisers may withdraw patronage. Television advertising is mainly of consumer goods that are readily subject to organized boycott. During the McCarthy years, many advertisers and radio and television stations were effectively coerced into quiescence and blacklisting of employees by the threats of determined Red hunters to boycott products. Advertisers are still concerned to avoid offending constituencies that might produce flak, and their demand for suitable programming is a continuing feature of the media environment.[63] If certain kinds of fact, position, or program are thought likely to elicit flak, this prospect can be a deterrent.

The ability to produce flak, and especially flak that is costly and threatening, is related to power. Serious flak has increased in close parallel with business's growing resentment of media criticism and the corporate offensive of the 1970s and 1980s. Flak from the powerful can be either direct or indirect. The direct would include letters or phone calls from the White House to Dan Rather or William Paley, or from the FCC to the television networks asking for documents used in putting together a program, or from irate officials of ad agencies or corporate sponsors to media officials asking for reply time or threatening retaliation.[64] The powerful can also work on the media indirectly by complaining to their own constituencies (stockholders, employees) about the media, by generating institutional advertising that does the same, and by funding right-wing monitoring or think-tank operations designed to attack the media. They may also fund political campaigns and help put into power conservative politicians who will more directly serve the interests of private power in curbing any deviationism in the media.

Along with its other political investments of the 1970s and 1980s, the corporate community sponsored the growth of institutions such as the American Legal Foundation, the Capital Legal Foundation, the Media Institute, the Center for Media and Public

Affairs, and Accuracy in Media (AIM). These may be regarded as institutions organized for the specific purpose of producing flak. Another and older flak-producing machine with a broader design is Freedom House. The American Legal Foundation, organized in 1980, has specialized in Fairness Doctrine complaints and libel suits to aid "media victims." The Capital Legal Foundation, incorporated in 1977, was the Scaife vehicle for Westmoreland's $120-million libel suit against CBS.[65]

The Media Institute, organized in 1972 and funded by corporate-wealthy patrons, sponsors monitoring projects, conferences, and studies of the media. It has focused less heavily on media failings in foreign policy, concentrating more on media portrayals of economic issues and the business community, but its range of interests is broad. The main theme of its sponsored studies and conferences has been the failure of the media to portray business accurately and to give adequate weight to the business point of view,[66] but it underwrites works such as John Corry's exposé of the alleged left-wing bias of the mass media.[67] The chairman of the board of trustees of the institute in 1985 was Steven V. Seekins, the top public-relations officer of the American Medical Association; chairman of the National Advisory Council was Herbert Schmertz, of the Mobil Oil Corporation.

The Center for Media and Public Affairs, run by Linda and Robert Lichter, came into existence in the mid-1980s as a "non-profit, non-partisan" research institute, with warm accolades from Patrick Buchanan, Faith Whittlesey, and Ronald Reagan himself, who recognized the need for an objective and fair press. Their *Media Monitor* and research studies continue their earlier efforts to demonstrate the liberal bias and anti-business propensities of the mass media.[68]

AIM was formed in 1969, and it grew spectacularly in the 1970s. Its annual income rose from $5,000 in 1971 to $1.5 million in the early 1980s, with funding mainly from large corporations and the wealthy heirs and foundations of the corporate system. At least eight separate oil companies were contributors to AIM in the early 1980s, but the wide representation in sponsors from the corporate community is impressive.[69] The function of AIM is to harass the media and put pressure on them to follow the corporate agenda and a hard-line, right-wing foreign policy. It presses the media to join more enthusiastically in Red-scare band-wagons, and attacks them for alleged deficiencies whenever they fail to toe the line on foreign policy. It conditions the media to expect trouble (and cost increases) for violating right-wing standards of bias.[70]

Freedom House, which dates back to the early 1940s, has had interlocks with AIM, the World Anticommunist League, Resistance International, and U.S. government bodies such as Radio Free Europe and the CIA, and has long served as a virtual propaganda arm of the government and international right wing. It sent election monitors to the Rhodesian elections staged by Ian Smith in 1979 and found them "fair," whereas the 1980 elections won by Mugabe under British supervision it found dubious. Its election monitors also found the Salvadoran elections of 1982 admirable.[71] It has expended substantial resources in criticizing the media for insufficient sympathy with U.S. foreign-policy ventures and excessively harsh criticism of U.S. client states. Its most notable publication of this genre was Peter Braestrup's *Big Story*, which contended that the media's negative portrayal of the Tet offensive helped lose the war. The work is a travesty of scholarship, but more interesting is its premise: that the mass media not only should support any national venture abroad, but should do so with enthusiasm, such enterprises being by definition noble. In 1982, when the Reagan administration was having trouble containing media reporting of the systematic killing of civilians by the

Salvadoran army, Freedom House came through with a denunciation of the "imbalance" in media reporting from El Salvador.[72]

Although the flak machines steadily attack the mass media, the media treat them well. They receive respectful attention, and their propagandistic role and links to a larger corporate program are rarely mentioned or analyzed. AIM head, Reed Irvine's diatribes are frequently published, and right-wing network flacks who regularly assail the "liberal media," such as Michael Ledeen,[73] are given Op-Ed column space, sympathetic reviewers, and a regular place on talk shows as experts. This reflects the power of the sponsors, including the well-entrenched position of the right wing in the mass media themselves.[74]

The producers of flak add to one another's strength and reinforce the command of political authority in its news-management activities. The government is a major producer of flak, regularly assailing, threatening, and "correcting" the media, trying to contain any deviations from the established line. News management itself is designed to produce flak. In the Reagan years, Mr. Reagan was put on television to exude charm to millions, many of whom berated the media when they dared to criticize the "Great Communicator."[75]

## 1.5.  Anticommunism as a Control Mechanism

A final filter is the ideology of anticommunism. Communism as the ultimate evil has always been the specter haunting property owners, as it threatens the very root of their class position and superior status. The Soviet, Chinese, and Cuban revolutions were traumas to Western elites, and the ongoing conflicts and the well-publicized abuses of Communist states have contributed to elevating opposition to communism to a first principle of Western ideology and politics. This ideology helps mobilize the populace against an enemy, and because the concept is fuzzy it can be used against anybody advocating policies that threaten property interests or support accommodation with Communist states and radicalism. It therefore helps fragment the left and labor movements and serves as a political-control mechanism. If the triumph of communism is the worst imaginable result, the support of fascism abroad is justified as a lesser evil. Opposition to social democrats who are too soft on Communists and "play into their hands" is rationalized in similar terms.

Liberals at home, often accused of being pro-Communist or insufficiently anti-Communist, are kept continuously on the defensive in a cultural milieu in which anticommunism is the dominant religion. If they allow communism, or something that can be labeled communism, to triumph in the provinces while they are in office, the political costs are heavy. Most of them have fully internalized the religion anyway, but they are all under great pressure to demonstrate their anti-Communist credentials. This causes them to behave very much like reactionaries. Their occasional support of social democrats often breaks down where the latter are insufficiently harsh on their own indigenous radicals or on popular groups that are organizing among generally marginalized sectors. In his brief tenure in the Dominican Republic, Juan Bosch attacked corruption in the armed forces and government, began a land-reform program, undertook a major project for mass education of the populace, and maintained a remarkably open government and system of effective civil liberties. These policies threatened powerful internal vested interests, and the United States resented his independence and the extension of civil liberties to Communists and radicals. This was carrying democracy and pluralism too far. Kennedy was "extremely disappointed" in Bosch's rule, and the State Department "quickly soured on the first democratically elected Dominican President in over thirty years." Bosch's overthrow by the military after nine months in office had at least the tacit support of the United States.[76] Two years later, by contrast, the Johnson administration invaded the Dominican Republic to make sure that Bosch did not resume power.

The Kennedy liberals were enthusiastic about the military coup and displacement of a populist government in Brazil in 1964.[77] A major spurt in the growth of neo-Fascist national-security states took place under Kennedy and Johnson. In the cases of the U.S. subversion of Guatemala, 1947–54, and the military attacks on Nicaragua, 1981–87, allegations of Communist links and a Communist threat caused many liberals to support counterrevolutionary intervention, while others lapsed into silence, paralyzed by the fear of being tarred with charges of infidelity to the national religion.

## Notes

1.  Media representatives claim that what the government says is "news-worthy" in its own right. If, however, the government's assertions are transmitted without context or evaluation, and without regard to the government's possible manipulative intent, the media have set themselves up to be "managed." Their objectivity is "nominal," not substantive.

    In early October 1986, memos were leaked to the press indicating that the Reagan administration had carried out a deliberate campaign of disinformation to influence events in Libya. The mass media, which had passed along this material without question, expressed a great deal of righteous indignation that they had been misled. To compound the absurdity, five years earlier the press had reported a CIA-run "disinformation program designed to embarrass Qaddafi and his government," along with terrorist operations to overthrow Quaddafi and perhaps assassinate him (*Newsweek*, Aug. 3, 1981; P. Edward Haley, *Qaddafi and the United States since 1969* [New York: Praeger, 1984], p. 272). But no lessons were learned. In fact, the mass media are gulled on an almost daily basis, but rarely have to suffer the indignity of government *documents* revealing their gullibility. With regard to Libya, the media have fallen into line for each propaganda ploy, from the 1981 "hit squads" through the Berlin discotheque bombing, swallowing each implausible claim, failing to admit error in retrospect, and apparently unable to learn from successive entrapment—which suggests willing error. See Noam Chomsky, *Pirates & Emperors* (New York: Claremont, 1986), chapter 3. As we show throughout the present book, a series of lies by the government, successively exposed, never seems to arouse skepticism in the media regarding the next government claim.

2.  James Curran and Jean Seaton, *Power Without Responsibility: The Press and Broadcasting in Britain*, 2d ed. (London: Methuen, 1985), p. 24.

3.  Quoted in ibid., p. 23.

4.  Ibid., p. 34.

5.  Ibid., pp. 38–39.

6.  Alfred McClung Lee, *The Daily Newspaper in America* (New York: Macmillan, 1937), pp. 166, 173.

7.  Earl Vance, "Freedom of the Press for Whom," *Virginia Quarterly Review* (Summer 1945), quoted in *Survival of a Free, Competitive Press: The Small Newspaper: Democracy's Grass Roots*, Report of the Chairman, Senate Small Business Committee, 80th Cong., 1st session, 1947, p. 54.

8.  Note that we are speaking of media with substantial outreach—mass media. It has always been possible to start small-circulation journals and to produce mimeographed or photocopied news letters sent around to a tiny audience. But even small journals in the United States today typically survive only by virtue of contributions from wealthy financial angels.

9. In 1987, the Times-Mirror Company, for example, owned newspapers in Los Angeles, Baltimore, Denver, and Hartford, Connecticut, had book publishing and magazine subsidiaries, and owned cable systems and seven television stations.

10. Ben Bagdikian, *The Media Monopoly*, 2nd ed. (Boston: Beacon Press, 1987), p. xvi.

11. David L. Paletz and Robert M. Entman, *Media . Power . Politics* (New York: Free Press, 1981), p. 7; Stephen Hess, *The Government/Press Connection: Press Officers and Their Offices* (Washington: Brookings, 1984), pp. 99–100.

12. The four major Western wire services—Associated Press, United Press International, Reuters, and Agence-France-Presse—account for some 80 percent of the international news circulating in the world today. AP is owned by member newspapers; UPI is privately owned; Reuters was owned mainly by the British media until it went public in 1984, but control was retained by the original owners by giving lesser voting rights to the new stockholders; Agence-France-Presse is heavily subsidized by the French government. As is pointed out by Jonathan Fenby, the wire services "exist to serve markets," and their prime concern, accordingly, "is with the rich media markets of the United States, Western Europe, and Japan, and increasingly with the business community. . . ." They compete fiercely, but AP and UPI "are really U.S. enterprises that operate on an international scale. . . . Without their domestic base, the AP and UPI could not operate as international agencies. With it, they must be American organizations, subject to American pressures and requirements" (*The International News Services* [New York: Schocken, 1986], pp. 7, 9, 73–74). See also Anthony Smith, *The Geopolitics of Information: How Western Culture Dominates the World* (New York: Oxford University Press, 1980), chapter 3.

13. The fourteenth annual Roper survey, "Public Attitudes toward Television and Other Media in a Time of Change" (May 1985), indicates that in 1984, 64 percent of the sample mentioned television as the place "where you usually get most of your news about what's going on in the world today . . ." (p. 3). It has often been noted that the television networks themselves depend heavily on the prestige newspapers, wire services, and government for their choices of news. Their autonomy as newsmakers can be easily exaggerated.

14. Quoted in Curran and Seaton, *Power Without Responsibility*, p. 31.

15. Ibid., p. 41.

16. ". . . producers presenting patrons [advertisers] with the greatest opportunities to make a profit through their publics will receive support while those that cannot compete on this score will not survive" (Joseph Turow, *Media Industries: The Production of News and Entertainment* [New York: Longman, 1984], p. 52).

17. Noncommercial television is also at a huge disadvantage for the same reason, and will require a public subsidy to be able to compete. Because public television does not have the built-in constraints of ownership by the wealthy, and the need to appease advertisers, it poses a threat to a narrow elite control of mass communications. This is why conservatives struggle to keep public television on a short leash, with annual funding decisions, and funding at a low level (see Barnouw, *The Sponsor*, pp. 179–82). Another option pursued in the Carter-Reagan era has been to force it into the commercial nexus by sharp defunding.

18. Bagdikian, *Media Monopoly*, pp. 118–26. " 'The dominant paper ultimately thrives,' Gannett Chairman Allen H. Neuharth says. 'The weaker paper ultimately dies' " (Joseph B. White, "Knight-Ridder's No-Lose Plan Backfires," *Wall Street Journal*, Jan. 4, 1988).

19. Quoted in Curran and Seaton, *Power Without Responsibility*, p. 43.

20. "Advertising and the Press," in James Curran, ed., *The British Press: A Manifesto* (London: Macmillan, 1978), pp. 252–55.

21. Ibid., p. 254.

22. *1984 CBS Annual Report*, p. 13. This is a further refinement in the measurement of "efficiency" in "delivering an audience." In the magazine business, the standard measure is CPM, or "costs per thousand," to an advertiser to reach buyers through a full-page, black-and-white ad. Recent developments, like CBS's CAP, have been in the direction of identifying the special characteristics of the audience delivered. In selling itself to advertisers, the *Soap Opera Digest* says: "But you probably want to know about our first milestone: today *Soap Opera Digest* delivers more women in the 18–49 category at the lowest CPM than any other women's magazine" (quoted in Turow, *Media Industries*, p. 55).

23. William Evan, *Organization Theory* (New York: Wiley, 1976), p. 123.

24. Turow asserts that "The continual interaction of producers and primary patrons plays a dominant part in setting the general boundary conditions for day-to-day production activity" (*Media Industries*, p. 51).

25. Quoted in Todd Gitlin, *Inside Prime Time* (New York: Pantheon, 1983), p. 253.

26. Pat Aufderheide, "What Makes Public TV Public?" *The Progressive* (January 1988).

27. "Castor oil or Camelot?" December 5, 1987. For further materials on such interventions, see Harry Hammitt, "Advertising Pressures on Media," Freedom of Information Center Report no. 367 (School of Journalism, University of Missouri at Columbia, February 1977). See also James Aronson, *Deadline for the Media* (New York: Bobbs-Merrill, 1972), pp. 261–63.

28. According to Procter & Gamble's instructions to their ad agency, "There will be no material on any of our programs which could in any way further the concept of business as cold, ruthless, and lacking in all sentiment or spiritual motivation." The manager of corporate communications for General Electric has said: "We insist on a program environment that reinforces our corporate messages" (quoted in Bagdikian, *Media Monopoly*, p. 160). We may recall that GE now owns NBC-TV.

29. Barnouw, *The Sponsor*, p. 135.

30. Advertisers may also be offended by attacks on themselves or their products. On the tendency of the media to avoid criticism of advertised products even when very important to consumer welfare [e.g., the effects of smoking], see Bagdikian, *Media Monopoly*, pp. 168–73.

31. This is hard to prove statistically, given the poor data made available by the FCC over the years. The long-term trend in advertising time/programming time is dramatically revealed by the fact that in 1929 the National Association of Broadcasting adopted as a standard of commercial practice on radio the following: "Commercial announcements . . . shall not be broadcast between 7 and 11 P.M." William Paley testified before the Senate Commerce Committee in 1930 that only 22 percent of CBS's time was allocated to commercially sponsored programs, with the other 78 percent sustaining; and he noted that advertising took up only "seven-tenths of 1 percent of all our time" (quoted in *Public Service Responsibility of Broadcast Licensees*, FCC [Washington: GPO, Mar. 7, 1946], p. 42). Frank Wolf states in reference to public-affairs programming: "That such programs were even shown at all on commercial television may have been the result of FCC regulation" (*Television Programming for News and Public Affairs* [New York: Praeger, 1972], p. 138; see also pp. 99–139).

32. Barnouw, *The Sponsor*, p. 134.

33. For Alcoa's post-antitrust-suit sponsorship of Edward R. Murrow, and ITT's post-early-1970s-scandals sponsorship of "The Big Blue Marble," see Barnouw, *The Sponsor*, ibid., pp. 51–52, 84–86. Barnouw shows that network news coverage of ITT was sharply constrained during the period of ITT program sponsorship.

34. Barnouw, *The Sponsor*, p. 150.

35. Mark Fishman, *Manufacturing the News* (Austin: University of Texas Press, 1980), p. 143.

36. Ibid., pp. 144–45.

37. Gaye Tuchman, "Objectivity as Strategic Ritual: An Examination of Newsmen's Notions of Objectivity," *American Journal of Sociology* 77, no. 2 (1972), pp. 662–64.

38. United States Air Force, "Fact Sheet: The United States Air Force Information Program" (March 1979); "News Releases: 600,000 in a Year," *Air Force Times*, April 28, 1980.

39. J. W. Fulbright, *The Pentagon Propaganda Machine* (New York: H. Live-right, 1970), p. 88.

40. Ibid., p. 90.

41. An Associated Press report on "Newspapers Mustered as Air Force Defends B1B," published in the *Washington Post*, April 3, 1987, indicates that the U.S. Air Force had 277 newspapers in 1987, as compared with 140 in 1979.

42. "DOD Kills 205 Periodicals; Still Publishes 1,203 Others," *Armed Forces Journal International* (August 1982), p. 16.

43. Its nine regional offices also had some public-information operations, but personnel and funding are not readily allocable to this function. They are smaller than the central office aggregate.

 The AFSC aggregate public-information budget is about the same size as the contract given by the State Department to International Business Communications (IBC) for lobbying on behalf of the contras ($419,000). This was only one of twenty-five contracts investigated by the GAO that "the Latin American Public Diplomacy office awarded to individuals for research and papers on Central America, said a GAO official involved in the investigation" (Rita Beamish, "Pro-contra Contracts are Probed," *Philadelphia Inquirer*, July 22, 1987, p. 4A).

44.   The NCC's news services are concentrated in the Office of Information, but it has some dispersed staff in communications functions elsewhere in the organization that produce a few newsletters, magazines, and some videotapes and filmstrips.

45.   In 1980, Mobil Oil had a public-relations budget of $21 million and a public-relations staff of seventy-three. Between 1976 and 1981 it produced at least a dozen televised special reports on such issues as gasoline prices, with a hired television journalist interviewing Mobil executives and other experts, that are shown frequently on television, often without indication of Mobil sponsorship. See A. Kent MacDougall, *Ninety Seconds To Tell It All* (Homewood, Ill.: Dow Jones–Irwin, 1981), pp. 117–20.

46.   John S. Saloma III, *Ominous Politics: The New Conservative Labyrinth* (New York: Hill & Wang, 1984), p. 79.

47.   MacDougall, *Ninety Seconds*, pp. 116–17.

48.   Thomas B. Edsall, *The New Politics of Inequality* (New York: Norton, 1984), p. 110.

49.   Peggy Dardenne, "Corporate Advertising," *Public Relations Journal* (November 1982), p. 36.

50.   S. Prakash Sethi, *Handbook of Advocacy Advertising: Strategies and Applications* (Cambridge, Mass.: Ballinger, 1987), p. 22. See also Edsall, *New Politics*, chapter 3, "The Politicization of the Business Community"; and Saloma, *Ominous Politics*, chapter 6, "The Corporations: Making Our Voices Heard."

51.   The April 14, 1986, U.S. bombing of Libya was the first military action timed to preempt attention on 7 P.M. prime-time television news. See Chomsky, *Pirates & Emperors*, p. 147.

52.   For the masterful way the Reagan administration used these to manipulate the press, see "Standups," *The New Yorker*, December 2, 1985, pp. 81ff.

53.   Fishman, *Manufacturing the News*, p. 153.

54.   See note 43.

55.   On January 16, 1986, the American Friends Service Committee issued a news release, based on extended Freedom of Information Act inquiries, which showed that there had been 381 navy nuclear-weapons accidents and "incidents" in the period 1965–77, a figure far higher than that previously claimed. The mass media did not cover this hot story directly but through the filter of the navy's reply, which downplayed the significance of the new findings and eliminated or relegated to the background the AFSC's full range of facts and interpretation of the meaning of what they had uncovered. A typical heading: "Navy Lists Nuclear Mishaps: None of 630 Imperilled Public, Service Says," *Washington Post*, January 16, 1986.

56.   The Harvard professor in charge of the program, Harvey Mansfield, stated that the invitation to White had been a mistake anyway, as he "is a representative of the far left," whereas the forum was intended to involve a debate "between liberals and conservatives" (*Harvard Crimson*, May 14, 1986).

57.   See Edward S. Herman and Frank Brodhead, *The Rise and Fall of the Bulgarian Connection* (New York: Sheridan Square Publications, 1986), pp. 123–24.

58.   Mark Hertsgaard, "How Reagan Seduced Us: Inside the President's Propaganda Factory," *Village Voice*, September 18, 1984; see also "Standups," cited in note 79 above.

59.   Stephen L. Vaughn, *Holding Fast the Inner Lines* (Chapel Hill: University of North Carolina Press, 1980), p. 194.

60.   Bruce Owen and Ronald Braeutigam, *The Regulation Game: Strategic Use of the Administrative Process* (Cambridge, Mass.: Ballinger, 1978), p. 7.

61.   See Edward S. Herman, "The Institutionalization of Bias in Economics," *Media, Culture and Society* (July 1982), pp. 275–91.

62.   Henry Kissinger, *American Foreign Policy* (New York: Norton, 1969), p. 28.

63.   See above, note 28.

64.   See "The Business Campaign Against 'Trial by TV,' " *Business Week*, June 22, 1980, pp. 77–79; William H. Miller, "Fighting TV Hatchet Jobs," *Industry Week*, January 12, 1981, pp. 61–64.

65.   See Walter Schneir and Miriam Schneir, "Beyond Westmoreland: The Right's Attack on the Press," *The Nation*, March 30, 1985.

66.   An ad widely distributed by United Technologies Corporation, titled "Crooks and Clowns

on TV," is based on the Media Institute's study entitled *Crooks, Conmen and Clowns: Businessmen in TV Entertainment*, which contends that businessmen are treated badly in television entertainment programs.

67. John Corry, *TV News and the Dominant Culture* (Washington: Media Institute), 1986.

68. See S. Robert Lichter, Stanley Rothman, and Linda Lichter, *The Media Elite* (Bethesda, Md.: Adler & Adler, 1986). For a good discussion of the Lichters' new center, see Alexander Cockburn, "Ashes and Diamonds," *In These Times*, July 8–21, 1987.

69. Louis Wolf, "Accuracy in Media Rewrites News and History," *Covert Action Information Bulletin* (Spring 1984), pp. 26–29.

70. AIM's impact is hard to gauge, but it must be recognized as only a part of a larger corporate-right-wing campaign of attack. It has common funding sources with such components of the conservative labyrinth as AEI, Hoover, the Institute for Contemporary Studies, and others (see Saloma, *Ominous Politics*, esp. chapters 2, 3, and 6), and has its own special role to play. AIM's head, Reed Irvine, is a frequent participant in television talk shows, and his letters to the editor and commentary are regularly published in the mass media. The media feel obligated to provide careful responses to his detailed attacks on their news and documentaries, and the Corporation for Public Broadcasting even helped fund his group's reply to the PBS series on Vietnam. His ability to get the publisher of the *New York Times* to meet with him personally once a year—a first objective of any lobbyist—is impressive testimony to influence. On his contribution to the departure of Raymond Bonner from the *Times*, see Wolf, "Accuracy in Media Rewrites News and History," pp. 32–33.

71. For an analysis of the bias of the Freedom House observers, see Edward S. Herman and Frank Brodhead, *Demonstration Elections: U.S.-Staged Elections in the Dominican Republic, Vietnam, and El Salvador* (Boston: South End Press, 1984), appendix 1, "Freedom House Observers in Zimbabwe Rhodesia and El Salvador."

72. R. Bruce McColm, "El Salvador: Peaceful Revolution or Armed Struggle?" *Perspectives on Freedom* 1 (New York: Freedom House, 1982); James Nelson Goodsell, "Freedom House Labels US Reports on Salvador Biased," *Christian Science Monitor*, February 3, 1982.

73. For a discussion of Ledeen's views on the media, see Herman and Brodhead, *Bulgarian Connection*, pp. 166–70.

74. Among the contributors to AIM have been the Reader's Digest Association and the De Witt Wallace Fund, Walter Annenberg, Sir James Goldsmith (owner of the French *L'Express*), and E. W. Scripps II, board chairman of a newspaper-television-radio system.

75. George Skelton, White House correspondent for the *Los Angeles Times*, noted that in reference to Reagan's errors of fact, "You write the stories once, twice, and you get a lot of mail saying, 'You're picking on the guy, you guys in the press make mistakes too.' And editors respond to that, so after a while the stories don't run anymore. We're intimidated" (quoted in Hertsgaard, "How Reagan Seduced Us").

76. Piero Gleijeses, *The Dominican Crisis* (Baltimore: Johns Hopkins University Press, 1978), pp. 95–99.

77. Jan K. Black, *United States Penetration of Brazil* (Philadelphia: University of Pennsylvania Press, 1977), pp. 39–56.

# Chapter 31

# PIERRE BOURDIEU

# ON TELEVISION AND JOURNALISM

**P**IERRE BOURDIEU WAS A DOMINANT figure in French sociology during the last part of the twentieth century. He coined or popularized terms like social, cultural and symbolic capital, the idea that people live within a complex web of social relations and specific forms of "capital" could be "invested" to allow them to gain an advantage in specific situations. In perhaps his most well-known work, *Distinction: A Social Critique of the Judgment of Taste*, Bourdieu argues that social class in many ways determines aesthetic tastes and, in turn, taste serves as a marker for social class.

*On Television* is a devastating critique of television journalism. Originally delivered as a series of lectures televised internally at Paris's College de France as a protest boycott against the manipulation of the broadcast profession, Bourdieu examines ways in which journalism imposes limits on the public's vision of what constitutes both reality and politics. He draws attention to the media's predilection for spectacle, disasters, and human interest stories rather than analysis of political and social issues, and he demonstrates how journalists give precedence to the "game" of politics rather than the effects of these games. When this profound yet accessible book first appeared in France during 1996 it became an immediate best seller due to the huge media controversy that it generated. The excerpt presents Bourdieu's views on the constraints and limits on autonomy of those in television, in addition to a defense of the sociological analysis of television.

## In Front of the Camera and Behind the Scenes

I'd like to try and pose here, on television, a certain number of questions about television. This is a bit paradoxical since, in general, I think that you can't say much on television, particularly not about television. But if it's true that you can't say anything on television, shouldn't I join a certain number of our top intellectuals, artists, and writers and conclude that one should simply steer clear of it?

It seems to me that we don't have to accept this alternative. I think that it is important to talk on television *under certain conditions*. Today, thanks to the audiovisual services of the College de France, I am speaking under absolutely exceptional circumstances. In the first place, I face no time limit; second, my topic is my own, not one imposed on me (I was free to choose whatever topic I wanted and I can still change it); and, third, there is nobody here, as for regular programs, to bring me into line with technical requirements, with the "public-that-won't-understand," with morality or decency, or with whatever else. The situation is absolutely unique because, to use out-of-date terms, I have a *control of the instruments of production* which is not at all usual. The fact that these conditions are exceptional in itself says something about what usually happens when someone appears on television.

But, you may well ask, why do people accept such conditions? That's a very important question, and, further, one not asked by most of the researchers, scholars, and writers—not to mention journalists—who appear on television. We need to question this failure to ask questions. In fact, it seems to me that, by agreeing to appear on television shows without worrying about whether you'll be able to say anything, you make it very clear that you're not there to say anything at all but for altogether different reasons, chief among them the desire to be seen.

[. . .]

## Invisible Censorship

But let me return to the essential point. I began by claiming that open access to television is offset by a powerful censorship, a loss of independence linked to the conditions imposed on those who speak on television. Above all, time limits make it highly unlikely that anything can be said. I am undoubtedly expected to say that this television censorship—of guests but also of the journalists who are its agents—is political. It's true that politics intervenes, and that there is political control (particularly in the case of hiring for top positions in the radio stations and television channels under direct government control). It is also true that at a time such as today, when great numbers of people are looking for work and there is so little job security in television and radio, there is a greater tendency toward political conformity. Consciously or unconsciously, people censor themselves—they don't need to be called into line.

You can also consider economic censorship. It is true that, in the final analysis, you can say that the pressure on television is economic. That said, it is not enough to say that what gets on television is determined by the owners, by the companies that pay for the ads, or by the government that gives the subsidies. If you knew only the name of the owner of a television station, its advertising budget, and how much it receives in subsidies, you wouldn't know much. Still, it's important to keep these things in mind. It's important to know that NBC is owned by General Electric (which means that interviews with people who live near a nuclear plant undoubtedly would be . . . but then again, such a story wouldn't even occur to anyone), that CBS is owned by Westinghouse, and ABC by Disney, that TF1 belongs to Bouygues,[1] and that these facts lead to consequences through a whole series of mediations. It is obvious that the government won't do certain things to Bouygues, knowing that Bouygues is behind TF1. These factors, which are so crude that they are obvious to even the most simple-minded critique, hide other things, all the anonymous and invisible mechanisms through which the many kinds of censorship operate to make television such a formidable instrument for maintaining the symbolic order.

I'd like to pause here. Sociological analysis often comes up against a misconception. Anyone involved as the object of the analysis, in this case journalists, tends to think that the work of analysis, the revelation of mechanisms, is in fact a denunciation of individuals, part of an ad hominem polemic. (Those same journalists would, of course, immediately level accusations of bias and lack of objectivity at any sociologist who discussed or wrote about even a tenth of what comes up anytime you talk with the media about the payoffs, how the programs are manufactured, made up—that's the word they use.) In general, people don't like to be turned into objects or objectified, and journalists least of all. They feel under fire, singled out. But the further you get in the analysis of a given milieu, the more likely you are to let individuals off the hook (which doesn't mean justifying everything that happens). And the more you understand how things work, the more you come to understand that the people involved are manipulated as much as they manipulate. They manipulate even more effectively the more they are themselves manipulated and the more unconscious they are of this.

I stress this point even though I know that, whatever I do, anything I say will be taken as a criticism—a reaction that is also a defense against analysis. But let me stress that I even think that scandals such as the furor over the deeds and misdeeds of one or another television news personality, or the exorbitant salaries of certain producers, divert attention from the main point. Individual corruption only masks the *structural corruption* (should we even talk about corruption in this case?) that operates on the game as a whole through mechanisms such as competition for market share. This is what I want to examine.

So I would like to analyze a series of mechanisms that allow television to wield a particularly pernicious form of symbolic violence. Symbolic violence is violence wielded with tacit complicity between its victims and its agents, insofar as both remain unconscious of submitting to or wielding it. The function of sociology, as of every science, is to reveal that which is hidden. In so doing, it can help minimize the symbolic violence within social relations and, in particular, within the relations of communication.

Let's start with an easy example—sensational news. This has always been the favorite food of the tabloids. Blood, sex, melodrama and crime have always been big sellers. In the early days of television, a sense of respectability modeled on the printed press kept these attention-grabbers under wraps, but the race for audience share inevitably brings it to the headlines and to the beginning of the television news. Sensationalism attracts notice, and it also diverts it, like magicians whose basic operating principle is to direct attention to something other than what they're doing. Part of the symbolic functioning of television, in the case of the news, for example, is to call attention to those elements which will engage everybody—which offer something for everyone. These are things that won't shock anyone, where nothing is at stake, that don't divide, are generally agreed on, and interest everybody without touching on anything important. These items are basic ingredients of news because they interest everyone, and because they take up time—time that could be used to say something else.

And time, on television, is an extremely rare commodity. When you use up precious time to say banal things, to the extent that they cover up precious things, these banalities become in fact very important. If I stress this point, it's because everyone knows that a very high proportion of the population reads no newspaper at all and is dependent on television as their sole source of news. Television enjoys a de facto monopoly on what goes into the heads of a significant part of the population and what they think. So much emphasis on headlines and so much filling up of precious time with empty air—with nothing or almost nothing—shunts aside relevant news, that is, the information that all citizens ought to have in order to exercise their democratic rights. We are therefore faced with a division, as far as news is concerned, between individuals in a position to read so-called "serious" newspapers (insofar as they can remain serious in the face of competition from television), and people with access to international newspapers and foreign radio stations, and, on the other hand, everyone else, who get from television news all they know about politics. That is to say, precious little, except for what can be learned from seeing people, how they look, and how they talk—things even the most culturally disadvantaged can decipher, and which can do more than a little to distance many of them from a good many politicians.

[. . .]


## Show and Hide

So far I've emphasized elements that are easy to see. I'd like now to move on to slightly less obvious matters in order to show how, paradoxically, television can hide by showing. That is, it can hide things by showing something other than what would be shown if television did what it's supposed to do, provide information. Or by showing what has to be shown, but in such a way that it isn't really shown, or is turned into something insignificant; or by constructing it in such a way that it takes on a meaning that has nothing at all to do with reality.

On this point I'll take two examples from Patrick Champagne's work. In his work in *La Misère du monde*, Champagne offers a detailed examination of how the media represent events in the "inner city."[2] He shows how journalists are carried along by the inherent exigencies of their job, by their view of the world, by their training and orientation, and also by the reasoning intrinsic to the profession itself. They select very specific aspects of the inner city as a function of their particular perceptual categories, the particular way they see things. These categories are the product of education, history, and so forth. The most common metaphor to explain this notion of category—that is, the invisible structures that organize perception and determine what we see and don't see—is eyeglasses. Journalists have special "glasses" through which they see certain things and not others, and through which they see the things they see in the special way they see them.

The principle that determines this selection is the search for the sensational and the spectacular. Television calls for *dramatization*, in both senses of the term: it puts an event on stage, puts it in images. In doing so, it exaggerates the importance of that event, its seriousness, and its dramatic, even tragic character. For the inner city, this means riots. That's already a big word . . . And, indeed, words get the same treatment. Ordinary words impress no one, but paradoxically, the world of images is dominated by words. Photos are nothing without words—the French term for the caption is *legend*, and often they should be read as just that, as legends that can show anything at all. We know that to name is to show, to create, to bring into existence. And words can do a lot of damage: Islam, Islamic, Islamicist—is the headscarf Islamic or Islamicist?[3] And if it were really only a kerchief and *nothing more*? Sometimes I want to go back over *every* word the television news-people use, often without thinking and with no idea of the difficulty and the seriousness of the subjects they are talking about or the responsibilities they assume by talking about them in front of the thousands of people who watch the news without understanding what they see and without understanding that they don't understand. Because these words do things, they make things—they create phantasms, fears, and phobias, or simply false representations.

Journalists, on the whole, are interested in the exception, which means whatever is exceptional *for them*. Something that might be perfectly ordinary for someone else can be extrordinary for them and vice versa. They're interested in the extraordinary, in anything that breaks the routine. The daily papers are under pressure to offer a daily dose of the extra-daily, and that's not easy . . . This pressure explains the attention they give to extraordinary occurrences, usual unusual events like fires, floods, or murders. But the extra-ordinary is also, and especially, what isn't ordinary for other newspapers. It's what differs from the ordinary and what differs from what other newspapers say. The pressure is dreadful—the pressure to get a "scoop."[*] People are ready to do almost anything to be the first to see and present something. The result is that everyone copies each other in the attempt to get ahead; everyone ends up doing the same thing. The search for exclusivity, which elsewhere leads to originality and singularity, here yields uniformity and banality.

This relentless, self-interested search for the extra-ordinary can have just as much political effect as direct political prescription or the self-censorship that comes from fear of being left behind or left out. With the exceptional force of the televised image at their disposal, journalists can produce effects that are literally incomparable. The monotonous, drab daily life in the inner city doesn't say anything to anybody and doesn't interest anybody, journalists least of all. But even if they were to take a real interest in what goes on in the inner city and really wanted to show it, it would be enormously difficult. There is nothing more difficult to convey than reality in all its ordinariness. Flaubert was fond of saying that it takes a lot of hard work to portrary mediocrity. Sociologists run into this problem all the time: How can we make the ordinary extraordinary and evoke ordinariness in such a way that people will see just how extraordinary it is?

The political dangers inherent in the ordinary use of television have to do with the fact that images have the peculiar capacity to produce what literary critics call a *reality effect*. They show things and make people believe in what they show. This power to show is also a power to mobilize. It can give a life to ideas or images, but also to groups. The news, the incidents and accidents of everyday life, can be loaded with political or ethnic significance liable to unleash strong, often negative feelings, such as racism, chauvinism, the fear-hatred of the foreigner or, xenophobia. The simple report, the very fact of reporting, of *putting on record* as a reporter, always implies a social construction of reality that can mobilize (or demobilize) individuals or groups.

Another example from Patrick Champagne's work is the 1986 high school student strike. Here you see how journalists acting in all good faith and in complete innocence— merely letting themselves be guided by their interests (meaning what interests them), presuppositions, categories of perception and evaluation, and unconscious expectations—still produce reality effects and effects in reality. Nobody wants these effects, which, in certain cases, can be catastrophic.

[. . .]

### Contradictions and Tensions

Television is an instrument of communication with very little autonomy, subject as it is to a whole series of pressures arising from the characteristic social relations between journalists. These include *relations of competition* (relentless and pitiless, even to the point of absurdity) and *relations of collusion*, derived from objective common interests. These interests in turn are a function of the journalists' position in the field of symbolic production and their shared cognitive, perceptual, and evaluative structures, which they share by virtue of common social background and training (or lack thereof). It follows that this instrument of communication, as much as it appears to run free, is in fact reined in. During the 1960s, when television appeared on the cultural scene as a new phenomenon,[5] a certain number of "sociologists" (quotation marks needed here) rushed to proclaim that, as a "means of mass communication," television was going to "massify" everything. It was going to be the great leveler and turn all viewers into one big, undifferentiated mass. In fact, this assessment seriously underestimated viewers' capacity for resistance. But, above all, it underestimated television's ability to transform its very producers and the other journalists that compete with it and, ultimately, through its irresistible fascination for some of them, the ensemble of cultural producers. The most important development, and a difficult one to foresee, was the extraordinary extension of the power of television over the whole of cultural production, including scientific and artistic production.

Today, television has carried to the extreme, to the very limit, a contradiction that haunts every sphere of cultural production. I am referring to the contradiction between the economic and social conditions necessary to produce a certain type of work and the social conditions of transmission for the products obtained under these conditions. I used math as an obvious example, but my argument also holds for avant-garde poetry, philosophy, sociology, and so on, works thought to be "pure" (a ridiculous word in any case), but which are, let's say, at least relatively independent of the market. There is a basic, fundamental contradiction between the conditions that allow one to do cutting-edge math or avant-garde poetry, and so on, and the conditions necessary to transmit these things to everybody else. Television carries this contradiction to the extreme to the extent that, through audience ratings and more than all the other milieux of cultural production, it is subject to market pressures.

By the same token, in this microcosm that is the world of journalism, tension is very high between those who would like to defend the values of independence, freedom from market demands, freedom from made-to-order programs, and from managers, and so on, and those who submit to this necessity and are rewarded accordingly . . . Given the strength of the opposition, these tensions can hardly be expressed, at least not on screen. I am thinking here of the opposition between the big stars with big salaries who are especially visible and especially rewarded, but who are also especially subject to all these pressures, and the invisible drones who put the news together, do the reporting, and who are becoming more and more critical of the system. Increasingly well-trained in the logic of the job market, they are assigned to jobs that are more and more pedestrian, more and more insignificant—behind the microphones and the cameras you have people who are incomparably more cultivated than their counterparts in the 1960s. In other words, this tension between what the profession requires and the aspirations that people acquire in journalism school or in college is greater and greater—even though there is also anticipatory socialization on the part of people really on the make . . . One journalist said recently that the midlife crisis at forty (which is when you used to find out that your job isn't everything you thought it would be) has moved back to thirty. People are discovering earlier the terrible requirements of this work and in particular, all the pressures associated with audience ratings and other such gauges. Journalism is one of the areas where you find the greatest number of people who are anxious, dissatisfied, rebellious, or cynically resigned, where very often (especially, obviously, for those on the bottom rung of the ladder) you find anger, revulsion, or discouragement about work that is experienced as or proclaimed to be "not like other jobs." But we're far from a situation where this spite or these refusals could take the form of true resistance, and even farther from the possibility of collective resistance.

To understand all this—especially all the phenomena that, in spite of all my efforts, it might be thought I was blaming on the moderators as individuals—we must move to the level of global mechanisms, to the structural level. Plato (I am citing him a lot today) said that we are god's puppets. Television is a universe where you get the impression that social actors—even when they seem to be important, free, and independent, and even sometimes possessed of an extraordinary aura (just take a look at the television magazines)—are the puppets of a necessity that we must understand, of a structure that we must unearth and bring to light.

### Making Everything Ordinary

To return to the problem of television's effects, it is true that the opposition between news and analysis existed before, but never with this intensity. (You see here that I'm steering between "never-been-seen-before" and "the-way-it-always-has-been.") Television's power of diffusion means that it poses a terrible problem for the print media and for culture generally. Next to it, the mass circulation press that sent so many shudders up educated spines in earlier times doesn't seem like much at all. (Raymond Williams argued that the entire romantic revolution in poetry was brought about by the horror that English writers felt at the beginnings of the mass circulation press.[6]) By virtue of its reach and exceptional power, television produces effects which, though not without precedent, are completely original.

For example, the evening news on French TV brings together more people than all the French newspapers together, morning and evening editions included. When the information supplied by a single news medium becomes a universal source of news, the resulting political and cultural effects are clear. Everybody knows the "law" that if a newspaper or other news vehicle wants to reach a broad public, it has to dispense with sharp edges and anything that might divide or exclude readers (just think about *Paris-Match* or, in the U.S., *Life* magazine). It must attempt to be inoffensive, not to "offend anyone," and it must never bring up problems—or, if it does, only problems that don't pose any problem. People talk so much about the weather in day-to-day life because it's a subject that cannot cause trouble. Unless you're on vacation and talking with a farmer who needs rain, the weather is the absolutely ideal *soft* subject. The farther a paper extends its circulation, the more it favors such topics that interest "everybody" and don't raise problems. The object—news—is constructed in accordance with the perceptual categories of the receiver.

The collective activity I've described works so well precisely because of this homogenization, which smoothes over things, brings them into line, and depoliticizes them. And it works even though, strictly speaking, this activity is without a subject, that is, no one ever thought of or wished for it as such. This is something that is observed frequently in social life. Things happen that nobody wants but seem somehow to have been willed. Herein lies the danger of simplistic criticism. It takes the place of the work necessary to understand phenomena such as the fact that, even though no one really wished it this way, and without any intervention on the part of the people actually paying for it, we end up with this very strange product, the "TV news." It suits everybody because it confirms what they already know and, above all, leaves their mental structures intact. There are revolutions, the ones we usually talk about, that aim at the material bases of a society—take the nationalization of Church property after 1789—and then there are symbolic revolutions effected by artists, scholars, or great religious or (sometimes, though less often) political prophets. These affect our mental structures, which means that they change the ways we see and think. Manet is an example: his painting upset the fundamental structure of all academic teaching of painting in the nineteenth century, the opposition between the contemporary and the traditional.[7] If a vehicle as powerful as television were oriented even slightly toward this kind of symbolic revolution, I can assure you that everyone would be rushing to put a stop to it . . .

But it turns out that, without anyone having to ask television to work this way, the model of competition and the mechanisms outlined above ensure that television does nothing of the sort. It is perfectly adapted to the mental structures of its audience. I could point to television's moralizing, telethon side, which needs to be analyzed from this perspective. André Gide used to say that worthy sentiments make bad literature. But worthy sentiments certainly make for good audience ratings. The moralizing bent of television should make us wonder how cynical individuals are able to make such astoundingly conservative, moralizing statements. Our news anchors, our talk show hosts, and our sports announcers have turned into two-bit spiritual guides, representatives of middle-class morality. They are always telling us what we "should think" about what they call "social problems," such as violence in the inner city or in the schools. The same is true for art and literature, where the best-known of the so-called literary programs serve the establishment and ever-more obsequiously promote social conformity and market values.[8]

Journalists—we should really say the journalistic field—owe their importance in society to their de facto monopoly on the large-scale informational instruments of production and diffusion of information. Through these, they control the access of ordinary citizens but also of other cultural producers such as scholars, artists, and writers, to what is sometimes called "public space," that is, the space of mass circulation. (This is the monopoly that blocks the way whenever an individual or member of a group tries to get a given piece of news into broad circulation.) Even though they occupy an inferior, dominated position in the fields of cultural production, journalists exercise a very particular form of domination, since they control the means of public expression. They control, in effect, public existence, one's ability to be recognized as a *public figure*, obviously critical for politicians and certain intellectuals. This position means that at least the most important of these figures are treated with a respect that is often quite out of proportion with their intellectual merits . . . Moreover, they are able to use part of this power of consecration to their own benefit. Even the best-known journalists occupy positions of structural inferiority vis-à-vis social categories such as intellectuals or politicians—and journalists want nothing so much as to be part of the intellectual crowd. No doubt, this structural inferiority goes a long way to explain their tendency toward anti-intellectualism. Nevertheless, they are able to dominate members of these "superior" categories on occasion.

Above all, though, with their permanent access to public visibility, broad circulation, and mass diffusion—an access that was completely unthinkable for any cultural producer until television came into the picture—these journalists can impose on the whole of society their vision of the world, their conception of problems, and their point of view. The objection can be raised that the world of journalism is divided, differentiated, and diversified, and as such can very well represent all opinions and points of view or let them be expressed. (It is true that to break through journalism's protective shield, you can to a certain extent and provided you possess a minimum of symbolic capital on your own, play journalists and media off against one another.) Yet it remains true that, like other fields, the journalistic field is based on a set of shared assumptions and beliefs, which reach beyond differences of position and opinion. These assumptions operate within a particular set of mental categories; they reside in a characteristic relationship to language, and are visible in everything implied by a formulation such as "it's just *made* for television." These are what supplies the principle that determines what journalists select both within social reality and among symbolic productions as a whole. There is no discourse (scientific analysis, political manifesto, whatever) and no action (demonstration, strike) that doesn't have to face this trial of journalistic selection in order to catch the public eye. The effect is *censorship*, which journalists practice without even being aware of it. They retain only the things capable of *interesting* them and "keeping their attention," which means things that fit their categories and mental grid; and they reject as insignificant or remain indifferent to symbolic expressions that ought to reach the population as a whole.

## Notes

1.  I thought it useful to reproduce this text, which has already been published in *Les Actes de la recherche en sciences sociales*, in which I had set out, in a more tightly controlled form, most of the themes discussed in a more accessible fashion above.

2.  See for example the work of Jean-Marie Goulemot and Daniel Oster, *Gens de lettres: écrivains et bohèmes, l'imaginaire littéraire 1630–1900*, (Paris: Minerve, 1992), which gives numerous examples of observations and remarks by writers themselves that constitute a sort of spontaneous sociology of the literary milieu. They do not, however, derive the basic explanatory principle, largely because of their efforts to objectify their adversaries and everything they dislike about the literary world. But the picture that emerges of the functioning of the nineteenth-century literary field can be read as a description of the concealed or secret functioning of the literary field today (as Philippe Murray has done in "Des Règles de l'art aux coulisses de sa misère," *Art Press* 186 [June 1993], (pp.55–67).

3.  [Raymond Williams, *Culture and Society, 1780–1950* (New York: Columbia University Press, 1958).—T.R.]

4.  On the emergence of this idea of "objectivity" in American journalism as a product of the effort of newspapers worried about their respectability to distinguish news from the simple narrative of the popular press, see Michael Schudson, *Discovering the News* (New York: Basic Books, 1978). On the opposition between journalists oriented toward the literary field and concerned with style, and journalists close to the political field, and on what each contributed, in the French case, to this process of differentiation and the invention of a "job" of its own (notably, with the advent of the reporter), see Thomas Ferenczi, *L'Invention du journalisme en France: naissance de la presse moderne à la fin du 19ᵉ siècle* (Paris: Plon, 1993). On the form that this opposition takes in the field of French newspapers and news magazines and on its relationship with the different categories of reading and readers, see Pierre Bourdieu, *Distinction: A Social Critique of the Judgement of Taste* [1979] trans. R. Nice (Cambridge: Harvard University Press, 1984), pp. 442–51.

5.  [Television in France developed comparatively late: in 1963, France had some 3 million TV sets against 12 million in Great Britain. It has since caught up so that by 1984 there were television sets in 93 percent of French households and 94 percent of homes in Great Britain.—T.R.]

6.  [See Raymond Williams, *Culture and Society, 1780–1950* (New York: Columbia University Press, 1958).—T.R.]

7.  [See Pierre Bourdieu, "The Institutionalization of Anomie," in Randal Johnson, ed., *The Field of Cultural Production: Essays on Art and Literature* (New York: Columbia University Press, 1993), pp. 238–53.—T.R.]

8.  For example, the long-running show of Bernard Pivot, popular host of *Apostrophes*, a book review. The American equivalents are found on PBS.—T.R.]

# Permissions

## Section I: The Development of Journalism

1. Schudson, Michael (1978). From *Discovering the News*. New York: Basic Books, 12–31. Copyright © 1978 by Basic Books. Reprinted with permission of the publisher.
2. Mills, Kay (1988). From *A Place in the News*. New York: Columbia University Press, 15–34. Copyright © 1990 Columbia University Press. Reprinted with permission of the publisher.
3. Carey, James W. (ed.) (2009). "Technology and Ideology: The Case of the Telegraph" from *Communication as Culture: Essays on Media and Society*. New York: Routledge, 155–157, 162–177.
4. Washburn, Patrick S. (2006). From *The African American Newspaper*. Evanston: Northwestern University Press, 143–159. Reprinted with permission of the publisher.
5. Chapman, Jane (2005). From *Comparative Media History*. Cambridge: Polity, 147–150, 184–187, 214–216, 227–229, 231–233, 257, 261–263. Reprinted with permission of the publisher.
6. King, Elliot (2010). From *Free for All: The Internet's Transformation of Journalism*. Evanston, IL: Northwestern University Press, 251–268. Reprinted with permission of the publisher.

## Section II: Doing Journalism

7. Gans, Herbert (1979). From *Deciding What's News*. New York: Pantheon, 182–186, 188–192, 201–203. Copyright © 1979 by Herbert J. Gans. Reprinted by permission of the Northwestern University Press.
8. Gellhorn, Martha (1986). From "The Besieged City" and "The Bomber Boys" from *The Face of War*. London: Virago Press, 31–40, 91–96. Copyright © 1936, 1988 by Martha Gellhorn. Used by permission of Grove/Atlantic, Inc.

9.   Roberts, Gene and Klibanoff, Hank (2006). From *The Race Beat*. New York: Alfred A. Knopf, 159–170, 174–183. Copyright © 2006 by Gene Roberts and Hank Klibanoff. Used by permission of Alfred A. Knopf, a division of Random House, Inc.

10.  Knightley, M. Phillip (1975). From *The First Casualty*. Baltimore: The Johns Hopkins University Press, 402–421. Copyright © 1975, 2000, 2002, 2003, 2004 by Phillip Knightley. Reprinted by permission of the author.

11.  Bernstein, Carl and Woodward, Bob (1974). From *All the President's Men*. New York: Simon & Schuster, 9–26, 334–336. Copyright © 1974 Carl Bernstein and Bob Woodward. Reprinted with the permission of Simon & Schuster, Inc.

12.  Robertson, Nan (1993). From *The Girls in the Balcony*. New York: Random House, 99–105, 108–113. Copyright © 1993 by Nan Robertson. Reprinted by arrangement with Robert Levey and The Barbara Hogenson Agency. All rights reserved.

## Section III: Biography

13.  Morris, James McGrath (2010). From *Pulitzer: A Life in Politics, Print and Power*. New York: HarperCollins, 204–215, 219–220. Copyright © 2010 by James McGrath Morris. Reprinted by permission of HarperCollins Publishers.

14.  Steffens, Lincoln (1931). From *The Autobiography of Lincoln Steffens*. New York: Harcourt Brace, 169–179, 392–406. Copyright © 1931 by Harcourt, Inc. and renewed 1959 by Peter Steffens. Reprinted by permission of Houghton Mifflin Harcourt Publishing Company.

15.  Goldberg, Vicki (1986). From *Margaret Bourke White: A Biography*. New York: Harper & Row, 172–195. Copyright © 1997. Reproduced with permission of Victoria L. Goldberg via Copyright Clearance Center.

16.  Sperber, A.M. (1986). From *Murrow: His Life and Times*. New York: Freundlich Books. 594–595, 603–604, 610–611, 431–443. Copyright 1998 © by Liselotte Sperber. Reprinted by permission of Fordham University Press. All rights reserved.

17.  Rowan, Carl (1991). From *Breaking Barriers*. New York: Little, Brown, 314–323, 324–327. Copyright © 1991 by Carl T. Rowan. Reprinted by permission of Little, Brown and Company, and with the support of the Oberlin College Archives.

18.  Graham, Katherine (1998). From *Personal History*. New York: Vintage Books, 444–455, 458–459. Copyright © 1997 by Katharine Graham. Used by permission of Alfred A. Knopf, a division of Random House, Inc.

## Section IV: Classic Reporting

19.  Wells–Barnett, Ida B. (1892). "The Malicious and Untruthful White Press" and "Lynched as a Scapegoat" from *Southern Horrors: Lynch Law in All Its Phases*. New York: New York Age.

20.  Tarbell, Ida (1904). From *A History of Standard Oil*, Vol. 1, pp. 54–69, Vol. 2, pp. 267–271, 287–292. New York: McClure, Phillips & Co.

## Section V: Journalism and Society

# Index